W9-AZF-988

THE
MOB

THE
MOB

200 Years of Organized Crime in New York

Virgil W. Peterson

Green Hill Publishers, Inc.
Ottawa, Illinois

10 9 8 7 6 5 4 3 2 1

Copyright © 1983 by Virgil W. Peterson

Printed in the United States of America. All
rights reserved. No part of this book may be
used or reproduced in any manner without written
permission, except in the case of brief quotations
embodied in critical articles or reviews.

Copies of this book may be purchased from the
publisher for $18.95. All inquiries and catalog
requests should be addressed to Green Hill
Publishers, Inc., 722 Columbus Street, Ottawa,
Illinois 61350. (815) 434-7905.

ISBN: 0-89803-123-0

To
Clydie
Edward, Sharon,
Alan and Bryan

Acknowledgments

Numerous persons were most helpful to me during the several years that I was engaged in the preparation of this book. I am particularly indebted to Nat Cosnow who was my loyal and conscientious assistant during most of the twenty-eight years I headed the Chicago Crime Commission staff. Mr. Cosnow read each chapter as it was completed and made valuable suggestions.

The late John F. O'Connell, formerly chairman of the New York State Liquor Authority and before that the chief investigator for prosecutor Thomas E. Dewey, furnished me with over a dozen volumes of important transcripts of testimony taken by official agencies during hearings in New York. This testimony was extremely valuable in providing an inside picture of organized crime in New York. Also furnishing me with highly significant documents relating to the activities of some underworld bigwigs was the late Downey Rice. Mr. Rice, an attorney, was one of my associates in the late 1930s when I headed the Boston FBI office. Later he served on the staff of the celebrated Kefauver U.S. Senate committee.

To Gus Micek, a retired FBI agent with whom I was associated when I headed the St. Louis office in 1937, I am indebted for a search of New York newspaper files and forwarding to me pertinent data regarding a New York organized crime leader during the turn of the century. Also helpful in supplying me with information regarding a former influential underworld figure in Kansas City and Sicily was Frank Maudlin, previously the managing director of the Kansas City Crime Commission.

Most helpful were various pertinent items furnished to me by Chicago Crime Commission staff members including my former secretary, Virginia Barski, investigator Myke Novotnak and chief investigator Walter Devereux.

For arranging some important interviews for me at Harvard University, I am grateful to Bob Tonis, then head of security at Harvard and before that an FBI agent for many years.

Also sincerely appreciated was the efficient and painstaking typing of the manuscript by Agnes Barber Laidlaw. As far back as the 1930s she had served as my secretary when I headed the Milwaukee office and before that she had typed reports I prepared in the Chicago FBI office when assigned to the John Dillinger investigation.

Also deeply appreciated is the encouragement to write this book that I received from Professor Fred E. Inbau of Northwestern University Law School and Lloyd Wendt, noted author and previously the editor and publisher of a major Chicago daily newspaper.

And I am deeply grateful to my wife for her constant encouragement and for the sacrifices she has made while this book was in preparation.

V. W. P.

CONTENTS

INTRODUCTION

Organized crime has existed in America throughout much of its history. However, a broad public awareness of the problem started with the televised hearings conducted by a special committee appointed by the U.S. Senate in 1950 to investigate organized crime in interstate commerce. Headed by Senator Estes Kefauver, the committee held hearings in many sections of the country. Citizens throughout the land were glued to their television sets as they observed some of the nation's most powerful and sinister underworld leaders take the witness stand and, in most instances, refuse to testify on the grounds that their testimony might incriminate them. Particularly shocking was the irrefutable evidence examined by the committee that some of the gangland bosses not only controlled the rackets in their communities but were actually the behind-the-scenes political rulers as well. In many instances, the evidence clearly substantiated the boast once made by the infamous underworld leader Benjamin (Bugsy) Siegel: "We don't run for public office. We own the politicians."

In the three decades following the Kefauver committee hearings, numerous congressional committees have conducted investigations and held hearings on the role of organized crime in such diverse activities as narcotics traffic, securities thefts and frauds, waterfront racketeering, penetration of legitimate business, control of labor unions, and professional boxing.

Almost daily, newspapers as well as magazines feature stories on organized crime. Presidents of the United States have listed organized crime as one of the nation's pressing problems. Local, state, and federal prosecutors, attorneys general of states, mayors of numerous cities, and members of state legislatures decry the prevalence of organized crime. And federal, state, and local task forces are formed to deal with it.

Although almost everyone denounces organized crime, the exact meaning of the term varies. To many, organized crime is simply the Mafia; to others, the national crime syndicate; and to still others, La Cosa Nostra. In some localities an organized crime group is referred to as the crime syndicate, the mob, or the gang.

In the last analysis, organized crime may be defined as a continuing conspiracy for profit that perpetuates itself through violence or threat of violence and by arranging for immunity through the corruption of officials.

Frequently definitions have emphasized organized crime's role in providing the public with goods and services prohibited by law. Such definitions are entirely too restrictive. Organized crime is engaged in legitimate business on a wide scale and has taken over control of many labor unions. Of course, the modus operandi of organized crime is exactly the same whether it is engaging in activities prohibited by law or conducting a legitimate business or managing the affairs of a labor union. In each instance, organized crime imposes its will by generating a fear of violence and by making arrangements for immunity through the corruption of officials. It is through violence and threat of violence that the underworld maintains rigid discipline within its own ranks, eliminates rivals, and discourages the general public from making complaints to officials or testifying in court.

The present book is made up of two parts, plus three appendices. Part I traces the history of crime and politics in New York City and the development of organized crime in that metropolis. The first president of the United States, George Washington, was inaugurated in New York City in 1789, the same year usually given as the date of origin of Tammany Hall. Originally a patriotic, social, and benevolent organization with laudable objectives, Tammany Hall soon became enmeshed in partisan politics and its very name became a symbol of corruption throughout the world.

Among the early political leaders who exerted a strong influence on Tammany Hall was Aaron Burr. From the days of Aaron Burr in the late 1700s until the overthrow of the last big Tammany boss, Carmine G. DeSapio, in the 1960s, the Tammany organization had a continuous existence. During much of this long period, it dominated politics in the city.

From its early days, close ties were cemented between underworld leaders and influential Tammany politicians. These alliances were mutually beneficial. The underworld provided campaign funds and election workers that aided Tammany leaders in achieving and retaining political power. On some occasions the underworld ensured the success of its political patrons by engaging in violence at the polls and by organizing gangs of repeaters. The underworld, in return, was afforded iron-clad protection. Such alliances between the underworld and political leaders are the backbone of organized crime everywhere.

Of course, the underworld has not confined its political ties to Tammany politicians. The underworld is not interested in party labels or political ideologies. It seeks to forge ties with those who possess the power to afford it protection. And for many decades Tammany leaders usually occupied this position of power. There were times when an underworld boss also became the actual boss of Tammany Hall. And many persons with ambitions to become mayor or prosecutor or judge found it expedient to seek the support of the underworld boss directly.

Underworld-political alliances are not peculiar to New York City. In my earlier book, *Barbarians in Our Midst* (Boston: Little, Brown, Atlantic Monthly Press Book, 1952), I traced the history of crime and politics in Chicago and the development of organized crime in that city. The basic pattern of criminal-political alliances in Chicago and New York City is the same. The identical pattern is present wherever organized crime has become firmly established and flourishes.

Part II of this book carefully examines the testimony given by the prison inmate Joseph Valachi before a U.S. Senate committee in 1963, and chronicles the activities of organized crime and its "family feuds" into the 1980s. Valachi's revelations about an Italian criminal organization that he called La Cosa Nostra created a sensation. La Cosa Nostra was depicted by Valachi as a rigidly structured criminal organization composed exclusively of full-blooded Italians. New members are subjected to elaborate initiation rites and are required to take solemn oaths of allegiance. It is La Cosa Nostra, he asserted, that controls organized crime throughout America.

Valachi was a relatively insignificant figure in the organized crime setup in New York City. His experience and firsthand information were limited to New York City and environs. Yet this testimony was accepted as gospel by the Senate committee, the then attorney general of the United States, and a presidential commission. His revelations made a tremendous impact on the literature relating to organized crime. For many years following Valachi's disclosures, there was a spate of books, magazine articles, and newspaper stories on the underworld in America. And with few exceptions, Valachi's version of the structure of organized crime was accepted as accurate. In some instances authors have also attributed to Valachi statements that he never made.

A considerable portion of Valachi's testimony, particularly about individuals, can be verified. Much of this information had been related previously by other informants and had appeared in literature on organized crime. However, the interpretations given some events by Valachi are at variance with the versions of earlier informants. In some instances, Valachi's testimony indicates that he either was ignorant of the truth or deliberately lied. And his portrayal of organized crime in the United States as being under the control of a single rigidly structured organization composed exclusively of some twenty-odd Italian families (gangs) with ultimate rule vested in a small commission dominated by a few New York City Italian gang leaders does not mesh with known facts.

The three appendices deal with the Mafia. In the United States, perhaps no other term is used more frequently than *Mafia* to depict organized crime. The term is widely misused because it is generally misunderstood.

The appendices will perhaps help correct the misunderstanding. They describe the Mafia in Sicily—its origin and development, the sources of its power, and its organizational structure. The close relationship between the Mafia and politics in Sicily is similar to the criminal-political alliances in America, alliances that are the backbone of organized crime here. However, those alliances are not an imported product of the Mafia in Sicily. They were deeply embedded in American urban life long before the Sicilians and Italians became important in crime or politics here.

In the appendices I examine the findings of many of the foremost authorities on the Sicilian Mafia. Among those authorities is Luigi Barzini, a noted author and a former member of the Italian Parliament who had served on the Italian Anti-Mafia Commission. Mr. Barzini graciously read the first draft of the appendices and made a number of suggestions, for which I am grateful.

PART I

DEVELOPMENT OF ORGANIZED CRIME IN NEW YORK CITY

Tammany Hall from
Aaron Burr to Carmine G. DeSapio

1

TAMMANY HALL—ORIGIN AND EARLY CORRUPTION

George Washington was inaugurated as the first president of the United States in New York City in 1789, and City Hall, remodeled and renamed Federal Hall, became the seat of government for the fledgling nation. During colonial days the struggle between classes had reached greater intensity in New York than in any other colony. At the close of the Revolutionary War, members of the more affluent classes returned to power in New York City. Voting privileges were limited to those who could meet restrictive property qualifications. Poor soldiers who had fought valiantly for independence were disenfranchised because of poverty.

Still raging was the controversy over the Federalists' advocacy of a highly centralized national government. And an additional irritant to the masses was the Society of the Cincinnati, founded by officers of the Continental army just before disbandment. Initially, it was provided that the eldest male descendant of an original member was entitled to wear the insignia of the order and enjoy the privileges of the Society, thus creating an hereditary aristocracy. Among the numerous opponents of aristocratic tendencies was the Tammany Society in New York City.[1]

The first Tammany Society was formed in Philadelphia on May 1, 1772, and was named after the Indian chief Tammanend, who signed one of William Penn's treaties which resulted in the purchase of a portion of Philadelphia. During the Revolutionary War Tammanend became a pseudo-saint to the officers and men of the line of the colonial army. The name Tammany stood as a symbol for liberty. Several societies bearing his name were patterned after the one in Philadelphia. In New York City a Tammany Society was formed in City Hall by William Mooney, who ran an upholstery shop at Twenty-three Nassau Street. Its first celebration was held on May 12, 1789, which is usually listed as the date of origin of the Tammany Society in New York City. At the tercentennial celebration of the discovery of America by Christopher Columbus, the Tammany Society also became known as the Columbian Order.[2]

Patriotism and adherence to the principles of republicanism were principal

3

motives that prompted William Mooney to form the Tammany Society. As each member was initiated, he was required to promise that he would "sustain the state institutions, and resist a consolidation of power in the general government."[3] The Society was also intended to be a social, charitable, benevolent, and fraternal nonpartisan organization.

In the beginning the Tammany Society was divided into thirteen tribes representing the thirteen states. Each tribe was given a name, such as Eagle, Otter, Panther, Bear, and Rattlesnake. Aboriginal titles were adopted and the head of each tribe was called a sachem. Heading the Tammany Society was the grand sachem, chosen from the thirteen sachems who were the equivalent of trustees of the organization. The secretary was called the scribe, the doorkeeper the wiskinskie, and the meeting place the wigwam. In its early years the office of kitchi okemaw, or the great grand sachem, was conferred upon the president of the United States.[4] Several presidents maintained close ties with Tammany and leaned heavily on the Society for support in furthering their political ambitions.

For some time, meetings of the Tammany Society were held in Barden's Tavern at Lower Broadway. In 1798 the Society moved its quarters to the Long Room on Nassau Street, a one-story frame building attached to Martling's Tavern. Its proprietor, Abraham Martling, was elected a sachem on several occasions and members of Tammany were often called Martling Men.

The Tammany Society soon engaged in partisan politics and the Federalists contemptuously referred to Martling's Long Room as the Pig Pen. In 1809 Tammany felt the need for its own quarters and the sachems, led by Jacob Barker, a large shipbuilder, raised $28,000 for a new wigwam. The money was obtained through subscription and by means of a lottery. In 1811 the first Tammany Hall was opened at a site not far from Martling's. Indian ceremonies accompanied the opening. The grand marshal for the opening celebration was Sachem Abraham M. Valentine, who several years later was removed from the office of police magistrate for malfeasance. Beginning in 1811 the Society became generally known as the Tammany Hall political party.[5]

The founder of the Tammany Society, William Mooney, was a man of mediocre talents. Although patriotism was given as a principal motive for organizing the Society, there were unconfirmed charges that Mooney had deserted the American army in New York on September 16, 1776, joined the British forces, and for a year worn the king's uniform. His lifelong friend, Aaron Burr, was the guiding genius behind the scenes, the man who determined the true destiny of Tammany Hall. Although never a sachem, Burr was credited with having transformed the Tammany Society into a political club. A powerful grand sachem of Tammany, Matthew L. Davis, stated that "Burr was our chief." Burr's control over the Tammany Society lasted from 1797 until many years after he had fallen into disgrace. On July 11, 1804, when Burr shot and killed Alexander Hamilton in the celebrated duel at Weehawken, a township in New Jersey opposite New York City, two Tammany chiefs, Nathaniel Pendleton and William P. Van Ness, accompanied Burr to the field. One was his second. Another Tammany chief, John Swartwout, remained at Burr's home awaiting his return from the conflict. Until about 1835, Burr's protégés, nearly all of whom were involved in private or official peculations, were highly influential in Tammany affairs.[6]

In the early 1800s only a few city offices were elective—state senators, assemblymen, and aldermen. The Common Council was made up of the aldermen. From 1800 to 1809 most of these offices were filled by Tammany men. The important offices of mayor, sheriff, recorder, justices of peace of counties, and nearly all civil and military offices—from heads of departments and justices of the supreme court to auctioneers—were all filled by the powerful body in Albany known as the Council of Appointment. This council was composed of the governor and four state senators chosen by the Assembly. Through amendments to the state constitution, the Council of Appointment was abolished in 1822 and the selection of the mayor of New York City was vested in the city's Common Council. It was not until 1834 that the mayor was elected directly by a vote of the people. City elections, until 1840, lasted for three days. Throughout this era, law enforcement was woefully weak and for protection from criminals the city relied primarily on a few night watchmen, most of whom had other jobs during the daytime.[7]

The Tammany Society resorted to devious means as well as outright fraud to win elections and place its men in office. To circumvent the restrictive property qualifications for voting privileges in New York, Tammany engineered a practice of collective purchase of property. In 1801 it was Tammany that reputedly furnished the money for thirty-nine penniless students and mechanics to purchase collectively a house and lot in the Fifth Ward. Thus thirty-nine men became freeholders and entitled to vote. An additional seventy votes were secured in the Fourth Ward through the joint purchase of a house and lot at Fifty Dey Street. These newly created voters enabled Tammany to elect a majority to the Common Council. Among those who engaged in the Fifth Ward collective property purchase scheme were Daniel D. Tompkins, later a governor of New York and vice president of the United States; Richard Riker, subsequently a recorder of New York City; William P. Van Ness, later a United States district court judge; and several future powerful Tammany Hall leaders including Teunis Wortman, William A. Davis, Robert Swartwout, and John L. Broome.[8]

During a three-year period ending in 1809, a series of scandals caused the removal of several Tammany sachems from city offices. Even Tammany's founder, William Mooney, had caught the spirit of the time. In 1808 he had been appointed as superintendent of the almshouse at an annual recompense of $1,000 and the support of his family, providing it would not exceed $500. In the summer of 1809 an investigation disclosed that in addition to his salary, Mooney had spent nearly $4,000 on himself and family and had taken city supplies worth about $1,000. When he could give no satisfactory explanation for his extravagance, Mooney was discharged. His public disgrace did not affect his standing in the Tammany Society, which afterward named him its grand sachem on several occasions. Other men of Tammany who were publicly exposed for dishonesty during this period were Benjamin Romaine, who was subsequently elected grand sachem in 1808 and 1813, and Matthew L. Davis, who was named grand sachem in 1814 and reelected the following year. Thus the pattern of corruption by Tammany leaders was early established.[9]

The city was growing rapidly. Its population had jumped from 33,131 in 1790 to 58,000 in 1798 and 96,373 in 1810. Yet, it furnished very few services to its inhabitants. As late as 1815 there was but one public school, which was maintained by public subscription. Water was supplied chiefly by the Manhattan Company by means of bored wooden logs laid underground from the reservoir in Chambers Street. There was no fire department and every blaze brought terror to the people. The city did not clean the streets and only two or three were fit for carriages to be drawn over.[10]

The prestige of Tammany Hall was greatly enhanced during the War of 1812. Wholeheartedly supporting the conflict, Tammany Hall was considered the resort of the war party. President James Madison conferred favors on many Tammany leaders including Matthew L. Davis, who reaped profits of $80,000 from a single government contract while the office of U.S. district attorney, held by Nathan Sanford, yielded as much as $30,000 a year. By the end of the war, Tammany Hall had become the predominant political force in the state.[11]

In the early 1800s the Tammany Society was bitterly anti-Irish. It had a deep-seated prejudice against "adopted citizens" mingling in politics. The Irish, in turn, regarded the wigwam as a center of bigotry and politically supported DeWitt Clinton, an archfoe of Tammany. Originally, Clinton had been a member of Tammany but resigned because he could not stomach Aaron Burr's influence on the society. In 1815 Tammany arrogantly demanded that the Council of Appointment remove Clinton as mayor of New York City. Since 1803 Clinton, a nephew of the state's first governor, George Clinton, had served ten one-year terms as mayor and had a large following throughout the state. Governor Daniel D. Tompkins, who headed the Council of Appointment, was reluctant to offend Clinton's adherents and delayed meeting the Society's demands. Tammany became furious and issued threats of political reprisal. Clinton was removed. Still Tammany was not satisfied. A few years later, in 1824, it forced the removal of Clinton as canal commissioner, a post he had held with distinction and without pay. The general public was outraged throughout the state and Clinton's prestige became greater than ever.[12]

In 1817 the Irish sought the nomination of Thomas Addis Emmett, an Irish orator and a close friend of DeWitt Clinton, for Congress. Tammany had no intention of considering this proposed nomination but the Irish refused passively to submit to the dictates of the Society. When the General Committee was in session on April 24, some two hundred Irishmen marched in a body to the wigwam, broke into the meeting room, and a free-for-all erupted. Furniture was broken and used as weapons, windows were smashed, and heads battered. The mutual hostility that existed between the Irish and Tammany Hall at this time was anything but permanent. Before many years had elapsed, Tammany was dominated by the Irish.[13]

Beginning in 1817, Tammany Hall was hit by a new series of public scandals resulting from the ever-present corrupt practices and greed of its leaders. Ruggles Hubbard, once a Tammany sachem, was sheriff of New York. When his honesty was questioned, a subservient Common Council dutifully found his accounts in good order. A short time later, on August 15, 1817, Hubbard fled, and it was then discovered that substantial funds from his office were missing. Another Tammany sachem, John L. Broome, was removed as city clerk by the Council of Appointment because he had failed to take the necessary securities from Hubbard. On November 14, 1818, John P. Haff, a powerful Tammany leader and once a grand sachem, was removed from the office of surveyor of the port by President James Monroe because of corruption and general unfitness. In 1820 still another Tammany stalwart, Robert Swartwout, a U.S. Navy agent, was charged with a defalcation of $68,000. The government took a mortgage on his property for $75,000 to cover his peculation. Aided by the mortgage and by political influence, he escaped prison and continued as a trusted Tammany leader.

Tammany leaders were also participating in legalized-lottery swindles, then prevalent. This fact came to light in 1818 as a result of a famous libel suit in New York City. Testimony in the case undermined confidence in state regulation and supervision of lotteries in New York and caused reverberations throughout the nation.

In September 1818 Charles N. Baldwin, editor of the *Republican Chronicle,* publicly charged the managers of the Medical Science Lottery with fraud. In particular, he named the acting manager of the lottery, John H. Sikles, as a participant in the swindle. Baldwin was sued for libel and public hearings were held on November 11, 12, and 13, 1818, before a court composed of Mayor Cadwallader Colden and two New York City aldermen. The public was shocked by the testimony, which established collusion between one of the lottery managers and Napthali Judah, a former Tammany sachem who, incidentally, was to be elected a sachem again, in 1819. It was established that on the first day of a lottery drawing, Judah had received the lion's share of a $100,000 winning ticket. He was not the beneficiary of luck—the drawing had been rigged. Affidavits also revealed the presence of a corrupt understanding between Judah and Alderman Isaac Denniston in another fraudulent drawing of the Oswego Lottery; the collusion enabled the alderman to "win" $35,000. Also implicated in the scandal was John L. Broome. Another Tammany leader, Teunis Wortman, was indirectly involved and publicly disgraced.

The revelations in court shocked the citizenry, which had believed the lotteries were honest. Since the lotteries were authorized and purportedly supervised by the state, the entire situation was examined by the Assembly. A New York legislative committee concluded that the whole legalized lottery system was in a sorry mess. Fraud was commonplace. High-pressure sales tactics enticed women, children, servants, and the poorest and most ignorant people to buy lottery tickets. Defalcations by lottery directors had resulted in losses to the state of over $109,000. The legislative committee report was followed by an act passed by the Assembly on April 13, 1819, which was intended to reduce abuses and fraud. In 1820 the New York Constitution provided that "no lottery shall hereafter be authorized in this state." This was the first actual prohibition of lotteries in New York but it failed to apply to those already in operation.[14]

In 1819 the Tammany Society publicly decried the prevalent spirit of speculation and, in particular, singled out the distress caused by the multiplication of banks incorporated by the state legislature. At the time the Society was making its pompous pronouncement, which included suggestions that the legislature take steps to abolish such institutions, Tammany leaders were in Albany lobbying for charters for banks of which they were to become presidents or directors. Banks of the period yielded fortunes to their owners. They issued currency, which invariably depreciated, and this bad private money often worked hardships on the laboring classes.[15]

Almost from its inception, Tammany leaders had been engaged in the corrupt purchase of charters from the state legislature. In 1799 Aaron Burr had engineered through the Assembly a bill that incorporated the Manhattan Company. Purportedly this company was to engage in the laudable function of supplying pure water to New York City and thus prevent yellow fever. The company did provide city water but its charter also included a carefully worded clause, apparently not understood by the legislators, that vested it with banking powers. The Manhattan Bank thus came into being. As a pro-Tammany bank it became an extremely useful tool of the Society and aided in furthering the personal ambitions of Aaron Burr.[16]

A joint legislative committee reported in 1824 that the promoters of the

Chemical Bank had set aside $50,000 worth of stock at par value to buy votes from members of the Assembly. A lobbyist for the Chemical Bank charter was Tammany leader Robert Swartwout, the former U.S. Navy agent charged with a $68,000 defalcation in 1820. Other testimony before the committee revealed that stock in the Aetna and Chatham Fire Insurance companies had been given to legislators to obtain their charters. Among those involved in this chicanery was William J. Waldron, a Tammany grand sachem who gave $20,000 worth of stock to State Senator Jasper Ward.[17]

In New York City everything appeared to be for sale and everybody had a price. By 1820 the city's population had reached 123,706 and the demand for public services was growing rapidly. The Common Council in May 1823 granted the first gas company of the city exclusive rights for thirty years to light all streets south of Grand Street. The city received nothing in return for this valuable charter. Repeatedly, to raise needed revenue, aldermen sold ground owned by the municipality in the heart of the city. This land was increasing in value by leaps and bounds. And the lucky purchasers were usually aldermen themselves or Tammany leaders.[18]

Individual politicians were becoming affluent while city expenses were soaring. The law prohibited aldermen from being directly or indirectly interested in any city contract but violations of this statute were the order of the day. Allegations were made that city streets were sunk, raised, and lowered again to enable politically connected contractors to make large claims against the city. A report of the Common Council finance committee on January 10, 1820, disclosed that the city would soon be in debt to the extent of $1,300,000. Services performed by the city were minimal. The streets were described as an "abomination of filth." Despite a public clamor for pure water, the city turned a deaf ear. Reliance was still placed on a private company for the supply of water, which was impure and unhealthy. Because of filthy streets and bad water, cholera had several times wreaked havoc in the city.[19]

2

GANGS OF THE FIVE POINTS
AND THE BOWERY

Several areas of the city had deteriorated into centers of vice and crime. This was certainly true of the Five Points district, which was to become known throughout the world as a breeding place for violence and the home of gangsters. Actually, violence marked the history of this district long before it received the label Five Points. In 1741 the Common Council of colonial New York City, then a town of 10,000, offered a reward of one hundred pounds for information about a rumored plot by Negroes to burn the town and massacre the white people. A serving maid, Mary Burton, then in prison for thievery, began repeating the rumors and naming alleged conspirators. Based largely on her uncorroborated story, 154 Negroes and twenty-four whites were imprisoned between the spring and the following August 1741. Four white persons, including a clergyman, and eighteen Negroes were hanged, seventy-one Negroes were transported, and fourteen more were mercilessly burned to death in a hollow in the wood which many years later became known as Five Points.[1]

The Five Points district received its name from five streets—Little Water, Cross, Anthony, Orange, and Mulberry—that entered an area of about an acre in extent. In the center was a small triangular space known as Paradise Square and opposite this park was Coulter's Brewery, erected in 1792. Converted into a tenement building in 1837, it was known as the Old Brewery and became the center of a poverty and vice seldom seen elsewhere in the world. Subsequently, the routes of the five streets were altered and their names changed. However, this area continued to be known as the Five Points district.[2]

During the first two decades of the nineteenth century, the aristocrats of Five Points were the butchers. Notoriously heavy drinkers, the butchers reveled in such forms of entertainment as bull baiting. These sadistic events attracted large, boisterous crowds and huge sums of money were wagered on the number of dogs the bulls would gore. On the streets surrounding Paradise Square were scores of dance halls that attracted more than a fair share of unsavory elements. Nevertheless, the district was relatively peaceful until about 1820, when the character of Five Points changed decidedly for the worse. Respectable families moved to other parts of the city. Immigrants, predominantly "low-class Irish," swarmed into the district and lived in crumbling, broken-down tenement houses. During the next twenty years Five Points became the most dismal and evil slum section in America.[3]

From the tenements, saloons, and dance halls of the Paradise Square district emerged the original Five Points gangs. The early gangs were of a spontaneous character, without strong organization or leadership. However, well-organized gangs directed by fearless leaders of ability began making their appearance as cheap green groceries sprang up around Paradise Square and nearby streets that led into it. These green groceries displayed racks of decaying vegetables outside and in the back rooms dispensed liquor at prices lower than those in the saloons. The back rooms of the green groceries served as headquarters for gangs of thugs, pickpockets, thieves, and murderers.

The first green-grocery "speakeasy" was established about 1825 by Rosanna Peers in Center Street south of Anthony Street. The back room of this place became the headquarters and meeting place for a gang known as the Forty Thieves, headed by Edward Coleman. Also making its headquarters in the Rosanna Peers green-grocery speakeasy was a gang called the Kerryonians, so named because its members were natives of county Kerry in Ireland.

Springing up in other green-grocery speakeasies were such gangs as the Chichesters, Roach Guards, Plug Uglies, Shirt Tails, and Dead Rabbits. The Roach Guards gang was named after a Five Points liquor dealer. Internal dissension developed and in the midst of a howling, angry meeting, a dead rabbit was hurled into the center of the room. The dissident group formed an independent gang called the Dead Rabbits. The Shirt Tail gang was so named because its members habitually wore their shirttails outside their trousers. The most colorful gang, the Plug Uglies, was named after the oversized plug hats worn by its members. As the gangsters charged into battle, their hats were stuffed with wool and leather. With the plug hats pulled down over their ears, they became effective helmets that warded off damaging blows to their heads. Each Plug Ugly was generally equipped with a brick bat in one hand, a bludgeon in the other, and a pistol in reserve in his pocket. He was a fearsome character indeed.[4]

The gang leaders were the overlords of Paradise Square and the Five Points district became the sanctuary for purveyors of vice, gambling, crime, and debauchery. Not only was the Five Points one of the toughest districts in the nation; it served as the training ground for some of the most powerful organized crime leaders in America.

Crime and violence were not a monopoly of the Five Points, however. In several areas of the city there was an overabundance of street toughs, rowdies, bullies, and criminals. Violence was not uncommon. Some streets were studded with disreputable saloons. Vice and gambling flourished. Beginning about 1825 well-organized criminal gangs added to the city's problem. And the security of the public was vested in law-enforcement machinery that was inadequate in numerical strength, professionally incompetent, and completely inept.

In the daytime the only police force consisted of two constables in each ward and some marshals. The backbone of the city's law enforcement was watchmen who were on duty only at night. The watch force worked independently of the daytime constables, and communication between the night watchmen and the constables was virtually nonexistent. An official committee appointed to investigate the watch service reported on April 24, 1826, that the total force on duty each night consisted of 200 watchmen, including three captains and three assistant captains. The men were deployed in the three districts into which the city was then divided. The committee concluded that the number of watchmen was wholly insufficient to guard the city.

The watchmen were appointed by the politicians of the various wards. The watch service was largely a ward affair and there were no systematic citywide organization and regulation. When on duty, each watchman wore an old-fashioned fireman's leather hat, bereft of its upright front plate. Because of this headgear, the watchmen became known as leatherheads. Other than the hat and a thirty-three-inch club, the watchman had no badge of office. The ranks of the watchmen were made up of jaded stevedores, teamsters, and mechanics. Their political jobs as night watchmen merely served to augment their incomes from their regular daytime employment. The public gave them little respect and often they were the objects of derision and the butt of practical jokes and pranks. Robbers, thieves, and burglars, or the gangs of rowdies who often attacked innocent bystanders, had little to fear from the city's guardians of law and order. On the contrary, as one historian noted, "The watchmen of the period stood in wholesome terror of the lawbreakers they were supposed to keep within proper subjection."[5]

Politics controlled the entire system of law enforcement and the administration of justice. The mayor, deputy mayor, recorder, and aldermen were ex-officio justices of the peace and were empowered to hold courts of General Sessions. The mayor, recorder, and aldermen were justices of oyer and terminer. The mayor, deputy mayor, and recorder could preside over the court of common pleas.

Federal court was held in rooms provided in City Hall. During the early 1820s, William P. Van Ness, a Tammany leader, became a United States district court judge. Van Ness, who had won notoriety as a companion of Aaron Burr at the Alexander Hamilton duel, took it upon himself to move his federal court permanently to Tammany Hall, a highly unlikely place in which to dispense evenhanded justice. Under his ingeniously conceived plan, the government was to pay rent to Tammany Hall for the use of the courtroom. Although the public had become calloused to all sorts of political chicanery, the transfer of a U.S. court to Tammany Hall created a furor. Following an investigation, Van Ness was ordered to return his court to City Hall.[6]

In 1826 an historic amusement center made its appearance in New York City. The Bowery Theater was erected on the site of the old Bull's Head Tavern, which had occupied a conspicuous place on Bowery Lane long before the Revolution. In the 1600s the wandering wooded lane between the Dutch bouweries (farms) was known as Bouwerie Lane, and for many years its principal use was to connect the outlying farms to New Amsterdam. Through the efforts of Peter Stuyvesant, the irascible director of the Dutch West India Company, the lane was greatly improved. When the English gained control of the colony, Bowery Lane became an important highway and a link to the outside world. This was particularly true, beginning in 1732, when the first stagecoach began making regular trips over the lane en route to Boston.

The once somber Bowery Lane blossomed into life when the English introduced horse races, cards, and pleasure driving. During the Revolution, the British army of occupation encamped along the Bowery. Drinking shops and places of low amusement sprang up and remained long after the English soldiers had disappeared. The Bull's Head Tavern was located near a slaughter yard and it remained a gathering place for butchers and drovers until it was torn down in 1826. The Bowery Theater, which replaced it, seated three thousand persons. It not only was the largest theater of its time but also had the first stage to be lighted by gas. The management hoped to attract a fashionable audience from the respectable people who still resided in the Seventh, Tenth, and Fourteenth wards.[7]

Before long other theaters located near the Bowery and within a few years the area was filled with playhouses, concert halls, saloons, huge beer gardens, and basement dives. The Atlantic Gardens, next door to the Bowery Theater, was the most famous of the beer halls. The Bowery beer gardens offered their patrons such diversified amusements as music, dice, cards, and sometimes rifles for target shooting. Eventually these places became the resorts of gangsters and criminals of all sorts.[8]

The Bowery gave birth to gangs of ferocious rough-and-tumble fighters. Predominantly Irish, these gangs gave no quarter when engaged in battle with their rivals from the Five Points. Most noted of the early gangs were the Bowery B'hoys. Believed to have been offshoots of the original Bowery Boys were such gangs as the True Blue Americans, the American Guards, the O'Connell Guards, and the Atlantic Guards. Members of the misnamed True Blue Americans gang never became thoroughly Americanized. They remained Irish to the hilt. Wearing stovepipe hats and frock coats that reached to their ankles, they devoted much of their time to standing on street corners denouncing England.

All of the Bowery gangs joined hands in their numerous fights with gangs from Paradise Square of Five Points. Originally, the Bowery Boys were not as criminally motivated as their counterparts from Five Points. Some historians have attached a certain amount of glamour to the Bowery Boys, describing them as "ready for a lark, eager for a spree, reckless of consequences, and unreckoning of the future," and have even imputed to them qualities of heroism found on the western frontier. Such appraisals undoubtedly exaggerated their virtues and ignored their evil traits. Fearless they certainly were but their fearlessness was characterized by ruthlessness and brutality. From the ranks of the Bowery Boys emerged many celebrated brawlers and gangsters as well as politicians of note. Fires were a source of keen excitement to the Bowery Boys, who affiliated with the political voluntary fire companies of the day. Frequently, at fires they engaged in brawls with rival volunteer fire companies while the building was consumed by flames.[9]

Although it may have been coincidental, regular gambling houses were established in New York City around 1825, the same period that organized criminal gangs under capable leadership were formed. Historically, professional gambling has always been a favorite occupation of criminals and has usually served as the backbone of organized crime. Gambling, particularly in taverns, had been commonplace since colonial days. The volume of gambling greatly increased, however, following the exodus of sharpers from New Orleans and other Mississippi River towns to New York City, an exodus that began about 1803. These men found the pickings good. They set up games in saloons, hotels, racetracks, and vacation resorts. Their operations were brazen, conducted by the rule "Never give the sucker a break." By the time the Medical Science Lottery scandal broke in 1818, professional gambling was flourishing in New York City.

The first successful full-scale gambling house opened near Wall and Water Streets in 1825 and was highly profitable. Within the next few years, at least a dozen regular gambling houses were in operation. Among the gambling-house proprietors of the time was George Rice, a leader of the Bowery Boys and a notorious rioter and bully. During the following century, the professional gamblers and the politicians were to work hand in hand. Their alliances would not only contribute to corrupt government but also make the city one of the most important strongholds of organized crime in America.[10]

3

THE IMMIGRANT VOTE—
FRAUD AND VIOLENCE

By the mid-1820s Tammany's attitude toward the city's growing foreign population had made almost a complete turnabout. The change was based not on idealism but expediency. Instead of excluding immigrants from mingling in politics, it now adopted a policy of using them to win elections. In the November 1827 election, aliens exerted a powerful influence on its outcome.

Although it was a year before the presidential election, Tammany Hall was committed to advancing the candidacy of Andrew Jackson, who had actively sought the wigwam's support. As far back as February 23, 1819, Jackson had attended a Tammany banquet in New York City at the invitation of the grand sachem and founder of the society, William Mooney. In September 1827 Martin Van Buren, a member of Tammany Hall, had spent time in New York City in behalf of Jackson. He returned to Washington assured of the solid backing of the Tammany Society.

The fraud and violence that attended the November 1827 election exceeded anything ever witnessed in the city before. Cartloads of men, including immigrants ineligible to vote, were used as repeaters in different wards. In one instance, a cartload of six men voted at six different polling places. In a predominantly foreign ward, a native American found it impossible to vote at all. If he persisted in attempting to cast his ballot, he was arrested, his vote taken from him, and a vote for a Jackson supporter placed in his hand. Citizens of both parties, Whigs and Democrats, were stunned. And "to the revelations of this election can be traced the origin of the Native American Party," which was to insist that political privileges should be the exclusive right of natives of this country.[1]

Following Andrew Jackson's inauguration in 1829, Tammany Hall men were appointed to every federal post in New York City. The important position of collector of the port went to the powerful and venal Tammany leader Samuel Swartwout. As far back as 1823 Swartwout had served as Jackson's direct representative in obtaining the organization's support for his presidential aspirations.[2]

During this period the poor people suffered from many social injustices. Neither Tammany Hall nor the Whigs had shown any real concern. Until the early 1830s, more than ten thousand persons, mostly unfortunate laborers, were thrown into loathsome prisons each year because they were unable to pay their debts. New York City had a long, ignominious history of imprisonment for debt, dating back to colonial times. In fact, when the city's first jail (the New Gaol) was built in 1756, it soon became known as Debtors' Prison because most of its inmates were there for nonpayment of bills. Workingmen and reformers had constantly agitated, without success, for repeal of the law that permitted imprisonment of debtors. It was not until 1831 that Tammany leaders were finally goaded into giving their approval to a bill, introduced in the Assembly, that would abolish imprisonment for debts for everyone except nonresidents.[3]

In 1831 there was agitation for the direct election of the mayor by the people. Since 1822 the power of selecting the mayor had been vested in the Common Council. Tammany Hall vigorously objected to the proposed reform. During a public discussion on April 8, 1831, a Tammany alderman, Thomas T. Woodruff, boldly asserted that the people could not be trusted with the selection of such an important official as the mayor.[4]

By 1830 the population of New York City had soared to 202,589. The problems of health and public safety had continued to grow as well. The dreaded cholera made one of its numerous visits to the city in 1832. Following the death of a man in the road at Harlem, a coroner's inquest was held. Of twenty persons attending the inquest, nine died of cholera within the space of a few days. In September 1832 Philip Hone, who had served as the city's mayor from 1826 to 1827, deplored the thousands of immigrants arriving in New York City. Wrote Hone in his diary, "They have brought the cholera this year, and they will always bring wretchedness and want."[5]

Also viewing the nature of the huge immigrant population with alarm was the eminent French observer Alexis de Tocqueville, who wrote that the lower ranks of such cities as Philadelphia and New York City constituted "a rabble even more formidable than the populace of European towns . . . . A multitude of Europeans who have been driven to the shores of the New World by their misfortunes or their misconduct; and they bring to the United States all our greatest vices, without any of those interests which counteract their baneful influence." Tocqueville regarded this kind of population "as a real danger which threatens the future security of the democratic republics of the New World" and predicted the need for the creation of an independent armed force to repress expected excesses and violence.[6]

The rough-and-ready street toughs, including the gangsters from Five Points and the Bowery, made up a portion of New York City's rabble population that Tocqueville believed a threat to the nation's security. With these bruisers, violence was a way of life and riots were not uncommon. Over a period of years, theaters hosted much of this tumult.

In October 1831 an English actor was scheduled to appear in the opera *Guy Mannering* at the Park Theater. During his passage from England he had made insulting remarks about the Yankees and had quarreled with the ship's mate, who gave him a flogging after landing in New York. When the English actor appeared at the Park Theater on October 13 and 15, 1831, apples, eggs, and various missiles were hurled onto the stage. The street in front of the theater was filled with a mob bent on destruction. On Sunday, October 16, groups of idlers milled in front of the theater. After dark the crowd increased. Theater windows were broken and front doors battered. The next day a large crowd also appeared in front of the theater; order was finally restored when the mayor personally appeared in the company of numerous watchmen.[7]

Five years later the Park Theater was the center of another riot. J. Watson Webb, editor of the *Courier and Enquirer,* had charged an actor named Wood with a lack of gallantry toward a woman singer. Wood denied the charge. The editor then wrote an inflammatory article in his paper on May 27, 1836, calling upon the populace to go to the theater that evening and drive Wood off the stage. The appeal had the desired effect on gangsters from the Five Points and other brawlers unable, naturally, to tolerate a lack of chivalry. They appeared at the theater in force—and with intentions of violence.[8]

The Bowery Theater was the target of a riot on July 9, 1834. An actor had made uncomplimentary remarks about America. An hour after the performance opened, a mob broke open the doors, occupied every part of the theater, and hissed and pelted the actor. Not satisfied with the damage done at the theater, the mob then marched to the home of Lewis Tappan, who had been spotted at detested abolitionist meetings. The ruffians broke into Tappan's house, smashed windows, and carried furniture into the street, where it was set afire. The inept watchmen arrived after the destruction had been completed.[9]

On July 7, 1834, mobs attacked the Chatham Street Chapel as well as the Bowery Theater. Three days later, on July 10, gangs of ruffians damaged several residences while another mob, composed mostly of gangsters from Five Points, spread terror around Paradise Square. A dozen buildings were sacked and torched. Five houses of prostitution were burned. The girls were stripped and parceled out among the gangsters, who subjected them to shameful mistreatment. During the night blacks were tortured and an all-black church on Center Street destroyed. The mob grabbed an Englishman, gouged out both of his eyes, and tore off his ears. Troops were called to restore order.[10]

The riots in July 1834 had been directed primarily against the abolitionists.

They occurred only a few weeks after the outbreak of serious violence during the spring elections.

Almost as soon as criminal gangs were well organized in New York City, Tammany Hall began using their talents in winning elections and controlling the city. Criminal-political alliances were commonplace. Many ward and district leaders actually acquired title to green-grocery speakeasies in which Five Points gangs made their headquarters. Other ward and district leaders operated saloons and dance halls along the Bowery. Political leaders gave protection to the gangs' gambling places and houses of prostitution. Gangs from Five Points, as well as the Bowery Boys, figured prominently in the 1834 spring election riots.[11]

The 1834 election was the first one in which the people voted directly for the mayor. It began on April 8 and lasted three turbulent days. "The Sixth Ward remained true to its title of 'the bloody ould Sixth,' party strife running even more than usually high, giving rise to a series of brawls and riots." When the mayor and a strong body of watchmen attempted to restore order, they were attacked and overwhelmed. Several watchmen were severely wounded and eight were taken to a hospital for treatment. As a last resort, the National Guard was called in to quell the riots. Not unexpectedly, perhaps, the Tammany candidate, Cornelius W. Lawrence, was elected mayor.[12]

During the following year widespread dissension emerged within the ranks of Tammany Hall. Candidates for state offices had been proposed by Tammany who were obnoxious to the Equal Rights or Anti-Monopolist faction of the Society. The Tammany nominating committee called a meeting for the night of October 29, 1835, to ratify its slate of candidates. Members of the Equal Rights party started a march from headquarters in the Bowery and unceremoniously stormed into the Tammany meeting. Tammany leaders were unable to control the assemblage, which degenerated into a melee. The Tammany regulars withdrew from the meeting and their janitor turned off the gas lights, leaving the hall in darkness. However, the Equal Rights men were prepared for such a contingency. Each removed from his pocket a candle and a lucifer or Loco-Foco match. With the lighted candles, they continued the meeting and named their own ticket of candidates. From this incident, the Equal Rights men were dubbed Loco-Focos, a name subsequently applied by Whigs to the entire Democratic party. Within two years the Equal Rights party had returned to the Tammany fold and no longer existed as a separate organization.[13]

The health, safety, and economic security of New York City's population were often threatened because of the failure of the government to provide basic public services. Catastrophe struck the city twice in 1835 because of the lack of an adequate water supply coupled with inefficient firefighting facilities. At 2 AM on August 12 a fire broke out in a building occupied by bookbinders at 115 Fulton Street and swept through that section of the city, leaving a path of vast destruction. Five persons were killed. Many of the buildings destroyed were new five- and six-story structures. Philip Hone described it as one of the most destructive fires that had ever occurred in New York City. Yet within four months the city was hit by a holocaust that made the August fire seem insignificant.

About nine o'clock on the evening of December 16, 1835, a fire broke out in a store on Merchant Street. It was cold. Water froze in the hydrants, and the fire engines and hose failed to function properly. The flames became unmanageable. Some seven hundred stores in a thirteen-acre area were left in ashes. The blaze was seen as far away as New Haven and Philadelphia. Firemen became exhausted and their engines disabled. On December 18, four hundred Philadelphia firemen rushed to New York City to provide some relief. The gutted area served as a magnet to attract thieves and human scavengers, many of whom became drunk on the wine and liquor that had been piled on the streets. Soldiers were called in to stand guard while citizen patrols were formed in each ward. Property losses were estimated from $20,000,000 to $40,000,000; insurance companies were ruined. Despair hovered over the whole community.[14]

Recovery from the disaster was rapid, however. On December 16, 1836, the anniversary of the Great Fire, Philip Hone recorded in his diary that the entire area devastated by the conflagration had been "rebuilt with more splendor than before." The business community, at least, was hopeful for the future.

Following an established practice, the Tammany mayor, Cornelius W. Lawrence, held open house on January 2, 1837, to usher in the new year. It had been customary at such affairs for gentlemen to call at the mayor's home, drink a glass of sherry, eat a morsel of pound cake, pay the compliments of the day, and depart. But the rowdies, who had been gaining the ascendancy to the inner circles of Tammany Hall, were not accustomed to such mundane niceties. When the mayor's doors opened at ten that morning, a crowd bolted into the house and took the place by storm. Bottles of spirits were emptied in a moment, the food was promptly devoured, and furniture was soon in disarray. Men grabbed pieces of turkey and beef with their hands, wiped their greasy fingers on the curtains, and spat on the carpet. The place was a bedlam; the guests quarreled and became drunk. Finally, in desperation, Mayor Lawrence, aided by his police, cleared the house and locked the doors.[15]

As the year 1837 began, the economic situation appeared bright. Yet, within a few weeks the appearance of prosperity was gone. A financial panic engulfed much of the United States and New York City was hit hard. Unemployment soared. Rents, foodstuffs, and fuel were costly. Prices were inflated. In February 1837 an angry mob of two hundred men battered down the doors of a New York City flour warehouse. Nearly five hundred barrels of flour and a thousand bushels of wheat were taken from the place and strewn in the street. By May almost two hundred fifty business failures had been reported in the city. There were runs on banks. The president of the Mechanics Bank died of "mental excitement and apoplexy." The banks, unable to withstand the runs, were forced to suspend specie payments. Confidence was shattered as bankruptcy and want overspread the nation.[16]

Even Tammany Hall suffered a temporary political setback in the spring elections of 1837. Aaron Clark, a Whig, who had made a fortune from lotteries, was elected mayor. Tammany also lost control of the Common Council, which proceeded to remove Tammany men from various offices.[17]

At the beginning of 1838 almost one third of the laborers in New York City were substantially or wholly out of work. At least ten thousand persons were reduced to utter poverty. And while the Whig party kept at a distance from the poor, Tammany Hall embarked on a relief program. Tammany leader John M. Bloodgood collected food from charitable citizens and distributed it to the needy. Other Tammany men provided clothing, food, and sometimes money to the destitute.[18]

In the 1838 elections, brazen frauds were perpetrated by both Tammany Hall and the Whigs. Aliens, ineligible to vote, were brought to the polls to cast their votes. Repeaters voted in several wards. Robert Swartwout, once an influential Tammany leader and now a Whig, arranged for the transportation of two hundred bullies from Philadelphia to New York City to vote in the election. Each man was paid $22 and given a bonus of $5 for voting in several wards. Inmates in the House of Detention were brought to the polls, and cabins of vessels along the wharves were combed for live bodies that could be rushed to the voting places.[19]

At the time that New York City was in the throes of economic and financial disaster, several Tammany chieftains were caught with their hands in the public till—a commonplace by now. Late in 1838 it was disclosed that Tammany leader Samuel Swartwout, who had been appointed collector of the port by President Jackson, had systematically manipulated government accounts and stolen $1,222,705.69. This onetime lieutenant and colleague of Aaron Burr thereby gained the dubious distinction of being the first American to steal a million dollars. He had used much of the loot to invest in Texas land, gold mines, and various get-rich schemes. Tammany sachem Jesse Hoyt, who succeeded Swartwout as collector of the port, was involved in defalcations amounting to $30,000. And the accounts of still another Tammany stalwart, the brawling William M. Price, U.S. district attorney in New York City, revealed that he had stolen $72,124.06. At the time Swartwout and Price were named to their high federal positions, neither could have obtained "credit upon his personal responsibility for a hundred dollars." Both Swartwout and Price fled to Europe. Price escaped on the

British steamer *Liverpool* on December 6, 1838, just an hour or two before his peculations were made public. As an indication, perhaps, of the morals of the time, the *New York Herald* on December 10, 1838, unashamedly stated that "defalcations are no crime."[20]

The general demoralization of society, the venality of politicians, and the ineptness of the police provided an ideal climate for the underworld to flourish and become organized. Since the early 1800s, the gambling business had prospered in the city. The *Niles Weekly Register* on January 8, 1831, observed that "New York is infested by an extensive gang of accomplished gamblers and their depredations are to an enormous amount." The *New York Herald* on July 30, 1835, reported the presence of "splendid" gambling halls in which young men with property were being sent to perdition in no time. These places were elegantly furnished and provided their patrons with sumptuous meals prepared by dexterous cooks and served by waiters and cunning porters. Such places were never molested by the authorities.[21]

Conditions in New York City were also favorable for gamblers from other parts of the country. For instance, gamblers from Mississippi River towns swarmed into New York City following citizens' uprisings in the summer of 1835. The gamblers had formed the backbone of a vicious underworld that had become intolerable. A mass meeting held in Vicksburg, Mississippi, declared, "For years past, the gamblers have made our city their place of rendezvous . . . no citizen is ever secure from their villainy." Notices were posted giving the gamblers twenty-four hours to leave the place. Five gamblers were lynched and their bodies were left hanging in doorways for twenty-four hours "as a warning against those that had escaped." There were uprisings in Natchez and other river towns and law-and-order committees were formed in communities from Cincinnati to New Orleans.[22]

The outlaw gamblers and sharpers found New York City congenial, prospering as never they had before. Confederates of the blacklegs roamed the streets and lured suckers into games where they were mercilessly swindled. Working arrangements were maintained between gambling places and prostitution houses. But the most important alliance was that with political leaders.[23]

Money needed to finance political campaigns and to line the pockets of greedy politicians came from gamblers, prostitution houses, saloonkeepers, and gunmen, as well as from aspiring candidates and officeholders. An official document of the Board of Aldermen for 1836–37 acknowledged the presence of a "great number of gambling houses in the city" and revealed that in one year 2,937 saloon licenses had been granted—almost one to every hundred inhabitants. A statement published in 1838 charged that $600,000 was yearly collected from dives, gambling houses, and prostitutes, and extorted from prisoners in the Tombs and police courts. By 1838 the reliance of political leaders on the underworld for campaign funds had become an established practice. And that practice was the solid base for organized crime.[24]

Criminals could easily become organized because law enforcement remained disorganized. The principal police agency, the watch service, was entirely too small and its ranks were filled with incompetent political hacks. A report of the Committee on Police presented to the Common Council on February 12, 1838, revealed that the watch service had been subjected to little supervision; virtually no regulation or order existed in the service and there were no rules covering the entire department. Practically, each watch district functioned as a separate entity. Each captain laid down rules for his district which might be contrary to those promulgated by captains of other districts. An incompetent watchman discharged for neglect of duty could proceed to another district, where he would probably be hired with no questions asked.[25]

The weak, disorganized law-enforcement setup in New York City could not hope to offer any effective resistance to the underworld, which had been growing stronger nearly without interruption. And other government agencies were little better prepared to cope with serious problems affecting the health and welfare of the people. The prevalence of filth and unsanitary conditions resulted in periodic threats of yellow fever and cholera. In July 1839 the distinguished civic leader and diarist George Templeton Strong lamented, ''The whole city's one huge pigsty, only it would have to be cleaned before a prudent farmer would let his pigs into it for fear of their catching the plague.''[26]

Most unhealthful of all, perhaps, was the corrupt and incompetent political leadership of the city. And coming to the fore, as future rulers of the metropolis, were men showing little promise of lifting the city out of its mire. In 1839 the chairman of the Young Men's General Committee of Tammany Hall was Fernando Wood and its secretary was Richard B. Connolly. Within a few years, Wood, aided by effective alliances with the gangster element, was to become boss of Tammany Hall and the mayor of New York City. Connolly would make history as one of the infamous leaders of the Tweed Ring, which systematically plundered the city of millions of dollars.[27]

Disasters from fires continued to plague the city. After three destructive fires within an eight-day period early in 1840, the *Weekly Herald* on February 15 reported that almost 150 fires, as well as nineteen riots, had occurred during the previous ten months. The fire losses amounted to $7 million.

The fire department was shamefully incompetent. The engines were not sufficiently powerful to throw water to any great height; the hydrants were unable to furnish an adequate supply of water; and much of the available water was dissipated because the hoses were full of rips and holes. The fire engines were manned in part by the lawless elements, including members of such gangs as the Bowery Boys. Rivalry between engine companies was bitter. Engines were sometimes stolen and fights broke out between the rival companies. Clubs, wrenches, and pipes were used as weapons and many of the melees ended with broken skulls.[28]

Although many citizens often voiced complaints about conditions in the city, Tammany Hall showed little interest in reform of any kind. It was concerned solely with winning elections and satisfying the greed of its rulers. Because of flagrant frauds at the polls, the legislature introduced a bill in May 1839 providing for the registration of voters and penalties for illegal voting. Tammany Hall promptly labeled the bill an effort to deprive the poor man of voting privileges. The Common Council on March 16, 1840, denounced the proposed measure as inquisitorial and a reproach to New York City.[29]

Since 1823, foreigners had been used successfully by Tammany Hall to help swell its pluralities at the polls. Beginning in 1840, however, corralling the immigrant vote was turned into an efficient system. A special committee was established in the wigwam to aid aliens in obtaining naturalization papers and, of course, to convert them to loyal adherents of Tammany Hall. Between January 14 and April 1, 1840, Tammany Marine Court judges issued naturalization papers to 895 immigrants.[30]

In 1840, for the first time, New York City elections were held on one day only. Previously the elections lasted for three days. At the spring election on April 14, Tammany elected its candidate for mayor, Isaac L. Varian, and also continued its control of the Common Council. The fall election was held on November 4, 1840. Many aliens participated in the electioneering. On the night of November 3, "A mighty army of . . . banditti paraded the streets . . . attacking every place where the Whigs met. National Hall, in Canal Street, the conservative headquarters, was besieged. . . . All the windows of this large building are broken, bushels of brickbats cover the floors, and the doors show where the ruffians endeavored to gain admission by setting fire to the house." Thus wrote Philip Hone, who pessimistically concluded: "Scenes of violence, disorder, and riot have taught us in this city that universal suffrage will not do for large communities."[31]

It is very unlikely that Hone sympathized with Thomas Jefferson's conviction about the essential "goodness and wisdom" of the common man.

4

GANGS ACHIEVE POLITICAL IMPORTANCE

During the 1840s the gangs became entrenched in the political life of the city. They played an important part in the election of Tammany leader Robert H. Morris as mayor in 1841 and in his reelection in 1842. In advancing his candidacy, fighting had been heavy in the bloody Sixth Ward, the home of the Five Points gangs. Members of gangs were on such familiar terms with the mayor that they felt free to pat him on the shoulder and affectionately call him Bob.[1]

One gang leader, Mike Walsh, appeared with his retinue of plug-ugly followers at a meeting of the General Committee of Tammany Hall on November 1, 1842, and boldly demanded that he be nominated for a seat in the Assembly. Overawed by this show of brute force, Tammany Hall placed his name on the ticket. Although he was subsequently defeated, Walsh had demonstrated that an aspiring candidate, backed by a band of fearsome gangsters, could easily secure a nomination at the wigwam. Other ambitious politicians emulated Walsh and assembled gangs of their own as part of their strategy to control their wards. They became the absolute masters of their domain and advanced to positions of such influence in Tammany Hall that all office seekers, reputable and disreputable, found it necessary to curry their favor if they hoped to be elected.[2]

It was during this period that Captain Isaiah Rynders was rising to a place of great influence in the inner circles of Tammany Hall. He had arrived in New York City in the mid-1830s following a turbulent career as a gambler, as well as a pistol and bowie-knife fighter, along the Mississippi River. He still bore the battle scars of knife wounds on his head and other parts of his body. Once a bullet from an adversary's gun had pierced his hat. During a gambling operation on a Mississippi River steamboat, the loser in a faro game attempted to kill the winner. Rynders grabbed a red-hot poker and chased the assailant from the steamboat saloon. After taking leave of the Mississippi River, Rynders landed in Washington, D.C., where he was arrested as a suspect in the theft of valuable U.S. Treasury notes.

Rynders found New York City an ideal place in which to develop his talents. He became a saloonkeeper, a perfect vocation for an aspiring political boss of a ward. He owned a half-dozen green groceries, then the base of many gang operations. For some time he made his headquarters at the well-known Sweeney's House of Refreshment at 11 Ann Street. Both sides of the street were filled with low-class gambling houses and eating places and the area attracted rowdies, gamblers, thieves, and criminals of every description. Rynders became the owner of a saloon called the Arena at 28 Park Row. In 1843, he organized the Empire Club at this address. It became the headquarters for gangsters and at the same time it was from the Empire Club that Rynders governed the politics of the Sixth Ward and made arrangements to keep his henchmen out of jail. His rule over the Five Points gangs was absolute.[3]

Rynders' followers included prizefighters, most of whom were allied with the underworld. In fact, many pugilists owned interests in gambling "skinning" houses. When prizefights were staged, mainly in Staten Island, Westchester, and along the North River, crowds of several thousand attended the matches. Wagering was brisk. Between bouts, the gamblers often used known fighters as cappers (decoys) to lure heavy wagers on specified contestants.

One of the most celebrated prizefights of the era was held on the bank of the North River in Hastings, New York, on September 13, 1842. Tom McCoy and Chris Lilly, an employee of a notorious gambler, Jack Wallis, and a henchman of Isaiah Rynders, battled with their bare fists for 119 rounds. During the fight, which lasted two hours and forty-three minutes, McCoy was knocked down eighty-one times before he fell dead in the ring. Lilly evaded arrest but three men who had served as seconds during the fight were taken into custody. One was the well-known Yankee Sullivan, whose real name was James Ambrose, reputedly an escaped convict from Australia. At a trial in Westchester, New York, on November 28, 1842, a jury brought in a verdict of "guilty of manslaughter in the fourth degree." Lilly had fled to England, arriving in Liverpool on October 30, 1842. Before long he returned to New York City, where he enjoyed the protection of Isaiah Rynders and was never molested by the police. In 1848 Lilly went to New Orleans, where he organized gangs of repeaters, Tammany-style, to help the Democratic politicians control that Mississippi River city.[4]

For a number of years, Isaiah Rynders, the boss of the Five Points gangs, steadily gained influence in Tammany Hall politics. His Empire Club, shortly after its organization, staged thirty-three political parades and was hired to aid the cause of the Democratic party in Albany, Trenton, and other cities. On occasion, rival political clubs were encountered and fighting invariably erupted. In 1844 the importance of Isaiah Rynders was dutifully acknowledged when he was made a member of the General Committee of Tammany Hall.[5] This underworld boss was now solidly ensconced among the ruling elite of the dominant political organization of the city. A pattern of organized crime had been firmly established. And this pattern was to prevail, almost uninterruptedly, for the next hundred years.

By 1844 the population of New York City had grown to about 350,000. In addition, there was a floating population of an estimated 50,000 persons, many of whom were described at the time as "wicked and debased." Riots were frequent, many persons were killed, and property losses were high. A special committee of the Board of Aldermen in 1843 attributed many of the evils and misfortunes of the city to a police system that had become paralyzed through incompetence, inefficiency, and political control.

Actually, the very nature of the police system created an impossible situation. In the daytime, policing the city was entrusted to sixteen officers appointed by the mayor plus 108 Sunday officers and 100 mayor's marshals who served the courts and were authorized to act as general peace officers. Thirty-four constables were also elected, two from each ward. This disjointed day police force was thus entirely political in character. City administrations were elected for one-year terms; hence police personnel were subject to constant change.

Completely independent of the day police force was the night watch service. The night watch was divided into six districts, each of which had two captains and four assistant captains. Assigned to the captains and assistant captains in the six districts were 1,096 watchmen, who were appointed and controlled by members of the City Council. Only one half of the force was on duty each night since each watchman, as well as captains and assistant captains, served only on alternate nights.

For many years, criminals and mobs had enjoyed little restraint in New York City. As one police historian, Raymond B. Fosdick, noted, "A handful of unorganized 'day policemen' or a few ward watchmen could not hope to contend with serious conditions of disorder" then prevailing.

The ineffective method of policing that existed in New York City existed in all American municipalities. The first practical step to remedy the situation was taken by the New York legislature in 1844, when it passed a law creating a unified "day and night police" force for New York City. This act abolished the watch service and established a force of eight hundred men, who were to serve under the direction of a chief of police, appointed by the mayor with the consent of the council. The New York Act of 1844 formed the basis for modern police organization in America. Within a few years, unified day and night police forces were established in many other cities.

The commonsense approach of the New York legislature was not readily acceptable to the New York City politicians, however. Because of local official bickering, the city ordinance necessary for the law to become effective was not passed until May 23, 1845. And the new law perpetuated basic evils of the old system. All policemen, including captains and assistant captains, were appointed for one year and only upon nomination by the aldermen and assistant aldermen of the wards in which they belonged. The New York City Police Department thus remained "a ward affair, used to satisfy the demands for district patronage, and the chief of police was a figurehead with no authority and little honor."[6]

In the spring election of 1844 Tammany suffered one of its temporary setbacks. Flagrant, widespread abuses, including the exploitation of foreigners to win elections, had led to a reform movement that threw its support to the Native American party. James Harper, the Native American candidate, was elected mayor. In the 1844 fall election campaign, Tammany Hall went all out to carry the city for its favorite presidential candidate, James K. Polk. During an electioneering torchlight parade on November 1, 1844, Tammanyites carried banners with such pro-Polk slogans as "Polk and Texas" and a prejudicial anti-Negro streamer reading "Down with the Coons." Another banner declared "Americans Shan't Rule Us!" Polk, who became the eleventh president of the United States, undoubtedly was grateful for the support he had received from Tammany Hall. During a visit to New York City two years later, Polk was escorted to the wigwam on June 26, 1847, and formally initiated into the membership of the Tammany Society.[7]

Year after year, the population of New York City was swelled by the thousands of immigrants who arrived from Ireland, Germany and other European countries. During the period 1847–52, 1,339,999 immigrants landed in the port of New York. Many continued on to other cities in America but a large portion settled in New York City. Misrepresentations by unscrupulous agents had deceived thousands of Europeans into spending their last penny for passage to the New World; they thus arrived friendless and destitute. On one ship, the *Garrick*, which landed in New York in January 1847, twelve persons had died during the passage. Others passed away after arrival. Of the thousands of foreigners settling in New York City, many were not only ignorant and penniless but vicious as well. Philip Hone expressed the fear that New York had arrived at the state of society to be found in the large European cities, which were overburdened by a population consisting of two extremes—those living in luxury, expensive establishments and improvident waste and others existing in squalid misery and hopeless destitution.[8]

Only about "one minute's walk from that Broadway point of wealth, commerce, and enjoyment" was a center of degradation—the Five Points district. One tenement building, known as the Old Brewery, housed over three hundred human wrecks—thieves, pickpockets, prostitutes, neglected children. A filthy narrow path on one side of the structure was appropriately known as Murderer's Alley. Extending throughout the building were dark winding passageways. Double rows of rooms were entered by alleyways. The rooms were stark and barren. Newspapers were pasted on walls to take the place of the plaster that had long since crumbled away. When the place was visited in 1850, old men were observed trying to keep warm by burning a few sticks, unfortunate women were suffering from horrible diseases, and a young lad was sitting at a gaming table with old ruffians. In one basement room of less than fifteen feet square, twenty-six persons had been living together. People slept on the bare floor or on piles of filthy rags. The stench in the place was unbearable. The tenement building was a headquarters for vice, drunkenness, sickness, crime, violence, and misery.[9]

There were, of course, many districts in the city besides Five Points in which destitution and misery were commonplace. Such areas served as breeding places for violence and illness. In 1849 cholera again reached epidemic dimensions in the city. An official report in July disclosed that during the preceding week, deaths from cholera had exceeded one hundred each day. It was not until September that the epidemic was brought under control.[10]

Many of the "men of violence" used by Tammany Hall to win elections came from the city slums in which depravity abounded. The Five Points gangs, under the iron-clad rule of Isaiah Rynders, were important cogs in the Tammany machine, helping it build pluralities at the polls. And it was a rare occasion, indeed, when disapproval of such tactics was voiced by anyone from within Tammany itself. However, following a Tammany defeat in 1849, a politician of note, W. D. Wallach, mounted the rostrum in the wigwam and spoke out frankly about the reasons for the loss of voter support. He said that men of dishonesty, aided by bullies and loafers, not only had crept into the organization but had wielded great power at Tammany primary elections. And such elections, he said, everybody knew had been arranged "upon the assumption that by a free application of money, violence, and roguery, the people could and should be controlled." With violence and fraud notoriously attending the activities of the Tammany nominating committees, it was no wonder, Wallach said, that thousands of respectable Democrats had ceased to bow to the authority of regular nominations.[11]

With some segments of the population, violence continued to be a way of life. Uncontrollable riots broke out over seemingly minor and trivial incidents.

For a number of years, bitter professional jealousy had existed between William Macready, a British actor, and Edwin Forrest, an American tragedian who was the hero of the Bowery Boys and other ruffians. On May 7, 1849, Macready appeared on the stage at the Astor Place Opera House and was greeted by an angry mob of rowdies who threw eggs and hurled chairs. Under this barrage, the British actor was forced to withdraw from the stage, and he announced that his future engagements in the theater were being canceled. Many, however, persuaded him to make another effort to play Macbeth at the Astor Place Opera House on May 10. The opportunity for another assault on the British actor was not lost on such worthies as Captain Isaiah Rynders and other leaders of the hoodlums. The city was flooded with inflammatory placards. Some alleged that the British crew of a ship then in port intended to support their countryman with arms. Others urged Americans to defend their country against foreign insult.

On the night of May 10 the theater was packed, and thousands of men looking for trouble milled outside. As the play opened, wild disorder broke out. Theater windows were smashed and doors demolished. A detachment of troops—sixty cavalrymen and some three hundred infantrymen—was rushed to the theater. Brickbats and rocks were hurled at the troops and several were injured. Finally, out of desperation or fear, orders were given to fire. Twenty-two persons were killed and many others were wounded. Throughout the night and following day, the theater was guarded by troops. The police force was augmented by a thousand special constables stationed throughout the area. The Astor Place theater riot was among the most celebrated in New York City history, and its chief architect, say some historians, was the underworld boss and political leader Captain Isaiah Rynders.[12]

One of the most turbulent sections of New York City during the 1840s and 1850s was a short block on Ann Street between Broadway and Nassau Streets. Both sides of the street were lined with vicious gambling dens and low-class restaurants. Constantly milling from curb to curb were gangsters from the Five Points and the Bowery, brawling volunteer firemen, shoulder-hitting bruisers from Tammany Hall around the corner, pickpockets, thieves, confidence men, and gamblers.

Many of the gambling houses in the district were known as wolf traps. Owners of such places provided the gambling paraphernalia and sold chips to faro dealers, who set up their own games, with the house receiving a percentage of the winnings. Patrons consisted almost exclusively of gangsters, thieves, and bullies. "Bonneting," a form of robbery, was commonplace. Several ruffians standing around a game would suddenly throw a blanket over the dealer. While he was attempting to extricate himself, his money and chips were stolen. The proprietor of the joint would cash the chips even though he knew they had been obtained through robbery.

Somewhat superior to the wolf traps in accommodations were the second-class "skinning houses" that flourished in the city. Many were located on Broadway, the Bowery, and Chatham Street and served as sites for fake auctions. Although an estimated hundred second-class gambling resorts were in operation, the more prosperous dens were controlled by only a few sharpers, including Jack Wallis, who had ties to Isaiah Rynders. After Wallis acquired control of a resort on Park Place in the 1840s, it became a congregating place for prizefighters. Nightly, the pugilists, thieves, confidence men, and other underworld characters rubbed elbows at the same gaming tables with clerks, mechanics, and merchants.

Also plentiful in the city were the so-called first-class gambling establishments. Many were elaborately furnished and provided the players with sumptuous dinners and costly wines. Patrons included merchants, clerks, lawyers, politicians, and officers of the army and navy. Most of the first-class gambling resorts were owned by less than a score of men. Each of these individuals had an interest in several establishments. The most successful, as well as the most opulent, of the gambling entrepreneurs was Reuben Parsons, who had come to New York City from New England in the 1830s. For twenty-five years his principal partner was Henry Colton. Several protégés of Parsons became big gambling-house proprietors. Among them were Sam Suydam, once a follower of the Bowery Boys, and Joe Hall, who eventually became known as the gambling king of New York City.

Cheating was flagrant at all gambling resorts, including the first-class establishments. Ropers were used to lure suckers into these places, where they were diligently plucked. Defaulters from banks and mercantile concerns often helped swell the profits of the gambling-house owners.

All of the city's gambling resorts operated with assurance of official protection. Typical was the case of a man who appeared before a police magistrate in January 1849 and complained that he had been cheated in a den on Park Place. The judge refused to issue a warrant for the dishonest proprietor. Instead, he threw the complainant in jail. The victim was able to gain his release only by agreeing to withdraw his charges.

During the 1840s, policy gambling was a well-organized business in New York City. For about fifteen years, John Frink owned or controlled over three hundred wide-open policy shops scattered up and down Manhattan Island. Although known as the policy king, Frink was merely the front man for Reuben Parsons, who remained behind the scenes and pulled the strings in the city's far-flung policy operations.

The *New York Herald* in 1850 declared editorially that New York City was "the great headquarters of the gamblers in this country." Horace Greeley in the *New York Tribune* reported that throughout the metropolis the gamblers were "numerous, daring, and most pernicious." He charged that the chief of police and his department knew where five hundred gambling halls nightly operated but that he had failed to take any action.

A group of prominent citizens held public meetings to discuss the gambling situation, now grown intolerable. On July 1, 1850, the New York Association for the Suppression of Gambling was formed and several influential citizens, including Horace Greeley, were elected officers. A reformed gambler, Jonathan Green, was employed as executive agent. A mass meeting featuring such speakers as Greeley was held at the Broadway Tabernacle on February 20, 1851. The association committed itself to an energetic campaign to get enacted a bill that would provide prison terms and substantial fines for gambling. Such a bill, previously defeated by the gambling interests, was enacted by the state legislature on July 10, 1851.[13]

During this period many sections of the city were breeding places of degradation, vice, and misery. Countless women and men endured long hours of monotonous drudgery to eke out a bare subsistence. Hordes of persons existed by thievery. Numberless children virtually lived on the streets. The diarist George Templeton Strong wrote in 1851 that "no one can walk the length of Broadway without meeting some hideous troop of ragged girls, from twelve years old down, brutalized already beyond redemption by premature vice, clad in the filthy refuse of the rag picker's collections, obscene of speech, the stamp of childhood gone from their faces, hurrying along with harsh laughter and foulness on their lips . . . with thief written in their cunning eyes and whore on their depraved faces, though so unnatural, foul, and repulsive in every look and gesture that that last profession seems utterly beyond their aspirations. On a rainy day such crews may be seen by dozens. They haunt every other crossing and skulk away together, . . . the most revolting object that the social diseases of a great city can produce."[14]

5

EMERGENCE OF THE BOSSES

During its first sixty years of existence, the Tammany Society had established a continuing pattern of gross corruption. No single individual, however, had been able to exercise boss control over the Society or the city. This picture was to change in the early 1850s when Fernando Wood, a crook and a demagogue, became the first of a long succession of absolute monarchs over Tammany Hall.

Fernando Wood, the son of a dry-goods merchant, Benjamin Wood, was born in Philadelphia on June 14, 1812. During the panic of 1816 and 1817 the father's business failed; and apparently because of financial reverses, he suffered a nervous breakdown in 1819. Following a doctor's advice, the family traveled in the South and even visited in Cuba. While on this trip, Fernando's brother, Benjamin, was born in Shelbyville, Kentucky, on October 13, 1820. About one year later, in 1821, the Wood family settled in New York City.

When only twenty years of age, Fernando opened his own "Wine and Segar" shop at 322 Pearl Street. He became so absorbed in the game of politics that the business failed within three years. About 1836 he opened a grocery and grog shop at the corner of Washington and Recter Streets, one block from the busy waterfront.

On July 11, 1836, Fernando Wood became a member of Tammany Hall and within three years was named chairman of Tammany's Young Men's General Committee. Through the Society's backing Wood was elected to Congress in 1840 for one term but was defeated when he ran for reelection in 1842.

In the meantime, Wood's grog shop was a highly profitable enterprise. He sold bad liquor to members of stevedore gangs, who were employed on ships lying at nearby docks. Wood had arranged with the employers of the gangs to have them paid off in his groggery. The amounts owed for liquor were deducted from the wages of the men. Undoubtedly Wood padded the liquor bills, but in any dispute his word was accepted by the stevedores' employers. It was a good arrangement, particularly for the unscrupulous Wood. Profits from the business were exorbitant and before long Wood purchased three sailing vessels, subsequently adding other ships to his fleet.

In 1849 Wood's ship, the *John W. Carter,* filled with supplies, was one of the first to reach San Francisco following the discovery of gold in California. Enormous profits were realized from this venture, which was undertaken jointly with Wood's brother-in-law, Edward E. Marvine, who learned, to his chagrin, that he had been defrauded. After Wood had made the purchases to outfit the ship, he arranged to have the invoices altered to show that he had paid considerably more than his actual outlay for the merchandise. These bills were presented to Marvine, who paid Wood his share of the inflated prices on the invoices. Marvine learned of the swindle through some of the merchants who had sold the goods to Wood and he filed a suit in the New York State Supreme Court asserting that Wood had defrauded him of $8,000. The court appointed three referees, who recommended damages and overcharges aggregating more than $15,000 in Marvine's favor. The civil suit was followed by an indictment, which charged Wood with having obtained money under false pretenses. Wood beat the criminal case by pleading the technical defense that the statute of limitations had expired. A friendly recorder, F. A. Tallmadge, held that the indictment had been returned one day too late, thus barring Wood's prosecution. Later it was charged that Tallmadge had cashed a Wood check for $500 in a city bank shortly after he had rendered his decision.[1]

Wood was a man of great personal ambition and his immediate primary political goal was to become mayor of New York City. Under a new charter, the mayor's term of office had been lengthened to two years. Tammany Hall had also adopted the convention system in selecting candidates. The first general convention was held in October 1850 and Wood received the nomination for mayor. This action outraged many decent citizens, including Philip Hone, who wrote indignantly in his diary on October 16, 1850, "Fernando Wood, instead of occupying the mayor's seat, ought to be on the rolls of the state prison." The unsavory personal character of Wood, as well as of many other Tammany candidates, caused many Democrats to revolt against the Tammany ticket in the November 1850 election. Thus Wood was defeated by the Whig candidate, Ambrose C. Kingsland, who became the new mayor of New York City.[2]

At the next mayoral election in 1852, Tammany Hall found it expedient to bypass Wood and nominate a wealthy and respectable shipbuilder, James A. Westervelt, who was elected. Tammany was also concerned with the presidential election that year, and among the delegates it sent to the Democratic convention in Baltimore were gang leaders Isaiah Rynders and Mike Walsh.

At the primaries in August 1852, almost every voting place was the scene of violence and fraud. In some instances, one faction took possession of the polls and physically prevented opponents from voting. Numerous ballot boxes were half filled with "properly marked" ballots before the voting even started. In some wards with less than a thousand legal Democratic voters, two thousand votes were counted. Aldermen had their gangs of lawbreakers on duty at the polls. The same aldermen also appointed the policemen, who, if they expected to retain their jobs, could ill afford to notice any violation. If by chance a gang member was arrested, he was tried in the mayor's court, where aldermen sat as justices.[3]

The average citizen viewed the situation with disgust and a feeling of hopelessness. George Templeton Strong wrote in his diary in July 1852 that "the Common Council is notoriously profligate and corrupt; the police force partly awed by the blackguards of the brothel and groggery, partly intimate with them. And if some drunken ruffian is arrested, he's sure to be discharged by some justice or alderman, who feels that it won't do to lose the support of the particular gang to which he belongs." With protected crime, violence and corruption getting more and more out of hand, citizens were discussing privately the desirability, as a last resort, of forming vigilante committees.[4]

On February 26, 1853, a grand jury handed down a presentment that revealed that the city was honeycombed with corruption. Bribes totaling more than $30,000 had been paid in 1852 by grantees of the Third Avenue Railroad franchise. Of this amount, $3,000 went to Alderman William M. Tweed, then a member of the aldermanic board aptly characterized as the Forty Thieves. The grand jury found that huge bribes had been paid to obtain ferry leases, pavement contracts, and pier leases. Applicants for the police force were required to pay money to the aldermen who appointed them. Almost every saloon served as the headquarters for some gang, a gang that was active in corralling votes and winning elections. Both the aldermen and the police personnel regularly collected money from the saloons. It was disclosed that although twenty-nine aldermen were at one time under judgment of contempt of court and some were under indictment for bribery, they had, as provided by law, continued to act as judges in the criminal courts.[5]

The police department, controlled by the corrupt aldermen and assistant aldermen, was largely a big joke, a conglomeration of ragtag misfits. Refusing to wear uniforms because they were considered "undemocratic" and "un-American," officers of the law were indistinguishable from the average man on the street. If a policeman were needed suddenly by day or night, a writer in 1853 asked, where would you look for him? "Look at their style of dress," he said, "some with hats, some with caps, some with coats like Joseph's of old, parti-colored. If they were mustered together they would look like Falstaff's regiment. . . . They inspire no respect, they create no fear." And, he observed, "Hardly a day passes but the thief or felon turns around and attacks the policeman."[6]

Following the grand-jury presentment in February 1853, clamor for reform peaked. The legislature passed a new charter for New York City, which was submitted to popular vote on June 7, 1853, and adopted by a margin of 36,000 to 3,000. Under the new charter, the Board of Assistant Aldermen was abolished. Created to take its place was a Board of Councilmen, to be made up of sixty members. The Common Council was to consist collectively of the Board of Aldermen and the Board of Councilmen. Also abolished was the right of aldermen to sit as judges in the court of sessions and the court of oyer and terminer.[7]

A special target of the reform movement in 1853 was the New York City Police Department. The new charter placed the power of appointment and dismissal of members of the force in the hands of a newly created Board of Police Commissioners consisting of the mayor, the recorder, and the city judge. For the next forty-eight years the police department was to be under the legal control of some form of a police board. The legislature purportedly intended the police board setup to eliminate partisan political control of the department. Yet policemen were still appointed for one year only and political faithfulness remained the principal guideline for appointment or dismissal.[8] A regulation also mandated that New York City police officers wear uniforms but the regulation was meaningless. Some members of the department donned uniforms, others refused. And each ward decided upon its own special style of uniform. The New York City Police Department, as of July 1, 1853, consisted of 1,004 officers: the chief of police, 20 captains, 40 lieutenants (previously called assistant captains), 79 sergeants, and 864 policemen.[9]

The reform measures of 1853 were of little concern to the wily politician and demagogue Fernando Wood. He was busy laying plans to take over the rule of the city and had his eyes fixed on the 1854 mayoral campaign. Figuring prominently in his grand design were the Five Points gangs, controlled by Isaiah Rynders, political boss of the Sixth Ward. Also arriving on the scene during this period was the colorful gang fighter, professional pugilist, and gambler John Morrissey. For a quarter of a century he was to be a dominant figure in New York's gambling racket as well as a leader in politics. While his gambling houses served as resorts for criminals of every variety, Morrissey was to become a member of the state legislature, a congressman, and, for a time, a coleader of Tammany Hall.

Born in Ireland, John Morrissey was three years old when in 1834 he was brought to America by his parents. The family settled in Troy, New York, where Morrissey's father raised gamecocks. While still a teenager, Morrissey became a bartender in Troy. Before long he was the master of the saloon, which was a resort for notorious gamblers, thieves, and dissolute persons. Eventually the authorities closed the place. In the barrooms of the Hudson River boats, Morrissey became an accomplished rough-and-tumble fighter. He also ran afoul of the law on several occasions in hometown Troy. By 1849 he had been indicted twice for burglary, once for assault with intent to kill, and assault and battery. Following a conviction for burglary and assault, he was sentenced to sixty days in jail. Several years later, in 1857, in New York City three indictments were returned against Morrissey charging him with felonious assault with intent to kill.[10]

During one of Morrissey's visits to New York City in the late 1840s he was hanging around Isaiah Rynders' Arena Saloon on Park Row. He boldly asserted that he could lick anybody in the place. Then in the saloon, according to one version, were Tom Hyer, reputed American heavyweight champion, and "Bill the Butcher" Poole, head of a gang of West Side bruisers and terrorists. They accepted Morrissey's challenge. Although beaten, Morrissey put up such a fierce fight that he won the admiration of Rynders, who suggested that he settle permanently in New York City. Another version asserted that the fight took place between Morrissey and Tom Burns, Mike Murray, and six others in the saloon. They reputedly grabbed clubs, bottles, and anything handy as they rushed at Morrissey. An earthen spittoon hurled at Morrissey struck him under the ear and felled him.

Morrissey did not require too much encouragement to settle in New York City permanently and join the Rynders forces. He was without funds and was infatuated with Kate Ridgely, who kept a fashionable brothel at 14 Duane Street. After the big fight in Rynders' saloon, Morrissey returned to Troy but by 1850 was back in New York City working as a shoulder hitter for Rynders. During a local election Morrissey organized a gang of fifty thugs from the Five Points. When Bill the Butcher Poole and his gang arrived at the polls to control the voting, they observed that they were badly outnumbered by the Morrissey forces and diplomatically retreated. As a result of this exploit, Rynders reputedly placed Morrissey in charge of the Dead Rabbits gang and he won the acclaim of Tammany leaders, who provided him with funds to open a small gambling house.[11]

By nature Morrissey was a violent man and that trait was aggravated by excessive drinking. On one occasion Morrissey and a companion, after a drinking spree, entered the barroom of the Girard House on Chambers Street and West Broadway. Morrissey decided that he and his friend should have exclusive use of the barroom and started to clear out the place. He grabbed a water pitcher, which he hurled at the bartender. When a waiter tried to restrain him, Morrissey drew a revolver. The waiter turned on his heels and ran. Morrissey fired blindly. A bullet crashed through the window and pierced the top hat of a businessman walking by the place at the time. In the meantime, the waiter returned to the barroom with two policemen. Morrissey whipped out a dirk and threatened to "rip out the belly" of the first person who came near him. The policemen wisely retreated but returned with reinforcements. By this time the effects of the liquor were wearing off and Morrissey and his companion surrendered peacefully.[12]

In 1851 Morrissey temporarily left New York City and spent some time in San Francisco. He and a stranded artist began operating a faro game in San Francisco and amassed a substantial bankroll. A heavy loser at the game thought he had been cheated and challenged Morrissey to a duel. Morrissey appeared on the field of honor with a pair of butcher's cleavers under his arms and the challenger fled in terror.[13]

At the Democratic convention in 1854, Fernando Wood packed the meeting with his henchmen, who dutifully nominated him for mayor. His opponents in the mayoral election were James W. Barker of the Native American or Know-Nothing party, John J. Herrick, a Whig, and Wilson G. Hunt of the City Reform party.

During the campaign, Wood had the solid support of the saloonkeepers, the gamblers, and the underworld generally. Financial support was given him by prostitutes and female abortionists, including the notorious Madam Restell, who made a practice of contributing to all campaign funds. Serving as principal lieutenants to Wood during the campaign were Isaiah Rynders and John Morrissey.[14]

On the day before the election, George Templeton Strong observed in his diary that candidate Wood apparently had been involved in gross fraud and swindling; his opponent, Barker, had been accused of having set his store afire about eight years earlier in order to cheat an insurance company; and Homes, running for alderman in the First Ward, was then in the Tombs on a charge of murder, having stabbed a policeman to death. "Pretty commentary," wrote Strong, "on republican institutions and representative government as practically exhibited among us."[15]

The *New York Times* attacked Wood as "utterly unfit" and said "it would be a disgrace to the city to elect him mayor." Nevertheless, Wood won the election by a narrow margin and became mayor of New York City on January 1, 1855.[16]

In 1855 crime and rowdyism were rampant in the city. In many sections it was unsafe to walk at night. Men armed with clubs, knives, slingshots, and revolvers roamed the streets at will. Prostitutes wandered up and down Broadway, openly plying their trade. It was estimated that by 1855 thirty thousand men in New York City were in league with gang leaders who in turn were closely allied with influential politicians of Tammany Hall or the Know-Nothing party.[17]

On the night of February 24, 1855, the fighter and saloonkeeper Bill the Butcher Poole, a leader in the Know-Nothing party, stopped at Stanwix Hall for a pint of champagne. Also entering the place about the same time were John Morrissey and several companions, who had been making the rounds of neighborhood bars and were "well-liquored up." An altercation started between Morrissey and Poole. Arriving on the scene at this time were Lewis Baker, California Jim Turner, and "Pargene" McLaughlin, all in a drunken condition. They began hurling insults at Poole, who retorted that he could whip any one of the three men in a fair fight and offered to wager one hundred dollars in gold that he could do so. Turner responded by shooting at Poole twice and hitting him once in the leg. Poole, unarmed, crumpled to the floor and pleaded for his life. Baker then shot the helpless Poole twice in the chest and fled the premises in the company of Turner and McLaughlin. Poole died from his wounds several days later and was deemed a martyr by the Know-Nothing party. In the funeral cortege, some six hundred Know-Nothing party men followed Poole's coffin draped with an American flag. In the huge procession respectable men of the community walked beside notorious gamblers and thugs including Isaiah Rynders, who marched at the head of his gang. In his diary entry for March 13, 1855, Strong records that "two hundred thousand people, they say, were in Broadway; the street was crowded from Bleecker Street to the Ferry." The funeral of Poole surpassed the demonstrations given at the deaths in 1852 of the statesmen Henry Clay and Daniel Webster.[18]

By the second year of Wood's first term as mayor, corruption had permeated every facet of government. City Hall was a marketplace in which every job was for sale. N. Hill Fowler, corporation attorney, later testified that on the night of his appointment he delivered $4,000 to Wood. Pursuant to an agreement, Fowler was required to turn over to Wood his first year's salary and to divide with him the perquisites of the office for the balance of the term. The perquisites amounted to $10,408, which Fowler shared equally with Wood.[19]

Wood was greedy for power and money. Because he refused to give some Tammany leaders a sufficiently large share of the spoils he incurred their disfavor. On September 27, 1856, New York City newspapers published a statement made by secretaries of the Tammany General Committee, J. Y. Savage and Peter B. Sweeny, later an important member of the Tweed Ring. The statement denounced Wood's manipulations and charged that the primary system had become "so corrupt as to be a mere machine in the hands of unprincipled men, by which they foist themselves before the people as the nominees of a party for office in defiance of public sentiment." Sweeny and Savage charged that at primary elections the ballot boxes were stuffed and detachments of police were stationed at every polling place to aid Wood's agents and to bully his opponents.

Wood was renominated by the city convention at an hour when most of his enemies on the General Committee were absent. His Tammany Hall opponents countered by nominating another candidate, James S. Libby. When the Wood ratification meeting in the wigwam took place, a free-for-all erupted. Planks were taken from the platform and used as weapons. The Wood backers physically drove the Libby supporters from the room and chased them down the stairs.[20]

Wood was well fortified with funds to wage his reelection campaign. All city employees under his control were subjected to assessments. Each police officer was required to contribute a minimum of $25. From the police force alone, Wood collected from $8,000 to $10,000. Principal sources of campaign funds were the wide-open brothels and gambling dens that featured marked cards and crooked roulette wheels. The mayor also had a testimonial drawn up and signed by bankers, merchants, and property owners. Among those who signed the statement, which described Wood as the best mayor in New York City history, was William B. Astor, the city's wealthiest man and its largest real estate owner.[21]

On election day, rioting reached staggering dimensions. Staunchly supporting Wood were the gambling-house keepers and the saloon interests. Directing the underworld forces to ensure Wood's victory was the like of Isaiah Rynders and John Morrissey. The Dead Rabbits, the largest and most powerful of the Five Points gangs, and sluggers from the waterfront were solidly in Wood's corner. The Bowery Boys were backing the Know-Nothing candidate, Isaac O. Barker. In the Sixth Ward, the heart of the Five Points, the Bowery Boys succeeded in driving the Dead Rabbits gang patrols from polling places. The Dead Rabbits temporarily retreated to recruit reinforcements from the dives and tenements of Paradise Square. Armed with knives, clubs, axes, brickbats, and pistols, the Dead Rabbits returned to the fray and routed their enemies. At the height of the battle, the police barricaded themselves in a vacant house and restricted their action to firing an occasional shot through the windows. The Fourth Ward was the scene of vigorous street fighting. Some ballot boxes were seized and destroyed. In the First Ward, the nose of a voter was shot off. An unsympathetic bystander shouted that the victim looked better without it. In some instances, citizens called on the police to quell the disturbances, but the minions of the law were allies of Wood and refused to respond. It was charged that ten thousand fraudulent votes were cast, with Wood benefiting the most from the illegal ballots.[22]

Fernando Wood was reelected mayor and took office, a second time, on January 1, 1857. Only a few days later, on January 6, 1857, Governor John King, in his annual message to the legislature, offered some radical proposals to cope with misgovernment in New York City, now a metropolis of 820,000 inhabitants and growing rapidly. He pointed out that the administration of the city "under the present charter" had failed and asked the legislature to give serious consideration to this problem. In particular, the governor stated, a "new police system for the city of New York is . . . required," and added, "Experience renders it certain that the legislature will not entrust the management of that system to the mayor alone."[23]

The need for a more efficient police department was evident to everyone. Street crime was rampant. Garroting was commonplace. Tradesmen were being attacked in broad daylight and robbed. Citizens feared to walk the streets at night and many bought revolvers for protection.[24] Organized criminal gangs—the Dead Rabbits, Empire Club, Mike Walsh's Spartan Band, and others—fought in the streets, often with fatalities. Brawls between fire companies were frequent. Thieves, prostitutes, and cutthroats infested great areas of the city. The members of gangs as well as criminals and vicemongers of all descriptions had close ties with the police and important politicians, and operated with impunity.[25]

On April 15, 1857, the state legislature enacted a bill that created a Metropolitan Police District, which embraced the counties of New York, Kings, Westchester, and Richmond. The new Metropolitan Police District was placed under the control of a Board of Commissioners, five in number, to be appointed by the governor, with the consent of the Senate. The mayors of New York City and Brooklyn were to be ex-officio members of the board. The act declared that the present police force in New York and Brooklyn was to be assimilated by the Metropolitan force and that the local authorities were to be divested of all control. For the next thirteen years the police force of New York City was to remain under state rule. It was not until the charter of 1870 abolished the Metropolitan Police District that the force was returned to municipal control.[26]

Other important measures were enacted by the 1857 legislature. The number of aldermen in New York City was reduced from twenty-two to seventeen and aldermen were now to be elected from the regular assembly districts instead of the wards. The number of councilmen was also reduced, from sixty to twenty-four. The councilmen were to be elected on the basis of six from each senatorial district. The new charter specified that elections for mayor and Common Council were to be held on the first Tuesday in December. The legislature also provided for a new municipal charter election to be held in December 1857, thus cutting Wood's second term as mayor in half![27]

Fernando Wood had no intention of relinquishing control over his municipal police force. The Board of Aldermen supported the mayor's position and directed him to ignore the legislative act that had created the Metropolitan Police District. Thus Mayor Wood refused to recognize the legality of the new Metropolitan Police Department and declined to surrender police property to it or to disband his municipal police force as required by the state legislative act of 1857. As a result, New York City now had two police departments—the municipal force under Wood and the Metropolitan department controlled by the state.

Naturally, the law-enforcement situation was chaotic and a serious clash between the two police forces was inevitable. This occurred on June 16, 1857, when Daniel Conover, whom the governor had appointed as street commissioner, arrived at City Hall to take over his new office. Mayor Wood had supported Charles Devlin for the same post. In fact, there were allegations that Wood had sold the office of street commissioner to Devlin for $50,000. At any rate, Wood ordered his municipal police to throw Conover out of City Hall. Conover promptly obtained a warrant for Mayor Wood's arrest, handed it for service to George Walling, chief of the Metropolitan Police, and accompanied him to City Hall.

Walling entered the mayor's office and informed Wood that he had a warrant for his arrest. Wood belligerently replied, "I do not recognize the legality of the service or the existence of the Metropolitan Police. I will not submit to arrest . . . or concede that you are an officer at all." Walling then told Wood that he would have to take him forcibly. As he walked around the desk to seize Wood, the mayor hit a bell on his desk that summoned a captain and several patrolmen of the municipal force. They grabbed Walling and threw him out of the building. At this juncture, about fifty members of the Metropolitan Police Department arrived and started to march up the City Hall steps. However, they were promptly confronted by almost eight hundred members of the municipal department. The Metropolitan officers were so greatly outnumbered that they felt obliged to retreat temporarily. But they soon regrouped and valiantly charged. Officers of the opposing forces were swinging their clubs wildly at one another. Some men rolled helplessly down the City Hall steps. In the meantime, the battle had attracted a crowd of spectators. Many of the onlookers added to the overall confusion by attacking the Metropolitan officers from the rear. While the battle was raging, the Seventh Regiment happened to be marching down Broadway to board a boat for Boston. The Metropolitan Police appealed to General Charles W. Sanford, the commanding officer of the regiment, who marched his men to the City Hall green and lined them up in parade formation. The appearance of the soldiers ended the battle and restored quiet at City Hall.[28]

The feuding between the two rival police departments presented a tragicomedy—a boon to the criminal classes and a disaster for the decent citizens. Almost invariably when a burglar or robber was arrested by an officer of the Metropolitan department, a municipal policeman would appear on the scene and challenge his rival's jurisdiction. While the two officers were flailing away at each other with their clubs, the criminal would walk away unmolested. This situation prevailed much of the summer while the validity of the act creating the Metropolitan Police District was being challenged in the courts. Finally, the New York Court of Appeals upheld the law. Wood then reluctantly disbanded the municipal force and the Metropolitan department took over law inforcement in the city.[29]

July 1857 was marked by the most disgraceful violence in the city since the Astor Place riots of 1849. The trouble began about two in the morning on July 4, 1857. The Dead Rabbits gang decided to start the Independence Day celebration early by raiding the headquarters of their detested foes, the

Bowery Boys. Proceeding to the Bowery, the Dead Rabbits, armed with clubs and stones, broke windows in a building that had been occupied by their adversaries. Several persons were injured. When police arrived from the Tenth and Thirteenth wards, the Dead Rabbits retreated but their violence continued. As they reached a place near the Five Points, they viciously attacked a group of men, one of whom was mortally wounded. At sunrise many rioters took positions atop houses. There they shot pistols and muskets and showered brickbats and stones on their enemies below. As the day progressed, the fighting intensified. Casualties were heavy. Stretcher bearers were kept busy carrying away the wounded. In Mulberry and Bayard Streets, the Dead Rabbits and Bowery Boys fired at one another from behind barricades of furniture, carts, and wagons.

Early on Sunday, July 5, 1857, the Dead Rabbits, armed with paving blocks and iron bars, swarmed into a Bowery clubhouse and tore it apart. The Bowery Boys rushed to the scene in force and the two gangs again joined battle on Bayard Street at the corner of Chatham Street. A squad of Metropolitan Police attempted to march to the battle grounds but the two feuding gangs temporarily joined hands to fight off any police interference. As the police retreated, the residents of Bowery and Bayard Streets pelted the officers with stones and brickbats from windows and rooftops. At one point came a lull in the fighting, during which screaming hussies from the Five Points district taunted the Dead Rabbits with charges of cowardice. The Dead Rabbits, spurred by the taunts, attacked again. At the height of the conflict, an estimated thousand rioters were involved in the bloody melee. Many of the men who fell wounded on a sidewalk or street were trampled upon. Two days of fighting passed, and the police remained helpless. An attempt was made by Isaiah Rynders, political boss of the Five Points district, to intervene and restore peace. His efforts failed and he was injured in the process. As darkness approached, the rioters set fire to several houses. Finally, as a last resort, the police appealed to General Charles W. Sanford for help. General Sanford ordered three regiments of the militia to the troubled area. With the arrival of soldiers, the rioting ended. Casualties during the two days of disorders included ten killed and eighty wounded.[30]

The smoke of the bloody battles of July 4 and 5 had barely subsided when a new uprising erupted. On July 13, 1857, a mob of about five hundred armed persons, mostly Irish with a sprinkling of Germans, attacked the Metropolitan Police. To quell this new outbreak, it was necessary to call into action over four hundred policemen, and the militia was again placed under an alert. In all of the July disturbances, discharged members of Wood's municipal police force were involved.[31]

Adding to the civic woes in 1857 was the financial panic that struck the metropolis in August and gradually spread throughout much of the country. The financial crisis peaked in mid-October when tremendous runs on almost all banks forced a suspension of specie payments until December 14, 1857. Hundreds of thousands of laborers, skilled workers, and clerks were thrown out of work. Unemployment reached dangerous heights. In the Sixth Ward alone, as many as ten thousand hungry mouths were fed in a single day. In the Seventh Ward money was collected to aid the needy. Of the donors, William M. Tweed headed the list with a gift of $500. Charity now became an established practice and an integral part of Tweed's strategy in achieving and maintaining political power.[32]

Living conditions for large segments of the city's population were deplorable. Thousands of homeless children slept in the hallways of tenement houses, under porches, in cellars, in stables, or among bales of merchandise on the wharves. Crime and disorder were prevalent during broad daylight. At times as many as six murders or murderous assaults would be reported within a twenty-four-hour period. Mayor Wood had made a proposal to employ some of the starving unemployed laborers on a public-works project. However, his meritorious suggestion was accompanied by an appeal to the rabble, an appeal that alarmed many citizens. On November 10, 1857, a mob of disreputable elements, including members of criminal gangs, seized a part of City Hall as well as space in the park. About three hundred policemen were placed on duty inside to protect the building, its occupants, and records. Elsewhere in the city, some one hundred fifty U.S. soldiers and marines were posted in the customhouse and adjoining assay office to protect the treasury of the federal government. Mayor Wood was frightened. Mob orators denounced him as a humbug who had promised aid he could not deliver.[33]

Many decent citizens of New York City strongly felt that the corrupt Wood must be driven from office. The sentiment was spreading inside Tammany Hall, particularly among political opportunists and rivals of Wood. A reform group in Tammany Hall, headed by Samuel J. Tilden, John McKeon, and Isaac V. Fowler, succeeded in nominating Daniel F. Tiemann for mayor. Being sufficiently ingenious, however, Wood was able to bring about his own renomination at a Democratic convention in Tammany Hall. He had the solid support of gamblers, brothelkeepers, and the underworld generally. Working against Wood's reelection was William M. Tweed, who regarded the mayor as a threat to himself and his friends in Tammany Hall. At the election on December 1, 1857, Tiemann received 43,216 votes and Wood 40,889. Although Wood was defeated, the large vote he garnered from the underworld portended ill for government in New York City for many years to come.[34]

Just one week following the election, a meeting of the Democratic General Committee was held in the wigwam on December 8, 1857. Until his defeat for reelection, Wood had controlled this important committee, the chairman of which was Isaiah Rynders, noted gang leader, thug, political boss, and now United States marshal. It was evident that Rynders, who presided over the meeting, was now anti-Wood, and that the defeated mayor was no longer in command of the General Committee.[35]

At a meeting of the Tammany Society in April 1858 it was announced that 212 members had pledged to vote for anti-Wood sachems at the Tammany election, to be held six days later. Heading the anti-Wood ticket within Tammny Hall were Isaac V. Fowler and Nelson J. Waterbury. Wood was thus forced to withdraw from Tammany Hall, but his political power had not been destroyed as Tweed and his cohorts had planned. On April 13, 1858, Wood announced that he was setting up his own political organization, with headquarters in Mozart Hall, at the corner of Bleecker Street and Broadway. Aiding Fernando in establishing the new Mozart Hall Democracy was his brother, Benjamin Wood, the owner of lotteries and the publisher of the *New York Daily News*.[36]

The year 1858 gave New Yorkers a respite from the large-scale rioting and violence that characterized 1857. Attracting wide attention were efforts in the summer months to complete laying the Atlantic cable. Since 1854 the people of New York City had been keenly interested in the project. What especially enlivened their interest was the participation of New Yorkers Cyrus W. Field, Peter Cooper, and Moses Taylor in the monumental undertaking. Thrice the cable had broken but on the fourth attempt it was successfully laid, on August 5, 1858. The accomplishment was wildly hailed in Great Britain as well as in America. In New York City so many fireworks were exploded during a celebration of the affair that the overenthusiastic participants "set the City Hall on fire, burned up its cupola and half its roof, and came near destroying the county clerk's office and unsettling the titles to half the property in the city."[37] The wild demonstrations turned out to be premature. By October 1858 the cable had broken down, and the Civil War was to intervene before a permanently successful cable was laid.

In October 1858 reams of publicity were given to the prizefight scheduled between John Morrissey and John C. Heenan. The fight took place at Long Point in Lake Erie, about eighty miles from Buffalo. It took Morrissey but twenty-one minutes to knock out Heenan. Following his victory over Heenan, Morrissey retired as a professional prizefighter and devoted all of his energies to politics and the development of his gambling enterprises. He was on the threshold of becoming the most powerful gambling-house proprietor in New York City as well as one of the city's highly influential political leaders.[38]

As the year 1859 opened, gloom hung heavily over the business and financial community. Many factories were closed; much shipping was idle; wages, rents, and profits were low. The national administration headed by James Buchanan was held generally in contempt.

In December 1858 Strong had pessimistically recorded in his diary that the signs of the time were blue indeed. The "imminent pressing peril," he said, was "simple barbarism." From a glance at the city's long record of constant, widespread rioting, savage violence and unrestricted corruption, Strong's gloomy outlook was understandable. He suggested that the city had been gravitating toward barbarism for at least twenty years. He said, "Life and property grow less and less secure. Law, legislature, and judiciary are less respected; skepticism spreads as to the existence anywhere of anybody who will not steal if he have official opportunity. Our civilization is decaying."[39]

There was ample evidence to show that vice and crime had been well organized for some time and received iron-clad protection from political leaders such as Isaiah Rynders and Fernando Wood. Even official reports revealed the prevalence of conditions that invariably nurture organized crime. The deputy superintendent of the Metropolitan Police, Daniel Carpenter, in his quarterly report for the period ending January 31, 1859, disclosed that there were 7,779 places where intoxicating liquor was sold at retail. In nineteen precincts there were 496 known houses of prostitution and 84 houses of assignation. There were also 170 lager-beer and drinking saloons combined with houses of prostitution and 185 low-type groggeries in which thieves and prostitutes congregated each day and night.[40]

In addition to disreputable drinking places and vice resorts mentioned in official police reports, it was known that the city was honeycombed with gambling establishments. In 1859 John Morrissey, one of Wood's principal lieutenants, opened, in partnership with Matt Danser, a highly profitable gambling house at Broadway and Great Jones Street. Within five years Morrissey had an interest in sixteen gambling establishments in Manhattan.[41]

The saloonkeepers, vice-resort owners, and gamblers—the usual backbone of organized crime—constituted a major source of Fernando Wood's political strength. His ties with some well-organized criminal gangs had been so notorious that citizens, such as Strong, referred to him disparagingly as the King of the Dead Rabbits. In the 1859 mayoral campaign, Wood ran as the nominee of his Mozart Hall Democracy. His Tammany Hall opponent was the reputable William F. Havemeyer. However, on the Tammany ticket were a half-dozen nominees for councilmen who were under indictment for various crimes. During the campaign, Wood catered to the foreign-born, particularly the Irish voters, and to the numerous southern sympathizers who lived in New York City. But it was his underworld support that played the chief role in his winning the election.[42]

As Wood began his third term as mayor of New York City on January 1, 1860, the crisis between the North and the South was rapidly approaching the point of no return. On May 18, 1860, Abraham Lincoln was nominated for the presidency at the Republican convention in Chicago. In New York City the suave, dapper Republican politician A. Oakey Hall believed it would be a personal disgrace for him to remain in a party that could nominate the unsophisticated Lincoln. Eventually, in a dramatic move, Hall publicly renounced Lincoln and the Republican party and turned Democrat. William M. Tweed promptly embraced the renegade and brought him into Tammany Hall.[43] Both Hall and Lincoln were to gain immortality—Hall by dying in disgrace as a member of the infamous Tweed Ring, and Lincoln by distinguishing himself as one of America's greatest statesmen.

One of the leaders of the movement to force Wood out of Tammany Hall ran into difficulty in 1860. Isaac V. Fowler, grand sachem of Tammany, had been postmaster since his original appointment by President Franklin Pierce several years earlier. Auditors discovered that Fowler had embezzled $155,000 in postal receipts. On May 10, 1860, a federal warrant for Fowler's arrest was handed to Isaiah Rynders, then serving his last year as United States marshal. Rynders, with federal warrant in hand, proceeded to Fowler's hotel, where he stopped at the bar. With every drink he purchased, Rynders loudly announced that he had come to the hotel to arrest Fowler as an embezzler. Not unexpectedly—and probably by design—while the garrulous Rynders tarried at the bar, Fowler escaped and fled to Mexico, where he lived for several years. He returned to America, and died in Chicago in 1869. Succeeding Fowler as postmaster in New York City was General John A. Dix. In August 1860 a delegation of prominent Democrats visited Dix and demanded that he discharge a subordinate who had said "Fowler was little better than a thief."[44]

In the fall of 1860 the prince of Wales, later King Edward VII, made a highly publicized tour of America. He visited the White House, planted a tree at Washington's tomb, and attended balls and dinners given in his honor. In New York City he was cordially received by almost everyone except the Irish. In fact, the Irish Sixty-ninth Regiment under the command of Colonel Michael Corcoran refused to parade in his honor.

Climaxing the prince of Wales' visit to New York City was a grand ball held at the Academy of Music on October 13, 1860. Various dignitaries, including Mayor Fernando Wood, and the "cream" of New York society were invited guests. Serving on the reception committee were such distinguished citizens as Cyrus Field and George Templeton Strong.

As the various guests were being presented to His Royal Highness, the floor suddenly collapsed in two places and a couple of beams over the stage broke. Panic-stricken people fled from the dangerous region and the area was quickly roped off. Within fifteen minutes a crew of carpenters was frantically hammering away to repair the damage. About two hours later, at midnight, the repairs were completed and the dancing started. Although the affair could hardly be called an artistic success, a social fiasco had been partially averted.[45]

A few weeks later, in December 1860, another event of social significance took place. The forty-eight-year-old mayor, Fernando Wood, married Alice Fenner Mills, the sixteen-year-old daughter of a wealthy businessman. The marriage took place one year after the death of the second Mrs. Wood. The new bride had been schooled in Europe and the marriage enhanced Wood's social prestige.[46]

6

THE CIVIL WAR ERA

Just a little over three months before fighting broke out between the states, Fernando Wood, in a message to the Common Council on January 7, 1861, proposed that New York City secede from the state and the Union and set itself up as a free city. Wood had strong bonds with the South. He espoused slavery and reportedly he and brother Benjamin owned lotteries with charters from southern states. In his message to the Common Council, Wood stressed the city's friendly relations with and sympathy for "our aggrieved brethren of the slave states." Benjamin Wood's *Daily News* naturally praised the "free-city" proposal, but most of the local press treated it with contempt. The *Tribune* on January 8, 1861, stated: "Fernando Wood evidently wants to be a traitor; it is lack of courage only that makes him content with being a blackguard."[1]

At the outbreak of the Civil War, both Tammany Hall and Wood's Mozart Hall militantly opposed Lincoln and attempted to subvert the policies of the national administration. Locally, Wood's third term as mayor was steeped in corruption even more disgraceful than that of his previous two administrations.

In the December 1861 election, Wood failed in his bid for a fourth term as mayor. In a very close race George P. Opdyke, a Republican running on the nonpartisan People's Union ticket, was elected. He received only 613 more votes than C. Godfrey Smith, the Tammany candidate, and just 1,213 more votes than Wood. During this period William M. Tweed was gradually gaining control of Tammany Hall. In 1862 an agreement was reached between Tammany Hall and Mozart Hall whereby nominations would be divided between the two organizations. As part of the deal, Wood was to relinquish control over the city, but he and his brother, Benjamin, were to receive seats in Congress.[2]

At the September 1862 Democratic convention in Albany, Horatio Seymour, a fierce opponent of the Lincoln administration, was nominated for governor. Seymour had opposed the emancipation of the slaves and had asserted that the North could never subjugate the South. Henry J. Raymond of the *New York Times* declared that "every vote given for Seymour is a vote for treason." The disloyal and dissatisfied elements rallied behind Seymour and he was elected governor; the Wood brothers were also elected, to Congress.[3]

During the first two years of the Civil War, northern partisans received little news to buoy their hopes or relieve growing feelings of frustration and disappointment. Finally, on July 4, 1863, President Abraham Lincoln announced that on the preceding day the Battle of Gettysburg had ended triumphantly for the Union. Also on July 4 General Ulysses S. Grant captured Vicksburg.

On the day that Lincoln's pronouncement was giving the North a renewed optimism, Governor Horatio Seymour made a Fourth of July speech in the Academy of Music in Brooklyn. A biographer very favorable to Seymour conceded that "as regards the time of its delivery, this speech was probably the most unfortunate of his whole career." Although the address was made on the day after Lee's armies had been repulsed in Pennsylvania and Grant had captured Vicksburg, Governor Seymour failed to allude to these significant events. Instead, he opened his remarks by attacking the Lincoln administration for its "broken promises" of victory and for violating the civil rights of citizens in time of war. The administration, asserted Seymour, should set a good example, warning that the "bloody," "treasonable," and "revolutionary" doctrine of "public necessity" could be used "by a mob as well as by a government."[4]

Only a little over a week later, New York City was the scene of wild mob action—the most shameful disorders in the city's history. And critics of Seymour charged that the "mob" had been given encouragement by his Fourth of July speech.

The Conscription Act had been signed on March 3, 1863, and was to be put into effect in New York City in July. On Saturday morning, July 11, 1863, a drawing of the names for the draft was held at the headquarters of Charles E. Jenkins, provost marshal of the Ninth Congressional District, located at the corner of Third Avenue and Forty-sixth Street. The names of the men chosen in the draft were published in the press on Sunday, July 12. In his diary George Templeton Strong accurately predicted: "We shall have trouble before we are through. . . . That soulless politician [Governor Horatio] Seymour will make mischief if he dare. So will F'nandy Wood . . . and other reptiles."

Although there were no disturbances on Sunday, the draft was under constant discussion and feelings of resentment against it were running high. This was particularly true among the foreign-born people living in the Ninth Congressional District. Most of them were Democrats and Democratic newspapers and politicians had constantly drummed away on the theme that the acts of the Lincoln administration were highhanded, oppressive, and unconstitutional. Of the city's population then, 203,740, or roughly one fourth, were Irish, and most had settled in the Five Points and Mulberry Bend districts. There were also 119,984 Germans, and they lived mainly along the Middle East Side. Particularly offensive to the poor people was the provision in the Conscription Act that enabled men of financial means to hire a substitute by the payment of $300. And adding fuel to the fires of resentment was the presence of thousands of Negro freedmen who had recently immigrated to New York City from the South. The day laborers, particularly the Irish, felt the competition of these men for jobs and hatred of blacks was intense.

As Sunday wore on, unrest intensified. Sensing an opportunity for violence, members of criminal gangs were busily engaged in collecting brick-bats, paving stones, and other weapons. Saloons in the Five Points and along the waterfront were visited by southern sympathizers, who helped inflame feelings against the draft.

On Monday morning, July 13, 1863, a mob gathered at the draft head-quarters at Third Avenue and Forty-sixth Street. The original mob swelled as factory workers and employees of the street railroads joined the throng. The avenue soon became filled with a mass of angry humanity that hooted at the police and cursed the Negro race. Included in this angry throng were members of Volunteer Engine Company No. 33, all accomplished street brawlers. Their leader's name had been drawn in the draft the preceding Saturday.

Suddenly the mob surged forward and attacked the band of policemen that had been stationed in front of the provost marshal's building. The police were overwhelmed and were forced to retreat into the building. A hurricane of rocks and other missiles assailed the windows and doors. The mob rushed into the building but the provost marshal and his clerks escaped through the rear. The policemen found their positions untenable and also fled. All of the furniture in the place was demolished and then the mob set fire to the building. Before long, flames had enveloped buildings in the entire block from Forty-sixth to Forty-seventh Street.

Several hours later that day, John A. Kennedy, superintendent of the Metropolitan Police, made an appearance near the original scene of violence to check on conditions. The superintendent was unarmed and not in uniform. Someone recognized him and yelled, "There's Kennedy." A ruffian struck him from behind and knocked him down a six-foot embankment. The superintendent made every effort to flee. As he emerged on Forty-seventh Street, mobsters rushed at him. Again he was knocked to the foot of the embankment, and there a hoodlum beat him over the head with a club. Kennedy ran toward Lexington Avenue and a deep mudhole. Pursuing rioters screeched, "Drown him! Drown him!" A tremendous blow sent Kennedy flying into the mudhole where his face received lacerations from stones embedded in the bottom of the mire. Kennedy was now in great pain and nearing exhaustion. He was rescued by an influential citizen, John Eagan, who convinced the mobsters that the police superintendent was dead. Eagan was permitted to place the prostrate Kennedy on a common feed wagon and drive him to headquarters. A police surgeon found seventy-two separate bruises on his body plus a score of cuts. Although seriously injured, Kennedy recovered.

During the afternoon of July 13, rioting spread to many sections of the city. By evening much of the Upper Side was in the hands of men crazed by drink and uncontrolled passions. Negroes were special targets of the mob and were attacked indiscriminately wherever found. About four o'clock in the afternoon, a mob of about three thousand hoodlums descended upon the Colored Orphan Asylum on Fifth Avenue between Forty-third and Forty-fourth Streets. The main building was four stories high and the wings were three stories tall. Besides the officers and matrons, about two hundred Negro children were in the place when the mob arrived. The children were successfully evacuated through rear doors before the mob succeeded in battering down the barricaded doors. The building was ransacked. Every movable object of value was stolen. Then the building was set afire and within an hour in ruins. Property loss to the society that operated the orphanage was $80,000.

Mobs were attacking everywhere. A large armory at Twenty-first Street and Second Avenue was seized and torched. Some mobsters who had barricaded themselves in the drill room were trapped as the flames surged through the building. Many leaped from the building and were injured as they hit the pavement. Others perished as the building collapsed.

Buildings on Broadway and Lexington Avenue were pillaged, sacked, and burned. Jewelry stores were looted. Several hundred guns were stolen from hardware stores. Police stations were besieged. An effort was made to take over the *Tribune* building but the mob was repulsed and a fire that had been started in the place was extinguished. The postmaster's house on West Eighty-sixth Street was burned down. Six hundred rioters attacked a house at Baxter and Leonard Streets in which twenty Negro families were housed. On Thirty-second Street, between Sixth and Seventh Avenues, a Negro was hanged and his body burned. In one place where three Negroes took refuge on a roof, the rioters set the house afire. By nightfall New York City had virtually fallen into the hands of the mob. From all quarters came reports of small detachments of police meeting defeat and fleeing from the rioters.[5]

Shortly before midnight on Monday, a thunderstorm hit the city and a brisk rain helped to scatter many of the rioters. On Tuesday morning, July 14, 1863, rioting was resumed with a vengeance. After an all-night orgy of drinking and carousing in the dives of the Five Points and the Bowery, several hundred half-crazed men and women entered Clarkson Street before dawn. When William Jones, a Negro, attempted to defend his family and prevent the mob from burning his home, he was grabbed and hung to the limb of a tree. While he dangled from the tree, a fire was lighted under his body and hoodlums pelted the lifeless form with stones and bricks. A police station on East Eighty-seventh Street and numerous private homes in the vicinity were pillaged and burned.

It was during the second day of heavy rioting that Governor Horatio Seymour belatedly arrived in the city. Shortly after the disorders had broken out on Monday morning, Mayor George Opdyke sent telegrams, three in all, to Governor Seymour informing him of the insurrection in New York City and advising him to return immediately. The telegrams were sent to Albany. However, Seymour had been visiting at a home in New Brunswick, New Jersey, and the first word of the riots reached him about noon on Monday, July 13, when he was located and the telegram was handed to him. Although apologists for the governor stated that after receiving the message he caught the first train for New York City, it is obvious that he proceeded at a leisurely pace because he did not arrive in the troubled city until Tuesday morning, July 14.

After meeting with Mayor Opdyke at the St. Nicholas Hotel about noon, Governor Seymour issued two proclamations—one declaring the city and county of New York to be in a state of insurrection and the other stating that the riots "must and shall be put down." Seymour then proceeded to the City Hall, a little less than a mile away. From the City Hall steps Seymour made a speech to a crowd that had gathered in the park. Later there was disagreement whether the crowd consisted of innocent law-abiding citizens or was a segment of the mob. Horace Greeley's *Tribune* the following day reported that Seymour had started his speech to the "mob" with the salutation "My Friends." In his speech he also referred to himself as "Your friend and the friend of your families." That speech was to plague Seymour during the balance of his political career. He told his audience that he had sent his adjutant general to Washington, D.C., with a request that the federal government stop the draft. There was no cause for resistance, he said, because the draft had not yet been enforced. If the Conscription Act should be held unconstitutional, it would never be enforced, but if upheld by the courts, Seymour promised to see that inequalities would not be tolerated. After speaking from the City Hall steps, Seymour made a similar speech on Wall Street and then went uptown where he spoke for a third time that day. The substance of each of the three speeches was the same and each was greeted by loud cheering.

Seymour had been a bitter foe of Lincoln and his policies. He was a leader of the opposition party and had personal political ambitions. As a practical politician, he should have realized fully that his demands on the Lincoln administration to suspend the draft would carry no weight whatever.

There was every reason to believe that Seymour had been indulging in self-serving political speeches at a time when the city was on the verge of destruction by rioting mobs. The *New York Evening Post* on July 14, 1863, stated, ''Governor Seymour did not command the mob to disperse; he merely 'implored' them in dainty phrases to do him the kindness not to continue these violent proceedings, and at his side, while he was speaking, stood the man who had been encouraging the mob in an inflammatory address in front of the *Tribune* building. The governor's remarks seemed to give great satisfaction to the rioters.'' In view of the crisis facing New York City at the time, Governor Seymour's speeches were mild, indeed, whereas his vigorous opposition to the Lincoln administration and the draft served to encourage disloyal action. A fair appraisal of his conduct would probably conclude that Seymour had been fiddling with politics while the city burned.[6]

Throughout the day on July 14, the leaders of the mob sent out patrols, which cut telegraph lines and made it difficult for the police to keep the lines of communication open. Large sections of the Harlem and New Haven Railway tracks were ripped up. Fires were breaking out everywhere and when firemen appeared on the scene they were often attacked.

Along Ninth Avenue from Thirty-second to Forty-third Street, rioters cut down telegraph poles. These poles, together with carts and wagons, were bound with telegraph wire and served as formidable barricades across the avenue at Thirty-seventh and Forty-third Streets. When a saloonkeeper refused to turn over his stock of liquor to the mob, it set fire to the Weehawken ferry house on Forty-second Street; the house was destroyed by the flames. A bloody battle was fought on Catherine Street, where Brooks Brothers' clothing store had been entered and pillaged.

At Allerton's Hotel, on Eleventh Avenue between Fortieth and Forty-first Streets, rioters administered a beating to a body of soldiers and took their guns. Marauders sacked private residences along Forty-seventh Street. The primary purpose of mob action here was robbery. This entire section of the city was being terrorized by bands of hoodlums.

Early on Tuesday morning a contingent of two hundred fifty policemen marched through the streets en route to Second Avenue, where grave disorders had broken out. As the officers were marching between Thirty-second and Thirty-third Streets, they were assailed by a shower of bullets, bricks, and paving stones from the windows of houses. The police forcibly entered the houses and searched them from cellar to roof. Rioters found in the building were viciously beaten by the police. Policemen also converged on a liquor store on Thirty-first Street, from which the rioters were firing pistols and hurling stones. One of the hoodlums who had been using a gun was thrown from a window and killed.

On one occasion, while the police were engaged in a vigorous fight with the mob, Colonel H. J. O'Brien of the Eleventh New York Volunteers arrived with fifty men and two howitzers. At first the rioters were overawed, but before long they began an attack on the soldiers, who firing into the mob wounded several persons. The crowd scattered. About two hours later Colonel O'Brien returned alone to the place of earlier disorders. He was recognized and promptly attacked by hoodlums seeking vengeance. For several hours crazed rioters tortured and abused him. Finally the colonel died, after frenzied women had vented their fury against him late in the evening. Colonel O'Brien's corpse was almost unrecognizable when recovered after nightfall.

Although the backbone of the rioting was eventually broken on Tuesday, July 14, 1863, sizable mob action continued on Wednesday, July 15. George Templeton Strong recorded in his diary that the rioters on July 15 were "better armed and organized than those of Monday, and their inaction today may possibly be meant to throw us off guard. . . . They are in full possession of the western and eastern sides of the city, from Tenth Street upward, and of a good many districts beside." Strong reported that he could not walk four blocks eastward from his home without peril. The last sharp fighting occurred as late as July 16, when rioters were looting residences near Gramercy Park and were dealt with severely by United States armed forces.

The total number of casualties during the Draft Riots of 1863 was never determined with any degree of accuracy. The *Evening Post* declared that many of the slain rioters were buried secretly at night. Clandestine parties reportedly carried bodies across the East River where they were buried. More than one hundred buildings were burned down and two hundred others damaged and looted. Estimated casualties were over a thousand killed, and private property worth from $1.5 to $5 million was destroyed. Several months after the riots, John A. Kennedy, superintendent of the Metropolitan Police, asserted that at least 1,155 persons were killed. Eighty policemen were seriously injured and three died. Herbert Asbury has declared that casualties from the Draft Riots were as high as those of some important battles of the Revolutionary War and the Civil War. He quotes estimates of two thousand killed and eight thousand injured. Such estimates were very likely highly exaggerated.

In a biography of Horatio Seymour, Stewart Mitchell stoutly defended the role played by Seymour during the riots and attempted to minimize the gravity of the disorders. He stated, "The small number of persons who lost their lives in the riots cannot be determined exactly." The *New York Tribune*, he said, listed on July 20, 1863, the names of seventy-four persons killed in the riots for whom burial certificates had been obtained. The *Tribune* also asserted that many bodies were concealed in cellars uptown "awaiting removal." Four days later the *Tribune* estimated the number killed at three hundred to five hundred. The Metropolitan Police had already reported that one thousand had perished and Mitchell stated that Seymour carelessly used this figure in his second annual message to the legislature. Mitchell flatly asserts that "there is no evidence that any more than seventy-four possible victims of the violence of three days died anywhere but in the columns of partisan newspapers." He said the orgy of journalism covering the riots was followed by a scramble for fictitious damage claims against the city and county.

Although the exact number of casualties during the Draft Riots will never be known, the figure of seventy-four killed is probably far too low. However, judged by any civilized standards, the murder of seventy-four persons during a riot in any city would be declared a major catastrophe and would be headlined throughout the nation. It hardly justifies the assertion of Seymour's biographer that only a "small number of persons . . . lost their lives in the riots." And George Templeton Strong was recording in his diary on July 19, 1863, that "not half the history of this memorable week has been written. I could put down pages of incidents that the newspapers have omitted, any one of which would in ordinary times be the town's talk. Men and ladies attacked and plundered by daylight in the streets; private houses suddenly invaded by gangs of a dozen ruffians and sacked, while the women and children run off for their lives." Strong wrote of the "unspeakable infamy" of the persecution of the Negroes and said, "The outrages they have suffered during this last week are less excusable—are founded on worst pretext and less provocation—than St. Bartholomew's or the Jew hunting of the Middle Ages. This is a nice town to call itself a center of civilization!"

To bring the disgraceful riots under control, it had been necessary to utilize the services of about twelve hundred United States troops, two thousand regular policemen, and three thousand citizens who were given arms and voluntarily performed the duties of patrolmen during the emergency. By Thursday, July 16, about ten thousand veterans of the Battle of Gettysburg had poured into the city. And by the following day, thirteen regiments of regular soldiers had arrived, and they remained on duty until the draft was resumed without difficulty on August 19.

When the rioting first started, members of the mob were concerned mainly with breaking up the draft and wreaking vengeance on officials in charge of it. The draft, however, soon became a mere pretext for engaging in general lawlessness and violence. All elements of crime and disorder had joined forces and for almost three days and nights had imposed a reign of terror over the city. The eminent historian and poet Carl Sandburg observed that "never before in an American metropolis had the police, merchants, bankers, and forces of law and order had their power wrenched loose by mobs so skillfully led."[7]

Reports of the New York Draft Riots were received in the South with jubilation and gave encouragement to the rebel cause. Southern hopes were raised that the insurrection would spread to other northern cities and paralyze the war effort.

The role played by New York politicians had been ignominious indeed. If their actions had not aided in precipitating the riots, they certainly fanned the flames of unrest once the uprising started. Democratic aldermen, legislators, and judges, as well as the governor, were anxious to embarrass the Republican president and the Republican mayor of the city. While the riots were in progress, a Democratic police magistrate solemnly convened a special session of his court, held the federal draft to be unconstitutional, and urged people to resist it.[8]

Tammany Hall leaders had been proslavery throughout the crisis leading to the Civil War and vigorously opposed the Lincoln administration. Fernando Wood, exiled by Tweed to Congress, was allied with Clement Laird Vallandigham, Ohio politician and leader of the Copperhead Democrats. In a speech on May 1, 1863, Vallandigham had declared that the war was being fought not to save the Union but to free the Negroes and enslave the whites. The *Daily News,* owned by Fernando Wood's brother, Benjamin, constantly railed against Lincoln and the war. Benjamin was in communication with southern partisans who were based in Canada and plotting against the Union. During the assassination trials of 1865, proof emerged that Benjamin Wood "received a check for $25,000 from the treason fund of the rebel refugees and plotters in Canada." Governor Seymour's attacks against the president had been so vicious that Lincoln earnestly desired Seymour's defeat in the November 1864 election.

As the November 1864 elections approached, rumors were afoot of a plot to burn New York City. U.S. troops under the command of General Benjamin F. Butler were stationed in New York to prevent violence and fraud. Lincoln was reelected president by an overwhelming majority. In the New York race for governor, Horatio Seymour's chickens came home to roost. Many loyal citizens were of the opinion that his denunciations of the draft and attacks on Lincoln had been responsible, in part, for the riots. The voters rejected Seymour's bid for reelection and, instead, placed his opponent, Reuben E. Fenton, in the governor's chair.[9]

In March 1865 Abraham Lincoln, for the second time, took the oath of office as president of the United States. His second inaugural address was denounced and derided by Benjamin Wood's *Daily News,* as well as by the *New York World.* Some historians would later acclaim his second inaugural address as the most eloquent of his state papers and certain men of literature would accord it a place among the greatest English prose of all time.[10]

The North was elated on April 9, 1865, when General Robert E. Lee surrendered to General Ulysses S. Grant at Appomattox. But five days later elation turned to mourning when an assassin's bullets felled Lincoln as he was attending a Washington theater on the night of April 14. He died the following day.[11]

The war was nearing its end when the state legislature, in March 1865, passed a bill, long overdue, to create a paid fire department that would supersede the existing system of rowdy, brawling, and political engine companies. Members of the engine companies were enraged and many threatened not to turn out in case of fire.[12]

In the 1865 mayoral election Tammany candidate John T. Hoffman was successful. Although corruption was prevalent during his administration, Hoffman's name was not directly connected with scandal. Hoffman was chosen grand sachem of Tammany and in December 1867 was elected for a second term as mayor. Unsuccessfully opposing Hoffman in the 1867 election was Fernando Wood. Hoffman was working hand in glove with the Tweed Ring, into which his political fortunes were closely woven.[13]

New York City had grown into a huge metropolis. Awed by its size, a rebel prisoner remarked that if he had known New York was such a "hell of a big place," he "wouldn't never have fit agin it."[14] It was estimated that over a half-million persons were packed in dingy, foul tenement buildings. In fact, the city was plagued with multistoried overcrowded tenements, filthy streets, inadequate sewage disposal, and polluted milk and water. The prevalence of unsanitary conditions gave the city an outrageously high death rate. The state legislature in February 1866 created a metropolitan sanitary district under a board of health. The board's first report declared that hygienic conditions in the city were disgusting and horrible.

In May 1866 cholera again appeared in New York City. At first only a few cases were detected, but by July and August the disease had reached epidemic dimensions. By the time frost arrived, the city's death toll from cholera was some twelve hundred.[15]

Politically, William M. Tweed now controlled all Democratic nominations. As a practical matter, Mozart Hall, the brain child of Fernando Wood, had gone out of existence and the Tweed Ring had no Democratic opposition. Many offices provided opportunities for instant riches. One sheriff, it was proven, was, although a poor man when elected, worth $250,000, clear of all political assessments, when he retired at the end of a two-year term. Tweed looked upon the various offices of government as salable commodities. And candidates for office, including judicial aspirants, were required to shell out substantial sums of cash to the Tweed Ring. Judges, of course, were selected by the ring with an eye on their future decisions, decisions that would give Tweed and his cohorts a carte-blanche license to steal.

In July 1868 the Democratic National Convention was held in the new Tammany Hall on Fourteenth Street. During three days of balloting the leading candidates were George H. Pendleton and Winfield S. Hancock. Neither could muster sufficient strength, and it appeared that the time was ripe for a shift of convention votes to Chief Justice Salmon P. Chase, a man of long experience in national affairs and of considerable ability. However, on the twenty-second ballot a furor was created when some votes were cast for Horatio Seymour, who was serving as president of the convention. Seymour withdrew from the chair. The galleries were filled with seasoned wigwam shouters, who aided in creating a stampede for Seymour. The convention thus named Horatio Seymour as the Democratic nominee for president and Frank Blair as his vice presidential running mate. With Seymour's unsavory Copperhead reputation during the Civil War, he had virtually no chance of winning over the Republican candidate, General Ulysses S. Grant.[16]

At the state Democratic convention John T. Hoffman, Tammany grand sachem, received the nomination for governor. With Tweed in the chair the General Committee adopted a resolution urging the people to stand by Seymour and Blair. It proclaimed: ''We are united. We believe in our cause. It is the cause of constitutional liberty, of personal rights . . . and of the political supremacy of the white race and protection of American labor.''[17]

In November 1868 the electorate chose Hoffman as governor and Tweed was elected to the state Senate. By spending money lavishly, Tweed soon gained control of the legislature. Later Tweed stated that money had to be paid to get bills passed and, in fact, it was impossible to accomplish anything in the legislature without paying for it. With Tweed managing the legislature, and with his tool, Hoffman, in the governor's chair, the stage was set for unprecedented corruption.

7

THE TWEED RING

By 1870 the power of William M. Tweed and his cohorts was reaching its zenith. Tweed controlled the state legislature; his stooge, John T. Hoffman, was seated in the governor's chair; and another puppet, the elegant A. Oakey Hall, was mayor of New York City. Virtually all important city offices were held by men beholden to the boss. The police department and the judiciary were controlled by Tammany Hall, which was ruled by the grand sachem, Tweed. The Tweed Ring was master of all it surveyed and the stage was set for the plundering of a municipality on a scale never before witnessed in America.

The four principal members of the Tweed Ring were William M. Tweed, Peter B. Sweeny, Richard B. Connolly, and A. Oakey Hall. Each had long been trained in the school of venal politics.

William Marcy Tweed, son of a chairmaker, Richard Tweed, was born on April 3, 1823 at 1 Cherry Street in New York City. During his youth Tweed actively participated in the affairs of Volunteer Engine Company No. 33. Members of all fire engine companies of the time were deeply involved in ward politics. This was true of Company 33, which fell into disrepute because of the rowdy element attached to it and was eventually disbanded.

On January 1, 1849, Tweed was instrumental in organizing Americus Engine Company No. 6, and he became its foreman and "honored leader." The Big Six, as the company was later known, waged numerous battles against other companies, particularly Engine Company No. 8. It was Tweed's leadership of Americus Engine Company No. 6 that launched his political career. In 1851 Tweed was elected alderman of the Seventh Ward; while still serving as an alderman, he was elected to Congress in 1852 and reelected in 1854.[1]

As an alderman, Tweed tasted the heady wine of despotic power. He appointed the police of his ward, from the lowly patrolman to the commander of the precinct; he granted licenses to saloons; with his associates, he awarded ferry, bus, and streetcar franchises; he sat as a justice in the mayor's court and as a judge in the criminal courts. The aldermen also selected the thirty-six talesmen from which grand jurors were drawn.[2]

In 1857 Tweed was elected to the Board of Supervisors and in 1863 and 1864 served as president of the board. In 1861 he was elected chairman of the Tammany General Committee, and in 1863 was elected grand sachem of the Tammany Society. In 1863, through the good graces of Judge George G. Barnard, Tweed was admitted to the practice of law, including the right to try cases in the state supreme court and the New York Court of Appeals. "William M. Tweed, Attorney at Law" was imprinted in gold letters on the door of his office at 95 Duane Street. He was paid more than $100,000 for so-called legal services by the Erie Railroad, controlled by Jay Gould and James Fisk, Jr. Along with Fisk, Mayor Hall, and Comptroller Connolly, Tweed was a director of the Tenth National Bank, which became a depository for city funds. Tweed suffered a temporary political setback in 1861 when he was defeated for the office of sheriff. At the end of this unsuccessful political campaign he was dead broke financially. However, by the end of the Civil War, his ill-gotten gains had made him a millionaire. When Tweed arrived in Albany as state senator in January 1868, he had become a monarch with virtually unlimited power. And his physique was somewhat in keeping with his power. On his frame of five feet eleven inches, he carried a hulk of nearly three hundred pounds and was a man of commanding appearance.[3]

Although Tweed was head of the ring, he was ably assisted by Peter B. Sweeny, a lawyer of great natural shrewdness, who held the office of chamberlain and thus was in fact treasurer of the city and county. Often referred to as Peter (Brains) Sweeny, he was regarded as the most cunning and despicable of the entire gang. A master political tactician, he was credited with having arranged the deal that sent Fernando Wood of Mozart Hall Democracy to Congress and left Tweed's Tammany Hall in full control of the Democratic vote of the city.[4]

By the time the Tweed Ring reached the height of its power, Richard B. Connolly, known as "Slippery Dick," was the comptroller and was in charge of the city finances. A onetime auctioneer, he was particularly skilled in manipulating figures, a skill that was put to good use by the ring. Connolly was elected county clerk in 1851, although he had not yet been naturalized, and in 1859 he was elected to the state Senate. But it was not until he became comptroller that Connolly, an "unctuous, Uriah Heep–type book-keeper," utilized his talents to their fullest degree and became profitable to the ring.[5]

The most colorful member of the Tweed Ring was Mayor A. Oakey Hall. His wardrobe included frieze coats purchased from the most fashionable tailors, fancy vests of many colors, and ties of the finest silks. Pince-nez and a General Grant beard further distinguished him.

The mayor was born in the home of his maternal grandfather in Albany, New York, on July 26, 1826, and was named Abraham Oakey Hall. His mother's father, Abraham Oakey, served as deputy treasurer of the state of

New York for twenty-five years. His maternal grandmother, Alicia d'Assignie Oakey, had once been a refugee Huguenot countess. At the time of A. Oakey Hall's birth, his father, Morgan James Hall, was engaged in the wholesale grocery business in New Orleans and until 1830 young Hall lived there with his parents. The father died of yellow fever in 1830 and Hall's mother then returned to New York, where she provided for herself, her son, and her daughter by taking in boarders.

In the fall of 1840 Hall, then fourteen, matriculated at New York University. He graduated with a B.A. degree on July 2, 1844. A few months later he entered Harvard Law School but left at the end of one term, on January 17, 1845, and began reading law, first in a New York office and then in the office of John Slidell in New Orleans. He was admitted to the bar in Louisiana in 1846. In New Orleans Hall lived with his mother's brother, Samuel Oakey, a prosperous but eccentric businessman with a flair for the dramatic. After killing a cotton buyer in a duel, Samuel Oakey assumed the title Colonel and outfitted himself in an elaborate military uniform, which he wore when meeting celebrities who visited the city. He boasted of commanding the Bloody Forty-ninth Regiment, but the regiment existed only in his imagination.

Very probably, Samuel Oakey's love for the dramatic made a lasting impression on his young nephew. In 1848 A. Oakey Hall returned to New York. He eventually joined a law firm that had among its clients Jay Gould, then paving the way for the plunder of the Erie Railroad. On St. Valentine's Day, 1850, Hall married Katherine Louise Barnes, whose father, Joseph, was a wealthy man of power and an alderman of the Eighth Ward.[6]

Hall, originally a Republican, made friends with the leaders of that party in Albany. Among those friends were Thurlow Weed and William H. Seward, then a state senator. Hall served as counsel to various legislative commissions in Albany and was regarded as a lobbyist. In 1850 he was appointed an assistant district attorney in New York City, a post he held for three and a half years. In 1861 Hall was elected district attorney after having received the nomination of both the Republican party and Fernando Wood's Mozart Hall.

On February 1, 1864, Hall signed the registration book of the Tammany Society and was recognized as a member in good standing of Tammany Hall. Nine months earlier William M. Tweed had become grand sachem. Hall was district attorney when Tweed's man, John T. Hoffman, took office as governor on January 1, 1869. Aided by Tweed's manipulation, Hall then became the mayor of New York City and in November 1870 was reelected.[7]

Ably assisting the Tweed Ring in the perpetration of colossal frauds were corrupt members of the judiciary, particularly George G. Barnard, Albert Cardozo, and John H. McCunn.

Barnard ranked as one of the most venal judges ever to sit on the New

York bench. He was a strikingly handsome, tall man with dark, bright eyes and jet-black hair and mustache. After graduating from Yale, he went to California where he was employed as a shill for a gambling house. Upon his return to New York, he became active in politics. In 1857 Barnard, then twenty-eight, was elected recorder. Three years later he was advanced to a place on the state supreme-court bench.

During sessions in his courtroom, Judge Barnard, feet propped on the desk, whittled away on a pine stick and frequently gulped from his brandy bottle as he listened to witnesses or arguments of counsel. Subservient to Tweed, Barnard promptly dismissed the charges against any ring supporter who came before him. Before the 1868 elections, Barnard established a regular naturalization mill in the supreme court. During a fourteen-day period, October 8–23, 1868, Judge Barnard naturalized 10,093 citizens with the understanding, of course, that they would vote for the candidates of Tweed and company. When the Tweed Ring was finally exposed and impeachment of some of the judges was threatened, Judge Barnard defiantly retorted, "Impeachment be damned! We have enough money to buy up the legislature." Following the death of Barnard, more than one million dollars in bonds and cash were found among his effects.[8]

The most brilliant of the Tweed Ring judges, Albert Cardozo was born of a Portuguese-Jewish family in New York in 1830. Endowed with a keen mind, Cardozo was intensely industrious. Following his graduation from Columbia College with high honors, he turned to politics as a means of advancing his ambitions. Through ties with Fernando Wood, he became a judge of the court of common pleas. Subsequently, he shifted his allegiance to Tweed, who elevated him to the state supreme-court bench after the Civil War. Cardozo performed yeoman service for the Tweed Ring. He dismissed the charges against several hundred known criminals who were considered useful to the ring. Through his alliance with Tweed, Cardozo hoped to achieve his dream of an appointment to the United States Supreme Court. Instead, his career ended in ruin and disgrace. However, during the apex of the Tweed Ring's power in 1870, a son, Benjamin Nathan Cardozo, was born. And this son was appointed to the U.S. Supreme Court in 1932, and has been regarded as one of the nation's most illustrious and respected jurists.[9]

Also important as a Tweed Ring judge was John H. McCunn, who was not only dishonest but vulgar and ignorant as well. A poor Irish immigrant, he started his career on the tough city docks, entered politics, earned a law degree, and became in 1863 a judge. Thoroughly dishonest, McCunn, as an attorney, often sold his client's secrets to opposing lawyers.[10]

Although by 1869 the Tweed Ring controlled the chief offices of the city and state, it continued to grasp for ways of increasing its power. For many years there had been agitation for greater home rule for New York City.

The ring conceived the idea of giving the people a semblance of complete home rule while establishing virtual dictatorial control of the city. The vehicle through which this was to be accomplished was a bill titled ''An Act to Reorganize the Local Government of the City of New York,'' which was presented on the floor of the Assembly by a Tweed henchman in February 1870. Subsequently known as the Tweed Charter, it had the backing of well-intentioned New Yorkers as well as the enthusiastic support of the city's leading reform group, the Citizens Association. In fact, in principle the charter had many sound features to recommend it. [11]

In his drive to gain approval of the charter, Tweed found it necessary to buy the votes of many legislators. Some votes carried a high price tag and Tweed paid five Republican senators $40,000 each. Members of the ring considered the money spent a good investment. With the passage of the Tweed Charter on April 5, 1870, the ring was able to loot the city treasury without restraint.

The charter, believed to have been drafted by Peter B. Sweeny, created a Board of Audit, which passed on all municipal expenditures and managed the financial affairs of the city government. The Board of Audit comprised the mayor of New York City, A. Oakey Hall; the comptroller, Richard B. Connolly; the commissioner of public works, William M. Tweed; and the president of the Board of Parks, Peter B. Sweeny.

On May 5, 1870, the Board of Audit authorized payment of claims against the city amounting to $6,312,500, of which ninety percent were fraudulent. By 1871 the Board of Audit had approved payment of fraudulent bills totaling $15,750,000, and of this amount at least $12,500,000 was pure plunder. During the fifteen months between the passage of the charter in April 1870 and the public exposure of the ring by the *New York Times* beginning in July 1871, the boldness of the plundering of the city treasury by Tweed and company almost defies imagination. [12]

Also directly affected by the Tweed Charter was the law-enforcement structure of New York City. The state-controlled Metropolitan Police District, which had come into existence in 1857, was now replaced by a newly created police department for the city of New York under the control of the local government. The charter established a police board of four commissioners, who were to be appointed by the mayor for terms of eight, seven, six, and five years, respectively. With few exceptions, the persons connected with the Metropolitan Police were transferred to the newly created city police department. When the charter became effective in April 1870, the population of New York City was approaching one million. Its police force personnel numbered 2,325: 1 superintendent, 3 inspectors, 35 captains, 136 sergeants, 83 roundsmen, 1,992 patrolmen, and 75 doormen. [13]

Immediately following the adoption of the new charter, Tweed was looked upon as a civic benefactor in New York City. His popularity was enormous and his political power virtually unlimited.

Tweed and his family lived in a pretentious mansion at Madison Avenue and Fifty-ninth Street. They rode in elegant custom-built carriages drawn by stylish horses. The stables that adjoined Tweed's country home in Greenwich, Connecticut, had stalls built of the finest mahogany and reputedly cost $100,000. Tweed dressed ostentatiously. Enormous diamonds flashed on his fingers, his shirtfront, and watch chain.[14]

Although the Tweed Ring seemed impregnable, a cloud or two marked the horizon. A number of Tammany leaders complained that the boss had not properly rewarded them politically. Some were dissatisfied because they had not been permitted to share sufficiently in the plunder. Prominent in this recalcitrant group, which called itself the Young Democracy, were John Morrissey, James O'Brien, Henry W. Genet, Mike Norton, and others. Morrissey, the gambling king, had served Tweed and the ring well as an organizer of repeaters and was bitter when his ambition to become chamberlain had been denied. O'Brien, an ex-sheriff, had been refused payment of his claim to a third of a million dollars and was bent on revenge. Having been used by Tweed in his climb to the apex of his power, the leaders of the Young Democracy believed they could now successfully oppose and perhaps unseat him.[15]

Also somewhat disturbing to Tammany was the crusade against the ring that was being waged on the pages of the *New York Times*. And particularly irritating were the devastating cartoons by Thomas Nast in *Harper's Weekly*. It was Nast who created the Tiger as the political symbol for Tammany Hall.

The able George Jones had become the publisher of the *New York Times* in 1869. Rumors of ring corruption were prevalent, but at the outset Jones feared his own ruin if he started swinging at the powerful Tweed group and could not prove his charges. Indeed, one of the directors of the *Times,* James B. Taylor, was a business partner in Tweed's New York Printing Company, the beneficiary of a highly lucrative county printing and stationery business. But early in September 1870 Taylor died. Beginning on September 20, 1870, and continuing over a year, the *Times* daily railed against the Tweed Ring. For several months, the *Times'* charges were unsupported by any evidence and Tweed was perhaps not unduly worried.[16]

On October 18, 1870, at a meeting of the Tammany General Committee in the wigwam, corporation counsel Richard O'Gorman made a speech in which he labeled the *Times'* charges "false, scandalous and idle." The *Times* persistently demanded that the city's accounts be opened for public examination. In response, the comptroller, Richard B. Connolly, made available certain records to a group of prominent businessmen headed by John Jacob Astor. When the *Times* was hammering away the hardest, the

Astor committee reported it had found that the account books were being "faithfully kept" and concluded that the city's financial affairs were being administered in a correct, honest manner by Comptroller Connolly. A few days later Tammany swept the 1870 city elections.[17]

On New Year's Day, 1871, a throng of political bigwigs and lesser fry called on A. Oakey Hall to congratulate him on his second triumphant election as mayor of New York City. Everything looked bright and promising for the Tammany chiefs.

In March 1871 the proprietor of the *New York Sun* proposed erecting a statue honoring William M. Tweed. The adherents of the boss promptly pounced on this suggestion, formed an association, and sent out letters requesting donations for a statue that would commemorate Tweed's services to New York. With celerity, politicians pledged from $1,000 to $10,000 each. Tweed disapproved of the project in a letter that appeared in the *Sun* on March 14, 1871, under the headline "A Great Man's Modesty." The paper described Tweed as the great New York philanthropist and noble benefactor of the people.[18]

On May 31, 1871, Tweed's daughter, Mary Amelia, was married in Trinity Chapel on West Twenty-fifth Street to Arthur Ambrose Maginnis of New Orleans. All the prominent officeholders in the city and state, as well as merchants and financiers, were invited. The wedding gifts were displayed in a grand showroom and had a cash value of $700,000. Less than two weeks after the wedding, on June 10, the formal opening of the new clubhouse of the Americus Club, of which Tweed was president, took place. Resting on a cliff overlooking Long Island Sound at Indian Harbor, not far from Tweed's Greenwich country home, the clubhouse was built at a cost of $300,000 and described as one of the finest establishments of its kind in the world.[19]

In a sense, the formal opening of the Americus clubhouse was to be Tweed's last big triumphal hour. Only a few weeks later, the *New York Times* fired a broadside at the Tweed Ring. The ammunition was, for the first time, concrete evidence.

Oddly, it was a sleighing accident the previous January that indirectly led to the Tweed Ring's downfall. While driving a team of spirited horses hitched to a sleigh, James Watson, the county auditor and the ring's bookkeeper, collided with another sleigh in Harlem Lane at 138th Street. One of Watson's horses, valued at $10,000, was killed. Watson was kicked in the head and died about a week later. Before long Watson's job as auditor was given to Matthew O'Rourke, who was not taken into the ring's confidence. O'Rourke had once made a claim against the city which the ring had seen fit not to pay. This disgruntled bookkeeper meticulously copied explosive facts and figures from the ring's account books, and they were eventually passed on to the *New York Times*.[20]

The *Times* also received help from another unexpected source. James O'Brien, now prominently identified with the Young Democracy, had recently completed a term in the lucrative office of sheriff. Not satisfied with the handsome emoluments of the office, he had presented a bill to the city for about $350,000, which the ring refused to pay. O'Brien, who reportedly coveted Tweed's post as grand sachem of Tammany, was furious. He knew that members of the ring were looting the city treasury to the tune of millions. An O'Brien protégé, William Copeland, was employed as a clerk in the office of Comptroller Connolly. On O'Brien's instructions, Copeland copied records that established large-scale plunder by the Tweed Ring and turned his handiwork over to his patron. Armed with this dynamite, O'Brien collected $20,000 in blackmail from Tweed, who promised him additional payments totaling $130,000. However, O'Brien was interested more in revenge. His goal was the destruction of Tweed's power. O'Brien tried to peddle the explosive evidence in his possession to the *New York Sun* but that paper wanted no part of it. Then one hot night in July 1871 O'Brien dropped into the *New York Times* editorial office of Louis Jennings. After an awkward silence, O'Brien laid an envelope on Jennings' desk and said, "Here's the proof to back up all the *Times* has charged. They're copied right out of the city ledgers."[21]

Tweed and his pals learned that the *New York Times* possessed documents that would prove their colossal frauds. Comptroller Connolly offered George Jones, publisher of the *Times*, $5 million if he would forgo publication of the documents. Another bribe of a half-million dollars had been offered to cartoonist Thomas Nast to cease publishing his venomous drawings of the various members of the ring. Both Jones and Nast rejected the bribes. Rejection was itself an unusual experience for the ring.[22]

The *Times* found it expedient to postpone for a few days its documented series on the ring's peculations because the city's attention was being focused temporarily on another outbreak of violence. On July 12, 1871, the Orange Societies staged a parade. At Twenty-fourth Street a shot was fired from a window at the marchers. The Eighty-fourth Regiment promptly returned the fire and shots were fired also by the Sixth and Ninth regiments. Casualties included forty-seven dead and scores wounded.[23]

On July 22, the front page of the *New York Times* carried the bold headline "The Secret Accounts." The subheading read "Proofs of Undoubted Frauds Brought to Light." The *Times* then reported that Comptroller Connolly's books revealed an expenditure of $5,663,646.83 during 1869 and 1870 for purported repairs and furniture for the new courthouse. The warrants, explained the *Times*, "were drawn in different names, but they were all indorsed to 'Ingersoll & Co.'—otherwise, J. H. Ingersoll, the agent of the ring. Each warrant was signed by Comptroller Connolly and Mayor

Hall. . . . The bulk of the money somehow or other got back to the ring. . . ."[24]

On Monday, July 24, 1871, the *Times* reported a new set of figures, which revealed a payment of $2,870,864 in 1869 and 1870 for plastering, chiefly in the new courthouse but also in armories that in fact had never seen a coat of plaster. The recipient of the money was Andrew J. Garvey, who was dubbed the "Prince of Plasterers." For one day of plastering, he collected $45,966.99 and his bill for two months' work was $945,715.00. The records also showed that payment of $1,231,817.71 had been made for plumbing and gas fixtures in the new courthouse. The total cost for plastering, carpentry, and plumbing came to $9,789,482.00, and of this total more than eighty-five percent fraudulently went to the Tweed Ring. The huge courthouse expenditures were particularly remarkable; at the time construction of the courthouse was first authorized in 1858, the enactment law specified that the building and all its furnishings should not cost more than $250,000.

Records obtained by the *Times* revealed that an obscure carpenter, G. S. Miller, purportedly received $360,751.01 for one month's work. Some of the persons who received large payments were completely fictitious. A wholly unknown J. A. Smith was paid $750,000; a nonexistent T. C. Cash received $64,000; and a Phillipo Donnoruma was paid $66,000. The boodler who got this money had a sense of humor. He signed the warrant "Philip Dummy." When a reporter asked Tweed about the thefts, he defiantly retorted, "Well, what are you going to do about it?"[25]

The disclosures by the *New York Times* finally goaded the public into action. A meeting was called for September 4, 1871, at the Cooper Union. Presiding over a packed auditorium was former Mayor William F. Havemeyer. A leader at the gathering, Joseph H. Choate, then thirty-eight years old, advanced to the platform prominently displaying a scroll in his hand and declaring, "This is what we are going to do about it." Reading from the document, he emphasized that the acknowledged debt of the city had increased from about $30 million to over $113 million—over $83 million—during the few years A. Oakey Hall had served as mayor of New York City. A resolution was offered and adopted authorizing the president of the September 4 meeting to appoint an executive committee to take action against the Tweed Ring. Thus was born the famous Committee of Seventy, which was to bring about the downfall of the Tweed Ring. It was headed by Joseph H. Choate, Charles O'Conor, and Samuel J. Tilden. Mayor Hall scorned these civic efforts, telling a reporter that they were only gusts of reform, merely wind and chatter. He brazenly predicted, "Next year we shall all be in Washington."[26]

The Committee of Seventy designated a subcommittee to make an examination of the city's accounts. Upon attempting to carry out its assignment, the subcommittee was informed on the morning of September 11, 1871, that the comptroller's office had been burglarized the preceding night and all vouchers, thirty-five thousand in all, had been stolen from the glass case in which they were stored. Although $400,000 had been spent for safes, the vital records, so it was claimed, had been placed in an insecure glass receptacle. Later, the charred remains of the vouchers were discovered in an ash heap in the City Hall attic.[27]

At the elections on November 7, 1871, sentiment ran high against Tammany misrule in New York City. Of the anti-Tammany candidates, all of the judges, fifteen of the twenty-one assemblymen, four of the five senators, and all but one alderman were elected. Ironically, the wave of civic indignation was not immediately felt by the Boss himself. In the Fourth Senatorial District, where Tweed was a candidate for reelection as state senator, vote frauds and violence were prevalent. Many voters opposed to Tweed were assaulted, often with the aid of the police, and driven from the polls. Tweed was reelected by a majority of nine thousand votes, but measures were later taken that prevented him from assuming his office.

On November 20, 1871, Richard B. Connolly resigned as comptroller and was replaced by Andrew H. Green. Both Connolly and Mayor Hall saw the handwriting on the wall. To save their own skins, they deserted Tweed and played ball with the Committee of Seventy. On December 16, 1871, William M. Tweed was indicted and a few days later resigned as commissioner of public works. He also relinquished his post as grand sachem of Tammany and was succeeded by Augustus Schell, a wealthy and prominent lawyer.

Sweeny resigned from the Park Commission and fled to Canada, later joining his brother in Paris. Slippery Dick Connolly, who thought he had established good relations with the reformers, was shocked when he was arrested on January 2, 1873, and bail was set at $1 million. After arranging bail, Connolly fled to France with about $6 million. He spent the remainder of his days wandering from one country to another and never returned to New York City.[28]

Following bar association charges of misconduct against Tweed Ring judges George G. Barnard, Albert Cardozo, and John H. McCunn, a legislative committee was appointed and began its investigation in February 1872. Early in May 1872 Judge Cardozo filed his resignation with the secretary of state and thus removed himself from the probable penalty of impeachment. On May 10, 1872, articles of impeachment against Judge Barnard were filed by the Assembly with the Senate. In August a court of impeachment stripped Judge Barnard of his judicial robes and forever disqualified him from holding any office in the state of New York. Following his removal from office, Barnard shunned all of his acquaintances and wandered about, irritable and morose, until his death in New York City on April 27, 1879.

Judge John H. McCunn was also removed from office by a unanimous vote of the Senate. Immediately after the Senate rendered its decision, McCunn hurriedly left Albany. Upon returning home, he shut himself in his bedroom and scarcely permitted even his family to see him. After three days of almost total seclusion, McCunn died.[29]

The grand jury returned several indictments against Tweed, and his first trial, which started January 7, 1873, ended in a hung jury on January 30. The outcome was not particularly surprising. The commissioner of the jury, Douglas Taylor, was a Tammany sachem and a friend of Tweed. One juror was an ex-convict. Another was a hapless bum who had mysteriously been given a suit of clothes and accepted for jury service. Two known thugs, Nicholas Muller and Thomas Lynch, were observed entertaining some of the jurors at Delmonico's.[30]

At Tweed's second trial, the jury was carefully screened. On November 19, 1873, the Boss was found guilty of 204 counts charged in the indictments. The presiding Judge, Noah Davis, on November 22, 1873, imposed a cumulative sentence of twelve years in prison and a fine of $12,750. The Court of Appeals later ruled that a cumulative sentence was improper and no punishment in excess of that prescribed for one offense could be assessed. In Tweed's case this meant a prison sentence of one year and a fine of $250.

After completing his term of one year in prison, Tweed was released on January 15, 1875, but was promptly rearrested and placed in the Ludlow Street jail. A civil suit had been filed against him and bail was fixed at $3 million. Each day for nearly a year Tweed was taken for a drive by the warden and a keeper. Before returning to the jail, they always stopped at Tweed's home, where his wife had dinner awaiting them. Before dinner was served on December 4, 1875, Tweed told his friendly jailers that he was going upstairs to talk with his wife. His custodians were probably not too surprised when he failed to return and they discovered that the Boss had escaped.

For a time Tweed worked as a laborer in New Jersey. The civil suit against him was called for trial on February 7, 1876, and on March 9, 1876, the jury brought in a verdict against the Boss of nearly $6 million. Tweed now went on the lam in earnest. He fled to Florida and then to Cuba, eventually sailing as a seaman on a ship bound for Spain. The American authorities learned of Tweed's departure, but they had no official photograph of their prize fugitive to send to Spain. Hence they sent the Spanish authorities a copy of *Harper's Weekly* carrying one of Nast's cartoons. Tweed was thus identified, returned to this country on an American ship that arrived in New York City on November 23, 1876, and again lodged in the Ludlow Street jail.

Tweed was now broken in health and spirit. He faced thirteen criminal indictments with charges ranging from grand larceny to forgery. And he was suffering from heart trouble, diabetes, and bronchitis. His weight had dropped from over 280 pounds to 160. Under these circumstances, Tweed made overtures to the attorney general, Charles Fairchild. In return for his release, Tweed offered to make a full confession of his criminal activities and to turn over to the state all of his property. The attorney general, after having retained the confession for some time, returned it to Tweed and rejected his offer. Fairchild had become attorney general through Samuel J. Tilden's support, and indications were that the rejection of Tweed's confession was based on Tilden's advice. The confession implicated numerous high officeholders in the city and state, and they heaved a sigh of relief when the document was returned to Tweed without publicity.

In the meantime, Peter B. Sweeny had returned from Europe. On June 9, 1877, it was announced that Sweeny had settled with the state for $400,000 and the case against him was closed. The money reputedly came from the estate of his deceased brother.

Registering dissatisfaction with the state's action, the Board of Aldermen appointed a special committee to conduct an investigation of the Tweed Ring frauds. During the investigation by this committee, which lasted from July 19 to December 29, 1877, Tweed was one of numerous witnesses who testified. Sweeny, however, claimed that Attorney General Fairchild had given him immunity and he refused to cooperate in any way.

At noon on April 12, 1878, Tweed died of pneumonia in the Ludlow Street jail. He was given a modest funeral, attended by members of his family, some personal friends, and about twenty politicians, including "Honest" John Kelly, who was to succeed Tweed as boss of Tammany Hall. Tweed's last words reportedly were, "I hope Tilden and Fairchild are satisfied now."[31]

Understandably, Tweed had been the principal target of the investigations of the ring's plunder. Nevertheless, Judge Noah Davis, who had imposed sentence on Tweed, was critical of the tactics of Attorney General Fairchild, who had made the Boss the scapegoat while withholding evidence against others. Of the four principal members of the ring, only Tweed felt the ignominy of prison. Sweeny had made a money settlement on terms very favorable to him. Connolly fled with $6 million and never returned to America. The dapper mayor, A. Oakey Hall, was indicted for neglect of official duty but was allowed to remain in office until the end of his term on December 31, 1872. Hall's first trial ended with the death of a juror. His second trial ended with a hung jury, seven jurors voting for conviction and five for acquittal. At the conclusion of his third trial on Christmas Eve, 1873, Hall was acquitted.[32]

The debonair Hall, notorious punster, flashy dresser, and popular after-dinner speaker, was in some respects the prototype of future New York mayors Jimmy Walker and William O'Dwyer. Following his acquittal, Hall halfheartedly resumed the practice of law. In 1875 he tried his hand at writing a four-act play. Called *The Crucible,* it focused on an innocent man sent to prison for stealing. It opened at the Park Theater on Saturday, December 18, 1875, and, typically, the leading part was played by Hall himself. On opening night the theater was filled with Hall's friends, but two nights later, Monday, he was acting before an almost empty house. After twenty-two performances the play closed.

In 1877 Hall mysteriously disappeared from New York City and was finally located in London. The following year he returned to New York City and became editor of the *World.* After his discharge from the *World* in 1883, he purchased a penny newspaper called *Truth,* which he edited until December 5. The next year he returned to London. He was admitted to the Inns of Court and his principal client in London was James Gordon Bennett, Jr., proprietor of the *New York Herald.* Hall served as Bennett's London secretary and later headed the *Herald*'s London bureau. The former mayor returned to New York City on December 30, 1892. He lived in New York while his wife resided in Millburn, New Jersey. When his wife died on March 9, 1897, Hall was free to remarry, which he did. He and his second wife were converted to Roman Catholicism and were received into the Church of St. Paul the Apostle on March 25, 1898. His sponsors were Peter B. Sweeny and Sweeny's sister, Mrs. Mary L. Bradley. Hall died at the age of seventy-two on October 7, 1898. [33]

Emerging as one of the principal heroes in the fight to destroy the Tweed Ring was Samuel J. Tilden. The legend of Tilden as a white knight in shining armor furthered his political ambitions and made him a national figure. Yet, he had not always been a courageous foe of the Tweed Ring. As late as October 1870, when the Democratic state convention met in Rochester, Tilden, as chairman of the Democratic state central committee, was offered an excellent opportunity to attack the Tweed Ring. But in his opening address to the convention he never even mentioned the ring. In fact, Tilden's state central committee was herded into a secret session in Peter B. Sweeny's room and it approved the ring's program. During this period it was the *New York Times* and Thomas Nast who were crusading against the ring. In the November 1874 elections the Democrats swept Tilden into the governor's chair by a fifty-thousand majority. And cast in the role of the slayer of the Tweed Ring dragon, Tilden won the Democratic nomination for president at the national convention in St. Louis in 1876. He was defeated by his Republican opponent, Rutherford B. Hayes, in the most famous national election dispute in American history. [34]

During Tweed's rise to power, the Boss had been the recipient of invaluable aid from the underworld. Over a period of many years Tammany Hall had built up a virtual army of toughs, bullies, and criminals. Members of this army served as storm troopers, whose presence at or near the polls almost always ensured a Tammany victory. Somewhat typical was the gang headed by William Varley, also known as Reddy the Blacksmith, a thief and murderer who was powerful in the Fourth and Seventh wards. Varley's men beat up anti-Tammany voters and greatly aided Tweed in the elections of 1868, 1870, and 1871. Varley's sister was a notorious shoplifter, a fence, and a madam of a house of prostitution on James Street.[35]

Professional criminals who were engaged in vice, gambling, and confidence games were important tributaries of Tammany Hall and the Tweed Ring. They not only furnished repeaters at the polls, but were also sources of revenue to the political leaders who in turn provided them with iron-clad protection. The pattern of organized crime was very much in evidence. Underworld influence made itself felt throughout the criminal justice system. In December 1869 George Templeton Strong noted in his diary that the average New York judge was "as bad as the New York alderman, if not worse, because his office is more sacred. . . . Law protects life no longer. Any scoundrel who is backed by a little political influence in the corner groceries of his ward can commit murder with almost absolute impunity . . . a judge of our Supreme Court is *prima facie* disreputable. . . ." A few weeks later, in January 1870, Strong lamented that "crime was never so bold, so frequent, and so safe as it is this winter. We breathe an atmosphere of highway robbery, burglary, and murder. Few criminals are caught, and fewer punished. Municipal law is a failure in New York. . . ."[36]

By the time of the Tweed Ring's rule, the professional gamblers had become the dominant influence over the city's underworld. The gamblers were also powerful politically, and several judges were placed on the bench through their influence.[37]

During the Civil War period and for many years afterward, New York City was the principal gambling center in the United States. And for almost two decades following 1859, the man who dominated the city's gambling industry was the Tammany Hall politician and onetime brawler and prize-fighter, John Morrissey.

The gambling house that Morrissey and Matt Danser had opened in 1859 at Broadway and Great Jones Street proved to be a highly profitable venture. It was only a short time before they opened another establishment, at Twelve Ann Street, in the heart of a notorious gambling district. Before long, Morrissey withdrew from his partnership with Danser and took over a resort at Eight Barclay Street which he developed into one of the finest gambling emporiums in New York City. Under different managements, this place was to operate continuously as a gambling resort until 1902. One of the most celebrated gambling places in the city during the 1860s was located at Five West Twenty-fourth Street. It was owned by a syndicate consisting of John

Morrissey, Charles Reed, Albert Spencer, Johnny Chamberlain, and Price McGrath. In 1867 Chamberlain and McGrath quarreled with Morrissey and withdrew from the syndicate. For eight years Morrissey also was a principal owner of a place at 818 Broadway, an attractive four-story brownstone building that was elegantly furnished, and operated with complete immunity.[38]

Morrissey was not entirely satisfied with his role as New York City's most powerful gambler. In 1861 he decided to invade Saratoga Springs. After renting a house on Matilda Street, Morrissey brought gambling paraphernalia as well as croupiers from New York City and the doors of his place were thrown open for business. In August 1863, with the assistance of wealthy New York sportsmen, including William R. Travers, Morrissey opened a Saratoga horse-racing track known as Horse Haven. In 1867, he began building the Club House, which was to become the most famous gambling establishment in America. The Club House, elegantly furnished, was completed in 1869 at a cost of $150,000. Faro and roulette were featured on the first floor, while upstairs plungers usually played poker for huge stakes. Morrissey paid his chief faro dealer, Hamilton Baker, $4,500 a month with an occasional bonus of fifteen percent of the house winnings. Morrissey's policy was to keep native Saratogans out of the Club House. His patrons included U.S. generals, senators, and such well-known personalities as Cornelius Vanderbilt, Samuel J. Tilden, August Belmont, James G. Blaine, and Fernando Wood's brother, Benjamin. One author had written that in one game Benjamin dropped $120,000 to Morrissey. Another writer credits Wood with having broken the bank on one occasion, winning $124,000.[39]

Morrissey's political fortunes were rising simultaneously with his successful career as a big-time gambling entrepreneur in New York City and Saratoga. In 1866, with the support of Boss Tweed, Morrissey was elected to Congress from the Fifth New York District. While a member of Congress, Morrissey owned an interest in a gambling establishment called the Congressional Faro Bank, which occupied the second and third floors of a building on Pennsylvania Avenue near Fourteenth Street in Washington, D.C. In New York City, Morrissey was able, because of his strong political ties, to dominate the gambling industry and to levy tribute on fellow gamesters.[40]

A principal source of Morrissey's power was Tweed. In September 1877, during the investigation of the ring by the Board of Aldermen committee, Tweed presented a long statement regarding John Morrissey, whom he had known for twenty-four years. As an organizer of repeaters to win elections, Tweed said, Morrissey had no superior, and when the ring was in power such capabilities were always fully recognized. Tweed stated that Morrissey "has been a professional prizefighter and public gambler—a proprietor and owner of the worst places in the city of New York, the resort of thieves and persons of the lowest character. Perhaps one of the worst faults which can fairly be attributed to me, is having been the means of keeping his gambling houses protected from the police.'' The committee of the Board of Aldermen refused to make Tweed's statement a part of the official record. However, it was printed in the *New York Tribune* on September 19, 1877.[41]

Morrissey's gambling interests, which had flourished under the protective wing of Boss Tweed and Tammany Hall, were confined largely to casino-type operations. The poor people's ''casinos'' were primarily the policy and lottery shops, which had proliferated under the aegis of John Frink and Reuben Parsons during the 1840s and 1850s. By the end of the Civil War it was estimated that one fourth of the city's population played policy regularly and were patrons of six hundred or seven hundred policy shops, which were euphemistically called exchange offices. Hordes of runners were employed to make the rounds of the tenement districts twice daily, receiving as commissions fifteen percent of the wagers they brought in.

Shortly after the Civil War Zachariah Simmons, a New Englander, came to New York City with his three brothers and entered the policy racket. John Frink had disappeared from the New York policy scene and Parsons had abandoned policy and faro for the more dignified speculations of Wall Street. The time was ripe for a man of Simmons' capabilities to take over.

Simons formed an alliance with Tammany Hall and in return for protection he agreed to a division of the loot with Tammany statesmen. In midsummer 1870, some policy dealers indicated a reluctance to join the Simmons combination. Simmons promptly resorted to the usual ploy. Through Simmons' influence, the district attorney ordered the police to raid all recalcitrant policy shops in New York City. The policy dealers promptly capitulated and joined hands with Simmons, who then formed the Central Organization, which divided the city into districts, allotted policy privileges, and took most of the profits. By about 1871 Simmons and his brothers were in control of about three fourths of the policy shops in New York. They eventually extended their operations to twenty cities, including Chicago, Milwaukee, Philadelphia, Washington, and Richmond. One of Simmons' runners in New York City was Albert J. Adams, who later became a proprietor of numerous crooked gambling houses and eventually succeeded Zachariah Simmons as the policy king of New York City. In the middle and late 1870s Simmons was one of the managers of the Kentucky State Lottery and the Frankfort Lottery of Kentucky. Both were involved in fraudulent drawings.[42]

In addition to gambling, prostitution served as a rich source of revenue to Tammany Hall politicians. Until the close of the Civil War, prostitution was centered somewhat in the Five Points; the Bowery; and Water, Cherry, and other streets along the East River waterfront. After the cessation of hostilities, the prostitution industry began spreading to many parts of the city. Notorious madams made regular payments to the police, the district attorney's office, and the police justices. Some houses of prostitution maintained direct telegraphic communications with the police in order that officers of the law might be summoned in the event of a disturbance. [43]

In 1866 religious leaders publicly charged that prostitutes plying their trade in New York City totaled twenty thousand, almost one fortieth of the population. John A. Kennedy, the superintendent of police, angrily denied these figures and said that the police department records showed only 3,300 public prostitutes, who were distributed among 621 houses of prostitution and 99 assignation hotels. The police figures, he said, also included 747 waiter girls employed in concert saloons and dance halls.

Whatever their true number, the houses of prostitution and similar dives were numerous and served as congregating places for bank burglars, thieves, street brawlers, and criminals of every color, including members of ruthless gangs. The district around Broadway and Houston was unusually vicious and lawless. Thugs of this area attacked policemen at will. Finally a patrolman, Alexander S. Williams, was assigned to the district. He began challenging the toughest characters, and when they responded he knocked them unconscious with his nightstick. It was said that he averaged a fight a day for almost four years. And so skillful was he at wielding the nightstick that he became known as Clubber Williams, a nickname he was to bear until the end of his career.

In 1871 Williams was appointed a captain and was assigned to command the Twenty-first Precinct, one of the most turbulent sections of the city. Its stationhouse was located on East Thirty-fifth Street, between Second and Third Avenues. In 1876 Clubber Williams was transferred to command the Twenty-ninth Precinct, which extended from Fourteenth to Forty-second Street and from Fourth to Seventh Avenue. Many of the streets were lined with brothels, saloons, and all-night dance halls, which offered the opportunities for rich payoffs to corrupt policemen and politicians. A few days after Williams had taken over the command of this district, he remarked to a friend, "I've been transferred. I've had nothing but chuck steak for a long time, and now I'm going to get a little of the tenderloin." This area thus became known as the original Tenderloin District. [44]

Many of the most depraved dives in downtown New York were located in the immediate vicinity of police headquarters at 305 Mulberry Street. Only about a half block away was a gambling house that catered almost exclusively to the patronage of law officers. The saloon of the notorious bank robber and vice monger Shang Draper was located at 466 Sixth Avenue. In this saloon Draper employed about thirty women, whose duties consisted of enticing drunken men into a house located near Prince and Worster Streets. The men were relieved of their cash through the old badger game or were robbed by thieves who would creep into a room by means of hidden panels cut into the wall and steal a man's belongings while his attentions

were turned to his prostitute companion. Eventually, Draper became a partner of Al Adams, policy king. Draper and Adams at one time reputedly
owned about sixty percent of all cheap faro banks in New York and both
became influential in Tammany Hall politics.[45]

8

TAMMANY DABBLES IN REFORM

The downfall of Tweed and other members of the ring had no lasting cleansing effect on Tammany Hall. Waiting in the wings to assume the leadership of the Society were such worthies as John Morrissey, who had been associated with the Young Democracy revolt in 1870, and Honest John Kelly, a narrow-minded, suspicious, and vindictive martinet. Both had climbed the political ladder with the aid of Boss Tweed.

Kelly, born of poor parents on April 20, 1822, was brought up in one of the roughest districts in the city. When not working, he was fighting. He was a member of a volunteer fire department and participated in the violent politics of his ward. At night Kelly often hung out at the Ivy Green Saloon, where he met such important politicians as John Clancy, who was to become Tweed's secretary, and Peter B. Sweeny, a principal member of the Tweed Ring. In 1853 Kelly was elected alderman and two years later he defeated Mike Walsh for a seat in Congress by eighteen votes. Kelly served two terms in Congress and became a member of the Tammany Hall General Committee. While serving two terms as sheriff, 1859–61 and 1865–67, Kelly became a rich man. The *New York Times* accused Kelly of taking thousands of dollars more than he was entitled to for the care of prisoners and of charging the city 133 percent more than the legal rate for conveying prisoners to and from Blackwell's Island. In 1868 Kelly considered running for mayor against Tammany candidate A. Oakey Hall, but he withdrew from the race and went to Europe, where he was sojourning when the Tweed Ring was being pilloried in the press and investigated by the Committee of Seventy.[1]

In April 1872 the Tammany Society held its annual election. Recognizing the need for Tammany to project a public image of respectability, John Kelly and Augustus Schell, who had been named grand sachem upon Tweed's forced resignation, caused several men who had been identified with the reform movement to be selected as Tammany sachems. Particularly prominent in this group were Samuel J. Tilden and Charles O'Conor. Also brought into the fold of Tammany in 1872 to give the Society a new, clean look were Abram S. Hewitt and Edward Cooper. Like Tilden and O'Conor,

Hewitt and Cooper had been members of the Committee of Seventy. Hewitt was the son-in-law and Edward Cooper the son of one of New York's most illustrious citizens, Peter Cooper, the inventor, industrialist, and philanthropist who had founded Cooper Union. In 1844 he had taken both Hewitt and Edward Cooper into his new business venture of iron manufacturing. The Trenton Iron Company, as it was named, was highly successful. Samuel Tilden had been a stockholder, was elected a director in 1863, and became an intimate friend of Hewitt. It was only natural that he should encourage both Hewitt and Edward Cooper to enter the political arena. [2]

In 1873, William F. Havemeyer succeeded A. Oakey Hall as mayor of New York. His administration was characterized by good appointments. Ordinances dealing with health and security were enforced, streets were kept cleaner than before, the public-school system was improved, and criminal elements were deprived of the sway they had so long held.

By 1874 Honest John Kelly had established himself as the supreme ruler of Tammany Hall. He insisted that his crony and lieutenant Richard Croker be appointed marshal by Mayor Havemeyer. When Croker's appointment was announced, the mayor was "overwhelmed with a torrent of indignation" and a bitter quarrel broke out between Havemeyer and Kelly. In a public letter addressed to Kelly, Havemeyer charged that during Kelly's administration as sheriff he had obtained $84,482 by fraudulent and illegal receipts. Havemeyer characterized Kelly as "worse than Tweed, except that he was a larger operator. The public knew that Tweed was a bold, reckless man, making no pretensions of purity. You, on the contrary," said Havemeyer, "were always avowing your honesty and wrapped yourself in the mantle of piety. Men who go about with the prefix of 'honest' to their names are often rogues." Kelly brought a libel suit against Havemeyer, but on the date the suit was to be tried the mayor dropped dead in his office from apoplexy. [3]

In the 1874 elections Abram S. Hewitt was the Tammany candidate for Congress from the Tenth District. Opposing him was James O'Brien, running as an independent Democrat. Working in behalf of Hewitt's election was Kelly's protégé, Richard Croker. A native of Ireland, Croker had arrived in the United States when only three years old. As a youth he received training as a member of the notorious Fourth Avenue Tunnel gang and became a leader of the East Side roughs and of the volunteer fire department in his district.

On election day, November 3, 1874, Croker, George Hickey, and two other pals began wandering around the Tenth District in the early morning hours. In front of a saloon at Second Avenue and Thrity-fourth Street, Croker and his party encountered James O'Brien. Croker called O'Brien a dirty thief and O'Brien responded by labeling Croker a "damned cur" and stating, "I picked you out of the gutter and now you're supporting a rich man like Hewitt against me for Congress." Blows were exchanged and members of the Croker party drew revolvers. A shot struck John McKenna, an O'Brien adherent, in the head, mortally wounding him. Croker was arrested and charged with murder. Upon arraignment, John Kelly, mayor-elect William H. Wickham, and Abram S. Hewitt appeared in the defendant's behalf. Hewitt furnished $2,500 bail and Croker was released. When the case was tried, the jury was unable to agree on a verdict, and Croker was never brought to trial again. Actually, there was reason to believe that the fatal shot had been fired by George Hickey. Hewitt was elected to Congress by a close margin and, with the exception of one term, served there continuously until 1886.[4]

During this period, the prevalence of crime seriously concerned the people of New York City. In particular, numerous complaints said that the police were showing too much deference to the criminals and not adequately protecting the taxpayers. In 1875, the state Assembly appointed a select committee "to investigate the causes of the increase of crime in the city of New York." The committee focused on the Police Board, which had the responsibility of governing the New York City police force. The Police Board consisted of four commissioners, who selected one of their members to serve as president. The committee reported that "great abuses had sprung up in the past from individual commissioners issuing orders to the superintendent, and even to the superintendent's subordinates, without consulting him." The legislature had imposed on the Police Board a number of duties unrelated to police administration: the commissioners were charged with the responsibility for the management of the cleaning of streets; the commissioners controlled the Bureau of Elections, appointed the inspectors of elections (over two thousand), and designated all polling places. The president of the Police Board also served as a member of the Health Board. However, the select committee found that one of the greatest obstacles to the development of an efficient police force in New York City was "the continual intermeddling of politicians with the government of the force. Patrolmen have generally been appointed through political influence; promotions have been made on the same ground and even details for duty have frequently been regulated in the same manner." The select committee also attributed the increase in crime to the constant improper dismissal of criminals by the magistrates.[5]

The city's rapidly increasing crime rate was of no concern to Honest John Kelly. His main interest was solidifying his position as the new boss of Tammany Hall by eliminating any potential rival to the throne. Kelly's most troublesome foe within the ranks of Tammany was John Morrissey. In 1875 Morrissey was a candidate for state senator from the Fourth Ward, the Tammany stronghold that had previously elected Tweed to the Senate. Shortly before the election Morrissey and his friends were accused of being unresponsive to the demands of the Democratic party and were expelled from Tammany Hall. Although the Fourth Ward had always produced handsome majorities for the wigwam, Morrissey in 1875 defeated the Tammany candidate, John Fox, by 3,377 votes. Particularly rankling to Morrissey were the taunts that only a district that had elected Tweed would send a vicious thug and notorious gambler to the state Senate. Thus, in 1877 Morrissey determined to become a candidate for senator in the Seventh District, one of the most respectable and fashionable in the city. His opponent was Augustus Schell, a director of Vanderbilt railroads and grand sachem of Tammany Hall. During the campaign, Morrissey was publicly denounced as a gambler, ballot-box stuffer, and burglar. Nevertheless, when the ballots were counted, Morrissey was declared victorious by 3,874 votes. Having defeated Kelly-picked candidates in both the poorest and the most fashionable districts of the city, Morrissey's triumph over the Tammany boss was complete. The victory, however, turned out to be a hollow one. During the campaign, Morrissey contracted pneumonia. His health continued to fail and he died in Saratoga on May 1, 1878, before he was able to return to the Senate.[6]

Kelly's efforts to maintain an iron-clad rule over Tammany were not always accepted with abject docility. In 1875 a number of disaffected wigwam stalwarts denounced the Tammany General Committee and formed a rival organization—Irving Hall Democracy.

Kelly's suspicious and vindictive nature caused rifts with several of his political allies. His once cordial relations with Samuel J. Tilden had ended, and at the Democratic National Convention in St. Louis in 1876, Kelly organized a bitter, but unsuccessful, opposition to Tilden's presidential nomination. Upon gaining the nomination, Tilden was able to secure the election of his friend Abram S. Hewitt to the chairmanship of the Democratic National Committee; Edward Cooper was named treasurer. Hewitt served as campaign manager for Tilden during his unsuccessful quest for the presidency.[7]

In 1878 a coalition of anti-Tammany, pro-Tilden Democrats and Republicans elected Edward Cooper mayor of New York. Cooper was a man of recognized independence and character but proved to be indecisive. Within a short time, he alienated the independent voters by giving the appearance of being a Tilden henchman and he was outmaneuvered by Tammany and Republican politicians. The magazine *Puck* asserted that Mayor Cooper disgusted the public, angered the press, and pleased no one. It facetiously called on Peter Cooper to chastise his son. Later appraisals were more kind. His intentions, it was conceded, had been the best, but he had served as mayor under extremely difficult circumstances.[8]

A principal target of Boss Kelly's ire in 1879 was Governor Lucius Robinson, who had been elected three years earlier by Tilden Democrats. When Robinson was renominated, Honest John bolted the Democratic party.

Tammany Hall held a separate convention and nominated Kelly for governor. Kelly then campaigned throughout the state, vigorously attacking Tilden and jeering at Robinson. Through his perfidy, the Democratic party went down to defeat and Republican candidate Alonzo B. Cornell was elected governor. Kelly was satisfied—he had gained revenge on his political foes within the Democratic party.[9]

Boss Kelly's relations with Mayor Cooper were anything but cordial and the mayor's independence only added to the strain. Since 1876, Kelly had held the position of city comptroller. When Kelly's term expired in 1880, Cooper refused to reappoint him, thereby incurring Kelly's undying enmity. By this time the city's Democrats were divided into two factions, Tammany Hall and Irving Hall. From a list of names submitted in 1880 by Irving Hall, the Democrats chose William R. Grace as their candidate for mayor. He was elected and served as the city's chief executive during 1881–82.

In December 1880, anti-Tammany Democrats held a mass meeting at Cooper Union to discuss ways of regenerating the New York Democracy. Abram S. Hewitt was made chairman of a committee to draw up definite plans. A few months later, under the leadership of Hewitt and others, a new organization called the New York County Democracy was born. It was intended to oppose both Tammany Hall and Irving Hall. In the fall of 1881 the new County Democracy triumphantly carried the city elections. By the following year, however, the County Democracy had weakly compromised with Tammany in city affairs.[10]

The year 1884 was filled with disappointments for Honest John Kelly. At the Democratic National Convention in Chicago, Grover Cleveland was nominated for president over the bitter opposition of Kelly and his Tammany organization. The nominee's denunciation of Kelly and the Tammany organization helped to give Cleveland a national clean-government image, which garnered support for his candidacy. Kelly received another setback when his Tammany candidate for mayor in the 1884 election, Hugh J. Grant, was defeated by William R. Grace, a former mayor whose nomination had been agreed upon by both Irving Hall and the New York County Democracy.

The Board of Aldermen in 1884 was, as usual, notoriously corrupt. Twenty of the twenty-two aldermen shared in a $500,000 bribe to gain approval of a franchise for a surface railway on Broadway.

Following the 1884 political campaigns, Kelly broke down from physical and nervous prostration. From his home at Thirty-four East Sixty-ninth Street he continued to issue orders to the Tammany organization. As the end neared, he was able to sleep only with the aid of opiates. On June 1, 1886, the Tammany boss died. His reported fortune of a half-million dollars was deemed rather modest for one who had bossed the city for over a decade.[11]

Throughout Honest John's reign, assessments had been systematically levied upon all officeholders. Even those with salaries of only $1,000 were required to kick back as much as $250. Saloonkeepers, proprietors of prostitution houses, and small shopkeepers or grocers who wished to display their wares on the sidewalk were required to pay tribute to the political leaders of their district. Gangs were used in primary elections to stuff ballot boxes or to prevent opposition voters from entering the polling places. About three fourths of the aldermanic conventions in 1884 were held in saloons or friendly places next door. Reputable citizens who attended these conventions held their peace or ran the risk of being hurled down the stairs or thrown out the window. The police were under the thumb of Tammany Hall and refused to interfere with the activities of the gangs. Honest John had been a believer in a strong organization maintained by rigid discipline. One of his contemporaries declared that Kelly had found Tammany Hall a "horde" but had left it a "political army." Nevertheless, it is obvious that his policies, often based on vindictiveness, at times weakened his organization and spawned such rival groups as Irving Hall and the New York County Democracy.[12]

Upon the death of Kelly, the twenty-four Assembly district leaders which composed the Executive Committee of Tammany Hall announced that henceforth there would be no "boss." Instead, they said, Tammany Hall would be ruled by a committee of twenty-four. Not unexpectedly, cliques immediately arose. Richard Croker, the protégé of Kelly, gained the support of seventeen of the twenty-four leaders and soon became the absolute boss of Tammany Hall, a position he was to hold for a decade and a half.[13]

Richard Croker was born in Ireland on November 24, 1843, and was brought to America by his parents in 1846. Originally the Crokers were English and had landed in Ireland with Cromwell and his army of invasion. Eyra Coote Croker, Richard's father, came from a long line of Crokers noted for drinking, gambling, and squandering their fortunes at an early age. In America the elder Croker eventually obtained a steady job as a veterinary and for a time was assistant veterinary in the stables of a horsecar line.

Although the Croker home was not in the slums, it was on the edge of the notorious Gas House District. Like most boys, Richard joined a youthful gang and eventually became its leader. He disliked books but was interested in horses, dogs, and athletics. Although small of build, he possessed great strength and developed into an excellent boxer. When sixteen years old he left the Olney Grammer School, which he had entered four years earlier, and became an apprentice as a locomotive machinist in the shops of the New York Central Railroad.

At the age of twenty, Croker wrote his name on the rolls of Tammany Hall. He was active as a member of the Volunteer Fire Company, Engine 28, and it was his distinction with this company as well as his leadership of the youthful Fourth Avenue Tunnel Gang that launched his political career. By the time he had reached voting age, Croker expertly directed the activities of repeaters at the polls. In 1868 he became an alderman and for a time was the righthand man of Jimmy O'Brien, the district leader. Subsequently, through Honest John Kelly's influence, Croker was appointed marshal and a year later was elected coroner. He was the aide and protégé of Kelly and had been well groomed to take over Kelly's mantle as boss of Tammany Hall.[14]

At the Tammany convention on October 11, 1886, it was through the influence of Richard Croker that Abram S. Hewitt was nominated for mayor. If the strait-laced, honest, and public-spirited Hewitt was an unlikely candidate to be chosen by the wigwam, it was not because Croker and Tammany Hall had suddenly become idealistic. On the contrary, the Hewitt nomination was a move of political sagacity and expediency. A wave of labor unrest had been sweeping across America. The Knights of Labor had reached the apex of its power and numerous workingmen of New York City were eager to resort to political action. Tammany was frightened. It needed the best candidate it could get to avert political disaster.

Running against Hewitt in the 1886 mayoral election were the labor reform candidate, Henry George, noted economist, founder of the Single Tax movement, and the internationally famous author of *Progress and Poverty;* and Theodore Roosevelt, who had been chosen to head the Republican ticket. The historian Allan Nevins has stated that "never before or since have men of such ability contended for the prize." Hewitt was victorious, garnering 90,552 votes to 68,110 for George and 60,435 for Roosevelt.[15]

On January 1, 1887, Hewitt was inaugurated mayor of New York City. During the campaign he had visited every section of the city, frequently late at night. He had observed that no effort was being made to enforce the closing hours for saloons, either on weekdays or Sundays. Gambling dens, houses of prostitution, and other illegal establishments were operating wide open, and he properly concluded that these places were receiving official protection.

On the night of his inauguration the new mayor was stricken with a severe attack of sciatic rheumatism and was confined to his home for some time. However, he believed the lawless conditions in the city to be so serious that they demanded immediate attention. He summoned the superintendent of police, William Murray, to his home for a conference. He told Murray that the city was running wide open and that lawlessness in some districts was scandalous. Obviously, said Hewitt, such conditions prevailed because of general police graft. Without blinking an eye, Superintendent Murray conceded that everything Mayor Hewitt had said was true. When the mayor asked if the illegal places could be closed, Murray replied, "Certainly; it is only necessary to give the orders." When Hewitt inquired why such establishments existed at all, Murray suggested that it would be better if he put that question to some of his political friends. The mayor disclaimed any friendship with Tammany political leaders but asked if they were interested in such places. "Many of them," replied Murray, and warned the mayor that "if the order goes out, you will be attacking the men who were your best supporters in the last election and who put you in the mayor's chair." The police superintendent's frank remarks shocked Hewitt, but he instructed Murray that regardless of the interests of politicians, the illegal places must be closed.

Mayor Hewitt then launched a blunt inquiry into the personal wealth of his superintendent of police. Murray, a native of New York, had joined the police force in 1866 after having completed his military service as a private in the army during the Civil War. Advancing through the ranks from patrolman, roundsman, and sergeant, he was made a captain in the police department on October 2, 1876, and about eight months later was promoted to inspector. On June 9, 1885, Murray was appointed superintendent.

In a history of the New York Police Department published in 1885, Superintendent Murray's career was extolled as an example of a man rising to the top through honesty, perseverance, and ability. During his conversation with the mayor, Murray's acclaimed virtue of honesty began to appear somewhat clouded. Before becoming superintendent, Murray's highest salary in the police department was the $3,500 a year he had received as an inspector. He said he had never had any business other than that of a policeman. Yet, in response to Mayor Hewitt's specific question, Murray revealed that he was then worth $300,000. When asked about the wealth of police captains, Murray said he thought that most of them had made fortunes. As long as present conditions existed, he said, "there are plenty of opportunities." Hewitt thanked Murray for his frankness and said, "All I ask is that from this day you do your duty. If you are worth $300,000 you can afford to be honest."[16]

Hewitt also summoned Stephen B. French, the president of the Police Board, for a conference. The mayor advised French of his revealing conversation with Superintendent Murray. He told French that he expected the Police Board to lend its assistance in suppressing the dives then flourishing in the city. The response of French was anything but enthusiastic. In fact, he attempted to discourage the mayor by warning him that he was stirring up a hornet's nest and would ruin his chances for reelection. French stated, in what was judged to have been a jocular remark, that if the mayor left the system of political protection alone, he could receive a share of its benefits.[17]

The new mayor was determined to do everything in his power to clean up the city. Realizing that he could not place much reliance on his police department, he hired a private detective to explore and report to him on the underworld's operations. Thus, when he requested the police department to furnish him with a list of disreputable resorts, he could check it against information he was receiving from his private detective. On occasion, he would take the incomplete list furnished by the police department, make copious additions of addresses, and release the information to the press. Among the dives listed by the mayor were gambling houses, roulette establishments, panel houses, unlicensed concert-saloons, and places which specialized in handling stolen merchandise. Since many addresses furnished by the mayor did not appear on any list provided him by the police, he concluded in a letter to Superintendent Murray that there was "a want of knowledge on the part of the police authorities, which is possessed by citizens who choose to use ordinary observation in regard to the disreputable places of resort, commonly called dives, kept open in this city."[18]

The very organization of the police department with its control vested in the Police Board of four commissioners was disturbing to Hewitt. He observed, as had the state Assembly's select committee in 1875, that each commissioner thought himself empowered to give orders to the superintendent of police. This often resulted in an impossible conflict of authority. Also of grave concern to the mayor were the scandalous conditions prevailing in the police courts. The city then had eleven police magistrates, most of whom were ignorant political hacks completely subservient to Tammany bosses or saloonkeepers who controlled the vote. Justice was dispensed on the basis of political influence. Overwhelming evidence of guilt was ignored if the defendant had the backing of a political leader or a saloonkeeper. Frequently, of course, the political leader was himself a saloonkeeper.[19]

Within six months after Hewitt became mayor, New York City had become a cleaner and far more decent city, and remained that way throughout his term of office. Hewitt had an acid tongue and was frank and needlessly tactless. He aroused the enmity of the Irish by refusing to review a St. Patrick's Day parade. He was at odds with Grover Cleveland and openly stated he did not believe in his reelection. Although he unnecessarily made enemies at times, his high standards of integrity, his constant battle against corruption, and his efficient administration as the chief executive officer of the city were generally recognized and appreciated. When Hewitt stated during the first half of 1888 that he would not be a candidate for reelection, influential newspapers—*Times, Herald, Commercial Advertiser, World, Evening Post*—declared, in substance, that his services as mayor could not be spared and that the people should compel him to run again.

As might be expected, Tammany Hall was fed up with the impeccable and uncontrollable Mr. Hewitt. The need for a clean-image, window-dressing candidate was no longer urgent and Tammany Hall nominated Hugh J. Grant as its candidate for the 1888 mayoral election. The Republicans selected Joel B. Erhardt. Hewitt consented to accept the nomination of the County Democracy. At the election Grant was victorious, with 114,111 votes to 73,037 for Erhardt and 71,979 for Hewitt.[20]

9

CROKER RULE—A DECADE OF
INVESTIGATIONS

Hugh J. Grant, Boss Croker's protégé, was the first regular Tammany Hall man to be elected mayor since the days of the Tweed Ring. Grant promptly appointed Croker to the post of city chamberlain at a salary of $25,000 a year. The boss held this office until the beginning of 1890, when he resigned and took one of his numerous trips to Europe.[1]

In the same year, the New York State Senate Committee on Cities, headed by Republican J. Sloat Fassett, undertook an investigation of conditions in New York City. Testimony before the Fassett committee revealed that the various city departments were honeycombed with corruption; gambling houses made regular payments for protection and as much as $10,000 had been paid to obtain a single saloon license. The salary of every city office-holder was subject to an assessment ranging from five to ten percent, collected by the wiskinskie of the Tammany Society.[2]

A sensation occurred when Patrick H. McCann, a brother-in-law of Mrs. Croker, appeared before the Fassett committee. McCann, who had quarreled with the boss, testified that about six years earlier, Croker had shown him a satchel containing $180,000 in bills. This sum, he said, had been raised by Tammany to bribe members of the Board of Aldermen to confirm the appointment of Hugh J. Grant as commissioner of public works. However, the money was returned to the donors when Franklin Edson, mayor of New York City, 1883–84, refused to appoint Grant. Later, through Croker's influence, Grant became sheriff. He thereupon presented a number of en-velopes, each containing $5,000 in currency, to Croker's six-year-old daugh-ter, Flossie. When Grant was called before the Fassett committee, he admitted having made two such cash gifts totaling $10,000 because, he explained, he was Flossie's godfather and wanted to do something handsome for the child. Subsequently Croker conceded that he had not placed the money in trust for his daughter but had apparently used it himself.[3]

The Fassett committee revelations caused a public outcry. A combination of Republicans, Democrats, and Independents formed the People's Munic-ipal League for the specific purpose of removing Tammany Hall's grip on city government. Tammany promptly renominated Hugh J. Grant for mayor and in the fall elections of 1890 he was reelected.[4]

Croker's role as boss was highly lucrative and he made no effort to avoid an outward show of wealth. In 1890 he disposed of his modest home in Harlem and paid $80,000 for a residence at Five East Seventy-ninth Street, just off Fifth Avenue. With its elaborate furnishings, the total cost of the home exceeded $200,000. He maintained a retinue of servants and had his own private Pullman car. The following year, Croker purchased a stock farm at Richfield Springs together with a string of thoroughbred horses. In 1893 he paid $250,000 for a half interest in the Belle Meade Farm, recognized as one of the best stud farms in America. The boss also spent $100,000 more on race horses.[5]

On Sunday morning, February 14, 1892, the Reverend Charles H. Parkhurst of the Madison Square Church delivered a sermon that shocked many New Yorkers and eventually paved the way for a full-scale investigation of Tammany misrule. The minister had received some information on crime and corruption in New York City through his presidency for almost ten months of the Society for the Prevention of Crime, a civic agency originally organized in October 1878 by a number of distinguished citizens, including Peter Cooper.

Using as its text "Ye are the salt of the earth," Parkhurst's sermon was blunt, forceful, and undiplomatic, and, unfortunately, it contained charges not based on solid evidence. He accused the officials of protecting gambling and vice. In uncomplimentary terms, he mentioned the "mayor and his whole gang of drunken and lecherous subordinates" and charged that "while we fight iniquity, they shield and patronize it; while we try to convert criminals, they manufacture them. . . ."

A few days after Parkhurst's sermon, a grand jury issued a presentment in which it asserted that the clergyman's charges had not been based on evidence. Said the grand jury, "We desire further to express our disapproval and condemnation of unfounded charges of this character, which . . . can only serve to create a feeling of unwarranted distrust in the minds of the community with regard to the integrity of public officials, and tends only to hinder the prompt administraton of justice."[6]

Tammany officials, who very likely influenced the nature of the grand-jury presentment, smugly believed that they had muzzled the preacher. But Parkhurst, though taken aback by the criticism leveled at him, was not so easily subdued. If evidence they wanted, evidence they would get. With expert aid, from a member of his own church and some detectives, the clergyman proceeded to conduct firsthand investigations into conditions in the city. On March 13, 1892, Reverend Mr. Parkhurst mounted his pulpit. In the place usually occupied by a Bible and a hymnal was a bulky package of affidavits. This time the sermon dealt with specific facts. On the preceding

Sunday, five detectives utilized by Parkhurst had observed 254 saloons in twenty-two precincts operating in violation of the Sunday-closing ordinance. Investigators had visited wide-open gambling establishments and in just one precinct thirty-one houses of prostitution were doing a prosperous business. Parkhurst stated that all information in his possession had been reduced to written statements, which had been sworn to and corroborated, and were, he said, "subject to the call of the district attorney." The clergyman demanded that the authorities "take vigorous hold of the material . . . or quit their hypocritical clamoring after specific charges." Parkhurst asserted that "Tammany Hall is not a political party but purely a business enterprise. . . . The material in which it deals and from which it draws prolific dividends, is crime and vice, such as flourish in gambling resorts, disorderly houses, and corner groceries. The more material it can handle, the larger its profits, and therefore the policy which it steadfastly pursues is to foster crime and exercise guardianship over the criminals."[7]

Following the March 13 sermon, a grand jury insisted that the district attorney request the appearance before it of Dr. Parkhurst, his associates, and agents. In a presentment, the grand jury charged that the police department was either incompetent or corrupt but suggested corruption as the real reason for its ineffectiveness. A mass meeting regarding the city's crime and corruption was held at Cooper Union Hall in June 1892.

The grand jury indicted, among others, a notoriously corrupt police captain, William S. Devery. He was tried before a friendly jury and acquitted. The disreputable conditions in his precinct had received wide publicity and his acquittal outraged the public. On January 25, 1893, the chamber of commerce adopted a resolution calling for a thorough legislative investigation of the New York City Police Department. In response to this resolution, Senator Clarence Lexow obtained the authorization of the Senate to conduct the investigation. A committee headed by Senator Lexow was appointed and as a result of severe pressure exerted by the Reverend Mr. Parkhurst and his associates, the able John W. Goff was named general counsel.[8]

Boss Croker had a premonition of things to come and he wanted no part of it. In the spring of 1894 he ostensibly resigned his chairmanship of Tammany and sailed for Europe. Named as the deputy boss to mind the store during his absence was John C. Sheehan, who was also serving as a member of the Police Board. However, until his return over three years later, Croker continued to issue orders to Tammany Hall which were rigidly obeyed. While away the boss reportedly spent about $700,000 racing horses on English tracks.[9]

The Lexow committee began taking testimony on March 9, 1894. Evidence produced at the committee hearings clearly established that large-scale crime and vice flourished with the sanction and full protection of

Tammany Hall and the police. As in the marketplace, everything had a price.

Houses of prostitution were charged a rate, depending upon the number of inmates, ranging from $25 to $50 a month. Women of the streets paid the patrolman for the right to solicit. A woman who owned a number of houses of prostitution testified that over a period of time she had paid $30,000 for protection. A brothelkeeper on Chrystie Street testified that whenever a new police captain arrived in the precinct, the latter always called upon her, demanded an initial payment of $500 for the privilege of continuing business, and exacted a promise of $50 each month for protection. She named three police captains, including Devery, as having demanded and received the $500 "initiation" fee from her. All forms of gambling establishments were assessed high prices for their illegal concessions. Poolrooms were charged $300 a month and more than six hundred policy shops paid a monthly rate of $15. Saloons were assessed $20 a month in line with "established custom."[10]

Policemen and Tammany district leaders shared in the graft. Many became wealthy. The superintendent of police, Thomas Byrnes, admitted to the committee that he was worth $230,000. He attempted to explain that his wealth was derived from the stock market on tips given him by Jay Gould, who had died a few years earlier. The infamous Alexander S. (Clubber) Williams, who had been promoted to the rank of police inspector in 1887, told the committee that his personal fortune did not exceed $60,000. However, it was known that he owned a yacht as well as real estate in Manhattan and in Cos Cob, Connecticut, having an aggregate value of about $300,000. Williams declared that he had made his money from the sale of house lots in Japan.[11]

The Lexow committee hearings revealed that every phase of the police department was in the iron grip of Tammany Hall. James J. Martin, a powerful Tammany district leader who, conveniently, was a member of the Police Board, testified that of all the appointments, transfers and promotions he made, from eighty-five to ninety-five percent were recommended by Tammany leaders of the district in which the policemen resided. Police Captain Max F. Schmittberger testified that policemen were required to obey all orders from Tammany Hall, were compelled to pay money to Tammany politicians for their appointments as well as for any promotions, and had to contribute to Tammany Hall campaign funds. On the witness stand Captain Schmittberger revealed how a particular patrolman had approached him and said he wanted to be promoted to roundsman. Schmittberger got in touch with Captain Alexander (Clubber) Williams, who told him the price was $300. Schmittberger collected the $300, which he turned over to Captain Williams, and the patrolman became a roundsman. The same procedure was followed when the roundsman later paid $1,600 to become a sergeant and

$14,000 to become a captain. Another police captain, Timothy J. Creeden, testified that he had passed civil-service examinations on three or four occasions but was told he could not gain a promotion unless he paid for it. Finally he paid $15,000 for his promotion and the promise of an assignment to a "fat" precinct.[12]

By the time the Lexow committee had ended its hearings on December 29, 1894, it had issued 3,000 subpoenas, heard 678 witnesses, and taken 10,576 pages of testimony. Evidence disclosed a picture of widespread protected crime and corruption in New York City. The police department was under the absolute control of Tammany Hall, which used it to achieve and maintain political power as well as for financial enrichment. To all intents and purposes, the police department was in the business of issuing to criminals and vicemongers franchises that permitted them to operate with impunity.[13]

New Yorkers had not been so shocked at public revelations of crime and corruption since the 1871 exposure of the Tweed Ring. A Committee of Seventy, composed of representatives of all classes, was formed for the purpose of freeing the city from the grip of the Tammany machine. The committee nominated for mayor William L. Strong, a prominent dry-goods merchant and a Republican. Tammany Hall found it expedient to bypass its grand sachem, Thomas F. Gilroy, who was serving his first term as mayor. Instead, it returned to its old standby, Hugh J. Grant, who again became the wigwam's candidate. Strong was elected by a majority of 45,187 and was inaugurated mayor on January 1, 1895.[14]

Strong proved to be an efficient mayor and gave the city a good administration. In May 1895 Theodore Roosevelt became president of the Police Board and in the same month the wealthy superintendent of police, Thomas Byrnes, was replaced by Peter Conlin, who was given the title of chief of police. Theodore Roosevelt assiduously attempted to place the department on a sound basis by applying civil-service standards to appointments and reducing political control. At the time Roosevelt arrived on the scene, preparations were under way for the annual police parade. He canceled the affair, stating, "We will parade when we need not be ashamed to show ourselves."[15]

The accomplishments of the Strong administration were solid and merited the praise of independent observers. A genuine effort was made to maintain integrity in the various branches of city government. However, Strong's policy of strict law enforcement met with bitter opposition. This was particularly true regarding the detested law that ordered saloons closed on Sundays. Blamed in part for this law was the rural influence of upstate New York, which was labeled "hayseed tyranny."[16]

As Mayor Strong's term neared its end, Tammany Hall considered the city elections of 1897 of paramount importance. The state legislature had enacted the Greater New York bill, which provided for the merger into one city of the five boroughs of the metropolitan area—Manhattan, Kings, Queens, Richmond, and the Bronx. By this legislative action the population of New York City was nearly doubled, to 3,350,000. Beginning on January 1, 1898, one mayor would preside over greater New York. The new charter provided for the election of mayor in off years, when the elections for president or Congress did not take place. The powerbrokers of Tammany Hall saw in the new enlarged city great opportunities but they were aware of possible difficulties as well. In Brooklyn there existed a well-oiled political machine, Kings County Democracy, ruled over by a boss, Hugh McLaughlin, who was in the habit of issuing orders, not taking them.[17]

So important were the impending city elections that Boss Croker ended his voluntary three-year exile to England and returned to New York City on September 7, 1897. Tammany had awaited the return of the boss before naming its mayoral candidate. In fact, there were some rumors that Croker was considering running for mayor himself. Instead, he named an obscure judge, Robert A. Van Wyck, as the Tammany candidate and took charge of directing a sizzling campaign, which left no stone unturned to elect the man of his choice.[18]

The campaign was one of the most unusual in New York City history. Opposing Croker's candidate were General Benjamin F. Tracy, the Republican nominee; Seth Low, president of Columbia University, who was chosen by the Citizens' Union; and Henry George, who had made big waves in the 1886 election and was now representing a coalition of radical elements known as the Jefferson Democracy. At the height of the electioneering, George suddenly dropped dead of apoplexy. He was replaced on the ticket by his son, Henry George, Jr., but the Jefferson Democracy faded into the background.

Highlighting the bizarre campaign of 1897 was an invasion of Broadway by a Cook County Democracy delegation of several hundred politicians from Chicago. Most of the Chicagoans had never heard of Van Wyck, but they certainly embraced the ideals and motives of rapacious Tammany Hall. When Croker asked his intimate friend, Mayor Carter Harrison of Chicago, for electioneering help, Harrison herded several hundred of his loyalists onto a special train and headed for New York City. On the day the special train arrived, Tammany Hall staged a huge demonstration of welcome to its allies from the Windy City. By nightfall Fourteenth Street was packed with onlookers from Third Avenue to Union Square. For several hours the crowd was treated to fireworks, three marching brass bands, and numerous Tammany parading delegations followed by Carter Harrison's Cook County Democracy, which was accompanied by its own band headed by a gigantic drum major. The Chicagoans were decked out in their marching uniforms of long frock coats, dark trousers, silk hats, and white gloves. Among the prize representatives of Windy City statesmanship who participated in the gala affair were the incomparable rulers of Chicago's First Ward, "Bathouse John" Coughlin and Michael (Hinky Dink) Kenna. It was in their ward and with their aid that the notorious Capone organization had its genesis, was nurtured, and grew to power.[19]

As the bitter contest for the mayoralty progressed, it increased in intensity. During one fiery campaign speech, the chairman of Tammany Hall's legal committee and the wigwam's candidate for district attorney, Asa Bird Gardiner, defiantly shouted, "To hell with reform!" This expression struck a spontaneous note of approval with thousands of Tammany followers, who adopted it as a campaign slogan. On election day Tammany scored a smashing victory. Frenzied joy reigned in the wigwam and celebrations erupted on the streets. Impromptu parades occurred, and many of the participants carried placards that read "To Hell with Reform!" And snake-dancing young men chanted, "Well! Well! Well! Reform has gone to hell."[20]

On January 1, 1898, Robert A. Van Wyck became the first mayor of greater New York. But while Van Wyck held the legal title to the office, Boss Croker wielded the power and was the actual master of the metropolis.

Of all offices in the city, none was more important to Croker than that of chief of police. This post was held by John McCullagh, who for several months had been fighting graft in the department, crime in general, and the operation of gambling and vice establishments in particular. Obviously, McCullagh must go and orders were given to the Police Board to get rid of him. When the Republican commissioners refused to vote for McCullagh's ouster, the mayor removed them. The newly constructed Police Board then ousted McCullagh and Croker's friend, the venal William S. Devery, was named chief of police.[21]

The appointment of Devery as chief of police was an open acknowledgment that New York City was once again a wide-open town. The Lexow committee investigation of 1894 had established that the precinct Devery then captained was a cesspool of vice and corruption. It was Devery's philosophy that people wanted vice, gambling, and liquor, and that it was the prerogative of the police to tolerate vice and share handsomely in the profits. Devery's closest associate was Frank Farrell, formerly a Sixth Avenue saloonkeeper. With the aid of Devery, Farrell had established a string of poolrooms for horse-race betting and had taken the leadership of this kind of gambling away from James A. Mahoney, the owner of some one hundred thirty poolrooms. Another intimate of Devery was Al Adams, the boss of the policy racket in New York. Small wonder that in October 1898 a feature story in *Harper's Weekly* proclaimed, "New York is wide open once more. Tammany Hall has at last secured its 'terrible revenge'! Richard Croker and his associates have set in full operation a system of Tammany government under which vice flourishes openly for a price. . . . Tammany leaders are fattening their pocketbooks through the privilege of selling the right to violate the law and through extortion and forced tribute."[22]

Conditions in the city resembled those prevailing just before the Lexow committee began its investigation in 1894. Croker and his political machine were in control of every facet of municipal government and ruled with brazen arrogance. Predictably, in 1899 the state Assembly appointed a committee to investigate New York City. Known as the Mazet committee, its counsel, Frank Moss, had previously served as one of the commissioners on the Police Board and was well versed in Tammany manipulations of the police department.

Called as a witness before the Mazet committee was Boss Richard Croker, who admitted that he or his immediate associates had selected all the men who were appointed to important city offices after Van Wyck became mayor. Members of the Tammany Society became officeholders or favored contractors. Over $700,000 worth of city orders were given to favored contractors without bidding. Croker related that the Tammany organization was built not solely on political principles but on the way members of the Society sustained one another in business. Said Croker, "We want the whole business, if we can get it." During a cross-examination of Croker, committee counsel Frank Moss sarcastically asked, "Then you are working for your own pocket, are you not?" Croker snapped back, "All the time, the same as you!"[23] Croker's admission that he was working for his own pocket all the time had a public impact comparable to Tweed's arrogant rejoinder, "Well, what are you going to do about it?"

Testimony before the Mazet committee revealed that Croker and Tammany Hall maintained absolute control over the police department, which was thoroughly demoralized and inefficient. Vice was protected and the police shared in the proceeds not only of prostitution itself but also from robberies committed by harlots on men they had solicited. Saloons were required to make regular payments of $100 to $150 a month to the police for protection. In some districts, such as the Tenderloin, saloonkeepers also had to gain the approval of Tammany leader Bob Nelson and buy beer from Al Adams, the policy king, who owned the Karsh Brewery. Testimony was given the committee that a gambling syndicate was being operated by "Big Tim" Sullivan, a state senator and the Tammany leader of the Bowery district, Frank Farrell, the king of poolroom horse-race betting, and William S. Devery, the chief of police of New York City, who was a gambling-house partner of Sullivan.[24]

Croker admitted that judicial candidates were subjected to assessments in their districts. Other testimony noted that judicial aspirants had paid from $10,000 to $25,000 to secure their nominations. Croker told the Mazet committee that "the city would be better off without civil service" and labeled it "an obstruction to city government."[25]

As the Mazet committee sessions were nearing their end in April 1900, confidential agreements between the Tammany administration and the American Ice Company were brought to light. The company had been given a virtual monopoly on the sale of ice in New York City. Because of increased prices resulting from the monopoly, the really poor people of the city could not afford to buy ice. Just before the agreements were signed, the company had given blocks of stock to almost every influential Democratic politician in New York City. Among the stock beneficiaries were Croker, Mayor Van Wyck, and Hugh McLaughlin, the Brooklyn boss. The value of Mayor Van Wyck's stock alone was estimated at $500,000 to $700,000 before the committee disclosures destroyed the trust.[26]

At the conclusion of its investigation, the Mazet committee majority report summarized that the New York City government was responsible no longer to the people but to a dictator. "We see the central power, not the man who sits in the mayor's chair, but the man who stands behind it. We see the same arbitrary power dictating appointments, directing officials, controlling boards, lecturing members of the legislative and municipal assemblies. We see incompetence and arrogance in high places. . . . We see the powers of government prostituted to protect criminals, to demoralize the police, to debauch the public conscience, and to turn governmental functions into channels for private gain."[27]

Before the Mazet committee had completed its investigation, the *New York Times,* on March 9, 1900, reported that gambling in the city was under the rigid control of an unofficial secret gambling "commission" that collected $3,095,000 a year in graft. The powerful group consisted of a so-called commissioner, two state senators, and the dictator of the poolroom syndicate of the city. The *Times* reportedly received its information from a big gambling-house proprietor who became annoyed because he thought too many places were being given permission to operate. A scale of payoffs fixed by the commission required each of 400 poolrooms to pay $300 a month; each of 500 crap games, $150 a month; each of 200 small gambling houses, $150 a month; each of 20 large gambling houses, $1,000 a month; each of 50 envelope games, $50 a month; and an unspecified number of policy operators were assessed an aggregate of $125,000 a year. No new gambling place was permitted to open without the sanction of this unofficial commission. Before a gambling house could start operating, the proprietor was required to pay an "introduction fee" of $300 to the police captain of the district. The captain then made his report to the gambling commission on the applicant's ability to pay for protection on a regular basis. It was charged that of the big houses assessed $1,000 a month for protection, six were also required to share a part of their earnings with one of the state senators of the gambling commission. This was true of the place that had been only recently established by Richard A. Canfield at Five East Forty-fourth Street and that the *Times* described as "the finest place of its kind in this country if not in the world."[28]

Actually, at the very time the Mazet committee hearings were in full swing Richard A. Canfield was going ahead with plans to open in New York City the most exquisitely furnished gambling house in America.

Canfield, eventually known as America's greatest gambler, had come a long way since his release on January 16, 1886, from the Providence County Jail in Cranston, Rhode Island, where he and two associates had spent six months on gambling charges. Proceeding to New York City in June 1886, Canfield and William Glover, the owner of a pawnshop, began operating a poker house, equipped with six tables in a small room, on Broadway between Eighteenth and Nineteenth Streets. Profits for each partner amounted to $150 a week, hardly an improvement over his days in Rhode Island.

In May 1888 Canfield and David Duff, a cousin of Glover, opened the Madison Square Club at Twenty-two West Twenty-sixth Street. A four-story brownstone house with a monthly rental of $600, the club was only about a thousand yards from Delmonico's, which catered to the type of clientele that Canfield and Duff hoped to attract. At first they paid $200 a month for protection, but as the establishment prospered, they were required to turn over a percentage of the earnings. Duff went on a nightly drinking spree, which brought the place into ill repute, so Canfield forced Duff to sell out to him.

The Lexow committee in 1894 had issued two subpoenas to Canfield, but he refused to appear at the hearings. In the same year, Canfield paid Albert Spencer $250,000 for the Club House in Saratoga Springs, the place originally built by John Morrissey. Following the policy established by Morrissey, no local Saratogans were admitted to the gaming rooms. The restaurant connected with the casino gained an international reputation. The casino usually opened the last week in July and closed at the end of August.

In 1898 Canfield paid $75,000 for a brownstone house at Five East Forty-fourth Street in New York City. The title for the house was placed in the name of his mother-in-law, Maria Martin. In the summer of 1899 Canfield sailed to Europe. There he bought valuable art objects for his gambling house, and there he met American artist James A. McNeill Whistler, with whom he established a lasting friendship. Eventually Whistler painted his portrait. While abroad Canfield visited such noted casinos as the one in Monte Carlo. In the fall of 1899 he returned to New York City and placed the finishing touches to his place at Five East Forty-fourth Street, which had been converted into a beautiful art gallery–gambling house. The gambling rooms on the second floor had the appearance of a noble hall and contained elaborate layouts for roulette, faro, baccarat, and *rouge et noir*. Servants tended to every want of the patrons, who were served the costliest of foods and the rarest of wines. The clientele, while not large, was wealthy. Reginald Vanderbilt reputedly lost $405,000 in five nights. A well-known banker of New York City left his check for $75,000 after one night's play. Although the place operated only a little over two years, it formed the basis of a fortune for Canfield.[29]

The disclosures of the Mazet committee had convinced many citizens, including important businessmen, that the need for a municipal overhauling was urgent. Poor people had been outraged at the Ice Trust revelations; they were incensed by the widespread prevalence of well-organized, protected vice and crime. So strong were the public protests that Boss Croker realized some kind of a sop must be made to reduce citizen anger or Tammany would suffer defeat in the city elections the following year. Thus, in November 1900 Croker appointed a Committee of Five, all well-known Tammany men headed by Lewis Nixon, to investigate and report on the vice situation in the city. Croker's action aroused bitter opposition among those Tammany leaders whose principal source of wealth was the tribute they collected from vice and crime. Leading the fight against Croker's vice crusade was Big Tim Sullivan, Tammany district leader of the Bowery. Big Tim made it clear that he would not tolerate any outside dictation by Croker or anyone else.[30]

Next to Croker, Sullivan was the most powerful leader in Tammany Hall. His exalted place in the Tammany hierarchy had been achieved during the three-year sojourn of Croker in Europe, from 1894 to 1897. Big Tim, also known as "Dry Dollar" and "Big Feller," was born in a tenement in the old Sixth Ward in 1863. At an early age, he had become affiliated with the Whyos, a vicious gang of thugs, thieves, and murderers that came into existence after the Civil War. The gang was an outgrowth of the Chichesters of the old Five Points and reached its zenith as a criminal organization during the 1880s. Two of the gang's principal leaders were hanged in the Tombs in 1888 and by the middle 1890s the Whyos had been mostly exterminated. It was through the influence of the Whyos that Sullivan, when only twenty-three, was elected to the state legislature on an anti-Tammany ticket.[31]

At Albany Sullivan became friendly with an East Side Tammany leader, Tom Foley, who brought Big Tim into the folds of the wigwam. In 1890 Croker made Sullivan the leader of the Bowery district, a region of cheap amusement resorts, lodging houses inhabited largely by vagrants, petty criminals, and common laborers, and a tenement area that had recently been overrun by Jewish and Italian immigrants. Big Tim promptly mobilized the vicious and criminal elements of his district into an army that could be relied upon to win elections through the wholesale use of repeaters and the exercise of terrorism at the polls.

Among the underworld leaders most helpful to Big Tim during his climb to power was the notorious gunman Monk Eastman, whose organizing genius had enabled him to weld a number of East Side gangs of thugs and thieves into an efficient federation. The prostitution and vice interests in the Bowery were important segments of Sullivan's organization, and Big Tim headed a gambling syndicate that enabled him to exercise a dominant influence over the flourishing gambling industry throughout the city. By a series of alliances with other district leaders and underworld bosses, Big Tim had by the late 1890s established a vice and crime empire that controlled most of the city south of Fourteenth Street.

Sullivan's political formula, which relied heavily on underworld alliances, was obviously successful during a long career. It made him a state senator. He served one term in Congress, where he was seldom in his seat at roll call, made no speeches, and distinguished himself only by winning the pinochle championship of Congress. Besides becoming the second most powerful politician in New York City, he became a millionaire.[32]

A number of events in late 1900 and early 1901 Sullivan viewed as a threat to his empire. He had been outraged when Croker defied him by appointing his Committee of Five to investigate vice. Only a few weeks later Theodore Roosevelt, in one of his last official acts as governor, removed Asa Bird Gardiner as district attorney. Asa had won the hearts of Tammany in 1897 with his speech "To Hell with Reform." Appointed to replace Gardiner was an independent Democrat, Eugene A. Philbin, who promptly ordered a series of sensational gambling raids. Then in February 1901 the state legislature ousted William S. Devery by the simple expedient of abolishing the office of chief of police. That was the last straw for Sullivan. He got in touch with Croker, who was abroad, as usual, and issued an ultimatum. He threatened that unless remedial steps were taken promptly, the vice and gambling interests would desert Tammany in the coming elections and thus ensure the defeat of the wigwam's ticket. Croker bowed to Big Tim's demands and ordered Mayor Van Wyck to appoint Devery to the position of deputy police commissioner. In his new post, Devery appeared to be as powerful as before.[33]

In the Second District primary election on September 17, 1901, there was an indirect confrontation between Croker and Big Tim. In a fight for district leader the contestants were Paddy Divver, long a sturdy friend and lieutenant of Croker, and Big Tom Foley, who had the active support of Sullivan. In this polyglot district the large Italian vote loomed important. During the campaign, both Divver and Foley had attended Italian christenings and funerals, and presented gifts to newly married Italian couples. On primary day, Big Tim Sullivan played his trump card. Through arrangements with the infamous gang leader Paul Kelly—real name Paolo Vaccarelli—a steady stream of Italian gunmen poured into the Second District. As early as two o'clock in the morning gunmen were stationed in front of nearly every polling place. By nine that morning, a huge vote for Tom Foley had been cast, while many Divver supporters had found it impossible to reach the polls. Naturally, Foley won the election by a large margin and Big Tim emerged in Tammany Hall stronger than ever.[34]

Croker returned from Europe to direct the mayoral campaign of 1901. Four years earlier the slogan "To Hell with Reform" had served to rally the forces of Tammany to a sweeping victory. Now Tammany needed to show a receptiveness to reform. Official investigations had established that Tammany had been the instrument of protecting gambling, prostitution, and crime, and had engaged in shady, lucrative business transactions. The public was fed up.

Croker found it expedient to choose a respectable lawyer, Edward M. Shepard, as the Tammany candidate for mayor. The opposing Fusion ticket offered Seth Low for mayor and William Travers Jerome, a justice of the court of special sessions, for the office of district attorney. Jerome had been one of the first to crusade against protected vice, gambling, and police corruption. During the campaign the Fusionists directed their attack against three main targets: protected vice, William S. Devery, and Richard Croker. The dullness of the dignified Seth Low was offset by Jerome's lively thrusts, which so galled Devery that he finally lost his poise. Spouting off to reporters, Devery asserted that Jerome was unsound mentally and was going around insulting everybody. Said Devery, "He's like the rhinoceros up in the park. Every time he goes down under water he comes up with a gulp and blows it all over everybody." Devery blurted that it wouldn't take him ten minutes to grab Jerome by the back of the neck and lock him up. His sally, which also included a boast that he would not be thrown out of his police position, was a political mistake and upset candidate Shepard as well as Boss Croker. On election day Low won the mayoralty by a plurality of 31,636 and Jerome was elected district attorney. Once again Tammany had been ousted from power.[35]

Almost as soon as Seth Low was seated in the mayor's chair, Croker revealed that he was permanently retiring as the boss of Tammany Hall. On January 13, 1902, it was announced publicly that Croker had selected Lewis Nixon, then forty-one, as his successor and had made him chairman of Tammany Hall's finance committee, a position always held by the boss. The appointment of Nixon, a graduate of the U.S. Naval Academy, a naval contractor, and formerly head of Croker's Committee of Five to investigate vice, was intended to give the Society respectability. After attending Nixon's installation, Croker sailed for England, where he expected to live on his estate at Wantage. He told reporters that he intended to devote himself to winning the English Derby, a feat he was to accomplish in 1907, when Orby, a colt reared by Croker on his stud farm at Glencairn, near Dublin, was the winner at Epsom Downs.[36]

Nixon's reign as boss of Tammany Hall was short-lived, indeed. After but four months Nixon, on May 14, 1902, resigned. He asserted that he had been hampered at every turn. Before district leaders would carry out his orders they would get advice from the self-exiled Croker. During his past numerous absences abroad, Croker's reign was what reporters called "government by cable." And Nixon revealed that he had received a cablegram direct from Wantage ordering him to place certain men on the Board of Sachems. Said Nixon, "I could not retain the leadership of Tammany Hall and at the same time retain my self-respect." With his resignation, Nixon vanished permanently from Tammany politics.

For a few months, Tammany was under the control of a triumvirate of district leaders, Charles F. Murphy, Daniel F. McMahon, and Louis Haffen. Rule by committee naturally created an impossible situation. Big Tim Sullivan of the Bowery was now the most powerful individual in Tammany Hall but he did not want to become the boss. Sullivan threw his support to Charles F. Murphy and on September 19, 1902, Murphy became the real successor to Croker as the boss of Tammany Hall.[37]

Charles Francis Murphy was born in New York City on June 20, 1858. While a youngster, he worked in an East Side shipyard. Fighting his way among virile youths of the Gas House District, Murphy developed physical prowess and leadership qualities. In 1879 Murphy became the owner of a small saloon on Nineteenth Street, east of Avenue A, and became active in Tammany politics. Later he opened another saloon, at Twentieth Street and Second Avenue, which served as the headquarters for the Tammany district organization called the Anawanda Club. By 1890 he was the owner of four prosperous saloons. In 1892 Murphy was chosen the Tammany leader of the Eighteenth Assembly District. As leader of this "Gas House District," Murphy could be found every night from 7:30 to 10:00 leaning against a lamppost at the northwest corner of Twentieth Street and Second Avenue. Everyone knew where he could be found and it was from this lamppost that he conducted much of his business as district leader. Murphy combined the business of politics and saloon operations. One of his brothers was a member of the police force, another was an alderman, and still another later became an alderman. When Robert A. Van Wyck was elected mayor, Charles F. Murphy was appointed a dock commissioner. By that time he was worth about $400,000, which he had accumulated from the saloon business and politics over a period of about eighteen years.[38]

Murphy was never troubled by interference from Croker, who now was spending most of his time at his stud farm in Ireland or at the race courses of England. Two of Croker's sons died in 1905. One was killed while driving his racing automobile at Palm Beach, Florida. The other died on a train in Kansas, from narcotic poisoning caused by smoking opium. For some time Croker had been estranged from his wife, Elizabeth, whom he had married in 1873. However, when she died in 1914, Croker returned to New York City for the funeral. A few weeks later, Croker, then seventy-three, married Bula Benton Edmondson, a twenty-three-year-old direct descendant of Sequoya, a Cherokee Indian chief. The bride, whose Indian name was reported as Kotaw Kaluntuchy, had appeared at a New York threater the preceding summer in a spectacle in which she, while wearing an Indian costume, rode across the stage on a horse and sang our national anthem in the Cherokee language. Croker spent the remaining years of his life with his second wife on his Irish estate. When he died on April 29, 1922, his estate, valued at more than $5 million, was left to his wife.[39]

About eleven months after Charles F. Murphy had ensconced himself in the boss's chair in the wigwam, vicious gang warfare involving scores of gunmen broke out on the city streets. This widely publicized affair in August 1903 was embarrassing because the gang leaders of the opposing factions had been closely allied with Tammany Hall leaders and had received their protection.

For several years, two principal federations of criminal gangs under skilled and ruthless leadership had more or less divided Manhattan Island into well-defined kingdoms. The Five Pointers, successors to the Dead Rabbits, the Plug Uglies, and the Whyos of earlier Five Points fame, had several hundred members under the leadership of Paolo Antonini Vaccarelli, commonly known as Paul Kelly. The Five Pointers ruled the area between Broadway and the Bowery, and Fourteenth Street and City Hall Park. The New Brighton Dance Hall on Great Jones Street near Third Avenue was owned by Paul Kelly and served as the congregating place for the Five Pointers. Here they held their social functions and planned raids against their enemies.

A rival federation of gangs, also with a membership of several hundred, was led by Monk Eastman and dominated the area from Monroe to Fourteenth Street and from the Bowery to the East River. Headquarters for the gang, known as the Eastmans, was an unsavory dive on Chrystie Street near the Bowery.

The leaders of the two factions presented a study in contrasts. Paul Kelly was a soft-spoken man of below average height and was usually clothed in a neat and conservative manner. He rarely engaged in rough-and-tumble fighting, although for a time he had been a bantamweight professional prizefighter of modest skill. Kelly had indulged in a certain amount of self-education and had acquired a smattering of cultural tastes. He was an efficient organizer and commanded respect and sometimes emulation as a leader. Among the numerous groups affiliated with Paul Kelly was the James Street gang headed by Johnny Torrio, then a young man in his early twenties. Kelly became Torrio's idol. A few years later Torrio was to go to Chicago, where eventually he used his talents to establish, with the help of Al Capone, a criminal organization that became known throughout the world.[40]

Monk Eastman, whose real name was Edward Osterman, was the son of a respectable Jewish restaurant owner and was born about 1873 in the Williamsburg section of Brooklyn. He was a typical-looking gangster. His bullet-shaped head was usually bedecked with a derby hat, entirely too small for him, which sat atop bristly, unruly hair in need of trimming. His jowls sagged, and his short bull neck, as well as his face, carried the knife scars of many a battle. A broken nose and cauliflower ears added to his ferocious appearance. As he lounged around his Chrystie Street headquarters, Eastman did not wear a shirt, collar or coat.

Both Kelly and Eastman had maintained close relations with Tammany Hall politicians. At the polls the gangs furnished repeaters in wholesale lots and, when necessary, violence. The members of both gangs had interests in houses of prostitution and in stuss games, which flourished on the East Side. Stuss games operated by members of the Eastman gang were held up and robbed by Five Pointers, and similar games controlled by Five Pointers were raided by the Eastmans. The gang leaders directed the operations of pickpockets and loft burglars, and occasionally furnished murderers for hire.

In 1901 Eastman was set upon in the Bowery by a half-dozen Five Pointers armed with blackjacks and revolvers. He was shot in the stomach, but recovered. A Five Pointer was killed in retaliation.

Warfare between the Eastmans and Five Pointers continued month after month. Much of the turmoil centered around stuss games operated by members of one gang and raided by gunmen of the rival gang. Around eleven o'clock on a hot night in mid-August 1903, several Five Pointers were about to raid an Eastman stuss game on Rivington Street under the Allen Street arch of the Second Avenue elevated railroad. Six Eastmans appeared on the scene and opened fire, killing a Five Pointer. The Five Pointers sought cover behind pillars of the elevated structure and the Eastmans followed suit. Reinforcements for both gangs arrived. By midnight scores of gunmen, evenly divided between Eastmans and Five Pointers, were blazing away at each other from behind elevated pillars. Three gunmen were slain and many were wounded. Policemen who first appeared at the battle site were forced to retreat in disorder. A short time later, officers from several police stations were rushed to the field of conflict. Several gunmen were arrested and others were driven away. Among those arrested was Monk Eastman, who gave the name of Joseph Morris. When he was arraigned the following morning, a magistrate promptly discharged him.

The wide publicity given the big battle upset Tammany politicians, who agreed that steps must be taken to stop the "Wild West" gunfighting on the East Side. A meeting was arranged between Paul Kelly and Monk Eastman. Appropriately, Tammany district leader Tom Foley, the pal of

Big Tim Sullivan, acted as mediator. The two gang leaders agreed to a cessation of hostilities and Tom Foley gave a ball to celebrate the peace treaty. At the height of the festivities, Kelly and Eastman appeared in the middle of the dance floor and shook hands.[41]

As might be expected, the celebration was premature. It was only a short time before hostilities between the two gangs were in full swing again. Politicians arranged for another meeting between Kelly and Eastman; this one was to take place in the presence of neutral observers. To settle the question of supremacy, the two gang leaders agreed to meet in the prizefight ring. On the specified night Eastman and Kelly, each accompanied by about fifty men, proceeded to a barn in the Bronx for the fight. At the outset Kelly's experience, gained as a onetime bantamweight boxer, gave him an advantage. But Eastman's greater size and ferocity offset Kelly's skills. After two hours of fighting both Kelly and Eastman were exhausted and the fight was pronounced a draw.[42]

The big gang battle between the Eastmans and the Five Pointers in 1903 merely continued the warfare that had been going on intermittently for three quarters of a century. As far back as the 1820s, gangs from the Five Points sallied forth to engage in bloody combat with their rivals in the Bowery. On July 4 and 5, 1857, deadly fighting between the Dead Rabbits of the Five Points and the Bowery Boys was halted only through military intervention, and only after ten persons had been killed and scores wounded.

But if the gangs of the Bowery and Five Points in 1903 represented a continuation of the past, they were also a link to the future. For many years, Paul Kelly remained the political ally of Tammany Hall leaders Big Tim Sullivan and Big Tom Foley. Kelly also became an influential labor-union boss, and he maintained strong connections with many Italian gunmen, including his close friend Ciro Terranova. Those acquaintances were to play prominent roles in the deadly gang wars of the 1920s and 1930s. And Big Tom Foley continued to serve as the political patron of all East Side gangsters, including Joe the Boss Masseria, who was slain in a celebrated 1931 gang killing in which Terranova and Charles (Lucky) Luciano reportedly participated. With the aid of underworld backing, Foley eventually became the most powerful man in Tammany Hall, next to Boss Charles F. Murphy.[43]

10

EARLY 1900s—A POLICEMAN EXECUTED,
A GOVERNOR IMPEACHED

The mayoral election of 1903 was the first political campaign directed by Charles F. Murphy as boss of Tammany Hall. Running for mayor as the Tammany candidate was the physically attractive, thirty-eight-year-old lawyer George B. McClellan, Jr., the son of the controversial Civil War general who unsuccessfully opposed Lincoln in the 1864 presidential election.

Long a staunch Tammany organization man, George B. McClellan, Jr. originally had been a protégé of Boss Richard Croker. It was Croker who had made McClellan president of the Board of Aldermen in New York City in 1893–94. When selected for this $3,000-a-year post, he was only twenty-seven years old, and Croker told him that he was assessing him only $300 because he realized he did not have much money. From 1895 to 1903, McClellan served five consecutive terms in Congress, where, through the influence of Boss Croker, he gained a coveted place on the prestigious Ways and Means Committee. Before entering Congress, McClellan had also been a sachem of the Tammany Society and an ex-officio member of its Executive Committee.[1]

McClellan was elected mayor and took office on January 1, 1904. Most of the other Tammany candidates for the principal elective offices in the city were also successful, and once again the Tiger was in firm control of the city government.

Many observers viewed McClellan merely as a front man for Boss Charles F. Murphy. A *London Times* story reported that on the eve of the 1903 election, the gamblers and brothelkeepers of New York City had gathered in front of McClellan's headquarters to acclaim his victory. The underworld characters were addressed by "the unspeakable Bourke Cockran," who congratulated them on the return of "the wide-open town." McClellan branded this story fiction. W. Bourke Cockran, he said, had not participated in the mayoral campaign at all. Strained relations had existed between Cockran and the new mayor ever since McClellan had been given Cockran's seat in Congress nine years earlier. Nevertheless, McClellan later admitted having received a call shortly after the election from Boss Murphy, who stated, "Bourke Cockran was anxious to have a talk" with him that same evening. Arriving with Bourke Cockran were Murphy and J. Sergeant Cram, a constant companion of the boss. At this meeting, said McClellan, Bourke Cockran "proceeded to 'demand on behalf of the millions of our cosmopolitan citizens' that I throw the town wide open. I asked him if this included prostitution, liquor, and gambling and he replied that it did." When McClellan turned down the demand for a wide-open town, Cockran called him a "narrow-minded puritan" and left.[2]

Immediately after taking office, McClellan had to fill the positions in his cabinet. For advice he turned to Boss Murphy. Said McClellan, "I had great respect for his judgment and felt perfectly sure that he would not 'let me down.' My disillusionment came later. . . ." The cabinet members recommended by Murphy deemed him to be their chief and regarded the mayor only as a necessary inconvenience. The mayor learned that some of these men made daily reports to Murphy as to what was transpiring in the mayor's office. At the beginning of McClellan's administration, the suspicions that the mayor-elect merely was a front man for the boss of Tammany Hall were being confirmed.[3]

Of the cabinet posts not named by Boss Murphy, the most important was the office of commissioner of police. McClellan selected William McAdoo, whom he had known in Washington. There McAdoo had served as assistant secretary of navy under President Grover Cleveland. McClellan's commissioner of police (not to be confused with William Gibbs McAdoo of the Woodrow Wilson administration) was a lawyer and had served two terms in the House of Representatives from New Jersey. Subsequently, McClellan labeled McAdoo a failure as commissioner of police, stating that he lost control over the department, that it was being run by the police inspectors. Actually, it was the Tammany Hall politicians, particularly the district leaders, who ran the department.[4]

With Boss Murphy pulling the strings of government, his relatives, friends, and political associates were in a position to make hay and they overlooked few opportunities. The New York Contracting & Trucking Company had been incorporated about 1901 by John Murphy, a brother of the boss; James E. Gaffney, an alderman; and Richard J. Crouch, a political lieutenant of the boss. This firm was seeking a $2 million contract for excavating the site of the new Pennsylvania Railroad station in New York City. Before the contract was let, there was the usual behind-the-scenes maneuvering. The Pennsylvania Railroad was required to secure a franchise from the Board of Aldermen to use the streets for its terminal in Manhattan as well as for its tunnel approaches. Rumor had it that the aldermen were demanding $300,000 to act favorably upon the franchise. Originally leading the opposition to granting the franchise were Gaffney and "Little Tim" Sullivan, Tammany leader in the Board of Aldermen. (Little Tim and Big

Tim Sullivan were cousins. Boss Murphy once remarked to McClellan that Big Tim ''will sometimes tell the truth'' but Little Tim ''never does.'')

John F. Ahearn, president of the borough of Manhattan, confided to the mayor that Boss Murphy had instructed him ''not to give the Pennsylvania people their permits to dig the foundations of their new station unless they gave the contract to his brother Johnny.'' Actually, Ahearn asserted, the boss was a secret partner in the company. Suddenly, orders were given to approve the franchise and it was Alderman Gaffney who rallied support for a favorable vote. The New York Contracting & Trucking Company received its $2 million contract, although it was later learned that its bid was $400,000 higher than a competitor's. By 1905 it was estimated that the New York Contracting & Trucking Company or its offshoots had received contracts aggregating $15 million from companies that depended upon favors from the city government.[5]

For several years the dilatory tactics of the Board of Aldermen in awarding franchises had aroused considerable resentment. As a result, the state legislature passed an act vesting the power to grant franchises in the Board of Estimate and Apportionment, which was composed of eight officials: the mayor, the comptroller, the president of the Board of Aldermen, and the five borough presidents. This board became one of the most powerful instruments in the government of New York City.[6]

A major problem at the turn of the century was the impossible congestion on the busy thoroughfares of New York. Before the McClellan administration, some efforts had been made to enforce what might be called the common law of the road and a few safety islands had been introduced. However, meaningful traffic regulations of any kind were nonexistent. The driver of every truck, trolley, motorcar, or vehicle of any kind was on his own, and to make progress on the streets he relied solely on his nerve and bullying tactics.

Shortly after taking office, McClellan sent a police captain, John J. O'Connor, abroad to study traffic regulations in the principal cities of Europe. Upon his return, the Traffic Bureau was organized for the first time. A mounted squad now appeared on the streets and somewhat captured the fancy of the public, but the ostacles in initiating a system of traffic rules were almost insurmountable. Drivers of all types of vehicles rebelled against any traffic regulations, which they regarded as infringements on personal liberties. And Boss Murphy, inspired by the truck drivers' union, was outraged that anyone should be fined for refusing to obey the orders of a traffic policeman. In Brooklyn, Justice William Jay Gaynor, who would become mayor in a few years, issued a permanent injunction against Mayor McClellan on the ground that any regulation of traffic was a curtailment of individual constitutional liberties. Almost a year elapsed before the Court of Appeals overruled Gaynor and permitted the traffic laws to be put into effect in Brooklyn.[7]

In spite of vigorous opposition to innovation, McClellan was later able to boast that "during my administration the city bought its first motor fire engine as well as its first motor ambulance and its first official motorcar, and licensed its first cab, a horse-drawn hansom, equipped with a taxi meter."[8]

In 1905 public attention was diverted for a time from the usual machinations of Tammany Hall to scandals in the big life-insurance companies. Demands for an investigation of reputed abuses became so persistent that they could no longer be ignored. The state legislature appointed a committee of three senators and five assemblymen, headed by Senator William Armstrong, to conduct an investigation. Named as counsel for the committee was a brilliant lawyer of unquestioned integrity, Charles Evans Hughes. Only recently Hughes had distinguished himself when he handled the Gas Trust investigation. During this inquiry he had shown an unusual capacity for patient and persistent probing for the facts.

With Hughes directing the investigation, the insurance business was rocked to its very foundation. It was shown that the New York Life Insurance Company had contributed $48,702.50 to President Theodore Roosevelt's campaign fund and had made similar gifts to the Republican party in 1896 and 1900. Witnesses stated that Mutual Life Insurance Company had contributed $40,000 to the Republican party in 1904, Equitable had donated $50,000, and smaller companies had given lesser amounts. The public was indignant when it was learned that policyholders' funds were being spent for political purposes. Hughes prepared a comprehensive report with sweeping recommendations for legislation to curb abuses. By April 1906 the state legislature had enacted laws that gave New York the best insurance legislation ever known.

As Hughes was conducting his relentless questioning of insurance company executives, the Republican bosses were irate. Hughes, a Republican, had tied his party to the life-insurance scandal. The 1905 elections were approaching and the Republican leaders advanced the name of Hughes as the logical candidate for mayor. Hughes regarded his proposed candidacy in another light; he believed it to be a plot to break up the insurance investigation and he attempted to withdraw his name from consideration. Nevertheless, on October 6, 1905, a delegation of party leaders called upon Hughes and informed him that he had been nominated for mayor. Hughes remained adamant and stated that in his judgment, he had no right to accept the nomination. "A paramount duty," he said, "forbids it." The proposed candidacy of Hughes for mayor was reluctantly abandoned.[9]

The 1905 city elections loomed big in the eyes of Tammany Hall. Under the provisions of a revised charter, the term of the incoming mayor would be four years. And the Tiger certainly had no intention of losing control of the city for that length of time. Relations between Mayor McClellan and the boss had become strained. Murphy would have preferred to dump McClellan, but such a move was now politically inexpedient; the mayor had indicated an intention of running as an independent if denied the Tammany renomination. The election was certain to be hard-fought. An avowed enemy of Boss Murphy, William Randolph Hearst, the publisher, was the Municipal Ownership League candidate and would be a tough opponent. McClellan emerged victorious, with 228,407 votes to 224,929 for Hearst and 137,184 for the Republican candidate, William M. Ivins. William Travers Jerome, whom the bosses had declined to renominate for district attorney, ran as an independent and was reelected.[10]

George B. McClellan, Jr. began his second term as mayor on January 1, 1906. Without delay, Boss Murphy appeared at McClellan's home with his slate of suggested cabinet appointments. Although McClellan had announced that if reelected he would run the mayor's office independently of Boss Murphy, no one, including the boss, took him seriously. Murphy had been imbibing freely and, according to McClellan, was in the condition known as "fighting full." McClellan turned down Murphy's recommendations for the posts of corporation counsel and commissioner of police. He attempted to impress upon the boss that he would resist his efforts to control the mayor's office.[11]

McClellan removed his commissioner of police, William McAdoo, who left office on January 1, 1906. Shortly after his dismissal, McAdoo wrote realistically that "a combination of interests which thrive on the nonenforcement of law or make large profits by allying themselves in a business way with criminal and vicious groups, can bring a more concentrated and personal pressure to bear for the removal of a police commissioner than an army of law-abiding honest citizens, who may be even enthusiastically in favor of the policy he is pursuing. . . . [F]rom the day of his entrance until the day he leaves, an honest police commissioner must expect a perpetual conspiracy against his continuance in office or the success of his administration."[12]

For McAdoo's replacement, McClellan again turned to a former Washington, D.C., acquaintance. This time the man selected for the post of commissioner of police was General Theodore A. Bingham, a retiree from the army after the loss of a leg in an accident. In Washington he had been in charge of buildings and grounds and had acted as a sort of chief of protocol at the White House.

McClellan, who had tagged McAdoo a failure as commissioner of police, eventually complained that General Bingham gave him more trouble than any other man who served under him. Admittedly, Bingham was a man of great ability, energetic, and honest, but McClellan decried his lack of tact and charged him with disloyalty, an accusation that competent observers said was untrue. General Bingham, who remained as commissioner of police until he was removed by Mayor McClellan about July 1, 1909, soon learned that politics dominated the entire department. He later wrote of the far-reaching baneful influence that Tammany district leaders exerted over the police force. Some district leaders, he said, visited police stations where they had more authority than the executive head of the department. They issued orders to police captains and lieutenants, arranged for disciplinary action against policemen who showed signs of political independence, and made the lives of such officers miserable. Before Bingham was removed, McClellan, with the support of Senator Patrick H. McCarren, the Brooklyn boss, had launched a futile campaign to take over the leadership of Tammany Hall. During this period, the political influence in some Manhattan precincts became so bad that Bingham "had to make radical changes in the personnel of those districts." Perhaps it was this action that aroused the bitter animosity of McClellan and caused him to accuse Bingham of disloyalty.[13]

In addition to the ever-present pernicious influence of politics on the police department, conditions prevailing in some sections of the city made good law enforcement almost impossible. Shortly after his removal as commissioner of police, William McAdoo wrote in 1906: "Considering the fearful congestion of the population, the great number of families housed in each house, the closeness of the living quarters, the narrowness of the streets, and the mixture of races, the Lower East Side presents undoubtedly the most complex and difficult police problem of any similar place on earth."

In the crowded tenement houses of the Lower East Side, conditions were incredibly bad. The streets were always crowded. "The roadway," said McAdoo, "becomes a footpath, and wagons, automobiles, and trolley cars thread their way through dense masses of men, women and children." It was estimated there were five thousand licensed and unlicensed pushcarts in this one region. The pushcart peddlers sold anything from a pair of shoestrings or a stick of candy to a dressed goose, an oil stove or fresh fruit and vegetables. From the windows of many of the tenement houses, residents hurled refuse into the crowded streets below. In the Jewish sections, the noise made by live chickens and geese that were confined in coops before being kosher-slaughtered added to the overall confusion and noise of the district.[14]

In the Italian districts of the Lower East Side, there were many armed gunmen roaming the streets. Black Hand extortionists aroused intense fear among the Italians and Jewish victims were sometimes panic-stricken. For the specific purpose of dealing with vicious Italian criminals, Commissioner of Police McAdoo created a special squad headed by Detective-Sergeant Joseph Petrosino and staffed by Italian-American policemen. Petrosino had already established a reputation for solving crimes committed by Italians, and his squad performed meritorious service throughout greater New York.

McAdoo acknowledged the presence of desperate groups of criminals who resorted to violence if their extortionist demands were not met. However, wrote McAdoo, "That there is such a thing as a thoroughly organized, widely separated secret society which directs its operations in all parts of the United States from some great head center, such as the Mafia or Black Hand is pictured, I have never believed in the light of the facts presented to the police."[15]

Joseph Petrosino continued to head the Italian squad after McAdoo was removed as police commissioner and eventually was promoted to the rank of lieutenant. It was publicly announced by Commissioner of Police Bingham on February 19, 1909, that Petrosino, as head of a newly formed secret-service squad, had departed for Italy and Sicily to procure important information about Italian criminals who had come to America. On March 12, 1909, as Petrosino was waiting for a trolley near the Garibaldi Station in the Piazza Marina in Palermo, Sicily, two men suddenly fired four shots at the New York City lieutenant and he was instantly killed. The gunmen were never identified, but a widely accepted version attributed the murder to the Sicilian Mafia under the direction of its chief, Don Vito Cascio Ferro.[16]

During the early 1900s, there were several significant changes in New York City's underworld leadership. Monk Eastman, once the ally of powerful Tammany Hall leaders, had fallen into disfavor with his patrons and had lost his prestige and power. On November 2, 1904, Eastman and an associate had attempted to hold up a well-dressed man who was staggering down the street. The intended victim turned out to be a Pinkerton detective, who drew a gun and began firing. Eastman fled, but ran into a policeman who clubbed him into unconsciousness. He was charged with robbery and felonious assault and was sentenced to ten years at Sing Sing. Following his release on parole in June 1909, Monk returned to the East Side. There his efforts to regain his position of underworld leadership were unsuccessful. He even failed as a petty criminal, once receiving an eight-month sentence for smoking opium and on another occasion a two-year term in Dannemora following a robbery conviction. During World War I, Eastman enlisted under the name of William Delaney in the 106th Infantry of the New York National Guard. On December 26, 1920, his bullet-riddled body was found on the sidewalk on East Fourteenth Street. He had encroached on the territory of a bootlegger and narcotics peddler, who shot him five times, thus ending the career of the once powerful gang leader.[17]

After Monk Eastman's arrest in 1904 and his imprisonment, two of his lieutenants, Kid Twist and Richie Fitzpatrick, tried to assume leadership of the gang. Before long, jealousy developed and Kid Twist, whose real name was Max Zweiback (or Zerbach), suggested a conference to settle their differences. Actually, the proposed meeting was a ruse. Almost as soon as Fitzpatrick arrived at the designated back room of a Chrystie Street dive to meet Kid Twist, the lights were extinguished, a revolver blazed, and Fitzpatrick was slain. Everyone fled. When the police arrived, only the body of Fitzpatrick was there.

Kid Twist now looked covetously on one of the most prosperous stuss games on the East Side—that operated on Suffolk Street by a Five Pointer known as the Bottler. Kid Twist and an associate, Kid Dahl, visited the Bottler, who was flatly informed that henceforth Dahl was to be his partner and the profits were to be divided equally. The Bottler had the choice of accepting the arrangement or death. He agreed to the partnership. A few weeks later Kid Twist sent word that he had assigned the Bottler's share in the stuss game to a Twist adherent known as the Nailer. This was more than the Bottler could stomach and he declared that he would not capitulate to the new demands. Kid Twist promptly obtained the services of Vach Lewis, also known as Cyclone Louie, to kill the Bottler. Cyclone walked into a stuss game and fatally shot the Bottler. The game reopened a few days later, with Kid Dahl and the Nailer in charge.[18]

While Kid Twist was arranging for the demise of the Bottler and was attempting to solidify his position as the leader of the Eastman gang, trouble was brewing for the boss of the Five Pointers, Paolo Vaccarelli, better known as Paul Kelly. A onetime Kelly henchman, James T. (Biff) Ellison, and Razor Riley, a proficient gunman, became obsessed with a self-imposed mission to kill the head of the Five Pointers.

One night Ellison and Riley, each half drunk, headed for Paul Kelly's New Brighton Dance Hall. Upon entering the place, they observed Kelly seated at a table in the rear with Bill Harrington, Rough House Hogan, and Harrington's sweetheart. Clutching revolvers, Ellison and Riley rushed on the dance floor and walked toward Kelly's table. Harrington, sensing trouble, warned of the approaching gunmen. Riley shot and killed Harrington. Kelly instantly ducked under the table but immediately emerged from the opposite side with a revolver in each hand. The lights at the New Brighton were turned out, and for several minutes guns blazed away in darkness. Three bullets struck Paul Kelly. Friends carried him from the place and rushed him to Harlem, where he remained in seclusion for a month. When police arrived at the scene of the gun battle, the New Brighton was in darkness. Everyone had fled. Only the body of the slain Harrington remained. Significantly, hanging on the bar mirror was a portrait of the powerful Tammany leader Big Tim Sullivan, a close ally of Kelly. The New Brighton was never opened after the bloody incursion by Ellison and Riley. Paul Kelly started another place, Little Naples, but it was closed during the latter part of 1906 as a result of pressure by reform elements.[19]

Kelly, nevertheless, continued to be a powerful underworld leader in the area for several years. He also began looking at a new source of personal fortune—the labor unions.

Along the waterfront Kelly brought together some groups of unorganized workers into the Garbage Scow Trimmers Union, and in time became the leader of a number of influential harbor unions. After organizing the rag-pickers on the dumps at East River and 108th Street, Kelly became their business agent. He called a strike, which ended in violence. Three men were murdered during the conflict.

Eventually Kelly moved out of the Lower East Side and took up residence in a house at 352 East 116th Street, which was owned by his gangland associates, Ciro Terranova and members of the Morello family. Politically, he was recognized as a man of importance by Tammany Hall leaders. At a political meeting in the Bowery, Big Tim Sullivan found it advantageous to boast publicly that through his influence with the courts, he had saved Paul Kelly from at least twenty years in prison in the Harrington murder case. The declaration was intended to ingratiate himself with the Italian voters in his district. Following Big Tim's death, Kelly's patron was Big Tom Foley. [20]

Favorite gangster hangouts, particularly during the summer evenings, were the drinking and dining places of Coney Island. On the night of May 14, 1908, a nineteen-year-old Five Pointer, Louis Pioggi, known as Louis the Lump, entered a Coney Island dance hall where Carroll Terry, a girlfriend of Kid Twist, was employed. Pioggi danced with Carroll and asked her to return to Manhattan with him after her workday had ended. A short time later Kid Twist and Cyclone Louie appeared on the scene, sat down at a table, and were joined by Carroll Terry. Pioggi left the dance hall in a rage, visited a saloon, and heavily imbibed straight whiskey. Kid Twist and Cyclone Louie followed Pioggi to the saloon and there proceeded to humiliate him. Pioggi departed and made a telephone call requesting reinforcements. About six Five Pointers hurried to Coney Island. A hoodlum was sent into the saloon with a false message for Kid Twist that Carroll Terry wished to see him outside. The Kid fell for this ruse and when he stepped outside, Pioggi shot and killed him. Cyclone Louie, who had followed Kid Twist from the saloon, attempted to run but guns of the Five Pointers mowed him down. During the furor, Carroll Terry was on her way to the saloon to meet Kid Twist. A bullet struck her shoulder. As Pioggi was fleeing the bloody scene, a policeman made an appearance. Again Pioggi fired, and a bullet from his gun pierced the policeman's helmet. Pioggi went into hiding. After politicians interceded in his behalf, Louis the Lump pleaded guilty to manslaughter and was sentenced to eleven months in the reformatory at Elmira, New York. [21]

After the murder of Kid Twist, an important segment of the old Monk

Eastman gang was controlled by William Alberts, commonly known as Big Jack Zelig. Born of respectable Jewish parents in 1882, he started his criminal career when only fourteen years old as a pickpocket, and gradually moved up the ladder to the status of gunman and gang leader. By the time of Monk Eastman's downfall in 1904, Zelig ranked next to Kid Twist and Richie Fitzpatrick in the esteem and confidence of Eastman.[22]

During the early 1900s, incessant warfare marked the garment industry, which was scattered throughout the East Side. In sweatshops maintained in tenement houses and loft buildings, workers were abused and exploited. Frequently the laborers rebelled; picket lines were set up; thugs were hired to fight the pickets; and pickets, when the opportunity arose, administered beatings to their bosses. Constant turmoil in the garment industry offered lucrative opportunities to East Side gangs. Expert in the art of violence, they sold their services to the highest bidder.

Two of the most important gang leaders of the time who engaged in mercenary thuggery were Big Jack Zelig and Dopey Benny Fein. Growing up in their service were such future underworld "greats" as Little Augie Orgen, Hyman (Curley) Holtz, Louis (Lepke) Buchalter, and Jacob (Gurrah Jake) Shapiro. Before too many years had elapsed, Lepke and Gurrah were to impose their fearsome rule over the garment industry and achieve international prominence as underworld bosses. Also working for Big Jack were four gunmen, who within a few years were to play prominent roles in one of the most celebrated gang killings in New York history. These gunmen were Harry (Gyp the Blood) Horowitz, Louis (Lefty Louie) Rosenberg, Frank (Dago Frank) Cirofici, and Jacob (Whitey Lewis) Seidenshner.

During the first two decades of the twentieth century the Lower East Side was perhaps the most fertile breeding ground in America for underworld leaders who would gain national and sometimes international "renown." Ethnically, the criminal organizations of the East Side were predominantly Italian (including Sicilian) or Jewish. The West Side gangs and their leaders were largely Irish.[23]

In November 1906 the Bureau of City Betterment, predecessor to the Bureau of Municipal Research, issued a pamphlet denouncing the administration of a noted Tammany district leader, John F. Ahearn, president of the borough of Manhattan. John Purroy Mitchel, who had been appointed by Mayor McClellan to the office of commissioners of accounts, directed a thorough investigation, and on July 16, 1907, submitted a report that revealed inefficiency, waste, neglect, and corruption in the Ahearn administration. Inexcusably—but perhaps understandably—this was the first public investigation that had been conducted for eighteen years.

Only a few months earlier, in the 1906 state election, Charles Evans Hughes had been elected governor of New York on the Republican ticket. Charges against Ahearn were filed with Governor Hughes, who personally presided over hearings. On December 9, 1907, Hughes ordered the removal of Ahearn as borough president. Ten days later the Tammany-dominated Board of Aldermen elected Ahearn to succeed himself, but upon a judicial appeal the reappointment of Ahearn was declared illegal. The commissioners of accounts also filed charges with Governor Hughes against the powerful Tammany sachem Louis Haffen, president of the borough of the Bronx. Hughes also ordered the removal of Haffen. Subsequently, Joseph Bermel resigned as president of the borough of Queens when he was summoned by the governor to face his accusers.[24]

In 1907 a raid was conducted by the district attorney's men on the poolroom gambling syndicate's "clearinghouse" at 112 Fulton Street in New York City. Canceled checks and other records uncovered by the raiders established that a person designated variously in the syndicate's books as "Tommy," "T.G.," "T. Grady," and "Sen." had been paid more than $43,000 during the first two years of operations. There appeared to be little doubt that the beneficiary of this largess was Senator Thomas F. Grady, a close friend of Boss Murphy, a powerful democratic leader in Albany, and the chief orator of the Tammany organization.[25]

Senator Grady was one of the leaders of the opposition to Governor Hughes' dramatic battle in 1908 against racetrack gambling. Because of abuses stemming from gambling at racetracks, Hughes sought the repeal of the Percy-Gray law under which such gambling was flourishing, notwithstanding provisions in the state constitution absolutely prohibiting "any lottery, the sale of lottery tickets, pool selling, bookmaking, or any other kind of gambling." Instigated by Hughes, a bill was introduced to repeal the Percy-Gray law and the governor waged a vigorous fight to get this legislation enacted.

Progambling lobbyists swarmed through the corridors of the capitol in Albany. A subsequent legislative graft-hunt committee heard testimony that indicated a corruption fund of $500,000 had been raised to defeat the antigambling bill. Named in testimony as having received substantial sums of money from the corruption fund were James E. Gaffney, Senator Thomas F. Grady, and Senator Patrick H. McCarren, Democratic boss of Brooklyn and a close ally of Mayor McClellan. One jockey club had expended $33,000, seven other racing associations had spent similar amounts, and ninety-three bookmakers had subscribed $3,000 each to the graft fund. In the midst of the battle, Governor Hughes received a threat on his life. Republican leaders gave no support to Hughes but quietly sat on the sidelines and sneered. The governor took his fight directly to the people and through a series of hard-hitting speeches won wide support for his cause. The law prohibiting racetrack gambling was passed in June 1908 and Hughes hailed it a victory for law and order. Within twenty-four months, California, Texas,

Louisiana, and Georgia followed the example of New York by enacting similar antigambling legislation.[26]

As McClellan's last year as mayor, 1909, was nearing its end, he still entertained hopes of fulfilling high political ambitions. Figuring prominently in McClellan's plans was the Brooklyn Democratic boss, Patrick H. McCarren. Relations between the mayor and McCarren were close. Although their attempt to wrest the leadership of Tammany Hall from Boss Murphy had thus far failed, they had not given up the struggle.

But McClellan's political hopes received an unexpected blow with the sudden death of McCarren. At the funeral on October 26, 1909, McClellan marched in the procession as the chief mourner. "Certainly no one in the church that day," wrote McClellan, "had greater reason to mourn a loyal friend than I." The loss of McCarren left the mayor entirely on his own with his "prospects of success reduced to the minimum." McClellan's goal had been the governorship of New York, which he believed would have placed him in the running for the presidency of the United States in 1912. His break with Murphy had been irreparable and the man on whom he had pinned great hopes was dead.[27]

McClellan was one of the more interesting mayors of New York City. He was a lawyer, scholar, and politician, and after leaving the political arena, he was a professor of economic history at Princeton University for twenty years. While still a young man, he was politically ambitious. To reach his goals, he became a strong Tammany Hall organization man. He was a protégé of both bosses, Croker and Murphy. As he climbed the political ladder, he received the support of and gave his backing to some Tammany leaders who were known protectors of underworld elements. Later, McClellan observed, "The truth of the matter is that the game of municipal politics is not one that a self-respecting man can play with success under present conditions."[28]

In the city elections of 1909 Tammany candidate William J. Gaynor was victorious and took office on January 1, 1910. Gaynor, a sixty-one-year-old Brooklyn lawyer, had served as a New York Supreme Court justice since 1894 and had won acclaim for his frequent exposure of tyrannical conduct by policemen. He was an intelligent man of high integrity, with progressive views and unquestioned independence of character. But he was also highly eccentric. Even persons unflinchingly dedicated to Gaynor acknowledged that he was impatient, irascible, and unstable. He had a quick tongue and was a master at making statements that were widely quoted in the press. On occasion, he was compelled to make a humiliating public apology. Once an alderman sued him for libel. Gaynor directed his sleuths to investigate his antagonist's background and when it was reported that the man appeared to be honest, Gaynor sharply retorted, "He's an alderman—he can't be honest." Citizens who wrote letters of complaint to the mayor were publicly degraded through Gaynor's clever but highly insulting responses, which he gave to the press for publication.[29]

In August 1910 Maynor Gaynor and his son Rufus boarded the *Kaiser Wilhelm der Grosse* at Hoboken for a vacation trip to Europe. Before departure, several of the mayor's friends, members of his official family, and reporters were milling about the ship. Suddenly a disheveled man who had been lurking in the background pressed a gun to the back of the mayor's neck and pulled the trigger. The would-be assassin was James J. Gallagher, a discharged city employee who blamed the mayor for his troubles. Gaynor was rushed to a Hoboken hospital where he remained for three weeks. Later he spent several weeks recuperating at his summer home and finally returned to his office in City Hall on October 3, 1910. The bullet fired by Gallagher had lodged in Gaynor's throat and was never removed. For the rest of his days, Gaynor's voice was reduced to a rasping whisper. With his health impaired, the mayor became more impatient, unreasonable, and vindictive than before.[30]

By 1912 there were about eighty-five thousand regular employees on the city payroll. Of this number, 4,346 were firemen and 10,118 were policemen. Originally Gaynor had chosen James C. Cropsey as commissioner of police. Cropsey was a forceful, independent man of adequate competence. With corruption permeating the politically dominated police department, strong leadership was essential. Yet, Gaynor forced Cropsey to resign and appointed in his place a young socialite, Rhinelander Waldo, who had served as fire commissioner.

Waldo, the eighth police commissioner in eleven years, was a former army officer. Regarded as a man of high ideals and personally incorruptible, he was subservient to the mayor and had an unrealistic faith in the integrity of the policemen on his force. Whenever complaints were made against men in the department, they were referred to the accused themselves for investigation and report. Naturally, the accused officers always submitted reports in which they found that the complaints were groundless and exonerated themselves of any wrongdoing. Within the ranks of the department, Waldo was the butt of many jokes and was looked upon as a glorified Boy Scout who had little understanding of police work. When scandal rocked the department, the renowned Rabbi Stephen S. Wise unkindly called Waldo "a menacingly incompetent and incorrigibly stupid creature."[31]

In 1912 the principal gambling district of New York City began in the neighborhood of West Thirty-third Street and extended north on either side of Broadway to Fifty-ninth Street. Estimates had it that there were at least a half-dozen first-class gambling houses on almost every street between Fortieth and Fiftieth and from Fifth Avenue to Eighth Avenue. The gambling business, as always, operated under a system of official protection. Establishments that included roulette and faro were required to make an initial payment of $500 to open and $300 a month to continue operations with immunity. The gambling-house proprietors also necessarily maintained close relations with gang leaders, who had strong political and police connections. Violence or fear of violence was an integral part of the flourishing gambling industry in New York City.

Of the gang leaders who maintained alliances with Broadway gambling-house proprietors, none other was more important than the notorious specialist in violence Big Jack Zelig. He furnished some houses with gunmen for protection while he blackjacked their rivals. Reports abounded that some gambling-house proprietors paid Zelig sizable sums of money just to keep his gunmen out of their places. A principal competitor of Zelig for the business of violence in the gambling industry was the redoubtable Italian gang leader Paul Kelly. In 1910 Kelly had opened a place called the New Englander Social and Dramatic Club on Seventh Avenue, just north of what was known as the Roaring Forties. For two years several shootings and stabbings were attributed to Kelly gunmen.[32]

Among the numerous gambling houses in the district was the one operated by Herman Rosenthal at 104 West Forty-fifth Street. When he opened his establishment, Rosenthal received a loan of $1,500 from Charles Becker a police lieutenant. As head of the strong-arm squad, Becker had the specific duty of suppressing gambling, prostitution, and rowdyism and worked directly under Commissioner Rhinelander Waldo. Lieutenant Becker made the loan to Rosenthal on the condition that Jack Rose be taken into the place as Becker's representative and Rosenthal's partner. It was understood that Rosenthal was to pay Rose about twenty-five percent of the profits. Thus, Lieutenant Becker in effect became Rosenthal's partner, and from his relations with gambling-house proprietors it was obvious that Becker was prospering financially. During one period when his salary was only $1,687, Becker managed to deposit into his savings account $58,845. At the time Rosenthal opened the gambling place with the aid of Becker's loan, he also borrowed $2,000 from Big Tim Sullivan. Rumors were that Big Tim also had an interest in the establishment.[33]

In March 1912 relations between Rosenthal and Lieutenant Becker began to cool. Through Rose, Becker made demands upon Rosenthal for money. The gambler refused. In the meantime, complaints regarding Rosenthal's gambling establishment had been received at police headquarters and pressures were mounting on Becker and his strong-arm squad to take some kind of action. Becker instructed Rose to ask Rosenthal if he would stand for a "friendly" raid, a frequent procedure intended to appease the public and cause only temporary inconvenience to the gambler. Angered, Rosenthal refused to go along. On April 17, 1912, a police squad headed by Lieutenant Becker raided Rosenthal's gambling house. On this occasion Becker talked with Mrs. Rosenthal, advising her that he would cancel the $1,500 he had advanced to her husband. He explained that the raid was made only because he had been forced to take this action.[34]

Notwithstanding Becker's explanations and efforts at appeasement, Rosenthal was outraged by the raid, deeming it a double-cross by his partner, Becker. As a means of retaliation, the gambler threatened to "squeal" and reveal the true relationship between himself and the police lieutenant. Becker's position was becoming untenable and he determined to take action that would remove the Rosenthal threat permanently.

Big Jack Zelig had been arrested and was lingering in the Tombs. In June 1912 Lieutenant Becker sent his emissary, Jack Rose, to confer with Zelig. Rose promised Zelig his freedom provided he furnished gunmen to bump off Rosenthal and to see that the killing was properly handled. Throughout this period the feud between Rosenthal and the police gathered momentum. On July 11, 1912, Rosenthal proceeded to the West Side Police Court and protested the "oppression" by the police department, which had stationed a uniformed officer in his house constantly.[35]

As Rosenthal's anger mounted, he began talking for publication. About July 14, 1912, the gambler visited the offices of the *New York World* and dictated a statement in which he asserted that his fight was solely with the police and the only person who could "call him off" was his long-time friend Big Tim Sullivan. Rosenthal labeled untrue the charges that Sullivan was his gambling-house partner. However, he conceded that when he opened his gambling house with Lieutenant Becker as partner, he needed money and he turned to Big Tim Sullivan for a loan of $2,000. Said Rosenthal, "Big Tim didn't have the cash, so he signed a note for $2,000 for me and I got the money." Rosenthal not only talked freely to the press but had an appointment with District Attorney Charles S. Whitman for July 16, 1912, at which time he was expected to make a complete disclosure before a New York County grand jury.[36]

Just about eight hours before Rosenthal's scheduled grand-jury appearance, he was seated with a number of shady characters in the cafe of the Hotel Metropole on Forty-third Street near Broadway. A hoodlum entered the restaurant and told Rosenthal that a man wanted to see him outside. This was at 1:56 A.M. on July 16, 1912. Picking up several morning newspapers, which emblazoned his name in headlines, Rosenthal paused on the steps under the canopy lights of the Hotel Metropole. Four assassins sprang from an automobile, opened fire, and made their getaway. Rosenthal was killed instantly. A cabaret singer, Charles Gallagher, who was passing by the hotel recorded the license number of the killers' fleeing car and reported it to the police.[37]

District Attorney Whitman hurried to the scene and took charge of the murder investigation. Before dawn the automobile used by the assassins was located. The driver of the car gave the names of the men who had employed him. He insisted that when he agreed to drive the car, he believed the four men intended only to administer a beating and he knew nothing of their mission to commit murder. District Attorney Whitman broadcast an alarm and a few days later Jack Rose walked into police headquarters and surrendered. By July 29, 1912, Whitman was holding Jack Rose and three other gamblers—Harry Vallon, Bridgie Webber, and Sam Schepps—all of whom had turned informers. The men furnished details of the plot engineered by Lieutenant Becker to have Herman Rosenthal murdered. The four gunmen involved in the actual killing, all members of Big Jack Zelig's gang, were Louis Rosenberg, known as Lefty Louie; Harry Horowitz, known as Gyp the Blood; Jack Seidenshner, known as Whitey Lewis; and Frank Cirofici, known as Dago Frank. Jack Zelig testified before the grand jury and it was announced that he would be a witness at Becker's trial. However, as the trial was to begin Zelig was shot and killed.[38]

The four assassins and Lieutenant Becker were found guilty and sentenced to be executed. On April 13, 1914, Louis Rosenberg, Harry Horowitz, Jacob Seidenshner, and Frank Cirofici were electrocuted at Sing Sing.

Following his conviction on October 24, 1913, Becker was sentenced to death, but on February 24, 1914, the Court of Appeals granted him a new trial on the grounds that the presiding judge, John W. Goff, had made some prejudicial rulings. Goff had previously distinguished himself when directing the Lexow committee's investigation of police corruption in 1894.

Selected to preside at the second Becker trial was Judge Samuel Seabury, who would gain fame many years later for his investigation of official corruption in New York City. The defense attorneys who represented Becker were W. Bourke Cockran, the Tammany lawyer-politician-orator who had once demanded that Mayor McClellan adopt a policy of wide-open gambling and prostitution in the city, and Martin T. Manton, who later fell into disgrace when he was the senior judge of a U.S. court of appeals. As the tenth ranking jurist in the U. S., Manton was to make many indefensible decisions favoring some of the most powerful and vicious racketeers in the country. After he had spent twenty years on the bench, "he was convicted of selling his decisions on an over-the-counter basis." At the conclusion of the second trial, which started May 5, 1914, Lieutenant Charles Becker was again found guilty by a jury, and after the conviction was upheld on appeal, he was electrocuted at Sing Sing on July 30, 1915.[39]

For many years Big Tim Sullivan had been the dominant figure in New York City's gambling racket and had received wide publicity for his reputed interest in the Rosenthal establishment, but the scandal had no impact on him. In 1912 Big Tim went insane. For some time he was kept in a sanatorium but was later removed to a house on Eastchester Road, Williamsbridge, where several guards were hired to watch over him. Occasionally he eluded his guards and frequented his old haunts along Broadway and the

Bowery. Early in September 1913 Big Tim disappeared after he had exhausted his four guards by playing cards with them all night. His body was later found on the rails near the Westchester freight yards. The engineer reported that the man was dead before the cars passed over his body. The corpse reposed in the morgue for several days before it was identified. It was an ignominious ending for a man who had become, next to Boss Murphy, the most powerful leader in New York City politics.

At Big Tim's funeral over twenty-five thousand persons followed the body to the grave. Among those present to pay homage were three United States senators, a delegation of twenty members of the House of Representatives, justices of the New York Supreme Court, and judges of every other court in the city. Marching side by side at the head of the honorary pallbearers were Boss Charles F. Murphy and Edward E. McCall, Tammany candidate for mayor in the impending 1913 elections. Although much stock owned by Sullivan turned out to be worthless, he still left an estate with an actual value of $1,021,277.33.[40]

Not present at Big Tim's funeral was New York City's crusty mayor, William Jay Gaynor. In August 1913 the leaders of Tammany Hall had refused to renominate him on the Tammany ticket. This significant meeting was held in the luxurious suite of rooms maintained by Boss Murphy at Delmonico's fashionable restaurant at Fifth Avenue and Forty-fourth Street. It was here, amid ostentation and extravagance, that Murphy directed the affairs of Tammany Hall—a radical contrast to his days as district leader when he held important conferences by a lamppost on the street. Although rebuffed by Tammany, Gaynor, on September 4, 1913, accepted the nomination for mayor by an independent citizens' committee. The next day he boarded a steamship for a vacation trip to England. On September 10, while at sea, he dropped dead from heart failure.[41]

Before the Rosenthal-Becker scandal erupted, Boss Murphy had advanced the power of Tammany Hall throughout the state. In 1911 the Democratic party controlled the state legislature for the first time in nineteen years, and Tammany also controlled the Democratic organization in the state.[42]

At the time of Big Tim Sullivan's funeral and the sudden death of Mayor Gaynor, Boss Murphy was engrossed in a ruthless campaign to destroy a governor who would not bow to his every demand. He would demonstrate in that campaign an exercise of raw power seldom equaled in politics anywhere.

In 1912, through the backing of Tammany Hall, William Sulzer had been nominated and elected governor of New York. Murphy had thought him a safe candidate. After all, Sulzer had been a member of Tammany Hall for twenty-five years. As a young man, he had been one of Boss Croker's protégés and through Tammany support had been elected to the New York State Assembly, where he was made Speaker at a young age. Later, Tammany had repeatedly sent him to Congress and he had never shown any signs of insurgence.

Immediately before assuming the office of governor, Sulzer had a long meeting with Boss Murphy at Delmonico's. Murphy offered Sulzer money to pay his outstanding debts and to enable him to be free of financial worries while serving as the chief executive of the state. Sulzer declined the offer. The boss also demanded pledges from Sulzer regarding legislation and, especially, appointments to key departments and commissions of state government.[43]

Notwithstanding his long identification with Tammany politics, Sulzer, in his campaign for governor, had represented himself as a man of the people, a man independent of boss rule. He had begun to believe his campaign promises and looked upon himself as something of another Abraham Lincoln. As governor, he intended to serve the people's interests without dictation from Boss Murphy or anyone else.[44]

Governor Sulzer had received reports of widespread corruption in various branches of state government, including the highway department. Murphy was demanding that Sulzer appoint as state highway commissioner James E. Gaffney, a member of a contracting firm in which the boss reputedly was a secret partner. When Sulzer replied that he could make no promise, Murphy threatened, "It will be Gaffney or war." In the meantime, Sulzer had appointed John Hennessey to investigate corruption in several departments of state government. He disclosed that for every dollar the state was spending on roads, it received only thirty cents in value. And among those looting the treasure, he charged, was Charles F. Murphy of New York City.[45]

Murphy now launched an all-out offensive against the governor. The state legislature was controlled by Murphy and at his command refused to pass the regular appropriation bills necessary to keep the state government running. It even refused to appropriate money for the state prisons because Sulzer had declined to appoint one of Murphy's friends to the position of superintendent. The state government was paralyzed, and the boss refused to permit his henchmen from taking any action that would help the Sulzer administration in any way.

Still Murphy was not satisfied; he demanded that Sulzer be impeached. The boss held conferences with the Speaker of the Assembly, Alfred E. Smith, and the Democratic majority leader of the Senate, Robert F. Wagner, as well as with the top leaders of Tammany Hall. He cracked the whip, demanding action. The Assembly responded. In session throughout the night of August 13, 1913, it passed eight articles of impeachment by a vote of 79 to 45. The basis for the impeachment charges was the alleged omission of certain sums from Sulzer's statement of campaign expenditures and the use of those funds for personal expenses. Some of the contributors averred that no strings had been attached to their gifts and Sulzer was free to use them in any way he saw fit. In any event, the abuses of which Sulzer was charged were minor when compared with the wholesale corruption the governor's investigators had been uncovering. And it was these investigations into wrongdoing that had waked the ire of Murphy and his political cohorts.[46]

Charges against Sulzer were heard by the High Court for the Trial of Impeachments, which consisted of the state Senate and judges of the Court of Appeals. On October 17, 1913, by a vote of 43 to 12, Sulzer was convicted of three of eight articles of impeachment and was removed from office. The court found that Sulzer had filed with the secretary of state a false sworn statement of his campaign receipts and expenditures, had committed perjury in swearing to the truth of the campaign accounting, and had committed a misdemeanor in suppressing evidence. Significantly, Chief Justice Edgar M. Cullen of the Court of Appeals voted to acquit the governor on every article of impeachment. He flatly stated that Sulzer had committed no offense and there was no evidence of any deceit or fraud. The public clearly perceived that the real crime for which Sulzer had been punished was his refusal to take dictation from the boss of Tammany Hall and had sought to assert his independence of an organization long steeped in graft and corruption.[47]

On October 21, 1913, when Governor Sulzer and his wife arrived at Grand Central Station from Albany, an estimated fifty thousand people were present to welcome him. Sulzer was promptly nominated to the Assembly by the Sixth Assembly District of New York and was elected. Also elected by a large majority was the Fusion candidate for mayor, John Purroy Mitchel. On January 1, 1914, Mitchel took office as mayor of New York City and in Albany Sulzer became a member of the Assembly. In the fall of 1914, District Attorney Charles S. Whitman, who had won fame as the prosecutor of Charles Becker, was elected governor and was chief executive of the state when Lieutenant Becker was executed.[48]

Tammany's losses at the polls, particularly the mayoral election in 1913, created opposition to Boss Murphy's leadership that threatened to blossom into open rebellion. In the Democratic Club on February 2, 1914, there was introduced a resolution demanding that Murphy retire from all participation in the party's affairs. A few days later extracts of a letter written by the self-exiled Richard Croker from his European residence were made public. The ex-boss predicted that Tammany would never win under Murphy's management. And Croker, whose name had become synonymous with corrupt rule, expressed the hope that "some good man will get in and drive all them grafters . . . out."[49] Murphy defiantly weathered the storm and continued to direct the affairs of Tammany for over a decade.

11

THE RISE OF JIMMY HINES

New York City's new mayor, thirty-four-year-old John Purroy Mitchel, had been in office less than four months when he was the target of an attempted assassination. At noon on April 17, 1914, Mitchel, accompanied by Commissioner of Police Arthur Woods, corporation counsel Frank Polk, and tax comissioner George V. Mullan, left City Hall for lunch. Michael P. Mahoney, an elderly man and a psychotic with imagined grievances against the city, accosted the mayor and fired at him point blank. The bullet grazed Mitchel's ear and passed through Polk's left cheek, lodging under the corporation counsel's tongue. The wound, though painful, was not critical. The assailant was promptly seized and lodged in an insane asylum.[1]

Considerably more significant than the attempted killing of Mayor Mitchel was the assassination on June 28, 1914, of Archduke Francis Ferdinand at Sarajevo by an agent of the Serbian Society Union of Death, a Black Hand organization. The murder precipitated World War I. Before long the conflict would embrace America as a supplier of equipment and munitions and eventually as a belligerent.

In the early part of 1914 a garment-trades strike on the East Side erupted into violence. Among those hired to batter heads during the dispute were gangsters Dopey Benny Fein and Waxey Gordon. In March 1914 numerous persons were indicted on various charges of assault, rioting, and injury to property. Assigned to handle the preparation of many of the cases for trial was Assistant District Attorney Lucian S. Breckinridge, who stated that the investigation had uncovered "a use of gangsters and thugs in labor troubles, unparalleled in the history of this country." On March 23, 1916, before the trial and two years after the indictments were returned, Breckinridge resigned on the grounds that District Attorney Edward Swann's actions in these cases constituted "a travesty on justice, and an outrage to decency." A few months later, on December 30, 1916, Judge James A. Delehanty of the court of general sessions forwarded charges of misconduct against District Attorney Swann to Governor Charles S. Whitman. Judge Delehanty asserted that the Tammany district attorney, Swann, had obtained the discharge on bail of more than a score of defendants by presenting a false recommendation to a judge of the general sessions. And Judge Delehanty charged that District Attorney Swann had sought to have the indictments against these men dismissed even though seven of them offered to plead guilty.[2]

By the time that Judge Delehanty's charges were filed, the war in Europe had been raging for many months and the United States was finding it more and more difficult to avoid direct involvement in the conflict. Following Germany's submarine blockade of Great Britain, the American ship *Gulflight* was sunk without warning on May 1, 1915, and on May 7, 1915, the *Lusitania* was sunk about ten miles off the coast of Ireland with a loss of 1,198 lives, including 139 Americans. The sinking of the *Lusitania* brought the United States and Germany to the verge of war and America stepped up its shipment of equipment and munitions to the Allies.

The nation's most important spot for the transfer of munitions to Allied ships was Black Tom, a peninsula one mile long that jutted into the Hudson River from Jersey City and was just behind the Statue of Liberty. Freight cars loaded with military supplies were moved along tracks to the piers where their cargoes were transferred to barges that transported them to vessels in the harbor. On the night of July 30, 1916, about two million pounds of explosives were stored in railway cars, on piers, and barges alongside the dock. Beginning at 2:08 A.M., a series of tremendous explosions demolished the Black Tom terminal. New York skyscrapers and apartment houses quivered from the blasts. Windows by the thousands were shattered. Shock from the explosions was felt as far away as Pennsylvania, Maryland, and Connecticut. Within a radius of twenty-five miles, the explosions were responsible for damages estimated at $45 million, and property worth $20 million was destroyed at Black Tom itself.[3]

For several years before America's entry into World War I, a number of significant changes had been taking place in the political and underworld leadership in New York City.

After the death of Big Tim Sullivan in September 1913, Big Tom Foley reached the peak of his power. Big Tim Sullivan had always maintained strong alliances with important Italian gang leaders. In particular, he had worked closely with Paul (Paolo Vaccarelli) Kelly. Now Foley became Kelly's important patron. Through an agreement reached between Foley and Kelly, Harry C. Perry was made coleader of the assembly district that Big Tim Sullivan had ruled for so many years. The other coleader was Christopher D. Sullivan. Under the Foley-Kelly arrangement, Perry remained a district leader for over a decade.[4]

In rising to a place of political eminence, Thomas F. Foley had followed a route not uncommon for many Tammany leaders. Born on February 3, 1852, in a tenement house in the Williamsburg section of Brooklyn, he quit school at the age of thirteen to take a job as a butcher's errand boy. Two years later he became a helper and an apprentice in a blacksmith shop. By

1870 Foley had acquired an interest in a saloon on Bedford Avenue. When the place got into difficulty with the law in 1873, Big Tom moved from Brooklyn to Manhattan, where he worked in another saloon and joined Tammany Hall. By 1876 Foley was the owner of a bar at Walker and Oliver Streets and was on his way to becoming an influential figure in Tammany circles. In 1897 he became a member of the old City Council for one term and later served on the Board of Aldermen.

For several years Foley was the trusted lieutenant of Patrick J. (Paddy) Divver, boss of the old Second Assembly District. They had a falling out and in 1901 Foley succeeded in wresting the leadership of the district from Divver. Figuring prominently in Foley's defeat of Divver was Big Tim Sullivan, who in turn was significantly aided by Paul Kelly's Italian underworld forces. In 1907 Foley was elected sheriff by Tammany Hall.

For many years Foley's principal saloon was located at Center and Franklin Streets, across from the Criminal Courts Building and the Tombs. Naturally, Foley's place served as a hangout for politicians as well as for lawyers and friends of prisoners in the Tombs. In conjunction with his saloon, Foley maintained an office where he conducted a real estate business and was active in placing bail bonds. Serving as his errand boy was a young Italian, Michael N. Delagi, who carried messages to judges and prosecutors. At Foley's behest, Delagi labored over law books, and after taking the bar examination five times he finally succeeded in gaining admission to the bar. In time he became a magistrate.[5]

In 1915 Mayor John Purroy Mitchel backed Mike Rofrano, who engaged in a desperate and violent effort to oust Tom Foley as district leader. Gunmen participated in the contest and there were allegations that a plot was afoot to assassinate Big Tom. During the bitter conflict one of Foley's lieutenants, Michael Camara, was slain. Foley was successful in retaining the leadership of his district and, until he died in 1925, remained the powerful patron of East Side gangsters, including the up and coming Italian underworld leader Joseph Masseria.[6]

During this period, the political star of James J. Hines was rising. He had served a long apprenticeship in politics. His father, a blacksmith, and his father's father had been Tammany election captains. During Jimmy's childhood the family moved to a house near Eighth Avenue and 116th Street. Here Hines would spend the rest of his free life.

Young Jimmy, the second of eleven children, left school at the age of fifteen. While still a youth he became a blacksmith. About 1892, when Hines was only seventeen, his father became ill and young Jimmy assumed control of the blacksmith shop. At the same time he became a political canvasser in the election district. He was exposed early to a system in which ward politicians relied heavily upon the services of gangsters to win elections.[7]

In 1907 Hines became a candidate for alderman and James Ahearn, a plasterer, ran for leader of the Eleventh Assembly District. To stage his campaign, Hines raised $4,000, which he used to hire an army of mercenary thugs recruited with the aid of Harry (Gyp the Blood) Horowitz, who later died in the electric chair for the murder of gambler Herman Rosenthal. Also aiding the Hines cause was the Gophers gang. Hines was elected alderman and Ahearn became the district leader.

In 1910 Hines challenged Ahearn for the leadership of the Eleventh Assembly District. Both Hines and Ahearn conducted campaigns of terror. Hines' strong-arm men went after Ahearn's gangsters in a saloon, and by the time the melee ended there were several cracked heads. Ahearn's gang leader, Spike Sullivan, was seriously injured and was still confined in the hospital on voting day. Ahearn emerged victorious by forty-seven votes and the following year, 1911, won by a margin of only twenty-seven votes. In 1912, however, Hines won by fifteen hundred votes and his domain over the Eleventh Assembly District was to remain secure for decades. That year, 1912, Hines sold his interest in the blacksmith shop and entered the trucking business.[8]

It was a common practice for Tammany leaders to establish Democratic clubs and many of their clubhouses served as headquarters for rackets and racketeers. In 1910 Hines had founded the Monongahela Democratic Club, which was the outgrowth of the James J. Hines Association, established a year earlier. Beginning with the World War I period, Hines made the top floor of his club available for commercial gambling. The gambling concession was given to Arnold Rothstein, who paid $500 a month plus a small share of the house percentage for the privilege of conducting high-stakes crap and poker games in the clubhouse. The purpose of the commercial gambling operations was to bring money into the Hines organization without victimizing club members. Hence, eventually adopted was a rigid house rule that excluded all members of the club from the gaming tables. In principle this rule was similar to regulations prevailing in some of the European gambling centers, which prohibit local residents from patronizing the casinos.[9]

By 1916 the biggest gambler in New York City was Arnold Rothstein, who was rapidly becoming the most influential and powerful figure in the underworld. He had ties with almost every significant gangster in the city and supplied the financial backing for many of their illicit activities. Among the large-scale drug dealers with whom Rothstein maintained a long business association was Sidney Stajer. Records revealed that on November 16, 1916, Stajer transferred a racehorse named Virile to Rothstein and twelve years later (1928) was indebted in the amount of $28,868.51 to the gambling king.[10]

Rothstein's origins were respectable. His father was engaged in the wholesale cotton-goods business and Arnold was made a salesman for the firm. On a trip to Chicago he lost all of his money as well as his samples by gambling. Upon returning to New York City, he landed a job as a cigar salesman; the job took him into the horse-race poolrooms. Before long he gained employment in a poolroom and was launched permanently into a gambling career. From the very beginning he had the reputation for resorting to sharp practices.

In 1909, during the racing season at Saratoga, Rothstein, then twenty-six, married Caroline Greene, a showgirl. That year he also opened a small basement gambling establishment on West Forty-fifth Street but soon moved to a place on West Forty-sixth Street. Here, on a November night in 1910, Charles G. Gates, son of John W. (Bet a Million) Gates, dropped $40,000.[11]

In the early morning hours of May 16, 1917, Arnold Rothstein was operating a "traveling" crap game on the second floor of the Hotel Francis at 124 West Forty-seventh Street. Gunmen entered, lined the players against the wall, and stole their valuable jewelry and money. Urged by friends, Rothstein took the unusual step of reporting the robbery to the police. The gendarmes responded with remarkable speed and soon arrested two men, who were identified by Rothstein. The culprits were tried, and on August 23, 1917, a jury convicted them of robbery from the person. It is doubtful whether Rothstein ever again sought the aid of the police or assisted the authorities in their efforts to solve a crime.[12]

Several months later, on January 19, 1919, Rothstein's floating crap game, then operating in a fourth-floor apartment at 301 West Fifty-seventh Street, was raided by the police. When officers yelled, "Open up in there," they were greeted by three bullets crashing through the door. Two officers were grazed and the sleeve of a third policeman was pierced. When the officers finally gained entrance, they found twenty persons in the room, plus dice and large sums of money. Also present was Abe Attell, former featherweight champion and a personal attendant to Rothstein. On the fire escape the police observed Rothstein, who was believed to have fired the three shots. Two indictments were returned against Rothstein, charging him with felonious assault in the first degree and assault in the second degree. However, a subsequent motion to dismiss the indictments was granted, and throughout his lifetime Rothstein maintained a clean record insofar as any kind of conviction was concerned.[13]

In the fall of 1919, Arnold Rothstein and Abe Attell were principals in the infamous "Black Sox" scandal, in which gamblers had fixed the World Series between the Chicago White Sox and the Cincinnati Reds baseball teams. By this time Arnold Rothstein had become recognized as the big power in the underworld. He masterminded and financed huge bond robberies and bucketshop frauds. He was back of important organized gangs and was an engineer of an international dope ring. His advice, counsel, and financial backing were sought not only by leaders of the underworld, but by some of the city's most influential politicians and a number of important businessmen as well. Among the inner circle of criminals and corrupt politicians, he was known as the Brain.[14]

While Rothstein was reaching a position of preeminence in New York City's underworld, many other gang leaders and racketeers were also growing in stature. In the Lower East Side the most powerful and vicious gangs were made up largely of Italians or Sicilians.

During the early part of the century, the most influential leader in the Sicilian-Italian underworld was Ignazio Saietta, known as Lupo the Wolf. In 1899 Saietta, then twenty-two, murdered a man in his native town in Italy and fled to the United States. Settling in East Harlem, he was closely allied in criminal endeavors with Ciro Terranova, to whom he was related by marriage.

Lupo the Wolf and his cohorts engaged in extortion against their immigrant countrymen. They were involved in the Italian lottery. And in their diverse activities, they employed violence and terrorism to achieve their ends.

Saietta and his brother-in-law, Giuseppe Morello, were profitably involved in dope distribution. Headquarters for this operation was a place that eventually became known to the police as the Morello-Terranova "murder stable." Terranova and his allies brought mobsters to this place; there the guests either agreed to the demands of the Terranova forces or were eliminated. The police asserted that at least twenty-three men were put to death in the murder stable between 1900 and 1917.

During the first decade of the century Lupo the Wolf often came to the attention of the police, but evidence to support criminal charges was always missing. In 1903 Saietta was arrested as a suspect in a famous "barrel murder" mystery. In 1906 he was arrested on suspicion of possessing intimate knowledge regarding the kidnapping of Tony Bozzuffi, son of an East Side banker. In 1908 he attracted attention by suddenly disappearing when his wholesale grocery store at 210 Mott Street went bankrupt, leaving debts of $700,000.

Although Saietta's criminal and racketeering activities were highly profitable, money never rolled in fast enough to suit him. Thus he engaged in printing counterfeit bills in a plant in the Catskill Mountains. This was his undoing. Federal authorities convicted Saietta and eight other Italian criminals for counterfeiting. Lupo the Wolf received a sentence of thirty years and was incarcerated in the federal prison in Atlanta on February 21, 1910.

After spending ten years in prison, he was paroled on June 30, 1920. The next year, on October 30, 1921, Saietta received permission from Attorney General Harry M. Daugherty to make a trip to Italy. After several months' absence, Lupo returned to New York and engaged in the wholesale fruit business and bakery business with his son. Fifteen years later New

York State authorities determined that Saietta was in racketeering on a broad scale. He then controlled the Italian bakers in Brooklyn, ran an Italian lottery, and monopolized the grape racket. Following an appeal from New York Governor Herbert Lehman to President Franklin Roosevelt, Ignazio Saietta, then in his sixtieth year, was returned to the Atlanta prison.

At the time Saietta went to prison in 1910, Ciro Terranova was one of the principal bosses of the Italian rackets, particularly in Harlem and the Bronx. Advancing himself through strong-arm methods, he was feared and respected. He at one time cornered the market on artichokes and was dubbed in the press the Artichoke King.[15]

In the summer of 1916 Joe DiMarco, who ran a gambling joint at Fifty-four James Street, challenged Ciro Terranova's leadership. Terranova promptly called on Leo Lauritano, a saloon operator at 115 Navy Street, and commissioned him to remove DiMarco from the scene permanently. Lauritano gave the lethal assignment to Mike Fetto. Mike visited the DiMarco establishment but failed to recognize the intended victim. He returned having shot no one. Lauritano then dispatched another gunman, John Esposito, commonly known as Johnny Lefty, to the DiMarco gambling house and sent Mike Fetto along for company and perhaps to receive expert instruction from Johnny, a professional killer.

Esposito later testified that he had never seen DiMarco but that he was determined not to come away empty-handed. By mistake he shot and killed Charles Lombardi, who he thought was DiMarco. On the same visit Fetto, who was becoming more adept in the art of murder, shot and killed DiMarco.

Two weeks after the double slaying at Fifty-four James Street, followers of DiMarco called on Leo Lauritano and requested him to supply a gunman who would wreak vengeance on Terranova. Again Lauritano gave the job to Esposito. He shot down Nicholas Terranova, a brother of Ciro, as he was walking on Johnson Street in Brooklyn with a friend, Charles Umbriaco, who was also killed.

Ciro Terranova was charged with having instigated the murders of Joe DiMarco and Charles Lombardi. When the case was tried in 1918, Esposito freely testified about his role as a hired killer and related the details of the Lombardi and DiMarco murders. However, Judge Thomas C. T. Crain, later a Tammany Hall district attorney, dismissed the charges against Terranova on the ground that the testimony against him was given by coconspirators and accomplices and that the outside corroboration necessary under New York law was missing.[16]

It is doubtful if Terranova was ever able to reach the top spot in the Sicilian-Italian underworld. By the early 1920s that place was held by the short, fat, and somewhat piggish-appearing Giuseppe Masseria, who was to become known as Joe the Boss. Masseria's powerful political patron was Tammany leader Big Tom Foley.

Ciro Terranova was Masseria's ally in uptown New York and the Bronx. Closely allied with Joe the Boss in Brooklyn was Frankie Yale (Uale), and in downtown Manhattan Charles (Lucky) Luciano held sway. Before long Masseria would select Luciano as his overall assistant.[17]

On April 6, 1917, the United States declared war on Germany and thus became a combatant in World War I. This marked the beginning of a new era for American policy in international affairs. The year 1917 also marked the end of an era in public transportation in New York City. On July 26, 1917, the last two-horse streetcar made its final trip down Broadway. There were now, for the first time, more motor vehicles in the city than horses. Cars of various kinds numbered 114,717 as compared with 108,743 horses.[18]

Tammany Hall was busy laying plans to recapture the mayor's office at the city elections, which would be held near the end of the year. John Purroy Mitchel, whose four-year term as a Fusion mayor was coming to a close, had been an excellent chief executive of the city. He had a brilliant mind, was well educated, was honest, and before he was elected mayor had a background of city government experience. As commissioner of accounts, Mitchel had systematically investigated the presidents of the various boroughs and succeeded in having three of them removed. Upon becoming mayor, Mitchel created a confidential squad in the police department; it was charged with the responsibility of investigating police graft. Among those selected for this newly formed squad was the incorruptible Lewis J. Valentine. He was soon promoted to the rank of lieutenant and, after many years of ups and downs, eventually became famous as commissioner of police under Mayor Fiorello LaGuardia.

The government of New York City reached a new peak of efficiency under Mitchel. Almost every branch of city government—fire department, finances, schools, prisons—was well administered. Theodore Roosevelt stated that Mitchel had "given us as nearly an ideal administration . . . as I have seen in my lifetime, or as I have heard of since New York became a big city."[19]

Mitchel's principal weakness was a lack of tact; he thus made enemies unnecessarily. In the 1917 primaries he lost the Republican nomination and ran for reelection only on the Fusion ticket. His Tammany Hall opponent was John F. Hylan, often called Red Mike because of his red hair and mustache. Hylan was an ideal Tammany candidate. He represented mediocrity in its most abject form. A lawyer of average ability, Hylan had the political clout to become a Kings County judge. In the mayoral election of 1917, he had the backing of William Randolph Hearst. Hylan was described as a bumbling, empty-headed, ponderous man without wit, warmth, or wisdom. Yet he won the election, and took office on January 1, 1918. In 1921 he was reelected for another four-year term. Woodrow Wilson, in amazement, once asked how it was "possible for the greatest city in the world to place such a man in high office?'' Among Hylan's early acts as mayor was the removal of Lieutenant Valentine from the police department's confidential squad.[20]

After his defeat in the 1917 election, John Purroy Mitchel enlisted in the U.S. Army and received a commission as major in the air service. Frequently he suffered from excruciating headaches, which temporarily blinded him. He predicted to a friend that if he had a severe attack while flying it would be all over for him. On July 6, 1918, at Camp Gerstner, Lake Charles, Louisiana, Mitchel fell five hundred feet from his single-seated scout plane and was killed. An investigation disclosed that his safety belt had been unfastened.[21]

In 1918 New York City was visited by a devastating scourge of influenza, which was then plaguing all parts of the world. When the first few cases of influenza had been diagnosed as such, the city health commissioner, Dr. Royal S. Copeland, promptly assured the public that the city was in no danger of an epidemic. It soon became apparent that Mayor Hylan's health commissioner was greatly mistaken. Within a twenty-four-hour period, eight hundred persons died of influenza. The final death toll from the flu epidemic in 1918 was 12,562 in New York City, and in the United States about five hundred thousand persons died. Insurance firms of New York City paid out more money to the beneficiaries of influenza victims than to the survivors of soldiers killed in battle during World War I. Yet, in relation to total population, some of the earlier cholera epidemics in New York City—in 1832, 1849, 1854, and 1866—had been more deadly.[22]

While public attention was fixed on the events of World War I and on the influenza epidemic, a bitter fight was about to erupt between two of the most powerful figures in Tammany Hall, and erstwhile intimates—Boss Charles F. Murphy and district leader James J. Hines.

Early in 1918 Hines brought Louis N. Hartog to Boss Murphy with a moneymaking proposition. Hartog possessed a formula for combining malt with glucose to produce a substance he called Malto-dextrose, which brewers could use advantageously in making beer. A federal permit was required to obtain the necessary supply of glucose and it was believed that Murphy's influence was essential. Under Hartog's proposal, Murphy was to invest $175,000, which would be used in financing factory equipment and he would receive twenty-five percent of the profits. Murphy was also promised an additional fifteen percent of the profits without further investment. This largess was based on Murphy's expected help with the local brewers. As always, the brewers were deeply involved in politics and it was a fact of life that they could ill afford to ignore any firm with which Boss Murphy was affiliated.

The project was launched under the trade name North Kensington Refining Company. Although Hines knew nothing about the manufacturing process, he was given the job of overseeing the factory at a salary of $100 a week in addition to a share of the profits. The trucking contract was also awarded to the concern operated by James J. Hines and his brother, Philip.

From the outset the firm's operations were highly profitable. The federal permit enabled the company to draw five hundred barrels of glucose a day. When the establishment's gross daily income reached $46,000, with $5,000 a day in profit belonging to Murphy, the boss was not only overwhelmed but frightened. Imprinted on his mind were visions of Tweed's prison stripes and Croker's exile. Murphy decided to sever at once his affiliation with the North Kensington Refining Company. He demanded his accumulated profits and the repayment of his $175,000 investment. When Hartog turned down Murphy's ultimatum, the supply of glucose was shut off. The controversy resulted in a bitter falling out between Hines and Murphy.

The ill feeling between the two men reached its height in October 1918, when Hines, then forty-two, received a commission as a lieutenant in the Motor Transport Corps of the U.S. Army. He was sent to France, and there remained until July 1919, when he returned to New York City.[23]

While Jimmy Hines was in France, his district was in the trusted hands of his protégé, Edwin P. Kilroe. In furtherance of his feud with Hines, Boss Murphy induced Kilroe to make an attempt to take over the leadership of the district permanently. Naturally, this ruptured the relations between Hines and Kilroe. Also while Hines was out of the country, the Eighteenth Amendment to the Constitution was declared ratified on January 29, 1919. On October 28, 1919, the National Prohibition Enforcement Act (Volstead Act) was passed and it went into effect on January 16, 1920. Hines by then had cemented close relationships with important New York racketeers and the Prohibition era would enlarge his opportunities for lucrative alliances with the underworld.

Of the members of the inner circle of the New York City underworld during this period, Arnold Rothstein was by far the most feared and respected. The fear in which he was held by other criminals was clearly demonstrated by an incident that occurred in May 1920. Rothstein was then in the process of arranging bail for Jules Arnstein, better known as Nicky Arnstein, who had been charged with having engineered bond thefts in Wall Street totaling $5 million, of which Rothstein reputedly received $4 million.

On this occasion Arnstein, accompanied by actress Fannie Brice, to whom he was married, Arnold Rothstein, and lawyer William J. Fallon, brazenly rode in Rothstein's flashy blue Cadillac landaulet down Fifth Avenue at the tail end of the annual police parade. They were headed for Thomas F. Foley's old saloon, then a speakeasy. After parking the car in front of Big Tom's establishment, Fallon, Brice, Donald Henderson Clarke, a newspaper reporter, and Harold Norris, a professional bondsman allied with Foley, were imbibing some drinks while Arnstein and Rothstein went across the street to the Criminal Courts Building. Meantime, Rothstein's blue Cadillac disappeared. Fallon and Norris promptly jumped on Foley's henchman, Michael N. Delagi, and threatened him with dire consequences if he did not get the stolen car back in a hurry. Delagi made some telephone calls and informed the parties that the stolen Cadillac belonged to Arnold Rothstein. Within a half hour the fancy vehicle was returned by four gangsters, one of whom was the notorious Monk Eastman, who, incidentally, would be murdered only seven months later. Eastman apologized to the lawyer, Fallon, explaining that the thieves had not known the car was owned by Rothstein. Although the thieves had no qualms about stealing the car under the nose of the district attorney in the Criminal Courts Building, the mere mention of Rothstein's name got the car returned in short order.[24]

In the 1920 primary Boss Murphy made a determined effort to place his man Abraham Kaplan, an assemblyman, at the helm of the Eleventh Assembly District and wrest control from Hines. Gangsters were recruited by Hines to aid him in his battle to retain leadership. When the votes were counted, Hines had won forty-three of forty-five election districts. Murphy was shocked by Hines' political power.

Following his break with Kilroe, Hines made an alliance in 1920 with a lawyer, Joseph Shalleck, who had occupied desk space in the criminal law offices of the great mouthpiece William J. Fallon and his partner, Eugene McGee. The law firm of Fallon and McGee was established in 1918 and the elite of the underworld regularly sought the services of Fallon, who was never squeamish about resorting to any method, including jury fixing, that would free a client. Shalleck's apprenticeship under Fallon served him well. He had developed talents useful to Hines, and beginning in 1920 Hines and Shalleck were inseparable.[25]

In 1921 Joseph Shalleck, as campaign manager for Jimmy Hines, participated in a primary fight that was unusually bitter, even for New York City. Boss Murphy had selected Julius W. Miller as his choice to become the Tammany president of the borough of Manhattan. Hines decided to run for the same post and took it upon himself to beat the Murphy candidate. Working relentlessly for Hines were gangsters imported from New Jersey. The Murphy forces, in turn, included numerous gangsters from the Lower East Side of Manhattan.

As the votes were being counted on primary night, word was received at the Hines headquarters of gross fraud at a polling place next to Murphy's Anawanda Clubhouse on Second Avenue. Shalleck raced to the place in a taxicab. The entrenched Murphy forces had no intention of tolerating any interference from the Hines campaign manager. Although two policemen were present in the polling place, they made no effort to intercede when someone struck Shalleck on the jaw with a blackjack and knocked him down. As he lay helplessly on the floor, he was kicked repeatedly. As reinforcements arrived to aid Shalleck, a pistol was fired and a bullet struck the prostrate Hines lieutenant in the chest. Nearly fifty thousand votes were cast, and Hines lost the contest by 8,511 votes. Nevertheless, Hines did win control of the Thirteenth Assembly District, which was adjacent to his own Eleventh District, and he gained such fear and respect from the other leaders that in the years ahead all were hesitant to oppose him.[26]

The year 1921 was a highly profitable one for Arnold Rothstein. At Aqueduct on July 4, 1921, Rothstein engineered one of the most spectacular coups in American racetrack history. He had made arrangements to have his colt, Sidereal, run under the silks of Max Hirsch, whose brother-in-law, Willie Booth, was Rothstein's trainer. The Rothstein colt had been carefully nursed along in preparation for a big killing. In Sidereal's three previous races he was soundly beaten each time and had never finished in the money. His fast trial times had been carefully hidden. The odds against Sidereal opened at 30 to 1. Rothstein had borrowed all of the betting commissioners of the three biggest players on the tracks. Thus, he gained the services of a corps of expert bettors to work for him without his identity becoming known and he also borrowed the enormous credit of three wealthy friends. Rothstein had ordered his bettors to lay all the wagers they could make on Sidereal. The betting became frenzied and the odds were rapidly reduced. However, the winnings of Rothstein on Sidereal on July 4, 1921, totaled $800,000.[27]

Among Arnold Rothstein's seemingly endless sources of illicit income were Wall Street charlatans who operated bucketshops and defrauded would-be investors out of millions of dollars. Rothstein's protégé and lieutenant, Philip (Dandy Phil) Kastel, was the brains behind several lucrative bucketshop operations. This same Kastel was to occupy an important place in top-echelon organized crime activities the next four decades.

In pre–World War I days and before making the big time, Kastel had been a nightclub operator in Montreal. Later, in New York, Dandy Phil and his wife, Daisy, were charged with having worked the old badger game against a wealthy New Jersey manufacturer. Kastel was successfully defended by Arnold Rothstein's attorney, William J. Fallon. The close relationship between Kastel and Rothstein started about 1919 and continued until Rothstein was murdered almost a decade later. In addition to Rothstein, Dandy Phil's intimate associates included Nicky Arnstein and Big Nick Cohn.[28]

In March 1921 Daniel Dillon opened a brokerage office in New York City under the name of Dillon & Company. Dillon controlled the operation for one week only and then Kastel took over. Many of the company's patrons were out-of-town people, including numerous persons of little means who had poured their life savings into so-called investments with Dillon & Company. The firm failed, with losses of over $300,000. Dandy Phil promptly formed another bucketshop, Wilk & Company, and was the guiding genius behind other similar ventures. Finally, the authorities investigated and initiated prosecution. After three trials Kastel was convicted for bucketshop activities and was sentenced to prison in Atlanta.[29]

Perhaps the biggest bucketshop swindle of the period was conducted by E. M. Fuller & Company, operated by Edward Markle Fuller and William Frank McGee. The firm failed on the Consolidated Exchange, with losses exceeding $4 million. Fuller and McGee, who were brought to trial three times without a conviction, were represented by Rothstein's attorney, William J. Fallon. After Fallon had guided the defendants through a couple of jury disagreements, he was charged with jury bribery himself. Fallon had also been representing Dandy Phil Kastel in a bucketshop case. When Fallon was indicted for bribing jurymen, his place in the Kastel defense was taken by Hines aide Joseph Shalleck, who on that occasion won a disagreement for Dandy Phil.[30]

The records of E. M. Fuller & Company, examined after the firm's failure, revealed the names of a number of prominent New Yorkers. A check for $10,000 had been issued to Thomas F. Foley, the powerful Tammany leader and patron of influential underworld leaders. In June 1923 Big Tom had induced Charles A. Stoneham, then the principal owner of the New York Giants baseball team, to lend E. M. Fuller & Company $147,500 to stave off bankruptcy. Only $10,000 of the loan was ever repaid to Stoneham. Before soliciting Stoneham's aid, Foley had loaned McGee $15,000. The books disclosed that E. M. Fuller & Company had paid Arnold Rothstein more than $325,000. Rothstein contended that he had won all of this money from the partners of the firm at gambling.[31]

For many years Big Tom Foley had served as a principal source of political protection for many underworld leaders, including Rothstein. But Foley was growing old, and in the early 1920s Rothstein began to shift his allegiance from Foley to the younger Tammany leader, James J. Hines. It was during this period that the mastermind of criminals was ingratiating himself in many ways to members of the Hines family. He wrote a letter to John McGraw, manager of the New York Giants baseball team and a debtor to Rothstein, and demanded a season pass to the Polo Grounds for James J. Hines and his three sons, James Jr., Philip, and Eugene. Rothstein owned the Hotel Fairfield, which he made available, at his expense, to the wife of the Tammany leader. She entertained her friends there and warm notes of thanks written by Mrs. James (Geneva C.) Hines were found in Rothstein's correspondence files after his death.[32]

12

THE ROTHSTEIN ERA

During the 1920s Arnold Rothstein, who had cemented strong political ties, occupied a unique place of power and influence in the New York City underworld. He was the associate and financial backer of the influential. But perhaps more important, he was tutor to many of the up and coming young men who, within a few years, would constitute the elite of the ruling class of organized crime in New York City.

Among Rothstein's prize pupils was a young man destined to gain national notoriety under the name of Frank Costello. His real name was Francesco Castiglia, and he was born on January 26, 1891, in Lauropoli, Calabria, in southwest Italy. His parents, Luigi and Maria Saveria Aloise Castiglia, had six children—four daughters and two sons. In 1895 Luigi, accompanied by his four daughters and older son, Eddie, came to America. They were followed to the United States by Luigi's wife and young Frank in 1896.[1]

The Castiglia family settled in East Harlem, already a slum area. Eddie, ten years older than Frank, engaged in gang warfare and introduced his brother to this form of delinquency. During Prohibition, Eddie, like Frank, was a rumrunner and had ties with Arnold Rothstein. Records revealed that in 1925 Rothstein advanced $9,000 to Eddie.[2]

When only fourteen years old, Frank Costello, wearing a black handkerchief around his face as a mask, robbed the landlady of his parents' flat. The landlady recognized him and reported the holdup to the police. Frank concocted an alibi that the police accepted and he was turned loose. In 1908, and again in 1912, Frank was arrested on charges of assault and robbery, each time giving his name as Frank Castello. He won a discharge on both occasions. His early idol was Ciro Terranova, for whom he sometimes performed various chores. Ciro got Frank a job as a rent collector for an absentee landlord of the neighborhood.[3]

On the streets, where Frank spent much of his time, his intimate friends included Willie Moretti, later an important organized crime leader, and Dudley Geigerman. Dudley's parents had immigrated to the United States from Germany; they spoke with a distinct German dialect and were looked upon as foreigners. Of particular interest to Frank was a pretty girl in the

Geigerman family by the name of Loretta. That Costello was Italian and Roman Catholic did not present an insurmountable obstacle to his romance with a German-Jewish girl. In September 1914 Frank, twenty-three, and Loretta, affectionately known as Bobbie, were married in a Protestant church. In applying for the marriage license, the groom used the name Frank Costello, by which he would always be known in the future.[4]

Costello had been married only a few months when he again ran afoul of the law. The police, on March 12, 1915, arrested him for carrying a gun. The case was brought before Judge Edward Swann, who reviewed the defendant's previous skirmishes with the authorities and noted that he had from neighbors learned Costello had "the reputation of a gunman." The judge imposed a sentence of one year and Frank served ten months in prison on Welfare Island.[5]

In 1919 Costello and Harry Horowitz formed the Horowitz Novelty Company, which manufactured punchboards and kewpie dolls. The dolls were given as prizes to the winning players of the gambling devices supplied by the Horowitz firm. Within a year, the gross earnings of the company were more than $100,000 but Costello and Horowitz were not satisfied. They staged a successful bankruptcy. The attorney for the assignee told the referee in bankruptcy that the money owing the firm could not be collected since the debtors were "all East Side gangsters."

With profits secreted from the bankrupt firm, Costello invested in other punchboard companies and some real estate. But with the advent of Prohibition on January 16, 1920, a whole new avenue for huge profits was opened. And Frank intended to take full advantage of his opportunities.[6]

Costello's personal attorney for thirty years, George Wolf, asserts that it was Arnold Rothstein who served as the tutor for the embryonic underworld leader. Rothstein, he said, both financed Frank Costello when he was getting started and showed his apt pupil how to organize, cut costs, and eliminate competition, even by force, if necessary. The tutelage of Rothstein played an important role in developing Costello into a business brain. And it was through Rothstein that Costello nurtured new associates who were to figure prominently in his future. One such was Dandy Phil Kastel, whom he originally met through Rothstein. Kastel was to become Costello's partner and would guide the fortunes of Costello's gambling empire for several decades. The close relationship between Rothstein and Costello lasted for almost a decade. Records revealed that in 1928, the year in which Rothstein was murdered, he had loaned Costello $21,000.[7]

Among others receiving the financial backing, guidance, and protection of Arnold Rothstein was George Uffner, alias George Hoffman. In the years ahead, he would become one of Frank Costello's intimate friends and business associates. Uffner, who specialized in narcotics, owed his early success in the rackets to Rothstein. When Uffner was arrested in 1925, it was

Rothstein who paid the fee of an attorney, Samuel M. Reiss, to represent Uffner in court. But in his business dealings with his underworld accessories, Rothstein did not indulge in philanthropy. When he furnished financial aid he wanted assurance that the debt would be paid. On January 23, 1923, George Uffner took out two policies totaling $28,000 with the Union Central Insurance Company. Both were turned over to Rothstein and held by him as security for Uffner's debts.

In the late 1920s the gambler Frank Erickson was accepted into Rothstein's coterie of assistants. Rothstein retained the services of Erickson to handle his high-level bookmaking business and to deal directly with big horse-race bettors. Erickson's start with Rothstein led to his subsequent partnership in the gambling business with Frank Costello; the partnership flourished for over two decades and was featured in testimony before U.S. Senate committee hearings in the 1950s. Frank Erickson, Frank Costello, and George Uffner eventually became partners in oil leaseholdings in Wise County, Texas.[8]

Few criminals who received the tutelage of Rothstein achieved the international prominence of Charles (Lucky) Luciano.

In 1907, when about ten, Luciano, whose real name was Salvatore Lucania, was brought from Sicily to America by his parents, Antonio and Rosalia Lucania. The family settled in a cold-water flat on First Avenue, just below Fourteenth Street, on the upper rim of the Lower East Side.

In school Luciano was a chronic truant, and while a mere youth he engaged in gambling, borrowed money from loan sharks, and was arrested for peddling narcotics. After serving six months behind bars, he returned to the streets a confirmed criminal. In 1923 Luciano was arrested when he delivered morphine to a customer who turned out to be a federal narcotics agent. He then took the easy way out by becoming an informer. In return for his freedom, he directed narcotics agents to the address of 163 Mulberry Street, where they found a trunk filled with dope.

Luciano early demonstrated exceptional talent for organization. Joe the Boss Masseria, embroiled in a power struggle with the gang leader Salvatore Maranzano, was anxious to have him serve as his number one assistant. At the time Masseria was cajoling Luciano to become his overall assistant, Lucky was already closely associated with such future bigwigs in organized crime as Meyer Lansky, Frank Costello, Joe Adonis, Benjamin (Bugsy) Siegel, Vito Genovese, and Frank Scalise. Luciano conferred with these gangland associates and sought their advice before accepting Masseria's offer. According to a statement attributed to Luciano, this took place in 1927. During this period Luciano's associates also included Louis (Lepke) Buchalter and Jacob (Gurrah) Shapiro, who were rapidly becoming the foremost industrial racketeers in New York City and perhaps the nation. During the mid-1920s Luciano turned up as a member of the Jack (Legs)

Diamond gang of hijackers, which included such rising underworld leaders as Arthur Flegenheimer, better known as Dutch Schultz. In 1926 Luciano was arrested with Eddie Diamond, a brother of Legs and a member of his gang.

In addition to his affiliation with the Diamond mob, Luciano worked for a time for George Uffner, who, like the Diamonds, depended on Arnold Rothstein for financial backing. Luciano reportedly credited Rothstein with having immeasurably influenced his life—even his tastes in wearing apparel and appreciation of the social amenities. Luciano also bought liquor that Rothstein had brought to America from England and even boasted that he had backed some of Rothstein's poker games. The close relationship between Luciano and Rothstein was apparently known to the police, who picked up Lucky and Uffner for questioning following the Rothstein murder.[9]

Another illustrious Rothstein protégé was Irving Wexler, better known as Waxey Gordon, who had begun his career unpretentiously as a pickpocket on the Lower East Side. As he developed his criminal skills, Gordon advanced himself until his services were in demand as a slugger, particularly in connection with labor violence in the garment center. Once Gordon was tried for murder but was discharged. However, he did serve a term in Sing Sing for assault and robbery. For a time, before Prohibition, Waxey was a member of an East Side gang led by Dopey Benny Fein, a gang that included such worthies as Lepke Buchalter and Gurrah Shapiro.[10]

Rothstein was credited with having made rumrunning a huge industry along the East Coast. But it was Waxey Gordon who gave Rothstein the germ of an idea that he developed into a million-dollar business. Gordon, accompanied by Big Max Greenberg of Detroit, had approached Rothstein for a $175,000 loan to embark on a large-scale rumrunning venture. Rothstein mulled over the suggestion and made a counterproposal, which was put into effect. He created an organization to buy liquor by the shipload in England, transport it to America, and sell it to eager buyers in this country. Through Henry Mather, his European agent, Rothstein bought twenty thousand cases of Scotch whiskey and loaded them on a ship bound for America. Offshore, a fleet of small speedboats met the ship and brought the whiskey to Long Island, where trucks were waiting. Rothstein had made amicable, and profitable, arrangements with the Coast Guard and police, and on the last stage of the journey a motorcycle escort protected the convoy of trucks en route to the warehouses.[11]

After Rothstein's ship, loaded with liquor, had made ten ocean crossings without mishap, there were indications of trouble ahead. A new Coast Guard commander was stationed on Long Island at the Montauk Point headquarters with specific orders to seize the Rothstein ship. Rothstein was tipped off. He decided it was time to settle his accounts with Gordon and Greenberg and bring this particular smuggling venture to a close.[12]

By the mid-1920s, Waxey Gordon had made millions of dollars out of syndicate operations. A plush suite of offices on Forty-second Street and Broadway served as his business headquarters. He owned a brewery in New Jersey and had an interest in a large distillery in upstate New York. He lived luxuriously in an expensive apartment on Central Park West, owned a summer home on the New Jersey shore, and had a fleet of expensive automobiles.[13]

Waxey Gordon's phenomenal rise in the ranks of the underworld from a lowly pickpocket to an affluent racketeer dealing in millions of dollars was made possible, in part, by the financial backing, guidance, and protection of Rothstein. Records uncovered after Rothstein's demise disclosed that he had paid the premiums on Waxey Gordon's life insurance and was holding securities belonging to Gordon with a value of $25,521.25.[14]

Among Rothstein's minions none other was more colorful than the vicious gunman Jack (Legs) Diamond. Jack and his brother, Eddie, were products of the northeastern section of Philadelphia and arrived in New York City for the first time in 1913. Jack became a member of package thieves on the Lower West Side and made the acquaintance of some of the leading gangsters of the period, including Monk Eastman.

For a time Legs served as Rothstein's trusted bodyguard. Some writers state that his service in this capacity began before Prohibition. However, Lewis J. Valentine, the distinguished New York City police official, asserts it was following the killing of Little Augie Orgen in 1927 that Legs was placed on Rothstein's staff and was paid $1,000 a week to protect the Brain from poor losers at gambling and to persuade debtors to pay their bills.[15]

Although regarded by his peers as irresponsible, Legs Diamond was fearless and was open to new ideas. Late in 1921 Legs came to the conclusion that it was a waste of time and money to invest large amounts of capital in liquor, then smuggle it into the country, and pay off the local and federal law-enforcement officials. Instead, he reasoned, it would be simpler to hijack the cargo after it arrived in America. Of course, money was needed to buy trucks, rent warehouses, and secure police protection. Rothstein was willing to furnish Legs with the necessary cash and to make his organization available to dispose of the hijacked liquor.

Both Legs and brother Eddie had the backing of Rothstein, who paid their hotel bills and furnished expensive apartments for Eddie. When they became embroiled with the law, Rothstein arranged for their relase on bail and for lawyers to represent them in court.

Naturally, preying on liquor smugglers was a hazardous occupation but Legs Diamond seemed to lead a charmed existence. But in the fall of 1924 a carload of gunmen caught up with him at 110th Street and Fifth Avenue; there they opened fire and peppered the right side of his head with birdshot.

The wounded Legs Diamond drove himself to Mount Sinai Hospital, where he was treated and eventually recovered.

Rothstein and the Diamond brothers later had a parting of the ways and the Brain withdrew his protection. Big Bill Dwyer had become the biggest liquor smuggler and thus the chief target of the Diamond gang's hijacking enterprises. Conjecture had it that Dwyer may have been instrumental in turning Rothstein against the Diamonds. At any rate, without Rothstein's blessing, the Diamond gang began to fade.[16]

The list of powerful underworld leaders who received training and guidance at the knee of the master was formidable indeed. Rothstein's protégés would soon head some of the most prestigious criminal organizations in New York City and the nation. The impact of Rothstein on organized crime and its leaders was ensured for decades.

Politically, Rothstein was also a man of great influence. After his death his close ties with Tammany leaders and officeholders, including members of the judiciary, would come to the public eye and help precipitate a political upheaval.

On April 25, 1924, Charles F. Murphy, Tammany boss for twenty-two years, died. Although Murphy's post carried no salary, the sixty-five-year-old boss left an estate of almost $2 million. Selected to succeed Murphy as boss of Tammany Hall was Judge George W. Olvany.[17]

Murphy's demise in 1924 was followed by the death in 1925 of Big Tom Foley. Thus within a period of a few months death had ended the careers of two Tammany powerhouses. Succeeding to the leadership of Foley's district was Peter Hamill, who honored the alliance that had been formed between Foley and Paul (Paolo Vaccarelli) Kelly, a leader of the Italian underworld. Under this arrangement, Harry C. Perry, once a lieutenant of Big Tim Sullivan, was permitted to retain the coleadership of the Second Assembly District, provided that protection was ensured for the growing Italian underworld, which included such bigwigs as Ciro Terranova and Joe the Boss Masseria.[18]

The first major task facing Judge Olvany was the upcoming mayoral election. Tammany leaders were determined to get rid of the two-term mayor, John F. Hylan, and place in office a man who would be unalterably subservient to the Tiger. Hylan was anxious to obtain the renomination and serve a third term as New York City's chief executive. Strongly backing Hylan's aspirations was Brooklyn boss John H. McCooey. The political leaders of Queens and Richmond also opposed dumping Hylan, who had always gratified their patronage demands.[19]

On July 2, 1925, a delegation of five hundred noisy citizens called on Boss Olvany and urged him to support James J. Walker, then Democratic leader of the New York State Senate, for mayor. Walker was no stranger to Olvany. As young boys, Olvany and Walker had been playmates in

Greenwich Village and Walker's father had once been an alderman in Olvany's district.

The forty-four-year-old Walker had served sixteen years in the Assembly and the Senate in Albany. In debate he had a quick wit, and his rapierlike thrusts delivered telling blows to an opponent. His ability to push Tammany-sponsored bills through the Senate had been remarkable. Otherwise his public service had been undistinguished. His principal interests were in Broadway shows and showgirls, and his philandering was anything but a well-kept secret. He possessed great personal charm and was attractive in appearance. His weight, which never exceeded one hundred thirty pounds, was carried on a straight five-foot-eight frame. In dress he was somewhat of a dandy.[20]

At a meeting of the Tammany Executive Committee on August 6, 1925, Boss Olvany insisted that the Democratic party could not win the mayoralty if incumbent Hylan were on the ticket. His recommendation that James J. Walker receive the nomination was approved unanimously. In the Bronx a similar resolution was pushed through by the Democratic boss there, Edward J. Flynn. The enthusiasm for Walker was somewhat dampened by a well-grounded fear that as mayor he might have difficulty in keeping out of trouble. Nominated to run with Walker were Charles W. Berry for comptroller and Joseph W. McKee for the aldermanic presidency. It was hoped that Berry, a long-time friend of Governor Al Smith, and McKee, a Flynn protégé, would maintain vigilance over Walker and keep him in line.[21]

As the campaign got under way, Mayor Hylan charged that Walker intended to make New York an open city for gangsters, thieves, prostitutes, and dope peddlers. In particular, he asserted that Arnold Rothstein, the known link between Tammany politicians and the underworld, had actually dictated the nomination of Walker for mayor. In a masterful non sequitur, Governor Alfred E. Smith retorted that Daniel E. Finn, not Rothstein, had made the nominating speech for Walker at the wigwam. That response prompted loud laughter and the Rothstein charge was forgotten for the time being.[22]

In the primary fight, of the five borough leaders, John H. McCooey of Brooklyn, Maurice Connolly of Queens, and David Rendt of Richmond supported Hylan. Tammany Boss Olvany of Manhattan and Boss Edward J. Flynn of the Bronx endorsed Walker. Governor Smith actively participated in Walker's campaign and lent prestige to his candidacy.

Tammany leaders were concerned, however, that Walker's philandering might come to public notice and thus sabotage the political fortunes of the party. For a number of years, Walker, a married man, had been having an affair with Yvonne Shelton, whom he had met in 1917 when she was a singer and dancer with the Ziegfeld Follies. Walker and Vonnie met regularly in a private third-floor dining room at Leone's. Tammany Hall envoys now called on Vonnie Shelton and persuaded her to get out of sight during the campaign. Her disappearance, she was told, would be in Walker's best political interests. Vonnie dutifully took a trip to Cuba and did not return until after the primaries in 1925.[23]

Following Walker's victory in the primary, the noted socialist leader Norman Thomas stated that while he had never looked upon Hylan with any enthusiasm, never for one instant had he shared the delusion that the people would be better off under Walker. In fact, said Thomas, "there isn't anyone who does not know that under Walker, the underworld of New York will flourish as it never flourished under Hylan."[24]

Walker won the election handily, with a plurality of 402,123, and his running mates were also victorious. As Walker was sworn into office on January 1, 1926, a radio microphone was placed on the dais and the mayoral inaugural ceremony was broadcast for the first time in New York City history. A shallow playboy who admittedly knew nothing about many of the city's problems and who confessed that in his entire lifetime he had never read to completion more than fifteen books now became the chief executive and leader of a metropolis of almost six million people.[25]

The new mayor was the son of William H. Walker, a carpenter who had come to the United States in 1857 from county Kilkenny, Ireland. Toward the end of the 1870s, he married Ellen Ida Roon, the daughter of a saloon-keeper, James Roon. Mayor James John Walker, the second of four children, was born June 19, 1881. He had an elder brother, William H. Walker, Jr., a younger brother, George, and a sister, Anna.

By 1886 the father, William, was sufficiently affluent to move his family into a three-story brick house at Six St. Luke's Place, for which he paid $17,000 in cash. Eventually Jimmy would bring his own wife to this place, his home for four decades. Beginning in 1886, William Sr. served four terms as alderman from the old Ninth Ward of Greenwich Village. He was elected to the New York State Assembly for the 1892-93 term. And his political career ended upon losing his job as commissioner of public works when Governor Charles Evans Hughes removed John F. Ahearn as president of the borough of Manhattan.[26]

Young Jimmy attended St. Joseph's parochial school and St. Francis Xavier, a Jesuit preparatory school, where his academic record was undistinguished. His elder brother, William, entered medical school and the father was determined that his second son should become a lawyer. In 1902 Jimmy, without much enthusiasm, entered New York Law School. He was interested more in becoming a songwriter than a barrister. While attending law school, Jimmy met vivacious Janet Frances Allen, a singer and a chorus girl. Once she was the understudy to the leading lady of a show that flopped, whereupon she drifted back into vaudeville. For a number of years Janet sang Jimmy Walker's songs in various vaudeville halls. Walker's success as a songwriter peaked in 1905, when he wrote the lyrics for "Will You Love Me in December As You Do in May?" Janet had introduced Jimmy to Ernest Ball, who composed the music. At best, Walker never advanced beyond the rank of a third-rate songwriter, and by 1909 there were few demands for his talents. His older brother, William, was a doctor; his younger brother, George, was in the insurance business, and the father began increasing the pressure on Jimmy to pass the bar examinations and get into politics.[27]

Jimmy's first venture into politics as a candidate was in 1909, when he ran for the New York State Assembly and was elected. In Albany Al Smith took Walker in tow and attempted to give him guidance. Three years were to elapse before he finally passed the bar examinations in Albany. In April of that year, 1912, Walker, then thirty-one, married Janet Frances Allen, who had been patiently waiting for seven years. And at the wedding in St. Joseph's Church, Walker and his best man arrived more than two hours late. The ceremony was adorned musically with a mixture of "Here Comes the Bride" and Jimmy's masterpiece, "Will You Love Me in December As You Do in May?"[28]

As an assembly man, Walker was brash, witty in debate, and given to histrionics. Tammany Boss Charles F. Murphy was impressed with Walker's political potentialities and decided to make him a state senator. With Murphy's backing, Walker's election to the Senate in 1914 was ensured. In 1919 Walker became the Democratic leader in the Senate, a post he filled until he was elected mayor six years later. As early as 1923 Al Smith was becoming somewhat disillusioned with Walker. A good family man, Smith disapproved of Walker's philandering, some of his extracurricular activities, and his profligate spending. It also annoyed Smith that in matters of party policy, Walker followed the dictates of Boss Murphy, not Smith. Nevertheless, Smith campaigned effectively for Walker during the mayoral campaign of 1925.[29]

Upon taking the oath of office as mayor, Walker appointed George V. McLaughlin to the important post of commissioner of police. The appointment was a surprisingly good one. McLaughlin had served as state superintendent of banks and was a man of integrity and ability.

The tasks confronting the new commissioner of police were formidable indeed. Commercialized vice, gambling, and crime of every variety were flourishing. The underworld was widely involved in the manufacture, sale, and distribution of beer and liquor, which had been outlawed by Prohibition. Gang killings were commonplace.

And the use of guns was not confined to gangsters. Weapons were easily obtainable by almost everyone. McLaughlin was incensed when he learned that a young boy arrested by the police had purchased a pistol and ammunition through the mail for fourteen dollars. How could New York City make the Sullivan gun law effective, he asked, when other states were permitting the sale of guns by mail? Police laxity had also added to the gun problem. Weapons confiscated by the police were sold to pawnbrokers and were soon on the street and in the hands of criminals. Next to the easy availability of handguns, McLaughlin named drugs as the most serious cause of crime and violence. A half century later the problem was much the same.[30]

Of particular concern to the new police commissioner was the widespread corruption in the department. He determined to do something about it. Significantly, McLaughlin restored to good graces some of the honorable officers in the department who had been punished when they had refused to follow orders of corrupt Tammany politicians. One such man was Lewis J. Valentine, who had been passed over when examinations were held for the post of captain. On January 30, 1926, Commissioner McLaughlin restored Valentine to civil-service elegibility for the rank of captain; on February 26, 1926, he was made an acting captain, and a month later attained the top civil-service goal of captain. On July 1, 1926, Commissioner McLaughlin summoned Valentine to his office. He announced the re-creation of the confidential squad and placed it under the command of Valentine, whom he promoted to the post of deputy inspector.[31]

Valentine and his confidential squad declared war on the professional gamblers, who were doing a flourishing business throughout the city, and who frequently based their operations in the clubhouse of political leaders. Arnold Rothstein, Johnny Baker, Arthur Froelich, and Gus Mayo were only a few of the gamblers described by Valentine as menaces to law and order. "The plug uglies and hoodlums of an early day," said Valentine, "were mere fleas compared to the gamblers," who were accustomed to buying and paying for high police officials and who enjoyed the iron-clad protection of political bigwigs.

Huge sums of money were wagered at political clubhouse gambling games operated by professionals and patronized often by criminals. The operations of George McManus were based in the clubhouse of the city clerk, Michael J. Cruise, at 226 East Thirty-second Street; Johnny Baker's games found a haven in the clubhouse of Harry C. Perry, chief clerk of the city court, at Fourth Street and the Bowery; and the games of Froelich and Mayo operated in the clubhouse of Sheriff Thomas M. Farley at 369 East Sixty-second Street. In a 3 A.M. raid on Sheriff Farley's clubhouse, Valentine's men had to smash through steel-sheathed icebox doors and barred windows. Twenty-six men, including Froelich and Mayo, were arrested. On one occasion, two armed robbers took their loot of $12,000 to Harry C. Perry's clubhouse where they lost it in a crap game. Guns were pulled. Both robbers were fatally shot and their bodies dumped by a taxicab at Bellevue Hospital. When Valentine's squad arrived at Perry's clubhouse, two pistols were found on the blood-covered floor. A vicious gun battle had obviously occurred. No one from the club had notified the police about the shooting, nor would anyone discuss what had happened.

The Tammany leaders were shocked and enraged over the gambling raids, particularly when their holy of holies, the clubhouses, were unceremoniously subjected to police action. Tammany politicians ran to City Hall and complained bitterly. Growing pressure was exerted on Commissioner McLaughlin, but he remained firm. In fact, he responded to the pressure by promoting Valentine to the rank of inspector.[32]

On March 12, 1927, the commissioner of police authorized Valentine to raid three political clubhouses in Brooklyn. In the People's Regular Democratic Club, the district leader, Alderman McGuinness, and eight other men were arrested on charges of bookmaking. At least one hundred fifty others in the place were taken into custody for disorderly conduct. A safe labeled "Peter J. McGuinness, Private" contained records showing annual wagers of $600,000 with profits of over $60,000. Also raided was the clubhouse of a McGuinness political rival, John A. McQuade, who enjoyed the backing of Brooklyn Boss John H. McCooey. The McQuade clubhouse had long been a center of gambling operations.[33]

Those arrested had little to fear from the prosecutors and the courts. Almost as soon as Valentine's men brought the gamblers into court, charges against them were dismissed. Nonetheless, the raids had an unsettling effect on the prestige and vaunted power of the district leaders. During one raid, officers broke through the iron-doored clubhouse of Harry C. Perry and arrested several men while a gambling game was in progress. Italian underworld bosses who were receiving the protection of Perry scornfully questioned the power of a district leader who was unable to keep policemen out of his own clubhouse. Perry's prestige continued to deteriorate. He was deposed a few years later and a new leader, Albert Marinelli, took control of the district.[34]

As Valentine's confidential squad continued raids on gambling establishments, the protests by Tammany leaders to Mayor Walker grew in volume and intensity. By the end of March 1927 McLaughlin decided he had endured enough. He resigned the post of commissioner of police, which he had held under trying circumstances for fifteen months, and accepted the position of executive vice president of the well-known telegraph and cable firm, the Mackay Companies. His new job had fewer headaches and paid an annual salary of $75,000.[35]

Mayor Walker was not long in appointing his former law partner, Joseph A. Warren, to succeed McLaughlin as commissioner of police. Warren, a close friend of the mayor, had been serving in the Walker administration as commissioner of accounts. He was a Tammany man and Walker was confident that he could depend on him to follow the dictates of the political leaders. The mayor specifically instructed Warren to disband the confidential squad, demote Inspector Valentine, and transfer him to some remote spot in the city where he could cause no further trouble. Valentine knew the word was out that he must go, so when he was called to the new commissioner's office, he carried his letter of resignation. Valentine was therefore taken aback when Commissioner Warren bluntly told him, "Your duties are unchanged. I like your work." A few days later Valentine was promoted to the rank of deputy chief inspector. The new police commissioner was in failing health and under increasing political pressures. Nevertheless, Warren never faltered in giving his full support to Valentine and the confidential squad.[36]

Although Mayor Walker had appointed political hacks to many offices, his first two appointments to the post of commissioner of police were most creditable. To Tammany Hall politicians, however, they were disastrous. The selection of McLaughlin had been urged on Walker by Governor Al Smith, but Warren, the mayor's friend and former law partner, was apparently Walker's responsibility alone. In the face of protests by district leaders, Walker, for some time, enigmatically remained loyal to the men he had placed in charge of his police department.[37]

As mayor, Walker did not change his lifestyle. He was still the playboy, exuding charm and pursuing Broadway showgirls. On November 8, 1926, the musical *Okay,* starring Gertrude Lawrence, opened. Walker went backstage and met for the first time an uninhibited, vivacious, brown-eyed dancer, Betty Compton. By the summer of 1927, his relationship with Compton, twenty-three years his junior, had blossomed into a full-blown affair.[38]

Seldom rising before ten o'clock and at times suffering from a hangover, Walker usually was little inclined to tackle the real problems of the city. He was popular with City Hall reporters with whom he shot craps. When serious issues were debated by the Board of Estimate, they were often ignored by newspaper accounts while the mayor's wisecracks were given prominent space. Walker once mercilessly abused a citizen who took more than a few minutes of his time to discuss some proposed measure, but he hesitated not in keeping huge crowds waiting in board chambers while he dallied for an hour and a half over his lunch.[39]

Occupying a high priority in the mayor's scale of values was an immaculate personal appearance. He changed his clothes thrice daily—twice during the daytime and once for his evening activities. Wardrobes were maintained at several places in the city to enable him to change his garb frequently and conveniently.[40]

In his personal financial matters, the mayor woefully lacked a sense of propriety. He surrounded himself with a coterie of wealthy advisers, who lavished gifts upon him. One friend, Jules Mastbaum, paid $25,000 for the renovation and repair of Walker's Greenwich Village home. After Mastbaum's death in 1926, publisher Paul Block furnished Walker with a private railway car, presented him with a $15,000 coat, paid his hotel and other personal expenses, and opened a joint brokerage account with Walker, which benefited the mayor alone. In this curious transaction, Walker placed no money whatever into the brokerage account, but between March 9, 1927, and June 15, 1927, he withdrew $102,000 from it, and by the time the account was closed in August 1929 his withdrawals had totaled $246,000.[41]

What, if anything, Block expected to receive as a result of his generosity to the mayor was never definitely established. Interestingly, Block, Senator John A. Hastings, a Walker crony noted for expensive living and overindulgence, and Dr. Robert S. Beyer, a chemist, were chief stockholders in the Beyer Company. Once, Walker, Senator Hastings, Paul Block, his son Billy, and John H. Delaney, chairman of the board of transportation for the city, journeyed to Brooklyn to watch Beyer demonstrate his alleged process for changing copper into gold. Although some technical problems apparently prevented that transformation, the mayor was told the Beyer Company had developed a synthetic tile that could be used in the city's subways. Mayor Walker ordered chairman Delaney to look into the tile immediately. Apparently the Beyer Company, with the aid of the mayor and his cronies, had hopes of turning tile into gold through city contracts. However, the engineers for the board of transportation turned down the purchase of the Beyer Company title. By the time that decision was reached, Senator Hastings had sold his stock in the company, making a profit of $50,000.[42]

Many grave problems were facing the city and greatly needed was strong leadership from the chief executive. Such leadership could hardly be expected from Mayor Walker, a man of shallow intellect and questionable moral and ethical standards. New York, like all other American cities, was in the midst of a period of general lawlessness aggravated by Prohibition. And Walker, with paramour Betty Compton, often patronized nightspots in which the law was flouted. His personal example hardly inspired either the general public—which adored him—or law officers to curb those activities on which organized crime thrives.

Several months before he became mayor, Walker had served as defense lawyer for a low-ranking member of the Jacob (Little Augie) Orgen gang. During a strike of laundry workers in August 1923, the minions of Little Augie engaged in open conflict with the forces of Nathan Kaplan, commonly known as Kid Dropper, the acknowledged leader of the most notorious gang of Jewish gunmen in New York City and once a member of Paul Kelly's Five Pointers. While the conflict raged, Kid Dropper was arrested on a charge of carrying concealed weapons and arraigned in the Essex Market Court. Law-enforcement officials promised Dropper his freedom in return for his promise to leave the city. As the gang leader left the courthouse, over thirty policemen surrounded him to give him protection. Arriving at the street, Kid Dropper and Captain of Detectives Cornelius Willemse entered a waiting taxicab. An underling of Little Augie's gang, Louis Kushner, alias Louis Cohen, walked up to the rear window of the cab and fired three shots. One killed Kid Dropper instantly, another wounded the cab driver, and the third pierced the straw hat Captain Willemse was wearing. Kushner was immediately arrested and charged with first-degree murder. James J. Walker, then a state senator, appeared in court as counsel for Orgen, against whom there was no evidence. The court then appointed Walker to defend Kushner. The jury brought in a verdict of second-degree murder and Kushner was sentenced to twenty years to life.[43]

Industrial racketeering had for some time served as an important source of revenue for the leaders of powerful criminal organizations. Louis (Lepke) Buchalter and Jacob (Gurrah) Shapiro had become so influential in the garment industry that they opened a clothing manufacturing firm of their own. Greatly aiding Lepke and Gurrah in their rise to eminence in industrial racketeering were the working arrangements they maintained with Tammany leaders James J. Hines and Sheriff Tom Farley.[44]

In 1927 Lepke and Gurrah were involved in a confrontation with Little Augie Orgen. It erupted into deadly violence. Little Augie had accepted a fee of $50,000 from the boss painters' association of Brooklyn to end a strike then in progress. Little Augie's approach was to call upon the union leaders and threaten them with death unless the strike was ended immediately. A disagreement over policy caused bad blood to break out between Orgen and gang bosses Lepke and Gurrah. Little Augie believed in getting all the money he could as soon as he could, whereas Lepke and Gurrah insisted that much greater benefits could be reaped from a prolonged strike. Lepke and Gurrah were further enraged when Little Augie formed an alliance with Jack (Legs) Diamond and his brother, Eddie. Orgen gave the Diamond brothers one half of his $50,000 fee for their help in breaking the painters' union strike. Lepke and Gurrah deemed the Diamond brothers common thugs, unworthy of participating in the specialized field of labor racketeering.

On the night of October 15, 1927, the Lepke-Gurrah forces were on the prowl looking for Little Augie. About eight-thirty they located Orgen and Legs Diamond on the corner of Norfolk and Delancey Streets on the Lower East Side. As Gurrah jumped from a car, Legs wheeled around and pulled his gun. During the battle that followed, Little Augie was killed and Legs suffered many bullet wounds, including two just below the heart. Diamond was held in Bellevue Hospital as a material witness and slowly recovered from his wounds.[45]

Lepke and Gurrah were charged with murdering Orgen but won their freedom when all witnesses, including Diamond, refused to identify them. They thus emerged from the Orgen killing more powerful than ever. Whenever they had appeared in court, the police found it expedient to furnish a guard of fifty detectives and ten uniformed men under the command of a deputy inspector.

Lepke and Gurrah had amply demonstrated their ability to commit murder and get away with it. That fact was not lost on the one hundred thousand persons in the garment industry or on potential victims in other businesses. Lepke and Gurrah gained control of the truckmen's union; they organized trade associations, and through terroristic methods forced manufacturers and jobbers to join. The industrialists soon perceived that if they were to remain in business, they had to pay tribute of $5,000 to $50,000 to Lepke and Gurrah. Soon the entire garment industry was under their dirty thumbs.[46]

On July 1, 1928, about eight and a half months after the demise of Little Augie, a highly influential Italian underworld boss, Frankie Yale, was ambushed and slain gangland-style. His garish funeral was the most spectacular that New York had witnessed.

Yale's underworld credentials were excellent. He had been an intimate associate of Ciro Terranova and had served as an aide to Joe the Boss Masseria. He had been active in the affairs of the Unione Siciliana and for nearly a decade had been recognized as its national head.[47]

Among Yale's diversified business interests in Brooklyn were ownership of the Yale Cigar Manufacturing Company at 6309 New Utrecht Avenue, partnership with his brother in an undertaking establishment, involvement in the illicit liquor and beer traffic, and labor racketeering.[48]

During the early part of the century, Johnny Torrio, the protégé of Paul (Paolo Vaccarelli) Kelly, left his James Street interests and moved to Brooklyn. There Torrio and Yale became partners in a Coney Island waterfront dive named the Harvard Inn, on Navy Street near the Brooklyn Navy Yard.

About 1909 Torrio went to Chicago. There he became the bodyguard, aide, and eventual successor to Big Jim Colosimo, vice lord in the Windy City's First Ward. Yale continued to operate the Harvard Inn in Brooklyn and some time later hired a young hoodlum by the name of Al Capone to serve as a bouncer and bartender. Capone was a native of Brooklyn, having been born there on January 17, 1899. It was in the Harvard Inn that young Capone made offensive remarks to the sister of a petty felon, Frank Galuccio. Unclasping a pocketknife, Galuccio went for Capone's face. When the knife wounds healed, Capone's face was thrice scarred—across the cheek in front of his left ear, on his left jaw, and under his left ear on the neck. Later he would be known worldwide as Scarface Al Capone.[49]

On December 18, 1918, Capone married an Irish girl, Mae Coughlin, and the next year a son was born. Already Capone was a suspect in two murders and a third victim, stabbed by Capone during a dance brawl, was hovering between life and death. It was expedient for Capone to get out of New York. Frankie Yale got in touch with his erstwhile partner, Johnny Torrio, and arrangements were made to give Capone employment in Chicago. Capone was hired by Torrio as a bouncer in his Four Deuces, a four-story saloon, gambling house, and brothel at 2222 South Wabash Avenue in Chicago. Before long Capone was Torrio's chief lieutenant and eventually his successor as the underworld boss of Chicago.[50]

On May 11, 1920, Big Jim Colosimo was shot and killed in his nationally renowned Colosimo's Cafe, 2126 South Wabash Avenue, in Chicago. At the extravagant funeral given the vice lord, honorary pallbearers included three judges, an assistant state's attorney, two congressmen, a state representative, numerous aldermen, Mike Merlo, head of the Unione Siciliana in Chicago, and Johnny Torrio. Undoubtedly Torrio's grief was simulated. In fact, indications were convincing that he had imported Frankie Yale from New York to rub out Big Jim. On the day of the killing, Frankie Yale, who had been in Chicago for a week, was stopped by police as he was about to board a train for New York. There was no tangible evidence to connect him with the murder and he was permitted to go on his way.[51]

Following Colosimo's death, Torrio assumed the leadership of the crime organization in Chicago, which he would develop into one of the most powerful in the nation. Al Capone would soon serve as his chief lieutenant. And the friendly relations that had long existed between Torrio and Yale would continue.

On November 10, 1924, one of Chicago's more celebrated gang killings took place when the North Side underworld leader Dion O'Banion was slain in his flower shop at 738 North State Street. The murder may have stemmed from a dispute between O'Banion and Torrio over the operation of a Torrio gambling house in Cicero in which O'Banion had an interest. There were also rumblings that Dion O'Banion may have double-crossed Torrio when the police raided the Sieben Brewery in Chicago on May 19, 1924. Johnny Torrio was among numerous underworld figures arrested at that time. Whatever may have precipitated the slaying of the North Side gangster, it is clear that bad blood existed between O'Banion and the Torrio organization. And, although it may have been coincidental, Frankie Yale was in Chicago on the date O'Banion was murdered. He was stopped by Chicago police in the LaSalle Street railway station only a few minutes before his New York–bound train was scheduled to depart. Yale insisted that he had come to Chicago to attend the funeral of Mike Merlo, head of the Unione Siciliana in Chicago. Mike had died of cancer on November 8, 1924. His explanation was plausible and he was permitted to return to New York City.[52]

As a result of the Sieben Brewery raid, Torrio was convicted in a federal court in Chicago and sentenced to nine months in jail. On January 24, 1925, just before his commitment to jail, Torrio was ambushed and shot. He was rushed to a hospital, where he recovered. After serving his jail sentence of nine months, Torrio bequeathed his Chicago underworld throne to Al Capone. He then traveled extensively before returning to New York.[53]

Capone was soon to become the most renowned gang leader in the world. The organization he headed grew fat from the proceeds of commercialized vice, gambling, and liquor. Capone maintained alliances in many parts of the country—with the Purple Gang in Detroit, Max (Boo Boo) Hoff in Philadelphia, and Egan's Rats in St. Louis. On the East Coast, Capone turned to his former patron, Frankie Yale, who was a major figure in the bootleg industry, and had ties with a number of important syndicates, including the one headed by William Vincent (Big Bill) Dwyer. Yale had been a pioneer in bringing liquor into New York from rum fleets off the coast. In these operations Yale's righthand man and chief killer was Gandolfo Civito, commonly known as Frankie Marlow. Yale was also connected with Vannie Higgins, who operated some speedboats and headed a gang of hijackers that dominated the highways of Long Island.[54] In his arrangements with Capone, Frankie Yale was responsible for supervising the landing of liquor on Long Island and seeing that regular shipments were made to the Capone organization in Chicago. Beginning with the spring of 1927, a number of trucks engaged in transporting liquor to Chicago were hijacked before they were able to leave Brooklyn. Capone suspected a double-cross and dispatched one of his men, James Finesy de Amato, to Brooklyn to spy out the facts. De Amato's role was uncovered and he was gunned down on the streets of Brooklyn. Before he was killed, De Amato had sent information to Capone that confirmed the gang leader's suspicions. Furthermore, friction between Frankie Yale and Capone over control of the Unione Siciliana in Chicago had been intensifying for some time. Accordingly, the Chicago gang leader decided that the time had arrived when Yale must be treated as a double-dealer.

During the latter part of June 1928 a conference was held in Florida between Al Capone and several of his Chicago henchmen, including Charles Fischetti, Jack Guzik, and Dan Serritella. A few days earlier Capone had directed a Florida friend, Parker Henderson, to buy two .45-caliber revolvers and other guns from a Miami pawnshop. On June 28, 1928, six Chicagoans who had been visiting Capone in Florida boarded the Southland Express presumably for the return trip to the Illinois metropolis. At Knoxville, Tennessee, four of the men got off the train, purchased a used black sedan from a Nash agency for $1,050, and drove to New York City.

About midafternoon on Sunday, July 1, 1928, Frankie Yale was drinking in a Borough Park speakeasy when he received a telephone call. After hanging up the receiver, Yale rushed outside, entered his automobile parked nearby, and drove away. On Forty-fourth Street, a black sedan crowded the Yale car to the curb. Gunmen in the black sedan opened fire and Yale was killed instantly. The assassins abandoned the black Nash on Thirty-sixth Street between Second and Third Avenues. Inside the car police found several weapons, including two .45-caliber revolvers and a Thompson submachine gun. Through serial numbers the two revolvers were traced to Parker Henderson, who later appeared before a New York grand jury and admitted that he had purchased them for Capone from a Miami pawnshop. The Tommy gun was traced to the sporting-goods store of Peter von Frantzius in Chicago. This store had furnished machineguns and other weapons that had figured in some of Chicago's most spectacular gang killings of the time. The slaying of Frankie Yale was thus laid at the doorstep of Al Capone and his gang in Chicago, but no prosecution was ever instituted.[55]

Yale's funeral was befitting a ruler of his standing in the underworld. An estimated ten thousand persons attended the requiem mass for his soul at St. Rosalia's Roman Catholic Church in Brooklyn or rode in the cortege to the Holy Cross Cemetery or paid their respects at graveside, where his corpse, in a $15,000 nickel-silver casket, was lowered to its final resting place. Thirty-eight cars were required to carry the floral offerings. One eighteen-foot column of red and white roses bore the deceased's initials. Among the most demonstrative mourners were two women, who seemed to be vying with each other in a show of grief at graveside. Each was married to Yale and each claimed to be his rightful widow.[56]

Following the murder, Yale's Brooklyn enterprises were taken over by Anthony Carfano, also known as Little Augie Pisano. Carfano was the son-in-law of John DiSalvio, better known as Jimmy Kelly, a Greenwich Village nightclub proprietor and a Tammany election captain in the Second Assembly District. Important associates of Carfano were Joe the Boss Masseria and Joe Adonis, who enjoyed unusually good political connections in Brooklyn.[57]

The Frankie Yale killing was only one of numerous gangland murders in 1928. And in some instances, like Yale and Capone, old allies had become bitter adversaries. This was true of the relationship between Dutch Schultz and Legs Diamond. Schultz, as well as Lucky Luciano, had once been a member of the Diamond mob. But Diamond had been pushed out of the Bronx by the formidable organization built up by Dutch Schultz and his intimate friend Joey Noe. And Diamond had no intention of kindly accepting such a reverse.

Dutch Schutz was born Arthur Flegenheimer on August 6, 1902, at 1690 Second Avenue. Numerous German-Jewish immigrants had moved to this locality from the Lower East Side ghetto. With the advent of Prohibition, Dutch worked awhile for Otto and Jake Gass, who had a small trucking business that was converted into a beer-hauling enterprise. Schultz shrewdly learned the importance of making political connections and in 1925 was able to wangle an appointment as deputy sheriff from the incumbent sheriff, Edward J. Flynn, then boss of the Bronx. He was relieved of his badge the following year for his part in an embarrassing shooting at Jack Diamond's Bronx Club.

Apparently the first joint business venture of Dutch Schultz and Joey Noe was launched when they opened a speakeasy called the Hub Social Club. Before long they opened several other drinking places and then bought a few trucks, which they used to deliver beer. Eventually, the Arthur Flegenheimer–Joey Noe organization became powerful and was everywhere feared. It included such vicious apostles of violence as Bo Weinberg, Joey Rao, Fatty Walsh, Edward (Fats) McCarthy, and Vincent (the Mick) Coll and brother Peter. With such effective persuaders, business expanded prodigiously, and headquarters for the Schultz-Noe organization moved to an office building on East 149th Street.

On the night of October 15, 1928, Dutch and Joey visited a favorite haunt, the Swanee Club, located under the Apollo Theater on West 125th Street. There they tarried until dawn. Upon leaving, they gave a ride to two newspaper reporters, whom they dropped off on Fifth Avenue. Noe and Schultz parted. Schultz was believed to have visited the office of William V. (Big Bill) Dwyer and Noe headed for the Chateau Madrid, where he intended to straighten out some problem with Legs Diamond. About seven o'clock there was a fusillade of gunshots on West Fifty-fourth Street. Stretched out on the sidewalk in front of the Chateau Madrid was Joey Noe. The bulletproof vest he was wearing failed to prevent bullets from piercing his lower spine and his right breast. On him was found a new brass badge; he had recently been appointed a deputy sheriff of the Bronx. The police believed the ambush had been set up in front of the Chateau Madrid by Jack Diamond with the hope that both Schultz and Noe could be wiped out at the same time. Noe was taken to the Bellevue Hospital prison ward, where he lingered for over a month before dying on November 21, 1928.[58]

Joey Noe was still breathing, though unsteadily, when the mastermind of New York's underworld was slain. Reverberations from that would be felt for a long time.

On Sunday night, November 4, 1928, Arnold Rothstein was in Lindy's Restaurant, on Broadway at Fiftieth Street. About ten-thirty the cashier told him he was wanted on the telephone. The call to Rothstein had been made from room 349 in the Park Central Hotel, on Seventh Avenue between Fifty-fifth and Fifty-sixth Streets, about six blocks from Lindy's. After completing the telephone conversation Rothstein went outside on Broadway. There he talked to Jimmy Meehan, who later testified before a grand jury that Rothstein handed him a loaded revolver stating, "Hold this for me. George McManus wants to see me and I'm going up to his room. I'll be back in half an hour."[59]

At 10:47 P.M. Rothstein was observed staggering from the servants' areaway of the Park Central Hotel. Clutching his abdomen, he entreated, "Get me an ambulance. I've been shot." He was rushed to the Polyclinic Hospital, where he lingered in a semicomatose condition until he died about ten-twenty on the morning of November 6—election day.

Deputy Chief Inspector Lewis J. Valentine reported that when the police arrived in room 349 of the Park Central Hotel, the place reeked with tobacco smoke. In the closet they found a gray overcoat bearing a label with the name of George McManus.[60]

It was learned that on the night and morning of September 8–9, 1928, Rothstein had participated in a big poker game held in Jimmy Meehan's apartment on the northeast corner of Fifty-fourth Street and Seventh Avenue. Also having a hand in the game were George McManus and Nathan Raymond, both notorious gamblers. Rothstein's losses totaled $316,000 and he gave his IOUs totaling that amount to various players. The police believed that Rothstein welshed on those gambling losses and that McManus therefore shot him. On December 8, 1928, McManus and his payoff man, Hyman (Gil) Biller, were indicted for the Rothstein murder, but when the defendants were brought to trial by Tammany District Attorney Joab Banton, there was a directed verdict of acquittal because of weak evidence. Later, Tammany leader Jimmy Hines confided to Dutch Schultz's mouthpiece, J. Richard Davis, that he had done everything in his power to save his friend George McManus.[61]

Competent observers have expressed doubt that welshing on gambling debts caused McManus, if he was the slayer, to kill Rothstein. Instead, it has been suggested that the ambush slaying of Joey Noe a few days earlier precipitated the Rothstein murder. This theory calls attention to the warfare then raging between the Jack Diamond gang and the Dutch Schultz organization. Credited with having instigated the Noe shooting was Diamond, who had the backing of Arnold Rothstein. And it was speculated, the murderous Schultz mob killed Rothstein in retaliation for the attack on Noe.[62]

On the fateful Sunday night of November 4, 1928, Mayor James J. Walker and his vivacious girlfriend Betty Compton motored to the Woodmansten Inn, a suburban nightclub near the Williamsbridge Road, where the popular Vincent Lopez and his orchestra were playing. Betty was in a gay mood and while on the dance floor kicked off her satin slippers, which she retrieved and handed to Lopez to autograph. Other women followed suit. Sometime after midnight several men with known underworld ties who were sitting with their women at ringside tables apparently received a report of some kind that caused them concern. One man came over to the table where the mayor was sitting and whispered to him. Walker abruptly told Betty, "We're leaving." When Vincent Lopez asked him if he was all right, Walker replied, "Not exactly." Lopez volunteered that something must have happened since he noticed the "boys" were acting funny. The mayor answered, "Rothstein has just been shot," and with prophetic accuracy added, "That means trouble from here in."[63]

The Rothstein shooting meant trouble, indeed, for the Walker administration. Many recalled the charges of Mayor John F. Hylan in 1925, namely, that Arnold Rothstein had dictated the nomination of Jimmy Walker, and that Walker, if elected, would turn New York into an open city for gangsters. Tammany Hall spokesmen had met such charges with biting ridicule and open laughter. Now the public was not laughing. It was clamoring for a solution to the Rothstein murder. Newspapers headlined the case and a Republican political leader of Suffolk County, W. Kingsland Macy, called for a comprehensive state investigation.

As the public furor intensified, Mayor Walker realized that he must take some kind of action. After all, within a few months he would be campaigning for reelection and the Rothstein case would surely provide excellent political fodder for his adversaries. About mid-November Walker issued an ultimatum that gave Commissioner of Police Joseph A. Warren just four days to obtain more than hearsay information on the Rothstein murder. On the very day he was confronting Warren with the four-day time limit to solve the murder, the mayor paid a visit to Grover A. Whalen, general manager of the John Wanamaker department store, and urged him to become New York City's commissioner of police. At first, Whalen indicated a reluctance to accept such an assignment. Subsequently, Walker used his charm on some higher Wanamaker officials, who informed Whalen that if he accepted the city appointment his salary of $100,000 a year would be continued by Wanamaker's while he served as commissioner of police.

On December 13, 1928, Commissioner Warren resigned and was replaced by Whalen. Eight months later, in August 1929, Warren, only forty-seven, died of a paralytic stroke. The appointment of Whalen was a political move and the new commissioner of police was no stranger to politics. He had served as former Mayor John F. Hylan's secretary and as his commissioner of plant and structures. In the 1925 mayoral campaign, Whalen endorsed Walker's candidacy and upon his election had served as the mayor's impresario at public functions.

Exactly one day after Whalen became commissioner of police, he abolished the confidential squad, demoted Lewis J. Valentine to the rank of captain, and stationed him in Long Island City. Whalen, a skilled publicity artist, then embarked on a program designed to divert attention from the Rothstein murder. He organized traffic campaigns, encouraged anticommunist demonstrations, and, with the ever-present gardenia in his lapel, resorted to superb showmanship as chairman of the mayor's reception committee for distinguished visitors. He was to become known as the official greeter for the city.[64]

During the two days that Rothstein was lingering in the hospital before he died, his personal files were rifled. Some documents were removed and presumably destroyed, but left intact were numerous papers that proved highly embarrassing, if not incriminating, to many persons. Found in his files were documents that established that Rothstein had engineered the infamous "Black Sox" World Series scandal of 1919. Other papers revealed the close relations that had existed between Rothstein and Tammany Hall politicians, including the powerful Jimmy Hines and members of the Hines family. Also found were bills that a Rothstein attorney, Maurice Cantor, known for many years as "Hines' assemblyman," had submitted to the underworld mastermind for legal services performed for various men charged with crime. Disclosed was Rothstein's financial dealings with political figures, including judges, as well as with top-flight members of the underworld such as Frank Costello, Larry Fay, and many others. To aid him in conducting his far-flung business and financial transactions, Rothstein operated under a number of corporate entities, including the Rothmere Realty Company, the Rothmere Mortgage Corporation, and the Rothmere Brokerage Company.[65]

On November 21, 1928, the Tammany district attorney, Joab Banton, announced that Rothstein's files had been found and it was indicated that they would be examined by his office. Originally, Banton had been placed in office through the influence of Big Tom Foley, once Rothstein's staunch patron. Perhaps it is not too surprising that Banton soon had a change of heart. On November 22 he countermanded his orders for an inspection of the Rothstein files and stated his office had no interest in them. The United States district attorney's office promptly demanded the files.

Acting on information found in the Rothstein files, federal agents on December 7, 1928, seized narcotics valued at $2 million and arrested several men. On December 18, 1928, federal agents, still pursuing clues gleaned from the Rothstein files, seized a ton of narcotics on a Jersey City pier. Four men arrested by the agents were represented by Joseph Shalleck, the righthand man of Jimmy Hines. By examining the Rothstein files, federal agents had located and confiscated about $7 million worth of narcotics and uncovered a trail that led to Boston, Philadelphia, Detroit, Chicago, San Francisco, and foreign countries.[66]

By the time of Rothstein's demise, a number of New York and East Coast gang leaders had formed a loosely knit alliance that enabled them to pool their resources in the rumrunning and bootlegging business. The venture was the brainchild of Johnny Torrio, whose talents as an organizational genius were widely respected by the major gang bosses in the New York City area.

The cartel envisioned by Torrio established a cooperative buying, selling, and shipping pool, leased or purchased warehouses, and afforded protection to the members. Selected to run the combination, Torrio appointed a New Yorker, Frank Zagarino, as his field representative. Torrio maintained a low profile and Lucky Luciano was credited with being the ex-officio commander in chief of the alliance. A Newark house was selected for a radio installation. Vessels used by the group to unload ships were equipped with radio receivers and U.S. Coast Guard ships were monitored. Directing the combination's fleet of ships were two experienced smugglers, Jacob (Yasha) Katzenberg and Bert Erickson. Each gang in the combination retained its separate identity and agreed to stick to its own territory.[67]

Initially, the cartel was made up of seven mobs and thus became known as the Big Seven or the Seven Group. Newspapers reported the existence of the Big Seven but were not in complete agreement when identifying the original seven gangs. Many intimate details of the Big Seven's operations did not come to light until witnesses disclosed them during the income-tax trial of Johnny Torrio several years after the repeal of Prohibition. And Elmer L. Irey, chief of the Enforcement Branch of the U.S. Treasury, revealed it was not until the investigation of this tax case that Torrio's role in the Big Seven was known at all.[68]

According to information reportedly furnished by Luciano almost three decades after Prohibition ended, the original seven members of the cartel were: (1) the Bug and Meyer mob headed by Benjamin (Bugsy) Siegel and Meyer Lansky, which operated in New York, New Jersey, and surrounding areas; (2) the group headed by Joe Adonis, which held sway in Brooklyn; (3) the organization headed by Abner (Longy) Zwillman and Willie Moretti, which maintained a strong foothold in northern New Jersey, including Newark, Jersey City, and Fort Lee, as well as in western Long Island; (4) the group controlled by Irving Wexler (alias Waxey Gordon), Harry Stromberg (alias Nig Rosen), and Irving Bitz in Philadelphia; (5) Charles (King) Solomon, who ruled much of New England; (6) Enoch L. (Nucky) Johnson, boss of Atlantic City, who controlled the south New Jersey coast; and (7) Lucky Luciano along with Torrio himself. From other sources it appears quite certain that Frank Costello was also one of the ruling members of the Big Seven. He had become one of the most powerful rumrunners of the time and was an intimate associate of Siegel, Lansky, Moretti, Luciano, and other principals of the combination.

At the time of Luciano's active role in Big Seven affairs, he was also the chief assistant to Joe the Boss Masseria. Yet, neither Masseria nor the Italian mob he ruled had any connection whatever with the Seven Group.

The Big Seven cartel was so successful that by 1928 it had entered into cooperative alliances with twenty-two mobs from Maine to Florida and as far west as the Mississippi River.[69]

The Rothstein murder was only one of a series of gangland executions that had captured national headlines. On February 14, 1929, the infamous St. Valentine's Day massacre, engineered by the Al Capone forces in Chicago, shocked people throughout the civilized world. Several Capone gangsters, dressed in policemen's uniforms, entered a garage on Chicago's North

Side where seven members of the rival George (Bugs) Moran gang were awaiting the momentary return of their leader. The Capone emissaries, purporting to place the Moran hoodlums under arrest, ordered them to face the wall with their hands raised high. The seven helpless victims were then sprayed with machinegun bullets and mowed down like rats.

The barbaric savagery and ruthlessness that had characterized many gangland murders were arousing public indignation. Almost daily came demands for official action. The heat thus generated was believed to have prompted some of the nation's more powerful underworld leaders to take steps to reduce the killing. A three-day conference was scheduled for the President Hotel in Atlantic City, New Jersey, in May 1929.

Just who was responsible for initiating the Atlantic City conclave is not certain. Many observers, including George Wolf, long-time attorney for Frank Costello, insist that it was Costello who called the gangland leaders together. Some writers have credited Meyer Lansky with having inspired the get-together. Serving as elder statesman and adviser at the assemblage was Johnny Torrio. Undoubtedly, important roles were played by all three—Costello, Torrio and Lansky.[70]

The conference site assured America's premier underworld leaders a congenial atmosphere and protection from the prying eyes of any unfriendly officials. Boss of Atlantic City was Enoch L. (Nucky) Johnson, who controlled the numbers racket, provided casino and horse-parlor gambling, and protected a flourishing prostitution business. Having held the offices of sheriff, county treasurer, and clerk of the supreme court, Johnson was recognized as one of the most influential Republican politicians in the state. His capacity to afford iron-clad protection in New Jersey to gangland members was virtually unlimited. Johnson was an original member of the Big Seven cartel and under his watchful eye Atlantic County, New Jersey, had served as a haven where bootleggers landed shiploads of liquor from Canada, the Bahamas, and England. Johnson also often provided armed guards to protect liquor convoys, which were always in danger of being hijacked. Naturally, Atlantic City had become a favorite hideout for important criminals, including fugitives.[71]

No great effort was made to keep the May 1929 gathering of gangsters in Atlantic City a secret. In fact, a photograph of Nucky Johnson and Al Capone strolling on the famed boardwalk appeared in the newspapers. For Meyer Lansky the trip to Atlantic City served a dual purpose. He had been married to Anna Citron on May 9, 1929, and the business trip to Atlantic City also served as a honeymoon. In addition to Lansky, among those reportedly attending the convention from New York City were Frank Costello, Lucky Luciano, Johnny Torrio, Joe Adonis, Lepke Buchalter, Frank Erickson, and Dutch Schultz. The Brooklyn delegation included Albert Anastasia, Vince Mangano, and Frank Scalise. Chicago was represented by

Al Capone, his bodyguard, Frank Rio, Jack Guzik, and others. Also reported at the conference were Moe Dalitz and Lou Rothkopf from Cleveland; Joe Bernstein and other members of the Purple Gang from Detroit; Charles (King) Solomon of Boston; Max (Boo Boo) Hoff, Waxey Gordon, and Nig Rosen of Philadelphia; Longy Zwillman and Willie Moretti of New Jersey; and Johnny Lazia of Kansas City. Whether that list is accurate, or was perhaps padded through journalistic speculation, is impossible to determine. However, Luciano reportedly confirmed that all of those men were present. Absent from the meeting, and not invited to attend, were the Italian gang bosses Joe the Boss Masseria and Salvatore Maranzano.

Several gangsters attending the conference were important members of the Big Seven alliance. Quite likely the mobsters discussed combined operations that would eliminate destructive competition and violence. Concern was voiced over the large number of senseless killings. It was conjectured that joint efforts were made to put the clamps on Al Capone, whose vicious murders in Chicago had generated official heat on underworld operations everywhere.[72]

After the close of the Atlantic City meeting, Al Capone and his bodyguard, Frank Rio, proceeded to Philadelphia, arriving about seven o'clock in the evening. They attended a motion-picture theater at Nineteenth and Market Streets. When they emerged two hours later, two Philadelphia detectives, James (Shooey) Malone and John Creedon, were waiting for them. Both Capone and Rio were armed with .38-caliber revolvers, which they turned over to the detectives, who arrested them for carrying concealed weapons. Particularly mystifying is the fact that Capone had met Detective Malone at the Hialeah Race Track in Florida a year earlier, and a friendship had developed between the Chicago gang boss and the policeman. A Chicago newspaper account of Capone's arrest asserted that both Malone and Creedon had admitted having been Capone's guests at his Florida estate on one occasion.

Shortly after Capone had been taken into custody, he was interviewed by Philadelphia's director of public safety, Major Lemuel B. Schofield. Capone stated that he was tired of gang shootings and killings. And, he declared, it was with the idea of making peace among the gangsters that he had spent a week in Atlantic City and obtained the word of each leader that there would be no more shooting.

A few hours later Capone was arraigned before Judge John E. Walsh in the criminal division of the municipal court in Philadelphia. He pleaded guilty to the charge of carrying a concealed weapon and was given the maximum sentence of one year.

Only sixteen hours had elapsed between the time of arrest and his commitment to prison. Indeed incredible! Ordinarily, the gangster would have been represented by a battery of attorneys, who would have raised every legal technicality imaginable, and by appealing each ruling the final disposition could have been postponed for months, perhaps years.[73]

The entire affair—beginning with Capone's arrest by friendly officers who apparently were waiting for the infamous gang boss to emerge from the theater and his imprisonment within a matter of hours—gave rise to allegations that everything had been prearranged. Rumors were that at the Atlantic City conference Capone had been ordered to go to jail for a while to remove the heat from the underworld generally. There were also suspicions that increasing threats against his life moved Capone to protect himself by arranging for confinement. In either case, Capone was believed to have contrived with friendly detectives in Philadelphia for his arrest. With time off for good behavior, Scarface Al was released from Eastern Penitentiary on March 17, 1930.[74]

13

THE SEABURY INVESTIGATIONS

As the year 1929 opened, Tammany Hall was in the throes of internal conflict and intrigue. George W. Olvany, who had succeeded Charles F. Murphy as boss, had failed to hold the organization in line and his personal greed had aroused animosity. During his tenure as head of the Tiger, Olvany's law firm had received millions of dollars in fees, largely through handling cases before the Bureau of Standards and Appeals and in condemnation proceedings. Loyalist Tammany lawyers were annoyed because they had not been permitted to share in the loot. Olvany was persuaded to resign as Tammany boss on March 16, 1929, and a power struggle ensued to name his successor.

Mayor Walker summoned the district leaders of Tammany Hall to a conference and there made it clear that he wanted a new boss who was friendly to him. The three principal candidates to succeed Olvany were leaders Edward J. Ahearn of the Fourth Assembly District, Martin G. McCue of the twelfth, and John Francis Curry of the fifth. Ahearn was favored by Al Smith supporters; McCue was a former prizefighter who had served with Walker in the legislature; Curry, favored by Walker, was the least acceptable to Smith. On April 23, 1929, as a result of Walker's arm twisting, John Francis Curry was elected the new leader by a half-vote margin. Socialist Norman Thomas observed that the mask had been removed from Tammany. Said Thomas, "A district leader of the old school sits in the seat of Tweed and Croker. Jimmy Walker is mayor and Grover Whalen is police commissioner. The old gang is on the job."[1]

Not long after Curry had been named boss of Tammany, former governor Alfred E. Smith visited Walker in City Hall. During a heated conference lasting forty minutes, Smith attempted to extract a promise from the mayor that he would not be a candidate for reelection. Smith warned of great public indignation over the Rothstein murder scandal and of growing criticism of the city administration by ministers and taxpaying groups. He showed Walker a front-page article from the *New York Times* of March 14, 1929, which reported the absence from the city of several of its top executives and asked, "Who, if anybody, at the present moment is the acting mayor of New York?'' Smith also bluntly informed the mayor that his extramarital love affair was bothering a great many people. When Walker brusquely replied that he was going to run for a second term, Smith hotly retorted that he had better pray for a miracle and angrily stormed out of the conference.[2]

Facing the city were many serious problems, which should have received the undivided attention of the mayor. But Walker, as usual, was interested more in frills and personal enjoyment than in the business of his office.

A source of great annoyance to Franklin D. Roosevelt in the spring of 1929 was the constant unavailability of the mayor to meet with the governor during his visits to New York City. Much of Walker's time was taken up with Betty Compton and with a project to remodel the Casino Restaurant in Central Park.

Through Walker's machinations, the lessee of the old Casino had been forced out and a new lease was awarded to a corporation headed by the mayor's pal, Sidney Solomon. In May 1929 the announcement by the new management that on opening night the Casino Restaurant and ballroom would require a twenty-five-dollar cover charge touched off a heated controversy. The restaurant was intended to be a dining place for the ''fashionable and fastidious'' and also a hideaway for Walker and his paramour, Compton. Although Prohibition would not allow the Casino to serve intoxicants, on opening night Walker nevertheless drank champagne while Betty guzzled beer. The drinks were brought into the restaurant for them one bottle at a time from a car parked outside. At the same festivity, the band played for the mayor and his beloved ''Will You Love Me in December As You Do in May?'' The mayor responded by tipping the bandleader, Leo Reisman, $100 and later gave the hatcheck girl $200.[3]

Walker's legitimately earned income would hardly permit him to indulge in two-hundred-dollar tips to hatcheck girls. Yet, he seemed always to be surrounded by benefactors, some of whom were seeking city favors and who provided him with ready cash that enabled him to live extravagantly. Also aiding Walker's financial position somewhat was the action taken on December 17, 1929, by the Board of Estimate, an action that increased the mayor's annual salary from $25,000 to $40,000.[4]

About midyear, Walker summoned his commissioner of police, Grover A. Whalen, to City Hall for a conference. He wanted Whalen to arrange for the mayor to be drafted to run for a second term. It was suggested that Whalen prepare a list of so-called accomplishments of the Walker administration, a list that could be used in a petition urging the mayor to become a candidate for reelection. The petition, said Walker, should be brought to the Board of Estimate chamber by a committee of important persons. Walker instructed Whalen to manage the affair with ''your usual David Belasco skill, plus a bit of Phineas T. Barnum.''

On July 18, 1929, a committee of 682 well-known persons arrived at City

Hall armed with the petition lauding Walker. The group crowded into the Board of Estimate chamber where the mayor sat on a platform next to his wife, Janet (Allie), who was smiling as though Jimmy were still her devoted spouse. The petition, with forty "praiseworthy" points that had been assembled by Commissioner Whalen, was read by the committee chairman, August Heckscher, a venerable and beloved philanthropist. Walker was so touched by the sentiments expressed in the eulogy that he responded with a long speech assuring the petitioners that he could not turn a deaf ear to their supplications. He would, indeed, run for a second term.[5]

Tammany's slate of candidates for city offices in the 1929 elections was anything but encouraging to the advocates of efficient, honest government. Walker, who headed the ticket, had shown a remarkable degree of insensitivity to accepted moral and ethical standards insofar as the source of his personal finances was concerned. Although the *New York Times* editorially expressed confidence that Walker had in him the makings of a "remarkable chief magistrate" of the city, his track record indicated otherwise. He was fundamentally a playboy, who could not and would not seriously apply himself to the arduous task of running a great city. Some of the other Tammany candidates were even less promising than Walker.

The Tiger realized that District Attorney Joab Banton, who had been thoroughly discredited in the Rothstein murder scandal investigation, would have to be replaced. Chosen as the candidate for district attorney was a Tammany sachem, Thomas C. T. Crain, an unenergetic sixty-nine-year-old supreme-court justice. And to run for sheriff, Tammany selected Thomas M. Farley, the leader of the Fourteenth Assembly District. Farley was "well credentialed," having converted his clubhouse into an illegal, well-fortified gambling establishment, which had been subjected to raids by Walker's police department.[6]

The Republican party on August 1, 1929, named as its mayoral candidate Fiorello H. LaGuardia, a short, stocky, flamboyant Italian-American. The Little Flower, as he became known, had been a formidable vote getter on anti-Tammany tickets in New York City. With the exception of one term, when he served as president of the Board of Aldermen, LaGuardia had been in Congress since 1916.[7]

LaGuardia threw himself into the campaign with gusto. Many of the charges he hurled at his opponent were discounted by the public as political oratory. But some of his more serious accusations were later proven true.

Walker did not permit the campaign to interfere with his love life. Betty Compton, his girlfriend, was a member of the cast in the new show *Fifty Million Frenchmen*. During the show's trial run in Boston, the mayor virtually commuted between New York and the bean city. In the midst of a rehearsal, Walker jumped onto the stage, attempted to have Betty's part enlarged, and issued instructions to the orchestra how it was to play the numbers in which Betty appeared. When the show moved to New York City, Betty was enraged over the remote dressing room assigned her, and she put in a call to Jimmy. City officials soon arrived at the theater and menacingly pointed out to management the existence of fifteen building-code violations that could close the place. Management repented its oversight and took steps to make Betty's quarters more suitable. The city in turn forgot about the building-code infractions. The incident clearly casts light on Walker's priorities, and ethics, in running America's largest city.[8]

As the campaign progressed, LaGuardia pounded away at Walker, charging graft and mismanagement. He described the Casino Restaurant, which the mayor visited at least three times a week, as a "whoopee" joint and declared it was a source of revenue to Tammany officials.

The ghost of Arnold Rothstein made its presence felt throughout the campaign. LaGuardia ridiculed the statement of the Tammany district attorney, Joab Banton, that Rothstein's files contained no document to show any financial transaction between the underworld mastermind and any public official. LaGuardia produced a copy of a letter in the deceased gambler's files establishing that a loan of $19,940 had been made by Rothstein to Magistrate Albert H. Vitale, who was then actively campaigning in behalf of Walker. The caliber of judges in the magistrates' courts had reached an all-time low, charged LaGuardia, and he promised, if elected, to clean out the entire bunch of them.

LaGuardia asserted that Mayor Walker, as well as his police, knew who murdered Arnold Rothstein but did not dare to bring the killers to trial for fear they would tell everything, thus bringing to light a revolting scandal. Of the head of Walker's police department, Grover A. Whalen, LaGuardia said sarcastically, "It takes more than a silk hat and a pair of spats to make an efficient police commissioner."[9]

Boss John F. Curry skillfully marshaled all the troops under his command to assure a sweeping victory for the Tiger candidates. When the voters swarmed to the polls on November 6, 1929, most disregarded the charges against the Walker administration of widespread graft, corruption, and mismanagement of city government. Even the unsolved Arnold Rothstein murder case and evidence of the deceased gambler's intimate relations with influential Tammany leaders and officials of local government were largely overlooked. Jimmy Walker was reelected mayor by the overwhelming plurality of 497,165. Also swept into office were the inept Thomas C. T. Crain as district attorney and the corrupt Thomas M. Farley as sheriff. All would take office on January 1, 1930.[10]

During the closing days of the election campaign, ominous signs appeared on the economic front. Although business conditions had been unsatisfactory in 1929, stock prices continued to soar. Every Tom, Dick, and Harry had entered the stock market purchasing shares on margin. Paper profits were used to purchase more stock on margin. Finally the bubble burst. On October 24, 1929, Black Thursday, almost thirteen million shares changed hands. But the worst was still to come. On October 29, 1929, over sixteen million shares were traded. Stock prices collapsed. Bankers demanded repayment of money that had been loaned to purchase stock and brokers called in their margin accounts. With the stock-market crash of 1929, there began a downward spiral of prices, production, and employment, resulting in the Great Depression, which lasted for several years.[11]

During the mayoral campaign LaGuardia had brought to light Magistrate Albert H. Vitale's loan of nearly twenty thousand dollars from Rothstein. Before the year ended, Vitale's intimate relations with the underworld would again be in the limelight.

On December 7, 1929, the board of directors of the Tepecano Democratic Club gave a testimonial banquet honoring Magistrate Vitale. The affair was held in the upstairs room of the Roman Gardens, located in the Bronx at 187th Street and Southern Boulevard. Vitale was honorary life president of the club. Chairman of its board of directors was Michael N. Delagi, a former magistrate and protégé of Big Tom Foley. Of the club's membership of three hundred, about ten percent had police records. Vitale himself was long a known associate of gangsters; he protected them and they in turn ensured his political power.[12]

The December 7 banquet for Magistrate Vitale was attended by seventy invited guests, including two armed court attendants, John Monico and Dominick LaClare, as well as Arthur C. Johnson, a veteran of twenty years on the police department and also armed. Other invited guests included the powerful gangland boss Ciro Terranova, and six gunmen who were members of his mob—John Savino, James Savino, Joseph Catania (alias Joe the Baker), James Catania (alias Jimmie the Baker), Paul Marchione, and Daniel J. Iamascia. Each of the seven men had sizable police records, which showed charges ranging from burglary and robbery to felonious assault. Terranova, who rode around in a heavily armored bulletproof car, had recently been questioned about the gangland slaying of Frankie Marlow, with whom he had been feuding. All played not unimportant roles in New York City's organized crime. At one time or another the Savinos, the Catanias, and Marchione had ties with Dutch Schultz. Danny Iamascia was the Dutchman's bodyguard and later, on June 18, 1931, was killed when he and Schultz engaged in a shootout with police officers whom they mistook for rival gangsters. At the time a war between Schultz and his onetime trusted gunman, Vincent Coll, was at its peak. Danny would receive a lavish gangland funeral, replete with extravagant floral pieces from Ciro Terranova and other mob chieftains, and be laid to rest in a $10,000 coffin. Anthony Iamascia, a brother of Daniel and an officer of the Tepecano Democratic Club, was a bondsman who plied his trade around the court over which Magistrate Vitale presided.[13]

About one-thirty in the morning Vitale was making a speech to his distinguished guests and admirers when seven gunmen entered the banquet room of the Roman Gardens. Two men walked directly to the front of Vitale and kept their weapons pointed at him, while the others stood at the exits with their guns trained on the rest of the banquet guests. One gunman approached Detective Johnson and said, "So you're a cop, are you? Keep quiet and you won't get drilled." The bandits took the policeman's gun as well as the weapons from the two armed court attendants. The bandits then robbed the guests of jewelry valued at $2,500 and cash amounting to $2,000, including $40 from Vitale and $62 from ex-magistrate Michael N. Delagi. Strangely, the robbers met with no resistance of any kind from any of the guests, who included some of the toughest gangsters in the city.[14]

After the robbers departed, Detective Johnson hurriedly conferred with Vitale about their embarrassing predicament. Vitale instructed Johnson to say nothing; he would take steps to get some information. Within three hours Vitale called Johnson and told him to come to the Tepecano Democratic Club, located at 747 East 187th Street in the Bronx. Obviously, the magistrate's efforts had proven fruitful. Johnson's gun had been returned to Vitale, who gave it to the detective. When Johnson asked the magistrate if he knew who had committed the holdup, Vitale said he had an idea it had been staged by some of the "boys from downtown, around Kenmore Street." The reference was to gangsters from the political domain of Albert Marinelli, who later became the coleader of the Second Assembly District.

Marinelli and his brother operated a garage across the street from Celano's Restaurant. Here Joe the Boss Masseria and Lucky Luciano held meetings with their henchmen. From evidence later uncovered by a police investigation, almost certainly the leader of the bandits who held up the Vitale party was Trigger Mike Coppola, a gunman and murderer known to Magistrate Vitale and many other guests at the banquet. And adding to the bizarre character of the entire affair was the statement of Inspector Joseph J. Donovan, who said he had learned from police undercover agents that those in the inner circle at the dinner had known the robbery was to take place two hours before it did. Credited with having engineered the robbery was Ciro Terranova.[15]

The revelation that a magistrate had been honored at a banquet by some of the more insidious and powerful members of the city's gangland brought forth a howl of public indignation. The affair highlighted the close relationship existing between segments of the judiciary, the police department, and the underworld. Public pressure induced Police Commissioner Whalen to forward charges against Vitale to the bar association, which made a report to the appellate division of the supreme court. On March 14, 1930, the appellate division removed Vitale as a judge of the magistrates' courts. It was disclosed that during a period of almost five years of Vitale's tenure on the bench, he had made bank deposits exceeding $100,000, an amount well above his salary. Figuring prominently as a basis for Vitale's removal was the loan he had accepted from Arnold Rothstein.[16]

Only three months after Vitale's removal from the bench, he was given another testimonial dinner, on June 8, 1930, by the Federation of Italian-American Democratic Clubs at Ricciardi's Restaurant, 579 East Fordham Road. Among those who turned out to honor the deposed Vitale were Secretary of State Edward J. Flynn, General Sessions Judge John J. Freschi, Supreme Court Justices Salvatore A. Cotillo and Louis A. Valente, Magistrates Joseph Raimo and Thomas Aurelio, and the former magistrate Michael N. Delagi.[17]

The Vitale case served to crystallize a public awareness of scandalous conditions prevailing in the magistrates' courts and the press began demanding an investigation. On July 9, 1930, a *New York Times* editorial deplored the bad conditions in the city courts and stated that the hour had come for the mayor to summon both the demolition and the reconstruction crews. "It is not too late," said the *Times*, "for Mr. Walker, who has in no personal way been even slightly connected with any of these scandals, to voice the indignation of the community which has twice elected him." Overlooked were the mayor's improprieties, if not outright venality, in accepting huge financial gifts for his personal use and his general insensitivity to proper ethical standards. Walker was hardly in a position to adopt the stance of an indignant crusader. Instead, he was primarily concerned with having severe restrictions placed on the scope of any investigation that might be initiated.

Among the magistrates under fire at the time was George F. Ewald, accused of having paid $10,000 to Tammany district leader Martin J. Healy to obtain his judicial post. Evidence supporting the accusation was placed in the hands of the Tammany district attorney, Thomas C. T. Crain, who reluctantly presented the matter to the grand jury. Not surprisingly, the grand jury found that the charge was without foundation. The press denounced Crain's ineptness, and the ensuing public outcry made it expedient for Governor Franklin D. Roosevelt to order the attorney general, Hamilton Ward, a Republican, to take over the Ewald investigation. About the same time, U.S. Attorney Charles H. Tuttle announced that he possessed important evidence regarding Ewald and Healy. He further charged that Judge W. Bernard Vause of the Kings county court had accepted a fee of $190,000 for procuring a lease of two city-owned piers for a large steamship line. Later Vause was convicted on an unrelated charge of using the mails to defraud and was sentenced to six years at the federal penitentiary in Atlanta.[18]

A statement emanating from the attorney general's office revealed the intention of conducting an all-embracing investigation. Governor Roosevelt immediately announced he intended that Attorney General Ward's investigation be limited solely to the Ewald case. When Ward said that he would comply with the governor's wishes, Mayor Walker heaved a sigh of relief.

The very next day Walker invited Betty Compton to accompany him on a cruise departing from Montauk Point, Long Island. Along with a party of friends, they put out to sea on the yacht *Florida*. The yacht was beset by a heavy rainstorm and a strong forty-mile-per-hour wind, and the mayor became seasick. Upon returning to shore that evening, Walker and Betty visited a casino at Montauk. In the gaming room, hidden behind the kitchen, men and women in evening clothes were gambling with dice or playing the roulette wheel. Walker informed the manager that Betty wished to play hazard. While the mayor looked on, she accumulated $2,000 worth of chips. Shortly before midnight, law officers raided the gambling establishment. Walker hurriedly disappeared through a door leading to the dining room, but Betty and other patrons were taken into temporary custody and led outside. According to one version, as officers led Betty through the kitchen she observed that Walker had donned a waiter's apron and was calmly sitting at a table eating a plate of beans. However, a deputy sheriff, Max Mittenleifer, revealed that at the time of the raid, he had been called aside by Walker, who identified himself. At the mayor's request, the deputy sheriff gave him a "pass" and permitted him to return to his boat. Betty was taken to night court and when released a few hours later, inveighed her anger at Walker for having deserted her. The mayor justified his action by stating that he knew she would be released. And, he explained, after Governor Roosevelt had ordered the attorney general to limit the investigation to the Ewald case, he thought it unwise to tempt fate "by showing up in a rural hoosegow."[19]

While agitation for a full-scale investigation of the courts was mounting, Supreme Court Justice Joseph Force Crater was vacationing with his wife in Belgrade Lakes, Maine. The forty-one-year-old Crater, an intimate associate of U.S. Senator Robert F. Wagner, had been appointed to the bench the preceding April. On August 5, 1930, Justice Crater returned alone to New York City. There he spent some time at his official chambers and remained all night in his apartment at Forty Fifth Avenue. On August 6, 1930, he again visited his chambers, filled several portfolios with private papers, which he sent to his residence, and obtained $5,150 in currency, which represented the proceeds of two personal checks cashed for him by court attendants.

Justice Crater purchased a single ticket for a new show that had just opened at the Belasco Theater. Before going to the theater, Crater stopped at the Billy Haas restaurant on West Forty-fifth Street, a popular hangout for show people. There he ran into an attorney friend and a showgirl who asked the justice to join them. At 9:15 P.M., considerably after curtain time for the show at the Belasco, Justice Crater hailed a cab; as his friends waved goodnight, he was driven away and never seen again. He gained immortality by becoming one of the most celebrated and mysterious missing-person cases in American history.

Suspicions were strong that Crater's disappearance was related to the impending judicial inquiry. George F. Ewald was in trouble for having paid district leader Martin J. Healy $10,000 for his judicial post. Crater had once been the president of the Nineteenth Assembly District's Cayuga Democratic Club, the stronghold of Healy. About six weeks after Crater's appointment to the bench, he had withdrawn $7,500 from a bank account and sold securities for $15,779. The total of $23,279 was only slightly more than a supreme-court justice's salary of $22,500. It was commonly understood that a year's salary was the accepted price for a place on the bench.

It was also surmised that Crater may have feared exposure for the part he had played several months earlier in financial manipulations relating to the Libby Hotel on the Lower East Side. When the hotel went into bankruptcy, Attorney Crater was appointed referee to administer the property and supervise bids from prospective buyers. Although the Libby Hotel had been appraised at $1.2 million, it was sold on June 27, 1929, for $75,000 to the American Bond and Mortgage Company. On August 9, 1929, the property was sold to the city for $2,850,000, a profit of $2,775,000 on a $75,000 investment![20]

The press continued to clamor for a thorough investigation of the magistrates' courts and there were growing demands for a citywide inquiry as well. Governor Franklin D. Roosevelt refused to authorize any investigation beyond the Ewald matter, contending that a general probe of the magistrates' courts was within the province of the judiciary and only the legislature had authority over a citywide inquiry. Nevertheless, he succumbed to public pressure, and on August 21, 1930, the governor wrote the appellate division of the First Judicial Department and requested that the judiciary take the initiative in conducting an investigation of the magistrates' courts. The appellate division responded by ordering the probe and designating the impeccable Judge Samuel Seabury as referee to conduct the inquiry.[21]

Also on August 21, Joseph Clark Baldwin III, minority leader of the Board of Aldermen, made public a letter he had written to Governor Roosevelt, in which he urged the state's chief executive to investigate the office of Mayor Walker. The letter referred to such abuses as "salary grabs," a "dishonest budget," and "misrule." Walker promptly quipped that Baldwin was nothing but a "third-rate" politician, which explained why he always placed the Roman numeral *III* after his name.[22]

Mayor Walker's quips were insufficient to stem the tide of public opinion that had been steadily swelling over several months. Citizen indignation had its beginning with the Rothstein killing and its criminal-political ramifications. The indignation became outrage with the disclosures about Magistrate Vitale's testimonial dinner on December 7, 1929. With authorization to investigate the magistrates' courts, the first so-called Seabury investigation commenced in September 1930 and continued intermittently until summer 1931; the report, however, was not filed with the appellate division until March 1932. In the meantime, two additional "Seabury investigations" were in progress.

The City Club had filed charges against the Tammany district attorney, Thomas C. T. Crain, and asked for his removal on the grounds that he had failed to discharge his duties properly and had demonstrated general incompetency. On March 10, 1931, Governor Roosevelt appointed Judge Seabury as his commissioner to investigate and report on the charges against Crain. This second Seabury investigation took place in April and May 1931, and Seabury submitted his report to Governor Roosevelt on August 31, 1931.

On March 12, 1931, William J. Schieffelin, chairman of the Citizens Union, held a conference attended by nineteen civic-minded persons. From this conference came the New York Committee of One Thousand, with Schieffelin as chairman. Its purpose was to marshal public opinion in favor of a citywide legislative investigation. As a result, near the end of March 1931, the state legislature created a joint committee composed of twelve senators and assemblymen, and headed by Senator Samuel H. Hofstadter. Seabury was named counsel to the committee. Public hearings started on July 21, 1931, and continued intermittently until December 1932. Thus, Seabury was a referee for the appellate division in one investigation, a commissioner of the governor in another, and counsel to a joint legislative committee in a third inquiry.[23]

Samuel Seabury was an excellent choice to direct an investigation into corruption in the courts and the city generally. He came from a distinguished family, his father having been an eminent rector in New York City as well as a professor of canon law at General Theological Seminary. When only twenty years old, Judge Seabury graduated from law school and published a manual on corporation law. Eight years later he was elected a judge of the city court. In 1906, when thirty-three, Seabury became a state supreme-court justice and in 1914 was elected to the Court of Appeals. Two years later he won the Democratic party nomination for governor but was defeated by Charles S. Whitman. Seabury was idealistic, learned in the law, diligent, and objective. And one of the most highly respected men in New York City.[24]

The Tammany political system, which included the sale of judicial positions, was responsible for placing many venal, as well as incompetent, men on the bench. The Seabury probe into the magistrates' courts established that many judges were implicated in questionable fast-buck enterprises; some were associates of gamblers and other underworld characters; many performed their judicial functions with bias and were lacking in honesty and judicial temperament.

During three days of public hearings in November 1930, solid evidence emerged of the presence in the women's court of an infamous ring of policemen, bondsmen, lawyers, and an assistant district attorney engaged in wholesale extortion from women, most of them prostitutes. Participating in the vice ring were forty members of the police department's vice squad, twenty-three lawyers, and thirty-eight bondsmen. Particularly shocking was evidence that thousands of dollars had been extorted annually from innocent women who had paid from $250 to $1,180 each to gain their release from arrest and avoid public disgrace. One woman, Vivian Gordon, visited Seabury's office and recounted how she had been framed. She was told to return with evidence in her possession. Before she was able to revisit Seabury's staff she was found murdered.[25]

John C. Weston, an assistant district attorney who had spent eight years in women's court, admitted that bribes he received from six hundred cases involving nine hundred defendants totaled $20,000. The bribes had been paid by twenty-one lawyers although ninety percent had come from about six frequent practitioners in the court. Many police officers assigned to the vice squad were unable to explain how they had amassed large bank accounts. In a period of just five years, five members of the vice squad had saved a total of $550,000 above their salaries. One officer, James J. Quinlivan, who had deposited $80,000 in less than four years, was subsequently sentenced to federal prison for filing false income-tax returns.[26]

Sitting in women's court from three to six months each year was Magistrate Hortense Norris, the first woman ever to be elevated to the judiciary in New York City. Magistrate Norris, a widow, had been admitted to the bar on October 18, 1909. She was active in politics and by 1916 was coleader of Manhattan's Tenth Assembly District with George W. Olvany, who would later become boss of Tammany Hall. Originally appointed as a temporary magistrate by Mayor John F. Hylan on October 27, 1919, she was designated to fill a series of unexpired terms until June 30, 1930, when Mayor Walker named her for a full ten-year term. Magistrate Norris had pledged that the "poor unfortunate members of the weaker sex" who appeared before her would be dealt with in kindness and sympathy. The Seabury investigation disclosed that she had treated the defendants in her court with undue harshness, ignored their basic rights, and made improper, prejudicial rulings reflecting bias. And when cases were appealed, she altered the records to conceal her improprieties, thus deceiving the higher courts.

Magistrate Norris also owned stock in a surety company. Each day, as part of her official duties, she approved bail bonds written by this same firm. That constituted a violation of the Inferior Criminal Courts Act. She was constantly on the lookout for opportunities to make a fast buck. She sold a testimonial to a yeast company for $1,000 and posed in judicial robes for photographs, which were used in advertisements in a score of magazines and newspapers. Judge Seabury presented the evidence against Magistrate Norris in hearings before the appellate division, which rendered a unanimous decision that her conduct showed unfitness for judicial service and constituted cause for removal.[27]

Often presiding in the corrupt women's court was Magistrate Jesse Silbermann, who conceded that his selection to a judicial post had stemmed from his activity in politics. When his term was nearing expiration, Silbermann got in touch with his district leader, James W. Brown, who held the $20,000-a-year-job of Bronx County public administrator. Brown spoke to the coleader, Edward J. Flynn, then secretary of state, who "fixed it up downtown" and Silbermann's reappointment was ensured. Silbermann admitted that district leader Brown frequently interceded with him concerning pending cases—an estimated thirty-six to forty-eight times. On at least one occasion, district leader Brown actually sat on the bench with Silbermann as he was dispensing justice.

The hearings demonstrated that an intimate relationship existed between Magistrate Silbermann and Mark Alter, one of the lawyers who had played a dominant role in the systematic payment of bribes to Assistant District Attorney John C. Weston. When Silbermann was sitting in women's court, Weston, Silbermann, and Alter lunched together nearly every day. Alter's clients were consistently turned loose by the magistrate. In a shoplifting case, a girl was taken into custody with the stolen property on her person. She admitted to the two store detectives who arrested her that she had stolen the merchandise. Magistrate Silbermann discharged the girl. His friend Alter then had another lawyer file a suit for false arrest and imprisonment against the department store. Upon conclusion of the Seabury hearings, a unanimous decision was rendered that Magistrate Silbermann was unfit to remain on the bench.[28]

Evidence amassed by the investigation caused a few magistrates to resign rather than oppose Judge Seabury's legal action to remove them from the bench. One who resigned was Magistrate Francis X. McQuade, who was engaged in a number of questionable business activities. He had an investment in a Havana gambling casino and had promoted numerous professional prizefights. He also used the prestige of his judicial robes to endorse stock in a highly questionable speculative venture in which the investors suffered complete losses. On the morning that he was scheduled to appear for public examination, McQuade resigned. Magistrates George Washington Simpson and Henry M. R. Goodman also resigned while their judicial conduct was under investigation.[29]

Somewhat less sensational than the inquiry into the magistrates' courts was the Seabury investigation of Tammany's superannuated district attorney, Thomas C. T. Crain. Nevertheless, the investigation highlighted the general incompetency and ineptness of the prosecutor's office. Almost every important case handled by Crain and his staff had ended in failure.

In February 1929 the crash of the City Trust Company had wiped out the savings of some sixteen thousand depositors, most of whom were small wage earners. The City Trust Company, although insolvent, had been permitted to continue operations after bribes totaling almost $100,000 had been paid to the state banking commissioner. Implicated was General Sessions Judge Francis X. Mancuso, a Tammany stalwart who had been chairman of the trust company's board of directors. Only when forced by public opinion to do so, Crain reluctantly obtained an indictment against Mancuso. But Mancuso had little to fear. Through ineptness, the prosecutor's office lost the case.[30]

Early in 1930 public clamor forced Crain to conduct a grand-jury investigation of the magistrates' courts. He handled the matter in a perfunctory manner and uncovered no wrongdoing. Yet, only a few months later, the Seabury probe established that some of the magistrates' courts were veritable cesspools of corruption. Crain was also delinquent in bringing to justice men accused of engaging in stock frauds. The cases were permitted to languish in his office apparently because they were difficult and no one wanted to examine voluminous documents and files.

In conducting an inquiry into the racketeering that existed in the Fulton Fish Market, Crain failed to ask the chief witness the pertinent question whether he had paid money for protection. Later, Seabury, with limited power, established that criminals had extracted regular protection payments over a long period of time. The racket boss at the Fulton Fish Market was Joseph (Socks) Lanza, who controlled the United Seafood Workers local union and was in charge of labor negotiations. The Seabury investigation determined that fish firms made annual payments of $2,500 to Lanza to keep their plants nonunion and Lanza was actually on the payroll of one of the firms.[31]

Socks Lanza remained a powerful and evil influence at the Fulton Fish Market from the early 1920s until the mid-1930s. Two of his instruments of control were the Seafood Workers Union and the Fulton Market Watchmen's Protective Association, which he had formed. Dealers who visited the market and failed to have a Lanza watchman look after their vehicles usually found their tires slashed. Lanza had perfected a strong-arm organization that engaged in systematic shakedowns. In his rise to power, Lanza was aided by his political allies, Peter J. Hamill, leader of the eastern half of the First Assembly District, and Albert Marinelli, who eventually became the leader of half of the Second Assembly District.[32]

District Attorney Crain had justified his failure to prosecute millinery racketeers on the ground that witnesses would not testify. Seabury soon thereafter produced witnesses who testified that they paid as much as $100 a month for protection. Crain was also accused of failure to investigate properly the important cloth-shrinking business, allied with the garment industry. Racketeer Joseph Mezzacapo had dissolved the Cloth Shrinkers Union and established one of his own. Seabury investigators determined that within the preceding five years, Mezzacapo had deposited over $332,000 in a single bank account.[33]

Crain's sorry record as district attorney had been laid bare for the public. Yet, since corruption had not been proven, Judge Seabury recommended against his removal from office. In his report to Governor Roosevelt, Seabury stated: "In the absence of dishonesty or willful neglect or incompetency dangerous to the public welfare, removal of elected officials by the governor is not the remedy for public indifference in the nomination and election of public officers." To warrant removal, said Seabury, "There must be proof of neglect so general, or incompetency so gross, as to make such action necessary in the public interest." Judge Seabury recommended that the petition for Crain's removal be dismissed.[34]

The most dramatic evidence of widespread corruption in New York City was uncovered during the hearings conducted by the joint legislative committee headed by Senator Samuel H. Hofstadter. The city Democrats had opposed any inquiry that might prove embarrassing to Tammany Hall and resorted to obstructionist tactics to thwart the committee's efforts. Tammany Boss John F. Curry challenged the committee's power. Mayor Walker publicly ridiculed the committee and attempted to discredit it by attacking the motives of its members. Two of the committee's Democratic members, Assemblyman Louis A. Cuvillier and Senator John J. McNaboe, tried to sabotage the committee's inquiry in every way. McNaboe, who was known as Boss Curry's man on the committee, openly attempted to disrupt public hearings and his conduct was sometimes disgraceful. Ably assisting Cuvillier and McNaboe in attempting to thwart the investigation were ex-officio Democratic members of the committee, Senate minority leader John J. Dunnigan and Assembly minority leader Irwin Steingut.[35]

Under the direction of the committee's counsel, Samuel Seabury, the hearings produced solid evidence showing alliances between the underworld, political leaders, and city officials, including the judiciary. Testimony established that Thomas M. Farley, sheriff of New York County; Michael J. Cruise, city clerk; Harry Perry, chief clerk of the City Court of New York; and James A. McQuade, register of Kings County, all district leaders, had been protecting professional gamblers and had made their clubhouses available to them for their profitable commercial games. Naturally, official action taken against the gamblers was almost nonexistent. Of 514 persons arrested in gambling raids during 1926 and 1927, only five were held for the Court of Special Sessions. And district leaders Farley, Cruise, Perry, and McQuade, the allies of professional gamblers, had accumulated large amounts of unexplained wealth within a short period of time.[36]

Most of the police raids on gambling operations in political clubs were led by Acting Captain Ezekiel Keller, attached to the confidential squad headed by Lewis J. Valentine. Keller testified that he had led two raids on the clubhouse of the Thomas M. Farley Association. The place, he said, was strongly fortified with "icebox" doors. Outside the establishment, he observed "lookouts," whom he identified as employees of professional gamblers. One lookout had been arrested by Keller for gambling violations about twelve times previously. Inside the locked doors of the clubhouse, Keller saw Alderman Jerry O'Leary, who was directing men to upstairs rooms. After much difficulty, Keller and his officers gained entrance to the place, where they found numerous patrons, as well as the head of the club, Thomas M. Farley, then county clerk of New York County, and an attorney, Frederick L. Hackenberg, a member of the Assembly from Farley's district. A few days later Hackenberg resigned from Farley's club. He appeared before the Hofstadter committee and corroborated Keller's testimony. Keller testified that his men arrested "thirty or forty" men, who were taken to the police station. Farley came down to the station and arranged bail for the prisoners. Among the gamblers found in Farley's establishment were former associates of Arnold Rothstein and well-known gangsters with felony records.[37]

Naturally, Keller's raids on political clubhouses aroused the ire of Tammany Hall politicians. Only a few hours after Grover A. Whalen became commissioner of police on December 18, 1928, the ax fell on both Lewis J. Valentine and Ezekiel Keller. Demoted to his civil-service rank of lieutenant, Keller was transferred to a district occupied largely by a cemetery. To reach his new assignment from his home, Keller was obliged to travel by subway for two hours. Resenting this punishment, which he regarded as grossly unjust, Keller retired from the department.[38]

When Thomas M. Farley was on the witness stand, Judge Seabury confronted the sheriff with records of his huge bank deposits. In 1925 Farley's deposits were $34,824, as compared with his salary of only $6,500; in 1927, on a salary not exceeding $8,500, his deposits were $38,000; in 1928 his deposits totaled $58,177.75. When asked to disclose the source of these large bank deposits, Farley childishly explained that they consisted of "moneys that I saved" from a "tin box" kept in his home. Seabury asked, "Kind of a magic box, Sheriff?" Replied Farley, "It was a wonderful box."

In six years Farley had deposited $360,000, and he swore that this money had come from his wonderful tin box. Admittedly, with the exception of some real estate commissions amounting to less than $25,000, Farley had no souce of income during that six-year period other than his salary. As a result of his wondrous explanation for his newly acquired wealth, the sheriff gained immortality as Tin Box Farley.

Assemblyman Louis A. Cuvillier sought to have Farley's testimony about his financial affairs stricken from the record. Judge Seabury retorted: "Those accounts prove conclusively that while in office Sheriff Farley and County Clerk Farley was grafting. . . ." On December 29, 1931, Judge Seabury forwarded a transcript of the evidence against Farley to Governor Roosevelt with a letter asking for Sheriff Farley's removal from office. The governor responded by officially removing Farley on February 24, 1932.[39]

Records examined by the Hofstadter committee disclosed that large sums of money were rolling into the coffers of other district leaders whose club-houses served as centers for professional gambling operations. The club-house of James A. McQuade, register of Kings County, had been subjected to police raids after housewives had complained that their husbands' wages were being squandered on horse-race bets made to professional gamblers in McQuade's establishment. When McQuade took the witness stand, Judge Seabury asked, "Where did you get the $510,000 deposited in your ac-count?" McQuade replied, "Money that I borrowed." He then related a tale of woe about various deaths and mishaps in his family that left him with thirty-four McQuades to feed, clothe, and educate. To carry on his acts of mercy, he said, it was necessary for him to borrow money. Within a short time, the lender would demand repayment and he would borrow money again to pay off the loan. This procedure was repeated time after time, he explained, and this accounted for his huge bank deposits. Judge Seabury, however, took a rather dim view of McQuade's testimony, for McQuade could not remember the name of a single person who had lent him money and had no records of any kind to substantiate his story. When asked why professional gamblers were in his clubhouse when it was raided by the police, McQuade testified that they were "only reading books in the library I put in for the boys." As McQuade stepped down from the witness stand, he encountered three newspaper reporters, whom he asked, "How did my story go over?" In the fall election of 1931, McQuade was rewarded with the Democratic nomination for sheriff of Kings County and was elected.[40]

City Court Clerk Harry C. Perry was confronted with records that showed deposits of $135,000 between 1925 and 1931. During this period, his salary totaled $21,366.17, leaving a difference of $113,633.83. This amount, he explained, represented money he had borrowed. However, it was revealed that many, if not most, of his deposits were made in cash. As much as $7,500 in silver had been deposited in Perry's bank account on a single day. Another Tammany stalwart, City Clerk Michael J. Cruise, had made deposits of $217,246 over a six-year period, and concerning this amount he was unable to give any explanation as to the source of $80,758.76.[41]

The Hofstadter committee made inquiry into many phases of city government and almost everywhere it found evidence of gross corruption. Democratic politicians had always posed as champions of the poor and in 1931 the city had appropriated nearly $10 million for relief. The Hofstadter committee found that this appropriation was used to reward loyal party workers. Relief applications were handled by the Democratic political clubs. Among witnesses called by Judge Seabury was a recipient of city relief who owned four automobiles and was maintaining a staff of maids in his home. Also documented by the committee were the huge fees obtained by George W. Olvany, when he was boss of Tammany Hall, for handling cases before the Board of Standards and Appeals. On most occasions, an intermediary lawyer's name appeared on the official record but the major portion of the fee, usually paid in cash or cashier's checks, went to the Olvany firm. Also uncovered were scandals arising from the granting of permits, leases, and franchises by the city.[42]

Exposed by the committee as a grafter par excellence was Dr. William F. (Horse Doctor) Doyle, a veterinarian who made a fortune handling "nonanimal" cases before the Board of Standards and Appeals. Doyle had been active in politics since the early 1900s and once received an appointment as chief veterinarian of the fire department. Subsequently, Mayor John F. Hylan named Doyle to the post of chief of the Bureau of Fire Prevention. He was indicted for malfeasance when a building he had failed to check was destroyed by fire. The Horse Doctor then began practicing before the Board of Standards and Appeals, where he represented builders, contractors, and landlords. His success was phenomenal. Judge Seabury determined that in hundreds of cases Doyle obtained permits for garages in places where they were prohibited by law, gained approvals for applications for gasoline stations that had previously been denied by the Bureau of Fire Prevention, and in many cases induced the board to reverse previous rulings. Between 1922 and 1930 Doyle had deposited over a million dollars in his bank accounts and in one year alone, 1927, his fees amounted to $243,692.60. When Doyle persistently refused to answer questions about fee splitting, bribes, and bank accounts, the committee held him in contempt of court and Justice William Harman Black sentenced him to thirty days in jail. Tammany Boss John F. Curry then personally telephoned a more sympathetic judge of the appellate division, who was vacationing in Lake Placid, New York, about three hundred miles away, and obtained a stay of the order jailing Doyle. Because of this action, the legislature, in an extraordinary session called by the governor, enacted legislation that empowered the Hofstadter committee to grant immunity to witnesses in proper cases.[43]

During the Seabury hearings significant upheavals in the New York City organized underworld were occurring. In particular were outbreaks of violence from power struggles among gangland leaders.

At the time the top man in the Sicilian-Italian underworld was Joe the Boss Masseria, whose principal aide was Lucky Luciano. Indications were that Masseria was becoming resentful toward his main assistant. A confidential law-enforcement report disclosed that Joe the Boss had conferred with Joe Adonis, the Brooklyn bigwig in crime, and revealed his dissatisfaction with Lucky. Adonis, also known as Joseph Doto and Joey A, was a good friend of Luciano. Double-crossing Masseria, Adonis apprised Lucky of his talk with Joe the Boss.[44]

On April 15, 1931, Lucky and Joe the Boss spent the morning at a Masseria headquarters on Second Avenue in downtown Manhattan. According to Luciano's reported revelations many years later, they discussed plans for murdering several lieutenants of Masseria's bitter rival, Salvatore Maranzano. About noon, Luciano suggested that they drive to Coney Island and have lunch at a restaurant owned by Gerardo Scarpato, a friend of Lucky and many other mobsters. Scarpato's Nuova Villa Tammaro was crowded when Lucky and Joe the Boss arrived, but they were cordially greeted and seated by the owner himself.

By about three-thirty all of the customers, except Lucky and his guest, and most of the restaurant employees had departed. Luciano and Masseria settled down to play a card game. After one hand, Luciano excused himself to go to the men's room. The lavatory door had barely closed behind Luciano when the front door of the Nuova Villa Tammaro was flung open and four men with pistols blazing came charging at Masseria. Of the more than twenty shots fired, six bullets crashed into Masseria, who slumped over the table dead. Their mission having been completed, the four gunmen dashed out of the restaurant, entered a waiting car manned by a fifth accomplice, and sped away. Not until the shooting had ended and the assassins had fled did Luciano emerge from the washroom. After glancing at the dead Masseria, Lucky called the police. The officers arrived and a grief-stricken Luciano wondered aloud why anyone would want to harm poor Joe.

Many years later Luciano reportedly named Masseria's four assassins as Joe Adonis, Vito Genovese, Albert Anastasia, and Benjamin (Bugsy) Siegel. Waiting outside the restaurant in a car with the motor running was Ciro Terranova. When the gunmen jumped into the automobile, Terranova was so nervous that he was unable to get the car in gear. Siegel pushed Terranova aside, got behind the steering wheel, and drove away. With Masseria's demise, his affairs passed to the control of Lucky Luciano, the man who very likely was the architect of the slaying.[45]

About the time of the Masseria killing, trouble was brewing in the clothing industry. The huge Amalgamated Clothing Workers of America, embracing some fifty thousand members, was ripped with dissension fostered by the master of labor racketeering, Louis (Lepke) Buchalter. In an effort to combat the terroristic tactics of Buchalter's army of strong-arm men, an approach was made to Luciano to organize and head a counterforce. Luciano declined the offer because he did not want to battle his intimate associate, Buchalter. In the past, Lepke and Lucky had worked together in the field of labor racketeering in the cleaning and dyeing trade and in the motion-picture theater business.

When Luciano refused to participate in the clothing industry violence, the contract to fight Buchalter was given to Salvatore Maranzano. Before taking on the assignment, Maranzano conferred with Luciano and assured him that he was entering the fray solely for the money to be made and would not make trouble for Luciano's pals. His promises soon turned out to be empty ones. When Maranzano's sluggers threw rocks at the window of a clothing district shop, a manufacturer, John Ferrari, who just happened to be in the place, led a group of men who charged outside to do battle. A business agent of the Amalgamated Clothing Workers of America was shot. Maranzano blamed Ferrari for the trouble and ordered his men to take care of him. Through a blunder, Maranzano's thugs murdered the wrong man, John Ferrari's brother, Guido, who had been a noncombatant. Lepke called on Luciano and convinced him that action should be taken against Maranzano.[46]

According to statements attributed to Luciano many years later, he conferred with Meyer Lansky and plans were made for the extermination of Maranzano. A suite of offices was maintained by Maranzano in the New York Central Building at Park Avenue and Forty-sixth Street. On the door leading to his suite was a sign indicating that he was in the real estate business. Maranzano was always concerned about his tax returns and it was decided that assassins posing as federal agents could possibly gain entrance into the gang leader's office without arousing suspicion. Lansky made arrangements for the importation of three Jewish gunmen from other cities and placed them under the direction of his trusted aide, Sam (Red) Levine. As these plans were in progress, Frank Costello received an important call from Philadelphia from Harry Stromberg, known as Nig Rosen. Stromberg confided that he had learned of plans by Maranzano to have Costello, Luciano, Vito Genovese, Joe Adonis, Dutch Schultz, and others murdered. The contract to perform the executions, he said, had been given to Vincent (the Mick) Coll, who was then feuding with his former boss, Schultz.

On September 9, 1931, Maranzano telephoned Luciano and requested that Lucky and Genovese come to his office the following day at 2 P.M. for a conference. In the light of the information he received from Costello, Luciano assumed that Maranzano was setting a trap and he had no intention of falling into it. An objective observer would be justified in believing that it would be highly unlikely for Maranzano to arrange for his personal office to serve as the site for gangland executions. Nevertheless, whether Luciano's story was embellished or not, it appears that the larger portion of his account was true.

Just before two o'clock on September 10, 1931, four Jewish gunmen posing as police officers flashed badges, mumbled something about a raid, and entered the reception room to Maranzano's suite of offices. In the reception room at the time were Maranzano, his secretary, Grace Samuels, bigwig garment center racketeer Gaetano (Thomas) Lucchese, and five bodyguards. Two of the raiders shoved Maranzano into his private office. The other two raiders took charge of the persons in the reception room, lined them up against the wall, and disarmed the bodyguards. When Maranzano's captors pulled knives, the gang leader realized that his custodians were not law officers. He fought back desperately but was finally overwhelmed. He received four gunshot wounds and was stabbed six times before he died. In his office, legitimate policemen later recovered a knife and two pistols. As the four assassins fled the building, they met Vincent Coll, who was just arriving on the scene. He was warned that the cops were coming and he wasted no time in making a getaway.[47]

Of the four Jewish gunmen implicated in the Maranzano murder, undoubtedly one was Meyer Lansky's man, Red Levine. J. Richard (Dixie) Davis, attorney for Dutch Schultz, has quoted Bo Weinberg, a principal Schultz lieutenant, as having boasted that he killed Maranzano. Weinberg told Davis that after the murder he fled into Grand Central Station; there, while unobtrusively mingling with a large crowd waiting for a train, he slipped his gun, the murder weapon, into the pocket of an unsuspecting commuter. This makes a fascinating tale but the reputation of Dixie Davis for veracity was not particularly good, and either he or Bo may have invented the story. On the other hand, both Levine and Weinberg may have participated in the killing.

A popular version attributes the slaying of Maranzano to a purge of the Mafia bosses under a decree that all Mustache Petes (old-time Mafiosi) of any consequence throughout the nation must be killed. And it has often been claimed that beginning with Maranzano's murder on September 10, 1931, and within forty-eight hours thereafter, some forty Mafia executives were wiped out from coast to coast. Dixie Davis has placed the figure much higher. He quotes Weinberg as having said that at the very hour Maranzano was slain, ninety Italian gangsters were "knocked off" throughout the country. And, said Weinberg, "That was the time we Americanized the mobs." Luciano has labeled this "Night of the Sicilian Vespers" pure fiction and asserted that he did not know the name of a single "top guy in the Maranzano group" who was killed on the night of September 10, 1931, in New York, Chicago, or elsewhere. Beginning in 1919, the Chicago Crime Commission maintained for over fifty years an accurate record of gangland-type killings in the Chicago area. Those records show that only two such murders occurred during the month of September 1931. And neither victim was a top-flight underworld figure. Both were slain on September 16, almost a week after the Maranzano killing, and obviously were unrelated to it in any way.[48]

Following the murder of Maranzano, Luciano, according to Dixie Davis, changed the Unione Siciliana "from a loose federation of Italians into a close-knit national organization, affiliated with mobs of other national origin." The system of underworld cooperation between gangs, regardless of ethnic background, spread from coast to coast. Davis credits Luciano with having taken over the general leadership in the Unione Siciliana. However, he said, Lucky was specializing in the liquor and alcohol racket, in which he was an equal partner with Joe Adonis and the team of Bugsy Siegel and Meyer Lansky.

In his discussion of the events of 1931, Dixie Davis inaccurately refers to the Unione Siciliana as an "international secret society, composed of mobsters and of apparently legitimate businessmen." This society, he asserted, was the "modern version of the old-fashioned Mafia or Sicilian Black Hand." Even his inference that the Mafia and Black Hand are synonymous is incorrect.[49]

Three decades after the assassination of Maranzano, a different version was provided by a New York City underworld character, Joseph Valachi. Testifying before a U.S. Senate subcommittee in 1963, Valachi described the bitter warfare that raged between two major Italian-Sicilian underworld groups in 1930 and 1931. One group was led by Joseph Masseria, the other by Salvatore Maranzano. Masseria, it was reported, had decreed a death sentence on everyone in the United States who had originated from the locality of Castellammare del Golfo, Sicily. Thus, the bloody conflict became known as the Castellammarese War. From this warfare evolved a rigidly structured nationwide organization called La Cosa Nostra, in which membership was restricted to full-blooded Italians. In New York City, there were five Cosa Nostra families (criminal gangs), of which two stemmed from the Masseria group and three from the Maranzano group. Other than New York City, no municipality had more than one family.

Following the murder the Masseria on April 20, 1931, Maranzano proclaimed himself to be the Boss of all Bosses. And he personally designated the boss and underboss of each of the five New York City families. But Maranzano's reign was cut short by his assassination less than five months later. Recognized as his successor as head of the Italian underworld throughout the land was Lucky Luciano. According to Valachi, the structure of La Cosa Nostra as established in 1931 became permanent, and this Italian organization has since controlled organized crime throughout America.

Flaws can be found in the stories of both Dixie Davis and Joseph Valachi.

Nevertheless, established facts indicate that Luciano could view 1931 as a year of great personal triumphs. Not only had he helped engineer the demise of two top-flight Italian underworld leaders, Masseria and Maranzano; he played an important role in Tammany Hall politics as well. That year, not long after the murder of Masseria, Luciano decided it was time to replace Harry C. Perry, coleader of the Second Assembly District, with Albert C. Marinelli, a stooge of Lucky as well as other Italian criminal bosses.

The takeover was accomplished with remarkable ease. Luciano's gunmen approached Perry, menacingly fingered their guns, and said, "Lucky says you're through." It was explained to Perry that if he failed to get out of the district and turn it over to Albert Marinelli, his wife and children would be found in the river. Perry confided to his friends that he was terrified. He resigned and was immediately succeeded by Marinelli, who now became the coleader of the Second Assembly District with Christopher Sullivan. Some years later Christopher Sullivan would become the top man in Tammany Hall. Marinelli thus became the sole Italian district leader, a position he had attained through force. Truth is, of course, Luciano and his gangsters ruled the district and Marinelli was their willing servant.[50]

Marinelli quickly took steps to grab control of the western half of the First Assembly District, which had been ruled since 1925 by Big Tom Foley's successor, Peter J. Hamill. Upon Hamill's death on January 12, 1930, the leadership passed into the hands of his secretary, David A. Mahoney, and the situation was ripe for a change. Mahoney and Louis F. X. Santangelo, aldermanic candidate, loudly complained that Johnny Torrio, Joseph (Socks) Lanza, and other gangsters were taking over the district and giving it to Marinelli. With Marinelli's backing, Joseph Greenfield defeated Mahoney. And serving as alderman from the district was the physician Dr. Paul F. Sarubbi, who later was uncovered as a substantial stockholder in Johnny Torrio's liquor concern, Prendergast-Davis, Inc.[51]

Albert C. Marinelli was born of Italian parents in the Second Assembly District and served a long apprenticeship in politics before superseding Harry C. Perry as coleader. Originally, he became an election captain when Big Tim Sullivan was the district leader. In 1919 Marinelli was appointed to the position of port warden of New York, an office that was abolished in 1922. He then joined his brother Joseph in the trucking business, which was first located at Crosby and Spring Streets and later at Kenmore and Mulberry Streets. The latter location was in the center of the bootleggers' "curb exchange." Much contraband liquor was stolen from bonded government warehouses. The curb exchange enabled a hoodlum with an oversupply of Scotch, for example, to trade for bourbon. Across the street from the Marinelli brothers' garage was Celano's Restaurant, which had served as a headquarters for Masseria and Luciano.

After taking over the leadership of the Second Assembly District, Marinelli was able to have himself elected alderman in 1932. Two years later he became the county clerk of New York County. His followers frequented the political clubhouse of the Albert C. Marinelli Association, of which ex-convict Patrick J. Lupo was treasurer. In November 1932 Marinelli made Lupo a deputy commissioner of records in the city court.

Marinelli's political machine included numerous underworld characters. At one time, of 227 county committeemen who helped keep Marinelli in power, over one tenth were ex-convicts or persons who had been charged with crimes. And over one third of twenty-two election district polling places in his domain had been manned by ex-convicts or persons charged with criminal offenses. In addition to Luciano, Marinelli's intimate underworld associates included Luciano's aide David Betillo, Socks Lanza, Joe Adonis, Vito Genovese, Lupo, and others.[52]

The underworld-political alliance of Luciano and Marinelli formed a strong base for organized crime in New York City. But an even more formidable base arose from the ties between Frank Costello and Tammany leader Jimmy Hines, patron of many gangland rulers.

By 1929 Costello had emerged as the slot-machine boss of the East. Aided by ex-convict Dandy Phil Kastel, a swindler and extortionist whom he had met through Arnold Rothstein, Costello had built up an efficient organization which controlled the slot-machine racket in New York City. Of course, making it all possible was the protection of influential Tammany Hall politicians.

The largest manufacturer of slot machines in the nation at the time was the Mills Novelty Company of Chicago, and Costello arranged with Mills for a monopoly over the New York territory. The machines were made to dispense candy mints along with slugs that were redeemable in money. The purpose of this arrangement was to make it arguable before friendly judges that the one-armed bandits were actually vending machines. Most of the devices were built to receive nickels, but there were also quarter, half-dollar, and even silver-dollar machines.

Through the tutelage of Rothstein and experience gained in large-scale illicit liquor operations, Costello had become an expert at organization. In New York City he formed the Tru-Mint Company, with offices at 1860 Broadway. Acting as front men for this corporation were Jacob Jaffe and Edward K. Ellis, alias Henry Hunt, while the apparent operating head was Cecil J. Crabtree. Subsidiaries to the Tru-Mint Company were formed, each covering the territory of a police inspection division or a borough. The Village Candy Company serviced the First Police Division, the Monroe Candy Company the Second Division, which included the Lower East Side, and the Triangle Mint Company covered Brooklyn. Triangle was headed by Leo P. Byk, a friend of District Attorney F. X. Geoghan. The Costello organization's monopoly of slot machines was absolute. The freewheeling

Dutch Schultz always maintained one-armed bandits in his watering spots in the Bronx. But the Dutchman, like everyone else, was compelled to get his machines from Costello.

The slot machines were never sold but were placed in various establishments by the Costello organization, which presumably gave the location owner a percentage of the take. By 1931, 5,186 slot machines were on location in New York City. Favorite spots for the one-armed bandits were speakeasies, nightspots, cigar stores, stationery shops, candy stores and similar locations. The patronage of everyone, even young children, was encouraged. In some candy stores, small ladders were provided to enable the tiny tots to climb up, insert their nickel, and pull the machine lever. Outraged parents often ran to the police with complaints that their children were spending their lunch money by patronizing the one-armed bandits. The police seldom took any action. Costello, backed by Jimmy Hines and other Tammany politicians, had cloaked his operations with impenetrable immunity.

Whenever necessary, Costello could always depend on favorable rulings by friendly members of the judiciary. In the early 1930s a state supreme-court justice, Selah B. Strong, issued an injunction prohibiting the police from seizing the machines. The same Justice Strong had issued a gun permit to Joe the Boss Masseria in 1922. The permit, endorsed "unlimited," permitted Masseria to carry the gun in any part of the state. Justice Strong had also signed a pistol permit for the notorious Frankie Marlow, killed in gang warfare on June 24, 1929.

Occasionally, through a burglary or holdup, slot machines were stolen from locations. The Costello-Kastel organization maintained its own private law-enforcement branch, which usually recovered the machines and punished the offenders with typical gangland efficiency.[53]

Throughout 1931 considerable publicity was focused on the various rackets dominated by Owney (the Killer) Madden, who, like Costello, had strong ties with Tammany leader Jimmy Hines. A highly knowledgeable city editor of the period declared that Madden was "as authentic a bigshot as the underworld ever saw." Madden seemed to have his fingers in everything—illicit liquor, breweries, nightclubs, taxicabs, laundries, and cloakroom and cigarette concessions. Although a relatively young man by 1932, he was sometimes referred to as the Elder Statesman and the Grand Old Man of the New York City rackets.[54]

Born in Liverpool in 1892 as Owen Victor Madden, he came to the United States when he was eleven years old and settled in Hell's Kitchen, on New York City's West Side. Here he was leader of the old Gopher Gang and amassed a long record of arrests. Before reaching voting age, he had become known as the Killer. His name inspired fear and his services were in demand by politicians.

Principal rival to the Gophers was the gang known as the Hudson Dusters. Late on the night of November 6, 1914, Madden arrived at the Arbor Dance Hall at Seventh Avenue and Fifty-second Street. Eleven Dusters surrounded Owney, shot him five times, and left him for dead. Madden soon recovered and laid plans for gaining revenge. On November 28, 1914, William Moore, better known at Little Patsy Doyle, was lured into a saloon at Forty-first Street and Eighth Avenue; there two members of the Gopher Gang fatally shot him. Witnesses later testified that Madden had actually instigated the murder. He was convicted of manslaughter in the first degree and sentenced to ten to twenty years in Sing Sing Prison.

Released from prison in January 1923, Madden returned to New York City and found that his talents were in greater demand than ever. For a time he served as a straw boss, supervising a gang of strong-arm men employed by rumrunner Larry Fay, who had entered the taxicab business. Fay's men took over the preferred locations on the streets by raw muscle. Whenever a driver of a competing cab offered any resistance, a couple of Fay's goons usually appeared and put him in his place[55]

Madden had been out of prison almost a year when a warehouse watchman was overpowered, bound, and gagged, and a truckload of liquor worth $16,000 was stolen. Arrested in connection with this crime were Madden, George Jean (Big Frenchy) DeMange, and Harry Jacobs. Again, in January 1924, Madden and five other men were arrested on a truck loaded with stolen liquor valued at $25,000. Madden beat the rap in each case. In April 1924 the district attorney wrote the state superintendent of prisons advising that within a year Madden had been arrested on two occasions with men having long records for criminal violence and urged his return to Sing Sing. The district attorney's request was ignored.[56]

For a short time Madden and his gunmen preyed on the trucks of William Vincent (Big Bill) Dwyer, a liquor importer, manufacturer, and wholesaler. Dwyer maintained working arrangements with most of the big syndicates throughout the country—Florida, New Orleans, Cincinnati, St. Louis, Kansas City, Chicago. The organization headed by Dwyer was believed the largest and most affluent in the United States. It owned several seagoing rum ships and a dozen steel-plated speedboats armed with machineguns. On shore the ring maintained warehouses, trucks, garages, cutting plants, and wholesale outlets. Operating in the ring's offices were efficient departments to handle traffic, distribution, and bookkeeping. Highly important to the syndicate's success was the functioning of a separate department dealing with protection payments.

Dwyer readily recognized the talents of Madden and brought him into his syndicate in 1924. The basis for Owney's rapid climb to the rank of one of the city's most influential underworld leaders was thus established.

On December 4, 1925, the federal government announced that it had cracked the biggest ring of liquor smugglers in the country. Arrested were fifty-two persons, including Big Bill Dwyer, Frank Costello, and his brother Eddie. Most of the attention was focused on Bill Dwyer, who was described as "head of the international group." Listed as headquarters for the ring was 405 Lexington Avenue in New York City. Years later, Frank Costello's attorney, George Wolf, pointed out that it was Costello's office that had been described by the government as the headquarters for the ring. Many observers believed that Costello actually was the brains of the syndicate purportedly run by Dwyer. The trial of Dwyer started on July 27, 1926. Following appeals, Dwyer was incarcerated in the federal penitentiary in Atlanta on July 18, 1927, and remained there until August 13, 1928. The case against Frank Costello ended in a hung jury. While Dwyer was in prison the syndicate business continued to flourish. Particularly profitable was a brewery owned by Dwyer, Owney Madden, and Waxey Gordon.[57]

Madden furnished liquor to hundreds of nightclubs and speakeasies. For some time, an important customer of the Madden-Dwyer brewery was Dutch Schultz. Madden controlled the highly prosperous Cotton Club in Harlem. Arnold Rothstein owned an interest in this place as well as in the Silver Slipper. Partners in the Silver Slipper, also controlled by Owney, included William Duffy, a Madden henchman, and Frankie Marlow, whose real name was Gandolfo Civito. When the Plantation Club was opened as a rival to the Cotton Club, a gang of hoodlums, apparently inspired by Owney, descended on the place with a fury. The Plantation was demolished. In retaliation, a few months later Harry Block, one of Owney's partners in the Cotton Club, was shot and killed.

Owney's investments were highly diversified. He sank a quarter of a million dollars in a laundry but later deplored this kind of venture because big profits were not immediately forthcoming. He preferred the type of investment, he said, that would double itself within a week or two. With William Duffy and George Jean (Big Frenchy) DeMange as partners, Madden owned most of the giant Italian prizefighter Primo Carnera, who came to America in 1930. Carnera toured the country and scored a series of knockouts against "setup" opponents before eventually winning the heavyweight championship on June 29, 1933. Money from the numerous rackets in which Madden was involved flowed into his coffers in a steady stream. One of his attorneys estimated in the summer of 1930 that Owney the Killer was then worth more than a million dollars.[58]

During 1931 the psychopathic gangster Vincent (the Mick) Coll was on the prowl. On June 15, 1931, Coll and some associates drove a sedan to the Club Argonaut on Seventh Avenue where they observed the club's owner, Big Frenchy DeMange, standing on the street. The Coll gunmen kidnapped DeMange, a partner of Madden in numerous rackets, and held him captive for several hours. DeMange was released when Madden paid

$35,000 ransom to Coll. Rumors were that Coll was making plans to kidnap Madden as well.[59]

The events of 1931 were disquieting to Madden. Although he had a firm grip on his lieutenants whom he trusted, the threat was present that irresponsible Coll gunmen or some paid assassin might take him for a ride. Also troublesome was unwanted publicity that referred to him as the chief racketeer in New York City and compared him with Chicago's Al Capone. On January 23, 1932, Madden was ordered by the state parole board to report regularly. There followed a hearing on the laundry rackets and the parole board decided that Owney should be returned to Sing Sing Prison. After serving almost a year in prison, Madden was released on July 1, 1933. By 1935 Madden had left New York City behind him and settled permanently in Hot Springs, Arkansas, where he became a powerful gambling boss who enjoyed solid political backing. Over the years, many of America's most influential underworld bosses journeyed to Hot Springs. There they received the counsel, assistance, and sometimes the protection of Madden. On April 24, 1965, Madden, then seventy-three years old, died in a Hot Springs hospital.[60]

During the investigation of the magistrates' courts in 1931, Judge Seabury's assistant, Irving Ben Cooper, was assigned to interview two of Harlem's most prosperous policy racketeers, Wilfred Adolphus Brunder and Jose Enrique Miro. Brunder's bank books disclosed that between January 1, 1925, and December 31, 1930, he had deposited $1,753,342.33. To avoid public hearings and potential income-tax troubles, Brunder, a West Indian who had been engaged in policy operations since 1923, turned his business over to Joseph Matthias Ison and fled to Bermuda. An examination of the bank records of Jose Enrique Miro revealed that he had made deposits totaling $1,111,730.08 between July 7, 1927, and December 12, 1930. When Miro testified before Judge Seabury, he made contradictory statements and faced charges of perjury. Like Brunder, Miro turned his policy bank over to Joseph Ison and fled the jurisdiction.

With the Miro and Brunder operations under his wing, Big Joe Ison appeared to be sitting on top of the world insofar as the Harlem policy racket was concerned. His attorney, J. Richard (Dixie) Davis, a twenty-six-year-old son of a tailor from Romania, specialized in handling policy cases and was an eminently successful "fixer." Hence, Ison had little to fear from official interference with his business. However, trouble of a more ominous nature was brewing.

The highly efficient and ruthless organization of Arthur Flegenheimer, better known as Dutch Schultz, began casting covetous eyes on the lucrative Harlem policy racket. Two Schultz lieutenants, Abe (Bo) Weinberg and Abe Landau, took Joe Ison for a car ride, pressed a gun against his ribs, bluntly told him they wanted a piece of his business, and demanded an answer within a week. Ison ran to his attorney, Dixie Davis, for advice. Davis pragmatically advised his client that it would be useless to buck the powerful Dutch Schultz organization. He placed his client in touch with George Weinberg, a brother of Bo. George had once operated his own policy bank and was a former client and intimate friend of lawyer Davis. Through George Weinberg, it was arranged that Ison would pay $600 a week to the Schultz organization, which was now well under way in its campaign to take over the Harlem policy racket.[61]

The takeover of one policy bank after another was accomplished by following a simple and very effective pattern. A typical victim was the big operator, Alexander Pompez, who received a summons to appear for a meeting at the Cayuga Democratic Club in Harlem. There a Dutch Schultz spokesman and thug, Solly Girsch, told Pompez he would be given just two weeks to place his bank under the control of the Schultz combination. Subsequently, he received visits from Girsch, Bo Weinberg, and Bernard (Lulu) Rosenkrantz, who informed Pompez that the Dutchman wanted to see him. By this time the attorney Dixie Davis had become part and parcel of the Dutch Schultz organization, and the conference between Pompez and Schultz was held in the home of the lawyer's mother. While talking with Pompez, the Dutchman exposed a .45-caliber weapon he was carrying. He accused Pompez of lying because he had not turned over his business as he had allegedly promised, and threatened to make an example of him. The message came through to Pompez loud and clear and he capitulated. Before long all policy banks had been brought into the fold of the Schultz combination. However, Dixie Davis has asserted that Ciro Terranova held a twenty-five percent interest in the Schultz policy combination as well as his beer business.[62]

The Dutch Schultz policy operations flourished without serious interference from the authorities. Jimmy Hines, the powerful Tammany leader, actually was a part of the combination. For the greater part of four years, Hines was on the Schultz payroll, receiving from $500 to $1,000 a week. The money was delivered to Hines every Friday night by George Weinberg. And Hines was worth every cent he was paid. As lawyer Dixie Davis related, "Hines . . . could and did have cops transferred when they bothered the numbers. He had magistrates throw out good cases that honest cops had made against George Weinberg and Lulu Rosenkrantz. He gave his support to a district attorney who didn't bother us much."

As Schultz was busily engaged in taking over the policy racket, he became embroiled in a vicious shooting war with Vincent Coll. After having served as a trusted gunman for the Dutchman and his mob, Coll announced in the spring of 1931 that he wanted a piece of the beer business. Schultz responded with a flat no. Coll then went on a rampage hijacking beer trucks, and the war was on.

On May 30, 1931, Vincent's brother, twenty-four-year-old Peter, was mowed down by bullets and killed on a Harlem street corner. Vincent was filled with grief, and a lust for vengeance. Within the next few weeks four Schultz men fell before the blazing guns of Coll and his cohorts.[63]

On July 28, 1931, Coll gunmen drove a car into crowded East 107th Street in Spanish Harlem. Arriving in front of Joey Rao's place, the Helmar Social Club, the gunmen opened fire. Rao, a long-time ally of Dutch Schultz, was unscathed but five children playing on the street were shot. One child, five-year-old Michael Vengalli, was killed. The press promptly labeled Coll the "baby killer," as well as "Mad Mick" and "Mad Dog."[64]

The Wild West shooting sprees of Coll made Schultz jittery. On one occasion, the Dutchman walked into the detectives' squad room of the Forty-second precinct station in the Bronx. He confided to three detectives that Coll was driving him out of his mind and he wanted him killed. Magnanimously, Schultz offered to give a valuable home in Westchester to the officer who would bump off Mad Mick.

On October 2, 1931, Joe Mullen, a Schultz employee, was gunned down as he stood in front of a garage that served as a beer drop on Park Avenue in the lower Bronx. Eyewitnesses identified the Mullen killers as Dominic Odierno and Frank Giordano, former Schultz men who had switched allegiance to Coll. Subsequently, Odierno and Giordano were executed in the electric chair for the murder.[65]

On February 1, 1932, four Schultz toughs, with guns blazing, entered a dwelling on Commonwealth Avenue in the North Bronx where a card game was in progress. They sprayed the room with bullets and fled. Killed were Mrs. Emily Torrizello and two Coll triggermen, Patsy del Greco and Fiorio Basile. Basile's brother, Louis, and another woman were wounded. In the place at the time of the massacre were four children, including two babies in cribs, all of whom escaped injury. The Schultz gunmen had blasted into the residence on a tip that Coll would be there. The intended victim arrived a half hour after the shooting.

Eight days later, about twelve-thirty on the morning of February 9, 1932, Vincent Coll entered a telephone booth in a drugstore on Twenty-third Street near London Terrace, an apartment house in which Owney Madden resided. As Coll engaged in a protracted conversation, a limousine with three men pulled up to the curb outside the drugstore. One of the men entered the establishment, planted himself a few feet from the telephone booth, removed a Thompson submachine gun from under his coat, and opened fire. The victim's body was riddled with bullets and he was killed instantly. There were reports that Coll had been talking over the phone with Owney Madden, who deliberately kept him on the line long enough for the assassins to arrive and murder him. Dixie Davis asserted that the driver of the murder car was Dutch Schultz's trusted aide, Bo Weinberg.[66]

Less than two months before the Coll murder, the seemingly indestructible career of Jack (Legs) Diamond, another Schultz friend-and-associate-turned-enemy, finally came to an end. Diamond's record for surviving gunshot blasts had been remarkable, indeed. In the fall of 1924, he had been ambushed and shot at 110th Street and Fifth Avenue in New York City. He recovered. On October 15, 1927, he suffered many bullet wounds during a gun battle with the Lepke-Gurrah forces. He slowly recovered in Bellevue Hospital. Later, Legs was known as the Beer Baron of the Catskill Mountains. On October 13, 1930, gunmen invaded the Monticello Hotel in the Catskills where he was sharing quarters with a former showgirl. Four bullets were pumped into his body. Believed to be dying, Legs was taken to a hospital where he amazed surgeons by recovering. A short time later, as he was leaving an inn at Cairo, New York, a gunman blasted away at him with a shotgun. One slug struck Diamond's right lung, another pierced his liver, a third hit him in the back, and the fourth lodged in an arm. Again Legs recovered. Finally, on December 18, 1931, the myth of Diamond's invulnerability ended when gunmen shot and killed him in an Albany, New York, roominghouse. According to the version provided by the loquacious Dixie Davis, Bo Weinberg succeeded in having a duplicate key made for the room Legs had rented. Using this key, Schultz gunmen entered the room where Diamond was sleeping off a drunk and blasted him to death.[67]

The internal turmoil and violence that plagued the New York City underworld during 1931 and early 1932 took place in the midst of Judge Seabury's relentless exposure of the corruption then permeating city politics. Public interest in the hearings peaked when the inquiry focused on scandals directly involving the city's dapper mayor.

In response to a subpoena, James J. Walker appeared on May 25, 1932, in the Manhattan County Courthouse to testify before the Hofstadter committee. New Yorkers rushed to the courthouse by the thousands and about seven hundred squeezed into a hearing room intended to accommodate about half that number. When Walker arrived at the building, he was greeted with cries of "Good luck, Jimmy," "Atta boy," and "You tell him, Jimmy." The smiling and confident mayor responded by clasping his hands over his head like a victorious prizefighter and making other friendly gestures to his admirers.[68]

Under the grilling of Judge Seabury, it was disclosed that in July 1927 Mayor Walker had led the fight to force the Board of Estimate to approve the Equitable Coach Company bus franchise, even though the Service Bus Company, a rival applicant, was better equipped and offered superior terms. The Equitable Coach Company had been organized in 1925 by a few men, including Senator John A. Hastings, an intimate friend of Walker since their days together in Albany. Hastings not only was a stockholder but was also on the payroll of the company, receiving from $1,000 to $1,500 a month as a political contact man. Only about a day after the Equitable franchise was signed, Walker sailed for Europe. In his possession was a $10,000 letter of credit given to him by J. Allan Smith, a representative of the Equitable Coach Company. Subsequently Walker attempted to find invest- ment support for the Equitable but was unsuccessful, and eventually it became necessary to cancel the franchise because the firm was without necessary financial resources.[69]

The attempted "steal" by the Equitable Coach Company was probably concocted in the fast-working brain of Hastings, a constant promoter of get- rich-quick schemes who has been described as "all shoddy and a yard wide." Had the franchise become effective, the company earnings would have totaled $19 million in ten years. And Hastings, who had not invested a single dollar, would have received $6.3 million in dividends. Through his known friendship with Walker, Hastings was placed on the payroll of various firms that hoped to profit by doing business with the city. During most of the years that Walker sat in the mayor's chair, the sideline earnings of Hastings amounted to an estimated $54,000 annually.[70]

Judge Seabury also grilled Walker regarding his unusual financial rela- tionship with the publisher Paul Block. Evidence established that through a joint brokerage account set up by Block, and without any investment by Walker, the mayor had received $246,693 between February 1927 and August 1929. During this period, Block owned a substantial interest in a firm that was endeavoring to sell synthetic marble tile to city subway con- tractors. Senator Hastings was also using his talents in the promotion of this scheme. Of the total benefactions from Block, the mayor had received $102,000 within a period of five months in 1927. When Seabury asked the mayor how he had spent this large amount of money, Walker, in substance, replied that it was none of the committee's business. Seabury then confronted Walker with a $7,500 check he had carelessly drawn on the Block account in 1929 and turned over to Betty Compton. Walker testified that none of the money he had received from Block had been deposited in a bank. Instead, he said, it was kept in his home and "available for Mrs. Walker and myself."

After completing his first day on the witness stand, the mayor walked through a crowd that thunderously applauded him as he approached his waiting limousine. That same night he appeared before an audience of 18,000 persons attending the Police College graduation exercises at Madison Square Garden. The crowd whistled, stomped feet, and screamed in a show of enthusiastic approval. In his speech Walker charged that the Seabury investigations had virtually turned New York into a lawless city. The crowd wildly applauded his remarks, notwithstanding their patent absurdity.[71]

Walker returned for a second day before the Hofstadter committee on May 26, 1932. Seabury questioned the mayor about his relationship with an investment banker, J. A. Sisto, who owned a sizable interest in one of the big taxicab companies. Sisto had sought a limitation on the number of cabs that would be permitted to operate in New York City, and had presented to the mayor thirty-three bonds having an actual value of about $26,000. Following this handsome gift, there was established with Walker's approval a Taxicab Control Board, which in effect placed a limitation on the number of cabs and gave the big cab companies an advantage. Of the securities received by Walker, ten were Reliance Bronze & Steel Corporation bonds. This firm had received in February 1931 a $43,000 contract for traffic light standards on Fifth Avenue. Under the provisions of the city charter, an official was subject to removal if found guilty of owning stock in a corporation doing business with the city. Walker contended that he was unaware of Reliance's contract with the city and, furthermore, he had given the bonds of this company to his wife.[72]

Judge Seabury questioned Walker at length regarding the "mystery man," Russell T. Sherwood, who had fled the city rather than submit to an examination by the Hofstadter committee. Sherwood was once a $3,000-a-year accountant employed by Walker's law firm. When Walker was elected mayor, Sherwood became his personal financial agent. And it was through the mayor's backing that Sherwood was given a $10,000-a-year job with the Manhattan Trust Company.

Sherwood, in effect, maintained a joint checking account with the mayor and that account was used to pay Walker's personal bills. Also, throughout the mayoral years Sherwood shared a safe-deposit box with Walker. In March 1927 Sherwood opened a so-called brokerage account with a deposit of $100,000. This account was used solely for accumulating cash and not for stock trading. About four and one half months after it was opened, the account was closed when Sherwood withdrew $263,000 in cash. This money, presumably, was placed in the safe-deposit box he shared with the mayor.[73]

Other than the mayor, only Sherwood was in a position to explain Walker's shrouded money matters. As early as August 1931 Seabury had issued a subpoena for the mayor's personal financial agent to appear before the committee. Sherwood abruptly abandoned his job with the Manhattan Trust Company and fled the state never to return. When his presence was discovered in Atlantic City, Sherwood hastily departed for Chicago. From Chicago he scurried off to Mexico City, where he was married. In Mexico City Sherwood was served with an order of the New York State Supreme Court, which required him to appear before the Hofstadter committee. He refused to comply with the order and during his absence was adjudged in contempt of court. A fine of $50,000 was imposed against him.[74]

Through the questioning of Walker by Judge Seabury it was clearly shown that Sherwood had handled the mayor's personal financial matters. From the records of banks and brokerage houses, it was established that from the time Walker took office on January 1, 1926, until Sherwood fled in August 1931, the mayor's personal financial agent had handled some one million dollars. And of this huge amount, $720,000 had been in cash. Seabury asked Walker if he could give the committee any information regarding the source of the money handled by Sherwood. The mayor whined that the question was too general and, furthermore, claimed to know nothing about Sherwood's private affairs.[75]

Giving Walker the benefit of every doubt, the hearings had established that he had been guilty of a gross betrayal of a public trust. The committee had subpoenaed certain records that might have shed light on the mayor's mysterious financial dealings. But he refused to comply with the committee's subpoena. His testimony had been evasive and some of his statements were flatly contradicted by other witnesses. Nevertheless, when he walked out of the hearing room on his final day of testimony, he was met by a group of women who presented him with roses as a token of their loyalty, affection, and support. And as he left the courthouse to enter his limousine, a crowd applauded him only a little less vigorously than it had the day before.

A few days later, on June 1, 1932, the Hofstadter committee delved into the finances of the mayor's older brother, Dr. William H. Walker. Records disclosed that during the previous four years he had made bank deposits totaling $431,258. As a medical examiner for the New York City Board of Education he received a salary of $6,500 a year. He also received numerous fifty-dollar fees for serving as an official at various boxing matches. Obviously, these sources of income would account for only a small percentage of his huge bank deposits. Dr. Walker admitted that he had received over $100,000 of his deposits by splitting fees with four physicians who had been named by the city to treat municipal employees under the provisions of the Workmen's Compensation Act. The four doctors had been given a monopoly by the city to handle such cases. Evidence convincingly showed that they had padded their bills and then split their fees with Dr. Walker, who had never been designated by the city to treat workmen's compensation cases.[76]

As the Hofstadter committee hearings were nearing their conclusion, the Democratic National Convention was only a few weeks away. Franklin D. Roosevelt, the astute New York governor, had been laying plans to capture the presidential nomination and the Seabury investigation of the New York mayor presented him with a thorny dilemma. To act on his own initiative against Walker would alienate support from Tammany Hall and he did not wish this to happen. Yet, failure to act might be interpreted as bowing to the demands of the Tiger, thus creating a national image harmful to FDR's lofty ambitions. In the meantime, Albany was deluged with letters and telegrams asking for Walker's removal and praising the hard-hitting Judge Seabury. The acclaim of Seabury was particularly galling to Roosevelt since the judge had been mentioned in some quarters as a possible Democratic presidential nominee. Finally, the governor issued a blunt statement in which he asserted that if the joint legislative committee and its counsel believed they had sufficient cause, they should present the evidence to the proper authorities. It was pointed out that in the case of Sheriff Thomas M. Farley, "Judge Seabury asked the legislative committee to present the evidence to the governor. The committee refused. Judge Seabury sent it himself. I acted." And, said Roosevelt, "it is time for the legislative committee and their counsel to stop talking and do something. It is not the time for political sniping or buck passing."

On June 8, 1932, Judge Seabury forwarded to Governor Roosevelt a transcript of Walker's testimony and his analysis of the evidence considered by the committee. As in the case of Sheriff Farley, the joint legislative committee refused to present the case to the governor. Hence, said Seabury, "This record is presented to you by me in my individual capacity as a citizen of the state of New York." In commenting on the evidence, Seabury stated that "Mayor Walker, in his testimony before the joint legislative committee, was neither frank nor truthful. . . ." And Seabury charged that since Walker had assumed the office of mayor, his "conduct has been characterized by . . . malfeasance and nonfeasance . . . and he has conducted himself . . . in a manner so far unbecoming the high office which he holds, as to render him unfit to continue in the office of mayor."[77]

The case against the dapper, arrogant Tammany Hall mayor had now been placed squarely in the lap of Governor Roosevelt. And heretofore Roosevelt had never been a crusader against the Tiger. On the contrary, as the distinguished journalist Walter Lippmann had written in the *New York Herald Tribune* on January 8, 1932, Governor Roosevelt, through his patronage, had "supported the present powers in Tammany Hall." And, said Lippmann, based "on his record these last three years he will fight Tammany only if and when he decides it is safe and profitable to do so." In mid-June 1932 Lippmann again was highly critical of Governor Roosevelt's indecision in the Walker matter and wrote: "He seems to be mostly deeply irritated at the fact that the Seabury investigation has been producing testimony which compels him to choose between condoning corruption and striking it. He has displayed a singular petulance towards everybody who has had any part in putting him in a position where he might have to make a decisive choice between breaking with Tammany and surrendering to it. . . ."[78]

On June 21, 1932, Governor Roosevelt forwarded to Mayor Walker the charges made against him by Judge Seabury. On June 23, 1932, Walker responded by advising Roosevelt that he was leaving for Chicago to attend the Democratic National Convention and he would reply to the charges upon his return to New York.[79]

Of the numerous Tammany Hall delegates attending the convention, none other was more colorful than Mayor Walker. But among Tammany's most influential leaders at the time was James J. Hines, ruler of the Eleventh Assembly District and a dominant force in other districts as well. While attending the convention, Hines occupied a luxurious suite of rooms in Chicago's swanky Drake Hotel. Significantly, his roommate was Frank Costello, by now one of the most powerful underworld bosses in New York. Also rooming together in another plush suite in the Drake were Lucky Luciano and Albert C. Marinelli. Rooming together in still another suite in the Drake was the imposing trio of Thomas M. (Tin Box) Farley, the deposed sheriff; Louis Shomberg, also known as Dutch Goldberg, an influential New York racketeer; and Leon Scharf, a close ally of the feared Lepke Buchalter and Gurrah Shapiro. Occupying a suite by himself in the same hotel was Meyer Lansky. And Newark underworld bigwig Longy Zwillman, a close associate of Costello, Lansky, and Luciano, was practicing the art of national politics by flitting between the Drake and other hotels accompanied by delegates under his control from Nassau County in New York and the Newark area in New Jersey.[80]

Several of the New York underworld bosses attending the convention had close ties with top-ranking members of Chicago's powerful criminal organization, the Capone syndicate. In fact, in April 1932, only a few weeks before the convention, Lucky Luciano and Meyer Lansky had been seized by Chicago police officers in the company of Capone gang leaders Paul Ricca and Rocco Fischetti as they were leaving the Congress Hotel together.[81]

Principal contenders for the top prize at the Chicago convention were two New Yorkers, Alfred E. Smith and Franklin D. Roosevelt. On the fourth ballot, taken on July 1, 1932, Roosevelt received the presidential nomination. After flying to Chicago to accept the nomination, Roosevelt returned to Albany where he would have to resolve the sticky Walker matter.

Hearings on the removal charges brought by Judge Seabury against Mayor Walker were scheduled to start in Albany on August 11, 1932, in the executive chamber, a room adjacent to the governor's private office on the second floor of the state house. When Walker arrived in Albany, he was accompanied by his long-suffering wife, and was striving to give the impression that he and Allie were once again a devoted married couple. This gesture was looked upon as rank hypocrisy and fooled few observers.

Presiding over the removal hearings as judge, Roosevelt followed Seabury's brief as he questioned Walker about his weird financial dealings and his irregular code of public conduct. As the hearings progressed, the sessions grew longer, some lasting until almost midnight. On Friday afternoon, August 26, 1932, the hearings were ordered adjourned until the following Monday. In the meantime, Walker's brother, George, died and the mayor attended the funeral on September 1, 1932. He was downhearted and believed that Roosevelt intended to remove him. He asked the advice of Al

Smith, who suggested that he resign for the good of the party. Roosevelt also had been seeking advice regarding a proper disposition of the Walker case. He had toyed with the idea of letting the mayor off with a severe reprimand, but he realized that such a disposition, favored by the politicians, would give him the image of being weak. And he knew that an image of weakness would hardly aid him in his quest for the presidential chair. However, Roosevelt's dilemma suddenly disappeared. On the night of September 1, 1932, Walker sent a message to City Clerk Michael J. Cruise in which he resigned as mayor of New York City, the resignation to take effect immediately. The aldermanic president, Joseph W. McKee, became the acting mayor.[82]

A few days following his resignation, Walker sailed for Europe. He was met in Italy by Betty Compton. After whiling away time with Betty in Italy and Paris, Jimmy returned to New York for a brief stay, remaining incommunicado. Betty and her mother returned a short time later. On November 10, 1932, Walker, Betty, and her mother sailed once again for Europe, where the ex-mayor and Betty would live in grand style for almost three years.

Following an ultimatum from Jimmy, Janet Allen Walker tearfully filed for divorce in Florida on March 21, 1933. In April 1933 Walker, then almost fifty-two, married the twenty-nine-year-old Betty Compton at a civil ceremony in Cannes. Walker and Betty returned to New York in October 1935. The following March they adopted a baby girl and the next year a baby boy. In March 1941 Betty obtained a divorce from Jimmy, charging him with extreme cruelty. The next year Betty remarried, and in 1944, at the age of forty, she died of cancer. On November 18, 1946, Walker, then sixty-five, died of a clot on the brain, and ten years later, in 1956, his first wife, Allie, died in Florida at the age of seventy.[83]

The forced resignation of Mayor Walker in 1932 threw New York City politics into a turmoil. The acting mayor, Joseph McKee, insisted that he was entitled to serve out the remainder of Walker's term. This position was opposed by Tammany boss John F. Curry and Brooklyn boss John H. McCooey. McKee, a good family man, was handsome, intelligent, and very popular. During Walker's numerous absences, McKee had often sat in the mayor's chair during Board of Estimate meetings. However, McKee was a protégé of the Bronx boss, Edward J. Flynn, a confidant of Franklin Roosevelt. Curry and McCoeey feared that if McKee were in the mayor's office, Boss Flynn, with the backing of Roosevelt, would become the political leader of New York City.

Early in October 1932 the Court of Appeals ruled that a special election would be necessary to name a mayor for the unexpired portion of Walker's term. Under the leadership of Boss Curry, Tammany Hall selected a surrogate court judge, John P. O'Brien, as its candidate. O'Brien, a man of mediocre talents, had shown unswerving loyalty to the Tiger for thirty years. His principal attributes were his Roman Catholic piety and booming voice, often more noisy than sensible. At the election on November 8, 1932, O'Brien was successful but the results showed that Tammany was in deep trouble. An astounding 260,000 voters had come to the polls and cast write-in votes for McKee. That development gave impetus to the Fusion movement, which would successfully challenge Tammany Hall only a year later.[84]

14

THE DOWNFALL OF DUTCH SCHULTZ, LUCKY LUCIANO, AND JIMMY HINES

The Seabury investigations had firmly established that corruption permeated local government from top to bottom. The public was aroused and many demanded a civic housecleaning. Yet, an inept Tammany leadership failed to grasp the extent of the citizen uprising. In laying plans to capture the mayoral election in 1933, the Tiger boss, John F. Curry, and his cohorts nearsightedly clung to the bumbling John P. O'Brien as the mayoral candidate of the Democratic party and he was again nominated at the primary on September 19, 1933. Selected as the Republican and Fusion candidate to oppose O'Brien was the fiery archfoe of corruption, Fiorello H. La-Guardia.

The results of the primary were looked upon with alarm by President Franklin D. Roosevelt, who had been distressed with O'Brien's performance as mayor. Roosevelt had hoped that New York City would elect a Democratic administration friendly to him and was upset when Tammany insisted on reslating O'Brien. The day after the primary, President Roosevelt called his confidant Edward J. Flynn, the Bronx boss, to Washington for a conference. Roosevelt asked Flynn to urge Joseph McKee to enter the race for mayor and promised that he would publicly support McKee's candidacy.

During the campaign Flynn went to Washington to ask President Roosevelt to give his public blessing to McKee as he had promised. Flynn's entreaties were met with evasion. Later in the campaign, Flynn again unsuccessfully implored the president to make some kind of a statement in behalf of McKee. Roosevelt, an astute politician, had apparently concluded that "political expediency dictated doing nothing," and, a disappointed Flynn later wrote, "Nothing is what he did."[1]

In the November elections, voters swarmed to the polls in record numbers. LaGuardia won a sweeping victory, although the ballots cast for him were less than the combined vote for McKee and O'Brien. But candidates espousing reform were not the sole winners in the 1933 elections. In New York County, at the specific instance of Tammany leader Jimmy Hines, Magistrate William Copeland Dodge was slated for the post of district attorney and was elected. Through Hines, Dodge's campaign was generously supported by the vicious crime boss Dutch Schultz, the policy king. And also playing an indispensable role in the election of Dodge, as well as Tammany candidate for borough president, were the fraudulent votes cast by the thousands.[2]

In the Second Assembly District, Lucky Luciano's political protégé, Albert C. Marinelli, had prepared for the 1933 elections by naming George Cingola chairman of the local board of elections. Six years earlier, Cingola had been involved in an election law violation but was not convicted. Twice he had been arrested for assault, once he was charged with bootlegging, and on one occasion during a raid narcotics squad policemen found him asleep with two loaded pistols under his pillow. A federal investigation of the 1933 elections established that Marinelli's henchmen had aided their candidates by adding 4,534 votes to their totals and by stealing 3,535 votes from the opposition. A federal grand jury indicted Cingola but he disappeared and eventually the indictment was dismissed.[3]

On the evening of December 31, 1933, a number of civic leaders and their wives gathered in the second-floor library of Judge Samuel Seabury's townhouse. With the exception of LaGuardia, who was wearing a business suit, the male guests were attired in tuxedos. As the clock struck midnight, a black-robed New York State Supreme Court justice swore LaGuardia into office as the ninety-ninth mayor of New York City.[4]

The man who was to become New York City's greatest mayor was born of immigrant parents on December 11, 1882. His mother had been born in Trieste and his father in Foggia, Italy. When Fiorello was only a few months old, his father, a musician, joined the U.S. Army and became leader of the Eleventh U.S. Infantry band.

Early assignments of the elder LaGuardia included the Whipple Barracks near Prescott, Arizona. Fiorello's Arizona days made a lasting impression on him. The youth observed that although gamblers and saloonkeepers were an important adjunct to frontier life, they never became a part of the respectable community. The professional gamblers were known as "tinhorns," an appellation derisively used by LaGuardia when he became mayor to describe the bigwig gamblers in New York City. Almost every week, LaGuardia's mother would place a wager on a ten-cent policy slip. No one ever seemed to win. The policy game, young Fiorello concluded, was "nothing but petty larceny from the pockets of the poor." LaGuardia's antipathy toward the gambling profession would remain constant throughout his career.[5]

During the short Spanish-American War in 1898, LaGuardia's father became ill after eating diseased beef sold to the army by corrupt contractors. The illness caused a disability that resulted in his discharge from the service.

Accompanying his parents, Fiorello traveled to Trieste, where they lived with the family of LaGuardia's mother. There Fiorello's father died in 1901.

Young LaGuardia obtained a job as a clerk in the American consulate in Budapest and subsequently served for three years as a consular agent in Fiume, then an autonomous city of the Hungarian crown. Returning to New York City in 1906, Fiorello was employed awhile as a ten-dollar-a-week clerk by the Society for the Prevention of Cruelty to Children. After passing a U.S. civil-service examination, LaGuardia became an interpreter on Ellis Island. In 1907 he entered New York University Law School, attending classes at night during the first two years and working as an interpreter in the daytime. During the third year LaGuardia attended law school in the daytime and was assigned as an interpreter to night court, which handled commercialized vice cases. Here he gained firsthand information regarding police corruption.[6]

In October 1910 LaGuardia was admitted to the bar and for the next five years practiced law. In 1913 a clothing workers' strike involved about sixty-five thousand men. LaGuardia was retained as a lawyer by the Amalgamated Clothing Workers of America to fight picket cases and to explain the strike issues to the Italian clothing workers.

Taking an interest in politics but unable to stomach Tammany Hall, he joined the Republican party. Receiving an appointment as a New York State deputy attorney general, LaGuardia was assigned in January 1915 to the New York City Bureau of the Attorney General's office. During 1915 and 1916 Fiorello spent his spare time attending a flying school at Mineola, Long Island. In 1916 he was elected to Congress and was a member of that body when war was declared against Germany on April 16, 1917. Congressman LaGuardia promptly enlisted; he received a commission on August 16, 1917, as a first lieutenant in the aviation section of the Signal Corps. He was later promoted to the rank of captain and assigned to the aviation training center in Foggia, Italy, where Americans received flying instructions. LaGuardia flew on air-raid missions, was promoted to major on August 5, 1918, and returned to New York City on October 28, 1918, shortly before the congressional elections. With the exception of one term, 1920–21, when he served as president of the New York City Board of Aldermen, LaGuardia sat in Congress continuously until 1933.[7]

Within six months after LaGuardia's victory in the 1933 elections, John F. Curry was forced to resign as boss of Tammany Hall. In addition to the loss of the mayoralty, the Tiger had been feuding with the national administration and thus choice federal patronage was being awarded to Tammany's Democratic rivals. Earlier, under Curry's leadership, Tammany had opposed the 1932 gubernatorial nomination of Herbert H. Lehman; hence, the Tiger also found itself shut off from state patronage. Following Curry's ouster, Tammany was ruled temporarily by a triumvirate: James J. Hines, leader of the Eleventh Assembly District; Nathan Burkan of the Seventeenth Assembly District; and Edward J. Ahearn of the Fourth Assembly District. In July 1934, through the influence of James A. Farley, chairman of the Democratic National Committee, a district leader, James J. Dooling, became the chief of Tammany Hall. Before a year had elapsed, Dooling and Farley were at odds. However, Dooling was to remain the titular head of Tammany until July 1937.[8]

One of LaGuardia's first acts as mayor was to appoint Major General John J. O'Ryan as commissioner of police. O'Ryan had sought the Fusion-Republican candidacy for mayor but had stepped aside for LaGuardia. Significantly, during the first week of January 1934 LaGuardia sent word to Lewis J. Valentine to visit the mayor's home. The distinguished police officer was interrogated at length regarding the state of the department. At the conclusion of the briefing, LaGuardia revealed that he had instructed O'Ryan to designate Valentine the chief inspector, the second highest rank in the department, and to give him a free hand in eradicating corruption. Within an hour after becoming chief inspector, Valentine assembled his commanding officers and delivered a blistering message. "Be good or begone," he admonished. "This department has no room for crooks. . . . The day of influence is over. . . . I'll stand up for my men, but I'll crucify a thief." Further, said Valentine, "I'll be more quick to punish a thief in a police uniform than any ordinary thief. The thief in uniform is ten times more dangerous." Only a few months later, O'Ryan and LaGuardia differed on some matters affecting the police and O'Ryan resigned. On September 26, 1934, Valentine was sworn in as commissioner of police, a position he was to hold with distinction for almost eleven years.[9]

The very first day that the Little Flower occupied the mayor's chair, he declared open warfare against the underworld. He told the police it was their job to keep the crooks and racketeers out of New York City. In his zeal to combat the underworld, LaGuardia suggested to policemen that they adopt a "muss 'em up" policy, a suggestion looked upon with horror by civil rights groups.

The mayor's ire was particularly directed at the slot-machine industry ruled over by Frank Costello. Only a few weeks after his inauguration, LaGuardia resurrected an old law that gave the mayor the right to sit as judge in certain criminal proceedings. Suddenly the Little Flower appeared in the West 100th Street Police Station where he presided as magistrate and sentenced a slot-machine racketeer to jail. Only a week later, LaGuardia, sitting as a judge in Brooklyn, imposed a jail sentence on another gambler. To give his crusade publicity, the mayor posed for newspaper photographers as he smashed slot machines with a sledge hammer before they were dumped into the East River.[10]

Honest policemen had been handcuffed by a federal ruling obtained by the Costello forces, a ruling that enjoined them from seizing slot machines. The LaGuardia administration carried the fight against this ruling all the way to the U.S. Supreme Court and succeeded in having it set aside. In cooperation with the state's attorney general and various social agencies, the state penal code was amended on May 7, 1934, to allow more effective action against the one-armed bandits. By the end of 1934 most of the slot machines had been driven out of New York City. In many instances, however, they were replaced with pinball machines, which served as subterfuges for the slot machines and which were also operated by underworld interests.[11]

LaGuardia's successful drive against the one-armed bandits did not prove disastrous to the New York City slot-machine king, Frank Costello. Early in 1935 he made arrangements with Louisiana politicians that enabled the Costello–Dandy Phil Kastel combination to transfer its principal slot-machine operations to New Orleans. Costello subsequently gave sworn testimony to federal officials that he had entered into the deal with none other than U.S. Senator Huey P. (the Kingfish) Long, then the virtual dictator of Louisiana. Also involved in the slot-machine conspiracy, according to a federal investigation, was the flamboyant ex-convict James Brocato, better known as Jimmy Moran, intimate friend, playboy associate, and drinking companion of Huey Long.[12]

In July 1935 the Costello-Kastel combination, under the firm name of the Bayou Novelty Company, began operating 986 slot machines in New Orleans. On September 8, 1935, in the capitol in Baton Rouge, an assassin shot Senator Long and two days later the Kingfish died. Upon the death of Long, the New Orleans slot-machine industry was thrown into utter confusion. Costello's long-time personal attorney, George Wolf, has reported that the new mayor of New Orleans, Robert S. Maestri, promptly ordered the one-armed bandits closed down. Maestri then paid a visit to Costello's friend, Owney Madden, in Hot Springs, Arkansas. After a two-week vacation Maestri returned to New Orleans and the slot machines were permitted to resume operations. However, there are flaws in this version. At the time of Long's assassination, the mayor of New Orleans was T. Semmes Walmsley, a bitter enemy of the Kingfish. Maestri, then a conservation commissioner and an important cog in Long's organization, did not become the mayor of New Orleans until August 17, 1936.[13]

It has also been reported that because of the confusion prevailing in the ranks of the New Orleans underworld following Huey Long's murder, Owney Madden of Hot Springs hosted a conference attended by Frank Costello, Dandy Phil Kastel, Meyer Lansky, and a number of influential Louisiana politicians. The conferees decided that slot machines in New Orleans would continue to operate under the tight control of Costello's man, Kastel, who would receive the aid of a Long henchman, Seymour Weiss. After the Louisiana politicans had departed, Owney Madden, Frank Costello, and

Meyer Lansky transacted other business. Plans were made for expanding Madden's gambling resort in Hot Springs with financial backing by Costello and Lansky. This resort, bossed by Madden, was highly profitable and for decades served as a sanctuary for underworld leaders from all parts of the nation.[14]

A Huey Long biographer, T. Harry Williams, has stated that Costello's sworn testimony concerning his deal with the Kingfish to bring slot machines into New Orleans may be open to question. He suggests that Costello may have been trying to shield the identity of the person with whom he actually made his arrangements. Nevertheless, it is clear that politicians in Louisiana did afford the Costello-Kastel slot-machine combination iron-clad protection. And New Orleans was to serve as a base of operations for Costello and Kastel for many years.[15]

In 1937 a federal indictment was returned against Costello, Kastel, and four other defendants. They were charged with conspiracy to evade income taxes owed by Dandy Phil Kastel. Not surprisingly, they eventually beat the rap. The Bayou Novelty Company, which had been closed down, was reopened as the Pelican Novelty Company, a firm featuring pinball machines equipped with automatic payoff devices. Based on his New York City experience, Costello got a Louisiana court ruling that slot machines were legal if they paid off in mints. In 1942 the Louisiana Mint Company was organized. Partners in this firm were Frank Costello, Dandy Phil Kastel, Meyer Lansky's brother, Jake, and two others. In 1944 Frank Costello's wife, Loretta, was listed as the partner of Kastel in the Crescent Music Company, a juke-box corporation, and in December 1945 the Beverly Club, a plush gambling casino, was opened by Costello and Kastel in Jefferson Parish, just outside New Orleans.[16]

Developments in New York City early in 1935 undoubtedly convinced Costello that he had exercised sound judgment when he decided to transfer his slot-machine operations to New Orleans.

In mid-February 1935 it was publicly disclosed in a report prepared for the commissioner of accounts that seventy-seven bondsmen had committed perjury 1,584 times while procuring the release on bail of numbers racket runners. Allegedly, money for the bonds had been furnished by Dutch Schultz, whose numbers banks were taking in millions of dollars annually. Civic groups were incensed and demanded action. During this same general period, the *New York American* ran a series of articles by Martin Mooney; in them Mooney asserted that the Dutch Schultz organization was receiving top-level political protection from powerful Tammany leader James J. Hines. And a grand jury, through its foreman, Lee Thompson Smith, charged that every conceivable obstacle was being thrown in its way. Loss of confidence in District Attorney William Copeland Dodge was complete. The grand jury "ran away," ignored District Attorney Dodge, issued its own subpoenas for witnesses, barred Dodge's assistants from the grand-jury room, and demanded the appointment of a special prosecutor by Governor Herbert H. Lehman.[17]

On June 25, 1935, the governor forwarded to District Attorney Dodge the names of four outstanding Republican lawyers—George Z. Medalie, Charles E. Hughes, Jr., Charles H. Tuttle, and Thomas D. Thacher—and directed him to designate one of them special prosecutor. Each of the four lawyers declined to consider such an appointment. Instead, on June 26, 1935, in a joint statement to Governor Lehman, they unanimously urged that Thomas E. Dewey be named to the post. Initially, the governor rejected their recommendation on the ground that Dewey was not sufficiently well known. However, he reluctantly yielded to the pressure of the four lawyers and Dewey was appointed special prosecutor.[18]

Thomas E. Dewey was born in Owosso, Michigan, on March 24, 1902. In 1919 he entered the University of Michigan, which he attended four years. He studied voice and was an accomplished singer. In 1923 Dewey entered Columbia University Law School and upon completing his studies there, he was employed by a New York City law firm.

Early in Dewey's career, the law firm that employed him retained a distinguished lawyer, George Z. Medalie, to represent one of its clients. Dewey worked with Medalie in the preparation of the case and Medalie was greatly impressed with the young man's legal capabilities. On February 12, 1931, George Z. Medalie was sworn in as the United States attorney for the Southern District of New York and appointed Dewey to the post of chief assistant. The entire staff selected by Medalie was unusually able and included the brilliant lawyers Barent Ten Eyck, Murray I. Gurfein, William B. Herlands, and Jacob J. Rosenblum. All worked under the supervision of the youthful Dewey.[19]

As chief assistant U. S. attorney, Dewey gained invaluable experience in the preparation and trial of important criminal cases as well as in the administration of an important prosecutor's office. He also developed background information on the city's organized crime and the close relationship that existed between the racketeers and political leaders.

Among the cases in which Dewey participated were the income-tax prosecutions against the policy racketeers Henry Miro and Wilfred Brunder. Representing the defendants was lawyer J. Richard (Dixie) Davis. The government's evidence included sales slips that revealed that on July 22, 1930, Miro had paid $196.30 for one dozen monogrammed shirts delivered to Tammany leader James J. Hines. Sales slips dated December 19, 1930, established that Miro had made similar gifts to gangland chief Dutch Schultz, to Sam Kantor, a district leader, and to William Solomon, a political satellite of Jimmy Hines. In each instance, the gift was sent to the recipient in care of the Owosco Club. Miro was convicted for income-tax evasion and sentenced to three years in the federal penitentiary in Atlanta. Brunder pleaded guilty and was given a lighter sentence.[20]

Also prosecuted for income-tax evasion was Joseph Castaldo, the successor to Ciro Terranova as the Artichoke King. Both Castaldo and Terranova were related to the Morello clan of the infamous "murder stable." Terranova had turned over the artichoke business to Castaldo, who, with others, had organized the Union Pacific Produce Company in 1929. Dealers who failed to buy artichokes from Castaldo were beaten and their trucks hijacked. Castaldo was convicted and spent eleven months in jail. Some time later, Mayor LaGuardia personally initiated a drive against the artichoke racketeers and the federal government obtained indictments against several conspirators, who were charged with violation of the antitrust laws. In this case Castaldo was one of four defendants who pleaded guilty and he received a suspended sentence.[21]

The U.S. attorney's office in 1933 was ready to proceed with the income-tax prosecutions of two of the city's more affluent gang leaders, Arthur Flegenheimer, better known as Dutch Schultz, and Irving Wexler, commonly known as Waxey Gordon. Schultz, charged with evading payment of $92,103 in federal taxes on an estimated income of $481,000, went into hiding and could not be located for prosecution.[22]

On November 1, 1933, George Z. Medalie resigned as U.S. attorney and returned to the private practice of law. Through the authority of a seldom-used federal statute, a U.S. district court judge designated Thomas E. Dewey, then only thirty-one years old, to serve as the U.S. attorney until such time as his successor was appointed by the president.[23]

With Dewey personally handling the prosecution, the income-tax evasion trial of Waxey Gordon began on November 20, 1933. For the year 1930 Gordon had reported an income of $8,000, on which he had paid a tax of $10.76. The government showed that in 1930 Gordon had an estimated income of $1,338,000 from beer alone, and in 1931 the income from this source was $1,026,000. A life insurance agent, called by the defense, testified that a policy issued to Gordon had been canceled. This testimony was intended to show that Waxey was a poor man. Dewey exhibited a letter written by this witness in 1927 to his insurance company in which he certified that Gordon owned a half interest in the Paramount Hotel Corporation with a value of $3 million, a twenty-five percent interest in the Allied Hotel Construction Company with a value of $500,000, and a twenty-five percent interest in the Mansing Coal Corporation with a value of about $900,000. The vast holdings of Gordon included two breweries in New Jersey, which he took over after their ostensible owners had been killed in gang wars in 1929 and 1930. At the conclusion of a nine-day trial, Gordon was convicted on all counts and sentenced to ten years in prison, fined $20,000, and assessed $60,000 in costs.[24]

On November 25, 1933, President Roosevelt announced the appointment of Martin T. Conboy as the new U.S. district attorney, and at the end of the year Dewey returned to private law practice. It was only about a year and a half later, in June 1935, that Dewey, then thirty-three years old, was appointed special prosecutor for New York County.

The special prosecutor promptly recruited an unusually able staff composed of twenty deputy assistant district attorneys, ten investigators, and ten accountants, as well as process servers, stenographers, and clerical personnel. Selected by Dewey as his four chief assistants were young men who had worked under his supervision in the U.S. attorney's office—William B. Herlands, Murray I. Gurfein, Barent Ten Eyck, and Jacob J. Rosenblum. Joining the staff on July 26, 1935, was Frank S. Hogan, who in 1942 would succeed Dewey as district attorney for New York County and occupy that position longer than anyone in history.[25]

Office space for Dewey and staff was rented in the Woolworth Building, which was located across the street from the U.S. attorney's office, a block from City Hall and only a short distance from the Supreme Court Building, where the extraordinary grand jury was to hold its sessions. Designated to preside over the special grand jury was Justice Philip McCook, a courageous and honest jurist. On July 29, 1935, the grand jury was chosen and received the charge of Justice McCook. Thus was launched one of the more significant investigations in New York City history, an investigation that had the avowed purpose of destroying organized crime and racketeering.[26]

From the very outset Dewey received the wholehearted cooperation of Mayor LaGuardia and his administration. Commissioner of Police Lewis J. Valentine made available to the special prosecutor an acting deputy chief inspector and a squad of talented young policemen, most of whom had just completed their training at the Police Academy.[27]

As Dewey began his investigation, he had his sights set on one of the most powerful and ruthless underworld bosses in New York City—Dutch Schultz. Over a period of many years the Dutchman had built up a diversified criminal empire and had cemented close ties with Tammany Hall bigwig James J. Hines. Schultz had made a fortune from beer. He had gained control over the lucrative policy racket. He became involved in the bail bond business, which gained the prompt release on bond of numbers or policy operatives who were arrested. When the New York Department of Insurance, in January 1933, petitioned the New York Supreme Court to dissolve the Greater City Surety and Indemnity Company, it was disclosed that Johnny Torrio, with 1,667 shares, and Dutch Schultz, with 833 shares, owned two-thirds of this giant firm in the bail bond business.[28]

Early in 1932 the fertile brain of Dutch Schultz hatched a plan for systematic extortion from the restaurant industry. One of his henchmen, Julius Megilowsky, better known as Jules Martin, opened a cheap restaurant for the purpose of gaining a foothold in the business. Before long Schultz men took over control of two local waiters' unions, to which all restaurant employees were forced to pay dues. Schultz mobsters then created an employers' association, the Metropolitan Restaurant and Cafeteria Association. Restaurant and cafeteria owners were warned that failure to join the association would result in waiters' strikes, picket lines, and stench bombs. For membership in the association, Schultz mobsters assessed initiation fees ranging from $5,000 to $25,000, and levied heavy annual dues as well. As the racket flourished, Dutch learned that Jules Martin had failed to turn over to him about $30,000. This was an unpardonable sin. Early in 1935 five men, including Dixie Davis, Martin, and Bo Weinberg, boarded a train for Albany, where they were met by Schultz. It did not take long to dispose of Jules. His stabbed and mutilated body was found not long thereafter in the snow near his home in Troy, New York. Also found in the body was a bullet wound, the product of a gun fired by the Dutchman himself.[29]

For the greater part of two years Dutch Schultz remained in hiding to avoid standing trial on federal income-tax charges. During his absence many of his affairs in New York City were left in the hands of his lieutenant, Bo Weinberg, and lawyer Dixie Davis. Unexpectedly, on November 24, 1934, Dutch Schultz surrendered in Albany, New York, and entered a plea of not-guilty to a federal indictment charging him with having defrauded the government of $92,103.34 in taxes on an income of $481,637.35. On April 15, 1935, Schultz went on trial in Syracuse, New York, amid rumors of jury tampering. When the jury was unable to agree, the case was transferred to Malone, New York, for retrial. On August 1, 1935, the jury returned a verdict of acquittal. The presiding judge castigated the jury, stating that its verdict had shaken the confidence of law-abiding people and obviously was based on some reason other than the evidence.[30]

After his acquittal in Malone, Schultz saw obstacles in his path that made a prompt return to New York City at least injudicious. Mayor LaGuardia issued a public warning that New York City had no room for the Dutchman. The gang leader found Connecticut much more hospitable. In Bridgeport, where he frequented the bridlepaths, he was accepted by many socialites. A Fairfield riding master, Dudley Brothwell, later testified that Tammany leader James J. Hines visited Schultz at the stables. It was here that Dutch sadly informed Hines of the necessity to cut his weekly stipend in half. Schultz cited soaring expenses as the reason for the action. For a time, Schultz lived at the Barnum Hotel in Bridgeport, where he was also visited by Hines. On September 24, 1935, Schultz checked out of the Barnum Hotel and settled in the Robert Treat Hotel in Newark, New Jersey.[31]

For several weeks Schultz and an entourage of bodyguards and numbers racket workers met nightly in the back room of the Palace Chop House and Tavern located on East Park Street in Newark, just around the corner from the Robert Treat Hotel. In the front room was a sixty-foot bar. At the end of the bar to one side was a door leading to the men's washroom and in the back room, beyond the bar and men's room, were tables to accommodate persons who wished to dine in relative peace and quiet. Here, in this back room, Schultz and his lieutenants often discussed their business affairs over dinner.

About six o'clock on October 23, 1935, Schultz and two armed body-guards, Bernard (Lulu) Rosenkrantz and Abe Landau, arrived at the Palace Chop House and seated themselves around a table in the righthand corner of the back room. In addition to his weapon, Rosenkrantz had on his person a new Essex County, New Jersey, deputy sheriff's badge, which he had acquired when he began residing with Schultz at the Robert Treat Hotel.

During the course of the evening, Schultz had a number of visitors, including his twenty-one-year-old wife, Frances Flegenheimer, a former hatcheck girl who was the mother of the Dutchman's two children. At eight the night waiter arrived and served dinner to the Schultz party in the back room. By this time two new arrivals had joined the Schultz table. One was never identified, but the other was the mathematical wizard Otto Berman, frequently called Abbadabba. The numbers racket payoffs were based on racetrack pari-mutuel figures. Abbadabba was paid $10,000 a week by the Schultz organization to rig the racetrack pari-mutuel figures, thus increasing the Dutchman's profits and avoiding potential losses if certain numbers were receiving a heavy play. Abbadabba was worth every cent of his pay.

By 8:50 P.M. only four men remained at the Schultz table—the boss himself, Rosenkrantz, Landau, and Berman. They spent some time going over records, subsequently recovered, which disclosed that during a six-week period the policy banks had taken in $827,253.43 in bets and had paid out in winnings $313,711.99.[32]

At 10:15 P.M. two gunmen hurled open the front door of the Palace Chop House and headed straight for the back room. Only seconds earlier, Schultz had arisen from his accustomed place at the round table, put on his light top coat and gray fedora, and stepped into the men's room. One gunman, later identified as Charlie (the Bug) Workman, was a deadly mob executioner who was on the payroll of Lepke Buchalter. Workman was armed with a .38-caliber pistol and carried a .45-caliber revolver in reserve. He started firing away at the three men sitting at the Schultz table. Workman's con-federate, who he later stated was Mendy Weiss, removed a sawed-off shot-gun from under his coat and likewise blasted away at the Schultz lieutenants. A third confederate, known only as Piggy, who had been supplied by the New Jersey mob, was the driver of the getaway car. Apparently Piggy remained outside, although one version had him entering the place.

Lulu Rosenkrantz grabbed his .45-caliber Colt and attempted to return the fire. Seven slugs had ripped into Lulu's body. Otto Berman was struck six times and collapsed on the floor in a pool of blood. Abe Landau was shot from the back through his left shoulder; another bullet went through his upper left arm and a third struck his right wrist.

Initially, it appeared that the principal quarry had eluded the gunmen. However, Workman kicked open the door leading to the men's room. According to one version, Dutch Schultz was washing his hands. Another account had him standing at a urinal. Workman opened fire with his .45-caliber weapon. One steel-jacketed bullet entered Schultz's body just below the chest on the left side and tore the abdominal wall into the large intestine, gallbladder, and liver. Schultz staggered out of the men's room, headed for a table, stumbled down on a chair, and draped himself over the table top. Workman later asserted that when he shot the man in the washroom he had not recognized him as the gang boss but assumed he was a Schultz lieutenant.

As Workman was taking care of Schultz, Weiss, shotgun in hand, fled through the bar. Workman also started to make his departure but the path was not easy. He was pursued by a critically injured Abe Landau, who, with blood spurting from a severed artery in the neck, was trying to fire away at the departing gunman. Behind Landau stumbled Rosenkrantz, who collapsed on the tavern floor before reaching the door. During the exchange of gunfire, bullets crashed into walls, shattered a cigarette machine, and smashed a display of bottles. The place was a shambles. Once Landau reached the outside, his strength waned and he sat down on a garbage can a few feet away. When Workman arrived outside, he discovered that Weiss, as well as Piggy, the driver of the getaway car, had abandoned him and fled. Thus, Workman started running west toward Park Place and made his escape on foot.

Two radio cars sped to the Palace Chop House and Landau was rushed to the hospital in the first-arriving police emergency wagon. Three ambulances also called to the bloody scene transported Schultz, Rosenkrantz, and Abbadabba Berman to the Newark City Hospital. None of the victims would provide any information about the shootings or the identity of the assailants. (Subsequently, Charlie Workman gave his account of the massacre to Albert [Allie] Tannenbaum, a protégé of Gurrah Shapiro. The details of the story that Tannenbaum related to the authorities varied considerably from other versions of the affair.)[33]

Less than two hours after the carnage in the Palace Chop House in Newark, another chapter of the story was unfolding in New York City. Before midnight on October 23, 1935, Little Marty Krompier, a chief enforcer in the Dutch Schultz policy racket, made a stop at the Hollywood Barber Shop, next door to the Palace Theater in the subway arcade at Broadway and Forty-seventh Street. For a number of years Marty, along with such worthies as Bo and George Weinberg, had been a member of the Dutch Schultz inner circle. Obviously the talents of the enforcer and shakedown artist were appreciated by his boss. Records disclosed that Krompier was receiving a stipend of $1,500 a week. Bodyguards Rosenkrantz and Landau were each paid $1,875 a week.

At 12:01 A. M. a gunman armed with a .38-caliber pistol barged into the Hollywood Barber Shop and started blasting away at Little Marty. Four bullets struck their target—one in Krompier's chest, another in his abdomen, and one in each arm. Krompier was rushed to the Polyclinic Hospital, where he was expected to die. He defied the medical experts' predictions. After a series of operations over a nine-week period, he recovered.[34]

The Palace Chop House victims were less fortunate. At 2:55 A. M. on October 24, 1935, Abbadabba Berman died. Abe Landau succumbed at 6:30 A. M. Schultz lingered until 8:35 P. M. And Lulu Rosenkrantz followed his boss seven hours later.[35]

The motives stated for the assassination of Dutch Schultz were many. The most often-repeated version emanated from underworld sources, who asserted that the Dutchman was killed to prevent him from murdering special prosecutor Dewey. Although the Dewey investigation was only in its initial stages and its ultimate results problematical, the special prosecutor was feared by the underworld. During Dewey's earlier service in the U.S. attorney's office, he had been instrumental in obtaining an indictment against Schultz for income-tax evasion and had personally handled the successful prosecution of Waxey Gordon.

At two meetings of gangland bosses in New York City, Schultz reportedly had insisted that Dewey must be "bumped off." Between the two meetings, held a week apart, the daily movements of Dewey were charted and there was developed a plan for his execution in a drugstore telephone booth. Lepke Buchalter realistically pointed out that the murder of the special prosecutor would spawn a nationwide public crusade that would be disastrous for the underworld. Buchalter's position was backed by Lucky Luciano and the mob bosses decided against the rash proposal to kill Dewey. The Dutchman was unhappy with the decision and there were rumbles that he intended to murder the special prosecutor himself. The organized crime rulers, under the leadership of Buchalter, decided upon the execution of the Dutchman as a means of preventing the repercussions that would surely follow the murder of Dewey. Thus, the Buchalter henchmen Charlie Workman and Mendy Weiss were assigned to kill Dutch Schultz in Newark. The truth of this highly sensational story can be neither established nor disproven. Dewey, in an autobiography, has stated that he had no idea whether there was any truth to the story or whether it was merely underworld gossip.[36]

The usual underworld motives of double-cross and retaliation were also present in the Schultz assassination. When Schultz had fled the environs of New York City to go into hiding, he entrusted the immediate care of many of his affairs to his lieutenant, Bo Weinberg. Overtures were made to

Weinberg by both Buchalter and Luciano, who attempted to persuade him that his boss would never return. The picture changed, however, on August 1, 1935, when Schultz was acquitted in Malone, New York. The Dutchman had learned of Bo's friendly relations with Buchalter and Luciano and suspected, perhaps with some reason, that his lieutenant was double-crossing him. A conference with Weinberg did not allay his suspicions. On September 9, 1935, Bo disappeared and the underworld was convinced that he had been given a cement overcoat and dumped into the East River. Because of the murder of Weinberg on Schultz's instructions, a bitter enmity developed between the Dutchman and Buchalter. And there were suspicions that Buchalter ordered Schultz murdered in retaliation for the Bo Weinberg slaying. In any event, during the absence of Schultz, Luciano reportedly had made inroads in the Dutchman's policy operations and Buchalter had taken over portions of the restaurant racket. The bad blood thus generated would naturally result in warfare with gangland assassinations.[37]

There were also other possible motives. Well-founded rumors were prevalent that Schultz was a target of special prosecutor Dewey and was about to be indicted. Buchalter forces, in particular, feared that if Schultz were taken into custody, he would not "stand up" but spill everything he knew about the New York City mobs. Hence, it was said, Schultz was killed in order to silence him.[38]

Whatever the motives, it appears that two Buchalter gunmen, Charlie (the Bug) Workman and Mendy Weiss, mowed down the Dutchman and three lieutenants in the Palace Chop House on October 23, 1935. Workman eventually, in June 1941, was brought to trial in Newark for the Schultz murder. After a defense witness, on cross-examination, admitted that he had fabricated an alibi, Workman changed his plea to no contest—the equivalent of a guilty plea—and was sentenced to life imprisonment. After serving almost twenty-three years, Workman was paroled on March 10, 1964.[39]

The sudden demise of Dutch Schultz had denied Dewey the opportunity of initiating prosecutive action against this high-echelon crime boss. But numerous million-dollar rackets, including those controlled by the Schultz organization, were still flourishing in New York City and were receiving the concentrated investigative attention of the Dewey staff.

Only five days after the Palace Chop House bloodletting, Dewey revealed that in a single coordinated operation his men had arrested twenty-two loan sharks, who were being held on 252 counts in 126 indictments. Most of these moneylenders were gangsters and many were affiliated with potent criminal organizations. Borrowers unable to repay loans and the exorbitant interest rates imposed were ruthlessly beaten, slashed with knives, and subjected to a merciless reign of terror, which frequently drove them from their homes. By the time the Dewey investigation was completed, thirty-six loan sharks had been convicted and were sentenced to prison terms ranging from two to five years.[40]

Early in 1936, Dewey began laying plans to strike at one of New York City's most important underworld leaders, Charles (Lucky) Luciano. Lucky had been reaping huge monetary benefits from drug importation, the Italian Lottery, and the Dutch Schultz policy and numbers operation. Word had been received that Luciano was head of a combination controlling a lucrative prostitution racket.

Playing an important role in the prostitution business were the bookers, who assigned the girls to various houses where they remained for one week. At the end of that period, the girl called her booker, who gave her the address of the house where she would work the following week.

In 1933 the booking business was so lucrative that it attracted the attention of major racketeers. Four of the big bookers in New York City who also ran large chains of brothels were Pete Harris, Dave Miller, Nick Montana, and Cockeyed Louis Weiner. By the time of the Dewey investigation, Montana had been imprisoned and his business as booker was then in the hands of Jack Ellenstein, also known as Jack Eller. The business of Cockeyed Louis, also a convicted booker, had been taken over by his son, Al Weiner.

The girls usually lived with their pimps in roominghouses or hotels, and early each afternoon reported for duty at the houses of prostitution to which they had been assigned. The workday of the girls ranged from ten to fourteen hours. They received their pay at the end of each week, but promptly turned over one half of their earnings to the madam. From the remainder each girl was required to pay five dollars a week to a doctor for a medical examination, a substantial sum to the madam for meals, and ten dollars a week for the bond fund. Through the bonding arrangement, it was understood that as soon as a girl was arrested, a bondsman would appear on the scene and gain the prostitute's freedom on nominal bail. An attorney would also appear and coach her as to the testimony she was expected to give when the case was called for trial.[41]

In January 1936, Dewey investigators learned that the four major bookers in New York City had succumbed to tremendous pressures, particularly threats of violence, and had been taken over by a single combination. Reportedly, the boss of the combination was Lucky Luciano's underling, Little Davie Betillo, and the treasurer was Thomas Pennochio, known as Tommy the Bull. To ensure that everything ran smoothly, the combination had a strong-arm squad that included James Frederico (alias Jimmy Fredericks), Little Abie Wahrman, Ralph (the Pimp) Liguori, and Benny Spiller, who also ran a loan-shark business.[42]

At the stroke of midnight on Friday, January 31, 1936, Dewey's men quietly took into custody sixteen suspects who had been under surveillance for some time. On the following night, 160 policemen assembled in secrecy and received orders to make simultaneous raids on eighty houses of prostitution. Apparently because of police tipoffs, forty of the raids were failures. Nevertheless, the night's raids resulted in the arrests of a hundred prostitutes and madams, some of whom were the most notorious in the business.

All persons arrested were subjected to a thorough interrogation. Not only was valuable information supplied by madams and prostitutes but three of the four major bookers began to talk. The bookers asserted that through threats of violence they had been forced into the combination, which was headed by Luciano. Lucky maintained suites at the Barbizon Plaza, where he was known as Charles Lane, and at the Waldorf Towers, where he used the name of Charles Ross. His frequent meetings with members of the combination were observed by respectable hotel employees, some of whom later became highly important witnesses.[43]

The bond money was a constant source of trouble to the combination. Ralph Liguori, a holdup man, was assigned the task of disciplining madams who fell behind in their payments. Madams who resisted paying the bond money often had their heads bashed in. At one meeting, Little Davie Betillo complained about the trouble he was encountering in collecting the bond money. Luciano instructed Betillo to "wreck the joints" in order to bring the madams in line.[44]

Facts relating to the prostitution combination were presented to the grand jury, which returned a ninety-count indictment against Luciano and fifteen other conspirators. Luciano fled to Hot Springs, Arkansas, and placed himself under the protective wing of gambling boss Owney (the Killer) Madden. At Dewey's request, Luciano was arrested on April 1, 1936, in a Hot Springs gambling casino. Probably through Madden's influence, within an hour three of the city's most prominent lawyers had come to the aid of Luciano and secured his release on an insignificant bond of $5,000. Dewey, infuriated, burned up the telephone wires to Carl E. Bailey, the attorney general of Arkansas. Through Bailey's intervention, Lucky was arrested a second time and bond was fixed at $200,000. Also on orders of the attorney general, Luciano was transferred to the jail in Little Rock. Here a veritable army of lawyers, city officials, and members of the state legislature went into action with a view to gaining Lucky's release. It was reported that a bribe of $50,000 had been offered to the attorney general if he would permit Luciano to escape. A certified copy of the indictment was rushed to Arkansas and Luciano was ordered extradited to New York City.[45]

As the trial opened on May 13, 1936, the defense received a shattering blow. Three of the four major bookers—Dave Miller, Pete Harris, and Al Weiner—entered pleas of guilty and became witnesses for the prosecution. Luciano's strategy was to deny all charges. He insisted that, with the exception of Little Davie Betillo, who had once conferred with him about a gambling venture, he had never seen or heard of any of the codefendants in the case. They were, he said, complete strangers to him. When Ralph (the Pimp) Liguori took the witness stand he likewise declared he did not know a single one of the other defendants; and, he added, with the exception of Jimmy Fredericks, he had never seen any of the other defendants before. Yet, through a procession of hotel employees called as prosecution witnesses, all members of the combination, including bondsmen, were positively identified as frequent visitors of Luciano. Records of telephone calls also corroborated the testimony of bookers, madams, and prostitutes regarding the connections between Luciano and the other members of the combination.[46]

Among the more colorful madams who testified was Florence (Cokey Flo) Brown, the mistress of defendant Jimmy Fredericks. She told about her meetings with Luciano, Tommy the Bull Pennochio, Little Davie Betillo, and Fredericks. At one of these meetings, Luciano recommended that the houses of prostitution be organized like chain stores, the same as "A & P" establishments.

During the trial, testimony was given about numerous meetings of various defendants at Celano's Restaurant, long known as a Luciano headquarters. Lucky was also confronted with records of numerous telephone calls that had been made from his apartment in the Waldorf Towers to Celano's Restaurant. The calls to Celano's, Luciano explained, were made because he sometimes ate there. Celano's, of course, was located in the political stronghold of Luciano and his stooge Albert Marinelli. Although Luciano clung to his story that the other defendants were unknown to him, telephone record slips and the testimony of independent hotel employees served as a devastating rebuttal to his defense.[47]

On June 7, 1936, the jury returned verdicts of guilty against Luciano and his codefendants. Justice Philip McCook, who had presided over the trial, praised the jury's action as intelligent, courageous, and discriminating. He sentenced Luciano, found guilty on sixty-two counts of compulsory prostitution charged in the indictment, to a prison term of thirty to fifty years; Little Davie Betillo was sentenced to prison for twenty-five to forty years; Tommy Pennochio, twenty-five years; Jimmy Fredericks, twenty-five years; Little Abie Wahrman, fifteen to thirty years; Ralph Liguori, seven and one half to fifteen years; Jack Eller, four to eight years; Pete Harris, two to four years; Al Weiner, two to four years; and Dave Miller, three to six years. Upon appeal, the convictions were upheld by the appellate division and the Court of Appeals.[48]

Ten years after his conviction, Luciano's sentence was commuted and he was deported to Italy. In 1957 Dewey and his wife were traveling in Rome. Liguori, who had been visiting Luciano, sought out the former prosecutor and pleaded with him to "help the boss" get back to the United States. "Boss" accurately applied to Lucky at the time of his trial in 1936, although both Luciano and Liguori then brazenly denied ever having known each other. Luciano also always denied that he was ever connected with the prostitution racket. Nevertheless, in a statement made not long before his death, Luciano asserted that Liguori, Little Davie Betillo, and Tommy Pennochio had been his valuable and always loyal associates for many years before they started "to organize the whores." Lucky learned that these men, who had been running a string of houses of prostitution, had represented him as the boss of the operation. He instructed these underlings, he said, to cease representing him as boss, but they disobeyed his orders. The story is highly unlikely.[49]

At the time of Luciano's conviction, less than a year had elapsed since Dewey had been named special prosecutor and it was only a little over ten months since the first special grand jury had received its instructions from Justice McCook. By December 1935 the first special grand jury had examined more than five hundred witnesses and was exhausted. At the end of June 1936 the second special grand jury reported that it had been sitting six hours a day for six months and asked to be excused. Taking cognizance of the numerous investigations still in progress, a recommendation was made that two special grand juries should be sitting simultaneously. Governor Herbert H. Lehman thereupon authorized a second special term to be presided over by Ferdinand Pecora of the supreme court. Justice Pecora had distinguished himself while conducting a New York State Senate investigation a few years earlier. But Pecora was known as a political regular and had served as a long-time assistant in the offices of Tammany-backed district attorneys. Hence, his appointment was looked upon with apprehension by Dewey and his assistants.[50]

During the special grand jury's deliberations, it had become obvious that numerous witnesses were afraid to testify. In the summer of 1936, the grand jury issued a presentment recommending the formation of a citizens' organization that would provide support for law enforcement and ensure protection for witnesses. Thus was born, in the fall of 1936, the Citizens Committee on the Control of Crime in New York, which was patterned after the Chicago Crime Commission and other similar organizations then functioning in Baltimore and Cleveland. Among the members of the Citizens Committee were Lee Thompson Smith, who had served as foreman of the "runaway grand jury," George Z. Medalie, and Raymond Moley, noted professor of public law, author, editor, and expert on the treatment of criminals. Appointed to head the committee was Harry F. Guggenheim, former ambassador to Cuba. Originally formed to aid the Dewey investigation, the comittee continued in existence and issued reports on the crime situation in New York until 1943. [51]

The summer of 1936 also saw important developments in the field of politics. The American Labor party was birthed, and intended to provide support in New York City for the reelection of President Franklin D. Roosevelt. The founders of the new party included Sidney Hillman of the Amalgamated Clothing Workers, David Dubinsky of the International Ladies Garment Workers Union, Jacob Potofsky, Hyman Blumberg and Luigi Antonini of the garment-trades unions, and Alex Rose of the Millinery Workers. Although Roosevelt advisers James A. Farley and Edward J. Flynn originally were cool to the idea of forming a new party, Mayor LaGuardia, who had been close to the garment workers unions, heartily endorsed it. In the 1936 presidential elections, the American Labor party gave Roosevelt about 239,000 votes in New York City and became a leading minority party in the state. Having demonstrated its political virility, the American Labor party naturally began laying plans to participate in the 1937 mayoral election and to throw its support to its original friend, Fiorello H. LaGuardia.[52]

For many months most of the resources of the Dewey staff were tied up in the Luciano case. Nevertheless, during the same period, headway was made in the investigation of the restaurant and cafeteria shakedown racket, which initially had been organized by Dutch Schultz. Although death had claimed the Dutchman and his principal lieutenant in the restaurant extortion conspiracy, Jules Martin, the racket continued to flourish. Restaurant owners were forced to pay tribute to the extortionists. If they failed to do so, their establishments were closed by phony strikes or were victimized by ruinous stench bombs.

Indictments were obtained against ten defendants—two lawyers, six labor leaders and two gangsters—who were charged with conspiracy, extortion, and attempted extortion. Also named in the indictment as coconspirators were the deceased Dutch Schultz and Jules Martin. At the conclusion of a long trial, which began on January 18, 1937, the defendants were found guilty. Justice Philip McCook sentenced one defendant, Paul Coulcher, to a prison term of fifteen to twenty years and the other defendants to lesser terms, all in excess of five years. Upon appeal, all of the convictions were upheld.[53]

As the Dewey staff investigated the various industrial rackets thriving in New York City, the evidence clearly pointed to partners Lepke Buchalter and Gurrah Shapiro as the undisputed lords of this type of organized criminal activity.

Buchalter was born of respectable immigrant parents on February 12, 1897, in the Lower East Side of New York City. While quite young he was arrested several times for such offenses as grand larceny and burglary. He served a short term in a reformatory in Connecticut in 1915 and beginning in 1917 was twice committed to prison in New York. Following his release from Sing Sing in 1922, Lepke managed to avoid imprisonment for almost two decades. Buchalter, only five feet seven and of slender build, was usually attired conservatively and had the appearance of a respectable and successful businessman. His counterpart, Jacob (Gurrah) Shapiro, was short, heavy-set, and hoarse-voiced; his appearance did not belie his true character, a bullnecked thug.[54]

By the early 1930s, Buchalter had become the czar of industrial rackets in New York City. He commanded a force of some two hundred fifty sluggers and gunmen. His army excelled in shakedowns, murder, and helping win elections for Lepke's political allies. Money was rolling into the coffers of the rackets' czar. He maintained a plush apartment overlooking Central Square in Manhattan. Expensive, chauffeur-driven cars transported him to racetracks and nightclubs. In the winters he often sojourned in California and Florida. He visited Owney Madden in Hot Springs, Arkansas, as a member of a group that included Tammany Hall leader Jimmy Hines, Lucky Luciano, Meyer Lansky, and Joe Adonis.

Buchalter's influence was also felt in high judicial places. In 1933, because of racketeering in the fur industry, a federal grand jury indicted 158 persons, including Lepke and Gurrah, for violation of the antitrust laws. In 1935 both were convicted and each received the maximum sentence of two years in prison and a fine of $10,000. Federal Judge John C. Knox denied a request for release on bail pending appeal. Just two weeks later, the venal Martin T. Manton, senior judge of the U.S. circuit court of appeals, granted them freedom on bond and subsequently, with Judge Manton presiding, the circuit court of appeals reversed Lepke's conviction. On January 30, 1939, Manton was forced to resign from the federal bench because of well-founded charges of corruption that had been placed against him. Later he was prosecuted, convicted, and sentenced to two years in prison.[55]

By midsummer 1937 the authorities began closing in on Buchalter from all sides and he decided it was expedient for him to "take it on the lam." At the time of his flight, he was on the payroll of the Amalgamated Clothing Workers Union, had an interest in twenty-three dress firms, and was a partner in three large trucking concerns. For two years, while a nationwide manhunt was in progress, Albert Anastasia performed yeoman service by keeping the rackets' czar carefully hidden away in Brooklyn.[56]

In the midst of the investigation of industrial rackets, Dewey received letters offering full cooperation from the mother and wife of William (Billy) Snyder, who was president of Local 138 of the Flour and Bakery Drivers' Union when he was murdered on the night of September 13, 1934. That night the Flour Truckmen's Association, a known front for Lepke and Gurrah, was holding a meeting in a private room at Garfein's Restaurant on Avenue A in New York's Lower East Side. Among the fifteen men sitting around a table discussing a strike threat was Max Silverman, a senior associate of Buchalter and Shapiro and the boss of the combined group of truck owners and truck drivers. A vacant chair, with its back to the door, was awaiting the arrival of Billy Snyder, a union official who was in bad graces because of his refusal to truckle to the mob.

About ten o'clock, after Snyder had arrived and was seated at the conference table, Wolfie Goldis, the racketeer vice president of Snyder's union, got up from the table and walked out the front door. This served as a signal to a gunman waiting on the outside, who promptly entered the meeting room, shot Snyder thrice in the back, and walked outside and fled in an awaiting getaway car. Two witnesses identified Morris Goldis, a brother of Wolfie, as Snyder's slayer. The getaway car was traced through license plates to a man who admitted having rented the car with money given him by Morris Goldis. Before Snyder died he remarked that Wolfie's brother had shot him. The lawyer hired to represent Morris Goldis and the man who rented the getaway car was Charles A. Schneider, then an assistant attorney general of the state of New York. Suddenly the key witnesses recanted their identification of Morris and the case collapsed. Wolfie was elected president of Local 138 of the Flour and Bakery Drivers' Union, succeeding the murdered Snyder, and Wolfie placed brother Morris on the union payroll.

Dewey's staff initiated a thorough investigation of the Flour Truckmen's Association and its covert relationship with the union. Indictments charging conspiracy were returned against Harold Silverman, a son of Max, Wolfie Goldis, and Benjamin Spivack, attorney for the association. All were found guilty. And the Goldis brothers had another worry. They entertained well-grounded fears that the charge of murder was about to be filed against them. This fear mounted when they learned that Max Rubin, a long-time righthand man of Buchalter and an associate of Max Silverman, was talking with Dewey's investigators.[57]

Rubin, a silver-haired, well-educated labor organizer, appeared before the grand jury on September 27, 1937, and fully discussed activities on behalf of Lepke in the bakery racket. In the course of his testimony he cited facts that revealed the close ties that existed between the underworld and political leaders. In 1935, Rubin collected ten thousand dollars to settle a strike called by Local 138 of the Flour and Bakery Drivers' Union against the Gottfried Baking Company. The shakedown money, he said, was paid in the office of William Solomon, then a Tammany district leader in Harlem and a satellite of Jimmy Hines. On orders of Lepke, Rubin paid Solomon one thousand dollars, representing ten percent of the extortion money collected. Solomon, in turn, turned over five hundred dollars to Sam Kantor, a lieutenant of Solomon in the district.

On October 1, 1937, just four days after Max Rubin had testified before the grand jury, he got off the subway and was walking on Gun Hill Road when a Lepke torpedo stepped behind him and fired one shot into the base of his skull. The bullet went through his head and emerged between the bridge of his nose and eyes. After lingering in the hospital for thirty-eight days, Rubin miraculously recovered. Some time later he was able to give testimony that helped send Buchalter and his lieutenant, Mendy Weiss, to the electric chair on a murder charge.[58]

The brazen shooting of a grand-jury witness, Rubin, took place in the midst of a heated election campaign. On August 14, 1937, special prosecutor Dewey had accepted a draft by the Republican party to run for the office of district attorney of New York County. Also nominated by the Republican party was Mayor LaGuardia, who was seeking reelection. Dewey and LaGuardia also received the support of the Fusionists and the American Labor party.[59]

Both major candidates in the 1937 elections had excellent credentials to present to the electorate. During his tenure as special prosecutor, Dewey had amassed an incredible record of successful prosecutions. LaGuardia had taken over the management of a city that was in the throes of bankruptcy and had restored it financially. He had brought into his administration genuine career men of ability. From all city employees, the fiery mayor demanded a full day's work. Money honesty became a trademark of the entire LaGuardia regime. Almost every branch of city government had been improved. New Yorkers, accustomed to being ripped off by one Tammany administration after another, rallied to the support of the Little Flower and the kind of government he was giving them.[60]

In the November 1937 elections LaGuardia received a plurality of 450,000 and carried every borough in the city. Also elected were Newbold Morris, Republican candidate for president of the City Council, and Joseph V. McGoldrick, Republican nominee for comptroller. In New York County, Dewey defeated his Democratic opponent by over 109,000 votes.[61]

The election results were disastrous for Tammany Hall and its new county leader. In August 1937 the Tiger had chosen Christopher (Christie) Sullivan as its new boss, succeeding James J. Dooling. Christie, once a lieutenant of Big Tim Sullivan, was a coleader of the Second Assembly District with Albert C. Marinelli, the stooge of Lucky Luciano. And indications were that Marinelli controlled Christopher Sullivan.[62]

Tammany Hall was also anything but happy over the new city charter that became effective on January 1, 1938, the date LaGuardia began serving his second term as mayor. The charter, adopted by popular referendum in the 1936 elections, abolished the old Board of Aldermen and established a City Council as the new legislative body for the city. It provided for the election of councilmen by a system of proportional representation. Previously, the aldermen had been elected by districts, and through gerrymandering, Tammany Hall was able to dominate the legislative body and reduce the opposition to virtually nothing. In the last Board of Aldermen, Tammany had controlled sixty-two of sixty-five seats. The newly elected City Council, with a total membership of twenty-six, was made up of thirteen Tammany

Democrats, two independent Democrats, three Republicans, two Fusionists, and six members of the American Labor party.[63]

When Thomas E. Dewey took over his new duties on January 1, 1938, he brought his efficient special prosecutor's staff into the office of the district attorney of New York County. Of the sixty-four lawyers who had served under the inept district attorney William Copeland Dodge, only three were retained by Dewey. One of Dewey's first acts was to establish a new Rackets Bureau, with Murray I. Gurfein in charge. Also set up was a new Frauds Bureau, headed by Barent Ten Eyck. The Homicide Bureau, which was open twenty-four hours a day, was placed under the direction of Jacob J. Rosenblum. Named as Dewey's administrative assistant was Frank S. Hogan. Appointed to the post of chief investigator was the impeccable John F. O'Connell, who had distinguished himself on the special prosecutor's staff and before that with the FBI. Dewey's former chief assistant, William B. Herlands, had been selected by Mayor LaGuardia to become the commissioner of investigations for the New York City government.[64]

Dewey had barely settled into the New York County district attorney's office when he began laying plans to initiate prosecution against the Mr. Big of Tammany Hall, James J. Hines. Through his alliances with underworld kingpins, Hines had become the most powerful leader in Tammany and one of the most influential Democratic politicians in the entire state. Even before the death of Big Tom Foley in 1925, Hines had won recognition as the single most important patron to organized crime bosses in New York City. Over a long span of time, Arnold Rothstein, Frank Costello, Owney Madden, Lepke Buchalter, and Dutch Schultz were among the underworld stalwarts who had relied on the onetime blacksmith for protection.

The insidious influence of Hines had spread throughout the city government and many officials, including a number of judges, held him in awe. Long before he became mayor, LaGuardia sought assistance from an honorable judge of the court of general sessions, Joe Corrigan, to ensure police protection for laborers being brutalized by strong-arm thugs during a strike. Judge Corrigan was sympathetic but lamented to LaGuardia that if Jimmy Hines had any interest in the affair, he would be helpless to take any action against men in the police department, or for that matter, in any other branch of city government.[65]

Beginning in 1935 the Dewey staff engaged in a three-year investigation of the numbers racket. In July 1938, indictments were returned against Hines, Dixie Davis, George Weinberg, and other members of the Dutch Schultz policy organization. Hines, it was charged, had become a part of the Schultz combination, which had resorted to kidnappings, beatings, and other violence to force all independent policy operators into one combination. Hines' function was to control judges, police, and prosecutors, thus ensuring the continued operation of the numbers racket without interference from officials charged with enforcing the criminal laws in New York City.[66]

The trial of Hines opened on August 25, 1938, in the Supreme Court Building before Justice Ferdinand Pecora. Retained by Hines as his defense counsel was Lloyd Paul Stryker, one of the most outstanding criminal lawyers in the nation, a courtroom orator of renown, and a master in the art of cross-examination.

Early in the trial a succession of witnesses provided a detailed description of the policy business. Following the gangland slaying of Dutch Schultz in October 1935, one of his principal successors was Dixie Davis, who played a key role in perpetuating the Schultz policy organization. The so-called law offices of Davis occupied the entire floor of a skyscraper at 1450 Broadway. Davis maintained three residence addresses and supported in style a glamorous redheaded mistress, Hope Dare, once a rodeo rider and a former Ziegfeld girl. Indispensable to Schultz, and later to Davis, was Tammany leader Hines, who controlled District Attorney William Copeland Dodge, a number of key judges who presided over policy cases, and policemen.

Throughout the long trial, Justice Pecora's attitude indicated that he was out of sympathy with the prosecution's case. Finally, when defense lawyer Stryker objected to the propriety of a question Dewey asked a defense witness, Pecora declared a mistrial. But the troubles of Hines were far from ended. For a second time he was brought to trial, on January 25, 1939. Presiding over the second trial was a highly reputable judge, Charles C. Nott, Jr. On January 29 George Weinberg, a key witness for the state, committed suicide. However, the testimony he had given in the first trial was admitted into evidence.[67]

Testimony in the trials of Jimmy Hines set forth a blueprint for organized crime in American cities. George Weinberg related that he had met Hines during a conference in the apartment of Dutch Schultz. The Dutchman explained to the Tammany leader that he wanted to make certain there would be no drives by the police against his policy banks and he expected satisfactory dispositions of policy cases in the magistrates' courts. Hines assured Schultz that he could take care of the police department's sixth division in Harlem, where the numbers game flourished, and he could control the magistrates' courts. At the conference, Schultz paid Hines $1,000 and instructed Weinberg to make weekly payments of $1,500 to the Tammany bigwig. That arrangement continued, Weinberg testified, until June 1935, when, through mutual consent, Hines' stipend was cut in half because of "hard times."

The prosecution introduced evidence of telephone taps, which had been installed in an effort to locate Schultz when he was a fugitive. The taps had picked up calls made by Hines to Dixie Davis about his weekly payments.

A sister of Davis testified that she had delivered a $500 check to Hines and the check was introduced as evidence.

The control that Hines exercised over magistrates was demonstrated repeatedly. Once George Weinberg and fourteen other men were arrested in a raid on a policy bank. Weinberg testified that he overheard Hines tell Magistrate Hulon Capishaw to dismiss the charges and the judge obligingly replied, "I will take care of it."[68]

Essential to the protection of the Schultz policy combination was control of the district attorney's office. John F. Curry, boss of Tammany Hall until he was deposed in 1934, testified that as the citywide ticket was being put together in 1933, Jimmy Hines was interested in one office only—that of district attorney. It was at the insistence of Hines that Tammany slated and elected District Attorney William Copeland Dodge.

Weinberg testified that Schultz had contributed $30,000 to help ensure the election of Dodge in 1933. The money came from the policy banks of the Schultz combination and was turned over to Hines. A number of respectable businessmen and lawyers, as well as Dodge's 1933 campaign manager, testified that they had been sent to Hines for electioneering funds. When Dodge was called as a defense witness, he admitted his intimate friendship with Hines for over twenty years and conceded that when funds were needed in 1933, his manager had gone to Hines for help. Dixie Davis related how District Attorney Dodge had attempted to steer the 1935 grand jury away from the important rackets. His efforts failed when the grand jury became incensed and "ran way."[69]

It was through Hines that the Dutch Schultz organization actually controlled the law-enforcement machinery. Policemen who "cracked down" on Schultz policy banks were ordered transferred or reduced in rank. John F. Curry testified that frequently he had received calls from Hines requesting him to have "recalcitrant" officers transferred or demoted. As boss of Tammany, Curry would call the commissioner of police, who invariably ordered the transfers or demotions as dictated by Hines. A former chief inspector, John O'Brien, corroborated Curry's testimony.[70]

The influence of the politically powerful Hines in behalf of Schultz was apparent in many places. A Democratic county leader from Troy, New York, testified that he had received several calls from Hines asking him to stop the local police from "pushing Dutch Schultz around." Max D. Steuer, a noted defense attorney and a Tammany stalwart, testified that Hines personally asked him to help Dutch Schultz with his income-tax troubles with the federal government.[71]

The intimate relations between Hines and the gang leader were established by a number of independent witnesses. A bartender at the Embassy Club testified that Hines and Schultz were "steady customers" who often ate and drank together in his place. The proprietor of a Connecticut riding academy testified that when Schultz was a fugitive, Hines came to his stables for the express purpose of meeting with the gang leader. Mrs. Arthur Flegenheimer, the widow of Schultz, testified that she had been introduced to Hines by her late husband. She also had met Hines on many occasions with Dixie Davis.[72]

The brilliant defense attorney Lloyd Paul Stryker decided it would be disastrous to place Hines on the witness stand and subject him to a devastating cross-examination. Hence, the Tammany leader never testified. On February 25, 1939, the jury found Hines guilty on all thirteen counts in the indictment. Judge Charles C. Nott, Jr. sentenced him to a term of four to eight years in the state penitentiary. The Court of Appeals (*People* v. *Hines,* 284 New York 93) upheld the conviction and on October 14, 1940, James J. Hines entered Sing Sing Prison. He was granted a parole in August 1944 and died in 1957 at the age of eighty.[73]

As the Jimmy Hines prosecution was in progress, local and federal officers were intensifying efforts to locate the nation's most wanted fugitive, Lepke Buchalter. The reward for Lepke's capture was raised by New York City from $5,000 to $25,000. So much heat was being generated that the fugitive was persuaded to give himself up.

By prearrangement, on the night of August 24, 1939, Albert Anastasia, accompanied by Lepke, drove an automobile from 101 Third Street in Brooklyn to Manhattan and to a car parked near Fifth Avenue and Twenty-eighth Street. Seated in the automobile were Walter Winchell, the Broadway columnist, and J. Edgar Hoover, director of the FBI. Lepke stepped out of the Anastasia car, walked over to Winchell, and surrendered. Winchell turned Buchalter over to Hoover and thus the manhunt for Lepke came to an end.

Late in 1939, following a federal conviction for narcotics smuggling, Buchalter was sentenced to fourteen years in prison. Subsequently he was prosecuted by Dewey in the court of general sessions for his leading role in the flour and bakery racket and was given a prison term of thirty years to life. On September 15, 1941, Buchalter, Mendy Weiss, and Louis Capone, a front man for Albert Anastasia, were brought to trial in Brooklyn for the murder of Joseph Rosen. The victim had been forced out of his clothing trucking business by Lepke and had opened a small candy store. Lepke was warned by his trusted aide, Max Rubin, that Rosen was "shooting off his mouth" and was threatening to pay a visit to Dewey's office. Early on Sunday morning, September 13, 1936, Buchalter's minions descended on Rosen's candy store, pumped seventeen bullets into his body, and fled. Ironically, a key witness against Buchalter at the Rosen murder trial was Max Rubin, who, on orders of Lepke, had been shot in the head on October 1, 1937, but miraculously recovered. Buchalter, Weiss, and Capone were convicted of murder and sentenced to die in the electric chair. Following many appeals and much legal maneuvering, the three were electrocuted in March 1944.[74]

The Hines trial had focused attention on the office of New York County District Attorney William Copeland Dodge. It established that Hines, the political protector of the underworld, virtually owned and controlled the district attorney—Hines referred to Dodge, with justification, as "my man."

But the New York County district attorney's office was not unique. Similar conditions prevailed in the office of William F. X. Geoghan, who had served as the district attorney in Brooklyn since 1931. Among Geoghan's intimate associates was Leo P. Byk, a gambler and fixer. Until 1934 Byk had for some time been the Brooklyn manager of the Frank Costello–Dandy Phil Kastel slot-machine combination and enjoyed the protective services of Jimmy Hines.[75]

In 1938, charges were made that members of District Attorney Geoghan's staff were fixing cases. The Citizens Committee on the Control of Crime in New York, headed by Harry F. Guggenheim, examined some fourteen thousand Brooklyn cases handled since 1937 and reported an alarming number of irregularities. Mayor LaGuardia ordered his commissioner of investigations, William B. Herlands, to look into the matter. On October 10, 1938, Herlands petitioned Governor Lehman to supersede the Brooklyn district attorney. The petition was granted, an extraordinary special term was created, and John Harlan Amen was appointed to conduct an inquiry. Previously, as a special assistant to the United States attorney general, Amen had made an enviable record in obtaining convictions in rackets cases.

Just two days after Geoghan had been superseded, seventy-two hundred permanent police records contained in six volumes were stolen from the record room of the Seventy-eighth Precinct on Bergen Street. A thorough investigation by the commissioner of police, Lewis J. Valentine, resulted in the arrest, suspension, and eventual dismissal from the force of a police lieutenant.

Amen's investigation continued over a four-year period and uncovered much corruption in Geoghan's staff. One assistant district attorney, William F. McGuiness, pleaded guilty to accepting bribes and was sent to Sing Sing Prison. Two other assistants were disbarred. Also uncovered by the Amen investigation were a corrupt bail bond system, an abortion conspiracy, and a large gambling racket that flourished under police protection.

The scandalous conditions uncovered in the office of the Brooklyn district attorney received wide publicity. Hence, it became expedient for the Democratic party to drop Geoghan from its ticket in the 1939 elections. Named as the Democratic candidate for district attorney in Brooklyn was a county judge, William O'Dwyer. He was elected.[76]

O'Dwyer was a somewhat enigmatic personality. In many respects he was an updated version of A. Oakey Hall of Tweed Ring days. O'Dwyer possessed many talents but they were often useless because of his subservience to the demands of his powerful underworld supporters.

Born in county Mayo, Ireland, on July 11, 1890, O'Dwyer came to America at a youthful age. He was employed in the building trades, later became a bartender, and eventually received an appointment to the police department. As a patrolman for a while, he walked a beat in Brooklyn's tough gangster-dominated waterfront. On the side he attended Fordham University Law School, earned his degree, was admitted to the bar, and soon entered politics.

An early law partner of O'Dwyer was an alderman from a district controlled by Joe Adonis, who was rapidly becoming one of the most influential underworld leaders in New York City. Adonis was the proprietor of a restaurant that had for some time enjoyed the heavy patronage of bootleggers, gunmen, and ward politicians. Backed by a district leader who was a close friend of Adonis, O'Dwyer gained a place on the magistrates' bench on December 7, 1932. Later he became a county judge and in 1939 was the successful candidate for district attorney of Kings County.

As district attorney, O'Dwyer chose as his confidential assistant the venal James J. Moran, who was without any legal training whatever. Moran developed close ties to organized crime bigwigs, including Frank Costello, and exercised an unholy influence in the prosecutor's office. The sometimes unpredictable O'Dwyer also appointed such outstanding assistants as Burton B. Turkus, who was to gain fame as the prosecutor of members of the so-called Murder, Inc.

O'Dwyer was a man of personal charm. Complementing that charm was his ability to discourse on the poetry of Byron and Keats. But primarily, O'Dwyer was a student of practical politics—a man whose ambitions were closely linked to Tammany Hall–underworld alliances.[77]

The conviction of Jimmy Hines in 1939 was the culmination of a long series of setbacks for Tammany Hall. For over a decade following the assassination of Arnold Rothstein in November 1928, the Tiger had been under unrelenting assault by the forces of reform. An archfoe of Tammany, Fiorello H. LaGuardia had been placed in the mayor's chair. The untiring and effective prosecutions by Thomas E. Dewey had brought about the downfall of some of the city's more prominent underworld bosses, all of whom were closely allied with the Tiger.

Tammany was beset by other weakening influences. Its feud with the national administration resulted in a cutoff of badly needed federal patronage. James A. Farley, in 1937, had inspired the city's other Democratic organizations to wage a bitter primary fight with Tiger candidates. Not least was the development of the political combination of Boss Edward J. Flynn's machine in the Bronx and Frank V. Kelly's Brooklyn organization.

Although Tammany Hall was in a weakened condition, it was far from destroyed. In the past, periods of adversity had always been followed by a strong resurgence, and Tammany stalwarts had reason to face the future with confidence. In fact, it was during this low period that Frank Costello began his maneuvering to take over control of the Tiger organization. And within a few years, under Costello's leadership, Tammany would again place in the mayor's office in New York City the man of its choice—William O'Dwyer.[78]

**Boss William Marcy Tweed, whose
Tammany ring mulcted New York City
of millions.**

Photo: Culver Pictures

CAN THE BODY CAST OFF ITS SHADOW?
The Tammany Society has expelled TWEED as Sachem. —*Daily Papers.*

"WHAT ARE YOU LAUGHING AT! TO THE VICTOR BELONG THE SPOILS."

THE TAMMANY TIGER LOOSE—"What are you going to do about it?"

Some devastating Thomas Nast cartoons depicting Boss Tweed.

Photos: Culver Pictures

Can the Law reach him?—The Dwarf and the Giant Thief

THE "BRAINS"

That achieved the Tammany Victory at the Rochester Democratic Convention.

"WHO STOLE THE PEOPLE'S MONEY?"—DO TELL.NY.TIMES.   'TWAS HIM.

Photos: Culver Pictures

Mild-looking Albert Anastasia — chief executioner for Murder, Incorporated.

Photo: Culver Pictures

**Anthony Anastasia (Albert's brother),
who controlled the waterfront through
terror. 1943 photo.**

Photo: Culver Pictures

**Arnold Rothstein, king of New York's
organized crime in the twenties.**

Photo: Culver Pictures

**New York's affable boss of bosses,
Frank Costello, with his attorney
George Wolf, early 1940s.**

Photo: Culver Pictures

**The underworld king of New Jersey,
Joe Adonis.**

Photo: Culver Pictures

Old and New Tammany bosses in 1902: Boss Richard Croker, left, and Lewis Nixon.

Scarface Al Capone.

Photos: Culver Pictures

**Yvonne Shelton, showgirl and early
Jimmy Walker mistress.**

**Beautiful Virginia Hill, mistress of Joe
Adonis and later, Bugsy Siegel.**

Photos: Culver Pictures

**Playboy mayor Jimmy Walker and
his second wife and former mistress,
actress Betty Compton.**

Photo: Culver Pictures

**Bronx Democratic Boss and Franklin
Roosevelt confidante Edward J. Flynn,
who sometimes opposed Tammany.**

**Judge Samuel Seabury and an
unidentified woman. The impeccable
Judge Seabury's investigations were a
potent force in the struggle against
organized crime.**

Photos: Culver Pictures

**Governor Tom Dewey meets Governor
Earl Warren.**

**Tennessee Senator Estes Kefauver,
whose Senate hearings on organized
crime electrified the nation in the
early fifties.**

Photos: Culver Pictures

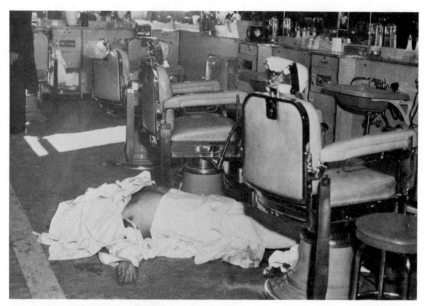

It wasn't a close shave for Albert
Anastasia. Soon after he had settled into
his chair at the Park Sheraton barber
shop on October 26, 1957, two
gentlemen plugged him.

A manacled Vito Genovese,
photographed in 1960.

Photos: New York Daily News

**Joseph Bonanno with his lawyer
in 1966.**

**Carlo Gambino, right, with his
chauffeur, James Failla, in 1973.**

Photos: New York Daily News

**The great Fiorello LaGuardia busts up
some one-armed bandits to publicize his
war on crime.**

Photo: Culver Pictures

15

THE O'DWYER YEARS—COSTELLO INFLUENCE

On February 2, 1940, Abe (Kid Twist) Reles, an arrogant, self-glorifying Brooklyn gang leader, was taken into custody for slaying a small-time hoodlum in 1933. The arrest of Reles was not deemed particularly momentous to the new Kings County district attorney, William O'Dwyer, who had taken office on January 1, 1940. After all, the police had arrested this thirty-three-year-old gangster forty-four times. Six times Reles had been charged with homicide but had always escaped conviction for that and other major crimes.[1]

On Good Friday, March 22, 1940, Reles, on the most recent murder charge, sought an audience with the Brooklyn district attorney. In an effort to save his neck, Reles offered to furnish inside information on a series of murders that would electrify the nation, he said, and make O'Dwyer the "biggest man in the country." A bargain was struck and Reles then proceeded to provide the details of about eighty-five killings committed in Brooklyn by a criminal organization that the press would dub Murder, Inc.

Born in East New York about 1907, Reles was solidly embarked on a career of racketeering, crime, and violence by the time he had reached voting age. Repulsive in appearance, he supported an obese body on a five-foot-two frame. Hard, piercing eyes were set in a round face marked by thick lips and a flat nose. Long, gangling arms completed his gorillalike shape. His temperament was unusually vicious. Once, when a Negro car washer in a Manhattan garage did not move fast enough to suit him, Reles stabbed and killed him. Not long afterward, in the identical garage, Reles and a companion beat another car washer to death for the same reason. In all, Reles was personally involved in at least fourteen murders.[2]

The talents of Reles were appreciated by such important organized crime leaders as Albert Anastasia, who became known as the chief executioner for Murder, Inc. And when Louis (Lepke) Buchalter was the object of a nationwide manhunt, it was often Reles, pistol in hand, who stood guard as Lepke was sleeping. Not only did Reles provide detailed information regarding scores of murders, but his testimony withstood the tests of grueling cross-examination and sent several of his erstwhile intimates to the death house. Among such were Harry (Happy) Maione, Frank (Dasher) Abbandando, Martin (Bugsy) Goldstein, and Harry Strauss, also known as Pittsburgh Phil and Pep.[3]

The first trial involving Murder, Inc. hoodlums ended on May 23, 1940, with the conviction of Happy Maione and Dasher Abbandando for the brutal slaying of George (Whitey) Rudnick in a public garage in the early morning hours of May 25, 1937. Rudnick became a candidate for death when it was learned that he had been "talking to the law." Weapons used in the killing included a meat clever and an ice pick. Rudnick's skull was shattered and sixty-three stab wounds were found in his body. Although the Court of Appeals reversed the convictions, Maione and Abbandando were again found guilty at a second trial and on February 19, 1942, were electrocuted.[4]

In the meantime, two other Murder, Inc. defendants, Harry Strauss and Bugsy Goldstein, had been executed on June 12, 1941, following conviction for the assassination of Puggy Feinstein on Labor Day, 1939. Puggy's gambling operations had encroached on the territory of Vincent Mangano, influential waterfront gang leader. Mangano's intimate associate, Albert Anastasia, awarded Pittsburgh Phil Strauss the murder contract for Puggy, who was slain after he had been lured to the home of Abe Reles. His body was hauled to a vacant lot, saturated with gasoline, set afire, and abandoned.[5]

In addition to recounting the gory details of scores of gangland murders in Brooklyn, Reles asserted that in 1934 a national crime syndicate had been formed. Organized along the lines of a cartel, every important mob in the United States was a member. The national organization was known by its members as the Combination. As far as Reles knew, no single man was in charge. When the national crime syndicate was formed, Lepke Buchalter's advice was highly respected among those on the governing board. Others named as influential in the national organization were Bugsy Siegel, Meyer Lansky, Lucky Luciano, Joe Adonis, Longy Zwillman, and William Moretti.

Although Reles purportedly gave the blueprint for the national syndicate or Combination, the specific information in his possession was confined to New York. When William O'Dwyer later testified before a U.S. Senate committee, he stated it was doubtful if Reles knew the names of the top men in the national syndicate. "He knew them around here in this neighborhood [New York]," said O'Dwyer, "but I doubt if he knew them all over the country."

In many cities of the United States there were groups of underworld characters known as troops. Each set of troops was under the direction of a single man. Allegedly, representatives of the troops in various cities conferred, agreed upon certain rules, and defined the jurisdictions of underworld enterprises.

To enforce edicts and to consider charges made against individual criminals, kangaroo courts were held in cities throughout the nation. Charges made against any member had to be substantiated in a kangaroo court, usually held late at night in some restaurant. Even if the accused hoodlum was absent at the trial, a gangster was assigned to defend him. Only one person was authorized to direct the troops of any locality to commit an execution. The sole gang leader who could order executions by the Brooklyn troops was Albert Anastasia. However, Joe Adonis was higher than Anastasia in the chain of command and was considered his boss.[6]

Following the death of Reles in November 1941, other underworld characters have provided varying accounts regarding a national crime syndicate. Usually, their stories can be neither verified nor disproved.

An informant, not identified, told author Hank Messick that the national crime syndicate was created at a meeting of gangsters in the Waldorf Astoria Hotel in the spring of 1934. According to his version, leadership at the meeting was provided by Johnny Torrio and Meyer Lansky, with valuable contributions made by Frank Costello and Joe Adonis. Actually presiding over the meetings was the wily Johnny Torrio. Other underworld chieftains attending the conference included Moe Dalitz from Cleveland, Dandy Phil Kastel from New Orleans, Anthony (Little Augie) Carfano from Miami, Abner (Longy) Zwillman from New Jersey, Paul DeLucia (better known as Paul Ricca) from Chicago, Harry Stromberg (alias Nig Rosen) from Philadelphia, Isadore Blumenfield (alias Kid Cann) from Minneapolis, and Hyman Abrams from Boston.

Under an agreement reached at the conference, the national crime syndicate would not be dominated by one boss. Instead, regional boards would be established to control all activities, and an overall commission would hear appeals and make final decisions. Regional bosses, all equals, would meet whenever required. Lepke Buchalter was authorized to create an enforcement arm for the national syndicate, which would eventually become Murder, Inc.[7]

Early in 1940 special prosecutor John Harlan Amen initiated an investigation of organized crime on the Brooklyn waterfront. In particular, the inquiry focused on six Italian locals of the International Longshoremen's Association that had a combined membership of eight thousand and maintained an office on President Street. The locals were controlled by Emil Camarda, a vice president of ILA and a man of influence in Brooklyn politics.

Camarda and Vincent Mangano had started the City Democratic Club, which had a clubhouse on property owned by Camarda. Active members of the club included Albert Anastasia and Gus Scannavino, who had served on the club's board of directors. Vincent Mangano and Phillip Mangano, both stalwart members of the club, were brothers of Scannavino's wife. Within the next eleven years Camarda and Phillip Mangano were murdered and Vincent Mangano, who had disappeared, was believed to have met a similar fate. Many of the crimes perpetrated by Murder, Inc. were plotted in the City Democratic Club. For some time the president of the club was Dr. Tom Longo, admittedly a good friend of District Attorney William O'Dwyer.[8]

Vigorously pursuing his waterfront investigation, Amen issued subpoenas for the books and records of the Camarda unions. After some litigation the New York State Supreme Court upheld the validity of the subpoenas. Interestingly, a brother of District Attorney O'Dwyer recommended to Emil Camarda an attorney who would institute proceedings in the supreme court for the purpose of attempting to vacate the Amen subpoenas. On the day after the supreme court had again rendered a decision upholding the Amen subpoenas, District Attorney O'Dwyer launched his own waterfront investigation and directed the unions to produce their books and records in his office, which they did.

O'Dwyer's waterfront probe began on April 30, 1940, and on a single night about a hundred witnesses were brought to his office for questioning. Their testimony was never transcribed. On May 10, 1940, special prosecutor Amen delivered to District Attorney O'Dwyer all the evidence in his possession, including the files of the New York City commissioner of investigation regarding the Brooklyn waterfront. Since O'Dwyer had taken over jurisdiction of the inquiry, Amen suspended and closed his investigation. Only a few days later, on May 15, 1940, District Attorney O'Dwyer enigmatically and abruptly ordered the discontinuation of the entire waterfront investigation. It was never reinstated. Later, when asked to explain his action, O'Dwyer weakly replied that his office was so engrossed in the more important Murder, Inc. cases that it became necessary to suspend the waterfront inquiry. Yet, there were strong connections between waterfront racketeering and the Murder, Inc. case itself. In fact, Albert Anastasia, who O'Dwyer conceded was the boss of the Brooklyn waterfront, was the chief executioner for Murder, Inc.[9]

The revelations of Abe (Kid Twist) Reles had created a sensation. The term *Murder, Inc.* became a byword throughout the land. Reles had established himself as an invaluable source of information on the intimate affairs of organized crime in New York and had proven to be a witness par excellence in court. Also being held in custody were three other highly important material witnesses: Allie Tannenbaum, once an ally of the Lepke Buchalter forces, Sholem Bernstein, head of an extensive stolen-car operation, and Mikey Syckoff, known as the shylock's shylock.

To afford protection to its prize informants and material witnesses, the Brooklyn district attorney's office rented the east wing of the sixth floor of the Half Moon Hotel, situated on the Coney Island oceanfront. For over a year, Reles, Tannenbaum, Bernstein, and Syckoff were kept under guard in this portion of the hotel, which was converted into an impregnable fortress. At the entrance to the east wing a steel door was erected that extended from wall to wall. Immediately behind the door was a short hall with rooms on each side; the hall ended in a double parlor. A room on one side, just behind the steel door, was used by police officers on duty around the clock to guard the entrance. Other rooms on each side of the hall served as bedrooms for the material witnesses. The prize stoolpigeon, Reles, occupied room 623, next to the parlor. To serve as guards for the material witnesses, a detail of eighteen police officers had been placed under the command of a New York City police captain, Frank Bals, the head of District Attorney O'Dwyer's investigative staff. On each eight-hour shift, there were five policemen on duty.[10]

During the evening of November 11, 1941, Reles was visited by his wife. They had a heated quarrel before she departed about eleven o'clock. About 6:45 the next morning, the assistant manager of the hotel heard a thud that sounded as if it had come from the roof of a kitchen extension on the ground floor. The noise was promptly forgotten by the hotel employee. Detective James Boyle later said he had made one of his periodic checks on room 623 at 6:45 A.M. and observed Reles in bed. Detective Victor Robbins made another routine check of the room about 7:10 and discovered that the star informant was missing. Rushing to the open window in the room, he saw the lifeless, fully clothed body of Reles sprawled on the kitchen extension roof five stories below. Fluttering about the dead man's body, lying about twenty feet from the hotel wall, were two bed sheets that had been knotted together. The sheets had been attached to four feet of insulated wire, which had been wound around the piping of the radiator in Reles' room. Several months earlier a hotel engineer had brought the wire into the room for the purpose of fixing a radio.

Speculation was that Reles intended to climb down the sheets, enter the room immediately below on the fifth floor, and make his escape. The weight of his body had caused the wire attached to the radiator to give way and Reles had plummeted five stories. Mysteriously, at the time of his fatal plunge, Reles was wearing a gray sweater that had not been a part of his wardrobe, and in his pocket was a new cap. The medical examiner reported that Reles had suffered a fractured spine as a result of his fall. The death was listed as accidental.

Although the police insisted they had discovered the dead body of Reles about 7:10, it was 7:46 A.M. when a Coney Island draft-board official happened to look out his office window and observed a body on the hotel kitchen extension roof. He called the hotel's assistant manager, who then remembered the thump he had heard an hour earlier and promptly telephoned the police guard on the sixth floor.

The sudden demise of Reles was front-page news throughout the nation.

The public was intrigued. How could Reles arise in the morning, dress himself, construct a makeshift rope of bed sheets and wire, climb out the window, and fall to his death while five policemen were supposedly keeping him under constant observation?

Charges of neglect of duty were filed against the five policemen—three detectives and two patrolmen. And at the police department trial, District Attorney O'Dwyer inexplicably appeared as a voluntary witness to testify in behalf of the five officers, whose negligence was responsible for the loss of one of the most important witnesses any prosecutor ever had. The accused officers were demoted and reassigned to the more mundane duties of patrolling the streets. No charges were filed against Captain Frank Bals, who was in charge of the detail assigned to guard Reles and the other witnesses. When O'Dwyer became mayor a few years later, he promptly elevated Bals to the position of seventh deputy police commissioner.[11]

Several theories were advanced concerning the fatal plunge of the star witness. The official position of District Attorney O'Dwyer was that Reles fell to his death while attempting to escape. Yet, time and time again O'Dwyer had asserted that Reles would be killed by the vengeful underworld the minute he left the protection of the fortified hotel. Captain Bals advanced the ludicrous and puerile theory that Reles was engaging in a prank. After descending on bed sheets to the room below, Bals suggested that Reles intended to return to the sixth floor and surprise his guards. Assistant District Attorney Burton B. Turkus, who actually handled the Murder, Inc. prosecutions, concluded that murder by one or two men was the most plausible theory advanced.[12]

In November 1941, the month of Reles' death leap, New York City was in the midst of a bitter city election. The Democratic nominee selected to oppose Fiorello LaGuardia was the ambitious William O'Dwyer. As the Brooklyn district attorney, he had received reams of publicity in connection with the Murder, Inc. cases, although credit for their successful prosecutions belonged to an assistant, Turkus. Helpful also to O'Dwyer's candidacy was the fact that he had not yet been identified in the public mind as a product of Tammany Hall. Instead, his principal allegiance belonged to the Frank V. Kelly machine in Brooklyn. Incidentally, Kelly, the Kings County Democratic chairman, had maintained a close friendship with Brooklyn underworld boss Joe Adonis for many years.

During the campaign O'Dwyer charged that LaGuardia had sought communist support, a charge vehemently denied by the Little Flower. Over the opposition of Democratic leaders in New York City, President Franklin D. Roosevelt openly and unqualifiedly endorsed the reelection of LaGuardia. The president asserted that the LaGuardia administration had given New York City the most honest and efficient government within his recollection. The 1941 election was close, with LaGuardia winning by a plurality of

132,000 votes. Indications were that the Little Flower's popularity was waning. He received fifty-three percent of the vote as compared with sixty percent four years earlier. Also reelected were Newbold Morris, president of the City Council, and Joseph D. McGoldrick, comptroller.[13]

November had been filled with front-page news stories, but they would soon be distant memories. On Sunday morning, December 7, 1941, Japanese naval and air forces attacked the U. S. fleet at the Pearl Harbor Naval Base in Hawaii. The toll was heavy: 19 ships sunk or disabled, 120 planes destroyed, 2,335 soldiers and sailors as well as 68 civilians killed, and 1,178 wounded. On December 8 Congress declared war on Japan, and three days later Germany and Italy declared war on the United States.

As America girded for an all-out war effort, priorities at the local and national levels of government were drastically altered. In the years ahead, Mayor LaGuardia would be overburdened with war-related duties. In addition to administering the affairs of New York City, he was to serve as director of the Office of Civilian Defense, which gave him the right to attend cabinet meetings. He was also designated chairman of the American section of the Joint Permanent Defense Board. His many duties in Washington, D.C., made it necessary for him also to maintain an apartment there. It was inevitable that his performance as mayor would suffer to some extent.[14]

Shortly after America's entry into the war, William O'Dwyer telegraphed President Roosevelt and offered his services in the national emergency. During the first five months of 1942, while O'Dwyer was waiting for his army commission to materialize, the affairs of the Kings County district attorney's office were conducted as usual. This meant that one of the most influential men in the administration of the office was James J. Moran, whom O'Dwyer had made chief clerk when he became district attorney on January 1, 1940. Moran was not an attorney. Nonetheless, he was one of the few men in the office who could authorize grand-jury proceedings. It was commonly understood among the policemen assigned to the district attorney's office that Moran was the spokesman for O'Dwyer. The policemen took orders from Moran. Occasionally an order issued by an assistant district attorney would be countermanded by Moran, whose word was final.

In April 1942 a police lieutenant received information regarding the whereabouts of the notorious Albert Anastasia and one of his associates, Anthony Romeo, a Brooklyn waterfront racketeer. Upon making inquiry at the Bureau of Criminal Investigation of the police department, he learned that in connection with a murder and extortion case, wanted notices had been filed for Anastasia and Romeo by the Kings County district attorney's office. On May 12, 1942, the same police lieutenant arrested Romeo and so notified the Bureau of Criminal Investigation. He was then informed that on May 4, 1942, the wanted notices for Albert Anastasia, Anthony Romeo, and another associate, Jack Parisi, had been removed on the orders of James

J. Moran. Two weeks after Romeo was released in Brooklyn, he was murdered and his body found in a river in Wilmington, Delaware. O'Dwyer later testified that he knew nothing about the removal of the wanted notices, and attempted to minimize their significance.

Anastasia was recognized as one of the most vicious killers in America. Assistant District Attorney Burton B. Turkus submitted an official memorandum in which he declared that it would be a travesty not to continue the Anastasia investigation. Yet, under O'Dwyer no grand-jury or prosecutive action of any kind was initiated.[15]

During the 1930s the Joe Adonis restaurant in Brooklyn was a major congregating place for politicians and the underworld. Both James J. Moran and William O'Dwyer were often observed there. Moran's acquaintance with Adonis went back to his childhood. And for about twenty years, Moran had known Irving Sherman, a shoddy character who was equally at home with Tammany district leaders and big-time mobsters.[16]

During the early months of 1942 an intimate comradeship developed between District Attorney O'Dwyer and Sherman. Sherman was a good friend of both Frank Costello and Joe Adonis, a fact well known to O'Dwyer. Even the glamorous and mysterious Virginia Hill, the onetime girlfriend of Joe Adonis and later the paramour of Bugsy Siegel, fell under Sherman's spell. In 1940 Hill, suspected of being a courier for top-echelon gang leaders, invested several thousand dollars in a nightclub on Broadway. Later she testified that she did not know the identity of her partners but that it was Irving Sherman who had talked her into investing in the venture.[17]

On June 1, 1942, O'Dwyer took a leave of absence as Kings County district attorney and entered the army as a major. Left in charge of the district attorney's office was O'Dwyer's assistant, Thomas Craddock Hughes, who became the acting district attorney. Also remaining in the district attorney's office was O'Dwyer's alter ego, James J. Moran, the chief clerk. During O'Dwyer's military service, he kept in close touch with Moran. In fact, Moran handled O'Dwyer's personal financial affairs, supervised his checking account, and paid some of his bills.

O'Dwyer's first army assignment was with the military police. Within a few weeks, on August 14, 1942, he was transferred to the procurement branch in the air corps and was particularly interested in contracts entered into with Wright Field in Dayton, Ohio. Promotions came rapidly for O'Dwyer, who rose to the rank of brigadier general within about two years. In 1944 he was sent to Italy to work with the Allied Control Commission, and in January 1945 President Roosevelt appointed him to head the War Refugee Board, a move probably intended to advance his political future.[18]

Throughout O'Dwyer's military service he maintained an unusually close relationship with Irving Sherman. Sherman had connections with a shirt manufacturing firm that did business with the navy. He also engaged in a "five percent" business. In this venture Sherman received fees for obtaining government contracts for clients—influence peddling.

Both Sherman and O'Dwyer were in and out of the nation's capital frequently. O'Dwyer later testified, "Every time I went to Washington I went looking for him [Sherman]." On a number of occasions in Washington, Sherman and O'Dwyer were joined by Vito Marcantonio, congressman from East Harlem and chairman of the American Labor party's New York County organization. Obviously, such meetings had a strong political flavor and probably were not unrelated to O'Dwyer's insatiable urge to become mayor of New York City. And as O'Dwyer traveled to many parts of the nation—from Los Angeles to Washington, D.C., and New York—he received numerous long-distance telephone calls from Sherman.[19]

In New York City Sherman owned the Arizona Bar and Grill on Broadway, which served as a hangout for sailors during the war and had the reputation of being a wild place. Sherman also had an interest in the Garment Center Fashion Club, which occupied the two top floors of a building at 1480 Broadway. A dining room and kitchen were located on the club's first floor. By opening a steel door and walking up a flight of stairs, patrons could enter a gambling room. The elevator in the building was equipped with a buzzer that enabled the operator to warn the club of the presence of any unfriendly policemen.

A bookmaker, Sam Gold, had introduced Sherman to John Francis McLaughlin, an employee of the New York Telephone Company for twenty-three years before he was discharged. Sherman put McLaughlin in touch with Frank Costello, who retained him for three months to check his telephone for taps. Sherman also made arrangements for McLaughlin to check the wires of Dandy Phil Kastel, who was staying at a New York City hotel. Eventually, at Sherman's insistence, McLaughlin checked the telephone in O'Dwyer's home in Brooklyn.[20]

Early in 1942 a battle loomed to determine who would succeed Christopher Sullivan as head of Tammany Hall. Over a period of time Frank Costello had cemented ties with several Tammany district leaders. And it was the district leaders controlled by Costello who named Michael J. Kennedy the new county chairman in April 1942. The obligations of Kennedy to the underworld boss were so deep that Costello in effect became the boss of Tammany Hall. Ironically, Costello had never voted in his life. Yet, politically, he had become one of the most powerful individuals in New York City.[21]

Inevitably, numerous aspirants to political office now began seeking Costello's approval and endorsement. William O'Dwyer, who coveted the mayor's office, was anxious to curry the underworld leader's favor.

Arrangements for a meeting between O'Dwyer and Costello were made by their mutual friend, Irving Sherman. And it was through the efforts of

Sherman that Costello hosted a cozy cocktail party in his apartment about mid-December 1942. Present were Kennedy, the new head of Tammany Hall; Bert Stand, the secretary of Tammany; Anthony P. Savarese, a recently elected judge; Sherman; James J. Moran; William O'Dwyer; and, of course, Costello. The host was generous with drinks and hors d'oeuvres and the affair was pleasant. Conversation was casual, although O'Dwyer and Judge Savarese talked together principally about the 1941 election campaign. Others occasionally volunteered comments on the same subject. At the conclusion of the cocktail party, most of the guests went to the Copacabana for dinner.

The congenial group in Costello's apartment was a microcosm of organized crime. Drinking and eating together in a spirit of conviviality and mutual respect were a top-flight underworld boss, leaders of the dominant political party, a district attorney, and a judge. The public did not learn of the party until a few years later. An embarrassed O'Dwyer then implausibly explained that he visited the Costello apartment on an official mission for the air corps. An anonymous letter, he said, reported rumors of involvement by Frank Costello and an associate, Joe Baker, in air corps contracts. The letter was mailed to O'Dwyer in care of the Brooklyn district attorney's office and turned over to him by James J. Moran. O'Dwyer promptly requested Sherman to make arrangements for the interview in Costello's apartment. No effort was made by O'Dwyer to have Costello come to the air corps office for an interview, which would have been the normal procedure. Instead, O'Dwyer gathered under his wing Sherman and Moran, neither of whom had any official military status, and the three traipsed off to Costello's apartment to complete a highly confidential military mission. Although the Joe Baker mentioned with Costello in the anonymous letter could easily have been located, no attempt was made to interview him. And O'Dwyer never disclosed his visit to Costello's apartment in any of his official reports to the air corps.

O'Dwyer's story is either fiction or the account of an incredibly incompetent military investigator. The gangland leader's attorney, George Wolf, has stated flatly that O'Dwyer visited Costello's apartment in 1942 for the purpose of getting his approval to run for the post of mayor of New York City at the next election. Few would question the basic soundness of this interpretation. [22]

All pilgrimages to Costello's domicile were not made by hungry office seekers. District leaders were often ordered to come to the Costello residence for conferences.

In 1942, about the time of the contest for the county leadership, Patrick Sullivan, a member of the New York State Assembly since 1930 and leader of the Seventh (formerly the Eleventh) Assembly District, arrived at the Costello apartment in response to a telephone call from the gangland leader.

Greeting him at the door was Joseph (Socks) Lanza, the czar of extortion in the Fulton Fish Market and the Lower East Side docks. Although Lanza remained in the apartment, he did not participate in the discussion between Costello and Sullivan. Costello told Sullivan to "go along" and promised, in return, to provide whatever help might be needed in a future primary fight.[23]

The underworld was exercising a menacing influence in the political affairs of New York City. In 1943, threats of violence were made against Warren Hubbard, the leader of the Sixteenth Assembly District, in an effort to force him to resign. Patrick Sullivan later testified, "I know he was afraid. . . . I remember discussing it with him . . . it seemed to me to be strange that a leader should be physically afraid."

Congressman James G. Donovan has related that once in 1943 he was present in the office of Phillip J. Dunn and the latter asked him to listen in on a telephone call from Warren Hubbard. Said Hubbard, "Phil, I got to get out as the leader. I can't take it anymore. The boys were in the clubhouse last night and stood me up against the wall, and for my own safety and safety for my family, I am going to resign."

A meeting of captains was held in the Pocasset Club of the Sixteenth Assembly District. Among those present were Samuel Martin and the infamous torpedo Mike (Trigger Mike) Coppola. Martin was informed that Mike Kennedy, county chairman and a Costello man, wanted Warren Hubbard replaced as district leader. At the meeting the name of a man suggested by Hubbard to be the new leader was given to the captains. Coppola interjected, "Just a minute and I will come back and give you the answer." After making a telephone call, Coppola returned with the message, "No, that won't do. We want Mancuso." It was well known to the captains that Francis X. Mancuso had been an intimate friend of Frank Costello for many years.

Waiting outside the clubroom were Mancuso and his bodyguard, John Gaudio, also known as John Avio Scupette, a hoodlum who had been arrested for burglary, felonious assault, homicide, and robbery. Upon leaving the clubroom, Martin walked down the stairs and was physically assaulted by Scupette. Martin's bloody and swollen face required first aid which was administered at a nearby drugstore.[24]

Thus, Francis X. Mancuso became the leader of the Sixteenth Assembly District in the spring of 1943 and would remain in that post for several years until he too was forcibly ousted by mob threats. Mancuso was admitted to the bar in 1912, then held such positions as assistant district attorney, city magistrate, and judge of the court of general sessions, from which he was forced to resign, under fire, in 1929. His friends included many important underworld characters; among them were Thomas Lucchese, whom he once represented on a murder charge, and Lucky Luciano, whom he visted just before the gang leader was deported. His intimate friendship with Costello spanned over three decades. During the years that Mancuso reigned as a district leader, Costello attended affairs of the Pocasset Club, and for several years Mancuso was a member of the inner circle of district leaders who were most influential in ruling Tammany Hall.[25]

The public was unaware that an underworld boss was playing a key role in the political affairs of the city. Then, on August 28, 1943, New York District Attorney Frank Hogan issued a formal statement in which he asserted that Frank Costello, an ex-convict and gang leader, had brought about the nomination of Magistrate Thomas A. Aurelio for justice of the New York State Supreme Court.

Aurelio had received the nomination of the Democratic party on August 23, 1943. A few days later, in keeping with a bipartisan arrangement intended to remove politics from judicial elections, the Republican party had also named Aurelio as its candidate.

The Hogan statement was based on authorized wiretaps that had been placed on Frank Costello's residence, a seven-room penthouse apartment at 115 Central Park West. Hogan's men had intercepted a telephone call made by Aurelio just a few hours after he had received the judicial nomination. The nominee expressed his thanks to Costello, who replied, "When I tell you something is in the bag, you can rest assured." Aurelio pledged his "undying loyalty" to the underworld leader and added, "Now we have to take care of Joe." "Joe" referred to another judicial hopeful, Joseph V. Loscalzo, an assistant district attorney in Queens. Once Loscalzo went to a golf course for the express purpose of meeting Costello and asking him to say a good word in his behalf to Tammany boss Mike Kennedy.

Unaware of the true relationship existing between Kennedy and Costello, District Attorney Hogan indignantly presented the facts to the Tammany leader in the presence of two distinguished members of the judiciary. Hypocritically, Kennedy professed shock, and said he would insist that Aurelio decline the nomination or he would repudiate him.

The Hogan statement exploded upon the public like a bomb. Demands for action were followed by a flurry of legal proceedings. A grand jury initiated an investigation and Costello testified before that body on October 14, 1943. Eleven days later, disbarment hearings against Aurelio were started before Referee Charles B. Sears in the appellate division of the New York State Supreme Court.

From testimony given in the various hearings, the public learned for the first time that Costello actually had made Michael Kennedy the leader of Tammany Hall, thus in effect making himself boss of the Tiger. His political power had grown to unbelievable and frightening dimensions. It was revealed that during the slate-making process, President Franklin D. Roosevelt had talked with Kennedy and urged him to place an Irish Catholic congressman, Joseph A. Gavan, on the judicial ticket instead of Aurelio. With pressure from the president, Kennedy began to waver. This was particularly disturbing to district leader Abraham Rosenthal, a Costello supporter and friend. Aurelio was a constituent of Rosenthal and the latter had urged his nomination. Rosenthal, together with some other district leaders, warned Costello that the Tammany boss was weakening on the Aurelio nomination. The gangland leader stormed over to Kennedy's office and angrily confronted the Tammany leader. In substance, he shouted, "Look, you made me a promise. Now, my word is my bond. Is your word good to me? Are you man or mouse?" The so-called boss of Tammany meekly replied that he would stand by his commitment and Aurelio would receive the nomination.

The testimony of Costello and others at the various hearings on the Aurelio matter had provided New Yorkers with a sordid lesson in civics. The leader of Tammany Hall had been caught between the president of the United States and Frank Costello, and the underworld boss had prevailed. It was anything but a pretty picture.

Legal action against Aurelio failed. He remained on the ticket and was elected easily, defeating write-in candidates.[26]

The public furor over the Aurelio revelations dictated that Tammany Hall take steps to improve its public image. Particularly untenable was the position of Michael J. Kennedy as titular head of the Tiger organization. He was removed and on January 29, 1944, Edward V. Loughlin, a leader of the Fourteenth Assembly District since 1935, became the new Democratic chairman.

The change in leadership did not reduce Costello's influence in Tammany affairs. During the Loughlin regime, two men playing key roles in the Tiger administration were Bert Stand, secretary of Tammany Hall, and Clarence Neal, leader of the Sixteenth Assembly District and chairman of Tammany's Committee on Elections. Neal had known Costello for about three decades and both Neal and Stand were close to Costello. Occasionally, Neal, Stand, and Loughlin visited the gangland leader's summer home in Sands Point. Abraham Rosenthal, leader of the Fourth Assembly District, testified that Loughlin was regarded as Costello's "man."

Following Kennedy's resignation, Clarence Neal had approached Irving Daniel Neustein, leader of the Sixth Assembly District, and instructed him to vote for Loughlin as the new Tammany boss. When he failed to do so, Neal threatened the captains of the district with the loss of patronage jobs unless they ousted Neustein and made Sidney Moses the assembly district leader. Moses soon succeeded Neustein. Moses developed a closeness to Frank Costello and within a few years would serve with three other Costello stalwarts on the steering committee of Tammany Hall. Some of the district leaders and captains asserted that during the regime of Loughlin, everyone around Tammany knew "the boss" referred to Costello.[27]

When the Aurelio story first broke, a *New York Times* article referred to Costello as a shadowy figure of whom little was definitely known. Now the image was shattered. He suddenly was a public figure whose every movement was deemed newsworthy.

On the night of June 14, 1944, Costello entered a taxicab at the New Yorker Hotel and was driven to the Sherry-Netherland Hotel. Shortly after the cab driver had discharged his passenger and was cruising around, he glanced in the vehicle's back seat and saw two envelopes. He pulled his cab over to the curb, retrieved the envelopes, and examined their contents. To his amazement, he found in the envelopes cash in the amount of $27,200. One of the envelopes bore a handwritten listing of the denominations of the bills, together with the initials *F.C.* The cabbie rushed over to a police station and turned the money over to the New York City police property clerk. News of the Costello taxicab bonanza spread quickly. Mayor LaGuardia telephoned the property clerk and threatened to fire him if he returned the money to "that tinhorn bum."

During legal action to recover the money, Costello testified that $15,450 had been sent to him by his Louisiana slot-machine partner, Dandy Phil Kastel, and the remaining $11,750 represented a loan from his brother-in-law, Dudley Geigerman, who was attached to the slot-machine corporation in Louisiana. Geigerman had delivered both envelopes to Costello at the New Yorker Hotel shortly before Costello left in the cab. At the conclusion of the trial, the court held that the $27,200 belonged to Costello but he was ordered to satisfy federal liens of $24,286.90 imposed in his New Orleans tax case and to pay court costs of $166.45. Since Costello had made a gift of $2,625 to the taxicab driver there remained only $121.65 of the huge sum he had carelessly left in the taxicab.[28]

In 1944 Costello's confederate, Joe Adonis, sold his home in Brooklyn and moved to Palisade, New Jersey. For many years Adonis had dominated Brooklyn politics. In underworld affairs he had received expert tutelage from gangland boss Frankie Yale, who was assassinated on July 1, 1928. Yale's immediate successor in Brooklyn was Anthony Carfano, known as Little Augie Pisano, but by 1931 Joe Adonis had become recognized as the boss of organized crime in Brooklyn.

What prompted Adonis to abandon his long-time residence in Brooklyn is not known. Perhaps he was influenced by his lucrative gambling interests in New Jersey where the political and law-enforcement climate was unusually favorable for wide-open gambling operations. Among the partners of Adonis in his various New Jersey gambling ventures were Jerry Catena, Salvatore Moretti, Anthony Guarini, James Rutkin, and James Lynch. Beyond New Jersey, in such diverse places as Saratoga Springs, New York, and Hallandale, Florida, the partners of Joe Adonis in plush gambling enterprises included Frank Costello, Meyer Lansky, Jake Lansky, and Frank Erickson, the most notorious bookmaker in America. With operations in every state in the union, Erickson maintained his business headquarters in New Jersey for several years.

In addition to his huge gambling interests in New Jersey, Adonis was a principal stockholder, as well as a director and vice president, of the Automotive Conveying Company of New Jersey, Inc. Beginning in the 1930s, this trucking company, a common carrier, had been used to transport assembled automobiles from the Ford Motor Company plant at Edgewater, New Jersey, and deliver them to agencies in nine states and the District of Columbia.

Among the more important lieutenants of Adonis was Albert Anastasia. In 1947 Anastasia, who had lived in Brooklyn for almost three decades, followed his boss to Palisade. Only three blocks separated the Adonis and Anastasia homes and the two gangsters saw one another almost every day. They often met at Duke's Bar and Grill, a favorite hangout for underworld bosses, in Cliffside Park, New Jersey. In the rear of this establishment was the inner sanctum of Joe Adonis, which served as a focal point for important underworld characters from New York and various parts of the nation. Influential lieutenants to Adonis in this gangster hangout were Albert Anastasia, Salvatore (Solly) Moretti and his brother Willie, and Anthony Strollo, better known as Tony Bender.

Adonis had been a real power in the Democratic party in Brooklyn, and now became influential in Republican politics in northern New Jersey. In Bergen County, New Jersey, Adonis and associates were big financial supporters of the Republican organization. And the support of Adonis and his crowd enabled the Republicans to control the state for several years.[29]

On May 7, 1945, Field Marshal Jodl signed the instrument of Germany's unconditional surrender in the Allied headquarters at Reims. World War II in Europe was over. A few months later, on August 6, 1945, an atom bomb leveled Hiroshima. On August 15, 1945, the Japanese accepted the Allied terms of surrender; they were formally signed by the Japanese premier and military leaders aboard the USS *Missouri* in Tokyo Bay on September 2, 1945. World War II was ended. American casualties were 322,188 killed and 700,000 wounded. In New York City, 891,823 men and women had entered the military service; 16,106 were killed in action, died of injuries, or were reported missing.[30]

In a sense, perhaps, Mayor LaGuardia was a casualty of the war. He had applied himself assiduously to the national defense effort while, at the same time, administering the affairs of the largest city in America. He had worked himself into a state of exhaustion. When the war ended, the Little Flower was in his twelfth year as mayor.

As might be expected, his popularity had eroded. No longer did his bombastic and theatrical style bewitch the public as in earlier days. In the spring of 1945 a *Daily News* straw poll on possible mayoral candidates showed Jimmy Walker leading with forty percent, William O'Dwyer second with thirty percent, and LaGuardia third with twenty-five percent. LaGuardia had never been popular with the professional politicians of either the Republican or Democratic party and for twelve years had denied them patronage. As the elections were approaching, leaders of both major parties were discussing privately the feasibility of putting up a bipartisan candidate who could beat LaGuardia. Perhaps LaGuardia saw the handwriting on the wall. In any event, he decided not to seek reelection in 1945.[31]

On September 15, 1945, Lewis J. Valentine resigned as commissioner of police after having filled that position with distinction for almost eleven years. His entire career had exemplified integrity. "There is nothing so pernicious in our city," he once said, "as the thief in the policeman's uniform." During his tenure Valentine dismissed hundreds of corrupt policemen and imposed fines on or rebuked thousands of others. Replacing Valentine as the new commissioner of police was Arthur W. Wallander, a career officer who had come up from the ranks. At the request of General Douglas MacArthur, Valentine went to Japan, where he helped reorganize the police, fire, and prison system.[32]

After about three years in the military service William O'Dwyer resumed his post as Kings County district attorney. He had been reelected in absentia in 1943. In August 1945 he resigned for the purpose of running for mayor. Appointed by Governor Dewey to succeed O'Dwyer was George J. Beldock, who was to become a candidate for district attorney in the fall elections. Beldock promptly fired chief clerk James J. Moran and convened a special grand jury that probed into the conduct of the district attorney's office under O'Dwyer.[33]

O'Dwyer's carefully laid plans to become mayor were beginning to bear fruit. At the outset, however, his quest for the Democratic nomination was not looked upon favorably by Boss Edward J. Flynn of the Bronx or Frank V. Kelly, chairman of the Kings County Democratic organization. Bert Stand, Tammany secretary, later told a Senate committee that "Mr. Loughlin, Mr. Neal, and I loyally supported O'Dwyer in his candidacy for mayor. . . . Even in the face of the outspoken opposition to his nomination by Edward J. Flynn and the late Frank V. Kelly, leader of his own organization, we successfully advanced his candidacy and worked vigorously for his election." Edward V. Loughlin, leader of Tammany at the time, later testified, "It was my vote that made him [O'Dwyer] mayor." Obviously, it was a Costello-dominated Tammany Hall that played a major role in gaining the Democratic nomination and eventual election for O'Dwyer.[34]

There were also indications that O'Dwyer was reaping the political dividends from his intimate association with Irving Sherman. Frank Costello conceded that Sherman had talked to him in behalf of O'Dwyer's candidacy. And the American Labor party, once in LaGuardia's corner, now endorsed O'Dwyer. Very likely this support was not unrelated to the convivial meetings in Washington, D.C., of Sherman, O'Dwyer, and Congressman Vito Marcantonio, chairman of the American Labor party's New York County organization. Since O'Dwyer's contrived meeting with Costello in December 1942, everything seemed to be falling into place according to plan.[35]

Opposing O'Dwyer in the 1945 mayoral election were Judge Jonah J. Goldstein, the nominee of the Republican and Liberal parties, and Newbold Morris, who was running on a "No Deal" ticket. Goldstein had been a lifelong Tammany Democrat. Upon his nomination, Morris bolted the Republican party and ran as an independent.[36]

As the campaign got under way, Goldstein charged that during the war O'Dwyer had met with Costello in the gang leader's penthouse apartment, a fact not then known to the public. He accused O'Dwyer of knowing Costello, Joe Adonis, and Irving Sherman. Goldstein asserted that records disclosed a large number of telephone conversations had taken place between O'Dwyer and the gangster-connected Sherman. There were strong implications by Goldstein that gangland bosses had brought about O'Dwyer's nomination and the underworld, he said, was behind O'Dwyer's bid for election. Although many of Goldstein's accusations were later proven true, they were discounted at the time as political oratory.[37]

Also looked upon as having been politically inspired were the findings of the special grand jury convened by District Attorney George J. Beldock in Brooklyn. The grand jury handed down two presentments, one in October before the election and the other in December after the election. The grand jury accused O'Dwyer of having interfered with the waterfront investigations launched by special prosecutor John Harlan Amen and the Department of Investigation. It looked into the strange conduct of chief clerk James J. Moran. It accused Moran with having improperly ordered the removal of wanted cards for Albert Anastasia and some associates. And the grand jury charged that based on testimony readily available from Abe Reles, O'Dwyer's office had a perfect murder case against Albert Anastasia. Yet, Reles was never brought before the grand jury to testify against Anastasia in the matter. In its second presentment, the special grand jury asserted that every case O'Dwyer's office had against Anastasia had been "abandoned, neglected, or pigeonholed."[38]

The O'Dwyer forces attempted to shrug off the charges of Judge Goldstein and the special grand jury as part of a political smear. Nevertheless, the accusations were worrisome. And especially worrisome was Irving Sherman, who, although helpful to O'Dwyer's political ambitions, was a potential source of trouble. As a precautionary measure, O'Dwyer persuaded Sherman to leave the city until the election was over, thus placing him beyond the reach of inquisitive newspaper reporters.[39]

O'Dwyer easily won the 1945 mayoral election with a plurality of 700,000 votes. On New Year's Eve, Mayor LaGuardia and some friends congregated at the home of Samuel Seabury as they had done twelve years earlier. At the stroke of midnight, a great era in New York City municipal government ended.

As LaGuardia stepped down as mayor, it was generally recognized that he had fulfilled his original promise of giving New York City a government without grafters or loafers. He had provided a police administration of integrity. He had fought crime and the gambling racket, which preyed upon the poor. He had restored the financial standing of the city while providing new facilities and services and expanding others. In all, he could say, with justification, to the people who elected him, "You gave me a job and I did it." He also warned, "I don't think they'll be able to break the city of New York in four years, but after that, watch."

The once vigorous and dynamic LaGuardia was now broken in health. Nevertheless, he served as director general of the United Nations Relief and Rehabilitation Administration and discussed its affairs with world leaders. The cancer from which he was suffering was incurable. And on September 20, 1947, the greatest mayor in the history of New York City died.[40]

William O'Dwyer took the oath of office as New York City's one hundredth mayor on January 1, 1946. He entered City Hall in a period of war-induced prosperity. Prevailing economic conditions pointed to a bright future for the city as well as the nation. The new mayor was a man of great personal charm and he actively sought the support of many influential citizens. For a short time he even succeeded in captivating some of his former political adversaries. But as Newbold Morris observed, O'Dwyer "never could shake off the sinister forces which helped him on his way." And those forces were evident in many of the appointments made by O'Dwyer while mayor.[41]

In the police department Captain Frank C. Bals was brazenly promoted to the post of seventh deputy commissioner of police. About four years earlier Bals had won notoriety as the officer in charge of the police detail that permitted Abe Reles to leap to his death from a hotel window. And a "perfect murder case" against Albert Anastasia went out the window with Reles. Actually, the post of seventh deputy commissioner of police had been unfilled for some time and was a sinecure. Nevertheless, a squad was assigned to Bals and ugly rumors persisted that gamblers seeking protection would be required to deal with him. Department inspectors and commanding officers throughout the city complained of a morale problem created by the activities of Bals and his squad. After two and one half months Bals was removed and went into retirement with the rank of deputy police commissioner. Thus he received a pension that exceeded by $1,000 a year, the largest salary he had ever drawn during his years in the department.[42]

To administer the fire department, Mayor O'Dwyer made two dubious appointments. Frank J. Quayle was named fire commissioner and the ubiquitous James J. Moran was designated first deputy fire commissioner. Both men occupied offices on the eleventh floor of the Municipal Building.

Quayle was a product of Brooklyn politics and an intimate friend of Costello's confederate, Joe Adonis. Quayle and Adonis enjoyed having dinner and attending the theater together. In the 1930s Quayle hung out at the Adonis restaurant; here many political careers were launched and nurtured. He was elected sheriff of Kings County and advanced politically with the aid of Adonis.[43]

Moran, before his appointment as first deputy fire commissioner, had been the mayor's man Friday for many years. He had known Adonis for about forty years and had developed a close friendship with Costello. Occasionally, he would drop into the entrance of the building in which Costello lived, announce himself, and proceed to the underworld leader's apartment, where the two men would visit and drink together.

Almost as soon as Moran got settled in his new office, he was in business. And he knew that he had something valuable to sell. John P. Crane, president of Local 94, International Association of Fire Fighters, later testified that Moran "was strong enough in his position in the O'Dwyer administration that if he said no, nobody could move O'Dwyer to say yes." And, said Crane, "Mr. Moran's friendship is very valuable to any man he considers a friend."

But Moran's friendship carried a high price tag, especially to those seeking political favors. In 1946, the first year that O'Dwyer was mayor, Crane handed Moran a gift of $5,000. In 1947 Crane on four separate occasions paid Moran $5,000 and wound up the year with a $10,000 payment. Subsequently, during the election year of 1949, Crane made two additional donations to Moran of $10,000 each. Thus, between 1946 and 1949 Moran received from Crane cash gifts of $55,000. Most of the payments were made in Moran's office in the Municipal Building. Crane testified that he also made a political contribution of $10,000 that he handed to Mayor O'Dwyer on the steps of Gracie Mansion, the mayor's official residence, about October 12, 1949.[44]

The post of first deputy fire commissioner opened up many opportunities to Moran and he was inclined not to overlook any of them. He became the "organizer, major beneficiary, and directing genius" of a huge shakedown racket. New Yorkers found it necessary to pay from five to thirty-five dollars to obtain approval of new oil-burner installations. It was estimated that this racket yielded as much as $2,000 a week.[45]

Not every person calling on Moran in the Municipal Building was concerned with fire department business. A frequent visitor of Moran was Louis Weber, once known as the policy king of Brooklyn, and a tough native Puerto Rican. Once Weber defied Lucky Luciano, who was then attempting to take over the Brooklyn policy racket, and survived a shotgun blast. A receptionist in the fire commissioner's office estimated that from late 1947 to early 1950, Weber visited Moran in his office about fifty times. Also paying personal visits or calling Moran over the telephone was Irving Sherman.[46]

The influence of Costello was evidenced in many of Mayor O'Dwyer's appointments. The public had been shocked in 1943 when it learned of the recorded tapped telephone conversation between judicial aspirant Thomas A. Aurelio and Costello. Aurelio had suggested to the gang leader, "Now, we have to take care of Joe," referring to Joseph V. Loscalzo. As mayor, O'Dwyer appointed Loscalzo a special-sessions justice.

One of Costello's staunch supporters in Tammany Hall was Abraham Rosenthal, leader of the Fourth Assembly District. Costello entertained Rosenthal in his home and attended the wedding of Rosenthal's daughter. Mayor O'Dwyer appointed Rosenthal an assistant corporation counsel. Previously, Rosenthal had been the chief clerk of the Board of Elections from 1943 to 1948 and had been placed in that position by Costello's man Mike Kennedy.[47]

Mayor O'Dwyer appointed Philip Zichello to the post of deputy commissioner of the Department of Hospitals. Zichello was a brother-in-law to Costello's intimate associate Willie Moretti, a notorious gangster who was assassinated on October 4, 1951. When asked by a Senate committee if he could have found someone for the hospital appointment who was not related to Moretti, O'Dwyer replied, "I could have found a hundred. But there are things you have to do politically if you want to get cooperation."[48]

Early in January 1946 Governor Thomas E. Dewey made the startling announcement that Charles (Lucky) Luciano was to be paroled and deported to Italy. Eight months previously, Luciano had filed a petition for executive clemency and freedom with the governor, who referred it to the state parole board. In support of the petition, representations were made that the gang leader had aided the military authorities during the war. In announcing the parole, Dewey stated that apparently Luciano had cooperated with the armed services, although the actual value of the information he provided was not clear.[49]

Luciano's contribution, if any, to America's war effort is still veiled in mystery. His attorney, Moses Polakoff, once explained to a Senate committee that in 1942 the New York County district attorney's office approached him on behalf of Naval Intelligence. It was believed that Luciano might aid that branch of the service and Polakoff was requested to act as intermediary. Polakoff agreed to undertake the assignment provided that he could have Meyer Lansky accompany him on his visits to Luciano. To make the visits more convenient, Luciano was transferred from Dannemora to the Great Meadow Prison at Comstock. During the course of the war years, Polakoff, always accompanied by Lansky and Naval Intelligence representatives, visited Luciano fifteen or twenty times. Other sources revealed that Naval Intelligence also sought the cooperation of Joseph (Socks) Lanza. Because of the influence of Luciano and Lanza over waterfront criminals, it was hoped that interference with the war effort on the docks could be prevented.[50]

On February 2, 1946, Luciano was removed from the Great Meadow Prison to Ellis Island, where he was held while final preparations for his deportation to Italy were completed. He was scheduled to sail on the *Laura Keene* from Pier 7 at Bush Terminal in Brooklyn on February 9, 1946.

Naturally, Luciano's deportation was a highly newsworthy event. The U.S. Bureau of Immigration arranged for a shipboard press conference and every newspaper, wire service, and news photograph organization in the metropolitan area sent representatives. About forty reporters and photographers were accredited to board the ship and were issued passes. They were shepherded into a group by an Immigration Bureau security officer, who was to bring the special guests aboard the *Laura Keene*. Everything had been carefully planned. But the government had failed to take into account the awesome power of the underworld, particularly the waterfront mobsters controlled by Albert Anastasia.

At the pier entrance, the newsmen encountered a solid phalanx of stevedores, each holding a sharp-pointed bailing hook. Notwithstanding their duly accredited passes, the newsmen were prohibited from entering the pier. Reporters who protested were threatened with bodily harm. On the other hand, these waterfront plug-uglies acted as an honor guard for Luciano and permitted his friends to enter the pier without hindrance. Each invited guest had been issued a card that depicted him as a stevedore and served as a pass. Many of the guests were laden with baskets bulging with food and champagne. Envelopes with money were also presented to the departing gang chieftain. A roisterous party lasted for hours.

Among those who visited Luciano before his departure—either on Ellis Island or aboard the *Laura Keene,* or both—were Frank Costello, Joe Adonis, Albert Anastasia, Meyer Lansky, Willie Moretti, Mike Lascari, Moses Polakoff, and Francis X. Mancuso, the powerful Tammany leader. Among others present to celebrate the gala affair, according to a statement reputedly made by Luciano many years later, were Bugsy Siegel, Longy Zwillman, Tommy Lucchese, Joe Bonanno, Carlo Gambino, Steve Magaddino, Dandy Phil Kastel, Moe Dalitz, and Owney Madden.[51]

As the *Laura Keene* sailed from New York and headed for open seas, some officials gave a sigh of relief, believing the final chapter on Luciano had been completed. But Luciano had no intention of idling away the rest of his days in Italy. Early in October 1946 he boarded a freighter bound for South America. At the freighter's first port, Caracas, Venezuela, Luciano disembarked, caught a plane for Mexico City, and after a short stay there chartered a private plane to fly him to Cuba. Arriving in Havana late in October 1946, the gang leader checked into a suite of rooms at the Hotel Nacional that had been reserved for him by Meyer Lansky. A few days later, Lucky moved to a spacious home in suburban Miramar.

Lansky was a man of influence in Cuba. For a number of years he had operated the racetrack and the Hotel Nacional casino. Although he once testified that these operations ceased when World War II broke out, indications were that Lansky—in collaboration with the dictator Fulgencio Batista, then living in Florida—was still running the casino in 1946. And Luciano reportedly paid Lansky $150,000 for a small interest in the casino.[52]

With Luciano in Havana, the Cuban capital became a mecca for the elite of the American underworld. Through testimony given before a Senate committee, it was established that Frank Costello, Lansky, Willie Moretti, Jerry Catena, and Vincent Mangano visited Luciano in Cuba. During an interview with Luciano many years later, the gang leader reportedly stated that Lansky had arranged for an underworld conclave at the Hotel Nacional beginning December 22, 1946. Those attending the conference, he said, included Lansky, Luciano, Costello, Moretti, Adonis, Albert Anastasia, Vito Genovese, Joe Bonanno, Tommy Lucchese, Joseph Profaci, Giuseppe Magliocco, Augie Pisano, Mike Miranda, and Steve Magaddino from the states of New York and New Jersey; Tony Accardo, and Charles and Rocco Fischetti from Chicago; Carlos Marcello and Dandy Phil Kastel from New Orleans; and Santo Trafficante from Florida.[53]

Luciano's reported story on the gathering of gang leaders at the Hotel Nacional does not quite ring true. He referred to it as a meeting of the Council of the Unione Siciliana. A principal subject for discussion, said Luciano, was Bugsy Siegel, who was building the Flamingo Hotel gambling emporium in Las Vegas. Suspicions were that money supplied by the underworld had been converted to his own use. Meyer Lansky proposed that Siegel be assassinated. However, Luciano declared that neither Lansky nor Kastel could vote because each was Jewish.

Many statements attributed to Luciano are replete with arrogance, exaggerations, and inaccuracies, and must be viewed with skepticism. For example, would Lansky be the leader in arranging a meeting of the Unione Siciliana? Moreover, Lansky, a long-time partner of Siegel, had a financial interest in the Flamingo Hotel. All of the officers and members of the board of directors of the Flamingo were Jewish. From Luciano's account, Lansky was the guiding genius behind the Hotel Nacional conclave and was one of the most influential of the mobsters present. In the face of known facts, the assertion that Lansky and Kastel were unable to vote because they were Jewish and not Italian is illogical and highly unlikely. Whether the Havana conference decided the fate of Siegel is not known. However, several months later, on June 20, 1947, Siegel was assassinated in a Beverly Hills house in one of America's most celebrated gangland killings. Following his death, Lansky's men, a Jewish group, took over control of the Flamingo.[54]

For the greater part of four months, Luciano's presence in Cuba was unknown to the general public. American authorities assumed the New York gangster was living quietly in exile in Italy. Then, late in February 1947, the *Tiempo de Cuba,* a weekly newspaper in Havana, proclaimed to the world that the infamous gang leader was residing in luxury in suburban Miramar. Following pressure exerted by the U.S. government on Cuban officials, Luciano was arrested on February 23, 1947, and lodged in the Tiscornia Immigration camp. Eventually, he was placed on board the *Bakir* and after an unusually slow voyage the ship docked at Genoa on April 11, 1947. This time, Lucky was to remain in Italy for the remainder of his days.[55]

During the few years that William O'Dwyer was mayor, the leadership of Tammany Hall changed hands frequently. Not long after he became the city's chief executive, he engaged in a running feud with the top moguls of Tammany Hall—Edward V. Loughlin, Bert Stand, and Clarence Neal. Although Loughlin was the county leader, Tammany affairs were largely directed by Stand and Neal. The mayor fought his adversaries by shutting off city patronage. Several of the district leaders became restless and concluded that Loughlin, as well as Stand and Neal, should be ousted. Some of the influential leaders approached Hugo Rogers, president of the borough of Manhattan, and asked him to replace Loughlin. When Rogers refused, Frank J. Sampson was elected county chairman in March 1947.

The position of Sampson as head of Tammany was a precarious one and before long he was in disfavor with the district leaders, who removed him in July 1948. Four of the most powerful district leaders—Francis X. Mancuso, Carmine G. DeSapio, Sidney Moses, and Harry Brickman—persuaded Hugo Rogers to become the new county chairman. It was explicitly understood that Mancuso, DeSapio, Moses, and Brickman, all intimate friends of Costello, would serve as a supervisory or steering committee and take care of patronage as well as many other important Tammany Hall affairs. The new head of Tammany had known Costello for twenty-five years. And when Rogers was elected borough president in 1945, Costello had hosted a congratulatory breakfast party for him in the underworld leader's apartment. During the one year that Rogers was the titular head of Tammany Hall, it was commonly understood that he was under the rule of Francis X. Mancuso, who was chairman of the Committee of Elections and Organization. In July 1949 DeSapio became the new leader of Tammany. Thus, since O'Dwyer had become mayor, four different leaders had been at the helm of Tammany and throughout that period the influence of Costello had been strong indeed.[56]

A few years later, Bert Stand declared to a Senate committee: "There is no doubt that O'Dwyer assumed office under a certain cloud and he craftily sought every opportunity to build himself up in the public estimation as a crusader to induce the public to forget the grave political charges made against him . . . concerning his official conduct as district attorney of Kings County. . . . O'Dwyer's actions were always confusing, contradictory, and irrational. He changed the leadership in Tammany Hall almost as often as he changed his mind. The public, however, was apparently misled by all his artful double-talk into believing that O'Dwyer sought to reform the organization when actually his only objective was to control it. . . ."[57]

Stand and O'Dwyer had become political enemies and Stand's views were hardly those of an impartial observer. Nevertheless, many of O'Dwyer's actions seemed to fit into the pattern described by Stand.

In the summer of 1948, O'Dwyer waged a fight against Eugene J. McManus, who had displaced Michael J. Kennedy as the district leader of Manhattan's Middle West Side. O'Dwyer charged that, in connection with a judicial nomination, McManus had "run over with the Costello crowd." The mayor indicated he was combating such sinister forces and henceforth was ignoring McManus and would recognize Kennedy as the leader of the district. He pompously proclaimed that he was interested in a new Tammany Hall, one composed of leaders who would provide a decent political setup in New York County. McManus had been tarnished because he had been identified with the Costello crowd. Yet, O'Dwyer had seen Costello hob-nobbing with Mike Kennedy in the gangster's home. He was aware of the Costello-Kennedy role in the Aurelio affair and knew that it was the underworld leader's influence that made Kennedy the head of Tammany in 1942. To say the least, O'Dwyer's actions in the McManus matter were "confusing, contradictory, and irrational." And his public declaration that he was seeking to reform Tammany could be categorized as "artful double-talk."[58]

In November 1948 a presidential election was held in America. Harry S. Truman had received somewhat less than an enthusiastic renomination at the Democratic National Convention and his principal opponent was the Republican candidate, Governor Thomas E. Dewey. Most political observers and analysts gave Truman little chance of winning. Truman embarked on a vigorous whistle-stop campaign, blaming the nation's ills on a "do-nothing" Congress. The nation was surprised, if not shocked, when Truman emerged victorious.

A large delegation of Democratic leaders from New York went to Washington for the inauguration early in 1949. A dinner for the important New

York politicos was held in the nation's capital. And gracing this affair by his presence was Frank Costello.[59]

For decades Costello had been able to command the loyalty and friendship of the top men in the underworld—Lansky, Adonis, Luciano, and Anastasia. He was influential in the councils of the dominant political party in New York City. Aspirants for office at every level of city and county government sought his approval and support. Yet, a coveted goal—respectability—eluded him. Since the Aurelio affair in 1943 his attorney, George Wolf, had attempted to change the gang leader's public image but had met with little success.

Early in 1949 Costello was presented with an opportunity that he believed would gain public approval for him. He was asked to sponsor an annual Salvation Army fundraising campaign dinner. Invitations were sent by the underworld boss to most of the important politicians in New York City and the rate of acceptance was very high. Printed tickets for this posh affair read, "Dinner and Entertainment Sponsored by Frank Costello, Vice Chairman of Men's Division, Salvation Army Campaign, Monday, January 24, 1949 at 6:30 P.M. at Copacabana, Ten East Sixtieth Street, New York. Entire Proceeds for Salvation Army Association. $100 Per Person. Dress Informal."

Acting as official hosts were George Wolf and his wife. Among those attending the dinner was Hugo Rogers, Tammany leader and president of Manhattan. Supreme-court justices present included Thomas A. Aurelio, Morris Eder, S. Samuel DiFalco, and Anthony J. DiGiovanna. Some time later George Wolf expressed surprise at the number of Costello's "friends" on the bench, in City Hall, and in Congress who were so anxious to help the Salvation Army by patronizing the dinner.

Publicity given the affair proved embarrassing to the Salvation Army and Costello withdrew from the campaign organization.[60]

Not long after Costello's unhappy incursion into the field of charity promotion, the political leaders of New York began laying plans for the city elections to be held late in the year. O'Dwyer seemed to be having some doubts about running for reelection as mayor. Some of his critics, including socialist leader Norman Thomas, suggested that perhaps his decision hinged upon the ultimate disposition of a murder case involving two waterfront racketeers, John (Cockeye) Dunn and Andrew (Squint) Sheridan, who were in the death house awaiting execution.

Dunn, a vicious ex-convict, had organized Local 21510 of the Motor and Bus Terminal Checkers, Platform, and Office Workers Union, and was its business agent. For over a decade, Dunn headed a gang that terrorized a large section of the Manhattan waterfront and controlled the rackets on about sixty piers in the Greenwich Village area. Regarded as the brain behind Dunn was his brother-in-law, Edward J. McGrath, whom Joseph P. Ryan, president of the International Longshoremen's Association, had appointed as an ILA organizer. A trusted lieutenant of the Dunn-McGrath gang was Squint Sheridan, an ex-convict who once had been a triggerman for Dutch Schultz. Another cohort, Daniel Gentile, also known as Danny Brooks, had been given the policy racket concession on the Greenwich Village piers. Both Dunn and McGrath were close associates of the elite of New York City's underworld and had ties with some of the city's most influential politicians.

Anthony Hintz, a hiring stevedore on Pier 51, North River, fell into disfavor when he refused to kowtow to edicts of the Dunn-McGrath mob. Early in the morning of January 8, 1947, Hintz was waylaid by three gunmen on the stairway leading to his Greenwich Village flat. Five bullets were fired into his body and he collapsed in a pool of blood. Before he died several days later, Hintz identified his assailants as Cockeye Dunn, Squint Sheridan, and Daniel Gentile.

District Attorney Frank Hogan's office launched a thorough investigation. It was learned that for a period of time before the Hintz murder, Dunn and Meyer Lansky had occupied a suite together in a seaside resort hotel in Hollywood, Florida. Records established that telephone calls had been made from this suite to Frank Costello, Dandy Phil Kastel, Bugsy Siegel in Las Vegas, Joe Adonis in New Jersey, Edward McGrath in New York, Dunn's wife in Queens, New York, and Lucky Luciano in the Hotel Nacional in Havana, Cuba. A few years later, in 1950, McGrath and Adonis shared a suite at the Arlington Hotel in Hot Springs, Arkansas, for three weeks. Obviously, Dunn and McGrath, waterfront racket bosses, had intimate ties with some of America's most powerful organized crime leaders.

Dunn, Sheridan, and Gentile were brought to trial for the Hintz killing and convicted of murder in the first degree. Upon appeal, the convictions were upheld. The governor commuted the sentence of Gentile because of his cooperation with the district attorney. Dunn and Sheridan were placed in the death house in Sing Sing.[61]

In the summer of 1949 Dunn let it be known that in return for a commutation of his death sentence he would expose the crime conditions existing on the New York waterfront. The offer of Dunn to talk may have been worrisome to the mayor in an election year. Four years earlier, in 1945, a special grand jury had charged that O'Dwyer, as district attorney in Brooklyn, had blocked a waterfront investigation and had failed to take any action against Albert Anastasia, the recognized boss of the waterfront rackets.

Although there may have been no connection between O'Dwyer's eventual decision to seek reelection and the waterfront murder case, the time table is fascinating. On June 10, 1949, O'Dwyer stated with finality that he would *not* become a candidate for reelection. Dunn, then in the death house, was attempting to avoid execution by offering to give evidence that would solve at least thirty waterfront murders and provide the names of policemen and politicians involved in waterfront graft. On July 7 Dunn and Sheridan were executed. Dunn went to his death without exposing waterfront criminals or their official protectors. On July 8 Joseph P. Ryan, president of the ILA, visited the mayor and urged him to run for reelection. Ryan, who had close ties with many waterfront underworld characters, had become a friend of O'Dwyer when the mayor was district attorney of Kings County. On July 9, 1949, O'Dwyer indicated a willingness to stand for reelection and five days later issued a formal announcement of his candidacy.[62]

The only major opponent of O'Dwyer in the mayoral election was Newbold Morris, who received the endorsement of the Republican, Liberal, and Fusion parties. Principal issues during the campaign included waterfront rackets, official corruption, and the prevalence of widespread gambling and bookmaking.

On October 27, 1949, the National Democratic Club, located at 233 Madison Avenue in New York City, tendered a preelection dinner in behalf of William O'Dwyer, Herbert H. Lehman, and Charles W. Froessel, Democratic nominees for mayor, U. S. senator, and judge of the Court of Appeals. O'Dwyer's presence caused a few raised eyebrows, for in the past he had assailed the club as a "cesspool" and charged it with contaminating the Democratic party.

At the entrance of the banquet hall, where the honored guests would make their appearance en route to the speakers' dais, was the table of Frank Erickson, the partner in gambling ventures with Frank Costello, Joe Adonis, and Meyer Lansky. Like Costello, he had once been associated with Arnold Rothstein. Erickson was regarded as one of the most notorious gambling tycoons in America, and his presence was no surprise. The seating list brazenly named "Frank Erickson and guests."

As the president of the National Democratic Club, James E. Brannigan, led the guests of honor into the dining room, Erickson arose and shook hands with Brannigan, Hugo Rogers, the Manhattan borough president, and the former governor Herbert H. Lehman. O'Dwyer ignored Erickson's proffered hand and gave a cool nod to Clarence Neal, seated at the gambler's table. The *New York Sun* reported: "Frank Erickson, the big-time gambler who has been known to make politicians do his bidding, demonstrated his power and acceptance in Democratic circles last night as he shook hands with former Governor Herbert H. Lehman, rubbed shoulders with Mayor O'Dwyer, nodded cordially to Police Commissioner William P. O'Brien, and partook of beefsteak with political leaders, judges, and party faithful." The news stories and photographs touched off a political furor but were soon forgotten.[63]

The Republican candidate, Newbold Morris, warned that if New York were to be saved from "plunder and corruption," the voters must throw

O'Dwyer out of office. The warning went unheeded. On election day, 1,266,512 votes were cast for O'Dwyer and 956,069 for Morris.

After the election O'Dwyer, a fifty-nine-year-old widower, flew to Stuart, Florida, where on December 20, 1949, he married Sloan Simpson, a beautiful thirty-three-year-old model. On January 1, 1950, O'Dwyer took the oath of office as mayor for the second time.[64]

As O'Dwyer embarked on his second term as mayor, he was about to face the most turbulent period of his political career. During the election campaign there had been rumbles of an embryonic scandal that might break out into the open at any time. In September 1949 Ed Reid, a *Brooklyn Daily Eagle* reporter, overheard a remark in a bar that a new boss, referred to only as Mr. G., had taken over the bookie joints and actually had been put in business by three top policemen. Reid wrote for the *Eagle* a series of articles that began appearing on December 11, 1949. Although Mr. G. was not identified, the articles reported widespread gambling and the payment of graft totaling millions of dollars.

At the request of Miles F. McDonald, district attorney of Kings County, Judge Samuel S. Leibowitz extended the term of the December grand jury for the express purpose of conducting a probe of gambling and corruption. On January 2, 1950, twenty-nine specially selected young policemen were congregated at the Hotel St. George in Brooklyn and briefed by McDonald on their assignment. Thus was launched one of the most far-reaching investigations of police corruption in New York City history. Directing the probe were District Attorney McDonald and his assistant, Julius Helfand. Both had worked for O'Dwyer when he was district attorney. Because of his arrogant, belittling attitude toward them at the time, little love was lost between O'Dwyer and his former assistants.[65]

The investigation established that a huge bookmaking ring, headed by Harry Gross, had been flourishing in Brooklyn with the aid of corrupt policemen. Gross had once operated a horse-race betting room in Bergen County, New Jersey, where gambling operations were under the tight control of Joe Adonis. Whether the earlier ties between Gross and Adonis played significant roles in the Brooklyn bookmaking ring's operations was never established, but it is reasonable to assume that they did. It was perhaps more than coincidental that a television store on Manhattan's Twenty-fifth Street was used by both the Gross syndicate in Brooklyn and the Adonis mob in New Jersey to purchase gifts for corrupt policemen on their payrolls. The same store also installed and serviced television sets in Duke's Bar and Grill and in the homes of such Adonis associates as Albert Anastasia and Tony Guarini.

Gross was an efficient organizer. He visited police officials in their offices, and there they conspired to divide up Brooklyn into bookie districts. On the payroll of Gross were the commanders and subordinates of at least six police divisions in Brooklyn and the Bronx as well as personnel of the police commissioner's squad, the chief inspector's squad, and, during the short time it existed, the so-called super squad headed by O'Dwyer's friend Frank C. Bals, seventh deputy police commissioner.[66]

Serving as the business manager of the bookmaking ring was James Reardon, a former New York City plainclothesman who had left the force after seven years to devote full time to the Gross operations. Handling the payoffs to the police was Willie Ricci. On some nights he would carry $50,000 on his person as he and Gross met policemen in various restaurants to pay them off. There were weekly meetings between Gross and policemen at a tavern called the Dug Out near Ebbets Field. Police bribes paid by Gross totaled almost a million dollars a year. He had become sufficiently powerful that he could cause the transfer of uncooperative policemen. And if any rival bookmakers attempted to compete with the ring, they were promptly arrested and driven out of business by officers on the Gross payroll.[67]

Policemen of every rank were called before the grand jury and interrogated. Many promptly retired or resigned. A few committed suicide. It was in April 1950 that McDonald first uncovered positive evidence that policemen were protecting the Gross ring. Within the next eight months, 376 policemen retired, resigned, or were discharged from the force.

Among the officers questioned by the grand jury on June 23, 1950, was Captain John G. Flynn, a policeman for twenty years. He was commanding officer of a precinct in which some Gross gamblers had recently been arrested by the district attorney's men. No incriminating evidence emerged and he was not told to make a second appearance before the grand jury. On July 16, 1950, Captain Flynn was on duty as the commander of the Fourth Precinct. He was alone in his office at 7:23 A.M. when he placed the barrel of his revolver against his right temple, pulled the trigger, and committed suicide. He left a note stating that his interrogation by the grand jury had not prompted him to shoot himself.

Mayor O'Dwyer had been using every means available to him to discredit and obstruct the grand-jury investigation. He believed that the Flynn suicide offered an opportunity to arouse public opinion against the McDonald probe into police corruption. Based on oral instructions given at the various precinct stations, every available policeman was told to appear early in the morning of July 21, 1950, at the funeral home at 63-17 Woodhaven Boulevard, where the body of Captain Flynn lay. Mayor O'Dwyer and his commissioner of police, William P. O'Brien, then headed a procession of more than six thousand policemen from the funeral home to the Church of the Ascension at Woodhaven Boulevard and Sixty-first Road. Policemen jammed the four corners of the intersection and the line of officers stretched back for eight blocks. It was the largest police funeral demonstration ever held in the history of New York. O'Dwyer pictured Flynn as a martyr who had been hounded to death by the Brooklyn investigation and labeled the probe a "witch hunt." When that characterization was given wide coverage in the press, O'Dwyer remarked to friends, "This ought to finish that knucklehead who used to work for me," referring, of course, to District Attorney McDonald. At a police department communion breakfast, Commissioner O'Brien piously declared that the police probe in Brooklyn had been inspired by the communists; it was a Red plot.[68]

The grand jury had exposed widespread police corruption. The mayor's constant efforts to belittle and actually hamper the probe caused a growing resentment in many New Yorkers. O'Dwyer was becoming a serious political liability to his party. The powerful Democratic leader Edward J. Flynn flew to Washington for a conference with President Truman. Flynn explained that O'Dwyer's continued presence in New York City could adversely affect the chances of Democratic candidates in the fall elections. It was Flynn's strong opinion that for the good of the party O'Dwyer should be removed from the New York scene, the farther the better. The president agreed. On August 14, 1950, the White House announced that William O'Dwyer would resign as mayor of New York City to take the important post of ambassador to Mexico. O'Dwyer tearfully explained his reluctance to leave New York City, but, he said, "my country needs me." He indicated that he had been tabbed to perform some unusually important and critical mission for his country in Mexico, a mission that could not be discussed publicly.[69]

O'Dwyer's resignation as chief executive of New York City took effect on September 2, 1950. Vincent R. Impellitteri served as acting mayor until November 14, 1950, when he took the oath of office as mayor, having been elected to the post at a special election.

In the last few days that O'Dwyer served as mayor, he made a number of speeches in which he stressed how faithfully he had served the city he loved. Usually before he came to the conclusion in his speeches, he was sobbing. He was also sentimental in other ways. At the last meeting of the Board of Estimate, which he attended as a presiding officer, O'Dwyer handed out raises amounting to $120,000 for some of his cronies on the city payroll. His two chauffeurs, policemen James Furey and Bernard Collins, who were drawing salaries of $5,000 a year, were appointed deputy police commissioners. Detective Joseph Boyle, the mayor's bodyguard, was also promoted to the rank of deputy police commissioner. The way was thus paved for the three men to retire on pensions of $6,000 a year. Citizens' groups were outraged. Following a civil suit, a court held that the promotions of Furey and Collins were tantamount to a gift of public funds to these officers through increased pension benefits, to which gift they were not entitled. Their annual pensions were ordered reduced to $2,575 each, the amount they would have received had they not been given phony promotions.

On the day before O'Dwyer left office, he appointed Lawrence Austin to the position of city marshal. Austin was a relative of Irving Sherman.

Of O'Dwyer's last-minute appointments, none other was more outrageous than the one he gave his alter ego, James J. Moran. It was common knowledge that Moran was deeply involved in graft. Nevertheless, the mayor presented him with a lifetime appointment to the post of commissioner of the Board of Water Supply at a salary of $15,000 a year. Obviously, O'Dwyer felt that he owed Moran very, very much.

According to the testimony of Harry Gross before a grand jury and at police department disciplinary trials, it was Moran who arranged for a meeting between O'Dwyer and about eight of the city's leading bookmakers during the 1949 mayoral campaign. Before the meeting, which he was unable to attend because of illness, Gross paid $15,000 to Moran for O'Dwyer's campaign. Four years earlier, in 1945, Gross had made a $5,000 gift to O'Dwyer's election fund.

O'Dwyer had been gone from New York just a little over six months when Moran's luck ran out. Mayor Impellitteri demanded that Moran resign his lifetime job because of his close and long-time association with Frank Costello and Brooklyn policy racketeer Louis Weber, and his acceptance of $55,000 from the president of the firemen's association. Moran yielded to pressure and on March 22, 1951, he resigned. A Manhattan grand jury later indicted Moran for having organized and directed a huge oil-burner inspection racket when he was first deputy fire commissioner. At the trial Moran was represented by Frank Costello's attorney, George Wolf. Some firemen implicated in the conspiracy testified that before the 1949 mayoral election, Moran had urged them to make extra efforts to collect graft money so O'Dwyer would have more funds for his campaign. On May 4, 1952, Moran was sentenced to twelve and a half to twenty-five years in state prison for extortion and three years in the city penitentiary for conspiracy.[70]

On the night of September 25, 1950, Commissioner of Police William P. O'Brien attended the graduation exercises of 496 probationary patrolmen at the Seventy-first Regiment Armory. In an address to the group, O'Brien stated that his position in the department had become untenable and he was retiring. About five minutes later, Mayor Impellitteri announced that the new commissioner of police would be Thomas F. Murphy, an assistant U.S. attorney who had won fame for his successful prosecution of Alger Hiss. Within minutes after O'Brien's announcement, numerous policemen of all ranks began submitting their retirement papers. Among the first to do so were Inspector John E. Flynn, head of the Confidential Squad, and Chief of Detectives William T. Whalen, an intimate friend of O'Dwyer.[71]

After his resignation as mayor, O'Dwyer left New York City with his bride for a vacation in California. A storm of protest arose in New York and Washington over his nomination to the post of ambassador. Letters and telegrams objecting to his confirmation poured into the White House and the Senate. However, President Truman made it clear that he wanted O'Dwyer to become the ambassador to Mexico and the Democratic-controlled Senate confirmed the nomination. In December the O'Dwyers went to Mexico City and moved into the embassy.[72]

On December 4, 1950, the Brooklyn grand jury returned a criminal information charging Gross and his associates with conspiracy to violate the gambling laws. Gross was also cited on sixty-five counts of bookmaking. Five former plainclothesmen were named as coconspirators but not defendants. When arraigned a month later in the court of special sessions, twenty-three confederates of Gross pleaded guilty and on February 19, 1951, they were sentenced to jail terms ranging from thirty days to three years.[73]

During the course of the long Brooklyn grand-jury probe, Judge Samuel S. Leibowitz and District Attorney Miles F. McDonald became convinced of the need for a citizens' watchdog organization. The head of the Chicago Crime Commission staff (the author of this book), upon the invitation of District Attorney McDonald, appeared before the grand jury in Brooklyn on December 6, 1950, and discussed how the Chicago commission had functioned since it was formed by leading citizens of the Windy City in 1919.

On January 31, 1951, one hundred prominent citizens of New York, including Admiral William F. Halsey and General James Doolittle, assembled in the courtroom of Judge Leibowitz, who read to them a grand-jury presentment that recommended the formation of a New York City citizens' crime commission. The commission, said the presentment, would "concentrate on purposeful and systematic observation of those who are duly entrusted with the conduct of our law enforcement, and on keeping the community informed of the results of this observation." The nonpolitical civic commission was to be financed by voluntary contributions and have no connection with any branch of government. District Attorney McDonald fully supported the grand-jury recommendation and the citizens assembled in the courtroom formed the New York City Anti-Crime Committee. Selected as chairman of the new organization was Spruille Braden, former assistant secretary of state. Subsequently, a highly competent staff was employed, and for the few years of its existence the committee focused attention on organized crime, particularly on the waterfront.[74]

The trial of Harry Gross and several bookmaking associates began in the court of special sessions on January 22, 1951. After listening to the testimony presented against him for over a day, Gross suddenly entered a plea of guilty and his codefendants followed suit. On September 27, 1951, Harry Gross was brought before three justices, who sentenced him to twelve years in jail. Earlier Gross had sabotaged the criminal bribery trial of some policemen when he refused to testify. Subsequently, he did testify against numerous officers in police department trials and eventually his sentence for book-making and conspiracy was reduced to eight years. By the time Gross had finished testifying, fifty-two policemen had been dismissed from the force after having been given departmental trials. And an additional four hundred or more had retired or resigned since the start of the inquiry.[75]

16

THE KEFAUVER COMMITTEE HEARINGS

The late 1940s witnessed an increasing concern over the growth of organized crime throughout America. Powerful criminal gangs were entrenched in many localities and in some places vicious underworld leaders had become political bosses. The problem was by no means new. In some areas it had prevailed for decades. But in the 1940s, there was a greater awareness of the problem, as well as an increased desire by many civic leaders to do something about it.

This attitude was in evidence at the 1949 annual conference of the American Municipal Association held in Cleveland, Ohio. On December 2, 1949, the author of this book, then operating director of the Chicago Crime Commission, addressed the closing luncheon session of the conference. Resolutions were adopted that were intended to lay the groundwork for effective warfare against organized criminal groups throughout the nation. Recognizing that organized crime operations are often interstate in character, the association called for a study of the problem as well as assistance by the federal government. Widespread publicity was given the Cleveland convention of the American Municipal Association, which represented over 10,000 municipalities in the United States.[1]

On January 5, 1950, Senator Estes Kefauver, Democrat from Tennessee, introduced Senate Resolution 202, which was intended to authorize a nationwide study and investigation of organized crime and particularly its use of the facilities of interstate commerce. The resolution was referred to the Committee on the Judiciary and for several weeks there was considerable back-room maneuvering to kill the proposal. The chairman of the Judiciary Committee was Senator Pat McCarran from the wide-open legalized gambling state of Nevada. He was up for reelection and did not want any federal snooping into gambling in his state, home to many casinos owned by powerful underworld figures. Also viewing the resolution with apprehension was Attorney General J. Howard McGrath. He feared that a vigorous inquiry into organized crime in several cities controlled politically by Democratic machines would prove embarrassing to the national administration.

Under public pressure for a full-scale investigation of organized crime,

Attorney General McGrath announced that a conference on organized crime would be held in the nation's capital on February 15, 1950. Invited to attend were representatives of the American Municipal Association, the National Association of Attorneys General, the National Institute of Municipal Law Officers, the United States Conference of Mayors, and all United States district attorneys. President Harry Truman addressed the opening session of the conference and urged federal, state, and local officials to cooperate in stamping out organized crime. The attorney general's conference lasted but one day. It accomplished nothing and many knowledgeable persons looked upon it as mere window dressing, a diversionary move to sidetrack demands for a thorough congressional investigation of organized crime.[2]

In the midst of the maneuvering to forestall the adoption of Senator Kefauver's resolution, an incident occurred which tended to melt effective opposition. On April 6, 1950, screaming headlines reported the twin gangland assassinations of Charles Binaggio and Charles Gargotta in Kansas City. Binaggio was the underworld gambling lord of Kansas City as well as one of the most powerful political bosses in Missouri, and his partner, Charles Gargotta, was a widely known and feared gangster. Significantly, their bullet-riddled bodies were found in the First District Democratic Headquarters in Kansas City. And since Kansas City was the political base of President Truman, it suddenly became inexpedient to oppose Senate Resolution 202. On May 3, 1950, the Senate approved the appointment of a Special Committee to Investigate Organized Crime in Interstate Commerce. Named to the committee a week later were Democratic Senators Estes Kefauver (Tennessee), Herbert R. O'Conor (Maryland), and Lester C. Hunt (Wyoming), and Republican Senators Charles W. Tobey (New Hampshire) and Alexander Wiley (Wisconsin). At the committee's first meeting on May 11, 1950, Senator Kefauver was chosen chairman.

Within the next twelve months, the Kefauver committee, as it was popularly known, took testimony from more than six hundred witnesses, including many of the nation's most influential underworld bosses as well as high officials of federal, state, and city governments. Hearings were held in fourteen cities: Washington, D.C., Tampa, Miami, New York City, Cleveland, St. Louis, Kansas City, New Orleans, Chicago, Detroit, Philadelphia, Las Vegas, Los Angeles, and San Francisco.[3]

Just a few days before the Kefauver committee came into being, a Senate subcommittee headed by Senator Ernest W. McFarland from Arizona conducted hearings in Washington, D.C., on the transmission of gambling information. Appearing as a witness on April 28, 1950, was Frank Erickson, who testified that he had been engaged in bookmaking for thirty years. Although he accepted wagers from individuals, primarily he handled layoff bets from bookmakers. In response to questions, Erickson admitted doing business in all forty-eight states and said his income in 1949 was about $100,000.[4]

Erickson's testimony before the McFarland subcommittee prompted New York County District Attorney Frank Hogan's men to raid the bookmaker's office at 487 Park Avenue on May 2, 1950. Records seized by the district attorney established that Erickson supplemented his bookmaking activities by a partnership with notorious underworld characters in lucrative casino gambling enterprises. In Hallandale, Florida, Erickson was one of eleven persons with an interest in the Colonial Inn Casino, which netted profits of $685,638 in one year. Partners in the Colonial Inn included Erickson, Joe Adonis, Meyer Lansky, Jake Lansky, Vincent (Jimmy Blue Eyes) Alo, a reputed agent for Frank Costello, and Mert Wertheimer, identified as a member of the Purple Gang in Detroit. Records also revealed that Erickson had loaned $50,000 to Costello's 79 Wall Street Corporation. As security, Costello had given Erickson two notes each in the amount of $25,000. Costello, Frank Erickson, his brother, Leonard Erickson, and ex-convict George Uffner were partners in oil lease ventures in several counties in Texas and Oklahoma. Uffner, an intimate associate of both Costello and Erickson, had been sentenced in 1933 to a prison term of four to eight years for forgery and grand larceny. Erickson's records showed that his receipts in 1949 were $343,869 and his admitted net profits $113,460. Between 1933 and 1945, Erickson's gambling operations had enabled him to make bank deposits of $22 million.

District Attorney Hogan called Erickson "the most notorious bookmaker in America" and brought him into court to face a criminal information containing fifty-nine bookmaking counts and one conspiracy count. The evidence against Erickson was overwhelming, and on June 19, 1950, he entered a plea of guilty to all sixty counts. He received a sentence of two years and was committed to Riker's Island Penitentiary, where he was confined from June 27, 1950, to October 26, 1951.[5]

When the Kefauver committee was formed and started functioning in 1950, New York City was in the midst of the Gross bookmaking–police corruption scandal. Before the year would end, not only would hundreds of policemen suddenly retire but the superintendent of the police department and the mayor of the city would find it expedient to resign.

For several months, committee hearings were held in numerous cities other than New York and were accorded front-page attention in the press nationwide. In many places, the committee produced evidence that established the existence of cozy alliances between underworld leaders and local political bosses. And through such alliances, vicious gunmen and reputed killers were able to operate various rackets with impunity. In some areas an organized underworld had a strong voice in formulating law-enforcement policies and actually naming key personnel to police agencies, prosecutors' offices, and the judiciary.

It was not until the early months of 1951 that the Kefauver committee was ready to hold public hearings in New York City. During February and March 1951, public hearings were conducted for eight days and private hearings were held in executive session for three days. Eighty-nine witnesses were heard by the committee and approximately five hundred other persons were interviewed. The committee staff had examined countless documents—books and records, income-tax returns, transcripts of authorized wiretaps, criminal records, transcripts of testimony in previous criminal and civil proceedings. This thorough preliminary investigation enabled the committee to confront witnesses with solid, irrefutable data and elicit meaningful admissions or explanations from them. The extent of the committee's preliminary investigation was underestimated by some of the key witnesses. At the outset, Frank Costello and his attorney indicated that the gang leader was thankful for an opportunity to testify before the committee and thus dispel prevailing stories about his underworld power. In February 1951 former Mayor William O'Dwyer communicated with the committee from his exile in the Mexican embassy and requested permission to testify in New York.[6]

The New York City hearings were televised; through a pooling arrangement with a station owned by the *New York Daily News,* three national networks picked up the hearings. Public interest was far greater than anyone had predicted. Seventeen times as many people viewed the morning telecasts as watched the usual programs. It was estimated that from twenty to thirty million people across the nation viewed the hearings.[7]

Evidence produced at the New York hearings clearly established that close associations and business relationships—legal and illegal—existed in several parts of the country between Costello, Adonis, Lansky, and many other powerful underworld leaders. For several years, Costello and his lieutenant, Dandy Phil Kastel, had been firmly entrenched in Louisiana. Also cashing in on the Louisiana bonanza were brothers Jake and Meyer Lansky. Partners in the Louisiana Mint Corporation, a big slot-machine venture, included Costello, Kastel, and Jake Lansky. Tax returns revealed that Costello's share of the earnings from this enterprise in 1944 amounted to $70,685.33. Managing the firm was Costello's brother-in-law, Dudley Geigerman.

Also highly lucrative was the Beverly Club, a plush gambling casino outside New Orleans in Jefferson Parish. For some time the owners of this place were Costello, Kastel, Meyer Lansky, A. G. (Freddie) Rickerfor, and Carlos Marcello, a notorious ex-convict.

In 1943 the Piping Rock gambling casino flourished in Saratoga Springs, New York. The committee examined a letter written by Meyer Lansky to his accountant. The missive explained that Frank Costello had a thirty percent interest in the place, and that other partners included Joe Adonis, Jake Lansky, and three other men.[8]

Until Benjamin (Bugsy) Siegel was murdered on June 20, 1947, the Flamingo Hotel casino in Las Vegas was owned by the Nevada Projects Corporation, of which Siegel was president and Louis Pokrass was vice president. Meyer Lansky, a long-time partner of Siegel, had a financial interest in the Flamingo. Subsequently, in New York, Pokrass formed a company, first called Consolidated Television and later Tele-King, which was intended to manufacture television sets for installation in bars. Stockholders in this company included Costello, Lansky, Adonis, and Pokrass. Each invested several thousand dollars in the venture, which eventually failed.

Initially, there was a close relationship between the proposed television project and Meyer Lansky's juke-box operations in New York City, New Jersey, and Connecticut. Lansky, together with Edward J. Smith and Wilbur A. Bye, had formed the Emby Distributing Company, chartered in New York on November 17, 1944. It was expected that the territories controlled by Emby Distributing and its experience in distributing juke boxes would aid Tele-King in placing television sets in bars. Emby also employed two mechanics who were believed qualified for television manufacture. The guiding genius behind Emby Distributing was Meyer Lansky, who served as vice president and secretary. One of four stockholders in Emby, Alvin J. Goldberg, was also president of a juke-box-distributing company in Chicago that had close affiliations with top-ranking Capone gangsters.[9]

In 1943 Costello had testified that at one time he was engaged in bookmaking. He explained that he accepted bets and handed them over to other bookmakers, and that he received a commission of five percent on the total of each wager. When questioned by the Kefauver committee, Costello insisted that for at least fifteen years he had severed all connections with bookmakers.

Costello's representations, at best, were only partially true. Perhaps, as he asserted, he was no longer a bookmaker. But his intimate personal and business associations with Frank Erickson, the best known bookmaker in America, had been fully documented. And from testimony elicited by the committee at the New York City hearings it was apparent that Costello exercised a mysterious, if not awesome, influence over many bookmakers.

In 1946, George Morton Levy, part owner of and attorney for Roosevelt Raceway, was warned by racing commissioner Benjamin Downing that if bookies were not cleared from his track its license would be removed. Levy promptly got in touch with Costello and asked him to use his influence to keep bookmakers away from the track. Costello testified that he frequented bars in such places as the Waldorf and in a half-dozen restaurants, in all of them spreading the word that bookmakers should stay away from Roosevelt Raceway. For this service, Levy paid Costello $15,000 a year from 1946 through 1949—a sum of $60,000. When the committee asked Costello what he did to earn this money, he replied, "Practically nothing." Nevertheless, he was unusually effective. Complaints against the presence of bookmakers at the track ceased as soon as Costello was placed on the payroll! It was all very mysterious. Or was it? Perhaps the committee's colorful Senator Tobey was not too far off target when he asked, "Don't you think the real reason that this bookmaking stopped out there is the magic of the name Costello, and when they heard Costello was against it, the rats ran to cover?" Replied Costello, "I don't think so, Senator." He failed to give any other explanation.[10]

From testimony given at the New York City hearings, it was apparent that bookmakers were not the only persons over whom Costello seemed to exercise absolute authority.

In 1943 Willie Moretti, a close associate of Costello, Joe Adonis and Lucky Luciano, was ill and had developed an uncontrollable tongue. Because he could not keep his mouth shut and might spill mob secrets, Costello sent Moretti to California on an extended trip. It happened that during this period District Attorney Frank Hogan's office had placed legally authorized wiretaps on Costello's telephones. Many telephone conversations were intercepted and transcripts of the calls were made available to the Kevauver committee.

When questioned by the committee, Costello denied he had sent Moretti to California to keep his mouth closed. He conceded, however, that he may have suggested to Moretti to "get a rest or go and recoup somewhere." The record of telephone conversations revealed that while Moretti was away, he called Costello 130 times during one five-month period. In some of the calls Moretti addressed Costello as "chief." Once Costello received a call from a man, identified only as Tommy, who asked about Moretti and wanted to know how much longer he would be in California. Costello replied, "Oh, I will keep him out there at least a month more." Even more revealing was a telephone call made to Costello by Solly Moretti, brother of Willie. Solly said, "I spoke to Will, and he is worried about his wife." It appeared that Willie had taken his wife to a country doctor but she was feeling worse. Pleaded Solly, "He wants to come back and take her to a doctor uptown." Costello bluntly replied, "No good. He can't come back now." And Costello's word was final.[11]

The New York hearings dramatically confirmed the tremendous influence that Costello exerted on the political life of the city. The record, said the committee, is replete "with evidence of persons in high political positions going to Costello's home at Costello's call." Hugo Rogers, until recently the leader of Tammany Hall and former president of the borough of Manhattan, confided to the committee during a private examination that "if Costello wanted me, he would send for me."

Responding to questions from the committee, Costello admitted knowing the leaders or coleaders, or both, in at least ten of the sixteen districts In Manhattan. His intimate friends included Carmine DeSapio, who had succeeded Rogers as leader of Tammany Hall, and Frank Mancuso, whom he had known for thirty years. Among other district leaders whom Costello counted as friends were Louis DeSalvio, the son of Costello's long-time pal Jimmie Kelly, and Vincent Viggiano, cousin of extortionist Joseph (Socks) Lanza as well as cousin of former leader Dr. Paul Sarubbi. Partaking of Thanksgiving dinner in Costello's home in 1950 were old friends, Sam Kantor, a district leader, and Al Toplitz, who had served as district leader as well as chief clerk of the Board of Elections. A predecessor of Toplitz in the important Board of Elections post was Abe Rosenthal, another intimate friend and supporter of the underworld leader. During his testimony, Costello characterized Mayor O'Dwyer's righthand man, James J. Moran, as a friend and admitted that he saw Irving Sherman with great frequency.

Based on evidence produced at the hearings, the Kefauver committee asserted that "Costello reached the height of his power in New York politics in 1942 when he unquestionably had complete domination over Tammany Hall." It was Costello who made Michael J. Kennedy the leader of Tammany. The gang leader controlled the votes of several district leaders and was able to influence the votes of others. "Without Costello's support, Kennedy would not have had a chance" of being elected head of Tammany. After Kennedy became the Tiger's top man, some district leaders actually bypassed the titular Tammany boss and approached Costello directly in order to bring about political appointments, including some to the bench. And Costello's great influence in Tammany remained long after Kennedy had been replaced as head of the New York County Democratic organization.[12]

Costello's testimony before the Kefauver committee furnished an invaluable insight into organized crime in New York City. But he provided a partial picture only. Naturally, he attempted to place himself and colleagues in the most favorable light possible. He made an effort to shield his friends who held influential positions. Often he answered questions evasively. When he knew the committee possessed documentary evidence of certain facts, he would make admissions grudgingly, give fanciful explanations, or resort to outright lies.

Somewhat characteristic were Costello's replies to questions about Johnny Torrio, previously the rackets boss of Chicago. Through independent sources, it was known that a close relationship had once existed between Torrio and Costello. George Wolf, long-time attorney for Costello, had also represented Torrio in 1939 and consequently knew both gangsters. Wolf has reported that when Torrio abdicated his underworld throne in Chicago and returned to Brooklyn, one of the first men with whom he got in touch in New York was Costello. And it was Costello, said Wolf, who at that time set up Torrio in the illicit liquor business in New York.

In response to questions by the Kefauver committee, Costello said he had met Torrio only once or twice, had never engaged in business dealings with him, and knew his reputation only through the newspapers. The committee confronted Costello with testimony he had given before a federal Treasury agent in 1938. On that occasion Costello said he had approached Torrio at the request of Irving Haim about the sale of a large liquor company owned by Torrio and had engaged in at least two conversations with the former Chicago crime boss in an effort to consummate the deal. Costello evasively informed the committee that he did not remember what his testimony might have been in 1938. On two subsequent occasions—during the Aurelio disbarment proceedings in 1943 and before the State Liquor Authority in 1947—Costello denied under oath that he knew Torrio at all. Attorney Wolf has stated that he never asked Costello "why he lied" about Torrio. The Kefauver committee reported that "Costello's answers with relation to Torrio are typical of his answers with relation to practically every other matter. He admits as much as he thinks he has to and does not hesitate to change his story to suit the occasion."[13]

Costello's carelessness with the truth was apparent when the committee interrogated him about his naturalization in 1925. There was conclusive evidence that Costello had engaged in the illicit liquor business both before and after 1925. On his application for naturalization, Costello listed two character witnesses as sponsoring citizens. Actually, these two men were in the bootlegging racket with him. Both were described in the citizenship application as being in the real estate business. The Kefauver committee grilled Costello in particular about one of his citizenship sponsors, Harry Sausser. When Costello denied that he had ever known Sausser as a bootlegger, the committee confronted him with contrary testimony he had given before the New York State Liquor Authority in 1947. On that occasion, he stated that Sausser was the person through whom he arranged for the importation of liquor from Canada. Costello unabashedly asserted that he knew two, perhaps three, men named Harry Sausser. And the individual who was in the bootlegging business with him was not the Harry Sausser, the real estate man, who had been the sponsor on his citizenship application. Apparently, as an afterthought, and making his story more confusing than ever, he said that the legitimate Harry Sausser was, in fact, a railroad man and not a realtor as listed on his naturalization papers. The irrepressible Senator Tobey referred to Costello's account as "the tale of the flying saucers."

Costello admitted to the Kefauver committee that in his application for citizenship he had deliberately omitted listing his alias, "Frank Severio." He said he feared that if he included this alias the immigration authorities might learn of his conviction under the name of Frank Severio for illegal possession of a gun and his application for citizenship might be jeopardized. The Kefauver committee expressed the opinion that Costello's naturalization should be revoked because of fraud.[14]

Originally, the attitude of Costello about appearing before the Kefauver committee differed from that of his confederate, Joe Adonis. Adonis made every effort to avoid accepting service of the committee's subpoenas. When questioned about his reluctance to testify, Adonis bluntly stated, "I did not have any desire to appear before this committee then or never [*sic*]." Costello, on the other hand, confidently believed he could parry all questions put to him by the committee and emerge in the public eye as a respectable businessman instead of an underworld boss.

Unfortunately for Costello, he had underestimated the effectiveness of the committee in developing solid information about his background, his associates, and activities. He was confronted with irrefutable evidence of his power as an underworld leader, his association with some of the most vicious gangsters in America, and his role as a kingmaker in Tammany Hall politics. He was unable to give satisfactory explanations for the contradictions that appeared in statements he had made previously under oath.

As the hearings wore on, Costello's credibility was damaged beyond repair and he lost his aplomb. His attorney objected to the presence of television cameras in the hearing room. When the committee ordered the cameramen to refrain from televising Costello, they complied, in part, by focusing exclusively on the gangster's hands. Thereafter, the television audience could not see his face but observed only his nervous, twitching fingers as they grasped a glass of water or played with a small ball of paper rolled between his thumb and index finger. Costello's fingers became unforgettable features of the hearings.

On the third day of his appearance, Costello complained of the heat, lights, and confusion in the hearing room. He asked for a postponement of his testimony, asserting that he was suffering from a throat inflammation and laryngitis. The committee was to expire at the end of the month and it viewed Costello's request as a ploy to avoid giving further testimony. When his plea for a postponement was denied, Costello, accompanied by his lawyer, walked out of the hearing room. On the following day the gang leader repeated his walkout before the television cameras. After opinions of doctors were presented to the committee, Costello was required to testify during shortened sessions each day.[15]

Next to Costello, the star witness at the New York City hearings was former Mayor William O'Dwyer, then ambassador to Mexico. Having resigned the mayor's office under pressure, O'Dwyer stated, "A lot has been said and written while my back was turned and I welcome an opportunity now to . . . talk to not only this committee but the people of this city and elsewhere that are listening in.''

Gray-haired and immaculately groomed in a blue pencil-striped suit, the former mayor exuded charm and was an impressive personality. He was equipped with a prepared statement, which took him an hour to deliver and also presented the committee with voluminous documentary material concerning his accomplishments as mayor. He emphasized his success in prosecuting the Murder, Inc. cases when he was district attorney, and his extensive building programs as mayor. As he delivered his time-consuming self-serving statement, the television audience became bored and many listeners telephoned to protest a continuation of his soliloquy.

After O'Dwyer had completed his prepared statement, the Kefauver committee launched into a thorough interrogation regarding his performance as district attorney in Brooklyn and mayor of New York City. The former mayor obviously was taken aback by the detailed preparation that had been made by the committee to question him. At times, he lost his composure, gave vent to his anger, and appeared evasive, illogical, or contradictory.

During one heated verbal exchange, O'Dwyer sneeringly charged that Senator Tobey of the committee had received funds for his New Hampshire primary and election campaign from New York. He implied that Tobey's support came from bookmakers and indicated he possessed evidence to substantiate his accusation. Senator Tobey was infuriated and when the committee chairman required O'Dwyer to produce his evidence, it turned out to be a form letter signed by Senator Tobey in which he had thanked a New Yorker, a stranger to Tobey, for his unsolicited campaign contribution through the reputable National Committee for an Effective Congress. O'Dwyer sheepishly conceded he had made his charge against Tobey in the heat of passion and there was ''nothing to it.'' The incident merely served to damage his stature as a responsible witness.

In his presentation to the committee, O'Dwyer related that from 1917 to 1924 he had been a member of the New York City Police Department. In 1924 he resigned from the police force and entered the practice of law. The advent of Prohibition, he declared, caused a disrespect for law and eventually brought about the efficient organization of criminals as well as the corruption of the police. O'Dwyer was appointed a magistrate in 1932. As he presided over magistrates' court, the ill-housed, ill-fed, and ill-clad slumdwellers appeared before him. He had an opportunity, he said, to observe the evil effects of the slot machines, which, he stated, he wholly eliminated later when he became mayor.[16]

Throughout O'Dwyer's days as a practicing lawyer and a politician in Brooklyn, underworld leader Joe Adonis was a very influential figure in the political life of the borough. For a number of years, until it was closed about 1935, the Adonis restaurant known as Joe's Italian Kitchen, 260–62 Fourth

Avenue at the corner of Carroll Street, served as a rendezvous for the most eminent politicians in Brooklyn as well as members of the underworld. During Prohibition the restaurant was also a profitable speakeasy. Adonis was on intimate terms with Brooklyn politicians at every level, including the chairman of the Kings County Democratic organization, Frank V. Kelly. Aspiring officeholders learned that the support of Adonis was extremely helpful in achieving their political ambitions.

When O'Dwyer started practicing law, his partner was George Joyce, who, he testified, "was and is one of my dearest friends." Joyce was the alderman from the Adonis district. Joyce and Adonis had known each other since their boyhood days. About six months after O'Dwyer and Joyce became law parners, Joyce received an appointment to the municipal court. O'Dwyer testified that subsequently Joyce was "elected to the municipal court, afterward to the city court, and now [1951] he is a judge of the county court."

In 1932 O'Dwyer actively entered the political arena and succeeded in obtaining an appointment as magistrate from Mayor Joseph McKee. The district leader who recommended O'Dwyer for this post was Kenneth Sutherland, who was close to Adonis. Accompanying Sutherland on his mission to visit Mayor McKee in behalf of O'Dwyer was Jerome G. Ambro, Democratic politician who had once served nine years as state asemblyman and was a former assistant state attorney general. Ambro testified that O'Dwyer was in the Adonis restaurant "very often" and, in fact, it was in the Adonis establishment that O'Dwyer asked him to intercede with Mayor McKee in support of his appointment to the judicial post of magistrate.[17]

In Brooklyn, the City Democratic Club was a hangout for Albert Anastasia, Vincent Mangano, Tony Romeo, and other important waterfront racketeers. Running the club was Dr. Tom Longo, who O'Dwyer testified was his good friend. Rumors were that many crimes committed by Murder, Inc. were actually planned in the club by Anastasia and his cronies.[18]

Obviously, the political climate in Brooklyn was most favorable for Adonis, Anastasia, and cohorts. O'Dwyer asserted that Anastasia directed all the killings committed by the Brooklyn "troops" and Anastasia's boss was Joe Adonis. The Kefauver committee interrogated O'Dwyer regarding his failure as Kings County district attorney to prosecute either Anastasia or Adonis. The 1945 grand jury, in its second presentment, declared that admittedly there had been available competent legal evidence sufficient to warrant the indictment and to obtain the conviction of Anastasia for murder in a matter "described by William O'Dwyer, himself, as a 'perfect murder case.'"

The victim in the case was Morris Diamond, business agent for a Teamster's local union. He had committed the grave sin of visiting Thomas E. Dewey's office in 1938 and providing information regarding the mobsters' stranglehold on the clothing industry through control of transportation. The Buchalter gang decided that Diamond must "go" and the murder contract was given to Anastasia. O'Dwyer's star witness, Abe Reles, had been with Anastasia when the details of the murder were planned. A teenage youth, whom O'Dwyer described as a small sickly boy, saw Anastasia's man, Jack Parisi, actually shoot Diamond. The "perfect murder case" went out the window with Reles when he took his fatal leap. Yet, Reles had been in the custody of the district attorney for twenty months. His grand-jury testimony had resulted in numerous murder indictments. But for some strange reason, the district attorney had never seen fit to bring Reles before the grand jury to testify against Anastasia for the Diamond murder.

O'Dwyer explained that he had not sought an indictment in this case because he feared gangsters might endanger the life of the young eyewitness to the slaying. And following the death of Reles, O'Dwyer stated he could not have obtained an indictment that would have stood up in court. Nevertheless, he said, the failure to prosecute Anastasia should not be attributed to him. Rather, the blame should be placed on his subordinates and Thomas Craddock Hughes, who was the acting district attorney when O'Dwyer was in the armed services.[19]

Of particular interest to the Kefauver committee was the intensely loyal friendship that prevailed between the former mayor and James J. Moran. This type of loyalty was not an embedded character trait of O'Dwyer, who had often demonstrated a capacity for petty vindictiveness and even wrath against former subordinates. He had also shown a proclivity to turn against erstwhile supporters whenever he deemed it politically expedient. Yet, O'Dwyer's confidence in his former righthand man never wavered although indications of Moran's venality and misconduct in office were overwhelming.

O'Dwyer was questioned at length about the propriety of Moran's orders to remove from police files the wanted cards for Anastasia, Romeo, and other racketeers. The former mayor would not concede that the removal of the wanted notices was of any significance.

In response to the committee's questions, O'Dwyer admitted that he could not think of any proper reason why the notorious convicted policy racketeer, Louis Weber, should have made regular visits to Deputy Fire Commissioner Moran's office. The committee informed O'Dwyer it had received evidence that Weber visited Moran an average of about once a week. When asked if such evidence would in any way affect his faith in his friend, the ex-mayor replied that it "would not be enough to shake my confidence in Moran." This blind trust was remarkable in the face of testimony that Moran had received $55,000, euphemistically referred to as gifts, from the president of the Uniformed Firemen's Association. It was also rather common knowledge that Moran was under an official investigation for having masterminded a shakedown racket in connection with oil-burner installations in New York City. When asked if he thought Moran did a good job in his fire department post, O'Dwyer replied, "I certainly do." In reply to Senator Tobey's queries about Moran, the former mayor blurted, "He was a friend of mine, and still is. . . . And I have no hesitation in saying that I hope the senator has as many good friends as Moran has been." O'Dwyer hotly insisted that he felt Moran had fully justified the repeated trust he had placed in him over a long period of time.[20]

O'Dwyer was questioned about his close association with Irving Sherman, whom he knew to be on intimate terms with Frank Costello and Joe Adonis. The former mayor admitted that Sherman had helped him throughout the 1945 mayoral campaign.

The committee was anxious to obtain the testimony of Sherman, who managed to stay out of reach of process servers until the hearings in New York City had been completed. Subsequently, Sherman, accompanied by his counsel, appeared before the committee in a public hearing in Washington, D.C.

Sherman testified that in the 1920s he was employed as an adjuster for the American Cloak and Suit Association. Exerting a powerful influence over the New York clothing industry at that time were the indomitable racket bosses Lepke Buchalter and Gurrah Shapiro. Sherman knew both Buchalter and Shapiro because, he testified, "You had to know them . . . they would make you do that." Between 1937 and 1940, Sherman was in California where he became very friendly with Bugsy Siegel. The two men visited racetracks and other places together.

In 1940 Sherman returned to New York City as the general manager of the Phono-Vision Company. This firm provided a slot-machine type of projector that enabled a customer to deposit ten cents and view a movie of his selection. Sherman said that he entered into negotiations with Frank Costello, who was interested in gaining the Phono-Vision distributorship in Louisiana for his partner, Dandy Phil Kastel. While the negotiations were in progress, Costello came to Sherman's office "once or twice a week for quite some time."

In addition to knowing Buchalter, Sharpiro, Siegel, and Costello, Sherman admitted knowing Meyer Lansky, Joe Adonis, James (Niggy) Rutkin, and Joe Stacher, among others. Obviously, his coterie of friends and acquaintances included a number of the most notorious gangsters in America.

Sherman testified that for several years he was very friendly with William O'Dwyer and attended the highly publicized meeting in Costello's apartment in 1942. He indicated that arrangements for this affair were made by Moran. It was not until afterward that he learned what the meeting concerned. Sherman related he was detained at the bar by Mrs. Costello and gained the impression that he was not wanted in the "huddle," which included Costello and O'Dwyer. During the war years Sherman and O'Dwyer socialized in Washington, D.C., and made arrangements to stay simultaneously at the Mayflower Hotel on fifteen occasions.

Sherman confirmed that he had worked strenuously in behalf of O'Dwyer's candidacy during the 1945 mayoral campaign. He urged people in the garment industry to do everything within their power to help O'Dwyer win the election. He also collected several thousand dollars, which were turned over to the O'Dwyer campaign fund.

Shortly before the election, Sherman received an urgent message from O'Dwyer asking him to leave the city immediately in order to make himself unavailable to the press. Sherman testified that O'Dwyer feared a newspaper "blast" would link Sherman to O'Dwyer on the one hand, and to Costello and Siegel on the other. On the very next morning, Sherman departed with his family on an extended trip that eventually ended in Florida, where he remained until the campaign was over. When asked why he would make such a sacrifice for O'Dwyer, Sherman replied, "Because the man asked me to, and I thought enough of him to do it."

Upon Sherman's return to New York City following the election, O'Dwyer refused to see his loyal friend. And when Sherman visited Moran in the Municipal Building, he used the fictitious name of Dr. Cooper. Sherman had helped O'Dwyer achieve his goal of becoming mayor and his immediate usefulness had ended. Apparently, the mayor feared that a continuation of his open association with Sherman, the known friend of underworld bigwigs, might prove harmful to his future political aspirations. Under such circumstances, O'Dwyer never had any qualms about turning against friends and erstwhile supporters. Moran seemed to be a notable exception.[21]

Following the New York hearings, the Kefauver committee observed that beginning with O'Dwyer's days as district attorney and through his tenure as mayor, a single pattern emerged from his official activities regarding gambling, waterfront rackets, murder, and police corruption: "No matter what the motivation of his choice, action, or inaction, it often seemed to result favorably for the men suspected of being high up in the rackets."

The committee also noted: "Toward other official agencies engaged in law enforcement or investigation, Mr. O'Dwyer exhibited a sometimes antagonistic attitude." He blocked the waterfront investigation by John Harlan Amen, the special prosecutor. He publicly branded District Attorney Miles F. McDonald's grand-jury probe into gambling and police corruption a "witch hunt," and created roadblocks intended to hamper the investigation.

The committee declared that at every stage in O'Dwyer's career, "the tendency to blame others for the ineffectualness of official efforts to curb the rackets and the ensuing corruption has also turned up very often. . . . ''

According to O'Dwyer, observed the committee, "California was to blame for not turning up sufficient evidence against Siegel. Amen had Adonis under arrest and had access to Reles; why didn't he act? Why didn't Amen resume the waterfront investigation after he, O'Dwyer, suspended it? Why did not his successor, the acting district attorney, move against the waterfront rackets? As mayor he depended upon his subordinates; if there was any laxity, they were at fault." Thus O'Dwyer attempted to place the blame for all failures on everyone but himself.[22]

From the New York City hearings, the Kefauver committee concluded that Frank Costello had "close personal friendships, working relationships, and mutual financial interests with leading racketeers in the city, state, and nation." And, averred the committee, Costello, Joe Adonis, and Meyer Lansky "formed the eastern axis of a combination of racketeers working throughout the nation."

Furthermore, said the committee, "There can be no question that Frank Costello has exercised a major influence upon the New York County Democratic organization, Tammany Hall, because of his personal friendships and working relationships with its officers, and with Democratic district leaders even today [1951] in ten of the sixteen Manhattan districts." He maintained helpful connections with some Republican leaders as well.

On several occasions following O'Dwyer's election as mayor in 1945, he made public statements deploring the sinister influences in Tammany Hall. And he admitted that Costello was a dominating influence behind venal Tammany leaders. However, the committee pointed out that despite O'Dwyer's frequent castigations of Tammany Hall and his acknowledgment of Costello's sinister influence, the former mayor had been "on terms of intimate friendship with persons who were close friends of Costello." Many of O'Dwyer's intimate friends were also close friends of Joe Adonis. And O'Dwyer "appointed friends of both Costello and Adonis to high public office."[23]

Based on its investigation nationally, the Kefauver committee concluded that "crime is on a syndicated basis to a substantial extent in many cities. The two major crime syndicates in this country are the Accardo-Guzik-Fischetti syndicate, whose headquarters are Chicago; and the Costello-Adonis-Lansky syndicate, based in New York. Evidence of the operations of the Accardo-Guzik-Fischetti syndicate was found by the committee in such places as Chicago, Kansas City, Dallas, Miami, Las Vegas, and the West Coast. Evidence of the Costello-Adonis-Lansky operations was found in New York City, Saratoga, Bergen County (New Jersey), New Orleans, Miami, Las Vegas, the West Coast, and Havana, Cuba. These syndicates, as well as other criminal gangs throughout the country, enter profitable relationships with each other. There is also a close personal, financial, and social relationship between top-level mobsters in different areas of the country."[24]

"In the *opinion* of the committee," there existed "a sinister criminal organization known as the Mafia operating throughout the country, with ties in other nations." This organization was described as the direct descendant of the Mafia that originated in Sicily, but it was explained that present-day membership is not limited to Sicilians. The committee referred to the Mafia as the binder which tied together "the two major criminal syndicates as well as numerous other criminal groups throughout the country."

It is significant that the committee's discussion of the Mafia was based on opinion and had no factual foundation. The committee also equated the Mafia in this country with the Black Hand and the Unione Siciliana, a viewpoint that is erroneous. It is conceded that "the committee found it difficult to obtain reliable data concerning the extent of Mafia operations, the nature of the Mafia organization, and the way it presently operates." Notwithstanding its inability to develop any reliable data whatever concerning the Mafia, "the committee is inclined to agree with the opinion of experienced police officers and narcotics agents who believe" in the existence of a nationwide crime syndicate known as the Mafia with international ramifications. Hence, it is obvious the committee, without supporting data, arrived at an opinion concerning the Mafia that was based on an opinion of others.[25]

The committee found that the tremendous profits made by crime syndicates stem from their ability to establish monopolies for the illegal operations in which they are engaged. The monopolies were secured by persuasion, intimidation, violence, and murder. In some cities "law-enforcement officials aided and protected gangsters and racketeers to maintain their monopolistic position in particular rackets. Mobsters who attempted to compete with these entrenched criminal groups found that they and their followers were being subjected to arrest and prosecution while protected gang operations were left untouched."

"Gambling profits," the committee said, "are the principal support of big-time racketeering and gangsterism." And, said the committee, "The legalization of gambling would not terminate the widespread predatory activities of criminal gangs and syndicates."

In many places, the committee determined that wide-open gambling operations and racketeering conditions were supported by "out and out corruption." Venal public officials had "the effrontery to testify before the committee that they were elected on 'liberal' platforms calling for wide-open towns." The committee believed "these officials were put in office by gamblers and with gamblers' money." In the few cases where the public was convinced that gambling was good for business, this myth, said the committee, "was deliberately propagated by the paid publicists of the gambling interests."

"Mobsters and racketeers," the committee said, "have been assisted by some tax accountants and tax lawyers in defrauding the government." And in different parts of the country, there are a number of lawyers "whose relations to organized criminal gangs and individual mobsters pass the line of reasonable representation. Such lawyers become true 'mouthpieces' for the mob. In individual cases, they have become integral parts of the criminal conspiracy of their clients."

The committee uncovered "evidence of the infiltration by organized criminals into legitimate business . . . particularly in connection with the sale and distribution of liquor, real estate operations, nightclubs, hotels, automobile agencies, restaurants, taverns, cigarette-vending companies, jukebox concerns, laundries, the manufacture of clothing, and the transmission of racing and sport news. In some areas of legitimate activity, the committee . . . found evidence of the use by gangsters of the same methods of intimidation and violence as are used to secure monopolies in criminal enterprise."

The committee also received "testimony showing that unions are used in the aid of racketeers and gangsters, particularly on the New York waterfront."[26]

THE NEW YORK WATERFRONT HEARINGS

For decades the New York waterfront had been a cesspool of lawlessness. Extortion, murder, wholesale thievery, and corruption abounded. It was a center of organized crime.

In 1948 Malcolm Johnson fired a journalistic broadside in a series of articles, "Crime on the Waterfront," which won him a Pulitzer Prize. Numerous responsible civic leaders had publicly deplored the conditions on the waterfront. Nevertheless, officials sat on their hands and did nothing. The 1945 grand jury had accused District Attorney William O'Dwyer of thwarting a waterfront investigation. And during the 1949 mayoral campaign, the waterfront became a political issue.

Following his reelection as mayor, O'Dwyer, in 1950, appointed a committee of about fifty persons to make a study of the waterfront. Known as the Mayor's Joint Committee on Port Industry, it made an examination of the physical and economic conditions prevailing at the port. Named as one of eleven members of a subcommittee on labor conditions affecting waterfront commerce was Joseph P. Ryan, life president of the International Longshoremen's Association (ILA). Ryan, artful in the dark mysteries of politics, had maintained close friendships with important figures at every level of government. He was the chief executive officer of the ILA locals, including those controlled by some of the most vicious criminals in America. It is not surprising that the subcommittee report signed by Ryan and four other men made no mention of crime conditions existing in the Port of New York.[1]

The Kefauver committee reported that racketeers were "firmly entrenched along New York City's waterfront with the resulting extortions, shakedowns, kickbacks from wages, payroll padding, gangster infiltration of unions, and large-scale gambling." And the committee named Albert Anastasia as the gangster who appeared to be "the key to waterfront racketeering in New York."[2]

Undoubtedly, the person who inspired the most fear on the waterfront was Umberto (Albert) Anastasia. Born in Italy, he was one of nine brothers, of whom five jumped ship in the United States, where they took up residence illegally. Albert informed the Kefauver committee that he was only fourteen years old when he came to this country from Italy in 1917. He never attended school. Instead, he worked as a longshoreman until about 1919. For twenty-nine years he lived in Brooklyn before moving to New Jersey.

Albert's brother Anthony testified that he was a sixteen-year-old seaman when he jumped ship in New York. He became a longshoreman, was active in the ILA, and eventually became a hiring foreman for the prestigious Jarka Stevedoring Company. At one time he was the proprietor of the A. A. Stevedoring Company, the "A. A." standing for Anthony Anastasia. Both Albert and Anthony were active in various waterfront affairs. The Long-shoremen's Clerks' and Checkers' Social Club was commonly known as Tony Anastasia's club. And the City Democratic Club was virtually owned by the Anastasia crowd. When it was formed all officials of the six Italian locals in Brooklyn were ordered to join. Souvenir programs for the annual City Democratic Club balls list Albert Anastasia as a committee head and disclose that he contributed money for full-page advertisements.

Anthony had been charged with such offenses as homicide and felonious assault but was not convicted. Because he had entered the United States illegally, he was ineligible to become a citizen. Hence, he took a trip to Italy, returned by way of Canada, and through the American embassy in Toronto he was able to make arrangements to reenter this country, legally. In 1940 he became a naturalized citizen.[3]

Another brother, Gerardo (Jerry), also a longshoreman, was active in the ILA and served as a business agent of Local 338-1, one of six Italian ILA locals reputedly under the thumb of brother Albert. About 1950 Gerardo was named an ILA delegate. At one time Gerardo was employed as a foreman by Anthony Anastasia in the A. A. Stevedoring Company. This firm, Gerardo testified, had a contract with the Army Engineers. Jerry Anastasia was involved in waterfront rackets and on three occasions was convicted of bookmaking.

A fourth brother, Joseph, upheld the Anastasia tradition when he won a discharge following his arrest for homicide in 1925. Although deported, he soon returned to American shores and with the help of his brothers became a boss of a pier on the North River. Cargo was stolen "by the ton" from this pier and Joseph was fired. But the ILA promptly forced his reinstatement.

Salvatore, another brother who came to the United States, was a priest and settled in New York City.[4]

Albert Anastasia, often labeled the boss of the waterfront, was a disciple of violence. Several times he had been charged with murder but always beat the rap. In the early 1920s he was actually convicted of murder and sentenced to death. Upon appeal, the conviction was reversed and the indictment against him dismissed. In 1923, after conviction for carrying a gun in violation of the Sullivan law, he received a sentence to a New York penitentiary for twenty-seven months.

In 1939 a crusading longshoreman, Peter Panto, began a drive to improve conditions on the Brooklyn waterfront. He attracted a substantial following and incurred the wrath of Albert Anastasia. Panto was garroted and buried in quicklime in Lyndhurst, New Jersey, where his corpse was located in 1941. Albert Tannenbaum, the prize Murder, Inc. informant, asserted that it was Albert who engineered the murder of Panto.[5]

In response to questioning by the Kefauver committee, Albert Anastasia insisted that he could not remember any job he had held between 1919 and 1942. In 1942 he volunteered for service in the U.S. Army. Notwithstanding his evil reputation and criminal background, he was accepted, was attached to the Eighty-eighth Division at Camp Forrest, Tennessee, and attained the rank of sergeant. When his unit went overseas, Albert was left behind at Indian Town Gap, Pennsylvania, were he was assigned to transportation. Because of his service in the army, Albert became a naturalized citizen in 1943.

Following his discharge from the army, Albert worked for his stevedore brother, Anthony, for about four to six months. He testified, "I was a stevedore superintendent, and hired people to work." Somewhat inconsistently, he explained, "A superintendent is above the hire foreman. The hire foreman designates the men in the gangs and the superintendent walks around the pier and sees that they do their work."

In 1948 Albert Anastasia and a partner, Harry Strauss, entered the dress manufacturing business under the firm name of Madison Dress Company in Hazelton, Pennsylvania. But Albert's principal business was murder—the chief executioner for the mob.[6]

In the fall of 1951 the Port of New York was paralyzed by the longest and most costly strike in its history. Freight was backed up for weeks and the economic repercussions were international in scope. In the midst of the crisis the New York City Anti-Crime Committee, on October 29, 1951, forwarded a dispatch to Governor Thomas E. Dewey in which it was urged that the governors of New York and New Jersey take bistate action to wipe out the gangsters and their corrupt associates in control of many ILA unions.[7]

On November 20, 1951, Governor Dewey ordered the New York State Crime Commission to conduct a sweeping investigation of conditions in the Port of New York. Pursuant to an agreement between Governor Dewey of New York and Governor Alfred E. Driscoll of New Jersey, close cooperation was to be maintained between the authorities of both states. Public hearings were held by the New York State Crime Commission beginning in December 1952 and ending in March 1953. And beginning late in March 1953 and ending in June 1953, hearings on the New York–New Jersey waterfront were conducted by a subcommittee of the Committee on Interstate and Foreign Commerce of the United States Senate.[8]

The Port of New York, the greatest in the world, has been described as an outlaw frontier. For many years, pier facilities representing an investment of almost a billion dollars were under the control of gangsters, many of whom were ex-convicts and murderers. At the time of the hearings, the waterfront of the port had over seven hundred miles of shoreline. Of some three hundred deep-sea piers, the city of New York owned 159. The port area included piers in the Hudson River, the East River, in Brooklyn, Staten Island, and New Jersey. In 1948, 19.3 percent in tonnage of all exports and imports of the United States passed through the Port of New York and represented a value of over seven billion dollars. During the course of a year, it was estimated that forty thousand individuals worked from time to time as longshoremen at the port.[9]

Men seeking work at the Port of New York were under the thumb of an antiquated and vicious "shape-up" system, which had existed from time immemorial. This system contributed greatly to perpetuating conditions of crime and racketeering on the waterfront.

At the shape-up, prospective dock workers would gather in a large semicircle around the hiring foreman at a pier. The hiring foreman selected the men he wished to hire and then "blew the whistle." The men hired would file into the pier and those not selected would drift away. At active piers there developed the procedure of hiring a gang as a unit at the shape-up. Under this method the composition of the group was determined by the gang boss. Upon the arrival of a vessel, the hiring foreman decided how many gangs he would need and at the shape-up would simply call out a gang number or the name of a gang boss.

A commonplace abuse that arose from the shape-up was a kickback racket. Men expecting to receive a favorable nod from a hiring foreman were required to kick back from ten to twenty percent of their wages. Workers on the piers were often in need of money. And always readily available to meet their needs were the rapacious loan sharks. These parasites were included in the ranks of the never-ending stream of racketeers who found the waterfront a lucrative field of operations.

Under the shape-up system, the key position on the pier was held by the hiring foreman. As a practical matter, it was in him that the dock workers' right of survival was vested. The prerogative to select and control the hiring foreman was of vital importance. And the contract between the New York Shipping Association and the ILA specifically provided that the employer had the sole discretion to designate the hiring foreman. But in practice this provision was meaningless.[10]

For a number of years the largest stevedoring company in the United States was the Jarka Corporation. Notwithstanding its contractual right to select its own hiring foreman, the Jarka Corporation was forced to hire Albert Anastasia's brother, Anthony, as a hiring foreman on a Brooklyn pier. Philip George O'Reilly, vice president of Jarka, testified, "We did not want him . . . we had a new client, Alcoa . . . and I went down to the pier. . . . There was just a chant of 'We want Tony. We want Tony' from the boys. . . . Now, the five gangs that were down there I fought for two days. . . ." O'Reilly was warned against trying to have the ship loaded unless Anthony Anastasia was named hiring foreman. And every top official of the ILA, including its president, Joseph P. Ryan, backed the demand that Anthony Anastasia be employed. Faced with the prospect of a prolonged work stoppage, the Jarka Corporation capitulated. Anthony Anastasia was accepted as its hiring foreman on the pier.

The Jarka Corporation also found it necessary to employ the notorious Albert Ackalitis as its hiring foreman on a pier in Manhattan. Insisting upon the employment of Ackalitis was Jerry Hickey, business agent of ILA Local 1258. Hickey himself had a record that included a conviction for possession of a gun and an arrest for grand larceny. Ackalitis had been a leading member of a gang of machinegunners and robbers known as the Arsenal Mob, which was rounded up by the police in 1936. He was sentenced to a term of seven to fourteen years in Sing Sing. Previously, sizable sentences had been imposed on him for receiving stolen property and attempted burglary. After his parole in 1948 Ackalitis became a hiring foreman for the Jarka Corporation at one of the busiest piers in Manhattan.[11]

The employment of Anthony Anastasia and Albert Ackalitis as hiring foremen merely continued a well-established pattern. With the backing of the ILA, many of the toughest criminals on the waterfront served as hiring foremen and held other key positions as well. This situation was well known to responsible officials. Following an inquiry into conditions on three North River piers, the commissioner of marine and aviation, G. Joseph Minetti, directed a letter to Mayor O'Dwyer on December 3, 1948. In it he stated, "The tenant does not have . . . freedom of choice in selecting the shaping boss, shipping and receiving clerks, and the checkers. As a result of this condition . . . the local union representatives are in a position to assume control of loading and unloading, and pier operations in general. This latter situation results in greater theft and pilferage because of the type of some of the men employed. . . . There is substantial theft and pilferage on the piers because of lack of control in hiring."[12]

Contributing greatly to racketeering on the waterfront were the public loaders. The pier loaders required shippers to pay them even though the actual loading was performed by the shippers' own employees. Father John M. Corridan, associate director of the Xavier Institute of Industrial Relations in New York City and a studious observer of the waterfront since 1930, testified, "The loading and the shape are . . . the two points of entry into which the racketeers came, starting with World War I. The key place on the waterfront is in front of the pier, that is, where the loading takes place. It is by and large a mob operation in many parts of the port.'' As far back as the early 1930s the chairman of the shippers' conference had charged that the ILA union loaders ''with the banner of God and their union in one hand, and an iron pipe in the other, stand between the merchants and their trucks and defy them to take away their freight.''

In a ''legislative findings of fact'' the legislatures of New York and New Jersey declared in 1953 that public loaders ''serve no valid economic purpose and operate as parasites, exacting a high and unwarranted toll on the flow of commerce in and through the Port of New York district, and have used force and engaged in discriminatory and coercive practices, including extortion against persons not desiring to employ them. . . . The function of loading and unloading trucks and other land vehicles at piers and other waterfront terminals can and should be performed, as in every other major American port, without the evils and abuses of the public loader system. . . .''[13]

The powerful International Longshoremen's Association, headed by Joseph P. Ryan, president, and affiliated with the American Federation of Labor, claimed jurisdiction over the loading and unloading operations of all floating structures in the United States and its possessions, in Canada, and in Central and South America. However, there was a chink in its armor. In 1936 Ryan had fired Harry Bridges as an ILA organizer of the Pacific Coast division. The West Coast longshoremen remained loyal to Bridges, seceded from the ILA headed by Ryan, organized the International Longshoremen and Warehousemen's Association, elected Bridges as president, and joined the Congress of Industrial Organization (CIO).[14]

Nevertheless, Joseph P. Ryan was one of the more powerful labor leaders in America. His career on the New York waterfront started in 1912, when he became a longshoreman. Within a few months he suffered an injury. Shortly thereafter he was elected financial secretary of Local 791 and never again performed any actual work on the docks. In 1927 Ryan was elected president of the ILA. From 1928 to 1938 he also served as chairman of the AFL Central Labor Council of New York. As a result, his prestige was enhanced locally as well as nationally. In 1943 he was named honorary life president of ILA, a title that was reaffirmed in the 1947 and 1951 ILA conventions.

Ryan was a shrewd politician and always maintained close relationships with Tammany Hall leaders and the national Democratic organization as well. Counted among his intimate associates were New York City mayors Walker, O'Dwyer, and Impellitteri. In 1923 Ryan had formed the Joseph P. Ryan Association, which was political in character and had as its chief purpose the promotion of Ryan's prestige. For some time the vice president of the association was James J. Boland, a New York City councilman and a Tammany district leader.

The Joseph P. Ryan Association staged annual dinners that were intended to honor and promote Ryan. In 1931 the principal speaker at the dinner honoring Ryan was Mayor James J. Walker. Listed as "honorary chairmen" of this affair were Franklin D. Roosevelt, then governor of New York, Mayor Walker, Mayor Frank Hague of Jersey City, and William Green, head of the American Federation of Labor. In 1948 the chairman of the reception committee for the Ryan dinner was Hugo Rogers, head of Tammany Hall and president of the borough of Manhattan. In addition to political dignitaries, the dinners were attended by important representatives of the underworld—gangsters and thugs with long criminal records.

One of Ryan's righthand men was Teddy Gleason, an ILA organizer and business agent of a checkers' local union. Gleason also promoted dinners for the benefit of the Teddy Gleason Association. At the 1939 Gleason dinner, a photograph was taken of Joseph P. Ryan posing with underworld notables John M. (Cockeye) Dunn and Danny Gentile. Both were later convicted for a gangland murder that traced to a waterfront conflict, and Dunn was sent to the electric chair. Ryan and Dunn were members of the arrangements committee for the Gleason dinner. Contributing a full-page advertisement to the souvenir program was Carmine DeSapio, then Democratic leader of the First Assembly District and later head of Tammany Hall.[15]

In Ryan was vested the power to hire and fire ILA organizers. And organizers appointed by Ryan constituted a veritable "who's who" in the New York City underworld. Eddie McGrath, an organizer from 1937 to 1951, was the brother-in-law and rackets partner of murderer John M. Dunn. McGrath, an intimate associate of Joe Adonis, had a criminal record that listed twelve arrests on charges ranging from burglary to murder, and on one occasion was committed to Sing Sing Prison. For many years the Greenwich Village piers from Fourteenth Street to Cedar Street were under the domination of the McGrath-Dunn gang.

Another Ryan appointee as organizer was Gus Scannavino. At the time of the waterfront hearings, Scannavino also held the title of a vice president of the ILA. Scannavino had been one of the founders of the City Democratic Club and was on warm terms with Albert Anastasia and Joe Adonis.

Scannavino's nephew, Mike Cosenza, was made business agent of an ILA local in Brooklyn. Although he moved to Arizona, he was kept on the payroll at a salary of $50 a week plus weekly expenses of $25. This arrangement continued for three years and Cosenza received almost $12,000 from the union, although he had performed no service whatever. Early in 1952 the Brooklyn local held a meeting. Cosenza felt no need to leave the comforts of his Arizona home. His uncle, Scannavino, was present and Cosenza was dutifully reelected business agent of the Brooklyn ILA local.

Also appointed by Ryan as a paid organizer was Harold Bowers, a cousin of convicted bank robber Mickey Bowers. Harold and Mickey Bowers headed a gang that controlled a section on Manhattan's Upper West Side under the jurisdiction of ILA Local 824, of which Harold Bowers had been a delegate. It was popularly known as the Pistol Local because of the frequent outbreaks of gunplay and numerous murders committed on its piers. Following the murder of Thomas Cullentine of ILA Local 824 on April 29, 1948, the district attorney called to his office one of Bowers' men for routine questioning. Less than an hour later, longshoremen on several piers in the Bowers gang territory walked off their jobs. ILA president Joseph P. Ryan called the district attorney's office to protest the questioning of Bowers' man and brazenly blamed the prosecutor for having caused a serious tie-up on the piers.

Still another organizer appointed by Ryan was a known mobster, Alex DiBrizzi, who had a record of convictions for gambling and liquor law violations and had been arrested on such charges as grand larceny and felonious assault.[16]

As an ILA organizer for northern New Jersey, Charlie Yanowsky, also known as Harry Alberts, was a Ryan appointee. Yanowsky had strong ties to the Democratic organization and was one of five trustees and incorporators of the Riverside Democratic Club of Hoboken. He was an intimate friend of John V. Kenny, leader in the Second Ward and subsequently the mayor of Jersey City. Regarded as a dangerous criminal, Yanowsky was a member of the old Arsenal Gang and had been arrested on such charges as kidnapping, felonious assault, attempted murder, and operating a gambling resort. In 1936 he was wounded during a gun battle with FBI agents, who attempted to arrest him as a bank robbery suspect. His prison alma maters included Alcatraz and Sing Sing. With the aid of politicians, Yanowsky ruled over the New Jersey docks and his word was law. Finally he overplayed his hand when he attempted to move in on a well-established gambling operation in Jersey City and was murdered on July 16, 1948.[17]

To succeed Yanowsky, Ryan appointed Edward J. Florio to the post of ILA organizer. By ILA standards he was well qualified. Florio had spent a year in a federal penitentiary for a liquor violation and had been arrested for such offenses as kidnapping, stealing from interstate shipments, and felonious assault.

To pay tribute to Florio's appointment, an impressive dinner was held in January 1949 at the New Union Club in Hoboken. Seven hundred guests were present to hear Florio lauded in speeches by ILA president Ryan and Hoboken's mayor, Fred DeSapio, a cousin of Tammany Hall leader Carmine DeSapio. Appropriately serving as a member of the dinner committee was

Florio's close friend John DeRobertis, who was then free on bail following an arrest on a federal narcotics charge. The dinner served public notice that Florio, with the backing of Ryan and Hoboken politicians, was the new boss of the Jersey docks.[18]

During the early 1950s the waterfront in Jersey City became a center of turbulence. The city's waterfront was located on the west side of the Hudson River and its several piers extended from Bayonne on the south to Hoboken on the north. Some were known as the Claremont Terminal Piers, which were opened up by the army in July 1951.

The most influential political figure in Jersey City at that time was John V. Kenny, successor to long-time boss Frank Hague. Kenny had long been active in waterfront affairs and witnesses named him the associate and protector of gangsters and pier racketeers. He had served as a ward leader on the waterfront, and when he was the successful candidate for mayor in 1949 he had received strong ILA backing. Kenny promised Anthony Marchitto, a shop steward of ILA Local 1247, that when he became mayor he would make Marchitto the business agent of Local 1247. Following the election, Edward Polo, then business agent of Local 1247, was called down to City Hall by Mayor Kenny and ordered to resign his union post. Apparently with Marchitto's acquiescence, Frank (Biffo) DeLorenzo became the new business agent. DeLorenzo was a brother-in-law of the slain Charlie Yanowsky and had close ties with the notorious Albert Ackalitis.[19]

One day in December 1950 DeLorenzo and Anthony (Slim) Liucy, secretary-treasurer of ILA Local 1247, were in the union offices when a reputed killer, Morris Manna, and four confederates barged into the place. A pistol was leveled at DeLorenzo's head and he was ordered to resign as business agent forthwith. He dutifully complied. Slim Liucy, also forced to resign his union post, was instructed to open the safe. When he refused, Manna struck Liucy in the mouth with his gun, knocking out his front teeth. He was also tortured by the mobsters, who burned his feet. On March 2, 1951, the ILA office was bombed. Several men were injured and required hospitalization. Because of the prevalence of constant strife and violence, ILA president Ryan, on April 21, 1951, placed Local 1247 in a trusteeship. Named as one of the trustees was Anthony Marchitto. On August 15, 1951, the trusteeship was dissolved and Marchitto became the business agent.[20]

Mayor Kenny looked upon the Jersey City waterfront as his bailiwick for patronage. He referred many of his constituents to union officials on the docks and the officials obligingly placed them on the payrolls. Kenny was the Democratic county leader and often the men he sent to ILA officials for employment were residents of Union City, Hoboken, and Bayonne. Marchitto testified that occasionally Mayor Kenny would direct him to come to City Hall and there pick up several hundred tickets for some political affair. Marchitto was instructed to sell the tickets and turn over the money to the mayor.[21]

When the army opened up the Claremont Terminal Piers in July 1951, a group of men under the direction of the influential underworld leader Anthony Strollo moved in from a number of Jersey City piers and took over control. These hoodlums had their hands in various waterfront rackets —gambling, narcotics, soft jobs, thefts, payroll padding. They received the assistance of officials of ILA Locals 1247 and 1478, which had jurisdiction over the Claremont piers.

After the Kefauver committee hearings, official action was taken against the organized crime overlord Joe Adonis. In New Jersey his power was on the wane and indications were that his successor as boss of crime and rackets on the Jersey City waterfront would be Anthony Strollo.[22]

Born as Anthony Strollo on June 14, 1899, he was commonly known as Tony Bender. When he was married to Edna Goldenberg, a participant in the ceremonies was the gangster Vito Genovese. In fact, the marriage was part of a double-wedding and Strollo testified that Genovese "stood up for me, and I stood up for him." The close relationship between Strollo and Genovese would last several decades. For many years Strollo resided with wife Edna in Palisade, New Jersey. Included among his close associates were Joe Adonis, Albert Anastasia, Frank Costello, Meyer Lansky, Anthony (Little Augie Pisano) Carfano, Michael (Trigger Mike) Coppola, Charles (Lucky) Luciano, and Salvatore and William Moretti.[23]

An important business associate of Strollo was Vincent Mauro, also known as Vinney Bruno, who was considered one of the principal dealers in narcotics in the Bronx. Bender and Mauro, friends since boyhood, formed a pinball-machine company called New Deal Distributors. The firm was on Tenth Avenue in New York City and Bender was vice president.

Bender was also associated with West Thirty-fifth Street Trading Company, 218 West Thirty-fifth Street, New York City. The company held a check-cashing license until it was canceled by official action on August 23, 1949. Other principals in this venture were Tony Bender's brother, Emilio Strollo, and John Robilotto, also known as Johnny Roberts. Following the gangland slaying of William Moretti on October 4, 1951, Robilotto was held for a time by Bergen County, New Jersey, authorities as a prime suspect.[24]

On July 26, 1949, Emilio was one of several persons arrested and subsequently convicted in New York City for operating a tristate crooked numbers racket. An official of the Cincinnati Clearinghouse, working in collusion with the ring, manipulated the daily figures to control the winning numbers. Indications were that Tony Bender was also implicated. He was arrested but the evidence was insufficient to convict him.

Until Duke's Restaurant, owned by John DeNoia, alias Johnny Duke, closed in 1951, Tony Bender was one of several influential underworld leaders who congregated there daily.[25]

The personnel of the Claremont Terminal Piers, opened in July 1951, clearly bore the imprint of Anthony (Tony Bender) Strollo. Employed as a day hiring boss for longshoremen was Frank (Red) Mitchell. Named as hiring boss for warehousemen was Augie DeAcutis. Both had criminal records. Particularly brazen was the designation of Bender's pal John DeNoia as the night hiring boss.

DeNoia promptly hired Dominick Strollo, the brother of Tony Bender, as a longshoreman. This was merely a stopgap arrangement. DeNoia liked to strut around the piers in a business suit and smoking a cigar. The stevedoring company rebelled and demanded his ouster. After working only three days as a longshoreman, Dominick Strollo became the new night hiring boss at the Claremont piers. DeNoia was placed on the payroll as a laborer. Anthony Marchitto, business agent of Local 1247, was the ILA official who recommended Dominick for the post of night hiring boss.

Through the influence of Tony Bender, the Claremont piers became a haven for the underworld. Hoodlums presented themselves at the docks with the message "Tony sent me" and were promptly placed on the payroll. Dominick's assistant night hiring boss was Pasquale Velenza, alias Anthony Valenza, who had been convicted on several occasions for bookmaking. Alfred Faccio, a friend of Tony Bender since their days together in public school, was named night warehouse foreman. Faccio previously had been convicted of manslaughter and had received a long-term sentence to Sing Sing. Frank Miano, the head day timekeeper and spot checker, had served a term for larceny in Elmira Reformatory. With Tony Bender controlling the hiring bosses and the ILA local union officials, it is not surprising that a U.S. Senate subcommittee determined that 156 men with criminal records were carried on the payrolls at the Claremont piers.[26]

By spring 1952 the situation on the Jersey City docks had become intolerable to Mayor Kenny. Perhaps his greatest concern was his loss of patronage. Jersey City police learned that Dominick Strollo was weeding out local men and replacing them with New Yorkers. Early in March 1952 Mayor Kenny publicly charged that New York mobsters were muscling in on the Jersey waterfront. Specifically mentioned by Kenny were Tony Bender, Trigger Mike Coppola and Joey Rao. Said the mayor, "We want no branch of Murder, Inc. established in Jersey City." He handed Anthony Marchitto, business agent of ILA 1247, a list of undesirables who, he declared, were not to be permitted to work on the docks. Jersey City police were utilized to enforce the mayor's edict. In particular, Kenny ordered Dominick Strollo off the Claremont piers as a hiring boss. Immediately, the piers were shut down by a strike reputedly instigated by Tony Bender. The strike lasted a few days and was ended only when brother Dominick was reinstated as a hiring boss.[27]

Although the strike had ended, the Jersey City docks were still the center of much turbulence. And Kenny was confident that the key to the situation was held by the infamous Tony Bender. About a week after the strike, arrangements were made for a surreptitious meeting between Bender and Mayor Kenny in the suite of entertainer Phil Regan in the Warwick Hotel in New York City. Among Regan's close friends in New Jersey were underworld bigwigs Abner (Longy) Zwillman and Doc Stacher. Obviously, he had good credentials to act as intermediary between Bender and Kenny.

About eleven-thirty on the night of March 14, 1952, Tony Bender entered the Warwick Hotel lobby holding a handkerchief in front of his face to conceal his identity. Kenny had arrived a few minutes earlier and was waiting for Bender in Regan's hotel suite. Bender and Kenny remained in conference until after one o'clock.

District Attorney Frank Hogan learned of the meeting and summoned Jersey City Mayor Kenny to appear before a New York County grand jury on March 25, 1952. Kenny denied that he had met with Bender at the Warwick Hotel. However, after leaving the grand-jury room, Kenny had second thoughts about his testimony and sought permission to correct it. On March 31, 1952, Kenny was brought before the grand jury in New York again and admitted having lied during his previous appearance. He explained that he had been embarrassed to confess he was powerless to deal with the waterfront situation unless he conferred with the underworld boss Tony Bender. Kenny was confident, he testified, that Bender had succeeded Joe Adonis as the top man in the Jersey City waterfront rackets. District Attorney Hogan charged that by meeting with Bender in New York City, Mayor John V. Kenny had surrendered to the underworld in order to keep peace on the Jersey waterfront.[28]

The ranks of the longshoremen in the Port of New York were honeycombed with men who had lengthy criminal histories. And the New York State Crime Commission investigation established that over thirty percent of the officials in the ILA had known police records.

Under such conditions it was not surprising that crime was rampant on the waterfront. When a cargo of furs worth $2 million arrived in the port from Eastern Europe, two ILA business agents in Newark extorted $70,000 from the lawful consignee before he was permitted to gain delivery of the cargo. And when a shipment of tulip bulbs, also worth about $2 million, arrived from Holland, the persons entitled to delivery were unable to obtain the cargo until they met the extortionist demands of ILA officials in the sum of $45,000.[29]

Of the numerous rackets flourishing on the New York waterfront, organized thievery was perhaps the most lucrative. During 1948 the Grace

Steamship Line alone suffered losses of almost $3 million, of which eighty percent occurred on its New York piers. An executive of the United States Line testified, with some indignation, that on one occasion ten tons of steel mysteriously vanished from a pier. Understandably, he said, "I was not only perturbed, but very angry."

Watchmen hired to uncover thievery were useless. An official of a stevedoring company testified that if a watchman caught a man stealing and "turned him in," the whole dock would walk out on strike.

In addition to losses on the piers, many trucks moving cargo between the docks and inland freight terminals were hijacked by armed robbers. Often accomplices of the hijackers were checkers and clerks on the piers, having been placed in their jobs through the influence of mobsters.[30]

Money also flowed into the coffers of the underworld from lucrative rackets on the piers—gambling, loan sharking, and traffic in narcotics. It was customary for ILA officials to hand out bookmaking and numbers game concessions to favored racketeers, who were required to kick back a percentage of their profits to the union bosses.[31]

Numerous ILA officials augmented their incomes by demanding under-the-table payoffs from stevedoring firms. Ruth M. Kennedy, secretary and treasurer of Daniels & Kennedy, a stevedoring, trucking, and warehousing company, testified that it had become an established practice to make such payoffs. She withdrew money by issuing checks payable to cash or to fictitious persons and placed the money in envelopes that were handed to the intended beneficiaries. Over a five-year period, 1947 through 1951, Daniels & Kennedy made payoffs of $7,500 to Joseph P. Ryan, president of ILA, and $3,500 to Gus Scannavino, an organizer and vice president of ILA. The New York State Crime Commission established that over a five-year period, this one firm had made payoffs totaling $27,850 to ILA officials.

From 1945 to 1951 the payrolls of the Huron Stevedoring Company revealed payments of $50 a week to Edward Ross. Actually, Ross was a phantom and money purportedly paid to him was delivered to Timmy O'Mara, a boss loader on North River piers. O'Mara's pedigree included convictions for larceny, burglary, and robbery. He had once received a five-year sentence to Sing Sing for attempted burglary and on another occasion was committed to Elmira Reformatory for grand larceny. O'Mara had been a friend of Owney (the Killer) Madden since boyhood days. Payments made to "Ross," for O'Mara, were $24,130.49. By making regular payments to O'Mara, Huron expected this ex-convict to keep men from going on strike.

A vice president of the Jarka Corporation revealed to the New York State Crime Commission that he had paid ILA organizer Edward Florio and a Florio stooge at least $12,000 during a two-year period. Admittedly, the payments were made to obtain Florio's "goodwill." Captain L. C. Howard, president of Nacirema Operating Company, another large stevedoring firm, disclosed that he had paid Florio $2,000 for allowing violations of the labor contract. Four waterfront firms owned by William J. McCormack, regarded as the Mr. Big of Port of New York politics, had paid out $840,000 in petty cash between 1947 and 1951. The firms were unable to give an accounting for their large petty-cash disbursements. Likewise, between January 1, 1947, and June 30, 1952, the petty-cash withdrawals of the Jarka Corporation were $489,582. It was a reasonable assumption that a sizable portion of the huge petty-cash withdrawals of these companies had been used to make payoffs.[32]

The hearings clearly revealed the influence exerted by the underworld on almost every phase of activity in the Port of New York. And throughout the hearings, there was evidence of the close relationships existing between the principal waterfront racketeers and some of the nation's most prestigious organized crime leaders.

Albert Anastasia, the key waterfront crime boss in Brooklyn, and Anthony (Tony Bender) Strollo, the dominant figure on the New Jersey docks, were friends of long standing. Both were intimate associates of Joe Adonis, Frank Costello, and Meyer Lansky.

For some time, John M. (Cockeye) Dunn and Eddie McGrath operated a lucrative numbers game on the New York waterfront. Daniel Gentile served as controller for the numbers game. Andrew Sheridan, one-time trigger man for Dutch Schultz and the main killer for the Dunn-McGrath mob, became the organizer for ILA Local 856. Both Dunn and McGrath were on intimate terms with Lansky and Adonis. Shortly before Anthony Hintz, a hiring stevedore, was murdered in New York City by Dunn, Sheridan, and Gentile on January 8, 1947, Dunn spent several days in Lansky's hotel suite in Hollywood, Florida.

Frequently McGrath was a dinner companion and golfing partner of Moe B. Dalitz, head of the powerful Cleveland syndicate that owned the Desert Inn gambling casino in Las Vegas, Nevada. For many years this syndicate exercised a dominant role in the plush legalized gambling fields of Las Vegas. Dalitz owned a yacht, the *South Wind,* and for several days in February 1952 McGrath was a guest of Dalitz on the yacht in Nassau. Included among other associates of Dalitz were Costello, Adonis, Lansky, Frank Erickson, Dandy Phil Kastel, and Longy Zwillman.[33]

As a result of the waterfront hearings, criminal prosecutions were instituted against more than thirty individuals and a number of corporations. ILA organizer Edward Florio was convicted of perjury in federal court and sentenced to eighteen months in prison. Joseph John Schultz, an ILA organizer and a relative through marriage of Joseph P. Ryan, pleaded guilty to a federal indictment charging tax frauds and was fined. Timothy J. O'Mara, boss loader on North River piers, pleaded guilty in federal court to an indictment charging tax frauds and was sentenced to three years in prison.

Among those convicted were close associates of Albert Anastasia. Anthony V. Camarda, formerly financial secretary of ILA Local 1199 in Brooklyn, pleaded guilty to an indictment charging him with grand larceny of union funds and was committed to prison for one year. The Camarda family had been influential in the affairs of six Brooklyn locals that were reputedly controlled by Albert Anastasia.

Another Anastasia pal, Michael Clemente, secretary and business agent of ILA Local 856, was convicted of perjury in New York County and sentenced to a term of five to ten years. Clemente, an ex-convict, was close to some of the nation's most influential racket leaders. Clemente's daughter was given a lavish wedding reception at the Biltmore Hotel in September 1951; invited guests included Albert and Anthony Anastasia, Willie Moretti, Joseph (Socks) Lanza, and many underworld characters from Las Vegas; Miami; Hollywood, Florida; and Hot Springs, Arkansas. Union officials attending the affair included Joseph P. Ryan and Thomas (Teddy) Gleason, ILA organizer and business agent. The wedding expenses, almost $11,000, were paid by a stevedore firm official. Clemente had reigned for several years as the boss of all Manhattan's East River piers.[34]

The prosecutions touched only a small representation of the underworld that held sway over the waterfront. More significant was the action taken by officials to strike at some of the basic ills at the port.

On May 23, 1953, Governor Thomas E. Dewey declared, "The public hearings . . . have disclosed the existence of conditions on the waterfront of the Port of New York which are a disgrace and a menace." He announced that he would hold public hearings on recommendations made by the New York State Crime Commission to eradicate the evils of the waterfront. Following these hearings, Governor Dewey, in a message to an extraordinary session of the legislature on June 25, 1953, urged the adoption of the Waterfront Commission Act and Compact, a counterpart of which was passed by the New Jersey legislature. The legislation was passed and approved by Governor Dewey on June 30, 1953. The compact received the consent of Congress by legislation, was approved by President Dwight Eisenhower, and became law on August 12, 1953.

To facilitate the elimination of racketeering, the Waterfront Commission Act and Compact required licenses for stevedoring concerns, pier superintendents, hiring agents, and port watchmen operating in the New York Port District. Longshoremen were required to register with the commission, which was authorized to deny registration to those with significant criminal records. The shape-up method of hiring longshoremen was eliminated. Instead, the commission was to operate employment information centers. Under the provisions of the compact, "public loading" was banned. The

Waterfront Commission of New York Harbor was given full authority to investigate racketeering on the waterfront and was vested with subpoena power in both New York and New Jersey.[35]

The formation of the Waterfront Commission was a giant step in the right direction, but it was not an instant panacea for all of the deep-seated ills. The Port of New York faced a long period of turbulence. For decades the criminal and gangster elements had been firmly embedded in the structure of the ILA. The underworld was reaping huge profits from payroll padding, phantom workers, organized pilferage, kickbacks, gambling concessions, and loan sharking. It had no intention of meekly abandoning such lucrative sources of income.

In unprecedented action, the American Federation of Labor ordered the ILA to purge its ranks of the criminals and gangsters who had been giving a bad name to the entire organized labor movement. When the ILA failed to comply, the International Longshoremen's Association was expelled in September 1953 from the AFL. A new longshoremen's union, intended to take the place of the discredited ILA, was formed by the AFL.[36]

Joseph P. Ryan, ILA president, was under mounting pressure from local and federal governments for the alleged offenses of misusing union funds and accepting payoffs from employers. At a convention in Philadelphia on November 18, 1953, Ryan resigned as president and his twenty-six-year reign ended. The delegates named Ryan president emeritus of the ILA and bestowed on him an "irrevocable" annual pension of $10,000. Elected as the new president of ILA was Captain William V. Bradley, who had headed ILA's tugboat division. Bradley singled out Teddy Gleason as the man most responsible for his election. During the waterfront hearings evidence emerged that Gleason had consorted with gangsters. And Gleason admitted that he had recommended the unsavory ex-convict Albert Ackalitis for the position of hiring boss on a North River pier. Gleason was to continue as one of the top men in the Bradley administration of ILA affairs.[37]

Under the auspices of the National Labor Relations Board, an election was held in December 1953 to determine whether the ILA or the rival union chartered by the AFL would serve as the sole bargaining agent for the longshoremen and other dock workers in the Port of New York. Hundreds of policemen were assigned to maintain order. Nevertheless, around the Brooklyn polling places in Anthony Anastasia's domain, violence was prevalent. Three AFL partisans were stabbed and a fourth received a severe head beating. In Manhattan, there was hand-to-hand street fighting and Harold Bowers, head of the "Pistol Local," suffered a broken nose. The ILA polled 9,060 votes, the AFL union 7,568, and 4,307 votes were challenged. Subsequently, the National Labor Relations Board set aside the December 1953 election on the ground that the ILA had won by means of fraud and violence.[38]

Beginning on March 5, 1954, the ILA tied up the Port of New York with a strike that lasted twenty-nine days. The situation became so critical that on March 27, 1954, a personal representative of President Eisenhower conferred with Governor Dewey and several federal and state officials for the purpose of mapping out a plan of action. In a joint statement, the conferees emphasized the "criminal nature" of the strike. The work stoppage, they said, was "not a legitimate labor strike at all" but primarily a criminal conspiracy. The ILA finally called off the strike on April 2, 1954, without having gained any concessions whatever.[39]

At another election the ILA defeated the rival AFL dock union and in August 1954 was certified by the National Labor Relations Board as the collective-bargaining agent for the pier workers in the Port of New York. In November 1954 the ILA negotiated a two-year agreement with the New York Shipping Association. During the preceding several months there had been an amalgamation of several locals and that further consolidated power in the hands of such ILA leaders as Harold Bowers, head of the Upper West Side's Pistol Local 824, and Anthony Anastasia, the Brooklyn dock overlord. In fact, Anastasia became an international vice president of the ILA and by 1956, through the merger of various Brooklyn locals, was in control of about twenty-four percent of ILA's membership.

On September 14, 1955, the ILA again walked out on strike and tied up the great port for eight days. No economic issues were involved and there was no dispute with employers or conflict with a competing union. The strike was directed solely at the Waterfront Commission, which the ILA hoped to cripple.[40]

Actually, the September 1955 strike ended with a victory for the Waterfront Commission. Since its formation two years earlier, the commission had achieved many reforms, including the abolishment of the public-loading racket, the reduction of payroll padding and the curtailment of organized theft on the piers. The veteran foe of crime on the waterfront, Father John M. Corridan, stated on September 27, 1955, that the bistate Waterfront Commission had been doing just about the best job that could be done considering the obstacles placed in its path by the ILA. Nevertheless, Father Corridan lamented that he could see no immediate hope for a real cleanup because the ILA was still firmly entrenched on the waterfront.[41]

18

TAMMANY BOSS DESAPIO'S HEYDAY—ERA OF GANGLAND TURBULENCE

When the Kefauver committee issued its final report in August 1951, it could assert, with justification, that "its activities have had a tremendous effect upon the whole field of law enforcement. Everywhere throughout the country citizens, made suddenly aware of the character and ramifications of organized crime, have risen up to demand greater vigilance in stamping out crime and corruption."[1]

In New York City public hearings were concluded by the Kefauver committee on March 21, 1951. A few days later, on March 29, Governor Dewey ordered the New York State Crime Commission to investigate the relationship between organized crime and any unit of government in the state. Public hearings began in November 1952. On November 20, 1951, the governor had also ordered the Crime Commission to conduct a sweeping investigation of the New York waterfront, a known center of organized crime. Public hearings on the waterfront were held several months later.

The rulers of what the Kefauver committee branded the Costello-Adonis-Lansky crime syndicate had long enjoyed absolute immunity. And perhaps the most influential "untouchable" of all was Frank Costello. It is understandable that when he had first appeared before the Kefauver committee he was confident he had nothing to fear. He did not yet realize the rules were being changed, and even more significantly, he no longer controlled the rules. When, in open defiance of the committee, he made his dramatic walkout during the hearings in 1951, the underworld leader's troubles began.

On April 4, 1952, Costello was found guilty on all ten counts of a federal indictment charging him with contempt of the U.S. Senate crime investigating committee. He was sentenced to a term of eighteen months and entered prison on August 15, 1952. Five months later, on January 16, 1953, the federal government filed tax liens against the gang leader's assets in an effort to collect alleged unpaid taxes of $486,722. After serving fourteen months and fifteen days on the contempt charges, Costello was released from prison on October 29, 1953. His troubles with the law were far from over, however. He had merely completed the first chapter in a long series of legal skirmishes with the authorities.[2]

In New Jersey hitherto apathetic officials were suddenly spurred into action against the multi-million-dollar gambling empire in Bergen County headed by Joe Adonis. On May 28, 1951, Adonis was sentenced on gambling charges to a term of two to three years in the New Jersey State Prison in Trenton. Also committed to prison at the same time were three Adonis confederates in the gambling syndicate—Arthur Longano, James (Piggy) Lynch, and Salvatore Moretti. Longano became involved in prison riots in 1952 and Moretti died in prison of a cerebral hemorrhage. His brother Willie was the victim of a gangland assassination on October 4, 1951. Frank Erickson once testified that he and Adonis had employed Salvatore and Willie to act as agents to arrange for telephone wire room locations in Bergen County.

In June 1953 immigration officials held hearings in the New Jersey State Prison regarding the citizenship status of Joseph Adonis. He had represented that he was born in Passaic, New Jersey, in November 1901 and therefore was an American citizen. Immigration authorities produced official documents, including a birth certificate, which established that Giuseppe Doto, the true name of Adonis, was born at Montemarano, Italy, on November 22, 1902. Thus, Adonis, an alien, was subject to eventual deportation. After spending twenty-six months in prison, Adonis was released on July 16, 1953, but was placed under bond immediately in connection with other charges pending against him. On August 5, 1953, U.S. Attorney General Herbert Brownell, Jr. ordered Adonis deported to Italy.[3]

Action, although weak, was also taken against Meyer Lansky, the third ruling member of the Costello-Adonis-Lansky syndicate. An extraordinary grand jury investigating gambling and corruption in Saratoga Springs, New York, returned an indictment on September 8, 1951, against Lansky. On February 18, 1953, Lansky pleaded guilty to five of twenty-one counts and on May 2, 1953, he received a slap on the wrist: three months in prison and a fine of $2,500. He was also placed on probation for three years. Subsequently, on December 28, 1953, Joseph (Doc) Stacher, who helped Lansky establish the Arrowhead Inn gambling casino in Saratoga Springs, was fined $10,000.[4]

In the aftermath of the Kefauver committee hearings, further prosecution was also instituted against Frank Erickson, the intimate associate and partner of Costello, Adonis, and Lansky. Erickson, who had recently served seventeen months in Riker's Island Penitentiary in New York City, was now charged with conspiracy to violate the New Jersey gambling statutes. The prosecution was based on his operation of wire betting rooms in Lodi and Cliffside Park. One of the wire rooms had been located on property owned by a police captain and the police commissioner of Lodi. Just as Erickson was about to be placed on trial on September 8, 1952, he unexpectedly entered a plea of *non vult* (no defense). On November 14, 1952, a Bergen County Superior Court judge sentenced Erickson to serve a term of twelve to fourteen months in the New Jersey State Prison, where his associate, Joe Adonis, was already incarcerated. Following his release on December 15, 1953, he began serving a six-month prison term for evading federal income taxes.[5]

The successful prosecutions of several New York City underworld rulers struck a critical blow to their prestige. For decades they had been untouchable, a testimony to their tremendous power. But now that power had been severely damaged, if not destroyed.

In the early 1950s rumors persisted that Frank Costello was to be replaced as the Mr. Big of the New York underworld by Thomas Lucchese. For years Lucchese, also known as Tommy Brown or Three Finger Brown, had been one of the more prestigious gangland leaders in New York City. This ex-convict had maintained long and warm relationships with many of the nation's top criminals. Yet he mingled socially with numerous influential politicians in New York City—prosecutors, judges, congressmen—and succeeded in projecting the image of a respectable businessman.

Born in Italy as Gaetano (Tommy) Lucchese in 1900, he came to the United States from Palermo, Sicily, in 1911. Physically, he was a small man, carrying about one hundred thirty pounds on a five-foot-two frame. His record indicates he did not eschew violence. On July 19, 1928, Lucchese was arrested with two men and charged with having shot and killed one Louis Cerasulo. Conveniently, eyewitnesses refused to identify the gunmen. Two years later, Lucchese was again charged with murder when the bullet-riddled body of Joseph Pinzolo was discovered on September 5, 1930. This time he was represented by attorney Francis X. Mancuso and eventually the charges against him were dismissed. In 1931 Lucchese was on the premises when gang leader Salvatore Maranzano was murdered. He ran out of the building before the police arrived. It was also in 1931 that Lucchese was arrested with Lucky Luciano and other gangsters in Cleveland, where they had attended the Stribling-Schmeling prizefight. In testifying before the New York State Crime Commission, Lucchese conceded that in the early 1930s, which he described as the "cabaret stages," he saw Luciano about once a week. Notwithstanding several arrests, Lucchese's sole conviction was on charges of grand larceny.[6]

Following the elimination of Lepke Buchalter from the dope racket, the New York office of the Federal Bureau of Narcotics determined that the center of activity in the narcotics traffic had shifted from the criminal gangs on the Lower East Side to what was commonly known as the 107th Street Mob in Harlem. Organizational charts prepared by the Federal Bureau of Narcotics for the 1940s listed Thomas Lucchese as the leader of the 107th

Street Mob and named Dominick Petrelli and Michael Coppola as his lieutenants. An earlier report in 1936 had carried Ciro Terranova as the leader and Thomas Lucchese as his lieutenant.

In the early 1940s federal narcotics agents and two New York City police officers raided the underworld hangout Duke's Bar and Grill, in New Jersey. Conferring in the place at the time were Lucchese, Willie Moretti and brother Salvatore, and a well-known narcotics violator, Salvatore Arcidiaco. Willie and Lucchese were close, visiting each other's home and attending family weddings. Other good friends of Lucchese included underworld bigwigs Frank Costello, Salvatore Shillitani, Joe Stracci, John and Tom Dioguardi, and Vincent John Rao. On the West Coast one of the kingpins of organized crime was Jack Dragna. Lucchese visited Dragna in California and once Dragna came east and stayed at Lucchese's home for almost two weeks. They also kept in touch with each other by long-distance telephone.

Lucchese's principal sphere of influence was in the garment center. He was a principal owner of Braunell, Ltd., a ladies garment manufacturing concern. Other Lucchese commercial interests included real estate, sand and gravel, reflecting lenses, a hoist company, a service firm, and wine bricks during Prohibition. His aides included Abe Chait, Joe Palisades, and Steve LaSalle. Almost without exception, his partners or associates in various enterprises were criminals; several trafficked in narcotics and at least one was a convicted murderer.[7]

Lucchese was active in political affairs and developed friends at every level of government. When he sought American citizenship, his principal adviser was Congressman Louis Cappozzoli, later a judge, who wrote letters in his behalf. Naturalization was granted to Lucchese in federal court in Newark, January 25, 1943.

A particularly close friend was Armand Chankalian, administrative assistant to the United States district attorney for the Southern District of New York. Lucchese and Chankalian attended political and social functions together. They visited Washington, D.C., and were registered jointly at the Mayflower Hotel. They took at least one trip together to Florida. It was probably through Chankalian that Lucchese was able to develop a friendly acquaintanceship with U.S. Attorney Myles Lane. When Lucchese made an application on September 19, 1945, for a certificate of good conduct, Chankalian served as a character witness. The certificate was granted by the New York State Parole Board on April 18, 1950.

It was Chankalian who introduced Lucchese to Assistant U. S. Attorney Thomas Murphy, who won national fame as the prosecutor of Alger Hiss in 1950. A friendship arose between Murphy and Lucchese that was to last for several years. The welcome mat was out for Lucchese at the Murphy residence and Murphy and his wife were entertained as dinner guests at the Lucchese home.[8]

Among Lucchese's more important political friends was the flamboyant congressman Vito Marcantonio. Originally, a protégé of Fiorello LaGuardia, Marcantonio, a lawyer, won his seat in the House of Representatives in seven of the eight elections between 1934 and 1948. He was chairman of the American Labor party's New York County organization. Consistently he espoused the Communist party line. Once he represented the Communist party before the Subversive Activities Board. The *Daily Worker* threw its full support to the American Labor party. And when Marcantonio died of a heart ailment on August 9, 1954, among the first to pay a glowing tribute to the deceased was William Z. Foster, national chairman of the Communist party.

But Marcantonio's major political strength was derived from the underworld, not the Communist party. In Harlem Marcantonio's word was law. He provided iron-clad protection for those engaged in the business of vice and crime, and in return received their solid political support. It was as a result of this underworld political activity that Marcantonio became a center of attention in one of New York City's most celebrated election murder cases. In 1946 criminal supporters of Marcantonio organized to help him win an election. John Scottoriggio, a Republican district captain and poll watcher, refused to cooperate with the conspirators. As Scottoriggio was walking to the polls at 5:45 A.M., he was waylaid on East 104th Street and beaten so savagely that he died six days later. Arrested as material witnesses and placed under bonds of $250,000 each were Trigger Mike Coppola and Joey Rao. The case aroused great public indignation and precipitated a congressional investigation of voter intimidation.[9]

The alliance between Marcantonio and Lucchese was important to the underworld and it had far-reaching effects politically. It was responsible for placing a protégé of the organized crime boss in the mayor's chair.

When William O'Dwyer resigned as mayor on September 2, 1950, he was automatically succeeded by the president of the City Council, Vincent R. Impellitteri, whose success story had its inception during the 1945 elections. At that time O'Dwyer had sat down with the five Democratic county leaders and the group decided on a ticket with a "perfect" geographic and ethnic balance. O'Dwyer, the Brooklyn Irishman, was slated for mayor; Lawrence Gerosa, a Bronx Italian for comptroller; and Irwin Davidson, a Manhattan Jew, for president of the City Council. All was harmonious until the unpredictable O'Dwyer suddenly declared that he would not run on the ticket he had helped put together. O'Dwyer had conferred with Congressman Marcantonio, who turned thumbs down on the proposed slate of candidates.

As head of the American Labor party in New York, Marcantonio's support was deemed a rich prize by O'Dwyer. After all, the mayoral aspirant had been wooing the congressman since the early 1940s, when O'Dwyer, Irving Sherman, and Marcantonio hobnobbed in Washington, D.C. Now, as a favor to Marcantonio, O'Dwyer came up with a substitute ticket, which named Impellitteri as the candidate for the presidency of the City Council. Impellitteri, an Italian from Manhattan, was virtually unknown. The most significant job he had ever held was the post of secretary to a New York State Supreme Court judge. Now, out of the blue, he was slated as a candidate for the position that would automatically place him in the mayor's chair if the chief executive should die or resign. Knowledgeable New Yorkers were flabbergasted. They suggested that his name must have been selected at random from the New York City green book (official directory). Actually, O'Dwyer had maneuvered the Impellitteri candidacy at the insistance of Marcantonio. And Marcantonio, in turn, had used his influence in behalf of Impellitteri as a favor to his lifelong friend Thomas Lucchese.[10]

The general public had heard little about Lucchese and knew nothing about the gangland leader's role in making Impellitteri mayor. But the significance of Lucchese as a behind-the-scenes kingmaker was not lost on either Tammany Boss Carmine G. DeSapio or Frank Costello. With Lucchese's man as mayor, DeSapio and Costello feared that their power would be undermined.

When Impellitteri took over the duties of mayor, he inherited a police department riddled by scandal. On September 26, 1950, he appointed Thomas Murphy, former assistant U. S. attorney, as the police commissioner of New York City. The friendship between Lucchese and Murphy was not generally known, and the selection Murphy to head the police department was widely acclaimed. Following the appointment, Lucchese paid a personal visit to the Murphy home to offer his congratulations to the new police commissioner.[11]

In making plans for the special November 1950 mayoral election, Tammany Boss DeSapio insisted that Impellitteri withdraw from the race. Impellitteri refused. His press secretary, whom he had inherited from O'Dwyer, charged that the acting mayor had spurned a $400,000 bribe offer from DeSapio to withdraw his candidacy.

Under DeSapio's guidance, New York Supreme Court Justice Ferdinand Pecora was selected as the Democratic organization candidate. Edward Corsi, state industrial commissioner, was chosen as the Republican standard-bearer, and Impellitteri ran as an independent. Corsi made a campaign issue of Impellitteri's connections with Lucchese. He charged that Tommy (Three Finger Brown) Lucchese was the power behind Impellitteri. These allegations, for the most part, fell on deaf ears. Impellitteri won the election handily, with 1,161,000 votes to 935,000 for Pecora and 382,000 for Corsi.[12]

During the campaign, Frank J. Sampson, formerly the boss of Tammany Hall, labored in behalf of the Impellitteri candidacy. Several other Tammany district leaders also defected to the Impellitteri camp and thus, in effect, had allied themselves with the Lucchese forces. Sampson demanded that all Tammany district leaders line up behind Impellitteri. Failure to do so, he warned, would result in a cutoff of their patronage. Following the election, Sampson became Impellitteri's patronage secretary.

Almost as soon as the votes were tabulated, Francis X. Mancuso, a longtime Costello stalwart, announced that he was joining the Impellitteri ranks. Costello was infuriated and considered Mancuso's defection a double-cross. Immediately, two notorious underworld chieftains, Joey Rao and Joseph Stracci, commonly known as Joe Stretch, called at Mancuso's clubhouse and ordered him to "get out" as district leader. An ultimatum from these gunmen was not to be taken lightly. Rao was still under bond for alleged involvement in the 1946 election day beating and murder of Scottoriggio. After Stracci and Rao had delivered their message to Mancuso, the election captains held a meeting. Pursuant to a directive from Costello, they ousted Mancuso as district leader.[13]

Less than a year after Impellitteri's election as mayor, he found it necessary to appoint a new police commissioner. Thomas Murphy, who had held that post since September 1950, was nominated for a place on the federal bench. Responding to an inquiry from the U.S. Senate Judiciary Committee, Murphy admitted in a letter of June 25, 1951, that he had known Thomas Lucchese socially for six years. It was not until 1950, he said, that he became aware of Lucchese's criminal record. Lucchese impressed him as being a respectable citizen who had paid his debt to society and was trying to raise his family in the American tradition. Murphy became a federal judge, and in July 1951 Impellitteri appointed George Monaghan as the new head of the New York City Police Department.[14]

A detailed study of the police department was initiated in 1951 by the Institute of Public Administration headed by an eminent authority on police administration, Bruce Smith. Following a survey lasting eighteen months, the institute reported on October 21, 1952, that the city's police force was riddled with politics and favoritism. Improper and careless recruitment methods had resulted in the appointment of some criminals, subversives, mentally unfit, and a few communists. Promotion within the department was said to be marked by favoritism, bargaining, and intrigue extending from stationhouse to headquarters. Discipline was characterized as a farce. Some men who had been guilty of violating almost every infraction in the books had been kept on the force after as many as twenty trials. The crime statistics released by the department were unreliable and in some instances false. The department had deteriorated to a state of ineptness, although more money had been spent on salary boosts and allied benefits than was the case in any other city. The institute warned that titanic efforts were needed to end the corrosive influence of politics on the department.[15]

The murder of a union official in 1953 touched off an investigation of labor racketeering that ultimately exposed a shocking harness racetrack scandal in New York. Politicians, legislators, underworld characters, and persons with close ties to organized crime leaders were uncovered as the hidden owners of racetrack stock worth millions of dollars. These insiders had been permitted to purchase stock for nominal or insignificant sums and reaped huge profits within a short period of time.

The catalyst for the sweeping investigation of harness racing was the murder of Thomas F. Lewis, president of Local 32-E, Building Service Employees Union, AFL. For some time Lewis had engaged in a struggle to gain control over the criminal-infested labor mart at Yonkers Raceway. One of his adversaries was John Acropolis, president of the Westchester Federation of Labor and head of Local 456, Teamsters Union, AFL. Lewis succeeded in forcing Acropolis out of the Yonkers Raceway labor picture. Local 32-E, headed by Lewis, obtained a closed contract, which covered pari-mutuel clerks, uniformed police, ushers, maintenance men, groundkeepers, and program sellers. On August 27, 1952, Acropolis was shot and killed but his murder did not cause any significant public reaction.

A year later, on August 28, 1953, a gunman, Edward (Snakes) Ryan, barged into the Lewis home at Fifty East 191 Street in the Bronx and shot and killed the union official. A nearby traffic patrolman heard the shots and when Ryan ran from the house, the officer pursued him. Ryan was headed for a getaway car, driven by William Howell, a longshoreman and a pari-mutuel clerk. The traffic officer and Ryan exchanged pistol shots and Ryan was killed. Howell was brought to trial about a year later and was convicted of second-degree murder.

At the Howell trial it was brought out that Lawrence (La-La) Lynch had been on the payroll of the Yonkers Trotting Association at a salary of $2,000 a month. His function was to combat excessive union demands. A brother, James, was an official of the union. Lewis caused the Yonkers Raceway to discharge Lawrence, and Howell informed a friend that La-La had ordered him (Howell) and Ryan to "knock off Lewis."[16]

Among the more lucrative sources of riches to union president Thomas F. Lewis at Yonkers Raceway were the health and welfare funds of Local 32-E. To handle the health and welfare insurance, Lewis established the Alcor Agency, Inc., of which he owned a half interest. His stock was held in the name of his wife, Mrs. Pauline Bender Lewis. Other stockholders were Alphonse Corcillo and Joseph P. Pizzo. Eventually Lewis and Pizzo had a falling out and just three hours before Lewis was shot, Pizzo received a certified check for $40,000 in settlement of his claims against Alcor. Pizzo had been active in politics and served as the Bronx campaign manager for Mayor Impellitteri during the 1953 primary campaign. The Alcor Agency had been succeeded by the Welfare Service Agency, Inc., which was also dominated by Lewis.

Within a five-year period ending May 31, 1953, employer payments made to the health and welfare funds of Local 32-E totaled $1,479,791. Of this, $412,634 had gone to Lewis and his associates for service fees, commissions, and salaries to Lewis's kinsmen attached to the agency staff. A nationally known consultant on welfare funds testified that $275,000 would represent a conservative estimate of overcharges during the five-year period.[17]

After the killing of Lewis, there were revelations of many abuses in the harness racetrack business in New York. Some of the evils were political and involved both Republicans and Democrats. The Democrats, however, hoped to saddle the Republican administration then in power with the liability of a racetrack scandal. Governor Dewey decided to take the initiative. Invoking the Moreland Act, originally passed in 1907, the governor appointed on October 8, 1953, a three-man commission to investigate every phase of harness racing in New York.

State-regulated harness racing with gambling had its inception in 1940, when legislation was enacted to set up pari-mutuels and provide for a three-man commission to license associations and allot racing dates. Some licenses were granted as early as 1940, but it was not until 1944 that harness racing had become established as a profitable venture.

When the scandal broke in 1953, the State Harness Racing Commission had issued licenses to eight associations for pari-mutuel racing. The two principal harness-racing tracks were Roosevelt Raceway and Yonkers Raceway.

The most influential man in the New York harness-racing industry was a lawyer, George Morton Levy, the close friend and golfing partner of Frank Costello and Frank Erickson. It was Levy who was the guiding genius behind Roosevelt Raceway, in Westbury, Long Island, which was owned by the Old Country Trotting Association.

Levy, together with a broker associate, started the Old Country Trotting Association in 1940 with $25,000 borrowed from a future track concessionaire. Obviously, Levy had the Midas touch. By 1953 the assets of the Old Country Trotting Association had a value of more than $14 million. Between 1944 and 1953 Levy had earned over $3 million in legal fees and stock gains through the Roosevelt track.

Yonkers Raceway was originally a thoroughbred-racing establishment called the Empire City Race Track. In August 1949 it was bought by a syndicate, Algam Corporation, and was converted into a harness racetrack. Members of the syndicate included Joseph Henschel, a garment manufacturer and former treasurer of Tammany Hall, and Arthur Lynch, former deputy city treasurer under Mayor William O'Dwyer. Henschel testified that he had paid $375,000 toward the purchase of the track. Of this amount he borrowed $150,000 on a note endorsed by Benjamin (Benny) Levine, a convicted racketeer and a former associate of Lepke Buchalter. Henschel, admittedly, had also known both Frank Costello and Thomas Lucchese for many years.

A hidden investor in Algam Corporation was Irving Sherman, the onetime crony of Mayor O'Dwyer and the friend of Frank Costello and numerous top-flight gangsters. Sherman sought to prevent his name from becoming publicly identified with the venture and his investment was made through a front, a raincoat manufacturer. Although the front was listed as the owner of 22,500 shares of stock and $40,000 worth of bonds in the Algam Corporation, Sherman owned eighty percent of this investment. In 1949 Sherman and his confederate purchased the Algam stock and bonds for $75,000. By 1953 these same stocks and bonds were worth $421,000.

On December 28, 1949, a tripartite agreement was signed between Old Country, Algam Corporation, and Yonkers. The pact gave George Morton Levy's Old Country control over Yonkers racing dates for twenty years. There also emerged an interlocking directorate between the Roosevelt and Yonkers tracks and eventually Old Country gained voting control over Algam.[18]

Throughout the investigation and hearings conducted by the Moreland Act Commission, it was apparent that George Morton Levy played a heavy role in many of the get-rich-quick stock deals. It was the same Levy who, admittedly, had paid Frank Costello $60,000 over a four-year period, ostensibly to use his influence to keep bookmakers away from Roosevelt Raceway. And several of Costello's friends and associates reaped rich profits from ''inside'' harness track stock purchases.

Levy testified that in 1942 he sold $5,000 worth of stock in the Old Country Trotting Association to William DeKoning, Sr., the labor boss of Nassau County. This stock was retained in Levy's name until about 1951, when DeKoning assumed ownership and placed it in the name of his wife. The $5,000 investment then had a value of $240,000.

DeKoning's interest in harness racing was not confined to stock purchases. In April 1954 he pleaded guilty to an indictment that charged him with having extorted $1 million from Roosevelt Raceway employees. He was sentenced to three concurrent terms of one year to eighteen months in Sing Sing Prison.[19]

In 1948 George Morton Levy made available 400 shares of stock in the Old Country Trotting Association to gambler Frank Erickson's son, Frank J. Erickson, and son-in-law, James Watson. The sale price was $14,000, to be paid in three easy installments over a two-year period. Stock splitting increased the shares to 3,360, and by 1953 they had a value of $100,000.

Levy testified that about 1946 he approached Irwin Steingut, Democratic minority leader of the New York State General Assembly, and asked him to oppose a particular bill. Steingut did oppose the legislation and it was defeated. At that time, 500 shares of stock in the Goshen Mile Track

Association were made available to Steingut's daughter for $250. When the Goshen Association was absorbed by the Yonkers Trotting Association in 1950, the stock owned by Steingut's daughter had a value of $45,000. Levy revealed that he, personally, had purchased 4,250 shares of Goshen Association stock in 1945 for $2,125 and sold it in 1950 for $300,000.

Also profiting handsomely from harness racetrack stock was the ex-convict Abraham Chait, a lieutenant of Thomas Lucchese. On March 27, 1952, Abraham's twenty-four-year-old son, Burton D. Chait, invested $40,000 in stock and $20,000 in debenture bonds in the Algam Corporation. It was charged that Burton was merely acting as a front for his father, who actually financed the transaction. At the time Chait paid $40,000 for the shares of stock, they had an over-the-counter value of $130,000.

The Moreland Act Commission hearings established that many prominent politicians had been favored with the opportunity of buying harness track stock at bargain prices. Often these shares were held in the names of friends or relatives. Some influential politicians had acquired substantial blocks of stock just before the time an association had received a license or had its racing dates extended.

Among legislators who had benefited from harness track stock were former Republican assemblyman Norman F. Penny and former Democratic state senator John J. Dunnigan. Penny and Dunnigan had coauthored the pari-mutuel law.

In November 1953 J. Russell Sprague of Nassau County resigned as Republican national committeeman to avoid causing embarrassment to his party. Over a period of eight years Sprague made a profit of over $500,000 on an original investment of $2,000 in harness-racing stock.[20]

The flagrant abuses highlighted by the Moreland Act Commission indicated that harness racing in New York was just one big racket operating for the benefit of slick promoters, politicians, men with close underworld ties, and corrupt labor bosses. Obviously, the three-man harness-racing commission established by the 1940 law had failed to protect the public interest. It was recommended that the three-man commission be replaced by one full-time salaried commissioner. The recommendation was followed and on December 21, 1953, Governor Dewey named the New York City police commissioner, George P. Monaghan, as the czar of the harness-racing industry. Following enabling legislation, Monaghan assumed his new post on February 2, 1954.[21]

In June 1953 the legislature had also created a permanent office of commissioner of investigation. This new watchdog post had been recommended by the New York State Crime Commission, which was scheduled soon to go out of existence. On December 28, 1953, Governor Dewey appointed William B. Herlands as the state's first commissioner of investigation. Herlands had held a comparable city position under Mayor LaGuardia and had been one of Dewey's associates during the famous rackets investigations in the 1930s.[22]

In the midst of the racetrack scandal in 1953, the political leaders of New York City were girding their loins for a heated mayoral campaign. In a broad sense, the forces of Thomas Lucchese were pitted against the DeSapio-Costello troops. After all, in 1950 Costello had played a vigorous role in taking punitive action against district leaders, such as Francis X. Mancuso, who had defected to Impellitteri. However, the Kefauver committee hearings and a stretch in prison had greatly diminished Costello's influence. With Impellitteri occupying the mayor's chair, the henchman of Lucchese had been inching nearer to control, a situation that was intolerable to both DeSapio and Costello.

Tammany Boss DeSapio named the Manhattan borough president, Robert F. Wagner, Jr., as his choice for mayor. In the primary he would face the incumbent, Vincent R. Impellitteri. As the battle lines were drawn, Impellitteri could count on the backing of the Democratic organizations in Brooklyn, Queens, and Richmond. Originally, Kenneth Sutherland, boss of the Brooklyn machine, had been inclined to back Wagner. But the influence of Lucchese on Sutherland was so strong that the Brooklyn boss threw the support of his organization to Impellitteri. Wagner had the solid backing of the Bronx Democratic machine and the boss of Tammany Hall in Manhattan. However, because of the defection of several Assembly district leaders in Manhattan to Impellitteri, DeSapio's control over the executive committee of Tammany Hall was rather shaky.[23]

In the primary campaign Wagner charged that the underworld was supporting Impellitteri. In particular, he noted that Impellitteri was receiving the backing of Generoso Pope, Jr., a close friend of Costello. Ironically, Wagner did not appear to be troubled with the fact that the man running his campaign, DeSapio, not only was a long-time friend Costello but owed much of his advancement to a position of political power to the Costello influence. Wagner also called attention to the association between Impellitteri and Thomas (Three Finger Brown) Lucchese, and asserted that Impellitteri's Bronx campaign manager, Joseph Pizzo, had been questioned about the murder of Thomas F. Lewis, the harness racetrack racketeer. Impellitteri responded that the responsible officials had not seen fit to hold Pizzo for the murder and that Pizzo would continue as his Bronx campaign manager.

The *New York Times* editorially took a dim view of both Impellitteri and Wagner. Impellitteri's record in office was described as dismally negative in nature. And although Wagner promised much, he failed to inspire confidence. The average voter appeared to be yawning and, said the *Times,* "we can't much blame him."[24]

Predictably, there was no great surge of voters to the polls come primary day, September 15, 1953. Emerging with a clear-cut victory was Robert F. Wagner, Jr., who received 350,484 votes to 181,295 for Impellitteri. But those who cast their ballots for Wagner represented only sixteen percent of the registered Democratic voters.

During the campaign twelve Tammany district leaders openly defected to Impellitteri and others worked secretly for his nomination. District leaders were elected by the county committee membership and the slates of committeemen arranged by DeSapio carried all sixteen Assembly districts. As a result, every district leader identified with the Lucchese forces was defeated. This represented a big victory for DeSapio and undoubtedly was savored by Costello as well. DeSapio's status as the undisputed boss of Tammany Hall was now secure. In the November election Wagner was the victor, with 1,022,626 votes. The Republican nominee, Harold Riegelman, received 661,591 votes and the Liberal party candidate, Rudolph Halley, who had won fame as chief counsel for the Kefauver committee, polled 467,105.[25]

On January 1, 1954, Robert F. Wagner, Jr. became the 102d mayor of New York City, a post he would hold for twelve years. Shortly before Impellitteri left office he appointed several DeSapio adherents to important offices. And almost as soon as Wagner took office, he appointed Impellitteri to the post of justice of the court of special sessions. The bitter rivalry of only a few days earlier was replaced with mutual back scratching.

Selected as the new commissioner of police was a highly respected lawyer, Francis W. H. Adams. On January 6, 1954, Adams called together four hundred ranking officers, who constituted the police brass. He stressed the need for eliminating the corruption that had resulted in scandals and a badly marred police image. He bluntly told the commanding officers they would be held responsible for any grafting policemen working under their supervision. And Adams laid down as the department's principal duty "the destruction of organized crime."

A few months after taking office, Commissioner Adams warned that New York City was on the verge of becoming a community of violence and crime. He declared that at least seven thousand additional policemen were needed to augment the existing force of 19,815.[26]

DeSapio had skillfully engineered the campaign of Wagner for mayor and the prestige of the Tammany boss had been enhanced tremendously. In the spring of 1953 Edward J. Flynn, the Bronx boss, died and DeSapio succeeded Flynn as a Democratic national committeeman. Thomas E. Dewey decided not to run for another term as governor and DeSapio believed the time was ripe for him to place a man of his choice in the office of the chief executive of the state. That man was Averell Harriman.

Franklin D. Roosevelt, Jr. was an avowed aspirant for the governorship. When he was passed over by the state Democratic convention and Harriman received the nomination, both Roosevelt and his mother, Eleanor, were bitter. However, young Roosevelt was given a consolation prize, the nomination for attorney general.

In the November 1954 election 5,110,351 cast votes for governor. Harriman squeaked through with a majority of only 11,125 votes over his Republican opponent, Senator Irving M. Ives. The sole loser on the Democratic state ticket was Franklin D. Roosevelt, Jr., who was defeated for the office of attorney general by a wide margin. DeSapio had played a major role in denying young Roosevelt the top spot on the ticket. Thus, Roosevelt's defeat merely added to the reputation of the Tammany boss for political acumen.

Carmine G. DeSapio had come a long way since he was made boss of Tammany Hall through the influence of underworld ruler Frank Costello. His prestige was at an all-time high. He had been responsible for the election of a mayor of New York City and a governor of the state, and was on intimate terms with each. When Harriman took office as governor on January 1, 1955, he named DeSapio to the ministerial post of secretary of state and enthusiastically hailed the Tammany boss as one of the great Democrats of "our generation."[27]

The outgoing governor, Thomas E. Dewey, originally had won fame following his appointment in 1935 as special prosecutor to investigate organized crime. When he left office on December 31, 1954, he had served three terms as governor (1943–54). The *New York Times* thanked Governor Dewey for the good government he had provided and referred to the period of service he had given to the people of New York as "extraordinary both for its length and fine quality." The course followed by Dewey was described as progressive and carefully thought out in advance. The state's fiscal position was kept sound, executive direction firm, and forward-looking. The citizen's liberties had been guarded diligently and his rights strengthened. From the beginning, Dewey had a gift for surrounding himself with able young men, and the result was energetic teamwork. "Thomas E. Dewey," said the *Times* editorial, "will surely be ranked high among this state's ablest governors, a fact usually conceded even by his political opponents. . . ."[28]

The new governor, Averell Harriman, had been in office but a few months when he became the target of criticism for his veto of legislation that provided for state supervision over union health and welfare funds. He was accused of kowtowing to labor-union politicians, who had supported him in his close race for governor the preceding November. And, it was charged, he was currying the favor of these union leaders to gain their support in his quest for the Democratic presidential nomination in 1956.

The need for supervision over health and welfare funds was apparent during the investigation that followed the gangland assassination in August

1953 of Thomas F. Lewis, president of Local 32-E, Building Service Employees Union. Over a quarter of a million dollars of the union's health and welfare funds had been siphoned into the pockets of Lewis, his relatives, or close associates.

Many labor leaders opposed any governmental scrutiny over union welfare funds. However, on July 4, 1954, David Dubinsky, president of the International Ladies Garment Workers Union and a leader in the fight against union racketeering, called on organized labor to support legislation designed to curb abuses in the administration of union welfare funds. Dubinsky realistically declared some union welfare funds were being squandered by racketeering elements and charged that criminals were muscling their way into trade unions for the express purpose of getting their hands on welfare funds.

A bill providing for the supervision of union trust funds was proposed after an inquiry by the former New York State superintendent of insurance, Alfred J. Bohlinger. He reported that of the union health and welfare funds investigated, many were properly administered, but thirty-four were riddled with serious abuses and thirty-seven were subject to "some criticism." The proposed legislation was passed, but vetoed by Governor Harriman.[29]

In the spring of 1954, the New York County Grand Jury, under the direction of District Attorney Frank S. Hogan, conducted an investigation of union health and welfare funds. Of particular interest were huge kickbacks made by a Newark insurance agent, Louis B. Saperstein, to a brother-in-law of ex-convict George Scalise, a notorious Brooklyn labor racketeer.

The criminal record of George Scalise extended back to 1913 when he was convicted under the White Slave Traffic Act and sentenced to four and one-half years to federal prison. For decades the associates of Scalise had included such top-flight gang leaders as Al Capone of Chicago, Frankie Yale and Anthony Carfano of Brooklyn, Lepke Buchalter, and Gurrah Shapiro. In the early 1930s Capone gangsters began taking over a number of the locals of the Building Service Employees International Union, which maintained its home office in Chicago. In July 1934 Scalise, reputedly on the recommendation of Carfano, was made eastern vice president of this international union and in 1937, through the influence of the Capone mob, he became its president. In May 1940 Thomas E. Dewey, then district attorney of New York County, obtained an indictment that charged Scalise with having stolen $60,000 from the union's treasury between May 1937 and March 1940. Following conviction, Scalise was sentenced to a term of ten to twenty years in prison. He was also sentenced to a three-year term on a federal indictment charging him with income-tax evasion.[30]

When Louis B. Saperstein was questioned by the 1954 grand jury about his kickbacks to Scalise's brother-in-law, he refused to cooperate. On May 17, 1954, District Attorney Hogan announced that the grand jury had voted an indictment that charged Saperstein with criminal contempt. The forty-eight-year-old Saperstein, once the secretary to the Newark Insurance Fund Commission, was then operating three insurance agencies in Newark, one in Chicago, and another in Los Angeles. On July 30, 1954, Saperstein was sentenced to a five-year prison term for criminal contempt. Later, after he had agreed to cooperate with the district attorney, his sentence was reduced to one year and he was released on bail pending the appeal of his conviction.

Saperstein had been an insignificant real estate and insurance broker until 1946, when he established a friendly connection with Abner (Longy) Zwillman, a powerful New Jersey organized crime personality. Zwillman's circle of intimate associates included the elite of the nation's underworld bosses—Frank Costello, Joe Adonis, Jerry Catena, Frank Erickson, and Lepke Buchalter. Evidence introduced at the Kefauver committee hearings established that Zwillman had telephoned Costello as many as seven times during the course of a single day.

Following his friendship with Zwillman, Saperstein's rise in the insurance business was meteoric. He began handling $5 million a year in health and welfare funds of several unions, chiefly the laundry workers and distillery workers unions. At a U.S. Senate committee hearing in 1955, insurance company representatives disclosed they had paid Saperstein commissions totaling $1.5 million in three years. When called before the committee, Saperstein invoked the Fifth Amendment and stated, ''I refuse to say whether I got the money. . . . I will say this—I didn't keep the money.''

With a contempt conviction hanging over his head, Saperstein cooperated with District Attorney Frank Hogan and testified before the grand jury regarding kickbacks of almost $300,000 he had made to George Scalise, Anthony Carfano, and Sol Cilento, former secretary-treasurer of the Distillery, Rectifying and Wine Workers International Union, AFL. He also gave $240,000 to Joseph (Doc) Stacher, a close associate of Longy Zwillman as well as Meyer Lansky.

On February 15, 1955, a bribery indictment was returned against Scalise, Carfano, and Cilento. On May 17, 1955, General Sessions Judge Jonah J. Goldstein dismissed the indictment, stating that the acts of the defendants were ''morally reprehensible and ethically indefensible'' but did not constitute a crime under existing law. He urged the state to enact remedial legislation promptly.[31]

On the evening of March 9, 1956, Louis B. Saperstein had dinner with members of his family in his home in an exclusive section of South Orange, New Jersey. About nine-thirty he told his wife, Irene, that he was going for a ride and drove away in his sporty convertible. Later, Saperstein and a woman companion, Mrs. Marie Benson, visited a number of nightclubs. About three-thirty the next morning, he parked his car in front of 54 Quitman Street in Newark and dozed off. Suddenly, a dark sedan with three or four occupants drove alongside the Saperstein convertible. One man jumped out, ran to the Saperstein car, opened the door to the driver's seat, drew his gun, and fired five shots. Two bullets entered Saperstein's head through his left ear, one through the mouth, one bullet pierced the neck, and the other shot went wild. Having completed their mission, the assailants sped away in their sedan. Mrs. Benson jumped out of the convertible and began screaming, which aroused a man and wife in a nearby home. The husband drove Saperstein, who was sprawled across the car seat in a pool of blood, to the St. Barnabas Hospital, only three hundred feet away. He was rushed to the emergency room. Physicians said his chances of recovery were very slim. Miraculously, Saperstein recovered. In a statement to the police, he declared that undoubtedly his testimony before the New York grand jury regarding union health and welfare funds had precipitated the attempted assassination. This view was also expressed by District Attorney Frank Hogan.

Saperstein's narrow escape from death in 1956 did not cure him of his penchant for dealing with mobsters. To finance a stock scheme several years later, he borrowed $400,000 at exorbitant rates from Angelo (the Gyp) DeCarlo and Daniel (Red) Cecere. When he failed to meet interest payments of $5,000 a week, he was savagely beaten and threatened with death. On November 25, 1968, Saperstein entered an Orange, New Jersey, hospital, complaining that "someone put silver stuff on my food." He died the following day and an autopsy revealed that his body contained enough arsenic "to kill a mule." Several months later, DeCarlo and Cecere were convicted of extortion and sentenced to twelve-year prison terms.[32]

Less than a month after the attempted assassination of Saperstein in 1956 the underworld struck again. This time the victim was a nationally known columnist and commentator on labor affairs, Victor Riesel. His syndicated column was then appearing in 193 newspapers throughout America.

In the early morning hours of April 5, 1956, Victor Riesel made a radio broadcast in which he denounced the prevalence of racketeering in Local 138 of the International Union of Operating Engineers on Long Island. In particular, he lashed out against the abuses of William C. DeKoning, Jr., who then headed Local 138, and his father, William C. DeKoning, Sr., who had recently been released from prison after serving a sentence for extortion. After his broadcast Riesel stopped at the popular Lindy's Restaurant at Fifty-first Street and Broadway. He walked out of Lindy's about three o'clock and shortly afterward was approached by a man on the sidewalk who hurled sulfuric acid in Riesel's eyes, causing permanent damage that left the columnist blind.[33]

A federal investigation established that the man who threw the acid in Riesel's face was a twenty-two-year-old hoodlum, Abraham Telvi, who had been hired for the job by Joseph Peter Carlino. The man who fingered Riesel for Telvi was Gondolfo Miranti. Both Carlino and Miranti were ex-convicts and had been active in the garment industry rackets.

Telvi had received a fee of $1,175 for hurling the acid. Allegedly, the fee was paid by John Dioguardi, commonly known as Johnny Dio, a onetime protégé of Lepke Buchalter and Gurrah Shapiro. The public furor that followed the attack on Riesel convinced Telvi that he had been grossly underpaid and he began dunning Dioguardi and other conspirators for more money. Finally, Telvi was told that he would be paid off in two weeks. He was! Exactly two weeks after receiving this promise, Telvi was slain in gangland fashion on July 28, 1956, on the Lower East Side of New York City.[34]

Testimony heard by a federal grand jury indicated that the acid-throwing attack had been plotted by John Dioguardi for the purpose of intimidating Riesel from testifying before a special federal rackets grand jury. On September 7, 1956, a federal indictment was returned that charged seven defendants with conspiracy to obstruct justice. Named as defendants were John Dioguardi, Charles Tusso, Domenico (Nick) Bando, Charles S. Carlino, Joseph Carlino, Gondolfo Miranti, and Leo Telvi a brother of Abraham.

In November 1956 three defendants—Domenico Bando, Gondolfo Miranti, and Leo Telvi—were brought to trial and convicted. Miranti and Bando each received a sentence of five years in a federal prison and Leo Telvi was given a two-year term. Miranti and Bando were expected to be key prosecution witnesses against Dioguardi and three codefendants. However, the imprisoned Miranti and Bando received underworld threats and were intimidated against testifying for the government. As a result, on May 27, 1957, United States Attorney Paul Williams announced that the prosecution against Dioguardi was being dropped.[35]

While the underworld was spewing vengeance against Saperstein and Riesel, judicial decisions were having effects on Frank Costello's future. On March 6, 1956, the United States Supreme Court upheld the conviction of Costello for income-tax evasion. Also facing the gangland boss were denaturalization proceedings instituted by the federal government with the view of eventual deportation. The basis for this action was false information Costello had provided under oath when he had applied for citizenship over three decades earlier. When the Supreme Court declined to review its decision on his income-tax conviction, Costello offered to leave the United States voluntarily if the government would suspend the five-year prison term that had been imposed on him. This offer was rejected and on May 14, 1956, Costello surrendered to begin serving his prison sentence.

Costello had been free on bail since a federal court in New York City had sentenced him on May 17, 1954. That sentence had an unsettling effect on the New York underworld. Organized crime bosses Albert Anastasia and Vito Genovese began vying for position with the objective of "taking over" once Costello landed behind bars. Costello's attorney, George Wolf, has related that during this period of uncertainty, Anastasia, flanked by two bodyguards, walked into an Italian restaurant on West Forty-eighth Street to meet with Costello. They shook hands and then sat down in a booth in the rear of the restaurant. During this conversation Anastasia complained that Vito Genovese had been "bad-mouthing" him by accusing him of muscling in on the Cuba business. In this respect, Genovese was not guilty of misrepresentation. Anastasia did enter into negotiations with Cuban officials over gambling concessions in Havana. According to Attorney Wolf, following the meeting between Costello and Anastasia in the Italian restaurant, word swept across the city that Anastasia was Costello's boy.[36]

Albert Anastasia, like Costello, was having trouble with the federal government over taxes. In November 1954, in a federal court in Newark, a five-day income-tax-evasion trial ended with a hung jury. An important witness at the trial was Charles Ferri, a Fort Lee, New Jersey, plumbing contractor, who had received $8,700 from Anastasia for work performed in the gangster's home. Ferri, regarded as a key witness, was expected to testify again during the upcoming second trial.

In April 1955 Ferri and his wife mysteriously disappeared from their blood-spattered home in suburban Miami, Florida. About a year earlier, Vincent Macri, an associate of Anastasia, was shot twice in the head and his body found stuffed in the trunk of a car in the Bronx. A few days later, Vincent's brother Benedicto, another close associate of Anastasia, disappeared and there was speculation that his body had been thrown into the Passaic River. Officials were convinced that the disappearances of Mr. and Mrs. Charles Ferri and Benedicto Macri, as well as the murder of Vincent Macri, were part of a plot intended to silence prospective witnesses and thus forestall a conviction of Anastasia.

The retrial of the tax case was scheduled in federal court in Camden, New Jersey, on May 23, 1955. Unexpectedly, the onetime chief executioner for Murder, Inc. entered a plea of guilty and on June 3, 1955, was sentenced to serve one year in the federal penitentiary in Milan, Michigan.[37]

Just a few weeks before Costello was convicted for income-tax evasion, his long-time confederate, Joe Adonis, was placed on trial in Washington, D.C., for perjury. Adonis had testified before the Kefauver committee that he was born in Passaic, New Jersey, in November 1901. The government produced an official birth certificate and other documentary evidence that established the gangster had been born in Italy on November 22, 1902. On March 25, 1954, a federal jury convicted Adonis of perjury and Judge Walter M. Bastian imposed a sentence of eight months to two years. Again, the once immune gangland boss had suffered a major defeat.

In October 1955 the Supreme Court rejected an appeal of the perjury conviction and Adonis was anxious to make a deal. Hanging over his head, in addition to a prison term, was a deportation order issued by the attorney general in 1953. Adonis offered to leave the United States voluntarily if the government would suspend his prison sentence. The offer was accepted and the gangster left American shores in style. Embarking for Italy on January 3, 1956, Adonis occupied one of the most luxurious suites on the Italian line's SS *Conte Biancamano*. Asked if he planned to see Lucky Luciano, Adonis replied, ''I have no plans to look him up and I hope he doesn't look me up.''[38]

Costello had met with a rebuff when he, imitating Adonis, had offered to go into voluntary exile in return for a suspended prison sentence. On May 14, 1956, Costello entered the federal penitentiary in Atlanta. In the meantime, he added to his legal staff a well-known criminal lawyer, Edward Bennett Williams, who raised a new legal point in the Costello income-tax case. Williams contended that Costello should have been sentenced under a section of the law that carried a maximum penalty of one year and a $1,000 fine. The U.S. Supreme Court agreed to hear this new appeal and on March 11, 1957, Costello was released on bail from prison. Several months later, the appeal was rejected and Costello was returned to prison to complete serving his five-year sentence. Not until June 29, 1961, did he gain his final release from the federal penitentiary.[39]

When Costello returned temporarily to New York City in March 1957, one of his intimate associates was a central figure in a parole scandal. The underworld was in a turmoil and within a few weeks the once all-powerful gangland leader and some of his colleagues would become the targets of violence.

Involved in the parole scandal that rocked state and local politics in 1957 was extortionist Joseph (Socks) Lanza, known as the czar of the Fulton Fish Market. Lanza, a frequent visitor at the Costello apartment, had once been influential in Tammany Hall politics. He was close to many Tammany Hall district leaders and his brother-in-law, Prosper Vincent Viggiano, was Tammany leader of the Second Assembly District and secretary to a state supreme-court justice. Lanza was no stranger to the Tammany boss, Carmine G. DeSapio. In fact, Bert Stand, former secretary of Tammany Hall, charged that DeSapio had used Lanza to oust Stand from his leadership in the Fourth Assembly District in the Lower East Side. The man who dismissed parole violation charges against Lanza under unusual circumstances was Parole Commissioner James R. Stone, an appointee of Governor Averell Harriman and a relative of Charles A. Buckley, Democratic leader of the Bronx. Obviously, the Lanza case was enmeshed deeply in politics.

Originally, Lanza had been sentenced on January 29, 1943, to a prison term of seven and one-half to fifteen years for extortion from a local Teamsters union. To operate in the Fulton Fish Market, the union was required to meet Lanza's demands for money. After spending over seven years and seven months in prison, Lanza was paroled on September 11, 1950. He retained his freedom until February 5, 1957, when he was arrested as a parole violator for consorting with criminals, living beyond his income, and gambling. He was lodged in the Westchester County Jail to await a hearing on the charges.[40]

As soon as Lanza landed in jail, political wheels were set in motion. Viggiano immediately sought the assistance of Thomas I. Fitzgerald, the recently appointed public administrator of New York County and from 1949 to 1953 the secretary of Tammany Hall. Fitzgerald, an intimate friend of Boss DeSapio, began burning up the telephone wires in an effort to reach Commissioner Stone. Within twelve hours after Lanza's arrest, Fitzgerald located Stone during the night at a motel near Auburn, New York, and talked with him by telephone about the Lanza parole. About two days later, Tammany Hall legislators from Manhattan, Senator Joseph R. Marro and Assemblyman Louis DeSalvio, called on Lee B. Mailler, chairman of the New York State Board of Parole, in Albany.

The parole board was composed of five men but a single commissioner was empowered to hear and decide parole violation cases. Lanza stalwarts were busily engaged in attempting to maneuver the hearing before a "friendly" commissioner. This was evident from surreptitiously tape-recorded conversations between Joseph Lanza, his brother Harry, and others who visited the parolee in the Westchester County Jail. Harry explained to Joseph that a different commissioner heard cases each week. He described the commissioner then hearing cases as "no good." This man was to be followed by Commissioner Phillip J. Hirsch, and, said Harry, "Then comes the other, the best friend of ours."

The tape-recorded conversations disclosed that many persons were working frantically in behalf of Lanza's release. Particularly intriguing were talks between the parolee and brother Harry in which references were made to expected help from "the little fella" and "the man with the glasses." And when a lawyer, Sylvester Cosentino, visited Lanza, he reported that he had seen "the little fella" and "the little fella" had seen "the man with the glasses." Cosentino also assured Lanza that "Fitzgerald's been working upstate, downstate, everywhere." In a report to Governor Harriman, the acting state commissioner of investigation identified "the little fella" as Tammany district leader Viggiano and Fitzgerald as a former Tammany secretary, Thomas I. Fitzgerald. There was good reason to believe that "the man with the glasses" was Tammany Boss DeSapio, who, because of an eye ailment, always wore dark glasses.[41]

Commissioner Hirsch had been scheduled to conduct hearings on February 19, 1957, but he decided to take the day off and so notified Commissioner James R. Stone. Without the knowledge of Hirsch or other members of the board, Stone constituted himself the parole trial commissioner on February 19 and promptly called the Lanza case.

In a report prepared by parole officials, it was asserted that Lanza, aided by his family and a combination, had continued to control the Fulton Fish Market through shakedowns of loaders, labor racketeering, and cornering the shrimp and halibut produce market. Not one fish boat could be loaded unless Lanza's combination received its cut. It was common knowledge in the market that Lanza's entourage included ten strong-arm men, payoff men, enforcers, and collectors. These hoodlums, mostly of Italian extraction, had been lifelong associates of Lanza. The report, approved by parole officers Israel Greenspan and John Clark, concluded that Lanza was not a fit subject for parole supervision. This document was turned over on February 19 to Commissioner Stone, who, nevertheless, immediately dismissed the charges against Lanza and ordered him restored to parole supervision. The decision created a public furor that touched off two official investigations: one by the Joint Legislative Committee on Government Operations, known as the Legislative Watchdog Committee, and the other by the acting state commisioner of investigation, Arthur L. Reuter.[42]

On March 31, 1957, Reuter summoned Parole Commissioner Stone to his office and bluntly told him that he was being given two choices: he could sign a letter of resignation to be effective immediately or face removal, also to be effective at once. Stone, formerly a career man in the parole service, resigned. Thus, he abandoned his pension rights as well as his annual $15,000 salary.[43]

For several weeks a steady stream of witnesses appeared at hearings conducted by the Legislative Watchdog Committee. Also made public were excerpts from official parole reports and transcripts of secretly recorded conversations between Lanza and visitors in the Westchester County Jail. Thomas I. Fitzgerald testified that Boss DeSapio had questioned him about his role in the Lanza case and was concerned over possible political repercussions. Fitzgerald revealed that on at least six occasions he had rehearsed the testimony he expected to give before the watchdog committee with DeSapio and lawyer friends. When first questioned by the committee, Stone denied that he had discussed the Lanza case with anyone outside the parole division. Subsequently, Stone conceded that Fitzgerald, P. Vincent Viggiano, and Assistant State Attorney General Vincent Marsicano had spoken to him about the matter. Marsicano testified that a law partner of Lanza's attorney had requested him to give false testimony before the watchdog committee. The hearings had, indeed, provided an insight into the machinations of the underworld and its political allies.

On April 18, 1957, Lee B. Mailler, chairman of the New York State Board of Parole, announced that the board had ruled Joseph (Socks) Lanza to be a parole delinquent and had ordered him returned to prison.[44]

But Lanza was not the sole loser in the parole scandal. There were serious political reverberations. Governor Harriman had relied heavily on Boss DeSapio for political advice and Commissioner Stone had been one of four Harriman appointees to quit or be forced out of office under a cloud within a two-year period. A *New York Times* article on April 14, 1957, realistically pointed out that the Lanza case was "posing an ominous threat to Carmine G. DeSapio's prestige as a national political figure" and was "likewise casting a dark cloud over Governor Harriman's future."

For several months, there had been indications of seething unrest in the underworld. That unrest surfaced in New York City on May 2, 1957, when an attempt was made to assassinate Frank Costello. It was Thursday night. Costello and his wife; Philip Kennedy, the manager of a modeling agency; Generoso Pope, the publisher of *Il Progresso,* an Italian-language newspaper; and others dined together at L'Aiglon, an East Side restaurant. After dinner someone suggested that the party go to the Monsignore Restaurant for a nightcap. All except Costello and Kennedy were receptive to the suggestion. Costello wished to return to his apartment to make some telephone calls and he hailed a taxicab. Accompanied by Kennedy, Costello proceeded by cab to his apartment building at 115 Central Park West. Standing in front of the building, Kennedy and Costello engaged in a short conversation before parting. In the meantime, a long black Cadillac had been driven to a spot near the entrance of the building. A huge man with a hat pulled down over his eyes jumped out of the car and hurriedly entered the place. Costello walked into the building, apparently unaware of any danger. The fat man who had been lurking in the shadows suddenly appeared. He leveled a gun at the gang leader's head and fired. Blood streamed from Costello's scalp as he crumpled to the floor. The gunman ran from the building, jumped into the waiting Cadillac, driven by another man, and sped north on Central Park West.

The bleeding Costello was placed into a taxicab and rushed through the Manhattan traffic to the Roosevelt Hospital, where he entered the emergency room at 11:08 P.M. The doctors determined that the bullet had struck behind the victim's left ear, burrowed under the scalp around the back of the head and emerged close to the right ear. The freakish course of the bullet had saved Costello's life. At 12:15 A.M. Costello, with a white bandage around his head and wearing a bloodstained shirt and jacket, was released from the hospital.

The shooting was front-page news throughout the nation. In New York City sixty-five detectives were assigned to the case. Costello insisted that he did not see his assailant and had no idea who might have had designs on his life. In fact, he solemnly asserted, he did not have an enemy in the world.

When Costello was receiving emergency treatment at the Roosevelt Hospital, police officers examined certain papers he was carrying at the time he was felled by a bullet. In a pocket of his jacket police found a puzzling note: "Gross casino wins as of 4-26-57 . . . $651,284.00." Other figures included "Casino wins less markers $434,695.00," "slot wins $62,844," and "markers $153,745." There were also listed payments to Mike, $150 a week, totaling $600; to Jake, $100 a week, totaling $400; to "L. $30,000"; and to "H. $9000." An examination of the note indicated that it bore the handwriting of two persons.

A grand jury initiated an investigation of the attempted assassination of the underworld leader and called him as a witness. In particular, he was asked to explain the note found in his jacket pocket. Costello invoked the Fifth Amendment and refused to answer any questions on the ground of self-incrimination. He was granted immunity and when he still persisted in his refusal to give any explanation regarding the note, he was held in contempt of court and sentenced to thirty days in the workhouse. After spending fifteen days in the Tombs, he gained his release pending an appeal of the contempt sentence.

Official investigations subsequently established that the note related to the financial affairs of the new Tropicana Hotel in Las Vegas, Nevada. During the first twenty-four days the Tropicana was in operation, its gross gambling receipts amounted to $651,284.00, the exact figure for casino winnings that appeared on the note.

Operating the Tropicana in Las Vegas was a firm called Conquistador, Inc., in which Costello's long-time partner, Dandy Phil Kastel, had been a principal investor. The Nevada Gaming Control Board, in February 1957, refused to approve Dandy Phil's connection with the Tropicana venture because of his known intimate ties with Costello, Meyer Lansky, and other crime bosses. Following conferences with the Nevada Gaming Control Board, Conquistador, Inc. signed an agreement in which Kastel supposedly relinquished his interest. His investment of $320,000 was to be repaid at the rate of $40,000 a year. The Tropicana Hotel opened on April 3, 1957, with Louis J. Lederer and Kel Houssels, Sr. in charge of the casino. According to Nevada official records, Tropicana stock valued at $180,000 had been issued to Lederer, and his long-time associate in Chicago, Charles (Babe) Baron, had stock holdings of $120,000. Later, it was revealed that Baron also had ties with Lansky in a gambling operation in Cuba.

Investigation by the Nevada Gaming Control Board established that the main portion of the note found on Costello was written by Michael J. Tanico, a Tropicana cashier who had been employed by Kastel in the lavishly furnished Beverly Club casino near New Orleans. Partners in the Beverly Club had included Kastel, Costello, Lansky, and Carlos Marcello. The remaining portion of the note was written by Lederer.

In New York City, officials developed information indicating that the hulking gunman who had attempted the assassination of Costello was Vincent (the Chin) Gigante. On July 17, 1957, Gigante, accompanied by his attorney, surrendered at the West Fifty-fourth Street police station. Later, at Gigante's trial, Costello turned out to be an excellent witness for the defense. He insisted that he had seen nothing at the time of the shooting and consequently could not identify his assailant. The doorman at the apartment building had a good opportunity to view the gunman but he was blind in one eye and had impaired vision in the other. The trial was brief and Gigante was acquitted. And giving a peculiar twist to the entire affair was a dinner party given by Costello in his apartment some time later. Among the honored guests was Vincent Gigante.[45]

Only a few weeks following the attempted assassination of Costello, underworld violence broke out again. On June 17, 1957, one of Albert Anastasia's righthand men, Frank (Don Cheech) Scalise, was slain by two gunmen as he was leaving a fruit and vegetable store in the Bronx. The assassins pumped four bullets into Scalise's neck and head and fled in an automobile. A onetime associate of Costello, Scalise counted among his intimate friends Lucky Luciano and Anthony Strollo, commonly known as Tony Bender. Scalise had ruled over the construction rackets in the Bronx and reputedly was involved in the international narcotics traffic.

Joseph Scalise, a brother of the victim, rashly vowed that he would avenge Frank's murder. On September 19, 1957, Joseph Scalise was reported missing by his son and was never seen again. It was rumored in underworld circles that he had been killed in the home of an Anastasia lieutenant, his body dismembered, and the pieces disposed of.[46]

The attempted assassination of Costello in May and the murder of Frank Scalise a few weeks later were but a prelude to more sensational underworld violence.

At 10:15 A.M. on October 25, 1957, Albert Anastasia, often dubbed the chief executioner of Murder, Inc., strolled into the Park Sheraton Hotel Barbershop at Seventh Avenue and Fifty-fifth Street. Cheerfully greeting the barbershop employees, Anastasia hung up his topcoat and sat down in chair number four, manned by John Bocchino. In the barbershop at the time were eleven persons in addition to Anastasia—five barbers, two other customers, two shoeshine men, a valet, and a manicurist. As Bocchino was using the clippers on Anastasia's neck, two men wearing scarves over the lower portion of their faces entered the front door. Each man promptly drew a pistol. Moving quickly behind the chair in which Anastasia was sitting, the gunmen opened fire. With the first spurt of bullets, Anastasia leaped forward, kicking the barber chair's footrest with such force it was torn away. He was standing unsteadily when a second burst of gunfire propelled him against the glass shelving in front of the mirror. Bottles crashed to the floor. The final shot hit him in the back of the head and he crumpled to the floor.

Other bullets had struck Anastasia's left hand, left wrist, right hip, and back. Of ten shots fired at close range at a stationary target, five missed completely—hardly expert marksmanship. Having finished their mission, the killers hurried out the front door and disappeared. Both pistols used by the assassins were abandoned nearby and recovered. When Anastasia entered the barbershop, his bodyguard had remained outside near the front door. Peculiarly, he had left his post and sauntered down the street just before the gunmen arrived and the shooting began.

A florist, whose place was next door, heard the shots and saw people running hysterically from the barbershop. He frantically dialed the police. Within minutes police radio cars converged on the barbershop while traffic policemen in the area rushed to the scene. A physician from a nearby hospital arrived, examined the prostrate body of Anastasia, and pronounced him dead. Word of the assassination rapidly spread through the city. A newspaper reporter telephoned Anthony Anastasia, vice president of the International Longshoremen's Association, at his office in Brooklyn. Anthony raced to the barbershop in Manhattan where he identified the body of his brother, Albert.

Attorney George Wolf has related that within hours after the murder, he was summoned to Costello's apartment where he found Costello and Anthony embracing each other and sobbing. Costello also expressed a fear that he would be next on the hit list.

Found among the personal effects of Albert Anastasia were papers that established he was then in the process of negotiating for a gambling casino in Havana, Cuba. A delegation from Cuba had been sent to New York City to meet with him and complete the deal.

Already solidly entrenched in Cuba's legalized gambling industry were several important organized crime leaders, who probably looked dimly upon Anastasia's efforts to gain a foothold in Cuba. The San Souci gambling casino in Havana was operated by Louis Trafficante, Jr. His father had been boss of the Tampa, Florida, rackets for many years. A partner of Trafficante in the San Souci was Luigi (Joe Rivers) Silesi, a New York gambler. The most powerful underworld leader in Cuba, however, was Meyer Lansky, who had been firmly entrenched in Cuban gambling ventures for many years. He put together a syndicate that was to control the plush gambling operations in the new Riviera Hotel. A report made by the U.S. consul general revealed that Lansky's associates in the Riviera were, among others, his brother Jake, Frank Erickson, Edward Cellini, Girodino (Dino) Cellini, Edward Levinson, Irving (Nig) Devine, and Charles (Babe) Baron, a stockholder in the Tropicana Hotel casino in Las Vegas.

The Anastasia murder ranked with the more sensational gangland-type killings of the century. Twenty-nine years earlier, the slaying of the powerful underworld boss Arnold Rothstein resulted in a political upheaval that rocked the city. Rothstein was fatally shot on November 4, 1928, at the Park Central Hotel, which later became the Park Sheraton, site of the Anastasia killing.[47]

Only three weeks after the sensational gangland killing of Anastasia, over sixty Italian and Sicilian underworld characters assembled on November 14, 1957, in central New York. The site of the meeting was the spacious home of Joseph Barbara in the hills behind the village of Apalachin, not far from the Pennsylvania border. The Barbara estate, with its picnic pavilion and huge barbecue pit, was well equipped for entertaining a big party.

The host, Joseph M. Barbara, Sr., president of Canada Dry Bottling Company of Endicott, New York, was born in Castellammare, Sicily, in 1905. He migrated to the United States about 1921 and became a naturalized citizen in 1927. For some time he lived in the Pittston, Pennsylvania, area where he was involved in the rackets. On two occasions, in 1932 and 1933, he was picked up as a suspect in gangland-type murder cases but was not prosecuted. His sole conviction was in 1944, when he was found guilty of illegal possession of 300,000 pounds of sugar.

For several years Barbara had been under the watchful eye of Sergeant Edgar D. Croswell of the New York State Police, Bureau of Criminal Investigation. Croswell's interest was first aroused in 1944, when he arrested a man stealing gasoline from one of Barbara's plants. Barbara came to the police station, arrogantly armed with a revolver for which he had a permit, and flatly refused to prosecute. Several times Croswell had observed men with known criminal ties visiting Barbara's home. And it was learned that on October 16 and 17, 1956, Barbara was registered at the Arlington Hotel in Binghamton, New York, with such underworld personages as Joseph Bonanno, Frank Garofolo, and John Bonventre. The hotel bills for all were paid by Barbara.

On November 13, 1957, Sergeant Croswell and partner, Trooper Vincent Vasisko, were in a motel investigating a bad-check case when Barbara's son came into the place and engaged three rooms for two nights for men who, he explained, were going to attend a Canada Dry convention. He declined to give the names of the men and departed with the keys. Croswell and Vasisko, who had remained out of sight during young Barbara's visit to the motel, became suspicious. They initiated an investigation by looking for strange cars in the vicinity. They were joined in their inquiry by two federal agents from the Alcohol-Tobacco Tax Unit. On November 14, 1957, Sergeant Croswell, his partner, and two federal agents drove to the Barbara estate. They were spotted and the Barbara party was thrown into utter confusion. Men started running in all directions. A road block was thrown up and New York State Police reinforcements were rushed to the scene. Some of Barbara's guests jumped into cars and attempted to drive away but were stopped by the roadblock. Other men ran into the woods but, as Croswell explained, there was no place for them to go. When they emerged from the woods they were picked up by officers who were patrolling the roads and taken to the state police substation in Vestal, New York, for questioning.[48]

When asked to identify themselves, most of the men reached into a shirt pocket and produced a driver's license. Although each man had from $2,000 to $3,000 on his person, very few possessed wallets. The money was carried loosely in a pants' pocket. The state troopers made public the names of the men they determined had attended the Apalachin conclave. It was revealed that previously several had been questioned by police regarding the Anastasia assassination. Most of the men known to have been present were from New York, New Jersey, and Pennsylvania. A few were from distant places, including Louis Trafficante, Jr., alias Louis Santo, originally from Tampa, Florida, but then the operator of the San Souci gambling casino in Havana, Cuba. A former part owner of the San Souci, Gabriel Mannarino of New Kensington, Pennsylvania, was also in attendance. Important New York underworld bosses present included Vito Genovese, Carlo Gambino, Gerardo (Jerry) Catena, Joseph Bonanno, Joseph Profaci, and Joseph Magliocco. Other influential organized crime figures at Apalachin included Natale Joseph Evola, Carmine Lombardozzi, Michele Miranda, John Ormento, Paul Castellano, Joseph Riccobono, and Alfred Rava.

The Apalachin conference was a remarkable assemblage of sinister underworld bosses and underlings. Most of the men had been arrested in the past on serious charges—murder, robbery, extortion, blackmail, counterfeiting, burglary, grand larceny, rape, possession of firearms, gambling, and narcotics. One of the few men present who had no known prior record was Charles Chiri, a former partner of Joe Adonis in the Automotive Conveying Company in New Jersey.

The Apalachin conference was front-page news throughout the nation. Speculation was rife as to the purpose of the conclave. Federal narcotics agents labeled the event a meeting of the grand council of the Mafia. No credible evidence was advanced to support this highly improbable thesis, even though it was widely accepted.

The Apalachin affair touched off numerous investigations and within the following several months public hearings were conducted by the State Joint Legislative Committee on Government Operations, the U. S. Senate Select Committee on Improper Activities in the Labor or Management Field, headed by Senator John L. McClellan, and the New York State Commission of Investigation.

In April 1958 an able New York lawyer, Milton Ralph Wessel, a special assistant to the attorney general of the United States, was named to head a group in the attorney general's office to spearhead a drive against organized crime. Under Wessel's direction, the Apalachin conference was thoroughly investigated and in May 1959 a federal grand jury in New York City returned an indictment that charged a conspiracy to obstruct justice. Twenty-seven men who had attended the Apalachin meeting were named as defendants and thirty-six were listed as coconspirators. The basis for the government's prosecution was an alleged criminal pact by the defendants to take affirmative steps to hide the purpose of the Apalachin meeting. The steps included perjury, giving testimony disguising the true nature of their activities, and thwarting the legitimate processes of federal grand juries. At the conclusion of a long trial on December 18, 1959, twenty defendants were found guilty. On January 13, 1960, the federal judge, Irving R. Kaufman, who presided over the trial, imposed sentences of five years on fifteen defendants, four years on four, and a three-year term on the remaining defendant. However, upon appeal, the convictions were reversed. And, notwithstanding exhaustive investigative efforts by both state and federal governments, the real purpose of the Apalachin conclave was never determined.[49]

The year 1957 had been an unusually eventful one in underworld annals. The parole scandal involving Joseph Lanza, the shooting of Frank Costello, the murder of Frank Scalise, the assassination of Albert Anastasia, and the Apalachin conclave of criminals had focused attention throughout the land on the forces of organized crime in New York City. Those events also had political connotations and 1957 was a political year. New York City was to be the scene of another mayoral election and the fortunes of the incumbent, Robert F. Wagner, would be guided by Tammany Boss Carmine G. DeSapio.

The Lanza parole scandal had tarnished DeSapio's political prestige. The shooting of Costello had a personal significance to DeSapio. After all, it was Costello's influence that had made DeSapio the head of Tammany Hall and had given him the opportunity for national political prominence.

The highly publicized underworld events of 1957 must have caused DeSapio some political uneasiness, an uneasiness that was aggravated by an act of personal carelessness. One morning in July 1957 DeSapio left his apartment, hailed a taxicab at Fifth Avenue and Eighth Street, and instructed the cabby to drive him to the Biltmore Hotel. After DeSapio had left the vehicle, the cab driver noticed a white envelope on the passenger seat. Upon opening the envelope, the driver observed that it contained bills, all in the denominations of $50 to $100, totaling $11,200. Additionally perplexing was the unusual condition of the bills. They were dirty and musty, giving the appearance of having been buried in some dank place. The cab driver delivered the envelope with the bills to the nearest police station.

The incident was reminiscent of the time Frank Costello had left two envelopes containing $27,200 on the back seat of a cab in June 1944. Then Costello had claimed ownership of the money, but by the time all legal action was completed, he had recovered only relatively little. Unlike Costello, DeSapio denied that the $11,200 found in the cab belonged to him.

He admitted having been a passenger in the cab but suggested the envelope must have been on the seat of the cab when he entered it. And because of his preoccupation with weighty matters, he explained, he did not notice it. Few accepted this highly unlikely story. It was commonly believed that DeSapio had left the money in the cab but could not afford, politically, to explain its source or why he possessed it. After a year had elapsed and no one claimed the money, it was turned over to the cab driver who found it.

The events of the year did not affect the cordial relations that existed between DeSapio and Mayor Wagner. DeSapio played a major role in engineering the successful reelection campaign of Wagner in 1957. When the votes were counted, Wagner received 1,508,775 votes to 585,768 for Robert K. Christenberry, the Republican opponent.[50]

19

END OF LINE FOR BOSS DESAPIO

On January 1, 1958, Robert F. Wagner began his second term as mayor of New York City. Both of his mayoral campaigns—in 1953 and 1957—had been directed with consummate skill by Tammany Boss Carmine G. DeSapio, who now looked with anticipation to the state elections of 1958. Having established himself as a kingmaker in city and state governments, DeSapio had visions of playing a similar role on the national scene two years later. And he expected the 1958 political campaigns to serve as a stepping stone for him to achieve this ambition.

The Democratic State Convention was to convene in Buffalo in September 1958. It was a foregone conclusion that Averell Harriman would be renominated as the Democratic candidate for governor. Hence, the key spot on the ticket to be filled was the nomination for U.S. senator.

In March 1958 Harriman had sent for his political mentor, DeSapio, and expressed the opinion that the Democratic ticket should be balanced by having a Catholic nominated for U.S. senator. But he made it clear that he did not want the nomination given to Mayor Wagner, who many politicians believed would make the strongest candidate. Wagner was not in a position to seek the nomination actively; during the mayoral race he had pledged that if reelected, he would not run for a higher office.

Harriman's choice as his senatorial running mate was Thomas E. Murray, Jr., a wealthy engineer who was a big contributor to the Roman Catholic church. Murray's proposed candidacy failed to inspire much enthusiasm among the county leaders either in New York City or upstate. DeSapio thereupon decided to back District Attorney Frank S. Hogan for U.S. senator. The Tammany boss also quietly lined up many leaders in the city and state to support Hogan. But there was no public pronouncement of DeSapio's selection and the Tammany boss took every precaution to preserve the fiction that he had no personal choice for the Senate nomination.

Adding further confusion to the preconvention manipulations, only a few days before the delegates were to meet in Buffalo, DeSapio was visited by Alex Rose, head of the Liberal party, and George Backer, a millionaire confidant of Governor Harriman. Rose and Backer urged that the Senate nomination be given to Thomas K. Finletter, a law partner of Adlai Stevenson. Finletter was expected to help Stevenson obtain a third Democratic nomination for the presidency two years hence. Governor Harriman entertained aspirations for the presidential nomination himself and indications were that Harriman and Finletter disliked each other.

As the 1,100 delegates gathered in Buffalo for the convention, DeSapio was still insisting publicly that he had no personal choice for the Senate nomination. He maintained this posture even in private hotel room conferences with Harriman and Wagner. But in the background DeSapio was pulling strings for his man Hogan. For three days and nights the various delegates were holding back-room meetings characterized by deals and bickering. Hogan was not invited to the meetings, nor was he a party to the behind-the-scenes machinations.

Harriman was maneuvered into accepting the renomination for governor before the convention had reached a decision on the balance of the ticket. Thus, the governor lost his bargaining power to name the man of his choice as his running mate on the ticket for the Senate nomination. The discord between Harriman and DeSapio on this issue now surfaced. Harriman reminded DeSapio that he was his secretary of state and should abide by his, the governor's, wishes. DeSapio rebuffed the governor and announced that he was for Hogan, who was then nominated by the convention. Harriman had suffered humiliation at the hands of the man he had once declared to be one of the great Democrats of "our generation."

The Buffalo convention served as a vivid example of bossism and presented a ready-made issue to the Republican opposition. In the November 1958 election, Nelson Rockefeller, Republican, defeated Harriman for governor by 573,000 votes and Kenneth B. Keating, Republican, was elected to the U.S. Senate, winning by 133,000 votes over Frank S. Hogan.

The internecine struggle over the Democratic senatorial nomination caused many raised eyebrows over the incongruous relationship existing between DeSapio and Hogan. The district attorney deservedly had won the appellation Mr. Integrity. Previously, he had exposed and fought the insidious political influence of Frank Costello. Why was Costello's protégé, DeSapio, so anxious to back Hogan for higher office? Some cynics suggested that the Tammany boss hoped to get the efficient Hogan out of the district attorney's office. On the other hand, DeSapio's record for choosing quality candidates had been reasonably good. Perhaps he expected that his selection of Hogan would redound to his credit as an enlightened political leader worthy to exert influence at the national level. Somewhat ironically, several years later, Hogan furnished evidence that aided in sending DeSapio to federal prison on a kickback conspiracy charge.

When the Democratic State Convention met in Buffalo, former Governor Herbert Lehman was vacationing in Switzerland. However, he was kept abreast of developments and was shocked and distressed by them. DeSapio's refusal to yield to Harriman's wishes regarding the Senate nomination was regarded by Lehman as a denigration of the office of governor, an office he held in high respect.

The Buffalo convention had served to unite the reform elements in the Democratic party. On January 22, 1959, Lehman held a press conference to announce that a new organization called the Committee for Democratic Voters (CDV) was establishing permanent headquarters at 120 East Fifty-sixth Street. The organization, he said, would function under the direction of a triumvirate consisting of Lehman, Eleanor Roosevelt, and Thomas K. Finletter. The main villain, according to Lehman, was Boss DeSapio, whom the CDV intended to oppose. Under Lehman's leadership, the CDV raised a half-million dollars to be spent on a drive to defeat DeSapio. A few philanthropists also provided funds, referred to as Adlai Stevenson money, to be used in an effort to defeat DeSapio as leader in his home assembly district in Greenwich Village. This was sound strategy, for only an assembly district leader could serve as head of Tammany Hall. The fight waged by the reformers in Manhattan became a personal issue. Considered as good guys were those who opposed DeSapio, whereas his supporters became the bad guys.

Some impartial observers noted, sardonically, that DeSapio and his tactics had been acceptable to the Democratic party and the Tammany boss had been hailed as a great leader, even by liberals, when he led the party to victory. It was only when the ticket met defeat that DeSapio suddenly became an ogre, the symbol of bossism, who must be stripped of all power at all costs.[1]

With the leadership of the reform movement in the capable hands of such Democratic notables as former Governor Lehman and Eleanor Roosevelt, DeSapio was faced with formidable opposition indeed. But all of DeSapio's supporters did not promptly abandon him. Mayor Wagner wished to keep in the good graces of both Lehman and Mrs. Roosevelt, but he still felt a need for DeSapio's services. At the 1959 annual dinner of Tammany Hall, Wagner referred to DeSapio as the best leader the party had ever had.

In the 1959 primary the reformers made substantial inroads, but the DeSapio forces still retained the upper hand. In DeSapio's home base of Greenwich Village, he was challenged for the assembly district leadership by Charles McGuinness, who ran under the banner of the Village Independent Democrats. DeSapio won the contest, 4,857 votes to 4,271. The Tammany Executive Committee then reelected DeSapio boss of Tammany Hall by a vote of ten to six. DeSapio was still kingpin of Tammany but it was obvious he would face tremendous opposition in the future.[2]

While the political fury raged in New York City in 1959, it may be questioned whether DeSapio's former patron, Frank Costello, was taking more than a casual interest in the developments. The man who was once the most powerful influence in Tammany Hall was still behind bars in Atlanta, serving a five-year term for income-tax evasion. In his judicial encounters Costello continued to fare badly. On February 20, 1959, a federal court divested him of his citizenship because at the time of his naturalization he had concealed his criminal activities. As an alien, Costello was now subject to deportation proceedings.[3]

Ill luck was also pursuing some of Costello's long-time intimate associates. On February 26, 1959, the body of Abner (Longy) Zwillman was found hanging from a plastic clothesline in his twenty-room mansion in West Orange, New Jersey. The fifty-four-year-old underworld bigwig had become despondent over a number of recent developments. The U.S. Senate Rackets Committee, headed by Senator John L. McClellan, was investigating the coin-machine industry. Jerry Catena, a partner of Zwillman in the cigarette vending-machine business, had already been called before the Senate committee and questioned. Just a week before the suicide, several persons had been indicted by a federal grand jury for bribing jurors who had served on the deadlocked panel that had tried Zwillman for income-tax evasion in 1956.[4]

Seven months after Zwillman's demise, the long career of another important underworld leader, Anthony Carfano, was suddenly ended by assassins' bullets. Carfano, commonly known as Little Augie Pisano, had been influential in gangland circles for several decades. In fact, immediately after the sensational murder of Frankie Yale on July 1, 1928, Carfano, a close associate of Joe Adonis, had taken over many of Yale's enterprises in Brooklyn. Carfano had also maintained strong ties with Tammany politics.

On the night of September 25, 1959, Carfano; Mrs. Janice Drake, a former beauty queen; Anthony Strollo, better known as Tony Bender; Vincent Mauro; and ex-convict Al Segal and wife dined at a restaurant on Lexington Avenue. In the midst of the meal, Carfano received a telephone call and hurriedly departed with Janice Drake. Several hours later, the bodies of Carfano and Drake were found in a 1959 Cadillac in Queens. Both had been shot in the back of the head, apparently by assassins who had been sitting in the rear seat of the Cadillac.

On September 29, 1959, an airplane bound from Houston to New York City disintegrated in flight over central Texas killing thirty-four persons. Found in the wreckage were loose diamonds valued at $200,000 and another undamaged case of diamonds. It was speculated that the diamonds belonged to George Uffner, one of the passengers killed when the ill-fated plane exploded. Uffner had been an intimate associate and golfing companion of Frank Costello. At one time the telephone in Costello's home in Sands Point was registered in George Uffner's name. Uffner, Costello, and Frank Erickson had been partners in valuable oil interests in Texas. During the 1920s

Uffner, Costello, Dandy Phil Kastel, and other underworld characters were on the payroll of Arnold Rothstein.[5]

For some time Vito Genovese had been growing in stature as one of the more powerful organized crime bosses in New York City. Although he had been arrested on charges ranging from felonious assault and burglary to carrying concealed weapons and homicide, he had shown an uncanny ability to beat the rap. But his status as an untouchable was coming to an end.

On April 17, 1959, Genovese was one of fifteen persons who received a lengthy sentence in federal court in New York City for conspiracy to violate the narcotics laws. During the trial, the government asserted that a multi-million-dollar international narcotics ring had been efficiently organized along the lines of a huge legitimate business. Genovese and aide Natale Joseph Evola were described as executives in the enterprise. Some of the conspirators specialized in the importation of the drugs, others served as distributors in the United States, and at the lower level were the peddlers or pushers who sold the narcotics to the consumers.

Genovese was sentenced to a federal prison term of fifteen years and Evola received a ten-year sentence. Each was fined $20,000. Both Genovese and Evola had been present at the conclave of criminals at Apalachin, New York, in November 1957.

Also convicted in the narcotics conspiracy trial was Vincent Gigante, the huge gunman who had been tried and acquitted of the attempted assassination of Frank Costello in May 1957. Residents of his community in Greenwich Village inundated the government with letters praising Gigante's work with juveniles and consequently he was given a sentence of only seven years.[6]

Only a few months after Genovese had been sentenced to prison, another prestigious gangland boss, John Paul Carbo, better known as Frank Carbo, received a setback in a court of general sessions in New York. Following a trial that began on October 29, 1959, Carbo was convicted on an indictment charging him with conspiracy, undercover management of prizefighters, and unlicensed matchmaking in bouts promoted by the International Boxing Club.

Assistant District Attorney Alfred J. Scotti called Carbo the "underworld commissioner" of boxing and declared, "The evil influence of this man has, for many years, permeated virtually the entire professional sport of boxing. . . . The name of Frank Carbo today symbolizes the degeneration of professional boxing into a racket." On November 30, 1959, Carbo was sentenced to two years in Riker's Island Penitentiary.[7]

Carbo's underworld credentials were formidable. On five occasions he had been arrested for murder. In 1924 he was charged with killing a cab driver in the Bronx. After hiding out for four years, he pleaded guilty to manslaughter and was sentenced to Sing Sing Prison for a term of two to four years. In September 1931 he was arrested for the killing of a Philadelphia beer baron in his room in an Atlantic City hotel. Again, in July 1936, Carbo was arrested in Madison Square Garden for the murders of Max Hassel and Max Greenberg, henchmen of Waxey Gordon.

Carbo also had Murder, Inc. affiliations. In 1939, at the direction of Lepke Buchalter, orders were given by his lieutenant, Mendy Weiss, to execute a disgruntled cohort called Big Greenie, otherwise known as Harry Greenberg or Harry Schacter. Big Greenie fled the New York area, eventually landed in California, and took cover in Hollywood. On Thanksgiving Day, 1939, he was located in Hollywood, "put on the spot," and assassinated. Indicted in Los Angeles for the murder were Carbo, Bugsy Siegel, Buchalter, Weiss, and Harry (Champ) Siegel. At a subsequent murder trial in Los Angeles, Allie Tannenbaum, a member of Murder, Inc. who had turned informant, testified that Carbo had fired five bullets into Big Greenie and Bugsy Siegel drove the getaway car. The trial ended with a hung jury and Carbo was not retried.

It was this same Carbo who cast an evil influence over the sport of professional boxing, an influence sometimes responsible for fighters taking a dive for the benefit of underworld gamblers. An outstanding middleweight fighter, Jake LaMotta, admitted to a U.S. Senate subcommittee that he had thrown a fight to Billy Cox in Madison Square Garden on November 14, 1947. Carbo, who arranged the fix, made $35,000 from wagers on that bout. How many fights were actually fixed will never be known, but the number was probably large.[8]

The boxing capital in America was New York City and the site of most of the important bouts was Madison Square Garden. In 1937 Mike Jacobs, a former New York ticket scalper, and three newspapermen had formed the Twentieth Century Sporting Club. For the next twelve years, most of the important fights in the United States were staged by Jacobs and his organization.

About 1948 Jacobs suffered a heart attack and it appeared to a wealthy Chicago sportsman, James D. Norris, that the Jacobs organization was about to fall apart. Norris, a member of the Chicago Board of Trade since 1928, his father, and Arthur M. Wirtz owned the Chicago Stadium, the Detroit Olympia, the St. Louis Arena, and held leases on the Indianapolis and Omaha coliseums. They were also substantial stockholders in Madison Square Garden. The Norris-Wirtz combination had brought hockey, boxing, wrestling, rodeos, ice shows, and other sporting events into the stadiums it owned or leased.

Norris raised thoroughbreds and raced them at major American and European tracks. He felt at home among the sporting element and was not always too choosy about some of his associations. He had maintained a long-standing friendship with Sam (Golfbag) Hunt, an organized crime bigwig with Capone gang affiliations in Chicago. During the period that gang warfare was commonplace in Chicago, Hunt gained the moniker "Golfbag" when it was discovered he carried a submachine gun in a golfbag. When questioned by a Senate subcommittee about his relationship with Hunt, Norris replied, "Well, I was very friendly with him. If he would want fight tickets, I would leave him fight tickets. If he wanted hockey tickets, I would leave him hockey tickets; and I had a very friendly feeling for Hunt. . . ." Beginning about 1930, Norris also developed a friendship with the bookmaker Morris Schmertzler, better known as Max Courtney. Courtney had important underworld connections and in the 1960s was placed on the managerial staff of a casino in the Bahamas by Meyer Lansky.

Following the illness of Mike Jacobs, Norris was anxious to step into the void created by the faltering Jacobs organization. With the blessing of Madison Square Garden, Norris, Wirtz, and a Chicago Negro attorney, Truman K. Gibson, Jr., formed the International Boxing Club of New York and the International Boxing Club of Illinois. Subsequently, the International Boxing Club of Michigan and the International Boxing Club of Missouri were also formed. James D. Norris became president of each International Boxing Club, and in June 1955 was made president of the Madison Square Garden Corporation as well. Originally, Gibson, who represented the famous heavyweight Joe Louis, was named secretary of the IBC of Illinois and the IBC of New York. In 1958 he was designated president of both clubs. The IBC entered into a contract with the National Broadcasting Company to televise weekly Friday night fights out of New York. Another contract was negotiated with Columbia Broadcasting System for televising weekly Wednesday night bouts.[9]

To fulfill its television commitments, it was imperative that IBC have access to a steady flow of fighters. Almost as soon as IBC started functioning in New York City, a large number of fight managers banded together to harass the new organization. At one of IBC's first championship fights, Madison Square Garden was picketed. Sometimes a fight manager would approach IBC a few hours before a scheduled fight, represent that his boxer was not in proper physical condition, and threaten to withdraw him from the match. Norris explained to a Senate subcommittee, "We felt it necessary to employ effective goodwill representatives to help us and we employed Jack Kearns, who was dean of fight managers. . . . We also employed Viola Masters, who subsequently became the wife of Frank Carbo." After a time, Norris placed the bookmaker Max Courtney on the payroll and between 1957 and 1960 he received remuneration of $76,000.

During the early stages of IBC operations, the key person approached directly by Norris was Frank Carbo, whom he had met many years earlier through Mike Jacobs. "Without question," Norris testified, "he was on friendly terms with more fight managers than anyone in boxing. He had done favors for many managers and knew them all." Gibson asserted that every important manager of boxing was linked directly or indirectly with Carbo. These managers were described by Gibson as either Carbo-controlled or Carbo-oriented. Gibson expressed a dislike for the gangster and despised the fact it had been necessary "to use the services of Carbo . . . he only did it to protect the programs and get fighters . . . it was the fact of life that he had to live with."

Intimately associated with Carbo was Frank (Blinky) Palermo, once a licensed fight manager in New York, Pennsylvania, Illinois, Maryland, California, and Florida. Regarded at one time as the Numbers King of Philadelphia, Palermo was an ally of Harry Stromberg (alias Nig Rosen), a partner of Carbo in a bookmaking establishment in Camden, New Jersey. Palermo also had close ties with influential members of the Chicago crime syndicate. On September 5, 1959, Cook County state's attorney's officers raided a Capone gang gambling establishment in Cicero. Among those seized in the place were Frank Palermo; Rocco Fischetti, a cousin of Al Capone and a powerful gambling king in Cook County for many years; Gus Liebe, a manager of Capone syndicate gambling establishments for decades; and Leslie Kruse, a notorious gambling-house proprietor. Kruse, in partnership with Tony Accardo, the organized crime boss in the Chicago area, had operated the infamous Owl Club in Calumet City, Illinois. Obviously, Palermo's underworld connections were first rate.

Among the fighters managed by Frank Palermo was Ike Williams, the former lightweight champion. Williams testified before the Senate subcommittee that Palermo had relayed offers to him totaling over $180,000 to throw fights. He was offered $100,000 if he lost to Kid Gavilan in 1949 and $50,000 if he lost to Jimmy Carter in 1951. Although he stated that he shunned these offers, he did lose both fights.[10]

For about a decade, Norris and Carbo enjoyed a cordial personal relationship. During this period Carbo visited the Norris Park Avenue apartment about twenty times. In 1957 Norris suffered a coronary attack and spent seven weeks in the Polyclinic Hospital in New York City. His hospital room became a meeting place for his friends. A regular visitor was Carbo. Among the numerous get-well floral pieces sent Norris was one from Albert Anastasia.

Usually, when Norris was involved in a boxing promotion in Philadelphia, he established headquarters at the Essex Hotel. Nearby, Carbo maintained a suite that served as a meeting place for gangsters who came from all parts of the United States to attend the fight. Presiding as hosts at this hospitality suite were Carbo and Frank Palermo.

Undoubtedly, the services rendered by Carbo aided the International Boxing Clubs in establishing a monopoly over professional fighting in America. Gibson testified that "during the period 1950 to 1959, practically all of the championships in the major weight categories were staged by one or the other of our organizations or in conjunction with our television presentations.'' He estimated that ninety-nine percent of such matches were handled by the International Boxing Clubs. In 1957, a federal court in New York City ruled that James D. Norris, Arthur M. Wirtz, Madison Square Garden, and the various International Boxing Clubs had violated the Sherman Act by creating a monopoly over the promotion of world championship fights in the United States. A decree was issued that required the dissolution of the monopoly. Following appeal, on January 12, 1959, the U.S. Supreme Court affirmed the decision sundering the IBC empire.[11]

Although the wealthy sportsman Norris headed the monopoly that controlled boxing, those close to the prizefight picture regarded Frank Carbo as the real boss, the man whose edicts were final. He was indeed the ''underworld commissioner'' of boxing, and maintained his rule, when necessary, by physical violence.

On the West Coast Jackie Leonard, a fight matchmaker, was associated with Donald Paul Nesseth in the management of Don Jordan, a Los Angeles welterweight. A championship bout between Jordan and another fighter was being planned when Carbo and Palermo bluntly declared that unless they were cut in for half ownership of Jordan there would be no fight. When Nesseth and Leonard objected to these demands, Carbo and pals went into action. From October 23, 1958, through September 22, 1959, Nesseth and Leonard were subjected to repeated economic and physical threats. Fully terrorized, they at last sought help from the police and the Federal Bureau of Investigation. On September 22, 1959, the federal grand jury in Los Angeles returned an indictment that charged Frank Carbo, Frank Palermo, Truman K. Gibson, Jr., and two notorious West Coast racketeers, Joseph Sica and Louis Tom Dragna, with conspiracy to violate the Federal Anti-Racketeering Act, extortion, and conspiracy. Following a long trial, the defendants were found guilty and on December 2, 1961, a sentence of twenty-five years was imposed on Carbo; Palermo received fifteen years; Sica got twenty; and Gibson was given a five-year suspended sentence. Each defendant was also fined $10,000. Upon appeal, the four convictions were upheld. Dragna had also been found guilty but his conviction was reversed.[12]

Just a few months before Carbo's encounters with the law in New York City and Los Angeles, ill winds were blowing against Meyer Lansky in Cuba.

On January 1, 1959, the Cuban government headed by Fulgencio Batista was suddenly toppled by revolutionary forces led by Fidel Castro. Batista fled Cuba for the Dominican Republic. Also fleeing Cuba was the dictator's client, Meyer Lansky, gambling king of Havana.

There was wild rioting on the streets of Havana with thirteen persons killed on January 1. Primary targets of the violence were gambling casinos owned by the American underworld. One victim was the Plaza Hotel on Calle Zulueta, which Cubans believed was once controlled by Albert Anastasia and was then being run by an American, Joe Rogers Stassi. The public was convinced, with justification, that the flourishing casino and slot-machine industries in Cuba were the products of gangsters, police protection, and the corruption of the Batista regime. The new Cuban leader, Fidel Castro, condemned the casinos and jailed a number of American gamblers before kicking them out of the country. Jake Lansky, brother of Meyer, spent twenty-five days in jail before he was released and permitted to return to the United States.[13]

After his flight from Cuba, Meyer Lansky began turning his attention to the Bahamas, where a group of white merchant-politicians, known as the Bay State Boys, ruled over a black majority. Leader of the Bay State Boys and the real boss of the Bahamas was Sir Stafford Sands, minister of finance and tourism.

Lansky appraised the Bahamas as a land of opportunity for big-time gambling operations. His evaluation was accurate. And with the arrival of big gambling, a scandal erupted that rocked the islands. The public learned that large sums of money had been paid to Sir Stafford for obtaining the necessary certificate of exemption (the equivalent of a gambling license) for the casino owners. It also came to light that influential members of the Bahamian government who approved the gambling license had been placed on the payroll of the gambling monopoly. The Progressive Liberal party made public charges of conflict of interest and an all-black government replaced the all-white government of the United Bahamian party. Sir Stafford left the Bahamas and settled in a castle in Spain. A Royal Commission of Inquiry was appointed to conduct hearings on the gambling scandal.[14]

Eventually, Sands appeared before the Royal Commission. He testified that in 1960 he was visited by Meyer Lansky, who offered him $2 million to obtain a gambling license in the Bahamas. Sands contended that he turned down Lansky's offer. However, in 1963 a gambling license was granted to Louis Arthur Chesler, a Canadian with whom Lansky had been associated in Canadian mining deals. Chesler had once operated nightclubs in Miami Beach, where Lansky also had strong ties. As soon as arrangements were completed for a gambling license, a check for $576,000 was issued to Sir Stafford. It was further agreed that in addition to all legal fees, Sands was to receive $50,000 a year from the gambling monopoly. Chesler also placed certain members of the Bahamian Executive Council on the payroll as consultants. Evidence presented to the Royal Commission revealed that a total of $714,118 had been paid to the consultants. The commission determined that Sir Stafford had been paid $1.8 million in fees, retainers, and expenses over a five-year period.

Chesler testified that he had consulted with Meyer Lansky about staffing the casino. It was on Lansky's recommendation that Chesler hired George Sadlo as the casino manager. A number of known Lansky veterans were placed in control of gambling operations: Frank (Red) Ritter was named general manager; Morris Schmertzler (Max Courtney) was appointed credit manager; Charles Brudner was made assistant credit manager; and Dino Cellini, an old standby who had been associated with Lansky in the Riviera in Havana, was designated supervisor.

When Ritter, the general manager, was called before the Royal Commission, he testified concerning meetings he had held with Meyer and Jake Lansky as well as with Trigger Mike Coppola and Charley (the Blade) Tourine.

Two years after Chesler had obtained a gambling license, Sir Stafford Sands filed an application for a certificate of exemption that would permit a casino on Paradise Island. Hired as manager of the casino was Eddie Cellini, a brother of Dino and a Lansky man at the Riviera in Havana. When unfavorable publicity forced the removal of Eddie as casino manager, he settled in Miami and was given the job of arranging for gambling junkets to Paradise Island. It was evident that the Meyer Lansky influence on gambling operations in the Bahamas was strong, indeed.[15]

In 1959 several important organized crime leaders suffered major reverses. Frank Costello's denaturalization had been followed by the deaths of Abner Zwillman, Anthony Carfano, and George Uffner. Meyer Lansky had been forced to flee from Cuba and to abandon his gambling empire there. In New York, Vito Genovese and Frank Carbo were convicted. And Carbo still faced the federal indictment pending against him in California.

In politics Carmine G. DeSapio, Tammany boss and Democratic national committeeman for New York, found himself under increasingly severe attack by the reform wing of the party led by Herbert H. Lehman, former governor and U.S. senator. A test of strength was to be provided in the upcoming primary.

Congressman Ludwig Teller, backed by DeSapio and the regular Tammany organization, was running for renomination in the Twentieth Congressional District on Manhattan's West Side. He was opposed by William F. Ryan, endorsed by the reform group. Ryan's running mate, Manfred Ohrenstein, was seeking the nomination for state senator and was opposed by the DeSapio candidate, Senator John H. Farrell. During the campaign both Ryan and Ohrenstein charged that Teller and Farrell were merely stooges for DeSapio. On some of Teller's campaign posters, the reformers pasted a sticker under his name which labeled him DeSapio's candidate. At the primary on June 7, 1960, Ryan and Ohrenstein won smashing victories over Teller and Farrell. The reformers' candidates for assembly nominations in the Eighth and Tenth Assembly Districts were successful also. The political prestige of DeSapio suffered a devastating blow. Even Mayor Wagner, who owed so much to the Tammany boss, was convinced that DeSapio's support was rapidly becoming a political kiss of death.[16]

DeSapio had aspired to be a kingmaker at the 1960 Democratic National Convention. Instead, he found himself fighting desperately to save his own political skin. During the presidential campaign DeSapio, Mayor Wagner, and the reformers all worked for the election of the John F. Kennedy ticket. But this show of harmony existed on the surface only. On election night, as soon as the votes were counted, former Governor Lehman went on the air and declared that the DeSapio rule in New York must be brought to an end for the sake of the legislative program of the incoming Kennedy administration.

In January 1961 Robert F. Wagner began making plans to run for a third mayoral term. He also decided to sever his political ties with DeSapio—the man who had engineered his victorious elections in 1953 and 1957, the man whom Wagner had described only a few months earlier as the best leader the party ever had. Replacing DeSapio as Wagner's political agent was the leader of the Liberal party, Alex Rose, who was on good terms with the reform group in the Democratic party. This created the anomaly of the leader of the Liberal party handling patronage for the Democratic party in City Hall. DeSapio was no longer welcome at City Hall and the mayor even refused to answer telephone calls from him. DeSapio had no intention of surrendering meekly. He announced that in the primary he would have a candidate of his own to oppose every district leader aspirant sponsored by the reformers. Mayor Wagner, for the first time, publicly called for the ouster of DeSapio as the leader of Tammany Hall.[17]

As a candidate for renomination and reelection, Wagner faced serious political obstacles. The City Club of New York declared that the record of the Wagner administration, especially in the second term, had been disappointing. It charged the mayor with having "a high tolerance for postponement and procrastination." The *New York Times* observed that Wagner's second term had been plagued by scandals involving graft and corruption. It was also noted that the Democratic party was split with dissension. And adding to the mayor's troubles were six days of public hearings in June 1961, conducted by the State Commission of Investigation. The commission concluded that New York City's school building program suffered from inefficiency, incompetency, payoffs, and shakedowns. Public concern was growing over crime in the streets. An opinion poll taken privately for the mayor indicated that only the issue of bossism offered him a chance of success. Bossism was thus adopted as Wagner's major campaign issue. And his onetime intimate political mentor and ally, Carmine G. DeSapio, was singled out for special attack as the embodiment of all the evils of bossism.[18]

Chosen by DeSapio and the other Democratic county leaders to oppose

Wagner in the primary was Arthur Levitt, the state comptroller. Levitt had an excellent record as an officeholder and as a vote getter. But Wagner virtually ignored Levitt in the campaign. Instead, the mayor flailed away at the evils of bossism. He charged that DeSapio and his gang had planned to take over City Hall and the Board of Estimate in 1961. The bosses, he said, were interested not in what was taught in the schools, but in who would get the construction contracts and the architects' fees. Wagner blasted DeSapio's relationship with Sydney Baron, the public relations expert who had built a lucrative business on boss influence peddling. Ironically, Baron had once been a part of the Wagner administration. Shortly after Wagner became mayor in 1954, Baron was named the deputy commissioner of marine and aviation. In fact, the evils of DeSapio's bossism and the influence peddling charged by the mayor occurred when Wagner was mayor and DeSapio was his righthand man. Thus, to an impartial observer, the mayor's logic appeared strained and his charges carried a hollow ring. In effect, the Wagner campaign for reelection consisted in blasting his own record as mayor and attempting to smash the political machinery that originally had placed him in office and kept him there for eight years.[19]

During DeSapio's rule over Tammany Hall, he had pushed through a number of reforms within the New York County Democratic organization. One provided for the direct election of assembly district leaders. Another reduced the county committee membership to a workable number. A third reform required that the county leader must be a district leader. By a twist of fate these reforms were to contribute to DeSapio's downfall in 1961.

To the reformers, the most important primary contest was to be waged in Greenwich Village, the home base of DeSapio. A defeat of DeSapio for the post of assembly district leader would automatically remove him as the county leader or boss of Tammany Hall, a major goal of the reformers. Selected as the candidate to oppose DeSapio was James E. Lanigan, a Harvard Law School graduate who had worked for Adlai Stevenson in his campaigns for the presidency in 1952 and 1956.

The primary of September 7, 1961, turned out to be a disaster for DeSapio. In Greenwich Village, Lanigan defeated DeSapio for district leader of the First Assembly District South by a vote of 6,165 to 4,745. Adding insult to injury, DeSapio was even defeated for the relatively insignificant post of county committeeman, receiving only 84 votes to his opponent's 100.

In the citywide contest for the Democratic mayoral nomination, Wagner defeated Arthur Levitt by a vote of 451,188 to 291,672. In Manhattan the reformers made heavy inroads by winning twenty-eight district leaderships. A *New York Times* editorial called the primary a "smashing defeat for New York City's hoary Democratic machine. . . . The campaign," said the *Times,* "was notable for its name calling, its bitterness, its generally low level, and not for any contribution it might have made to the future good government of this city. . . . The scars it has left on the Democratic party in New York are wide and deep. . . ."[20]

A few weeks after the primary, the *New York Times* declared in a forceful editorial that New York City needed a new mayor and urged the election of the Republican candidate, Louis J. Lefkowitz. Conceding the personal honesty of Wagner, the *Times* charged that "the mayor has not been able to keep corruption out of his departments. The scandals have bloomed, one after another. Mr. Wagner . . .has lacked force and moral indignation. . . . He has allowed the shakedowns to survive as a chronic feature of the city's political and governmental life . . . when he does move forward, it is usually because he has been impelled to do so by outside circumstances. . . . His fight against party bossism, against DeSapio, was an instance. Here he was battling for his own survival, not for the ideals of good government."

On November 7, 1961, New York City voters went to the polls and reelected Wagner to serve a third term as mayor. He received 1,234,533 votes as compared with 836,553 for Lefkowitz, and 321,996 for Lawrence E. Gerosa, a Democrat who ran under the Independent Citizens party label.[21]

Just a few days after the mayoral election, a notorious mobster, Joseph (Crazy Joe) Gallo was convicted of conspiracy and attempted extortion. On December 21, 1961, the thirty-two-year-old Gallo was sentenced to prison for seven and a quarter to fourteen and a half years. Assistant District Attorney Paul Kelly described Crazy Joe as a key figure behind the bloody gang warfare then raging in Brooklyn. Said Kelly, "There have been killings, shootings, and stranglings, kidnappings and disappearances, all directly involving the Gallos."

Running the infamous Gallo gang in Brooklyn were three brothers —Lawrence (Larry), Joseph (Crazy Joe), and Albert Jr. (Kid Blast). The father, Albert Gallo, Sr., was born in Naples in 1900, entered the United States illegally by jumping ship in Boston in 1920, and promptly became involved in the bootlegging racket. Later he was employed as a longshoreman.

Members of the Gallo gang were implicated in bookmaking, floating crap games, strong-arm activities, intimidation, and extortion. For some time the Gallo gangsters worked behind the front of a phony Teamsters Union, Local 266, called the Automatic Coin and Amusement Machine Employees Union. Owners of juke boxes, pinball, and other coin-operated machines were forced to pay an initiation fee of $25, monthly dues of $6, and 65¢ a month for each machine in operation. A juke-box distributor told a congressional committee, "They came out with steel bars and they split my skull open . . . and I was taken to the hospital."

Serving as headquarters for the Gallo mob was the Direct Vending Company, Fifty-one President Street, Brooklyn. By December 1961 this place had become what the press called a "besieged citadel." Gallo gangsters had "holed up" in the place as a means of protecting themselves from members of the criminal organization headed by Joseph Profaci. The Gallo brothers had nourished hopes of taking over some legitimate businesses as well as rackets controlled by the Profaci syndicate. Violent fighting broke out and much blood was spilled on Brooklyn streets.[22]

By engaging the Profaci forces in battle, the Gallo brothers were taking on a formidable foe. For many years, Joseph Profaci had ruled over one of the most powerful and deeply entrenched criminal organizations in Brooklyn.

Born in the province of Palermo, Sicily, on October 2, 1897, Profaci came to the United States in 1922 with a friend, Vincent Mangano, and Vincent's father, Gaetano. Eventually, both Vincent Mangano and Joseph Profaci were to become important underworld bosses. Before leaving his native land, Profaci was arrested twice and served a year in a Palermo prison for theft.

After settling in Brooklyn, Profaci prospered from numerous illicit activities and maintained ties with such underworld personages as Joe Adonis, Willie and Salvatore Moretti, and Albert Anastasia. On the West Coast he was friendly with Jack Dragna. In 1928 Profaci was one of several gangsters arrested in a Cleveland hotel where thirteen guns were confiscated by the police.

In the field of legitimate business, Profaci owned several companies, including the Mamiapro Realty Corporation and the Mamma Mia Importing Company. At one time he was regarded as the largest single importer of olive oil and tomato paste in the United States and was called the Olive Oil King. Allegations were that Profaci operated the olive oil business as a cover for his underworld enterprises. Among the Profaci-owned firms the Gallo brothers coveted were the Peerless Importers, Inc., the Alpine Wine and Liquor Corporation, and the Arrow Linen Supply Company. Those three companies grossed over $20 million a year from their business dealings with restaurants, bars, and nightclubs in the New York metropolitan area.

Profaci curried the favor of Italian prelates and maintained ties with influential politicians including judges. He attended the celebrated conclave of criminals at Apalachin, New York, in November 1957. When he appeared before the federal judge Irving R. Kaufman on January 13, 1960, the jurist aptly described Profaci as a "notorious member of the underworld. The perfect example of the trinity of crime, business, and politics that threaten the economy of the country."[23]

The Gallo-Profaci warfare in Brooklyn was probably only of casual interest to New Yorkers, compared with that created by the revelations of a judicial scandal that hit New York City in 1962. A sensational month-long trial in federal court highlighted an unholy relationship between an organized crime leader, a prominent member of the judiciary, and a federal prosecutor.

The case had its inception when a juke-box operator, Sanford J. Moore, pleaded guilty before the federal judge Leo F. Rayfiel to charges that by concealing assets he had defrauded a bankruptcy trustee out of $100,000. With a view to obtaining a lenient sentence for Moore, Anthony (Tony Ducks) Corallo, a top lieutenant of underworld boss Thomas (Three Finger Brown) Lucchese, paid a $35,000 bribe to New York State Supreme Court Justice James Vincent Keogh and Assistant U.S. Attorney Elliott Kahaner. Keogh and Kahaner, who shared the bribe, promised to use their influence on Judge Rayfiel to obtain a light sentence for the juke-box operator. The plot failed and Corallo, Keogh, and Kahaner were indicted for conspiracy.

Justice Keogh had been on the bench since 1951. A short, dapper man with an ever-smiling countenance, Keogh had served as an assistant district attorney on the staff of William O'Dwyer when he was district attorney of Kings County. During World War II, Keogh joined the navy and rose to the rank of lieutenant commander. In 1946 he was appointed United States district attorney for the Eastern District of New York and held that post until he was elected to the state supreme court. Keogh was ambitious politically and had aspirations to become mayor of New York. A younger brother, Eugene J. Keogh, was a congressman from Brooklyn and a close friend of President John F. Kennedy.[24]

Sharing top billing in the 1962 criminal trial drama was Anthony (Tony Ducks) Corallo, a nefarious organized crime bigwig. Corallo was born on February 12, 1913, and grew up in a tough neighborhood in East Harlem. He was short and stocky of build, and his piercing blue eyes, behind black horn-rimmed glasses, inspired fear in his adversaries. He had long been involved in gambling, bookmaking, traffic in narcotics, loan sharking, and labor racketeering. He had met with unusual success in "ducking" conviction and thus earned the moniker Tony Ducks. However, in 1941 Corallo was sent to the workhouse in Riker's Island for six months after police connected him with a cache of narcotics worth $150,000.

Corallo gained control of several labor organizations, including Local 239 of the Teamsters Union in New York City. In 1958 U.S. Senator John L. McClellan, chairman of the U.S. Senate Select Committee on Improper Activities in the Labor or Management Field, reported: "Our study into the New York phony local situation revealed an alarming picture of the extent to which gangsters led by John Dioguardi and Anthony (Tony Ducks) Corallo infiltrated the labor movement in the nation's largest city, using their union positions for purposes of extortion, bribery, and shakedowns. The fact that one of the nation's most powerful labor leaders, James R. Hoffa, the international president of the Teamsters, used Dioguardi and Corallo in his efforts to capture control of the union in New York City only serves to underline the importance of gangster infiltration in the labor movement."[25]

On January 25, 1961, both Corallo and Hoffa appeared as witnesses in

Washington, D.C., before a Senate subcommittee headed by McClellan. Evidence indicated that Corallo had siphoned from Local 239 funds amounting to $69,000. He did so by placing dummies on the payroll. When questioned by the Senate subcommittee, Corallo invoked eighty-three times the Fifth Amendment's protection against self-incrimination. The senators were fascinated with a recording of a court-authorized bugging of a New York City apartment. From conversation thus recorded, it appeared that Hoffa had given approval for Corallo to rob or steal from union funds so long as he did not get caught.[26]

The long conspiracy trial of Justice Keogh, Corallo, and Elliott Kahaner came to a close on June 16, 1962, when the three defendants were found guilty. Among the key witnesses who had been called to testify in the case was Judge Leo F. Rayfiel. He related that Justice Keogh had approached him with the suggestion of a light sentence for Sanford J. Moore, the jukebox operator involved in a fraudulent bankruptcy matter.

On August 2, 1962, Keogh, Kahaner, and Corallo appeared before the federal judge Edward Weinfeld, who sentenced each defendant to two years in prison. Regarding Keogh and Kahaner, the judge stated, "There are no mitigating circumstances. . . . The crime was calculated; it was deliberate. The motive for the corrupt effort to interfere with justice was venality and greed." Concerning Corallo, Judge Weinfeld noted his long history of involvement in illicit activities—bookmaking, gambling, labor racketeering, and narcotics. And within a few years, Corallo would again be a principal figure in another official corruption scandal that would rock the city and end with prison terms for the once powerful boss of Tammany Hall, Carmine G. DeSapio, and a city official who was an intimate friend and confidant of the then mayor of New York City, John V. Lindsay.[27]

About the time that Corallo was having troubles in federal court in August 1962, some of his confederates were being rounded up as members of a big narcotics conspiracy. Among those seized was Daniel (Pop) Smith, a close associate of Corallo. Smith was also a lieutenant of Carmine Locascio, whom the press dubbed the kingpin in the United States of a worldwide narcotics ring headed by Lucky Luciano. Locascio and ten of his lieutenants, including Smith, were seized in New York while three members of the gang were arrested by Italian authorities in Naples.

Luciano was no longer on the scene. On January 26, 1962, he had dropped dead of a heart attack at the Capodichino Airport in Naples. Just before his heart failure, Luciano had been conferring with Martin A. Gosch, an American film and television producer, about a proposed movie on the gangster's life.

Handling the funeral arrangements was a Roman Catholic priest, the Reverend Francesco Scarpati, who had been a close friend of Luciano since 1948. In February 1962 the priest's name was prominently mentioned when a slot-machine scandal erupted in Santanastasia. Cafe owners had rebelled against making monthly payoffs to the police for protection. Father Scarpati was questioned when the authorities learned that a hundred fifty slot machines in a warehouse were under his control.[28]

Luciano was only one of several important organized crime moguls whose careers came to an abrupt end in 1962. About ten o'clock on the night of April 8, Anthony (Tony Bender) Strollo informed his wife that he was going out to buy some cigarettes. He left his home at 1015 Palisades Avenue in Fort Lee, New Jersey, and was never seen again.

On June 7, 1962, Joseph Profaci died of cancer in the South Side Hospital, Bay Shore, Long Island. At that time, income-tax evasion claims against him totaled almost $1.5 million. Profaci's life of crime had paid well, indeed.

The ranks of the elder statesmen of organized crime were further depleted on August 16, 1962. The sixty-eight-year-old convicted swindler and gambling entrepreneur Philip (Dandy Phil) Kastel died from a self-inflicted bullet wound. His body was found in the bedroom of his ninth-floor Claiborne Towers apartment in New Orleans. He had been suffering from abdominal cancer and, in a note to his wife, expressed a fear of impending blindness.

Dandy Phil and Frank Costello, both protégés of Arnold Rothstein in the 1920s, had maintained a profitable association for over three decades. Kastel had served as Costello's righthand man in the slot-machine racket both in New York and New Orleans. Partners of Kastel and Costello in gambling casino operations in the New Orleans area had included Meyer and Jake Lansky and the New Orleans underworld chief, Carlos Marcello. In the late 1950s evidence indicated that Dandy Phil, Costello, and Meyer Lansky had joint secret interests in a Las Vegas casino. Although New Orleans remained Kastel's principal base of operations for years, his influence was felt in many places. Important underworld leaders from various parts of the United States, as well as influential politicians from such cities as Chicago, visited Kastel in New Orleans.[29]

In January 1961 Edward C. Jaegerman, director of special investigations for the Securities and Exchange Commission, had warned that the underworld was "invading the financial community." Counterfeiting of securities, travelers checks, and bank drafts was on the rise. The number of indictments obtained by the SEC for securities frauds had soared. Theft and fraud losses announced by the New York Stock Exchange were the largest in more than a decade. Criminal syndicates that were engaged in narcotics traffic, prostitution, gambling, and extortion appeared to be moving into some aspects of the securities business.

An influential mobster who was deeply implicated in crimes involving securities was Carmine Lombardozzi. He had attended the Apalachin conclave in November 1957 and later was described by a federal judge, Irving

R. Kaufman, as "an important member of loan-shark and gambling rackets in Brooklyn and an associate of premier criminals for most of his life." Reputedly, Lombardozzi was allied with a criminal organization headed by Carlo Gambino, successor to the slain Albert Anastasia.

In 1960 Lombardozzi and his partner, Arthur Tortorello, also known as Joseph Grasso and Artie Todd, were arrested for operating several stock swindles. They were convicted and in 1963 were sentenced to a federal penitentiary for violation of probation.

By making usurious loans to men in the securities business, Tortorello had succeeded in gaining control of several stock brokerage houses. One such firm, Carlton Securities, was used by Tortorello and associates to sell unregistered worthless oil stock for nearly $1 million. The same company, under Tortorello's direction, flooded the market with a million shares of worthless stock in an electronics corporation.

In 1962 the financial community was shocked when negotiable securities valued at $1,370,375 were stolen from the well-known brokerage firm of Bache & Company, Thirty-six Wall Street, New York City. Numerous persons were arrested, including Gordon A. Tallman, a Bache & Company stock record clerk. Allegedly, on June 12, 1962, Tallman walked out of the brokerage house with the stolen stocks tucked under his shirt. Among the persons arrested for attempting to dispose of the purloined securities was John Lombardozzi, a brother of Carmine. Solid information was also received that Carmine had distributed some of the stolen securities and they eventually found their way to banks in Switzerland.[30]

Testifying before a U.S. Senate subcommittee, Edward H. Wuensche, an ex-convict fence and a former Philadelphia numbers racketeer, revealed that between 1958 and 1963 stolen securities valued from $40 million to $50 million had been brought to his attention or actually passed through his hands. Said Wuensche, "In New York, I was introduced to and did business with, among others, Carmine Lombardozzi; Arthur Tortorello, also known as Artie Todd. . . ." Sometimes an associate, Jon Boran, aided him in disposing of the stolen securities in Switzerland. Wuensche testified, "Several times Jon Boran went to Swiss banks when I did not accompany him, but he carried to Switzerland stolen securities which I provided him. On one such occasion, I received stolen securities . . . from Carmine Lombardozzi. These securities, I believe, were part of a theft in 1962 from Bache & Co. They included shares of AT & T, General Motors, and Union Oil Co. I believe, in total, there were about 25,000 shares of stock which we got from Lombardozzi."

Wuensche expressed the opinion that the major portion of stolen securities was controlled by people connected with organized crime. He testified, "In the early sixties . . . Mr. Carmine Lombardozzi used to bear the title of 'The King of Wall Street.' . . . Carmine had more young clerks under his thumb who were either trapped because of indebtedness, gambling and otherwise, and if he said, 'Go get me XYZ,' they darn well went in and got it, because they were afraid of losing their lives.''

Wuensche identified numerous important traffickers in stolen securities with whom he was associated over a period of years. They included Thomas Eboli (alias Tommy Ryan), John Stassi, John Massiello, James Plumeri (alias Jimmy Doyle), Carmine Persico, Harry Riccobene, Charles Tourine, Joseph Zicarelli, Frank Basto, Vincent Alo, Carlos Marcello of Louisiana, Angelo DeCarlo of New Jersey, Angelo Bruno of Philadelphia, and Meyer Lansky's associate, Louis Chesler, in the Bahamas.[31]

For several months following the securities theft from Bache & Company, the Lombardozzi family had been feeling the pressure of federal investigations. In fact, John Lombardozzi had been indicted for the interstate transportation of some of the stocks stolen from the Bache firm.

On April 3, 1963, a funeral was held for Carmello Lombardozzi, the seventy-five-year-old father of Carmine and John, at the Church of the Immaculate Heart of Mary in Brooklyn. Just before the services, FBI agents and New York City detectives were standing on the public street observing persons entering the church. Suddenly, four men leaped from an automobile, seized FBI agent John P. Foley, beat him with a pistol butt until he crumpled to the sidewalk, stomped on the fallen agent, and fled into the church. Agent Foley was rushed to a hospital and underwent an emergency operation for a fractured skull. After the funeral John Lombardozzi was arrested as he was leaving the church and three other men were taken into custody at the Calvary Cemetery.

A federal grand jury in Brooklyn returned indictments against four brothers and two nephews of Carmine Lombardozzi. On November 26, 1963, three of Carmine's brothers—John Joseph, Camillo Charles, and George—were found guilty of the assault on FBI agent Foley. Another brother, Anthony, was acquitted. Also convicted were two of Carmine's nephews, Michael Joseph Zambello and Joseph Marino. Earlier, Carmine had been sentenced to a thirty-day jail term when he was called before a grand jury and refused to testify regarding the assault. Upon appeal, Carmine's sentence was set aside.[32]

Loan sharking has always been a lucrative source of income to organized crime. The New York State Commission of Investigation conducted an extensive investigation of the loan-shark racket and held public hearings for six days in 1964. Testimony disclosed that ''one hundred twenty-one of the high-echelon members of the five recognized criminal syndicates operating in greater New York were engaged in loan sharking.'' The leaders of the five syndicates were identified by the commission as Vito Genovese, Thomas Lucchese, Joe Bonanno, Carlo Gambino (Albert Anastasia's successor), and Joe Colombo (who had succeeded Joseph Profaci).

Although there were many exceptions, the commission concluded that the loan-shark racket as a syndicate venture was composed of three echelons. At the top level the underworld boss reigned supreme. Usually he served as the original source of the money to be placed on loan. He provided money for his chief lieutenants and underbosses, who made up the second echelon. Those in the second echelon paid the boss one percent a week "vigorish" (the underworld term for interest and other charges). The lieutenants and underbosses acted as middlemen and loaned the money to a third echelon composed of hoodlums, who dealt directly with the ultimate borrower. Criminals in the third echelon paid from one and one-half to two and one-half percent vigorish each week; and for loans they made to their patrons, they charged a minimum of five percent a week. That general pattern was not always present, however. Some of the major loan sharks in the New York area were syndicate lieutenants, and they handled their own distribution of money.

Another cog in the underworld moneylending apparatus was known as the "steerer," the individual who placed many prospective borrowers in touch with the loan sharks. Usually not a member of the syndicate, the steerer received a small fee for his service. The steerers, reported the commission, were "found in the vast army of doormen, elevator operators, bartenders, hatcheck girls, cab drivers, cigar stand operators, and others who have daily contact with many people."[33]

In testimony given before the State Commission of Investigation, Nicholas (Jiggs) Forlano was described by a reliable witness as the biggest loan shark in New York City. Forlano was known as a "shylock's shylock," a wholesaler of money who had established a reputation for moving money quickly and efficiently. Originally he was a member of the criminal organization headed by Joseph Profaci. But his loan-shark activities were not limited to those of a single mob. Several underworld bosses supplied him with money at the rate of one percent a week.

Forlano's partner was Charles (Ruby) Stein. The State Commission of Investigation reported that Forlano and Stein held "key positions in the intricate network of criminal usury operations in the New York area." To collect delinquent debts, Forlano utilized the brawn of the notorious Gallo gang in Brooklyn. As enforcers, the ruthless Gallo bothers and their minions had no peers.[34]

One of the city's more significant loan sharks during the early 1960s was Julio Gazia, a relative through marriage to underworld boss Vito Genovese and his brother Michael. Gazia, also known as Julie Peters, operated his loan-shark business under the high-sounding name of the First National Service and Discount Corporation with offices at 475 Fifth Avenue.

Gazia's major sources of money included Forlano's partner, Charles (Ruby) Stein; Thomas Eboli, a righthand man of Vito Genovese; and Joseph

DeNigris, alias Joe Ross, an aide to Eboli. Michael Genovese invested money in First National and profited handsomely from its operations.

Among Gazia's clients were doctors, stockbrokers, and even corporate executives who needed money desperately to cover gambling losses or to meet other emergencies. To make certain that these clients met their weekly vigorish payments of five percent, Gazia employed two hoodlum enforcers, Anthony (Junior) DeFranco and Anthony Scala, appropriately called the "leg breaker." Borrowers from Gazia lived in mortal fear that they or members of their families would be subjected to physical torture or death if they fell behind in their weekly payments.

In some instances, corporate executives who had become debtors of Gazia found that their firms had been taken over by the underworld. Typical was the experience of a businessman who fell behind in his vigorish payments that had grown to $1,425 a week. Conferences were held in such places as New Jersey and Florida between Gazia, Eboli, and Santo Trafficante. A decision was reached that placed Dominick Ferraro, a man with an extensive criminal record, in charge of the corporation's plant. Before long the firm's assets had been drained off and the company was thrown into bankruptcy.

Once Gazia himself was on the receiving end of threats from gangland bosses who had supplied him with money. Gazia was a heavy gambler and, typically, devised what he believed to be a foolproof system for wagering on baseball games. Under this foolproof system, Gazia's gambling losses were enormous and he owed Charles (Ruby) Stein about $150,000. Nicholas (Jiggs) Forlano barged into the offices of the First National Service and Discount Corporation and announced in a menacing fashion that he had been sent by Ruby Stein to collect the money owed by Gazia. Gazia went into hiding and sought the protection of Michael Genovese, who eventually worked out a compromise settlement.[35]

Hearings conducted by the State Commission of Investigation established that organized crime loan sharks had been able to enter the portals of the sacrosanct banking community. In some instances, through the collusion of bank employees and officers, bank funds were used by shylocks for their usurious moneylending operations. One bank located in the New York City garment center actually served as a base of operations for loan sharks.

The garment center was a fertile field for loan-shark operations. Manufacturers in the center frequently sought emergency cash loans. The need for immediate credit reached its highest point every afternoon between 1:30 and 2:30, a period appropriately known as the panic hour. It was during the panic hour, in particular, that members of the garment industry flocked to the bank in search of loans.

The head of the immediate credit department of a New York City bank testified that he had been friendly with a number of loan sharks who maintained accounts in his institution. Admittedly, he had received payoffs from loan sharks to the tune of thousands of dollars annually. During the panic hour, loan sharks loitered in the bank lobby. When the bank official turned down a garment manufacturer's request for a legitimate loan, he would give a signal to a loan shark indicating this person would be a good prospect. Sometimes the corrupt bank official would actually introduce the prospective borrower to the loan shark. Among those who received such preferential treatment at the hands of bank officials was Milton Kaufman, recognized as one of New York City's biggest shylocks. Affiliated with Kaufman as collectors and enforcers were mob strong-arm men Mike Camporetto and Lou DeFillipo.

The State Commission of Investigation "found that by various devices, loan sharks were able to obtain and use bank funds as part of their capital for usurious moneylending ventures." Testimony at the hearings featured the activities of John Massiello, identified as a member of the criminal organization headed by Vito Genovese. Witnesses revealed that through the collusion of the bank's loan officer, at least $1.5 million of the funds of a single bank branch had been made available to Massiello. And the commission reported that a large portion of the funds Massiello obtained at the bank would never be recovered.[36]

Public hearings on the loan-shark racket had touched only the tip of a gigantic iceberg. Nevertheless, it was shockingly clear that organized crime, through its usurious moneylending operations, had made miserable pawns of thousands of individual borrowers, had taken over and ruined countless legitimate business concerns, and had even gained a foothold in some financial institutions, including banks.

When Carmine G. DeSapio was defeated in the September 1961 primary for district leader in Greenwich Village, he was removed automatically as leader of the New York County Democratic organization, a post he had held since 1949. For several months, Tammany's executive committee engaged in behind-the-scenes squabbles in an effort to name DeSapio's successor. It was not until March 1962 that a trial lawyer, Edward Nazar Costikyan, the leader of Manhattan's Eighth Assembly District, was elected. Costikyan had received the tacit approval of Mayor Wagner but had been opposed by the reform group, which had backed John T. Harrington. Of the sixteen votes in the executive committee, nine and two thirds were cast for Costikyan and six and one third for Harrington.[37]

DeSapio had no intention of meekly departing the political scene. In the primary on September 5, 1963, DeSapio unsuccessfully attempted to regain the Democratic leadership of the First Assembly District South in Greenwich Village. He was defeated by a margin of forty-one votes by Edward I. Koch, a thirty-eight-year-old bachelor who was sponsored by the Village Independent Democrats. The *New York Times* editorially declared that DeSapio's defeat "had a symbolic as well as a practical meaning for politics and government. It rejects a tradition of bossism, of old clubhouse politics, of unwholesome alliances destructive to the long-time best interests of the community."[38]

Only a few days after the primary, Costikyan was reelected leader of the New York County Democratic organization. At a meeting of the county executive committee in the Chatham Hotel on September 26, 1963, a voice vote declared Costikyan reelected unanimously. However, when the vote was taken, the reform opponents of Costikyan were out of the meeting room attending a caucus and mapping strategy. The reformers realized that Costikyan had the votes necessary for reelection, but as a protest they had planned to abstain from voting. When they returned to the meeting room and learned that the vote had already been taken, they were indignant. Some of the reform leaders accused Costikyan of resorting to "DeSapio tactics."

Costikyan's tenure as leader of the New York County Democratic organization was relatively short. On November 5, 1964, Costikyan resigned abruptly with the announcement he was abandoning politics to devote full time to the practice of law. For some time there had been constant friction between Mayor Wagner and members of the party's faction-torn executive committee. Costikyan had found himself to be the man in the middle without power to restore party harmony.[39]

To all intents and purposes, when Carmine G. DeSapio was ousted as leader of the New York County Democratic organization, the last chapter in the saga of the Tammany Society as a force in city politics was ended. During the period that Costikyan served as county leader, even the name Tammany Hall largely disappeared.

Tammany Hall has been called the oldest continuous political organization in America. But even before the reform movement in 1961 destroyed the old Democratic party structure in New York City, Tammany Hall, as an organization, had been deteriorating for many years. Several times its adversaries had gleefully pronounced Tammany dead only to see it recover. Tammany had reeled from the blows it received from the LaGuardia Fusion administration, but the Tiger was far from dead. This was evident when President Harry S. Truman found it politically expedient to send his greetings to the Tammany Society.

When DeSapio became the leader of Tammany in 1949, there was a renewed interest in the Society, an interest that became dimmed as the boss began to neglect Tammany banquets. And Society meetings were stopped at the request of Averell Harriman, who was anxious to avoid having the Tammany label affixed to his gubernatorial candidacy. By the time of Tammany's 177th anniversary in May 1966, there were no active members and only one remaining officer of the Society: eighty-year-old Judge Edward McCullen, Tammany scribe.

In 1961 the New York County Democratic organization had moved from its old headquarters at 331 Madison Avenue to the Hotel Chatham. At that time the sole contents of the party safe were some cardboard boxes in which papers and documents relating to the Tammany Society had been packed. Among these documents were the charter of the Tammany Society and its bylaws, including a description of the initiation ceremony, secret handgrip, password, and song of the post–Revolutionary War patriotic and social club. Also found were minutes of Society meetings from 1891 to 1915 and scrapbooks containing correspondence, campaign material, and election forms for the period between 1921 and 1959. On February 8, 1965, Costikyan presented these papers to his alma mater, Columbia University. In a book, published in 1966, the former county leader noted that Tammany Hall had become the headquarters of a local of the International Ladies Garment Workers Union and, asserted Costikyan, there no longer existed any connection between the Society of Tammany and the Democratic party.[40]

Costikyan's successor as Democratic county leader was Councilman J. Raymond Jones, a district leader from Harlem and the first Negro to be advanced to this prestigious post. He was elected on December 3, 1964, after Mayor Wagner had called several district leaders and informed them that the Harlem politician was his choice. Following his election, Jones remarked, ''It's possible that some of the ancient sachems of Tammany Hall might be turning over in their graves.''

Jones, a smooth politician often called the Fox, headed the New York Democratic organization until March 1967, when he resigned. On July 7, 1967, the county Executive Committee elected Assemblyman Frank Rossetti as the new county leader.

A union official, Rossetti had been active in politics for many years. During the heyday of DeSapio, Rossetti had served as chauffeur and bodyguard for the Tammany boss. In fact, Rossetti and the city councilman John Merli were DeSapio's closest Tammany Hall cronies. Frequently, DeSapio, Rossetti, and Merli dined together at an Italian restaurant on Forty-eighth Street.

Within a few weeks after Rossetti was named county leader, his pal DeSapio became inextricably involved in an official corruption case that would end in ruin for the once all-powerful Tammany boss. Throughout all of DeSapio's troubles, Rossetti remained loyal to his old friend.[41]

In 1965 Robert F. Wagner decided against running for a fourth term as mayor. Comptroller Abraham D. Beame won the Democratic mayoral primary. In the election on November 2, 1965, Beame was pitted against the Republican candidate, Congressman John V. Lindsay, and the Conservative party nominee, William F. Buckley, Jr. Alex Rose, head of the Liberal party, threw his support to Lindsay with the understanding that if the Republican candidate became mayor, the Liberal party would receive half of the City Hall patronage.

During the campaign Beame attempted to rally support from the bitterly feuding elements of the Democratic party but was unsuccessful. Lindsay, a handsome man with an appealing style, attracted volunteer workers from all walks of life. Scores of persons zealously rushed to the Lindsay headquarters with offers to assist in his campaign. In a close contest, Lindsay was elected and took office as New York City's 103d mayor on January 1, 1966.[42]

Joining the new administration were several volunteer workers who had figured prominently in Lindsay's successful campaign. Of these, perhaps the most promising was handsome thirty-five-year-old James L. Marcus, a man with impeccable social credentials. His wife, Lilly, was the daughter of a former Connecticut governor, John Davis Lodge, and a close friend of Mayor Lindsay's wife, Mary. Marcus appeared to be a man of affluence—and no one bothered to look beyond this façade.

Marcus was given the responsibility of running the Department of Water Supply, Gas, and Electricity. Originally he was placed on the payroll with the nominal salary of one dollar a year. When trouble arose in the Sanitation Department, Marcus was directed to manage that agency as well. After a few months had elapsed, Marcus was officially appointed to the salaried post of Commissioner of the Department of Water Supply, Gas, and Electricity. Marcus had moved quickly from a crusading campaign worker to the inner circle of Lindsay confidants chosen to play key roles in running the city. He had handled his assignments with apparent diligence and efficiency. He was looked upon as a bright star in the new administration.

During the 1965 campaign Marcus had discussed with a fellow worker, Attorney Oscar Blaustein, the need for labor-union endorsements. Blaustein thereupon introduced Marcus to Herbert Itkin, a labor lawyer. Itkin in turn introduced Marcus to the underworld chieftain Anthony (Tony Ducks) Corallo, a powerful figure in Teamsters Union circles, and to Daniel Motto, president of Local 350, Bakery and Confectionery Workers Union. Thus was laid the groundwork for the unholy association of Marcus, Itkin, Corallo, and Motto that would end in a major scandal.[43]

James L. Marcus' image as a wealthy socialite was deceptive. Actually, he had lost money in dubious business ventures. In 1966 he had speculated heavily on margin in the stock of Xtra, a company engaged in the manufacture of piggyback railroad containers. In April 1966, when the Xtra margin call went out, Marcus was in deep trouble. He discussed his financial plight with Itkin, who arranged for a meeting in an East Side restaurant between Marcus and Corallo. At least the meeting had the outward appearance of class. Marcus was driven to the place in a limousine by a chauffeur, who patiently waited outside while the water commissioner and Tony Ducks transacted business. Corallo agreed to loan Marcus $10,000 on the basis of four to one—for every dollar advanced to Marcus, the loan shark was to receive four dollars' worth of stock. An agreement was also reached that all emergency cleaning contracts at the Jerome Park Reservoir in the Bronx would be awarded to a contractor friend, Henry Fried, president of S. T. Grand & Company.

On the very day that Marcus was named to the salaried post of commissioner, he left the ceremonies at City Hall for a cocktail conference with Henry Fried. It was agreed that an "emergency contract," without bidding, would be awarded to S. T. Grand for $835,000. In return for this lucrative contract, Fried promised to kick back $40,000. Part of the bribe was to be delivered immediately to Corallo and was to be applied to the loan he had made to Marcus.

The scheme was consummated with ease. To lay the groundwork, Commissioner Marcus and an unsuspecting Mayor Lindsay, attended by press-agent fanfare, were photographed at the Jerome Park Reservoir. It was explained that over the years debris had accumulated in the reservoir, and that since much city water passed through the reservoir, its present condition created a health hazard. Under the direction of Water Commissioner Marcus, the Lindsay administration intended to come to grips with this emergency immediately. The contract was awarded, without bidding, to S. T. Grand & Company, and Fried paid the $40,000 bribe, which was to be shared by Marcus, Corallo, Itkin, and the union official Daniel Motto.

Everything had proceeded without a hitch. But late in November 1967 the roof started to cave in. New York County District Attorney Frank S. Hogan received a letter from a Philadelphia lawyer who related that his client in Switzerland had given an American, James Marcus, $6,000 to invest in a stock called Xtra. The stock was never delivered and calls, as well as letters, to Marcus had gone unanswered. The complaint suggested that a stock fraud had been perpetrated and Assistant District Attorney Frank Rogers initiated an investigation. After Rogers had checked bank accounts and stock brokerage firm records, Marcus was asked to appear in the district attorney's office for questioning. The responses of Marcus were evasive and Rogers was convinced the city water commissioner was lying. The case was discussed with District Attorney Hogan, who recalled that a year earlier the name of James Marcus had been mentioned during the investigation of a lawyer, Herbert Itkin, who had been accused of implication in a $1.5 million mortgage swindle. Marcus had been described at that time as an investment partner of Itkin. Before any indictments were returned in the alleged mortgage swindle case, Hogan was advised that Itkin had been serving as a paid informant for the FBI and action was suspended temporarily.

After two unproductive sessions with Marcus, District Attorney Hogan angrily telephoned Mayor Lindsay and apprised him that one of his key assistants had been subjected to an interrogation. Lindsay called in Marcus, who explained that he had experienced some personal financial problems but that they did not affect the city. Nevertheless, Marcus suggested that it might be advisable for him to resign and devote his full time to straightening out his financial difficulties. On December 12, 1967, James L. Marcus resigned as water commissioner and cordial letters were exchanged between the mayor and Marcus. Lindsay praised the excellent government service Marcus had performed and mentioned the close friendship existing between the Lindsays and the Marcuses.

As Assistant District Attorney Rogers continued to question Marcus about his private business dealings, he became convinced that Marcus had fallen into the toils of loan sharks. During a session on December 15, 1967, Rogers asked Marcus if he knew Anthony (Tony Ducks) Corallo. Although Marcus denied knowing the underworld chieftain, it was evident from his reaction that the prosecutor had struck pay dirt. As soon as he left the courthouse, Marcus virtually ran to Itkin and explained that he was being questioned about Corallo. Itkin, the experienced federal informant, recommended that Marcus turn himself in to U.S. government officials, who, Itkin explained, would give him a better deal than District Attorney Hogan. Marcus got in touch with the Federal Bureau of Investigation and made a detailed confession. In discussing his loan from Corallo at the rate of four to one, Marcus disclosed that underworld pressure on him had been so great that he had contemplated suicide.

Following the confession of Marcus, the facts in the case were presented to a federal grand jury by Robert Morgenthau, U. S. attorney for the Southern District of New York. On December 18, 1967, just six days after Marcus had resigned as water commissioner, he was indicted and taken into custody. The federal indictment alleged that James Marcus, as commissioner of the Department of Water Supply, Gas, and Electricity in New York City, had received $16,000 of a $40,000 kickback on a contract to refurbish Jerome Park Reservoir in the Bronx. The indictment charged that Marcus had acted under the direction of Corallo when he awarded the Jerome Park Reservoir contract to S. T. Grand & Company without competitive bidding. In return, the indictment alleged, Henry Fried, president of the favored firm, was to kick back $40,000 to Marcus, Corallo, Herbert Itkin, a labor lawyer, and Daniel Motto, president of Local 350, Bakery and Confectionery Workers Union. Also charged with aiding in the plot was Charles J. Rappaport, a partner of Itkin.

The federal indictment and arrests created a sensation and proved highly embarrassing to the Lindsay administration. Particularly disturbing was the alleged role of an important organized crime bigwig, Corallo, as the guiding genius behind the bribery plot. Corallo had been a principal aide to Thomas (Three Finger Brown) Lucchese, who had died in July 1967 after a long illness. Government agents now asserted that Corallo was a candidate to head the Lucchese organization.

When the case was called for trial on June 3, 1968, James L. Marcus entered a plea of guilty. At the conclusion of the trial on June 19, a federal jury convicted Anthony Corallo, Henry Fried, and Daniel J. Motto. Charles J. Rappaport was acquitted. Marcus was sentenced to fifteen months in a federal prison. Fried and Motto each received a sentence of two years, and Corallo was given a three-year term.[44]

The return of a federal indictment and the subsequent prosecution of Marcus and codefendants intensified bitter feelings prevailing between Manhattan District Attorney Frank S. Hogan and U.S. Attorney Robert Morgenthau. Hogan's office had been in the middle of its investigation in December 1967 when, suddenly, federal prosecution was initiated and the defendants were taken into custody by the U.S. government. An angry Hogan believed that to all intents and purposes the federal prosecutor had "stolen" the case from him. At any rate, Hogan had no intention of dropping a matter that had originated in his office and members of his staff continued to question Marcus and others named as defendants in the federal indictment.

During an interrogation of Charles J. Rappaport, information was elicited that Carmine G. DeSapio was involved in the conspiracy. Hogan promptly called the former Tammany boss to his office for questioning. Beginning on January 8, 1968, DeSapio appeared on two occasions about a week apart. Without DeSapio's knowledge, the second interview was recorded. Later it was used against DeSapio when he was prosecuted in federal court.[45]

On December 20, 1968, a federal grand jury in New York City returned a four-count indictment against DeSapio, Corallo, and Henry Fried. The defendants were charged with having conspired to bribe Water Commissioner James L. Marcus and to shake down Consolidated Edison Company for construction contracts. Named in the indictment as coconspirators but not as defendants were Marcus and Herbert Itkin. When the case was brought to trial about eleven months later, the seventy-year-old contractor Henry Fried was granted a severance because of illness. Marcus had completed serving a fifteen-month sentence in a federal penitentiary at Lewisburg, Pennsylvania, and was the government's first witness in the prosecution of DeSapio and Corallo.[46]

Marcus testified that following the Jerome Park affair, Corallo suggested "other deals" could be profitable and mentioned Consolidated Edison Company as a prime target for shakedowns. Corallo estimated, said Marcus, that "Itkin and Corallo and I could share forty to fifty percent of the profits" if firms they selected received the contracts from Consolidated Edison. As commissioner of the Department of Water Supply, Gas, and Electricity, Marcus held absolute power over permits needed by Consolidated Edison. Thus, indirectly, Marcus was in a position to dictate the names of the firms with which Consolidated Edison entered into contracts.

Henry Fried, president of S. T. Grand & Company, previously had engaged in collusive bidding with some Consolidated Edison officials. However, there had been a change in top management personnel of the firm, which fact suggested to Fried the need for a new contact man. And chosen to serve as the intermediary between Fried, Consolidated Edison, and Commissioner Marcus was Carmine G. DeSapio. The selection of DeSapio was a masterstroke. The ex-Tammany boss certainly knew his way around in the sometimes shady realm of politics and business. Furthermore, Sydney Baron, who had been an intimate associate of DeSapio during the latter's halcyon Tammany Hall days, was engaged as a public relations consultant for Consolidated Edison.

In furtherance of the conspiracy, Fried wished to establish a close working relationship between DeSapio and Herbert Itkin. Fried therefore hosted a huge lawn party for associates and friends at his horse farm at Germantown, New York, on August 20, 1967. The bash, it was decided, would provide an ideal opportunity for a meeting between Itkin and DeSapio. The two attended and conferred about the proposed kickback scheme.

Not long after the Germantown party, Itkin informed Marcus that DeSapio "wants to handle our projects with Con Ed." Marcus replied, "Great, now maybe we can get somewhere." Consolidated Edison was seeking the approval of Commissioner Marcus to build a transmission line to Westchester County. Marcus withheld the letter of approval. Itkin testified that the plan was to force Consolidated Edison "so much against the wall" that the company would "welcome any help" it could get from any source.

In the fall of 1967 Itkin and DeSapio met several times for the purpose of formulating strategy to get Consolidated Edison construction work for Henry Fried's firm, S. T. Grand & Company. In return, DeSapio, Corallo, Marcus, and Itkin were to receive substantial kickbacks. The conspirators also had designs on the Consolidated Edison Storm King Mountain project. Con Ed would need city approval for its proposal to build a $167 million pumped storage hydraulic plant near Storm King Mountain at Cornwall, New York. The conspirators anticipated that they could extort payoffs amounting to over $5 million from this project alone.[47]

On November 10, 1967, an important luncheon meeting, arranged by Sydney Baron, was held at L'Aiglon Restaurant. Among those present were DeSapio and Max M. Ulrich, vice president of Consolidated Edison Company. Ulrich testified that at this meeting DeSapio boasted of his "experience in government work" and suggested he could be of assistance to Con Ed by acting as a sort of referee between the company and the commissioner of the City Water Department. The government charged it was this meeting that actually got the conspiracy off the ground.[48]

DeSapio was a key man in the conspiracy. The instructions he issued to Commissioner Marcus of the Water Department were relayed through Herbert Itkin. At a meeting between Itkin and DeSapio at the Biltmore Hotel,

DeSapio expressed doubt about the responsibility of Marcus. Itkin testified that DeSapio warned he must not "take a step or let the commissioner [Marcus] take a step without first consulting us."

The conspirators started collecting dividends after Marcus had dispatched a letter to Consolidated Edison Company granting approval of the construction of a transmission line to Westchester. Payoffs were handled through DeSapio. Itkin testified that beginning on November 24, 1967, he received three cash payments totaling $12,500 from DeSapio. The first payment was made to Itkin at DeSapio's apartment at Eleven Fifth Avenue and on two occasions the money was handed to him in DeSapio's office at 151 East Fifty-fifth Street. Itkin said that DeSapio named Henry Fried as a source of the payoff money.[49]

Testimony regarding DeSapio's role in handling the payoffs revived memories of the incident that had proved embarrassing to him in 1957. On that occasion DeSapio, then boss of Tammany Hall, got out of a taxicab at the Biltmore Hotel and carelessly left in the vehicle an envelope containing $11,200 in musty, worn bills. Mysteriously, DeSapio deemed it expedient to disclaim ownership of the bills and eventually they were turned over to the cab driver, who had found them.

By late November 1967 the kickback scheme was moving ahead with the efficiency of a well-oiled machine. The prospects for future payoffs were virtually unlimited. Then, on December 12, 1967, Marcus abruptly resigned as water commissioner and within a few days federal action was initiated against him and several confederates. The grandiose plan of the conspirators to collect kickbacks running into millions of dollars was ended.

On December 13, 1969, DeSapio and Corallo were found guilty by a federal jury in New York City in the bribery-conspiracy case. DeSapio appeared before Judge Harold Tyler for sentencing on February 10, 1970. Judge Tyler referred to the proof in the case as "overwhelming." DeSapio continued to protest his innocence and suggested that he had been the victim of a climate in which many people were concerned about organized crime. He insisted that he never had been connected in any way with organized crime. Notwithstanding these protestations, Corallo, who was convicted with DeSapio, was a top-echelon figure in the criminal organization headed for many years by Thomas (Three Finger Brown) Lucchese. And DeSapio's rise to the leadership of Tammany Hall in no small measure traced to the sponsorship and backing he had received from Frank Costello, one of the most powerful organized crime bosses in New York City.

Judge Tyler sentenced DeSapio to serve two years in prison and to pay a fine of $4,500. The U.S. Supreme Court rejected DeSapio's appeal on May 24, 1971, and on June 25, 1971, the onetime boss of Tammany Hall surrendered at the federal penitentiary in Lewisburg, Pennsylvania, to begin serving his sentence.[50]

The fall of Carmine G. DeSapio was now complete. Once the most important Democratic leader in New York, DeSapio had been stripped of his political power when he was automatically ousted as county leader in 1961. And ten years later came the humiliation of his conviction and prison sentence.

It was perhaps poetically fitting that the final episode in the downfall of DeSapio should be his conviction for conspiracy with the underworld chieftain Corallo.

For over a century and a half, Tammany Hall dominated New York City politics. That domination stemmed in part from the chummy alliances between Tammany leaders and the underworld. Political clubhouses were often the centers of organized crime. During the period that DeSapio was serving as a district leader and struggling to attain the top spot in Tammany Hall, almost half of Tammany's clubs were controlled by racketeers.[51]

Alliances between political leaders and underworld bosses are still with us. And they are still the very lifeblood of organized crime. They are not peculiar to New York City. On the contrary, they prevail wherever organized crime flourishes.

PART II

COSA NOSTRA
VALACHI'S TESTIMONY EXAMINED

20

JOSEPH VALACHI'S BACKGROUND

In 1963, the U.S. Department of Justice announced an "extraordinary intelligence breakthrough" on organized crime. Attorney General Robert F. Kennedy asserted that disclosures by Joseph M. Valachi, a federal prison inmate, had revealed for the first time "the whole picture" of organized crime, its organizational structure and initiation rites, which included sacred oaths and bloodletting.[1] Overnight, this relatively insignificant underworld character became an international celebrity whose testimony before a U.S. Senate subcommittee was widely accepted as the gospel on organized crime in America.

Joseph M. Valachi was born in New York City on September 22, 1903. His immigrant parents were born in the Naples section of Italy. Valachi's education in the public schools of New York ended when he was fifteen years old. Although he left school ostensibly to go to work, he admitted that his legitimate employment—working on sand boats—lasted only about a year before he turned to crime.[2]

When eighteen, Valachi was convicted in Jersey City, New Jersey, for carrying a loaded revolver, was fined $100, and placed on probation. Two years later he was sentenced to Sing Sing Prison in Ossining, New York, for attempted burglary. After a parole he was returned to Sing Sing on another sentence and reparoled in 1926. He managed to stay out of prison until 1956, when he was committed to the federal prison in Atlanta on a five-year narcotics sentence. Another sentence for a narcotics violation, this one for fifteen years, was imposed in 1959.[3]

While in the Atlanta prison yard on June 22, 1962, Valachi became panic-stricken when he saw inmate Joseph Saupp, a fifty-two-year-old inconsequential criminal. Under the delusion that Saupp was actually a syndicate hoodlum known as Joe Beck who had been hired to kill him, Valachi grabbed a pipe, attacked him from behind, and bludgeoned him to death.[4] Before Valachi's trial and conviction for the murder of Saupp, he was examined by Dr. Harry R. Lipton, a consulting psychiatrist in the Atlanta prison for twenty-six years. Dr. Lipton reported that Valachi was legally sane although he was suffering from a "paranoid state" characterized by "delusion of persecution.'' His comprehension and memory showed no defects and he had no hallucinations or suicidal tendencies. Valachi revealed that his brother had been a patient in a mental institution for thirty-one years and his two sisters as well as a grandmother had been patients in mental institutions. Valachi received a life sentence for the murder of Saupp and a short time later was removed from the Atlanta prison by federal agents, who questioned him thoroughly about his knowledge of organized crime.

In September and October 1963 Valachi testified before the U.S. Senate Permanent Subcommittee on Investigations headed by Senator John L. McClellan. Admittedly, Valachi's firsthand knowledge of organized crime was limited to New York City and environs. Much of his testimony related to gang activities of many years ago and a substantial amount of this history had previously appeared in books, magazine articles, and news items. None of Valachi's testimony could form the basis for successful prosecutions.

Attorney General Robert F. Kennedy, in referring to Valachi's disclosures, told the U.S. Senate subcommittee that ''for the first time, an insider—a knowledgeable member of the racketeering hierarchy—has broken the underworld's code of silence.''[5] Historically, this statement was inaccurate. Two decades earlier, Abe Reles, alias Kid Twist, provided inside information regarding the infamous Murder, Inc. in New York City. It was the testimony of Reles that resulted in the successful prosecution of numerous organized crime characters in New York. A considerable amount of Valachi's testimony was repetition of what Reles had disclosed many years earlier.

The most sensational phase of Valachi's revelations concerned a secret crime organization, which he called La Cosa Nostra (''our thing''). The Cosa Nostra, as an organization, was completely unknown before Valachi's testimony and there is some reason to believe that originally he may have been using the term in its generic sense rather than as the actual name of an organization. Nevertheless, within days, the term *Cosa Nostra* was used to depict crime syndicates everywhere in the United States. And Valachi's terminology was adopted throughout the land—a local organized crime group was referred to as a ''family,'' the adviser to the family boss as a ''consigliere,'' a lieutenant as a ''caporegima,'' and the run-of-the-mill member as a ''soldier.''

Eventually, the term *Cosa Nostra* became less frequently used and many law-enforcement officers as well as writers reverted to the use of *Mafia* to describe organized crime in America. In fact, it has often been contended that Cosa Nostra and Mafia are names that refer to the same organization. And some authors have flatly asserted that Joseph Valachi came forward and publicly stated he was a member of the Mafia. Yet, when Senator Edmund Muskie asked the witness point blank if Cosa Nostra is the same as the Mafia, Valachi replied, ''Senator, as long as I belong to this Cosa

Nostra. . .they never express it as Mafia.'' He said that only outsiders sometimes referred to it as Mafia but within the organization it was never called the Mafia.[6] Actually, Valachi, a Neapolitan, would have been barred from membership in the true Mafia, which is limited to Sicilians.

By the time Valachi was nineteen years old he was already an accomplished burglar and became associated with the 107th Street gang in New York. This gang of six to eight hoodlums became known to the police as the Minutemen because, as Valachi explained, "we got away from the burglary either in a minute's time or less." Although many of the stores victimized were equipped with burglary alarms, it would take the police from five to seven minutes to arrive after a window was crashed and the alarm went off. Valachi was the driver of the getaway car for the gang, which pulled two or three burglaries each week. Coats, jewelry, and other merchandise stolen by the gang were sold to fences, one of whom was Vincent Rao, who later became an important figure in organized crime.[7]

As Valachi was driving a getaway car about eighty miles an hour following a burglary on July 12, 1923, he was shot in the arm. About two months later he was picked up by the police and sentenced to Sing Sing. After his release on parole on August 20, 1924, Valachi promptly resumed his specialty in crime—burglary. Again, while driving a getaway car, Valachi was shot by pursuing police. He was seriously wounded in the head and his pals dumped him near 114th Street and Pleasant Avenue. About an hour later, his cohorts returned and brought him to a doctor, who, using only Scots whiskey as an anesthetic, removed the bullet from his head. He was then smuggled into a hospital on Eighty-sixth Street and subsequently moved to the Community Hospital at 100th Street and Manhattan Avenue, where he remained in a semiconscious condition for three months.[8]

After his release from the hospital, Valachi was associated with a gang known as the Irish Mob, although only two members of the group could have qualified as sons of Erin. A shootout occurred between the Irish Mob and the 116th Street gang, composed of Italians. No one was hurt and a peace meeting between the two gangs was held in 1924 at the Pompeii Restaurant. Influential at the conclave was William Moretti, already known as a ''big guy'' and later to become prominent as a gangland figure. On April 9, 1925, Valachi was sent back to Sing Sing to serve the unexpired term of his first commitment, after which an additional three-year sentence began. He received his discharge on October 8, 1926.[9]

While in Sing Sing Prison, Valachi read in the newspapers that one of his pals in the Irish Mob, Frank LaPuma, had been shot. A fellow inmate warned Valachi that the peace meeting at the Pompeii Restaurant had been a ''sellout'' and cautioned him to be careful when he was released from prison. It was learned that underworld boss Ciro Terranova, also known as Ciro Morello and the Artichoke King, had paid $100 to have LaPuma killed.

When Valachi hit the street, he approached Frank Livorsi, bodyguard and chauffeur for Terranova, and asked him to inquire about his status. Livorsi later told Valachi, "You mind your business and everybody else will mind theirs." Accepting Livorsi's report as assurance that his life was not in danger, Valachi organized a new burglary gang of about seven members, including Salvatore Shillitani, alias Sally Shields, who was to figure prominently in Valachi's future. This gang committed a burglary about every three weeks.[10]

In 1930 Valachi was approached by Dominick Petrelli, known as the Gap, and Bobby Santuccio, alias Bobby Doyle, to join another gang, some members of which were Sicilians. At first Valachi, a Neapolitan, was reluctant to become affiliated with this group. He knew of the historical hostility between Neapolitans and Sicilians and he recalled the warning given him by Alessandro Vollero when they were inmates in Sing Sing. Said Vollero, "If you hang out with a Sicilian twenty years and you have some trouble with another Sicilian, this Sicilian that you hang out with twenty years will turn on you. You can't trust him." However, Petrelli, whom Valachi called his "special friend," and Santuccio assured him that times had changed. The hostility between Sicilians and Neapolitans no longer existed, they said. When Valachi asked, "Who are we going to fight?" he was given the well-known underworld names of Ciro Terranova, Willie Moretti, and Dutch Schultz. After his original objections were overcome, Valachi affiliated with a new gang, headed by Tom Gagliano.[11]

21

CASTELLAMMARESE WAR

Assured that the age-old hatred between Sicilians and Neapolitans was a thing of the past, Joe Valachi became embroiled in gangland warfare based in part on this hostility. Powerful New York underworld leader Giuseppe (Joe the Boss) Masseria had decreed a death sentence on everyone in the United States who had originated from the locality of Castellammare del Golfo, Sicily. Thus, the bloody underworld conflict that broke out became known as the Castellammarese War.

The Castellammarese War began on February 26, 1930, when Masseria cohorts mowed down gangland boss Gaetano Reina with sawed-off shotguns. His underboss, Tom Gagliano, insisted upon avenging Reina's death and began recruiting new members for his organization. On August 15, 1930, the big boss, Peter Morello, alias the Clutching Hand, was murdered. He was succeeded by Salvatore Maranzano, who was believed responsible for the Morello killing.

Warfare erupted between two major groups of Italian and Sicilian underworld gangs. One group was headed by Joe the Boss Masseria and the other by Salvatore Maranzano. Allied with the Masseria forces were such prominent gang leaders as Lucky Luciano, Ciro Terranova, Dutch Schultz, Vito Genovese, and allegedly Al Capone of Chicago. All of the Castellammarese fought under the banner of Salvatore Maranzano, and one of his principal gang leaders was Tom Gagliano. However, the base of Maranzano's support was much broader than Sicilians who had originated from Castellammare del Golfo. Among those recruited by Gagliano to wage warfare on the side of Maranzano was Joseph Valachi, an American-born Neapolitan. The actual recruitment of Valachi to the Cosa Nostra organization followed the assassination of two Masseria gang leaders, Alfred Mineo and Steve Ferrigno, on November 5, 1930. By this time the war was nationwide in scope.[1]

Valachi's formal induction into the criminal organization, then headed by Maranzano, took place in 1930 in a private home about ninety miles from New York City. Valachi and two other neophytes, Nick Padovana and Salvatore Shillitani, were driven to this spot by Frank Callace, also known as Chick 99. Each inductee appeared separately in a big room where about forty men were seated around a table. Presiding over the group was Salvatore Maranzano, whom Valachi now met for the first time. Prominent on the table were a gun and a knife. Valachi was ordered to repeat some Sicilian words, which were explained to him to mean that members of the organization "lived by the gun and by the knife and you die by the gun and the knife." An oath was then administered to Valachi, who was given a piece of paper that was burning as he held it in his hand. Again words were uttered, meaning, "This is the way I burn if I expose this organization." After the ceremony, the men seated around the table drew numbers, and by this method Joseph Bonanno was selected to be the godfather of Valachi. The godfather, said Valachi, "pricks your finger. . .with a needle, and he makes a little blood come out, and in other words, that is the expression, the blood relationship. It is supposed to be like brothers. . . .Then they all shake hands, everybody gets up and shakes hands, and say a few more words together, which I can't recall. They also said it in Sicilian."[2]

Valachi was now a full-fledged member of the Cosa Nostra. At the time of his initiation, only two rules of the organization were pressed on him: the requirement of complete secrecy and the prohibition against violating any member's wife, sister, or daughter. Later he learned that "you can't hit another member with your fist." To do so would result in a trial, or as he expressed it, the offender would be "brought on the carpet."[3]

At the time of Valachi's testimony in 1963, he had been a member of Cosa Nostra for thirty-three years. During that period, he had sponsored others for membership in the organization. Yet, when asked by Senator Thomas J. McIntyre, "Were you ever present at any other initiation other than your own?" Valachi replied, "Right now I never remember being present, Senator. . . ." But regarding these initiation rites, Valachi insisted, "That is the same ceremony today, what I described in 1930."[4] To a casual observer, Valachi's testimony regarding Cosa Nostra's "hocus-pocus" initiation rites is not very convincing, particularly since over a span of three decades he never observed or attended initiation ceremonies other than his own.

After his induction into the ranks of Cosa Nostra, Valachi's first "contract" to murder involved Joe Catania, known as Joe the Baker. Catania had been hijacking Maranzano's alcohol trucks and the boss decreed that he must be assassinated. Valachi, Salvatore Shillitani, Nick Capuzzi, and a man identified only as Buster from Chicago were picked for the job. When the killers entered Catania's apartment, three men were painting the place. The intended victim was not present and Valachi proceeded to the getaway car parked nearby. About a half hour later, Catania appeared and was killed by Shillitani, Capuzzi, and Buster. Official records of the New York City Police Department revealed that at 11:45 P.M. on February 3, 1931, Joseph

Catania, age twenty-nine, was shot and killed fifteen feet west of 647 Crescent Avenue in the Bronx. While walking in front of that address, he had been shot six times in the head and body. Valachi testified that he did not get paid for his part in the killing. He was merely fulfilling his obligation as a member of the organization. He had received his instructions to murder and he had carried out his orders in the same manner as a soldier in the army.[5]

At the peak of the Castellammarese War, Maranzano's forces totaled about six hundred men. And as between nations, warfare among rival underworld organizations was costly. Tom Gagliano spent $140,000 to purchase cars and machineguns and to pay rent for apartments used by his men. The war was waged on a national basis and money was dispatched to Maranzano in New York by gang leaders in other cities. Valachi testified that $5,000 a week was received from boss Stefano (Steve) Magaddino of Buffalo and another $5,000 a week from Joe Aiello of Chicago. However, the money from Chicago stopped when Aiello was killed on October 23, 1930.[6] Aiello's murder took place a little over two months after Maranzano had succeeded Peter Morello as the big boss in New York City. Hence, Aiello's contributions to Maranzano's war chest, as related by Valachi, lasted only a few weeks during the early phase of the war.

As the conflict between the New York gangs intensified, Joe the Boss Masseria tried to make peace. Valachi testified that Masseria "offered himself to be a plain soldier. He will give up anything he had if they leave him alone. Maranzano refused." Masseria had lost much of his following but five or six men remained real close to him, including Vito Genovese, Lucky Luciano, and Ciro Terranova.

Yet, these same "friends" came to terms with Maranzano and double-crossed their leader. Genovese and Luciano lured Masseria to a restaurant in Coney Island on April 15, 1931, by telling him they wanted to sit down and discuss plans for killing Maranzano. As Masseria was seated in the restaurant, he was shot in the back and head six times and killed. Present at the killing, according to Valachi, were Luciano, Joe Stretch, Genovese, Terranova, and a man called Cheech. As the assassins fled from the Coney Island restaurant, Ciro Terranova became so nervous and shaky that he had trouble placing the "key in the ignition" and he was removed as the driver of the getaway car. Terranova thus "lost face" and was gradually stripped of his power. Eventually he was replaced by Mike Coppola.[7]

About five days after the murder of Giuseppe (Joe the Boss) Masseria, "there was peace. We closed this war. . . ." When asked by Senator John L. McClellan if he knew how many men were killed during the war, Valachi released one-sided figures typical of those of a combatant in a conflict between nations. Said Valachi, "The score was, we lost one and they lost from forty to sixty." When asked to give "the name of the one of your group who was killed," he replied, "We lost one in Chicago, Joe Aiello. . . .They told me Al Capone got him."[8]

It is true that Aiello was assassinated in Chicago by Capone gangsters. But Valachi's version that his murder was connected with the war between the forces of Maranzano and Masseria is highly improbable. Instead, Aiello was merely one of a long list of casualties resulting from Chicago gang wars. Before the Castellammarese War was initiated in 1930, Joe Aiello, one of seven brothers, had been a bitter enemy of Chicago boss Al Capone. In 1927, the Aiellos spread word that they would pay $50,000 to anyone who killed Capone.

Joe Aiello joined the forces of George (Bugs) Moran, who headed a gang of alcohol peddlers on Chicago's North Side. On Febraury 14, 1929, seven associates of Bugs Moran, an archenemy of Capone, were mowed down by Capone gangsters in the St. Valentine's Day massacre. The wholesale carnage did not intimidate Moran. Instead, it made him more determined than ever to seek vengeance against his foe. In 1930 the triumvirate of Moran, Aiello, and Jack Zuta were plotting to topple Capone from his Chicago underworld throne. On August 1, 1930, five gunmen poured bullets into Jack Zuta and he was instantly killed. A few weeks later, on October 23, 1930, Capone gangsters had established two machinegun nests covering the front and rear of the residence of Patsy Prestigiacomo, known as Patsy Presto, at 205 North Kolmar Avenue in Chicago. Presto and Aiello had been partners in a Chicago firm, the Italo-American Importing Company. As Aiello emerged from the Presto apartment, the waiting Capone gunmen opened fire and murdered him. Aiello's assassination was the sixty-first gang killing in the Chicago area since January 1, 1930. In 1926, four years before the Castellammarese War had even started, there were seventy-six gang killings in the Chicago area, the largest number in the history of the Windy City. In 1927, gang murders totaled fifty-one; in 1928, seventy-two; and in 1929, fifty-three. For an explanation of Aiello's murder, it is illogical to look beyond the local Chicago gang wars of the period.[9]

About a month after peace was restored in New York, through the murder of Joseph Masseria, a meeting, attended by four hundred to five hundred men, was held in a big hall on Washington Avenue in the Bronx. Presiding over this gathering was Salvatore Maranzano. He asserted that Joseph Masseria and his group had been killing people without justification. Now, he explained, things were going to be different and he outlined the new setup.

The supreme ruler over the entire organization was to be the Boss of All Bosses, a title he promptly conferred upon himself. Each family (gang) was to be headed by a boss; his assistant was to be known as an underboss. Next in rank were the lieutenants of a family, whom he called caporegime. Each caporegima was to be in control of a crew of soldiers, the lowest-ranking members of the organization. A proper chain of command was established and everything was to be handled through proper channels. Maranzano explained, "Now, if a soldier wants to talk to a boss . . . he must speak first to the caporegima, and the caporegima, if it is required and it is important enough. . .will make an appointment for the soldier. . . ."[10]

Maranzano also discussed realignments of families. He mentioned that since the war had ended, some men could return to the family headed by Tom Gagliano, and others could remain with him. Maranzano then asked for a show of hands by those who wished to remain with him. Valachi responded in this manner; he thus left the Gagliano family and became attached to Maranzano. This was the second family with which Valachi had been affiliated within the space of the few months he had been a member of Cosa Nostra.

Five Cosa Nostra families existed and Maranzano proceeded to designate the bosses and underbosses of each. One family was to be headed by Charles (Lucky) Luciano as boss and Vito Genovese as underboss; another family had Gaetano (Tom) Gagliano as boss and Gaetano (Thomas) Lucchese as underboss; another family boss was Vincent Mangano and his underboss was believed to have been Frank Scalise; the Newark boss at that time was Joe Bonanno (not identical with the Joe Bonanno of Brooklyn). In Maranzano's family the underboss was Angelo Caruso.[11]

A short time after the big organizational meeting was held in the Bronx, Maranzano promoted a five-day banquet. Each day men would arrive in the evening and leave between three and five o'clock in the morning. The purpose of this affair, said Valachi, was to raise money and to acknowledge Salvatore Maranzano as the Boss of All Bosses. Frank Scalise sat at a small table and as the men arrived they would throw money on the table. Each night piles of money contributed by those attending the banquet were turned over to Maranzano. Money also came in from other cities. Valachi testified that Maranzano sent out "a thousand tickets to Al Capone and Al Capone sent $6,000. He sent a thousand tickets to Buffalo, and they also sent $6,000. Luciano himself sent $6,000. Them were the big amounts, I know." The rest of the total of $115,000 collected came from the guests attending the banquet.[12]

The peace that followed the murder of Joe the Boss Masseria was a most uneasy one. When Valachi visited the home of Maranzano on Avenue J, the Boss of Bosses told him, "We have to go to the mattress again." During times of war the gunmen "hole up" in various houses and may be on the move at a minute's notice. In the meantime, they sleep on mattresses. In gangland parlance, going on the mattress means going to war. Maranzano told Valachi that "we can't get along" and rattled off the names of Al Capone, Frank Costello, Lucky Luciano, Vito Genovese, Vincent Mangano, Joe Adonis, and Dutch Schultz. Said Maranzano, "We have to get rid of these people."[13]

Pursuing his elimination program, Maranzano hired the Irish gunman Vincent Coll to murder Luciano and Genovese. Coll, known as the Mad Mick, had been a killer for the Dutch Schultz mob until the early spring of 1931, when they had a parting of the ways. Coll and his cohorts began raiding the Schultz mob beer drops and vicious warfare broke out. Coll was murdered by an employee of Schultz on February 7, 1932.[14]

Maranzano maintained a suite of offices in the Eagle Building Corporation, 230 Park Avenue at Forty-sixth Street in New York City. It was in these offices that he arranged for a meeting with Luciano and Genovese on September 10, 1931. It was planned to have Coll waiting to kill them when they arrived. However, Bobby Doyle (Santuccio) double-crossed Maranzano and tipped off the intended victims. Naturally, they did not show up at the appointed time. Instead, four gunmen, posing as policemen, entered the suite of offices. Several persons were there awaiting their turn to see Maranzano. The Boss of Bosses was killed and the murderers fled.

Bobby Doyle, present at the time of the killing, later recounted to Valachi: "There were four Jews went up there, and they posed as policemen. . . .Well, they (two men) brought Maranzano in the other room, while the other two stood with the crowd. . .they posed as policemen and showed them a badge. . . ." The men told Maranzano they wanted to talk business with him and he fell for this ruse. "But when they got in the other room, Maranzano seemed to have gotten wise. . . .Maranzano went for a pistol. . .and they were forced to use a shot on him before they cut his throat. . . ." Actually, the assassins shot Maranzano four times and stabbed him six times. The police recovered a knife and two pistols at the scene of the crime.

After performing their mission, the killers ran out of the building just as Vincent Coll and cohorts were arriving. Coll was warned to "Beat it, the cops are on the way." Bobby Doyle, who was rushing from the building as the police appeared on the scene, was arrested and held as a material witness. The four Jewish killers were allies of Meyer Lansky. Some time later, Red Levine, a Lansky affiliate, admitted to Valachi that he was one of the men who participated in the murder of Maranzano.[15]

In response to questions from Senator John L. McClellan, Valachi stated that neither Lansky nor the four Jewish gunmen who assassinated Maranzano were members of Cosa Nostra. In view of the impression left by Valachi's testimony that the killing stemmed from an Italian Cosa Nostra power struggle, it is understandable why the senator appeared somewhat confused. In referring to the four Jewish murderers, Senator McClellan asked, "How did they get into the picture?" Valachi replied, "Well, they were very close with Charley (Luciano) and Vito (Genovese) at that time. . ."[16]

Valachi's testimony that Luciano and Lansky were close associates is accurate. But this association had much broader implications than a fight for leadership of the Italian Cosa Nostra. During this period, there existed an alliance of rumrunners on the Atlantic Coast known as the Big Seven Combination. Among the influential underworld figures in the Big Seven were Luciano, Lansky, Bugsy Siegel, Frank Costello, Johnny Torrio, Longy Zwillman, Charles (King) Solomon, Lepke Buchalter, Jacob (Gurrah) Shapiro, Daniel Walsh, Frank Zagarino, Joe Adonis, Waxey Gordon, and Moe Sedgwick, better known as Moe Sedway. Through Ciro Terranova and the Tammany Hall leader, Jimmy Hines, the combination also had a working arrangement with Dutch Schultz. Designated as arbiter to settle differences between the gangsters was Henry Goldberg, also known as Dutch Goldberg, and Louis Shomberg. Luciano, Lansky, and Siegel engaged in an exchange of profits with Buchalter and Shapiro, who were kings of the industrial rackets with a stronghold in the clothing industry.[17]

According to Valachi, Maranzano had planned to use Vincent Coll, then a bitter enemy of Dutch Schultz, to bump off Luciano and Genovese. Some time after the Boss of Bosses had been murdered, Dixie Davis, attorney and cohort of Schultz, attributed the killing of Maranzano to Bo Weinberg, an important Schultz lieutenant.[18]

During Valachi's testimony, he revealed that Maranzano had hijacked Luciano's alcohol trucks as well as trucks containing clothing industry piece goods.[19] Naturally, such action would have placed Maranzano in direct confrontation with the Big Seven Combination. And the motive for Meyer Lansky to furnish four Jewish gunmen to wipe out Maranzano was clearly present.

Regardless of the motive, Maranzano's assassination on September 10, 1931, took place less than five months following the murder of Joe the Boss Masseria. And the killing of Maranzano, said Valachi, had to be justified to the other Cosa Nostra bosses. Valachi was asked to go to Chicago and explain to the bosses in the Windy City that Maranzano had planned to kill Luciano and Genovese. Thus the slaying of the Boss of Bosses was justified. Valachi admittedly knew no one in Chicago and asked Vito Genovese to be relieved of the assignment. As a result, Bobby Doyle was sent to Chicago in his place.[20]

The murder of Maranzano created a dilemma for Valachi. Boss Tom Gagliano wanted him to return to his family and he received overtures from the Luciano family as well. Valachi sought the advice of his best friend, Dominick Petrelli, whom he called the Gap. Valachi asked Petrelli, ''What should I do? I don't know what to do, and you give me advice. And he said, 'Go with Vito.' '' Thus, Valachi became a member of the Luciano family of which Vito Genovese was underboss. This was the same family that was headed by Joe the Boss Masseria before he was killed. As a result, Valachi had been attached to three Cosa Nostra families within the space of a few months. However, his membership in the family then headed by Luciano was to last over thirty years.[21]

Following the murder of Maranzano, Lucky Luciano became the overall boss of Cosa Nostra. His underboss was Vito Genovese, and Anthony Strollo, better known as Tony Bender, was an important lieutenant of his family. As top man, Luciano promptly initiated some reforms in the organization. He abolished the Boss of Bosses system and ordered that a consigliere be assigned to each family. In part, the purpose of the consigliere was to protect the rights of the soldiers. At that time, there were six Cosa Nostra families—five in New York and one in New Jersey. The consiglieri of the six families would meet as a council to decide important issues. If they were evenly divided in their deliberations, any family boss could be brought in and his vote would break the stalemate.[22] With these Luciano reforms, the general structure of Cosa Nostra as as organization was quite largely settled and has since remained intact.

22

COSA NOSTRA MEMBERSHIP

Valachi's testimony before the U.S. Senate subcommittee depicted Cosa Nostra as a highly formalized and restrictive organization. Membership is limited to full-blooded Italians only. Although birth in Italy is not a requirement for membership, Valachi said, "You have to be a full Italian. . .You can't be half Italian or half something else." Both parents must be Italian. Once a person is proposed for membership, he must be approved by the organization. Valachi boasted that of all the persons he proposed, "none of them was turned down."[1]

To become a member of Cosa Nostra, each man must undergo the elaborate initiation rites to which Valachi was subjected at the time of his induction in 1930. This includes the holding of burning paper in a cupped hand, bloodletting, the taking of a solemn oath, and the designation of a godfather. Although he was never present at initiation rites other than his own, Valachi insisted, "That is the same ceremony today, what I described in 1930."[2]

The member at the lowest rung of the ladder in the Cosa Nostra organization is called a soldier. All members are assigned to a particular Cosa Nostra family and the soldiers work as part of a crew under a caporegima or lieutenant. If a member moves to another city, he is required to continue reporting to his original family. After a period of six months, however, he may get a letter from the Cosa Nostra family in the city to which he has moved and thus gain a transfer there.[3]

In the Luciano-Genovese family in New York City to which Valachi was attached, there were from 450 to 500 members. The Genovese family had twenty to twenty-five lieutenants or caporegime. The number of soldiers working as a crew (regime) varied. In some instances, there were about thirty soldiers in a crew. However, Mike Coppola, a very important lieutenant in the Genovese family, had about sixty soldiers in his regime. Cosa Nostra members in New York City totaled about 2,000; in Newark, 100; in Philadelphia, 100; in Boston, 20; in Chicago, 150; in Los Angeles, 40; in Cleveland, 50; in Tampa, 10; in Buffalo, New York, 125; and in Utica, New York, 100. There were, Valachi stated, very few members in New

Orleans, and because he was unfamiliar with Detroit, he could not estimate the number of members there.[4]

If these estimates of membership, as given by Valachi to the Senate subcommittee, are approximately accurate, then Cosa Nostra is primarily an eastern organization, principally centered in New York City. Roughly ninety percent of the membership is located in the states of New York, New Jersey, and Pennsylvania with the remaining ten percent scattered from Tampa and Boston in the East to Cleveland and Chicago in the Midwest and Los Angeles in the far West.

Valachi testified that each Cosa Nostra member was required to pay dues of $25 a month. He paid his dues to Tony Bender, the Genovese family lieutenant in charge of his crew. Although he did not know the reason, the Genovese family stopped collecting monthly dues in 1959. However, all other Cosa Nostra families continued to extract dues of $25 a month from each member. Valachi related that while he was in the Atlanta prison from 1960 to 1962, several Cosa Nostra inmates were there. And with the exception of those in the New York Genovese family, all continued to pay dues even though they were serving prison terms. When Senator Jacob K. Javits asked if he knew that every member paid $25 a month dues, Valachi replied, "I know positively."[5]

From Valachi's description, Cosa Nostra is a dues-collecting organization resembling a country club or trade association. It was only natural that the Senate subcommittee asked him to explain membership benefits. His response was vague and not very revealing. Said Valachi, "I never earned anything from 'the family'. . .but I myself earned my own money." He explained that during World War II he sold ration stamps and at various times he was engaged in other rackets involving slot machines, pinball machines, numbers, and juke boxes. Whenever he was arrested, he said, "I got myself out." He arranged for his own lawyers and bondsmen and his family did not give him any protection. However, if he learned that one of his runners in the numbers racket had started working for some other group, Valachi could go to his Cosa Nostra lieutenant, who would see that the runner was returned to him. Senator Karl E. Mundt asked Valachi, "In other words, if I understand your answer, all you got out of your membership in this family, was protection from somebody cutting in on your racket?" Valachi answered, "That would be a good way to put it."[6]

Membership benefits, as originally explained by Valachi, are meager, indeed. However, in testimony before the Senate subcommittee five days later, Valachi stated that he never received any assistance because he had not been in trouble over something for which Cosa Nostra was responsible. He asserted that if a person is arrested or imprisoned because of carrying out orders, Cosa Nostra will then provide a lawyer and "support your family while you are away.'' The money for these services comes from the $25-a-month membership dues.[7]

According to Valachi, membership in Cosa Nostra is rigidly controlled. He became a member in 1930 and no members were admitted between 1931 and 1954, a period of twenty-three years. Valachi testified, "The books were closed in about 1931. They were reopened around 1954. . . the expressions 'books open' and 'books closed'. . .mean that no member can get in as long as the books are closed." After the books were reopened in 1954, they remained that way for four years only, until they were closed again in 1958.[8]

Thus, during a span of thirty-two years, from 1931 until Valachi testified in 1963, new members were barred for twenty-eight years. Certainly, attrition through death and other causes would have greatly decreased the numerical strength of Cosa Nostra during that long period. If Valachi's testimony is truthful, it is difficult to understand how Cosa Nostra maintained itself as a viable organization.

Between 1954 and 1958, Valachi testified, the powerful boss, Albert Anastasia, and his underboss, Frank Scalise, brought about two hundred new members into Cosa Nostra. It was learned that Anastasia and Scalise had "commercialized" memberships by charging some men as much as $40,000. Among those named by Valachi as having paid Anastasia and Scalise large sums of money to get into Cosa Nostra were Jimmy Squillante, Jimmy Jerome, Jerry Mancuso, Frank Rocci, Carmine Camarado, Jimmy Ward, Salvatore Bonfrisco, and the brothers Tony the Geep and Mike the Geep Sedotto. When asked why these men would pay Anastasia and Scalise huge sums of money to gain membership in Cosa Nostra, Valachi replied, "We were stunned. I really can't answer that. . .I really can't. Just that they wanted to be recognized. That is the only way I can describe it." He said that there were many tough men, particularly in the Bronx and Harlem, and those who paid for their memberships "felt they were equal to the tough guys. How else would you explain it?" Senator McClellan suggested that these men were mobsters and therefore they wanted to be in an organization. Valachi replied, "That is right."[9] The entire discussion by Valachi concerning membership in Cosa Nostra is not very convincing.

23

COSA NOSTRA FAMILY

The nucleus of the Cosa Nostra organization is the family or *borgata*. The term *family*, however, is not used in its usual sense of blood relationship. Rather, it is similar to a gang—a group of men bound together as a unit in racketeering or criminal activities as a part of the overall organization, La Cosa Nostra.[1]

Valachi testified that there are five Cosa Nostra families in New York City, and no other city has more than one family. The cities named by Valachi as having one Cosa Nostra family each were Newark, Boston, Chicago, Los Angeles, San Francisco, New Orleans, Tampa, Buffalo, Utica (New York), Philadelphia, Cleveland, and Detroit. When questioned about Las Vegas and Miami, Valachi described them as "open" cities or areas. Although there are no families in the open cities, members of various families from other parts of the country may go there and operate. However, the individual who operates in Las Vegas or Miami must "notify his boss that he is there." Valachi's information regarding the jurisdiction or operations of families outside New York was admittedly meager. When Senator Carl T. Curtis asked, "You do not know how the territory was handled outside of New York State?" Valachi answered, "That is right."[2]

The five families existing in New York City at the time of Valachi's testimony in 1963 evolved from the struggles beginning in 1930 between the gangs controlled by Joseph Masseria and those dominated by Salvatore Maranzano. Two families trace their origin to the Masseria group and three to the gangs under Maranzano. John J. Shanley, a New York City deputy chief inspector, informed the Senate subcommittee that the various families do not exercise exclusive control over geographical areas of the city. Instead, individual families have had a tendency to concentrate on a particular type of activity—one family is stronger in the beverage business while other families have specialized in the garment or trucking industries. The operations of a single family may touch all five boroughs in New York City and the metropolitan area generally.[3]

The makeup of the five Cosa Nostra families in New York City was set forth in elaborate charts introduced into evidence by the Senate subcommittee. Heavy reliance was placed on information furnished by Valachi and, said Inspector Shanley, the charts could not have been constructed without his aid. The 356 men listed on the charts had a total of 2,365 arrests. On the average, one out of four had been arrested for homicide, one out of two for assault, one out of two for narcotics, and four out of five for gambling. Based on the arrest information, it was obvious that the members of all five families had been deeply involved in murder, narcotics, assault, and gambling.[4]

Administratively, the most powerful man of a family is the boss, who is assisted by his underboss (*sotto capo*). The boss of each family receives the advice and counsel of a consigliere, a position established by Lucky Luciano. In New York the consiglieri of the five families in that city, together with the consigliere of the Newark family, meet as a council to make important decisions.[5]

At the operational level, the lieutenant plays an important role in the administration of family affairs. When a decision has been reached that a member must be killed, in almost all instances, the contract is given by a lieutenant to a soldier. The soldier is then responsible for making plans for the murder and is permitted to choose the men he wants to assist him in fulfilling the contract.

As the head of a crew engaged in numerous rackets, the lieutenant's position is a lucrative one. Various soldiers assigned to him give him tips regarding moneymaking schemes. Cash continues to roll into the coffers of the top-ranking men of a family, including the lieutenant. Valachi estimated that in the Genovese family alone, there were forty or fifty men who had become very wealthy. These men accumulated fortunes, which ranged from a half-million to over a million dollars. Even many soldiers have amassed fortunes.[6]

The ultimate control of the nationwide Cosa Nostra organization is vested in a commission. The Senate subcommittee asked Valachi, "The commission is the council of the bosses themselves over the whole United States or wherever the families are in the United States?" He replied, "Right." In his actual testimony before the subcommittee, Valachi made but few references to the commission and failed to provide much specific information about it. However, based on intelligence gathered from Valachi, Attorney General Robert F. Kennedy testified that the bosses of Cosa Nostra families in major cities are responsible to a commission of from nine to twelve men. The commission, he said, makes major policy decisions, settles disputes among families, and allocates territories of criminal operation.[7]

Valachi's testimony thus portrayed Cosa Nostra as an efficient nationwide organization with ultimate control in the hands of the few bosses who compose the commission. It is this Italian organization that many believe controls all organized crime in America. But Valachi's testimony clearly

24

THE "NO-NARCOTICS" RULE

In 1948, because of pressures created through investigations, prosecutions, and attending publicity involving the drug traffic, Frank Costello, then boss of the powerful Luciano family, laid down a rigid rule that prohibited any member of his family from dealing in narcotics. The rule, explained Valachi, governed members of the Costello-Luciano family only and he specifically stated it did not apply to members of other families. However, after the gang killing of another family boss, Albert Anastasia, on October 25, 1957, Valachi said, "All families were notified—no narcotics." This rule was then promulgated by the bosses themselves. After the hearings brought out that violations of the no-narcotics rule were commonplace, Valachi was asked, "Did some of the bosses violate the rule?" He replied, "Certainly, especially Albert Anastasia."[1] The subcommittee did not bother to inquire how Anastasia "especially" could have violated a rule that did not apply to members of his family until after his death! Not infrequently, during the hearings, Valachi's testimony was confusing as well as inconsistent.

At the very time of Valachi's appearance before the Senate subcommittee, he was serving prison terms for violation of the narcotics laws. Also in prison at that time for a narcotics violation was Vito Genovese, who had succeeded Costello as boss of the most prestigious family in New York City. Some bosses, said Valachi, entered into arrangements that permitted the soldiers of their families to deal in narcotics with the bosses sharing in the profits.

Valachi also described a unique situation in Chicago, which, incidentally, was viewed with skepticism by many knowledgeable law-enforcement officers. The Chicago Cosa Nostra family, said Valachi, paid soldiers $200 a week to stop dealing in narcotics. Later, when Valachi was in prison, he learned that Chicago had raised the weekly stipend to $250. This action in Chicago resulted in dissatisfaction among the soldiers in New York who had been ordered out of the narcotics racket without compensation. In Chicago the Cosa Nostra family taxed certain businesses it owned in the city to raise the funds to subsidize soldiers to stay out of the drug traffic. Soldiers who received the weekly payment and were caught dealing in narcotics were promptly put to death. Two soldiers were killed in Chicago for this reason. In discussing the Chicago situation, questions were raised by the subcommittee concerning its possible effects. It was suggested that possibly some soldiers, not previously dealing in narcotics, might enter the traffic in order to obtain a weekly check of $200 or $250 by promising to get out of the racket. Valachi replied, ''I don't think Chicago had any trouble at all. I don't think that they tried any phony business. They are pretty honorable. . . .''[2]

In the Genovese family in New York City, violation of the no-narcotics rule resulted in the imposition of the death penalty. It was because of an infraction of this rule that Joe DeMaca was murdered. However, of the four hundred fifty members of the Genovese family, Valachi estimated that as many as a hundred were engaged in the narcotics racket. He stated that the no-narcotics rule was still in effect when he left Atlanta prison in 1962. In view of the widespread involvement of members of the Genovese family in the drug traffic, Senator Edmund S. Muskie asked, ''With respect to this one rule, the family wasn't very effective in imposing discipline, was it?'' Valachi answered, ''That is right. No.''[3]

25

NARCOTICS CONSPIRACY

In his testimony Valachi related the details of a huge narcotics deal in which he was involved in the early 1950s. Obviously, the rigid no-narcotics rule was then in full force. Salvatore Shillitani, known as Sally Shields, a ring leader of the conspiracy, approached Valachi and asked him to participate. At Valachi's suggestion, Pasquale (Pat) Pagano was sent by Shillitani to Le Havre, France, where he was to meet one Dominick, who was to supply the heroin. Dominick, who was originally from America, said his wife was coming to the United States within a few months and upon arrival would get in touch with Pagano about the heroin shipment. Valachi left the impression that he did not know Dominick's last name and apparently the subcommittee was unable to identify him.[1] However, according to his testimony, it was Valachi who was responsible for having Pagano get in touch with Dominick in France. For many years Valachi's most intimate friend was Dominick Petrelli. And from other sources it is known that this same Dominick Petrelli was involved, directly or indirectly, with Salvatore Shillitani in heroin traffic in Europe during the early 1950s.

Dominick's wife did arrive in New York City as planned and telephoned Pat Pagano, who met her in a downtown hotel. She instructed him to make an advance payment of $8,000 on the narcotics transaction. Pagano relayed her demands to Valachi, who borrowed $8,000 from Anthony Strollo (alias Tony Bender), and Pagano was given this money to turn over to Dominick's wife.

A short time later, the boat carrying the contraband, fifteen kilograms of heroin, arrived in New York. By that time, Shillitani, the apparent architect of the conspiracy, had been arrested on counterfeiting charges and was unable to continue in the drug deal. Arrested with Shillitani were about twenty-five individuals, mostly Frenchmen, including Joseph Orsini. Tony Bender made arrangements to pay Pasquale Moccio the sum of $15,000 for getting the heroin off the boat. Bender now also bluntly informed Valachi that the profits from the heroin deal were to be divided among nine partners: Vito Genovese, Pat Pagano, Sandino Pandalfo, John Stoppelli (alias Johnny the Bug), Pasquale Moccio, Vinny Mauro, Tony Bender, Valachi, and another man whose name Valachi was unable to recall. Valachi was also informed by Bender that "Vito Genovese owed Frank Costello $20,000 and we will pay this debt for him." This amount was to be taken off the top before there was a division of the profits among the partners.[2]

The market value of the fifteen kilograms of heroin in the United States was $165,000. The purchase price of the heroin in France was $37,500, but apparently the only cash outlay was the $8,000 turned over to Dominick's wife and there remained an unpaid balance of $29,500. Other expenses totaled $16,000. Expected profits would have totaled $111,500, but since $20,000 was taken off the top for Frank Costello, there remained $91,500 to be divided among nine partners. Valachi testified, however, that of this amount about $71,500 was split between Vito Genovese and Tony Bender. For his share in the deal, Valachi received heroin valued at $20,000, which he turned over to Fiore Siano and Joe Pagano to sell for him. They gave Valachi only $5,000. Originally, Valachi had expected to make roughly $50,000, but the entire transaction was filled with double-crosses and cheating among the partners.[3]

How accurate or complete was Valachi's version of the narcotics deal that had been engineered by Salvatore Shillitani? Almost a decade before Valachi's testimony in 1963, a book by Sid Feder and Joachim Joesten gave a detailed and authentic account of Salvatore Shillitani's international exploits in narcotics and counterfeiting during the 1950–52 period. A partner of Shillitani in these ventures was Eugene (Gene) Giannini, whose criminal career was spawned in that part of Harlem where the 107th Street mob held sway. It was this same Giannini whose murder in 1952 was arranged by Valachi.

The schemes of Shillitani and Giannini included the printing of counterfeit money, which was peddled in Europe and America and which provided the funds used to purchase heroin. In the United States they were able to convert $100,000 of counterfeit money into $22,000 in legitimate currency. The counterfeit-for-narcotics operation extended from Rome to Paris to New York. Reportedly, the conspiracy was masterminded by a Frenchman, Joseph Orsini, while he was lingering in a cell on Ellis Island awaiting deportation for Nazi collaboration and treason.

In furtherance of the counterfeiting-narcotics plot, Giannini and his old Harlem pal Dominick Petrelli went to Milan, Italy, in April 1951. There they were arrested. Petrelli told the authorities that he was merely a traveling companion of Giannini, stating, "He brought forty thousand of the phony into Italy and asked me to take a ride to Milan with him." Giannini boasted to the police that he was working for the U.S. Bureau of Narcotics and when Petrelli left for Milan he accompanied him to see "who was in this thing." Giannini related that en route to Milan they had met two Swiss gentlemen and he saw Petrelli give them $10,000 in counterfeit money for four kilograms of heroin. In view of the conflicting stories, the Italian authorities threw both Giannini and Petrelli in prison.

A few weeks later, several members of the counterfeit-narcotics combination, including Salvatore Shillitani, were arrested in the United States. Giannini had spoken truthfully when he told the authorities in Milan that he had served as an informer for the federal Narcotics Bureau. But at the same time, he had been carrying on his own lucrative business as a smuggler and dealer in narcotics. In his role as informer, Giannini had supplied the tipoff resulting in the arrests of Shillitani, Joseph Orsini, and others. Giannini remained in jail for nearly a year before he was released and permitted to return to the United States.[4]

The U.S. Senate subcommittee hearings were completely silent about the relations that existed between Shillitani, Giannini, and Petrelli in the drug traffic during the period 1950–52. No mention was made of the arrest of Giannini and Petrelli in Milan, Italy, in April 1951.

Petrelli was Valachi's closest friend and confidant.[5] It was in Petrelli's presence that Giannini admitted to the Italian authorities that he was an informer for the federal Bureau of Narcotics. Giannini also provided the information resulting in numerous arrests, including that of Shillitani, a partner of Valachi in the drug deal that Valachi described to the Senate subcommittee. It is a foregone conclusion that Petrelli would have told his intimate friend Valachi of Giannini's admitted role as an informer. And Valachi would have had a personal motive for taking action against Giannini, a double-crosser. These facts obviously were unknown to the Senate subcommittee and Valachi's testimony was considerably less than forthright.

Late in the summer of 1952, Valachi testified, Tony Bender sent for him. Bender related that word had been received from Lucky Luciano in Italy disclosing Giannini as ''an informer.'' Realizing the underworld penalty for being a stoolpigeon, Valachi replied sadly, ''There goes my couple of thousand that he owes me. . . .'' About a month later Bender sent for Valachi a second time and told him that efforts to locate Giannini had been unsuccessful. From remarks made by Bender, Valachi feared that he might be accused of sheltering the intended victim. After all, a dead Giannini could not pay the $2,000 he owed Valachi. Hence, to prevent suspicion on himself, Valachi agreed to accept the contract to kill Giannini and the contract received the approval of boss Vito Genovese.

Thus, in his account to the subcommittee, Valachi pictured himself as having had a detached and impersonal role in the contract to kill Giannini. Dramatically, he explained, Luciano had sent word from Italy that Giannini was an informer. Therefore, Giannini must be killed and Valachi was given the contract for his murder, which he carried out as a good soldier who merely followed orders and performed his duty in a matter in which he had no personal interest. That version is contradicted by known facts and is patently incomplete and inaccurate.

According to Valachi, the full responsibility for executing the murder contract was placed on his shoulders and he selected as his aides Joe Pagano, Pasquale (Pat) Pagano, and Fiore Siano. Significantly, all had been involved with Joe Valachi in the drug deal instigated by Salvatore Shillitani. Before long, the would-be assassins learned that their prey, Giannini, was working for a crap game that was operated on 112th Street by Pauley Hamm, a member of the Lucchese family. On September 12, 1952, Giannini was mowed down by shotgun blasts and killed. His body was dumped in front of 221 East 107th Street in New York City. At the time of the actual killing, Valachi was in the Lido Restaurant, which he operated and the assassination was performed by his subordinates. After the murder Valachi was ordered to appear at the office of Vito Genovese in the Erb Scrapping Company. Pauley Hamm had complained that the murder had been committed so close to his crap game it had attracted the attention of the police and it cost $10,000 to straighten out matters.[6]

Dominick Petrelli was murdered by three armed men in a bar in New York City on December 9, 1953. The murder had the earmarks of a gangland killing.

26

VALACHI—MAN OF MANY TALENTS

During Valachi's career as a member of Cosa Nostra, a career that extended over a period of three decades, he engaged in a wide variety of activities. At one time he was a racehorse owner. Starting about 1938, he ran his horses on New England tracks. Said Valachi, "I raced in Lincoln Downs. I raced in Narrangansett, Suffolk Downs, and New Hampshire at Rockingham Park." The best horses he owned were Knight's Duchess and Son of Tarra.

It was while he was racing horses at these tracks that he became acquainted with the New England mobsters. Valachi's lieutenant, Tony Bender, recommended Valachi to Joe Bruno, who was described as the New England boss. Bruno later died and was replaced by Phil Bubona, who later retired. As early as 1938 Valachi met Raymond Patriarca, who was introduced to him as a member of Cosa Nostra. Several years later, when Valachi was in prison, he "heard about Raymond being the new boss in Boston."[1]

Valachi's testimony about the New England organized crime setup was contradicted in part by a version given some time later by Vincent Teresa, a mobster who once served as an aide to boss Raymond Patriarca and his underboss Henry Tameleo. Teresa turned government informer and his testimony resulted in the convictions of scores of underworld characters. Valachi was asked repeatedly by the Senate subcommittee if Patriarca was a member of Cosa Nostra and he replied in the affirmative. However, Teresa asserted that in New England the term *Cosa Nostra* was never used. He credited Valachi with having "coined the name Cosa Nostra to describe the mob." Teresa also stated that Valachi's terms *our thing,* depicting the organization, and *soldiers* or *caporegime,* denoting ranks of members, were never employed by the New England mob. The organization in New England, said Teresa, was known as the Office. The blood and fire initiation rituals described by Valachi were also unheard of in New England insofar as Teresa was aware.

Mobsters with the most clout became bosses of gangs. For two decades, until 1950, Teresa explained, the New England underworld was ruled by a coalition of Italian or Sicilian bosses. Reigning over this coalition was

Joseph Lombardo, the most powerful of all bosses. The various bosses surrounding Lombardo were not part of one crime family. Each had his own gang of underlings. When decisions were to be made affecting statewide or interstate criminal activities, the bosses met with Lombardo, whose word was final. Between 1930 and 1938, the period mentioned by Valachi in his testimony, Raymond Patriarca was a member of the Lombardo organization. In Rhode Island, a Patriarca stronghold, the undisputed boss for over thirty years was Frank (Butsey) Morelli, whose career ended in 1947 when Lombardo replaced him with Philip (Buccola) Bruccola. Bruccola retired and fled to his native Sicily. Eventually, Patriarca emerged as the top boss, or *padrone*, of the New England organized underworld. Second to Patriarca in importance was Henry Tameleo and the third-ranking man in the organization, according to Teresa, was Jerry Angiulo, the boss of Boston.[2]

World War II marked the end of Valachi's horse-racing endeavors. A ban was placed on racing and swamp fever killed one of his best horses. The War, however, opened up new opportunities. Valachi entered the black-market ration-stamp racket, which netted him profits of about $150,000. When asked how he was able to get ration stamps, Valachi testified, "Really, they came out of the OPA offices. In the beginning, they were robbing safes, the burglars. . . .When they caught up with that. . .the OPA members, themselves, was sneaking them out and selling them to individuals." He was asked if he could testify of his own knowledge that OPA members sold ration stamps and he replied, "Definitely."[3]

For about a dozen years, Valachi had a dress shop on Prospect Avenue. Said Valachi, "I never belonged in any union. If I got in trouble, any union organizer came around, all I had to do was call up John Dio or Tommy Dio and all my troubles were straightened out." John Dioguardi, commonly called Johnny Dio, had a criminal history going back to 1930 and was deeply involved in labor racketeering.[4]

Valachi was also in the restaurant business for many years. In 1950 his partner was Frank Luciano. Because of the criminal histories of Valachi and his partner, the license for the place was taken out in the name of Anthony Luciano, a son of Frank. When Valachi discovered that the restaurant was $18,000 in the red, he accused his partner of stealing the profits and struck him. A Cosa Nostra rule prohibits a member from striking another with his fist and Valachi was "brought on the carpet."

At the so-called trial the presiding official was Albert Anastasia, boss of the family of which Frank Luciano was a member. Valachi was represented by his lieutenant, Tony Bender. Luciano's lieutenant, Joe Riccobono, was not present but sent a substitute, Charley Brush. At the conclusion of the hearing, Albert Anastasia turned to Valachi and said, "After all, you have been in this life of ours twenty years. . . .You should know better. . . .You could start a war with this kind of thing you pulled." Continuing, Anastasia ruled, "Now, you two must split. . .you can't be together." He decreed that Valachi must pay Frank Luciano about $3,500 and then Valachi would "wind up with the place because Frank cannot buy you out." Anastasia also ordered Luciano to "see that your son keeps that license up there. . .until that place goes down to the ground, as long as Joe wants it." Pursuant to Anastasia's ruling, the license was maintained in the name of Anthony Luciano and Valachi continued to operate the restaurant for an additional six years.[5]

Restaurants and dress shops, however, were merely adjuncts to his more lucrative illicit enterprises. Typical of the average underworld character, Valachi was deeply involved in various kinds of gambling operations—the numbers racket, bookmaking, and casinos. He was less than forthright in discussing some important aspects of his gambling ventures. Senator Jacob K. Javits asked, "Do you know of any political tie-ins with political people or judges or police in this operation?" Valachi replied, "Senator, I didn't have any myself so I am not going to say anything. . . ." And regarding the people who worked for him in his bookmaking operations, Valachi said, "I don't know if they were paying. I never asked."[6] This was an incredible answer.

Through general conversation, Valachi learned that some of his Cosa Nostra associates had interests in gambling casinos in Las Vegas. These people, he said, "do a lot of business in Las Vegas." About the time that Fidel Castro was coming to power in Cuba, Valachi bought a "half-point" interest in the Capri gambling casino in Havana. Before the Castro regime, the casino operators were paying rent of $25,000 a year. Castro raised the rent to $50,000 and demanded fifty percent of the business. As a result, Valachi said, "They told him to take a walk and they all went out of Havana."[7]

Closely allied with the gambling business is the loan-shark racket. Valachi testified that he was engaged in shylocking for about fourteen years. Most of his loans were made to bookmakers and saloonkeepers. Loan sharks are usually stationed at dice games, which serve as an unusually lucrative field for their operations. The rate of interest at dice games, Valachi said, is "five percent for overnight borrowing." If a player has overextended himself or needs money to stay in the game, he turns to the ever-present loan shark. On a loan of $5,000, for example, he must return $5,250 to the shylock within twenty-four hours.

Valachi was a relatively small loan shark. As to individual sums advanced, he said, "The most I loaned was about $2,000 or $2,400." All loans were made for twelve weeks. When asked what interest he charged, Valachi replied, "Twenty percent. . . .If I gave you $1,000, you have to pay me $1,200, for 12 weeks $100 a week." Since Valachi's "twenty percent" interest rate covered a twelve-week period only, it is obvious that on an annual basis his interest rate was 86⅔ percent. Most patrons of loan sharks make reloans before the original debt is satisfied. On an original loan of $1,000 for twelve weeks, Valachi explained, "If you pay me $700 and you want a reloan. . .all I have to do is give you back the balance of that $1,000 and I charge you another $200." Reloans are the most profitable phase of the shylock racket.[8]

For some time Valachi's partner in loan-shark operations was John Robilotto, commonly known as Johnny Roberts. Tony Bender, Valachi's lieutenant in the Genovese family, had been associated with Robilotto in the ownership of the Hollywood Restaurant, the Village Inn, and other business ventures. Yet, Bender had been unable to get Roberts, whose brother was a policeman, accepted as a member of Cosa Nostra. Eventually, Albert Anastasia brought Roberts into Cosa Nostra and he became an influential Anastasia lieutenant.[9]

Referring to the time that he and Johnny Roberts were shylock partners, Valachi said, "We had forty-some-odd thousand dollars in the street. Johnny financed me. . . .He put up all the money. I worked and got customers." Apparently the profits were sufficient to attract Tony Bender, who indicated to Roberts that he wanted a piece of the business. Roberts relayed this information to Valachi, who expressed vigorous objections. Valachi told Roberts, "You talk for yourself, because I don't want to give anybody any part of this business." A short time later, Valachi received orders from Bender to appear at Duke's Restaurant, then a notorious hangout for powerful underworld leaders in Cliffside Park, New Jersey. Bender told him to collect all money due him from shylock operations because his partnership with Johnny Roberts was going to be broken up. Valachi followed these instructions, stating that he would rather dissolve the partnership than share any profits with Bender.[10]

27

NEW JERSEY RACKETS

Johnny Roberts was a prime suspect in one of the nation's most highly publicized gang killings of the 1950s. The victim, Willie Moretti, an associate of Frank Costello and other underworld bigwigs, had been an important figure in New Jersey rackets for many years. Valachi testified that "Willie Moretti had lots of men, about forty or fifty men. . .throughout Jersey. Some of them were members [of Cosa Nostra] and some of them were not, but they still were with Willie Moretti. He was like an independent, and he had his own little army."[1]

John J. Bergin, assistant attorney general and director of criminal investigations in New Jersey, informed the U.S. Senate subcommittee that following World War II until about 1950, a group of men called the Big Five engaged in extensive gambling operations in northern New Jersey, mainly in Bergen County. The principals in the gambling combination were Salvatore (Solly) Moretti, a brother of Willie; James (Piggy) Lynch; Arthur Longano; Anthony Reno, alias Tony Groan; Joe Adonis; and Frank Erickson. The hangout for these underworld characters, as well as many others, was Duke's Restaurant, on Palisades Avenue in Cliffside Park, New Jersey. Bergin stated that almost everyone mentioned by Joe Valachi in the Senate subcommittee hearings "at one time or another either telephoned Duke's Restaurant or was seen at Duke's Restaurant in the 1940s." The Big Five gambling combination was smashed in 1950 and members of the group were convicted and sent to jail. "Duke's Restaurant. . .owned by John De-Noia. . .went into bankruptcy, and about seven doors away a restaurant and bar known as Joe's Elbow Room and Joe's Restaurant became a hangout for these people on Palisades Avenue in Cliffside Park, New Jersey."[2]

Beginning in the late 1940s, Willie Moretti, whom Valachi described as a syphilitic, became unusually talkative and, from the standpoint of the underworld, irresponsible and dangerous. Frank Costello reputedly sent Moretti, accompanied by a male nurse, on a trip through the western part of the United States. The pilgrimage, however, did not cure him of his propensity to blabber. Assistant Attorney General Bergin, who knew Moretti personally, stated that the mobster became garrulous with newspapermen and was giving out interviews right and left.

About eleven o'clock the morning of October 4, 1951, six days before Moretti was scheduled to appear before a grand jury, three men were in the restaurant next door to Joe's Elbow Room. One customer departed momentarily and returned with Willie Moretti. Two restaurant employees in the dining area went into the kitchen. Suddenly there was gunfire. The three male patrons fled and Moretti, shot twice in the head, was lying on the floor. Two men's felt hats, apparently belonging to the assassins, had been left in the restaurant. One had a cleaning mark that was traced to a hat-cleaning place in New York City directly across the street from the building in which Johnny Roberts' brother resided. Waitresses in the restaurant tentatively identified a picture of Johnny Roberts as the patron who had left the place temporarily and returned with Moretti just before he was shot. Roberts was a lieutenant of boss Albert Anastasia. Indications were that Anastasia may have been involved in planning the murder. At the time of the killing Anastasia had used Moretti's chauffeur, Harry Shepherd, to drive him to a hospital in Passaic, New Jersey, where his back was X-rayed. Officials surmised that Anastasia had deliberately planned the X rays at that time to establish an iron-clad alibi to the murder. Johnny Roberts was picked up in Brooklyn and charged with Moretti's murder but was released because of insufficient evidence. Valachi was also questioned by the police, but he denied even knowing Johnny Roberts.[3]

When Valachi was questioned by the Senate subcommittee about Moretti's murder, he flatly stated that Johnny Roberts was one of the killers. At the time of the assassination, Valachi was in his Lido Restaurant. Later he heard over the radio that Moretti had been murdered. He said, "I. . .called up Tony [Bender] my lieutenant and he told me 'go about your business.' " Later that night, during Valachi's absence, Johnny Roberts came to the restaurant and waited a couple of hours for him. When Valachi failed to show up, Roberts left a message with a waitress and departed. Following Johnny's arrest, Valachi talked with him and asked about the hats found at the murder scene. Roberts said, "Don't worry. . .it ain't my hat. . .it belonged to the other guys." Valachi remarked to Roberts, "I am sorry I missed you up at the restaurant" on the night of the murder. Roberts explained that "he came up there to celebrate because he knew that Willie and I never got along."

Moretti's murder, said Valachi, "was supposed to be a mercy killing because he was sick, and he was supposed to be talking, and he was going to go to the radio, and all that kind of talk got around." When asked who ordered the murder, Valachi replied, "As long as they made it official, that he was sick. . .you could say (it) was by the commission. It means they all agreed."[4]

Throughout Valachi's lengthy testimony before the Senate subcommittee he mentioned the existence of the commission on only a few occasions. He described the commission in very general terms. His sole reference to action taken by the commission related to the Moretti killing. And this reference was extremely vague and indefinite. Based solely on his testimony before the subcommittee, it would appear that Valachi knew very little, if anything, about the commission and how it functioned.

28

LUCIANO–COSTELLO–GENOVESE FAMILY

Through Joseph Valachi's testimony, the Senate subcommittee traced the evolution of the five families in New York City from the warfare in 1930 and 1931 between the Masseria and Maranzano forces to the time of the subcommittee's hearings. Two families emerged from the gangs controlled by Joe the Boss Masseria and three from the Salvatore Maranzano group.

For over thirty years Valachi had been a member of the family originally headed by Joseph Masseria. As a soldier in this family, he had served under a succession of bosses—Lucky Luciano, Frank Costello, and Vito Genovese. His testimony, however, related mostly to Vito Genovese. The information he provided concerning Luciano was quite limited, and many of the facts about Lucky that did surface at the hearings were furnished by New York City police officers.

Luciano became boss of this family after he murdered Joseph Masseria on April 20, 1931. In June 1936 he was convicted of compulsory prostitution and sentenced to prison in New York, and there he remained until he was deported in 1946. Following Luciano's deportation, Valachi said, Frank Costello "automatically became boss."

Luciano's imposed residence in Italy did not mean that he lost touch completely with his former partners-in-crime in America. New York City police officials testified that they learned of many pilgrimages made by New York gangsters to Italy for the purpose of visiting Luciano.

In the early 1950s, Joseph Biando, subsequently the underboss in the Carlo Gambino family, made false representations in obtaining a visa to Italy. While there, he paid a visit to Luciano. Over twenty years earlier Biando had been arrested in Cleveland while attending a prizefight with Luciano and Gaetano Lucchese. Among other well-known gangsters who paid their respects to Luciano in Italy were Joe Adonis and Patchie Evelin.

In 1961, Tommy Eboli, one of the most influential members of the family, spent several days with Luciano in his hotel room in Italy. On January 26, 1962, Luciano died of a heart attack while waiting in a Naples airport. In Luciano's presence, until about three hours before he died, was Pasquale Eboli, alias Patsy Ryan, a brother of Tommy Eboli. On the same plane that returned Pasquale Eboli to America was Vinnie Mauro, who had been associated with Vito Genovese and Valachi in a narcotics conspiracy.[1]

In May 1945 Vito Genovese, after an absence of several years, was returned from Italy to New York City to stand trial for murder. He learned that the wealthy and powerful underworld leader Frank Costello was now boss of the family.

Costello, whose real name was Francesco Castiglia, already had a long career in crime and rackets. In 1908, when only seventeen years old, he was arrested for assault and robbery. In 1915 he was convicted for carrying a gun. He became proficient in rumrunning and gambling. By 1931 he had reached a stature that made him feared by Salvatore Maranzano, then the Boss of Bosses. In a conversation with Valachi, Maranzano named Costello along with Al Capone, Luciano, Genovese, Vincent Mangano, and Dutch Schultz as persons who must be eliminated.[2]

Costello's confederates included the elite of the New York underworld. Among Costello's associates mentioned by New York police officials during the subcommittee hearings were Joseph (Socks) Lanza, Tommy Lucchese, Willie Moretti, Albert Anastasia, and Anthony Carfano. Lanza controlled important New York waterfront rackets. Tommy Lucchese had big gambling interests. Once when Frank Costello was jailed for contempt of Congress, Lucchese took his place as a gambling overlord. Several of Costello's intimate pals were felled by assassins' bullets, among them Moretti in 1951 and Anastasia in 1957. Carfano, also known as Little Augie Pisano, had been arrested several times for carrying guns and once was charged with murder. He had strong connections in the gambling racket and, in addition to Costello, was close to Mike Miranda and Frank Erickson. On September 25, 1959, Carfano, accompanied by Janice Drake, was at a dinner party with Al Segal, Anthony Strollo (alias Tony Bender), and Vincent Mauro. Carfano received a telephone message and then departed with Janice Drake. A few hours later both were found shot to death in Queens.[3]

Costello has been mentioned frequently in connection with the well-known Copacabana Club in New York City. It was at the Copacabana in 1949 that he sponsored a highly publicized dinner for charity. Among those attending this affair was Vito Genovese. He was met at the door by Costello, who showered him with special attention reserved for an underworld personage of prominence and power. Many years later, when Valachi and Genovese were inmates together in Atlanta's federal prison, Valachi inquired if Joe Pagano owned a piece of the Copacabana. Genovese replied that "Frank Costello has the club back and it belongs to Frank and nobody else but Frank."[4]

Valachi testified that after Genovese returned to the United States in 1945, he was infuriated because Costello, together with Willie Moretti and Albert Anastasia, "had everything sewed up." It was also common knowledge that a huge gambling empire was operated by Costello independently of the family. This situation eventually became intolerable to Genovese and it was decided that Costello must be eliminated. Valachi asserted that he was approached to participate in a Costello assassination but declined. He refused to elaborate further in his testimony before the subcommittee.

On the night of May 2, 1957, as Costello entered the lobby of his apartment building at 115 Central Park West in New York City, a gunman brushed by the doorman and fired a shot that grazed Costello's head. He was rushed to a hospital where his wound was treated. Vincent Gigante was arrested and charged with the Costello shooting and bond was set at $100,000. Deputy Chief Inspector John J. Shanley of the New York City Police Department stated that Cross Suclair & Sons put up $76,000 to get Gigante released on bail. Tommy Eboli's close associate, Rocco Perretti, was a salesman for the Cross Suclair firm. Shanley indicated that Eboli may have driven the car used by the gunman in the attempted assassination of Costello. Although Costello recovered physically, the shooting marked the end of his reign as family boss and he was replaced by Vito Genovese.[5]

Genovese was the central figure and archvillain throughout Valachi's testimony before the Senate subcommittee. Valachi had maintained a more intimate relationship with Genovese over a longer period of time than he had with any of the other bosses. Shortly after the murder of Maranzano in September 1931, Valachi followed the advice of his friend, Dominick Petrelli, and joined the Luciano family, of which Genovese was the underboss and Tony Bender was a lieutenant. Only a few months later, in 1932, Valachi wed and Vito Genovese was the best man at the ceremony.[6]

In the mid-1930s Genovese, fearing arrest and prosecution, fled to Italy. Deputy Chief Inspector Shanley testified that in Italy, Genovese "became very close to the Italian government. . .and he was decorated by Mussolini for his efforts." In 1943 Carlo Tresca, an Italian-American antifascist leader and editor of the *Martello,* an antifascist publication, was shot to death in the streets of New York City by underworld assassins. According to Shanley, information was received that Genovese had ordered the murder of Tresca and given the contract for the killing to Mike Miranda.[7]

Genovese continued his racketeering activities in Italy and received preferential treatment from the authorities. During World War II he engaged in large-scale black-market operations until he was arrested and returned to New York in May 1945 to stand trial for murder. But when the murder trial was held in June 1946, Genovese had little to worry about. As Valachi related to the subcommittee, the all-important prosecution witness in the case, Peter LaTempa, had been found "poisoned in the Raymond Street jail while he was waiting to testify against Vito."[8]

After beating the murder rap, Genovese was a free man. For eleven years he served as underboss of the family until he succeeded in deposing Frank

Costello as head man in May 1957. After serving as boss of the family for about two years, Genovese was convicted of a narcotics conspiracy on April 17, 1959, and committed to the federal penitentiary in Atlanta. Even after imprisonment, however, he continued to be the top man in family affairs.

Throughout his long career in crime, Genovese had engaged in narcotics, gambling, shylocking, vending-machine operations, extortion, and murder. At one time, said Valachi, "Vito Genovese had a big. . .Italian lottery. In those days, it was very, very big." During a divorce proceeding, the wife of Genovese asserted that Vito's take from the Italian lottery was between $30,000 and $40,000 a year. She also revealed that he received kickbacks through his labor connections at a naval base in New York.[9]

Valachi stated that Genovese "has lots of interests in gambling like Las Vegas and Havana, Cuba, when it was there, and he has legitimate businesses." In Las Vegas gambling, Genovese was associated with Meyer Lansky. In fact, said Valachi, "Anywhere Meyer Lansky is, Vito Genovese is. . .they do everything together."[10]

In the mid-1950s Genovese moved to the Atlantic Highlands. He entered into a venture, said Deputy Chief Inspector Shanley, which attempted to provide "a steamboat service from the Atlantic Highlands to New York City, to take people from the city to the racetrack." The scheme backfired and Genovese reportedly lost $175,000.[11]

Among other interests of Genovese were several clubs in New York City; Valachi identified them as the Savannah Club on Third Street, the Groton Village on Eighth Street, the 181 Club on Second Avenue, the 82 Club on Fourth Street, and the Moroccan Village. He was also in the cigarette vending-machine and jukebox businesses. Serving as fronts for Genovese in various clubs he owned were Tony Petillo, a brother-in-law, and Steve Francis.[12]

Genovese always had his hand out and his appetite for money was insatiable. On one occasion, Philip Lombardo, alias Benny Squint, and Ben Turpin paid $25,000 for a hatchecking concession. At the end of one year they had made a profit of $30,000, which they reported to Genovese. Valachi testified that Genovese told them "he had a case pending. He took $30,000 and put it in his pocket and they did not get two cents."

Although Genovese received the lion's share of the loot, many of his underlings made handsome profits. There were about four hundred fifty soldiers and from twenty to twenty-five lieutenants in the Genovese family. Valachi estimated that about forty or fifty members of the Genovese family amassed wealth sufficient to place them in the millionaire class.[13]

When Valachi arrived in the Atlanta prison for the first time in 1960, Genovese was already an inmate there. Later Valachi was returned to New York to stand trial on a second narcotics case. Again, he was convicted and was sent back to the Atlanta prison.

During a conversation in prison Genovese told Valachi that Tony Bender had disappeared. To disappear, said Valachi, "meant in our language, that he [Genovese] had ordered his death." Genovese explained to Valachi that Tony "was a sick guy." He could not take a long prison term and his disappearance (death) was described as the best thing that could have happened to him.[14]

Valachi soon learned that it was not only Tony Bender who had fallen into the bad graces of the powerful boss. In the presence of another convict, Ralph Wagner, Genovese pointedly told Valachi, "You know, sometimes if I had a barrel of apples, and one of these apples is touched (partially rotten). . .it has to be removed or it will touch the rest of the apples." After delivering this parable Valachi said that "Genovese grabbed my hand and he gave me a kiss." Valachi realized that Genovese had accused him of being an informer and the kiss he received from Vito was the "kiss of death." For over thirty years he had held Genovese in the highest respect. Now, said Valachi, in a gross understatement of his feelings, he "was losing respect for him."[15]

In the Atlanta prison at this time were several associates of Genovese, including Joseph DiPalermo (alias Joe Beck), Charles DiPalermo (alias Charlie Beck), John Dioguardi, and Mike (Trigger Mike) Coppola, one of the most powerful lieutenants in the family. Following the kiss-of-death incident, Valachi was in constant fear that a Genovese associate in prison would kill him. When he saw inmate John Joseph Saupp walking in front of him, Valachi mistook the prisoner for Joe Beck. Grabbing a pipe, Valachi attacked Saupp from behind and bludgeoned him to death.[16]

Although Genovese was lingering behind prison bars, his iron-clad control over his organization was not broken. During his absence from New York, Tommy Eboli served as the acting boss of the family. He shared authority over family affairs with the underboss, Gerardo (Jerry) Catena. While serving as underboss to Genovese in Manhattan, Catena also had strong connections in New Jersey. For many years he had been associated with the powerful New Jersey underworld leader Longie Zwillman in the Public Service Tobacco Company, as well as in other ventures. The association ended when Zwillman committed suicide in his New Jersey mansion on February 26, 1959. Genovese's confidant and righthand man was Michele (Mike) Miranda, the consigliere. In conducting family business from prison, Genovese would manage to get messages delivered to his brother, Mike Genovese, who would relay them to Tommy Eboli.[17]

The rule of Genovese over his family was absolute. But his influence was not limited to his own family. As Valachi explained, "He not only has the power. . .in his family. . . .He controls the power in the Gambino family and the Lucchese family. In other words, they eliminated the boss of all bosses, but Vito Genovese is a boss of all bosses under the table."[18]

Within a decade following Valachi's testimony, death struck the top leadership of the Genovese family. On February 14, 1969, Vito Genovese, age seventy-one, died of a heart ailment in the federal prison medical center in Springfield, Missouri. Three days later he was buried in the St. John's Cemetery, Middle Village, in Queens, New York. Nearby were the tombs of Salvatore Lucania, better known as Lucky Luciano, and Joseph Profaci, once the powerful boss of another New York underworld family.[19]

On July 16, 1972, Tommy Eboli, sixty-one, was gunned down in traditional gangland fashion in a residential section in Brooklyn's Crown Heights. When shot, Eboli had a diamond ring on one finger and a gold crucifix around his neck. A pocket in his blue jacket contained $2,077 in cash. Until shortly before his murder, Eboli had been living with a woman in an $800-a-month apartment in Fort Lee, New Jersey. At the time of his demise, Jerry Catena was behind bars for refusal to answer questions during an official inquiry.[20]

Frank Costello, eighty-two, once called the prime minister of the underworld, died of a heart attack on February 18, 1973. He had lingered in a hospital for eleven days after having been stricken with a heart disorder at his home at 115 Central Park West in New York City.[21]

29

ALBERT ANASTASIA–CARLO GAMBINO FAMILY

The second New York City family that evolved from the 1930–31 Masseria group was headed by Carlo Gambino at the time of Valachi's testimony in 1963. Much blood had been shed before Gambino arrived at the helm of this family. In fact, all of his predecessors had been murdered.

The original family bosses, Alfred Mineo and Steve Ferrigno, were assassinated on November 5, 1930. After they had been marked for death, Valachi was given the assignment of keeping Steve Ferrigno's apartment under surveillance to set him up for the killing. Associated with Valachi in the bloody task were Joseph Profaci, Nick Capuzzi, and Buster of Chicago, whose true identity was never determined. Joseph Profaci was soon to become a family boss in the Maranzano group. He had originated from the Castellammarese area of Sicily. While working on the Ferrigno surveillance, Profaci explained to Valachi about the death sentence Masseria had imposed on all Castellammarese in America. On the day that Ferrigno and Mineo were killed at 750 Pelham Parkway in the Bronx, the assassins were actually waiting for Joe Masseria. When he failed to show up, they settled for the murders of Ferrigno and Mineo instead.[1]

Successors to Ferrigno and Mineo were Philip and Vincent Mangano, who lasted until 1951. Philip was murdered at the direction of Albert Anastasia on April 19, 1951, and Vincent, who is believed dead, disappeared about the same time. Succeeding the Manganos as boss of this family was Albert Anastasia, frequently labeled as the chief executioner for the infamous Murder, Inc. His underboss, Frank Scalise, had been a man of influence in Cosa Nostra affairs since the days of the Castellammarese War in 1930.

The activities of Anastasia ran the gamut of underworld operations—gambling, narcotics, extortion. His specialty, however, was murder. He directed or personally assisted in scores of assassinations. Some of his victims were mowed down by gunfire, others were strangled, and still others were chopped with ice picks.

Among Anastasia's numerous victims was Morris (Moish) Diamond, slain on May 25, 1936. The details of the Diamond murder, along with sundry others, were given to the Brooklyn district attorney by the celebrated informer Abe Reles. His testimony had stood up in court against scores of killers who were convicted. Reles was, indeed, a prize prosecution witness as well as informant.

To prevent retaliation by the underworld, Reles was kept in protective custody in the Half Moon Hotel in Coney Island. Heavy reliance was placed on his expected testimony in several pending gangland murder cases. Although policemen were assigned to guard him around the clock, on November 12, 1941, Reles somehow mysteriously climbed out the hotel window and fell to his death. The district attorney said that "the perfect case" he had against Anastasia for the murder of Moish Diamond "went out the window with Reles." The escape and death of Reles, supposedly under heavy police guard, created a scandal. Charges were hurled that Reles had been murdered to prevent him from testifying in cases pending against bigwig organized crime figures.

During the Senate subcommittee hearings, Valachi was asked if he knew how Reles fell out the hotel window. He replied, "They threw him out" to prevent him from testifying against Anastasia. New York police officials presented to the subcommittee a September 1951 Kings County grand-jury report, which found that Reles was only one of several accomplices in the Diamond murder case and was not an essential witness against Anastasia. The report concluded that Reles met his death while trying to escape. However, that grand-jury report was made ten years after the death of Reles and did little to appease skeptics who still believed, with Valachi, that Reles had been thrown from the hotel window and murdered to seal his lips.[2]

For some time, Anastasia and Frank Costello were looked upon with disfavor by Vito Genovese because he felt they were blocking his rise to power. About 1956 Genovese ordered his men to stay away from members of the Anastasia family. Once when Anastasia attempted to talk with Frank Costello, Genovese rebuked him, stating, "We will take care of our family and you take care of yours."

Friction among New York City underworld leaders erupted in violence during 1957. The unsuccessful attempt to assassinate Costello took place in May. A few weeks later, on June 17, 1957, Anastasia's underboss, Frank Scalise, was slain by two gunmen in the Bronx. On October 25, 1957, Anastasia was instantly killed by two gunmen as he was reclining in a barber chair in a New York City hotel.

When asked who arranged for Anastasia's murder, Valachi replied, "I believe that Vito Genovese worked hand in hand with [Carlo] Gambino and Joe Bandi. . .they have the right to do something like this. . . .Albert Anastasia was doing so much wrong and it was up to his own family to act." Gambino and Joe Bandi acted, said Valachi, with the assurance that Genovese was backing them up.[3]

The specific motive for the murder of Anastasia was not satisfactorily developed at the hearings. Charges against Anastasia, according to Valachi, included the sale of Cosa Nostra memberships to unworthy persons. Friction had developed between Genovese and Anastasia as a result of an apparent power struggle. It was indicated that these were the reasons for Anastasia's murder.

Not mentioned during the subcommittee hearings were some important facts that may have had a direct bearing on the Anastasia killing. Found among the personal effects of Anastasia after his death were papers reflecting that he was in the midst of negotiations for a gambling casino in Havana. Included among these papers was a handwritten letter on stationery of the Ronto de Hornedo Hotel of Havana. Although the letter was unsigned, it was probably written by the well-known Florida underworld boss, Santo Trafficante, a proprietor of the San Souci gambling casino in Havana. The letter did not pass through the mails but was hand-carried and delivered to Anastasia. It contained instructions to make arrangements for a three-bedroom and living-room suite at the Warwick Hotel in New York for the Cuban minister of public works and others who were coming to New York to negotiate for the casino operation. It was suggested that "Cappy" (believed to refer to Anthony Cappola, an Anastasia bodyguard) "get them women and whiskey as these people like to live it up." Among the Cubans coming to New York was Raul Gonzales, who had been associated with Trafficante in the San Souci casino. It was stressed in the letter that "we have to have complete control of the casino. Raul is not to have anything to do with running the casino. We have to take care of Raul in some small way as he has been very interested in this deal. . . ." Four Cubans, including Raul Gonzales, registered at the New York hotel on October 17, 1957, and departed on October 25, 1957, the same day Anastasia was murdered. Numerous organized crime bigwigs, including Meyer Lansky, were involved in Cuba gambling at the time. There were rivalries between important underworld leaders to control the legalized gambling industry in Cuba. And investigators close to the Havana scene at the time were convinced that Anastasia's murder was connected with his Cuba gambling casino negotiations.

Although not suggested as having a bearing on his killing New York police officials did testify concerning the gang leader's involvement in Cuba's gambling business. Among Anastasia's associates in Cuban gambling casinos was Aniello Dellacroce, a lieutenant in the Anastasia family and a pal of Meyer Lansky and Joe Silesi.[4]

Three weeks after Anastasia was slain, a secret conclave of at least sixty-five underworld leaders was held on November 14, 1957, in the stone mansion of Joseph Barbara in Apalachin, New York. The sudden and unexpected appearance of New York State troopers and federal agents disrupted the meeting. The names and addresses of fifty-seven racketeers at the conference were made public and the Apalachin crime conference was headlined throughout the nation. Among the underworld characters at the Barbara home were several who had been questioned previously by the police about the Anastasia killing. Exhaustive state and federal investigations were conducted but the real purpose of the Apalachin convention was never determined.

When interrogated by the Senate subcommittee, Valachi testified that the Apalachin conclave had been called by Genovese. Actually, he said, Genovese wanted the meeting held in Chicago, but Stefano Magaddino, boss of the Buffalo Cosa Nostra family, persuaded him to hold it in Apalachin. The hearings did not disclose why Genovese should have wanted the meeting held in Chicago. There was no information to indicate that Genovese, a New Yorker, had any close associations in Chicago. Of those known to have attended the Apalachin conference, most were from the eastern states, particularly New York, and none was from Chicago. The only person from Illinois who was positively established as having attended the conference was Frank Zito of Springfield, and his known connections with the organized underworld in Chicago were remote.

As to the purpose of the Apalachin conference, Valachi testified, "This meeting was held for two main reasons. . . . One was to talk about the justifying of the shooting of Albert Anastasia. The other one was that they were going to talk about eliminating some couple of hundred new members. . . ." These were the so-called unworthy members brought into Cosa Nostra by Anastasia and Scalise. State troopers appeared on the scene before a discussion on the elimination of members could be held. Another purpose of the conclave, averred Valachi, was to establish that Vito Genovese was now the boss of the whole country.[5]

Based on the information supplied by Valachi, Attorney General Robert F. Kennedy asserted that now, for the first time, "we know" the purpose of the Apalachin conference. It is possible that Valachi's version of the meeting may have conformed to the truth. However, Valachi was not present at the conference. His account was based on hearsay and rumor. It would hardly fall into the category of solid, factual information as indicated by the former attorney general.[6]

Following the Anastasia assassination, Valachi was anxious to have a talk with his intimate friend Johnny Roberts. He was fearful that Roberts, a lieutenant and close associate of Anastasia, might try to avenge the murder of his boss. Valachi visited Roberts at his club on Grand Avenue in Brooklyn. Roberts revealed that he had already received a warning from Genovese and Tony Bender against taking any action. Later it was learned that Roberts had actually made an agreement with Armand (Tommy) Rava and others to retaliate for Anastasia's death. Valachi related that when Roberts told

Rava, also a lieutenant in the Anastasia family, "he wanted to be counted out of it. . .they killed him because he was trying to declare himself out." Police records show that the body of John Robilotto, alias Johnny Roberts, then fifty-four years old, was found on September 7, 1958, near the corner of Utica Avenue and Kings Highway in Brooklyn. Multiple gunshot wounds in the face and head had caused his death. Rava was believed responsible for the murder of Roberts.

After Anastasia's demise, the new boss of the family was Carlo Gambino. His underboss was Joseph Biando, alias Joe Bandi. After Roberts was killed, Carlo's brother and lieutenant, Paul Gambino, visited Valachi in the Bronx. Paul said, "I have a lot of respect for your opinion regardless of how other people feel" and asked, "What should we do?" Valachi advised, "Go right ahead before they pounce on you." A few days later Rava and his friends were located in a club in Brooklyn; eighteen shots were fired and Rava was reportedly killed and buried. Although his body has never been found, New York City police officials presume that Rava is deceased.[7]

Carlo Gambino was born in 1902. As a stowaway he entered the United States at Norfolk, Virginia, in 1924. His sources of income have been varied and seemingly limitless. Valachi testified, "Gambino has been in every kind of business, butcher business, lottery, Italian lottery, shylocking. . . ." New York police officials have connected Gambino with the vending-machine industry, gambling, shylocking, labor racketeering, and illegal alcohol operations. He has been suspected of involvement in the narcotics traffic and the smuggling of aliens. His record includes sixteen arrests and six convictions. Through marriage, Carlo Gambino is related to the boss of another family, Tommy Lucchese.[8]

Many years ago Gambino made large profits from dealing in alcohol. According to Valachi, he would buy the alcohol in five-gallon tins from stills for $15, store it in warehouses, and, when ready to release it, charge $50 a tin.

During World War II Carlo and Paul Gambino, Sam Accardi, and Sam Stefman made a fortune in the OPA ration-stamp racket. Accardi, affiliated with the Newark Cosa Nostra family, told Valachi that Gambino and his cohorts made over a million dollars on one ration-stamp deal alone.

Gambino's close assoiciates included Max Block of the butchers' union and Paul Castellano, a relative and caporegima in his family. Castellano had a meat market and a fat-rendering business. It was through the brothers Paul and Peter Castellano that Gambino entered the meat business. One of the Castellano meat enterprises became implicated in a bankruptcy fraud.

For ten years Carlo Gambino was a partner in the labor-relations firm of SGS Associates, Inc., at 141 East Forty-fourth Street in New York City. His partners in this venture were Henry H. Saltzstein, a convicted burglar and bookmaker, and George Schiller. When businesses were threatened with labor difficulties, they hired Gambino's firm, which seemed to have excellent results in ironing out the troubles. In the wake of federal, state, and local investigations in 1965, the SGS firm ceased operations. Other New York underworld characters, such as Johnny Dioguardi, were also labor-relations experts. And no one Cosa Nostra family has preempted this field. Dioguardi and his brother Tommy were soldiers in the Lucchese family.[9]

30

LUCCHESE FAMILY

The family headed by Gaetano (Tommy) Lucchese, also known as Three Finger Brown and Tommy Brown, got its start with the Maranzano group. In fact, the murder on February 26, 1930, of gang boss Gaetano (Tom) Reina by the Masseria group was the first significant date in the Castellammarese War. The sawed-off shotgun blast that mowed down Reina touched off a series of gang killings. On September 9, 1930, Reina's successor, John Pinzola, was shot to death in the office occupied by his firm, the California Dried Fruit Importers, in the Brokaw Building, 1487 Broadway, in New York City. The lessee of the premises was Tommy Lucchese, and two days after the murder he was arraigned in homicide court and held without bail. The grand jury failed to indict Lucchese and he was released. Valachi testified that Bobby Doyle (Santuccio) told him that "he went down to Pinzola's office and he found him all alone and he killed him." Bobby Doyle was a member of the Gagliano gang.[1]

Valachi related that at the big meeting called by Maranzano in 1931, Gaetano (Tom) Gagliano was designated the boss of this family and Tommy Brown (Lucchese) was named the underboss. It was with the Gagliano gang that Valachi had served during the Castellammarese War. Gagliano's tenure as family boss lasted over twenty years, until he died of natural causes in 1953. Lucchese, who had served as underboss to Gagliano, then became boss and his underboss was Stefano (Steve) LaSalle.[2]

Gaetano Lucchese was born in Italy in 1899, immigrated to the United States in 1911, and was naturalized in 1943 in Newark. He was arrested on numerous occasions for such offenses as grand larceny, automobile theft, receiving stolen goods, and homicide. Deputy Chief Inspector John J. Shanley testified that Lucchese "got the right to vote in 1949 with a certificate of good conduct issued by the New York City police, removing a conviction, 1921." His income was in keeping with his prestige as one of the more powerful underworld leaders in New York. The U.S. government charged that he owed $162,000 in unpaid taxes for the five-year period 1947–51. The New York City police learned that when a prominent entertainer was in financial straits, Lucchese offered $150,000 for a ten percent interest in the celebrity.[3]

Over a period of many years, Lucchese was a big wheel in the gambling racket. Among those representing his gambling interests was Joe Lucchese (alias Joe Brown), a brother of the boss and a caporegima in his family. Another lieutenant, Joe Larratro, also known as Joey Narrow, was believed by the New York police to be Lucchese's overseer of gambling operations, including bookmaking and policy, in Queens. Still another important Lucchese lieutenant was Anthony (Tony Ducks) Corallo. Inspector Shanley stated that Corallo "is in gambling, labor racketeering, extortion, strong-arm, and murder." He had strong connections with Jimmy Hoffa's Teamsters Union. Only a few years after the Senate subcommittee hearings, Corallo was a key figure in a New York City scandal involving bribery and kickbacks; the scandal received national publicity. His coconspirators were Carmine DeSapio, once boss of Tammany Hall, and James Marcus, a member of the inner circle of Mayor John Lindsay's administration.[4]

When Valachi was asked about Lucchese's activities, he replied, "Three Finger Brown has been in the garment center." Although Valachi indicated that Lucchese's garment center interests included everything in the industry, apparently his specialty was the dress business. Police officials listed eight dress firms in New York City in which Lucchese was a part owner, and he had similar holdings in Scranton, Pennsylvania. Lucchese's New York City dress firms were nonunion and were, strangely, free from labor troubles. This was true even though the garment workers' union (ILGWU) pursued a very aggressive organizing policy. Inspector Shanley suggested that Lucchese's freedom from labor strife in New York City may have stemmed from his intimate relationship with Patsy Crapasano, trustee in Local Council 271 of the International Brotherhood of Teamsters.

The criminal record of Lucchese was produced at the hearings and Senator Jacob K. Javits observed that after an arrest for vagrancy on November 18, 1935, this important underworld boss had never been taken into custody during the following twenty-eight years.[5]

On July 13, 1967, four years after Valachi's testimony, Gaetano Lucchese, then sixty-seven, died in Lido Beach, New York. A few months earlier he had undergone surgery for a brain tumor and was also suffering from a heart ailment.[6]

31

JOSEPH PROFACI FAMILY

Another New York City family was headed by Giuseppe Magliocco at the time of the 1963 hearings. Originally, the boss of this family was Salvatore Maranzano. After Maranzano's assassination on September 11, 1931, Joseph Profaci became boss. Commonly referred to as the Old Man, Profaci served as boss for over thirty years, until he died of natural causes in 1962. He was then succeeded by his brother-in-law and underboss, Joseph Magliocco.

Profaci ruled his family with an iron hand. Valachi testified that even when Vito Genovese had reached the "under-the-table" status of boss of all bosses, he could never control the family in Brooklyn headed by Joseph Profaci.[1]

It was this iron-fisted rule that led eventually to open rebellion against Profaci by some of the young bloods in the family. They bitterly resented that Profaci doled out all lucrative operations to his contemporaries or relatives. Younger family members believed they were being left out in the cold. And insult was added to injury, for whenever they made a score on a burglary or robbery, they were forced to kick back some of their profits to the boss. Valachi related that while he was being tried on conspiracy charges in New York City, he was held in the Federal Detention House on West Street. Also in custody in that institution was Carmine Persico, Jr., who, Valachi said, "was very close to some friends of mine, even Tony Bender. . . .One day he was explaining to me about Joe Profaci. . . .He said, 'Even if we go hijack some trucks he taxes us. I paid up to $1,800.' "

Rebelling against such tactics, Nicholas (Jiggs) Forlano, a caporegima in the Profaci family, led about a hundred twenty-five men in a fight against the Old Man. Figuring prominently in the group of rebels were the brothers Lawrence, Albert, and Joseph Gallo, all soldiers in the Profaci family. Bloodshed and violence erupted and the conflict became known as the Gallo-Profaci war.

Five members of the Profaci family were kidnapped, including Joseph Magliocco and Frank Profaci, a brother of the boss. Responsible for the abductions, Valachi said, were the Gallo brothers and Carmine Persico, Jr. The victims were released, apparently on orders of Forlano. In a conversation with Persico, Valachi told him "that was a mistake. . . .If you went that far you were doomed anyway" and suggested the abducted men should have been killed.

Following the release of the kidnapped men, the rebels began to lose strength. The men that Forlano had recruited to fight Profaci "dwindled away and left the Gallos in the hole." The Gallos now, said Valachi, had "no support but maybe fifteen guys." Valachi observed Frank Costello and Carmine Persico, Jr. huddling together and he said, "I knew then that Frank was going to use his influence." Valachi testified, "I tried to convince Junior [Persico] to go back" with Profaci and "that is just what happened."[2]

On August 20, 1961, Lawrence (Larry) Gallo was invited to come to the Sahara Restaurant, 1201 Utica Avenue, Brooklyn, where he was to meet John Scimone. Actually, the invitation was a double-cross. Gallo arrived at the restaurant at the appointed time of 5 P.M., one hour before the place was open to the public. After exchanging greetings, Scimone excused himself. Suddenly, someone placed a rope around Larry Gallo's neck and an effort was made to strangle him to death. At that moment, a police sergeant and his chauffeur were passing by the restaurant in a radio car. The sergeant noticed that a side door to the restaurant was open, a suspicious and unusual condition for this time of day. He stopped and got out of the car to investigate. Sticking his head in the door, he saw the owner, Charles Clemenceau, behind the bar and asked if everything was all right. Clemenceau replied in the affirmative but the sergeant noticed the feet of Gallo protruding from the side of the bar. Later Gallo's father told Valachi that when the police accidentally arrived, Larry was blue in the face and on the verge of death from strangulation.

As the sergeant started to enter the premises, three men, one of whom was John Scimone, ran out of the place. Observing the men fleeing from the restaurant, the sergeant's chauffeur started to get out of the police car. One of the fugitives opened fire with a revolver and a bullet struck the officer on the right cheek. A police alarm was given and responding officers picked up John Scimone, who had been thrown by his companions from the hoodlums' getaway car. He told the police that a few blocks from the restaurant, he had been struck across the face with the butt of a gun and hurled from the fleeing car. Bruises on his nose, cheek, and eye tended to verify his story. Arrested for the attempted strangulation of Larry Gallo were Carmine Persico, Jr., John Scimone, Salvatore D'Ambrosio, and Alphonse Cirillo.

Casualties of the Gallo-Profaci war were numerous. Police records revealed that between August 17, 1961, and August 9, 1963, nine persons had been murdered and three missing persons were presumed dead. Scores of men had been assaulted. Some were wounded by gunfire, including

Nicholas (Jiggs) Forlano in October 1961 and Carmine Persico, Jr. on May 19, 1963.[3]

The Gallo-Profaci war was still in full swing when Profaci died and Joseph Magliocco became the new boss of the family. Both Profaci and Magliocco had attended the Apalachin crime conference in 1957. They were prosecuted and convicted for obstructing justice. The rebels in the Profaci family were hoping that the convictions would be upheld on appeal. With Magliocco and Profaci in jail, they expected to obtain concessions from new leaders or, perhaps, take over the leadership themselves. However, when the convictions were set aside, they turned to violence as a means of enforcing their demands.

Jiggs Forlano, a leader of the Profaci rebels, complained that they were not given sufficient opportunities in moneymaking schemes. Apparently, Forlano was not suffering personally from a lack of income. Two years after the Valachi testimony, an official report by the New York State Commission of Investigation on the loan-shark racket singled out Forlano as the biggest shylock in the five boroughs of New York. He obtained his money from various crime syndicate bosses and loaned it to other loan sharks, thus becoming known as a shylock's shylock. The partner of Forlano in his illicit moneylending activities was Charles (Ruby) Stein.[4]

Profaci's successor, Joseph Magliocco, was born in Italy in 1898, immigrated to the United States in 1914, and was naturalized in 1926. In 1928 Magliocco and Profaci were among twenty-three men arrested for carrying guns in Cleveland while attending a meeting of underworld figures. Many years ago Magliocco was engaged in the bootlegging racket and arrested on a liquor charge. After Prohibition he entered the liquor business. Because of his presence at the infamous Apalachin conference, Magliocco lost his alcohol license. Nevertheless, he continued to be a stockholder in a large, complex holding company, which owned a number of important wholesale liquor firms. New York police officials asserted that the Magliocco family was entrenched in the liquor business.

The underboss of the family, Salvatore Mussachio, also known as Sally the Sheik, was related to Magliocco through marriage. Like Magliocco, he first attracted attention as a bootlegger. In 1938 Mussachio was a suspect in the murder of two people. On May 6, 1963, when police received information regarding a possible shooting, they placed the home of Magliocco under observation. Mussachio was at the Magliocco home at the time, and when a gun was seen in his car he was placed under arrest. Mussachio has claimed to be a barber, represented himself as being in the fish business, and driven a car registered to a bakery.[5]

At the time of the Valachi hearings, indications were that the status of Joseph Magliocco as boss of the old Profaci family in Brooklyn was in jeopardy. Only a few months later, on December 28, 1963, Magliocco died of a heart attack in his Long Island home. The new boss of the family was Joseph Colombo, Sr.

Taped conversations in the office of underworld boss Simone Rizzo (Sam the Plumber) DeCavalcante in New Jersey revealed a belief that Magliocco had been poisoned by Joseph Bonanno, the boss of another Brooklyn family. Based on the taped conversations, a second autopsy was performed on Magliocco five years after his death. No trace of poison was discovered.

Before Profaci passed away, he was convinced that the revolt in his family, which culminated in the Gallo-Profaci war, had been inspired by two other bosses, Carlo Gambino and Gaetano Lucchese. His bitter feeling toward these two bosses was shared by Joseph Magliocco, whose sister was married to Profaci.

Cordial relations had always prevailed between the two Brooklyn bosses, Profaci and Bonanno. Following Profaci's death, Magliocco, an indecisive hoodlum, took orders from Bonanno as he had previously followed the commands of Profaci. Bonanno arranged for Magliocco to have Gambino and Lucchese killed. The contract was given to Joseph Colombo, Sr., who double-crossed Magliocco and leaked the scheme to Gambino and Lucchese. Unaccountably, they did not order the murder of Magliocco. Instead, they caused him to be deposed as boss and named Colombo as his successor. From taped conversations in the office of Sam DeCavalcante, it was apparent he believed that Joseph Bonanno had poisoned Magliocco to prevent him from disclosing Bonanno's role in the assassination plot.[6]

Joseph Colombo, Sr., at forty, was the youngest family boss in New York City. On the whole, his career in mob affairs had been undistinguished. On one occasion, he received recognition from Joseph Profaci, who appointed him to a five-man assassination squad, which also included Larry and Joe Gallo as members. However, Colombo had opposed the Gallos during the Gallo-Profaci war and thus remained in the good graces of Profaci. After serving as a muscleman at the piers and as an organizer of rigged dice games, Colombo engaged in big gambling operations in Brooklyn and Nassau County, loan sharking in Manhattan, and hijacking at Kennedy Airport. He represented himself as a real estate dealer and owned an interest in a flower shop and a funeral home.

Following the arrest of his son, Joseph Jr., in April 1970, Colombo led picket lines against the FBI and within a few months became the founder, unofficial leader, and chief promoter of the Italian-American Civil Rights League. He gave press interviews and appeared on a nationally televised talk show. He served as catalyst for ethnic pride. At an Italian-American Unity Day rally in New York City's Columbus Circle on June 29, 1970, almost forty thousand people gathered. Colombo was the central figure and addressed the crowd.

A second annual Unity Day rally was held in Columbus Circle on June

28, 1971. Colombo was again the center of attraction as he mingled with the crowd. Suddenly, a black photographer, Jerome Johnson, twenty-four, fired several shots at Colombo's head and neck. Immediately Johnson was shot and killed by an unknown person, who disappeared in the crowd even though policemen were everywhere in evidence. Speculation had it that underworld enemies of Colombo had hired Johnson to assassinate Colombo and then killed Johnson to make certain he could never divulge the plot to the authorities. Colombo was rushed to Roosevelt Hospital, where a bullet was removed from his cerebellum. The bullet wound left Colombo almost totally paralyzed and his chances for recovery were virtually nonexistent. After lingering in a semiconscious state for almost seven years, Colombo died on May 22, 1978. Colombo's rise to a place in the mob hierarchy and his publicity-seeking activities had earned him the bitter enmity of many important underworld characters, notably Joseph (Crazy Joe) Gallo.[7]

In the early hours of April 7, 1972, Joe Gallo, his bride of three weeks, her ten-year-old daughter by a previous marriage, a bodyguard, and others were celebrating Joe's forty-third birthday at a party in Umberto's restaurant in the Little Italy section of Manhattan. Four men entered the place and emptied their guns at Gallo and his bodyguard, Pete Diapoulas. Gallo was killed and Diapoulas wounded. The assassins escaped in an automobile waiting outside the restaurant.[8]

After the shooting of Joseph Colombo, Sr. in 1971, the family was run for a time by Vinnie Aloi, a godson of Carlo Gambino.

JOSEPH BONANNO FAMILY

The remaining New York City family mentioned by Valachi was headed by Joseph Bonanno and also evolved from the Maranzano group of gangs. In fact, Bonanno's father had been a close friend of Salvatore Maranzano in Sicily. That may have been one of the reasons why Maranzano, during the New York gang wars of 1930–31, selected Bonanno as one of his chief aides, along with Joseph Profaci, Joseph Magliocco, and Thomas Lucchese.[1]

In describing the heads of the various families, Valachi testified that in one part of Brooklyn the boss, until he died in 1962, was Joseph Profaci while "in the other part of Brooklyn it is Joe Bonanno." It was Bonanno who was selected as his godfather when Valachi was initiated into Cosa Nostra membership in 1930.[2]

Joseph Bonanno was born in Castellammare del Golfo in western Sicily in 1905. Still young, he fled Sicily and eventually landed in Cuba. From Cuba he entered the United States illegally through Florida in 1924. He came to New York and there lived with Pietre Bonventre, an underworld character.

Bonanno soon became a man of affluence. Chief Deputy Inspector John J. Shanley testified that in the early 1930s, Bonanno was part owner of an undertaking establishment. By 1934 he was vice president of the Brunswick Laundry. In 1937 he was part owner of the Morgan Coke Company. His partner in this venture was Philip Rapper, who ended up dead of a scalp wound in a Brooklyn gutter. Bonanno was also connected with the B & D Coke Company in the 1940s. At one time he was vice president of the Hilltop Hotel in Fort Lee. As the years rolled by, Bonanno's interests multiplied.[3]

Bonanno's original entry into the United States had been illegal, so he left the country in 1938 to return in a lawful manner. In an excellent biography of the Bonanno family by Gay Talese it is reported that the legal entry was made from Canada at Detroit. In 1945 Joseph Bonanno was naturalized and by that time he was a multimillionaire. His wealth stemmed from his investing money made from whiskey and the Italian lottery, in various legitimate businesses, including clothing factories and cheese firms.

In the 1940s, he was convicted and fined in Brooklyn for a violation of the Wages and Hours Act. He was charged with nonpayment of overtime to employees in a dress firm in which he had a one-third interest. Since the 1950s, Bonanno has spent much time in Arizona, where he had large real estate holdings, including a home in Tucson.[4]

The underboss to Joseph Bonanno was Carmine Galante, who was in jail on a narcotics charge at the time of the Senate subcommittee hearings. Galante had gone into hiding after Vito Genovese and thirty-five other defendants were indicted. He was eventually located in Barnegat Bay, New Jersey.

Galante's criminal history showed that he had excellent credentials to serve as a leader in the Bonanno underworld family. A native American, Galante was born in 1912. At the age of twenty Galante was arrested as a result of a gun battle following a stickup in which a patrolman was killed. Only four months later New York police officers interrupted another armed robbery. Again a gunfight occurred and a policeman was shot. Galante was apprehended and given a sentence of twelve years.

For some time, Galante was deeply involved with the Reed Cortner combination in an American-controlled gambling operation in Canada. During this period Galante was the proprietor of the Bonfine Restaurants in Montreal. He also had vending-machine and juke-box interests in Canada.

Among the more important lieutenants in the Bonanno family was Joseph Notaro, a close associate of Galante. Notaro was engaged in receiving and transporting stolen property, gambling, and alcohol operations.[5]

Joseph Bonanno's long tenure as family boss was nearing its end as the Valachi hearings were in progress in 1963. Some members of his family were becoming disenchanted with his leadership and he was meeting with stiff opposition from other family bosses as well.

During the summer of 1963, Salvatore (Bill) Bonanno, eldest son of the boss, moved with his wife and children from Arizona to New York. There he lived with his uncle, Joseph Magliocco, the successor to Joseph Profaci. He was still residing there at the time of Magliocco's death. Joseph Bonanno had been advancing his son in his organization and this had caused resentment and friction. Some bosses feared that Bill, whom they distrusted, would be a source of trouble. Bonanno, in turn, believed that some bosses were trying to undermine him. In particular, Bonanno was convinced that Stefano Magaddino, boss of the Buffalo Cosa Nostra family, was trying to take over control of his organization through the puppet leadership of Gaspar DeGregorio. Until he defected, DeGregorio, who was married to Magaddino's sister, had been extremely close to his boss, Joe Bonanno.[6]

The deep-seated troubles of Bonanno and his organization were revealed in FBI transcripts of conversations overheard in the bugged offices of an important underworld leader, Simone Rizzo DeCavalcante, commonly known as Sam the Plumber, who operated a plumbing and heating firm in Kenilworth, New Jersey. The FBI had concealed electronic eavesdropping devices in his office in 1961 and for almost four years recorded conversations that took place there. When DeCavalcante was placed on trial in federal court in Newark for extortion, his attorney moved that the electronic surveillance transcripts be made available to the defense. Unfortunately for Sam and the underworld generally, the attorney did not ask for the material to be sealed. The defense motion was granted. On June 10, 1969, thirteen volumes of transcripts were filed with the clerk of the U.S. district court in Newark and they became a public record. The revelations in the tapes created a sensation and undoubtedly jarred the underworld.

On August 31, 1964, Sam DeCavalcante was talking with one of his lieutenants, Joe Sferra, and mentioned the trouble then brewing in New York over Joe Bonanno. Sam said, "The commission don't like the way he's comporting himself. . .he made his son consigliere. . . .They sent for him and he didn't show up. And they want to throw him out of the commission. . . ." About a month later, in an effort to act as mediator, DeCavalcante had a meeting with Bonanno's son, Salvatore (Bill) Bonanno. In discussing this meeting with his underboss, Frank Majuri, DeCavalcante said, "His son [Bill] is a bedbug. I'm not afraid of him [Joe] so much as I am his son. . . ." He then stated, "Gasparino [DeGregorio] is the one that started the ball rolling. They're [the Bonannos] blaming him."[7]

Some time later DeCavalcante was talking in his office with his friend, Joseph Zicarelli, a member of the New York Bonanno family even though he lived and worked in New Jersey. Said Sam, "The commission doesn't recognize Joe Bonanno as the boss anymore. . . .I don't know what's the matter with this guy. . . .I done everything possible. . . .When Joe defies the commission, he's defying the whole world. . . .The commission was formed by people—all bosses—who have given the commission the right to supersede any boss. Joe knows that! He made the rules! . . .But this guy [Joe Bonanno] don't want to listen to reason. . . .He's causing so much friction against everybody. . . .They been looking for this man for over a year!"[8]

In the fall of 1964 several members of the Bonanno family went into hiding because of fear of rival gangs. On October 21, 1964, just a few hours before he was scheduled to appear before a federal grand jury, it was reported that Joseph Bonanno was kidnapped at gunpoint in front of a luxury apartment house on Park Avenue in New York City. Several weeks later DeCavalcante was overheard discussing this affair with one of his aides. Said Sam, "He [Bonanno] pulled that off himself. . .who the hell is he kidding? He kidded the government."

The absence of Bonanno did not improve conditions in his family. In February 1965 another taped conversation between DeCavalcante and an underling, Louie Larasso, revealed disenchantment with Gaspar De-Gregorio, who had been elevated to the position of boss. "I think it's going to his head," said DeCavalcante. And Larasso observed, "Gasparino looks. . .no good. . . .They should have waited a long time before they made a boss. 'Cause there's too much undercurrent."[9]

Many Bonanno soldiers deserted the ship and affiliated with other families. Bonanno's lieutenant, Joseph Notaro, remained loyal to his boss, but his position was precarious. It was revealed during one of DeCavalcante's recorded conversations that DeGregorio intended to kill him.

Only a few months after DeGregorio became boss, he suffered a heart attack. He appointed Sereno Tartamella, a union official, and Nicholas (Eye Glasses) Marangello, a former chauffeur for Joe Bonanno, to run the mob for him. Many members of the gang were in a state of rebellion and were uncontrollable. On January 28, 1966, about a hundred shots were fired during a bloodless shootout on Troutman Street. Carlo Gambino feared the outbreak of an all-out war. At his urging, DeGregorio stepped down and Paul Sciacca, an ally of Gambino, became the new boss of the Bonanno family.[10]

After an absence of almost nineteen months, Joseph Bonanno suddenly appeared, in May 1966, in federal court in New York City and was released on a $150,000 bond. Following his court appearance, Bonanno and several cronies celebrated the return of the boss by having lunch in LaScala's Restaurant. While the gaiety was in full swing, it was noticed that Joseph Notaro was slumped over the table. The trusted Bonanno lieutenant had suffered a heart attack and was dead.[11]

Following his return from exile, Bonanno attempted to reassert his authority over his family. His efforts met with stiff resistance and many gang killings ensued. Finally, he gave up the struggle and retired to his home in Tucson, Arizona, where he had spent much time during the preceding two decades.[12]

Within the space of a very few years, the leadership of the five New York City families as described by Joseph Valachi had changed drastically. Of the five bosses named by Valachi, only one, Carlo Gambino, was still in control by 1972. And Gambino had gradually taken control of the other families. Following the murder of Tommy Eboli on July 16, 1972, it was conceded that Gambino dominated the five New York City families and controlled the national commission. On October 15, 1976, the seventy-four-year-old Gambino died of natural causes in his Brooklyn apartment. At the time of his death he was regarded as the preeminent figure in organized crime in America. Named by New York police officials as Gambino's logical successor was Carmine Galante. On July 12, 1979, Galante and two other men were mowed down and killed by rival gunmen as they were dining on the patio of an Italian restaurant in Brooklyn.[13]

33

VALACHI KNOWLEDGE LIMITED TO NEW YORK

Valachi's testimony in 1963 was widely accepted as having provided an accurate picture of the structure of organized crime throughout the United States. Actually, his knowledge was limited strictly to New York and environs. And organized crime in New York is not limited to the Italian Cosa Nostra by any means. During the Senate subcommittee hearings, Senator Thomas J. McIntyre asked Deputy Chief Inspector John J. Shanley if the Cosa Nostra represented the core of organized crime in New York City. Shanley replied, "There are other elements in New York that are in organized crime. There are elements that are strong in the bookmaking field. There are elements that are strong on the piers; waterfront for instance." Shanley stated that the Cosa Nostra "is one specific aspect of organized crime in New York. . .that. . .[Valachi] is most familiar with. But there are other sections of it." When asked if the five Cosa Nostra families constituted all of the criminal element in New York City's organized crime, Shanley replied, "Positively not."[1]

The central figure running throughout Valachi's testimony was Vito Genovese. The importance of Genovese in the New York City underworld is undeniable. However, in virtually every important criminal incident discussed by Valachi, Genovese was always depicted as the guiding genius and the dominant influence.

Valachi's love and respect for Genovese lasted for thirty years. It was while they were cellmates in an Atlanta prison that Genovese gave Valachi the kiss of death. The love of Valachi for Genovese suddenly turned to fear and bitter hatred. In part, at least, it was a desire for revenge that caused Valachi to become a government informer. And the desire for revenge by an informer is not unlike the wrath of a woman scorned. It can lead to a twisting of facts or exaggeration in an effort to pin the role of villain on the target of scorn and hatred.

The last days of Valachi's life were spent in LaTuna Federal Correctional Institution, some twenty miles from El Paso, Texas. Here Valachi died of natural causes on April 3, 1971. He was then sixty-six. Also an inmate in

LaTuna was another mobster turned informer, Vincent Teresa. During the last eleven months of Valachi's life, Teresa and Valachi became close friends and spent considerable time together in prison. Teresa later said that Valachi talked incessantly, day after day, about how Genovese had given him the kiss of death. His bitterness toward Genovese had become an obsession with him. Teresa, who had played an important role in the New England organized crime group headed by Raymond Patriarca, asserted that Valachi had always been an opportunist. In earlier days whenever he was with Genovese he would knock Carlo Gambino and when he was with Gambino he would knock Genovese. According to Teresa, the mob had considered Valachi a "two-faced" Italian and long before he turned informer, no one trusted him.[2]

Throughout the more than thirty years covered by Valachi's testimony, Chicago was one of the principal centers of organized crime in America. Yet, in his testimony Valachi mentioned only three Chicagoans: a gunman whom he called Buster of Chicago, Joseph Aiello, and Al Capone. Buster had moved to New York City, where he was engaged in the rackets and his true identity was unknown, either by Valachi or by the Senate subcommittee. Valachi said that Buster was killed in a crap game argument shortly after Maranzano's murder in 1931, but that information could not be corroborated. Valachi attributed Joseph Aiello's murder in Chicago on October 23, 1930, to the Castellammarese War. Known facts, however, clearly indicate that his killing traced to the bitter rivalry then existing in Chicago between the Bugs Moran gang, of which Aiello was a member, and the Capone forces. This was strictly a Chicago-based fight between two gangs; it had resulted in much bloodshed and Aiello was merely one of a long list of victims. The only mention of Al Capone by Valachi related to his reported money contributions to New York during the Castellammarese War, which ended in 1931. Hence, Valachi's testimony is completely silent about any Chicago organized crime figures between 1931 and 1963.

Valachi asserted that there was only one Cosa Nostra family in Chicago, but he knew nothing about its territorial scope or jurisdiction. When asked by Senator Carl T. Curtis if he had ever been in Chicago, Valachi replied, "No, I stopped in Chicago on the way to Arkansas." Senator Curtis inquired, "Did you make any contacts with any of the criminal elements there?" Valachi answered, "No, no contacts." The senator then asked, "You do not know how the territory was handled outside of New York State?" Valachi said, "That is right."[3]

For several decades the most powerful crime organization in Chicago has been variously referred to as the Capone gang, the "mob," the "outfit," or the Chicago crime syndicate. Since the 1920s there has been a succession of bosses of this organization—Big Jim Colosimo, Johnny Torrio, Al Capone, Frank Nitti, and Tony Accardo. Remaining somewhat in the background but recognized as one of the most influential members of the ruling class of the syndicate was Felice DeLucia, commonly known as Paul (the Waiter) Ricca, who died October 11, 1972.

Throughout the syndicate's long history, the top echelon has included such non-Italians as Jack Guzik, Jewish; Murray Humphreys, English; Claude Maddox, Irish; and Gus Alex, Greek. Evidence has established that these men were not outsiders. They were integral parts of the hierarchy of the Chicago crime organization.

From the 1920s, until he died on February 21, 1956, Jack Guzik served somewhat in the capacity of business manager of the mob. For many years, Guzik and Hymie (Loud Mouth) Levin were in control of the syndicate's lucrative Loop (downtown) gambling operations. Official investigations disclosed that boss Tony Accardo and Jack Guzik shared equally in the profits of important illicit ventures. That fact indicates the importance of Guzik in the Chicago crime organization.

For almost forty years Murray (the Camel) Humphreys was a member of the ruling elite of the syndicate. For some time before his death on November 23, 1965, Humphreys was looked upon as an elder statesman of the mob. Not infrequently he had masterminded schemes in which Accardo was personally involved.

At the lower level of Chicago syndicate operations, various nationalities have always been represented. In 1962, FBI agents bugged a house rented in Florida by Jackie (the Lackey) Cerone, an aide and constant companion of Tony Accardo and Paul Ricca. The house served as a congregating place for Cerone, Dave Yaras, Fiore Buccieri, and other Chicago mobsters who were planning to murder an erstwhile pal, Frank Esposito, who had fallen from the syndicate's favor. The contract for his murder was withdrawn before it was consummated. However, during meetings in the Florida house, the mobsters were overheard discussing previous killings in which they had been implicated. Cerone mentioned how he and Johnny Whales had been partners in perpetrating gang killings in the "old days." Cerone explained, however, that Johnny finally "went off his rocker" and disappeared. Said Cerone, Johnny became afraid of the "Dagos" and feared that he might get hit himself. Cerone then turned to Dave Yaras, the Jewish racketeer present, and said, "You see, Dave, he didn't understand that we [Chicago crime syndicate] got Jews and Pollacks also. I told him this but he was still afraid." When Whales became obsessed with fear of the Italians, Cerone discussed the matter with Accardo, who asked if he wanted Johnny killed. Cerone said that he told Accardo he liked Whales too much to have him killed, but he assured the boss he would not have anything to do with him in the future. The presence of non-Italians in both the lower and upper echelons of the Chicago crime syndicate is a well-established fact.

Valachi's knowledge beyond New York was woefully limited and at times he exhibited unbelievable ignorance. Senator Curtis of Nebraska asked Valachi, "Do you know whether or not there are members of Cosa Nostra operating in Omaha?" Replied Valachi, "Senator, I never heard of Omaha, and I never heard anything about Omaha." When asked about Des Moines, Valachi inquired, "Where is that, Senator?" He was told, "That is in Iowa." Valachi retorted, "I never even heard of that."[4]

For many years Des Moines had served as the headquarters for the operations of Capone mobster Louis Thomas Fratto, commonly known as Lew Farrell. His Des Moines ventures received nationwide publicity during the Kefauver committee hearings in 1951. In addition to his gambling enterprises, Farrell was the Des Moines beer distributor for Alex Louis Greenberg, frequently called the financial wizard of the Chicago crime syndicate once headed by Al Capone. Greenberg was the victim of a gang killing in Chicago on December 5, 1955. Farrell was also the intimate associate of Charles Gioe, the important Capone gang lieutenant who was killed in gangland style on August 18, 1954. Valachi not only knew nothing about Farrell, but was unaware that such a place as Des Moines, the capital of Iowa, existed. Obviously, his credentials for providing a blueprint of organized crime and its structure throughout America were not overly impressive.

34

PRESIDENT'S COMMISSION ON LAW ENFORCEMENT

The President's Commission on Law Enforcement and Administration of Justice in 1967 quite largely accepted Valachi's version. The core of organized crime in America, said the commission, consists of twenty-four groups, known as families, which operate as criminal cartels in large cities across the nation. "Their membership is exclusively men of Italian descent, they are in frequent communication with each other, and their smooth functioning is ensured by a national board of overseers" known as the commission. The name of the organization is Cosa Nostra.

The twenty-four core families, which may be known in individual cities as the outfit, the syndicate, or the mob, work with and control other racket groups, whose leaders are of various ethnic derivations. And the thousands of employees who perform the street-level functions of organized crime in gambling, extortion, and other illegal activities represent a cross-section of the nation's population groups. The wealthiest and most influential core groups or families operate in New York, New Jersey, Illinois, Florida, Louisiana, Nevada, Michigan, and Rhode Island. Moreover, in many other states members of core groups control criminal activity, even though they do not reside there.

The President's Commission emphasized, "Recognition of the common ethnic tie of the 5,000 or more members of organized crime's core groups is essential to understanding the structure of these groups today." It concluded that "organized crime in its totality thus consists of these twenty-four groups allied with other racket enterprises to form a loose confederation operating in large and small cities. In the core groups, because of their permanency of form, strength of organization, and ability to control other racket operations, resides the power that organized crime has in America today."[1]

"The structure of the nationwide cartel and confederation which today operates the principal illicit businesses in America. . .came into being in 1931. These structures," says Donald R. Cressey in the President's Commission Task Force Report on Organized Crime, "resemble the national and local structure of the Italian-Sicilian Mafia, but our organization is not merely the Old World Mafia transplanted. The social, economic, and political conditions of Sicily,'' says Cressey, ''determined the shape of the Sicilian Mafia, and the social, economic, and political conditions of the United States determined the shape of the American confederation.''[2] In other words, Cressey has correctly pointed out that the Cosa Nostra is clearly an American organization of American origin in 1931 and is *not* the Mafia as so many writers have asserted.

Valachi's description of the organizational structure of Cosa Nostra was accepted by the President's Commission. Each of the twenty-four core groups is headed by a boss who has nearly absolute authority over his family. That authority is subject only to the national advisory body called the commission, which has overruling power. Beneath each boss is an underboss, and on the same level but functioning in a staff capacity is the consigliere, or counselor. Below the underboss are the caporegime, or lieutenants, who have direct communication with the soldiers and may serve as buffers between the top-level members of the family and the lower-echelon personnel. The lieutenants may also serve as chiefs of operating units. The members at the lowest structural level are the soldiers, who report to the caporegime. Beneath the soldiers in the hierarchy are large numbers of employees who are not members of the family and who need not be Italians.

The President's Commission report spelled out in detail the makeup of the so-called national board of overseers of organized crime in America. It asserted, ''The highest ruling body of the twenty-four families is the 'commission.' This body serves as a combination legislature, supreme court, board of directors, and arbitration board; its principal functions are judicial. Family members look to the commission as the ultimate authority on organizational and jurisdictional disputes. It is composed of the bosses of the nation's most powerful families but has authority over all twenty-four. The composition of the commission varies from nine to twelve men. . .there are presently nine families represented, five from New York City and one each from Philadelphia, Buffalo, Detroit, and Chicago. . . .The balance of power on this nationwide council rests with the leaders of New York's five families. They have always served on the commission and consider New York as at least the unofficial headquarters of the entire organization.''[3]

Thus, the President's Commission on Law Enforcement and Administration of Justice adopted Valachi's account of a highly formalized structure of organized crime in America with ultimate control vested in nine Italian bosses, mostly from the East. Of the nine members of the ruling body listed by the President's Commission, seven were from within the New York City orbit of influence—five from New York City, one from Buffalo, and one from Philadelphia. This version places the totality of organized crime in America in one neat, compact package. The explanation, however, is highly

35

ORGANIZED CRIME IN U.S. NOT CONTROLLED BY ONE GROUP

Regardless of ethnic background, the character traits of members and leaders of the organized underworld are much the same. They are defiant of laws as well as of accepted standards of morality and decency. By nature they are untrustworthy. They will lie, cheat, steal, double-cross, and even murder to achieve their goals. To assume that a single Italian organization with ultimate power in five New York bosses could control the conglomerate of organized crime groups of various ethnic derivation scattered throughout the United States is unrealistic. History reveals that the Italian Cosa Nostra has not been able to control effectively many of its own members, including some of the more influential bosses in the organization.

Valachi testified that in New Jersey, Willie Moretti had forty or fifty men who owed their allegiance only to him. Valachi described Moretti as an independent who "had his own little army."

For many years, Frank Costello was the boss of the most powerful Cosa Nostra family in New York. Yet, Costello built up and controlled a huge gambling empire that for decades flourished independently of the family he headed. It was this situation that eventually became intolerable to Vito Genovese and was said to have been one of the reasons for the attempted assassination of Costello in 1957.[1] Principals in the gambling organization controlled by Costello were such non–Cosa Nostra personages as Meyer Lansky, Frank Erickson, and Dandy Phil Kastel.

In the early 1930s, Costello and Lucky Luciano were members of a powerful organized crime group called the Big Seven Combination, which controlled liquor on the Atlantic Coast. Other members of the combination were Meyer Lansky, Bugsy Siegel, Moe Sedgwick (alias Moe Sedway), Charles (King) Solomon of Boston, and Daniel Walsh of Providence. The combination operated without any direction or control of the Cosa Nostra.

Lansky and Siegel headed a group of hoodlums in New York known as the Bugs and Meyer Mob. In the 1940s Lansky's pal Siegel launched the era of lavish gambling casinos in Las Vegas by opening the plush Flamingo Hotel. Until Siegel was riddled with bullets, in one of the nation's most celebrated gang killings, on June 20, 1947, Moe Sedway, a member of the old combination, was associated with him in the Flamingo. Indications were that Lansky had a hidden interest in the venture as well.

Meyer Lansky's underworld history covers the greater part of a half century. His gambling operations have extended to various parts of the United States, including Nevada, as well as to Cuba and the Bahamas. For many years he has been recognized as one of the most powerful organized crime leaders in America. Shortly before he died in February 1973, Frank Costello was interviewed by Peter Maas. Costello indicated that he did not hold in very high esteem some of the Italian leaders who were generally revered in the organization. Yet, said Maas, Costello "spoke with great regard about Meyer Lansky."[2] There is no reason whatever to believe that Lansky and his far-flung operations could be subjected to the control of a few Italian bosses in the Cosa Nostra commission.

The President's Commission in 1967 indicated that the twenty-four Cosa Nostra core families were able to control non-Italian gangs because of the "permanency of form" and "strength of organization" of the core groups. Few racket groups in America have had a greater permanency of form or achieved a stronger organization than the one known as the Cleveland syndicate, so called because of its original base in that city. Referred to as the Big Four in this predominantly Jewish syndicate were Moe Dalitz, Louis Rothkopf, Morris Kleinman, and Samuel A. Tucker. Originating during the rumrunning days of the 1920s, the Cleveland syndicate got a foothold in Las Vegas in 1950 when it began operating the Desert Inn. Before long it gained control of other casinos, and for many years dominated the Las Vegas gambling industry. Throughout its long existence, the Cleveland syndicate entered into friendly relations with powerful gang leaders of various ethnic backgrounds in all sections of the nation. However, it maintained its identity as a predominantly Jewish underworld organization and there is no evidence to indicate it ever fell under the control of the Italian Cosa Nostra.[3]

In 1970 the Pennsylvania Crime Commission, under the chairmanship of Attorney General William C. Sennett, submitted its official report, which concluded that organized crime "thrives throughout the Commonwealth and is a problem of tremendous and unrecognized magnitude. . . . Pennsylvania's organized crime is a conglomerate arrangement of criminal organizations. It is not a monolithic syndicate and is not dominated by a single individual. . . .The central, undeniable finding," said the report, "is that there are permanent ongoing criminal conspiracies operating in Pennsylvania which are controlled in large part, but not exclusively, by La Cosa Nostra families."

At the time of the Pennsylvania Crime Commission's investigation, it identified 142 Cosa Nostra members in the state. However, there were over a thousand major independent racketeers in Pennsylvania. The report stated that "many independent racketeers—usually in the largest cities—acquire wealth and power to rival the prestige of Cosa Nostra bosses." Under such circumstances, the report said, "a claim to monopoly over a territory by a Cosa Nostra boss would hold diminished weight."[4]

The official investigation in Pennsylvania thus establishd that Cosa Nostra families did not control all organized crime in the state and in some instances independent racket leaders acquired wealth and power Cosa Nostra leaders could not successfully challenge. And numerically, known major independent racketeers in the state outnumbered members of Cosa Nostra by a ratio of seven to one.

From Valachi's testimony, as well as the report of the President's Commission on Law Enforcement and Administration of Justice, it would appear that the ultimate control of organized crime in America is vested in a few Italian bosses who make up the Cosa Nostra commission, a so-called national board of overseers. When Attorney General Robert F. Kennedy appeared before the Senate subcommittee in 1963, he flatly stated, "We *know* that the commission makes major policy decisions for the organization, settles disputes among the families, and allocates territories of criminal operation within the organizations."[5]

About a decade later, in 1972, Henry E. Petersen, assistant attorney general and head of the Criminal Division of the Department of Justice, was asked whether the commission is a national policy-making body. Petersen, who had served as chief of the Organized Crime and Racketeering section of the Department of Justice for many years, replied, "No. That's probably too strong a term. . .each 'family' operates in a particular city or metropolitan area. By and large, the leadership in that area is responsible only to itself. The commission does not direct operations. . . .But when there are jurisdictional disputes—when the activities of one criminal group may impinge upon another group—then those disputes are referred to the national commission." Petersen was then asked to explain why numerous gang killings had recently taken place in New York City. He stated, "What's been going on in New York is obviously. . .a revolt of some kind, a refusal to follow the leadership of the commission."[6]

It is only natural, and logical, that underworld bosses, as well as many of their underlings, would defy a commission whenever they thought it would serve their purpose to do so. In Valachi's testimony, he revealed several instances of New York City bosses, all members of the commission, plotting and scheming against one another. The balance of power in the Cosa Nostra ruling body, said the President's Commission in 1967, always rests with the five New York City family bosses. And the evidence is clear that the Cosa Nostra commission has proven itself incapable of controlling effectively the New York members of the commission itself.

Joseph Bonanno, for many years a stalwart member of the commission, was openly defiant of the so-called ruling body when he was called upon to account for some of his acts. FBI tapes of conversations in Sam De-Cavalcante's office disclosed that for over a year Bonanno ignored pleas for him to appear before the commission. Bonanno was distrustful of the commission and not without reason. There were indications that a fellow commission member, Stefano Magaddino, boss of Buffalo, was involved in a conspiracy to take over control of the Bonanno family. From conversations overheard in DeCavalcante's office, it was obvious that some commission members not only were disgusted with Bonanno but also had very little regard for the commission. DeCavalcante once observed, "I've heard all of these guys talking. My father makes more sense than all of them. . . ."

In January 1965 a meeting of several Cosa Nostra bosses was held at the Villa Capri in Cedarhurst, Long Island. Among the commission members present were Carlo Gambino, Gaetano Lucchese, Joseph Colombo, Stefano Magaddino, and Angelo Bruno, the Philadelphia boss. Also present were Sam DeCavalcante, Tommy Eboli, Jerry Catena, and Mike Miranda. Subsequently discussing the meeting with two of his lieutenants, DeCavalcante lamented that the commission had become a "three-man thing" run by Gambino, Lucchese, and Magaddino.[7]

In the family of Joseph Profaci, a commission member, open warfare erupted as a result of rebellion against his leadership. Within a two-year period, twelve persons were killed while others were assaulted, wounded, and kidnapped. And while this violence constituted an open challenge to Cosa Nostra leadership and discipline, the commission stood idly by and was helpless to take any action whatever. With some justification, Profaci was convinced that the violence had been inspired by two other commission members, Gambino and Lucchese. Profaci went to his grave despising these men. Profaci's successor as family boss, Joseph Magliocco, died on December 28, 1963. Apparently through the influence of Gambino, the new family boss was Joseph Colombo, who also became a member of the commission.

Colombo was without stature in underworld circles and was deemed a stooge of Gambino. DeCavalcante remarked to his underboss, Frank Majuri, "I don't understand how a guy like that [Colombo] belongs on the commission." DeCavalcante indicated that Colombo was without experience in mob leadership and disparagingly remarked, "He was a bust-out guy all his life."[8] Although Colombo had little prestige even in the New York underworld, he was one of five bosses holding the balance of power in the commission, reputedly the ruling body over organized crime throughout the United States!

Colombo's career as a family boss was practically ended on June 28, 1971, when he was shot and completely incapacitated. Less than thirteen months later, on July 16, 1972, another New York City boss, Tommy Eboli, was assassinated by rival gangster's bullets. In the interval seventeen other gangland killings in New York City took place. Obviously, the commission has been ineffective in settling disputes or imposing its leadership or control over the New York City bosses. This was true even though such bosses were the most significant members of the commission itself. It should be evident that the commission would be even less effective in exercising any meaningful control over organized crime in other parts of the nation.

From the very beginning of the Cosa Nostra organization, the various bosses were plotting against one another. Salvatore Maranzano had barely established himself as Boss of Bosses when he revealed to Valachi that the bosses could not get along. He began laying plans to get rid of Frank Costello, Lucky Luciano, Vito Genovese, Al Capone, and other underworld leaders. Insead, Maranzano was murdered at the direction of some of the bosses he had been scheming against. Many years later, Genovese became the boss of all bosses "under the table" and was the most powerful man in the commission. Yet, said Valachi, Genovese was never able to control the Joseph Profaci family in Brooklyn. When the Cosa Nostra bosses laid down a rule prohibiting traffic in narcotics, it was generally ignored by the bosses themselves, and admittedly the rule was ineffective.

It is highly oversimplified to assume that organized crime in America is dominated by a single Italian organization functioning smoothly under the guidance and control of a national board of overseers, a commission that is actually under the thumb of five New York City bosses. Such a viewpoint is contrary to established facts. No single organization or ethnic group could possibly control organized crime in America in its totality.

Valachi made a remarkable impact on the literature relating to organized crime. In fact, it was Valachi who quite likely coined the name *Cosa Nostra,* using it to denote an Italian criminal organization. During the years following his revelations, the great majority of published books, articles, and news items that have attempted to describe the structure of organized crime in America clearly reveal a heavy reliance on Valachi. Likewise, his disclosures have been accepted without much questioning by many official agencies as well. On some occasions, writers have either misinterpreted portions of Valachi's testimony or attributed to him statements he never made at all.

Much information supplied by Valachi has been corroborated. On the other hand, some of Valachi's testimony was extremely vague, confusing, and inconsistent. Not infrequently, it would appear, he either withheld facts, which should have been known to him, or deliberately lied.

Valachi was a man of limited intelligence. He was provincially attuned only to New York, where he was a low man on the totem pole of organized crime. Notwithstanding his true significance as an informer, he was never in a position to provide an accurate blueprint of the structure of organized crime in the United States.

36

CONCLUSION: ORGANIZED CRIME IN AMERICA—AN OVERVIEW

The trademark of organized crime is violence. Each underworld boss, as in the animal kingdom, stakes out his territory and jealously guards his sovereignty. To infringe his domain means violence—killing, beating, or torture. Monopolies are established and competition is eliminated through violence or threat of violence.

Frequently, the will of organized crime bosses is imposed on the legitimate business comminity through fear. A businessman who refuses to purchase his supplies or services from a mob-controlled firm may be subjected to a thrashing or his establishment may be bombed or set afire.

Fear prevents prospective witnesses from testifying against the underworld or cooperating with the authorities. And this fear is not without justification. Numerous individuals considered prospective witnesses against organized crime bigwigs have been murdered and others have mysteriously disappeared and are believed killed. On rare occasions, the underworld has even been able to pierce the inner sanctum of a federal grand-jury room. A grand juror, indebted to syndicate gamblers or loan sharks, is coerced into keeping organized crime bosses informed of the investigations under progress, the identity of the witnesses, and the nature of their testimony.

It is also violence or fear of violence that maintains rigid discipline within the ranks of the underworld. Those who may defect or engage in a double-cross are summarily tortured or killed. And when a member of a crime syndicate furnishes information to officialdom, he is virtually signing his death warrant.

Although violence is a trademark of organized crime, the resort to violence, in itself, does not signify that a particular group is a part of organized crime. Terrorists seeking to bring about political change or youthful street gangs that often go on a rampage are disciples of violence but usually have no connection with organized crime.

Organized crime could never gain a strong foothold and flourish through the use of violence alone. Another essential ingredient is official corruption. Former Chief Justice Earl Warren of the U.S. Supreme Court once listed as a "rule of thumb" that corruption is the basis of organized crime.[1] And corruption, to be effective, must reach those in authority who have the power to provide the underworld with immunity.

Organized crime has often prospered when corruption has been limited to payoffs to the police. But such arrangements are usually considered less than ideal insofar as the crime bosses are concerned. After all, policemen do not work in a vacuum. In the last analysis, they are subject to political control. Thus, underworld bosses prefer to place on their payroll, not only police personnel, but political leaders who have the power to control the police, and in many instances, prosecutors and members of the judiciary as well.

From time immemorial, there have been political leaders who have been willing to furnish protection to criminals and racketeers in exchange for money—money used for personal wealth or for campaign funds or both. Also the criminal element may furnish election workers who will attempt to ensure victory at the polls for their political patron.

Criminal-political alliances have been a major factor in the development and growth of organized crime in this country. They have made it possible, at times, for the underworld to have a strong voice in formulating law-enforcement policies in a city and to place personnel of its choice in key positions in government. Sometimes the underworld boss has become the political boss as well.

Early in New York City's history, crime became organized. Strong alliances were forged between political leaders and the underworld. In the 1820s, gangs under effective leadership made their headquarters in green-grocery speakeasies owned by Tammany politicians. By the 1830s, reliance by political leaders on the racketeering and criminal element for campaign funds and election workers had become an established practice.

It was in the 1830s that Isaiah Rynders, a former Mississippi River gambler and gunfighter, arrived in New York City and became a saloon-keeper. From his Empire Club, Rynders governed the politics of the bloody Sixth Ward, the home of the Five Points gangs. Rynders' rule over the Five Points gangs was absolute, and with the aid of the underworld his political advance was rapid. By 1844 he was a member of the General Committee of Tammany Hall. Frequently presiding over the General Committee meetings, Rynders utilized gang members to maintain order and probably to control the vote. For twenty years Rynders was a sachem in Tammany Hall. Eventually he was appointed to the post of United States marshal, a position rather incongruous with a role of protecting gangsters.[2]

In 1852 Rynders and Assemblyman Mike Walsh, the leader of the Spartan gang, were sent by Tammany Hall to the Democratic convention in Baltimore to help select a presidential candidate. Eighty years later, Tammany district leader James J. Hines attended the Democratic National Convention in

Chicago. His roommate was the underworld boss Frank Costello. Rooming nearby in the same hotel were Albert Marinelli, Tammany coleader of the Second Assembly District, and his pal and political sponsor Lucky Luciano. Conditions had not changed much in eighty years.

A protégé of Rynders was John Morrissey, a notorious gambler, prizefighter, and onetime burglar. Morrissey won fame as an organizer of "repeaters" at the polls. Tammany Boss William M. Tweed admitted having afforded protection to Morrissey's gambling establishments, which Tweed described as resorts of thieves and criminals. Morrissey became a man of great influence politically. Once he was elected to the U.S. Congress and twice to the New York State Senate.

Beginning with Rynders there was a succession of powerful Tammany leaders who furnished protection to the underworld. For a period of more than a century, the clubhouses of many Tammany assembly district leaders were actually centers of organized crime operations. Three separate official investigations in the 1890s established that the New York City Police Department was honeycombed with corruption.

By 1902 Big Tim Sullivan, the district leader of the Bowery, was deemed the most powerful leader in Tammany Hall. His first big boost in politics occurred when he was elected to the state legislature through the influence of a criminal gang called the Whyos, an outgrowth of an old Five Points gang. Sullivan headed a huge gambling syndicate and for some time was allied with the notorious Monk Eastman gang. Among those whom Sullivan afforded protection was the Italian underworld leader Paolo Vaccarelli, also known as Paul Kelly. The assistance of Kelly was vital to Big Tim in winning elections.

Sullivan and Big Tom Foley, district leader of the Second Assembly District, were intimate friends and political allies of long standing. Following Sullivan's insanity in 1912 and death in 1913, Vaccarelli remained a close political ally of Foley. Among the criminal entrepreneurs who received the protection of Foley was the up and coming mastermind of the underworld, Arnold Rothstein. Eventually, with the exception of Boss Charles F. Murphy, Big Tom Foley became the most powerful leader in Tammany Hall. Retaining the leadership of the old Second Assembly District until he died in 1925, Foley continued to serve as the protector of many East Side gangsters, including Joseph (Joe the Boss) Masseria.

In the early 1920s, Arnold Rothstein shifted his principal allegiance from Foley to James J. Hines, who was rapidly becoming one of the most influential leaders in Tammany Hall. For many years Hines afforded protection to such underworld bosses as Rothstein, Dutch Schultz, and Lepke Buchalter.

The fatal shooting of Rothstein on November 4, 1928, detonated a political bombshell. Some of his personal records and papers located after his death revealed the close relations he had maintained with Hines and other members of the Hines family. Also disclosed were Rothstein's financial dealings with judges and other politicians as well as with various underworld bigwigs.

The impact made by Rothstein on organized crime in America was felt for several decades. Among his protégés were many who would gain national prominence as organized crime bosses or lieutenants—Frank Costello, Dandy Phil Kastel, Lucky Luciano, Frank Erickson, Waxey Gordon, George Uffner, and Jack (Legs) Diamond. Some of the associations developed under the tutelage of Rothstein would form the basis for criminal organizations that would flourish for over thirty years.

During the 1930s events took place that helped to undermine the power base of Tammany leader James J. Hines. In particular, the investigations and prosecutions conducted by Thomas E. Dewey were throwing fear into the ranks of the underworld and its political protectors. On October 23, 1935, gangland assassins fatally shot Dutch Schultz, who had been a major target of the Dewey investigations. Dewey then prosecuted Hines for his role in protecting Schultz and his policy operations. On February 25, 1939, a jury convicted Hines and he was sentenced to prison.

Meanwhile, Frank Costello, a close ally of Hines, was gradually becoming a powerful behind-the-scenes influence in Tammany Hall. Eventually, this underworld chief would actually name some of the bosses of Tammany. And aspirants to prestigious offices, including judges, would find it politically expedient to seek his support. In the 1945 elections a Costello-dominated Tammany Hall was responsible for placing William O'Dwyer in the major's chair. And it was Costello's influence that made it possible for Carmine G. DeSapio to be named boss of Tammany Hall and eventually to be recognized as the most powerful Democrat in New York City and in the state of New York.

Criminal-political alliances, the backbone of organized crime, have played a vital role in New York's history. But they are by no means endemic to New York. At one time or another they have been present in most American cities and in many rural communities as well.

For example, a crime syndicate headed by Abe Minker controlled Reading, Pennsylvania, for several decades. A dominant force in local politics, Minker ran a conglomerate of illegal activities, including a multi-million-dollar gambling empire. Directly beneath Minker in the ruling hierarchy of the syndicate was his nephew Alex Fudeman. Chief enforcer for the organization was John Wittig, a convicted murderer. Numerous Minker lieutenants operated various gambling enterprises.

As a means of controlling the juke-box racket, Minker brought about the formation of the Berks County Amusement Association, which was ostensibly headed by Fudeman. Juke-box operators were given the alternative of making payoffs to the association or going out of business. At the conclusion of an investigation by the attorney general of Pennsylvania in 1957 it was disclosed that $50,000 in extortion money had been paid to Fudeman. Indictments charging blackmail were filed against Minker and others. When key prosecution witnesses refused to testify, the state negotiated guilty pleas from Fudeman and Wittig, who were given suspended sentences.

In 1951 the Kefauver committee cited Reading as "a classic example of political strangulation of a police department at the behest of gambling interests seeking to thwart any interference with their activities." Ten years later, Abe Minker was convicted of evading over $130,000 in federal wagering taxes due on his multi-million-dollar gambling operations. Introduced at the trial were some of Minker's handwritten notes that detailed his payment of bribes to officeholders. In 1965 Minker and Mayor John Kubacki were convicted of extorting over $10,000 from parking-meter concerns that sought city contracts. At the trial, the city's top law-enforcement officer, Charles Wade, testified that he had purchased the post of chief of police for $10,000 from crime syndicate boss Abe Minker, and while serving as police chief he took orders from Minker in all matters relating to enforcement of the vice and gambling laws.

Obviously, crime boss Minker was also the political boss. He named the chief of police, whom he controlled, and was able to formulate the law-enforcement policies for the city.[3]

In New York City a new charter adopted in 1961 altered the power structure. Edward N. Costikyan, county leader of the New York County Democratic organization from March 1962 to November 1964, asserted that power is no longer in the hands of the political leaders. Instead, a growing civil-service bureaucracy increasingly rules city government without an effective counterbalance. And, said Costikyan, the growing puissance of the civil service has reached the point where civil-service unions have almost filled the power position formerly occupied by the political parties.[4]

The tremendous power wielded by police unions, for example, has been demonstrated in many places in America. And in several cities and suburban towns, local unions with close ties to underworld leaders have waged campaigns to organize the police. Obviously, a police department dominated by a union with underworld ties could very well be immobilized in dealing with organized crime. A somewhat parallel situation has occurred in a number of industrial plants in which organized crime bosses, in collusion with union shop stewards, have operated lucrative gambling rackets. The disruptive effects on plant productivity, coupled with complaints of employees' wives about their husbands' gambling losses, have sometimes presented serious problems to management. But company executives have often felt helpless to clean up the situation. To do so, they were warned, would result in a walkout that would close down the entire plant.

The takeover of numerous local unions in the United States by organized crime figures has been fully documented in evidence presented to congressional committees over the past several years. In April 1978, at congressional hearings in Washington, D.C., Peter Vaira, head of the U.S. Department of Justice Organized Crime Strike Force in Chicago, testified that nearly every major local of three international unions in the Windy City was controlled by the Chicago crime syndicate. And, said Vaira, the officers of these local unions answered directly to the Chicago underworld bosses. Recently, a local Teamsters Union chief steward at the McCormick Place exhibition center was convicted of labor racketeering and received a two-year prison term. The steward had placed crime syndicate figures on the payroll of McCormick Place. And the same local union had been engaged actively in attempting to organize the police departments in Chicago and suburban towns.[5]

In New Orleans, in February 1979, the police union, Teamsters Local 253, brought the city to its knees. Because of a protracted police strike, most of the famed Mardi Gras festivities were canceled. Tough negotiations with the city were directed by Teamsters Union troubleshooter Joseph Valenti, who was sent to New Orleans from Detroit. Police union leader Vincent J. Bruno is related through marriage to Carlos Marcello, one of America's most infamous organized crime bosses. During a conversation with reporters, Bruno threatened, "If the talks break down, we'll wreck the city." Both local papers ran front-page editorials denouncing the police conduct. A television poll revealed that within a period of two weeks, public support for the police dropped from sixty-seven percent to seventeen percent.[6]

In various cities the Teamsters Union has been particularly active in attempting to organize the police. And many Teamsters Union officials have maintained intimate relationships with organized crime bigwigs. In fact, influential organized crime figures helped James R. Hoffa gain control of the International Brotherhood of Teamsters. And it is generally believed that Hoffa's disappearance and probable murder in July 1975 were brought about by members of the underworld who had once been his allies.

Among the prime suspects in the Hoffa disappearance and murder was Anthony Provenzano, the onetime president of Teamsters Local 560 in Union City, New Jersey, and an affiliate of the Vito Genovese organized crime group in New York City. Provenzano had played an important role in establishing and maintaining Hoffa's power in the East.

From the very beginning of his career in the Teamsters Union, Provenzano enjoyed strong organized crime backing. An early sponsor was Anthony Strollo, also known as Tony Bender, an important aide to Vito Genovese. Strollo was a powerful underworld boss on the New York waterfront and controlled some Teamsters locals. In 1945 Strollo installed Provenzano as a shop steward in a trucking company. In 1950 it was Strollo who appointed Provenzano to the post of organizer for Teamsters Local 560 in Union City.

Strollo secured the assistance of longshoremen in smuggling heroin into the United States. And federal informants asserted that Provenzano was involved with Strollo in the drug traffic.

Within a period of ten years, Provenzano advanced from organizer for Teamsters Local 560 to its president and to a vice presidency of the International Brotherhood of Teamsters. In 1962 his original sponsor, Anthony Strollo, disappeared and presumably was murdered. But the loss of this ally did not interfere with the power of Provenzano in the Teamsters Union.

Under Provenzano's leadership, Teamsters Local 560 was a center of organized crime activites—loan sharking, numbers, and bookmaking operations run by shop stewards and business agents, and systematic pilferage of goods being trucked through the state. Eventually, Provenzano was prosecuted and convicted for having extorted $17,000 from a trucking company. During the extortion trial, efforts were made to intimidate the jury as well as witnesses. A prospective witness against Provenzano, Walter Glockner, was gunned down and killed. On May 5, 1966, Anthony Provenzano entered the federal penitentiary in Lewisburg, Pennsylvania, where he remained for four and a half years.

In the late 1950s and early 1960s Provenzano's rule over Local 560 met with some concerted opposition. A leader of a dissident group was viciously beaten and seriously injured on two occasions. The rebels also found themselves the targets of shotgun blasts and bombings.

During the turmoil in 1961 indications were that Anthony Castellito, then secretary-treasurer of Local 560, intended to oppose Provenzano for the presidency the following year. In June 1961 Castellito attended a Teamsters Union meeting, drove away in his union-purchased Cadillac, and was never heard from again. Several years later an indictment was returned in which Provenzano was charged with having directed Harold Konigsberg and Salvatore Briguglio to arrange for the murder of Castellito. Konigsberg, an affiliate of the Vito Genovese criminal organization, was a loan shark, extortionist, and organized crime enforcer. Briguglio, a business agent of Local 560, later was a major suspect in the disappearance and probable murder of James R. Hoffa in 1975. On March 21, 1978, Briguglio was shot and killed on Mulberry Street in Manhattan's Little Italy.

Following a trial and conviction in Kingston, New York, Anthony Provenzano was sentenced on June 21, 1978, to life imprisonment. A life sentence was also imposed on Harold Konigsberg, who was already serving a forty-year term for extortion.[7]

For some time organized crime was served well by the Central States Pension Fund of the Teamsters Union. Pursuant to contract with the Teamsters Union, the employers of some 450,000 Teamsters in the central, southeastern, and southwestern states contribute millions of dollars each month into the fund. By 1976 the fund was holding $1.4 billion in trust to cover the pensions of Teamsters Union members in those states.

For many years the most influential person in the management of the Central States Pension Fund was Allen Dorfman. It was Dorfman's father, Paul (Red) Dorfman, a close ally of important Chicago mobsters, who had introduced James R. Hoffa to organized crime bigwigs. This aided Hoffa in gaining control of the Teamsters Union. Allen Dorfman was murdered by gangland bullets on January 20, 1983.

Although it is axiomatic that pension funds should be protected through wise and conservative investments, the Central States Pension Fund has loaned huge amounts to organized crime interests. During the years 1959–61 the fund plunged heavily into loans to casinos in Las Vegas. One of the major recipients of such loans was the Cleveland crime syndicate headed by Moe Dalitz. Loans to Dalitz were used to finance the Stardust Hotel and Country Club, the Fremont Hotel, and the Desert Inn. Between 1965 and 1972, $20.4 million was loaned to Caesar's Palace in Las Vegas. By 1977 the Circus Circus Hotel and Casino in Las Vegas owed the fund over $26 million. It has been estimated by Steven Brill in his book, *The Teamsters,* that the Central States Pension Fund has made loans totaling $600 million to persons with organized crime connections. And although such individuals are considered high-risk borrowers, many received their loans at rates lower than those charged to persons with the highest credit rating.[8]

In defining organized crime, frequently the emphasis is placed on its role of providing goods and services prohibited by law. Such a definition is incomplete and inaccurate. Naturally, the underworld has a major interest in those activities that yield quick profits with a minimum of risk and negligible effort. Endeavors that meet these criteria are attractive to the underworld whether they are legal or illegal. Gambling, for example, has been attractive to organized crime whether it is unlawful or sanctioned by law. The role of important organized crime figures in the legalized gambling fields of Nevada, Cuba, and the Bahamas has been fully documented. And it has been established that in many instances the underworld has been a vital force, behind the scenes, in campaigns waged to get various forms of gambling legalized. It is the *nature* of the business that determines whether it is attractive to the underworld, not its legality or illegality.

It is true that gambling, narcotics, vice, and loan sharking have always served as important sources of revenue to the underworld. But there are a number of legitimate businesses that are particularly appealing to organized crime—nightclubs, bars, restaurants, parking lots, vending-machine operations.

For several years in many sections of the United States, the juke-box industry, particularly at the level of the distributors and operators, was in the hands of organized crime. Almost everywhere the pattern was the same.

The underworld would gain control of the juke-box operators association as well as the local union having jurisdiction over juke boxes. Territories were divided among the underworld operators and monopolies were established. Any attempt to challenge the monopoly resulted in violence and threats of violence. Often the victim was the relatively disinterested location owner—the restaurant proprietor or tavernkeeper in whose establishment the juke box had been installed. In addition to receiving threats of physical violence, the location owner would be warned by the mob-controlled union official that unless he followed orders a picket line would be thrown around his establishment and he would be driven out of business. The underworld also resorted to sabotaging the juke boxes of rival operators. Usually, the location owner decided to do business exclusively with the underworld operator. Numerous gangland-type murders, baseball-bat beatings, and bombings traced directly to the juke-box business.

Also attractive to the underworld has been the cigarette vending-machine business. In some places, the organized crime groups that controlled the juke-box industry also had a monopoly on cigarette vending-machine operations. At one time, some of the most powerful underworld leaders in America were involved in cigarette vending-machine operations—Meyer Lansky, Joe Adonis, Abner (Longy) Zwillman, Jerry Catena, Eddie Vogel, and Ralph Capone, a brother of Al.

The nationwide investigation of organized crime by the Kefauver committee in 1950 uncovered evidence of the infiltration of organized crime into some fifty areas of legitimate enterprise. A Kefauver committee staff report listed 514 names of individuals and companies involved in various forms of legitimate business that organized crime had penetrated.

The motives that prompt organized crime to enter the field of legitimate business are many and include: (1) making a fast buck by engaging in certain types of business particularly attractive to the underworld, (2) operating a lawful enterprise that can serve as a front for illicit activities, (3) laundering tainted money—investing untaxed profits from illegal gambling, narcotics, or loan sharking in a legitimate business, (4) showing revenue from a legitimate business as the source of income on tax returns to avoid accounting for profits from illicit sources, (5) providing an aura of respectability for the underworld figure and his family.

Whatever the motive, the infiltration of organized crime into the fields of legitimate business is widespread. In October 1969 Internal Revenue Commissioner Randolph W. Thrower revealed that the Internal Revenue Service had made a survey of 113 major underworld leaders in the nation. Of that number, 98 were involved in 159 individual businesses including 32 casinos and nightclubs, 17 land investment and real estate groups, 11 hotels and motels, 10 vending-machine companies, 8 restaurants, 8 trucking companies, 7 wholesale food distributors, 7 businesses in the sports and entertainment fields, and 6 financial institutions.

Commissioner Thrower warned that when members of organized crime get into legitimate endeavors, they resort to their usual methods of doing business: bribery of public officials, tax evasion, coercion, unfair competition, and monopolization. Serious threats are thus posed to the legitimate businessman and the consumer.[9]

Among the methods utilized by organized crime figures to acquire an interest in a legitimate business are: (1) investing profits from illicit activities, (2) accepting an interest in a business to settle the proprietor's gambling debts, (3) accepting an interest in a firm in payment of the proprietor's obligations to loan sharks, and (4) taking over a business through pure "muscle" or extortion. Ofttimes underworld characters have merely walked into an establishment and have declared themselves "in" for a certain percentage of the business. The victimized owner is threatened with physical torture or death if he reports the matter to the authorities, so frequently he accedes to the extortionary demands. The underworld thus acquires an interest in the business without the investment of any money.

Also primary targets of organized crime are various labor unions. In recent years it has been reported that union locals in twenty-five sectors of business and industry are under the effective control of the underworld.[10]

There are three principal motives for the invasion of labor unions by organized crime. First, bulging treasuries of many unions provide choice targets for looting. Particularly inviting are the union health, welfare, and pension funds that total billions of dollars in this country. Second, the control of a local union will enable the underworld to establish and maintain a monopoly over an entire business throughout a locality. Examples of this are numerous. In some cities, the underworld gained control of the Bartenders Union. Tavernkeepers and nightclub owners were forced to purchase beer and liquor from mob-controlled firms. And the union influence was not confined to intoxicating beverages. The union was able to dictate that all other goods and services, such as food and linen supplies, be purchased from concerns approved by the underworld. The threat of a strike was usually sufficient to keep everyone in line. If added emphasis became necessary, there were warnings of physical beatings, bombings, and arson.

Third, organized crime may utilize a labor union as a means of extortion, pure and simple. For example, in 1934 the Capone organization, aided by Lucky Luciano and Lepke Buchalter, succeeded in gaining control of the International Alliance of Theatrical, Stage Employees, and Motion Picture Operators. With this union under its thumb, the Chicago-based Capone syndicate extorted millions of dollars from theater owners from coast to coast. Either theater owners met demands for cash payoffs or their establishments were closed down by the union.

In America there is a widely held opinion that organized crime was spawned by the ill-fated Prohibition experiment. That opinion completely ignores the facts. For the greater part of a century before the Eighteenth Amendment was adopted, organized crime flourished in numerous places. For several decades before the Volstead Act became law, powerful criminal organizations engaged in gambling, prostitution, loan sharking, and other rackets were solidly entrenched in city after city nationwide. It is also true that long before the arrival of Prohibition, close ties between the underworld and the liquor interests were commonplace. From time immemorial saloons had served as hangouts and centers of operation for the underworld. Many gang leaders owned saloons. At times a single building had a bar, gambling operations, and rooms devoted to prostitution. In almost every city, saloonkeepers, many of whom had underworld ties, were actively engaged in politics. The saloon was a center of political activity. In 1884 it was estimated that three fourths of the aldermanic conventions in New York City were held in saloons or in friendly places next door.

Although the Noble Experiment was not responsible for creating organized crime, it did make a lasting impact on criminal organization. With the passage of the Volstead Act, the public demand for intoxicants remained high but the supply was suddenly cut off. The underworld was ready to fill this void. Many of the same organizations that had specialized in gambling, prostitution and extortion now entered the bootleg racket. Required, however, was a broader and more efficient organization. Involved were the manufacture, distribution, and sale of intoxicants. Numerous distilleries and breweries were operated by the underworld in every part of America. Thousands of individuals dwelling in tenement flats in the city were engaged to distill rotgut whiskey, which was sold to an indiscriminate thirsty public. Quality whiskey produced in foreign countries was smuggled into the United States on boats often owned and operated by the underworld. And the contraband—whether domestic or foreign—was transported on fleets of trucks manned by ruthless gunmen and frequently escorted by corrupt law-enforcement officers. The armed guards were essential because it became a common practice for rival gangs to hijack trucks loaded with liquor.

Consistent with long-established policies, the various gangs attempted to create and maintain a monopoly over a particular territory. Invasion by a competing organization resulted in gang warfare. Murders were commonplace. Some of the more intelligent leaders—such as Johnny Torrio—proposed the creation of alliances between a number of the principal organizations involved in the bootleg business. The purpose of the coalition was to increase efficiency of operation, augment profits, and reduce senseless killings as well as wasteful destruction of property. A major alliance was formed between East Coast rumrunners and included such influential underworld bosses as Torrio, Lucky Luciano, Meyer Lansky, and Bugsy Siegel. Working arrangements entered into between gangs during Prohibition were sometimes continued after repeal. And some of the associations cemented during Prohibition formed the nucleus for crime syndicates that were to flourish for several decades.

The ranks of organized crime have always been filled with individuals who once were members of youthful gangs. Although usually such gangs are not connected with organized crime, they have served as prime training schools for the underworld. In New York City the squalid Five Points district was a breeding place for gangs, and from them came some of the nation's most powerful organized crime leaders. Probably a high percentage of the personnel of organized crime received early training as members of neighborhood gangs.

The youthful gang usually is motivated primarily by fun and the mystique of adventure rather than by profit. Nevertheless, such gangs frequently engage in extortion and blackmail and thus receive early training in the fields of endeavor in which organized crime excels.

In Frederic M. Thrasher's classic study *The Gang*, he found that what organization exists has been developed as a result of natural selection. As the gang engages in various activities, "the positions within the group are defined and social roles become more sharply differentiated." As a result of this process, a somewhat efficient and harmonious organization develops, with one boy emerging as the natural leader.[11]

Likewise, the organization of many, if not most, underworld groups is the product of an evolutionary process. Through experience one man emerges as the one most qualified, by gangland standards, to lead and be recognized as the boss. Moreover, through experience, other roles in the organization become well defined.

Some of the basic codes of conduct followed in youth and adult gangs are quite similar. A universal requirement is loyalty to the group. Providing information to the authorities is considered an unpardonable sin. In youth gangs "squealing" may be punished by inflicting a severe beating of the offender or in extreme cases marking him for death. In adult organized crime groups, those suspected of talking to officials are executed. Frequently they are unmercifully tortured before being killed.[12]

In discussions of organized crime in America, there is a tendency to use labels that oversimplify and distort the total picture. Labels like *Mafia, Unione Siciliana,* and *La Cosa Nostra* give a decided Italian or Sicilian color to the image. It is true that numerous contemporary underworld leaders have Italian or Sicilian backgrounds. Yet, organized crime cannot accurately be circumscribed within an ethnic mold. In fact, the heads of many highly important criminal organizations are non-Italian and non-Sicilian. And it is only in relatively modern times that Italians or Sicilians have played dominant roles on the American crime scene.

From about 1820 to 1890 the rulers of the underworld in New York City were predominantly Irish. The gangs were so preponderantly Irish that in some quarters it was seriously suggested that the Sons of Erin were criminal by nature.

From about 1890 to 1930, a large number of Jewish gang leaders came into prominence. And for several years before his death in 1928, Arnold Rothstein was the most prestigious underworld leader in New York City. Interestingly, several of Rothstein's protégés were Italians who gained national and international fame as underworld bosses.[13]

In 1933 a conference of influential Jewish gang leaders was in progress in a suite of rooms at the Hotel Franconia when it was disrupted by a raid conducted by New York City police officers, headed by Captain Michael F. McDermott. Leading the conference were Lepke Buchalter and Gurrah Shapiro. In addition to Buchalter and Shapiro, the police arrested Joseph (Doc) Stacher, Bugsy Siegel, Harry Teitelbaum, Harry (Big Greenie) Greenberg, Louis (Shadows) Kravitz, Phillip (Little Farvel) Kovolick, and Hyman (Curly) Holtz. All were important characters in the organized underworld. Had they been Italian or Sicilian gangsters, the conference would probably have been tagged a Mafia meeting.[14]

Undoubtedly, the popular concept of organized crime in America has been influenced greatly by romanticized versions of the Mafia as they have appeared in books, magazines, and newspapers. Also influencing the general perception of organized crime has been the publicized disclosures of several criminals who decided to become informers. Particularly significant in this regard were J. Richard (Dixie) Davis, an attorney involved in the Dutch Schultz rackets in the early 1930s; Abe Reles, a murderer who gained renown as an informant for the Brooklyn district attorney's office in 1940; and Joseph Valachi, the federal informer whose testimony in 1963 created a sensation.

Dixie Davis wrote a series of articles that appeared in *Collier's* magazine in 1939. Davis related that in September 1931 the underworld boss Salvatore Maranzano was assassinated in his office at 210 Park Avenue by gunmen who posed as policemen. One of the assassins, he said, was Bo Weinberg, a lieutenant of Dutch Schultz. At the very hour that Maranzano was killed, ninety gunmen reputedly were murdered throughout the nation and, said Davis, the mobs were thus Americanized. However, the story of a national purge was not supported by the facts. The careful studies of one historian, Humbert S. Nelli, disclosed that there were not over four murders committed anywhere in the United States that could possibly have been linked to the Maranzano killing.[15]

According to Davis, in 1931 Lucky Luciano became the leader of the Unione Siciliana, which he used as a vehicle to create a system of underworld alliances throughout the United States. Luciano was thus able to force the underworld to cooperate on a national scale and to establish centralized control.

Under Luciano's direction, Davis explained, the more powerful underworld leaders got together, divided up the territories, and agreed to eliminate gang warfare as well as the competition of outsiders. It was comparable to the National Recovery Act of the New Deal, with the Unione Siciliana acting as a code authority.

Davis asserted that, following 1931, membership in the Unione Siciliana was not restricted to Sicilians. In fact, such Jewish gang leaders as Meyer Lansky and Bugsy Siegel were admitted into the highest councils of the Unione.

In New York City the Unione Siciliana was divided into districts, each headed by a minor boss known as a *compare* or godfather. Power in the Unione naturally came from New York, which had been a breeding ground for mobsters who became underworld bosses in various parts of the country. Luciano's alliance with the mobs headed by Buchalter, Lansky, and Siegel added to the prestige of New York as the power center of the underworld. Davis said that by 1936 the consolidation of control of the underworld had been completed and was dominated by the New York combination under the leadership of Luciano. And this control was so complete that no one could operate a gambling house in Saratoga Springs, New York, without the approval of the combination.

Long before the revelations of Davis or the emergence of Valachi's Cosa Nostra in the American crime lexicon, the Unione Siciliana was widely identified with the Mafia. Even the prestigious Kefauver committee erroneously asserted that the Unione Siciliana was merely another name for the Mafia. Actually, the Unione Siciliana had its origin in Illinois as a legitimate Italian fraternal mutual benefit society. In 1926 the charter of the Unione Siciliana was amended and its name changed to the Italo-American National Union. During Prohibition, prominent gangsters were identified with the Unione Siciliana and a number of its officers were assassinated.

The Unione Siciliana has sometimes been described as a society that controlled all organized crime in the United States. It was in this regard that Burton B. Turkus and Sid Feder, coauthors of the book *Murder, Inc.*, stated, "No one who really knows anything at all about the sharp clannishness of mob bosses with respect to nationalities and creeds would ever attempt to attribute to any one group the control over the whole." This observation is sound and applies to all other organizations that are depicted as controlling organized crime throughout the nation.[16]

In 1940 Abe Reles, under arrest for murder, turned informer to save his own neck. He boasted to the Brooklyn district attorney, William O'Dwyer, an ambitious man politically, that he would make him the "biggest man in the country."

In addition to furnishing information that solved scores of murders, Reles asserted that in 1934 an alliance of underworld bosses resulted in the creation of the national crime syndicate. Reles credited Johnny Torrio with having masterminded the formation of the syndicate. Others who played key roles were Luciano, Lansky, Adonis, Siegel, and Buchalter.

Under the setup, as described by Reles, the underworld bosses throughout the nation became members of one big powerful combination or syndicate. In effect, the national crime syndicate was a confederation of independent gangs—a cartel. Rule over the nationwide combination was lodged in a governing board composed of all gang leaders, all with equal power. The governing board was authorized to dictate policy, handle all intermob negotiations, and arbitrate intermob disputes. Members of the governing board were to sit as justices in kangaroo courts. Charges sufficiently serious to warrant the death penalty were to be brought before a kangaroo court and its decision was to be final and irrevocable. Killings were to be handled by an enforcement branch of the syndicate. At the outset, the Brooklyn group of gangsters known as Murder, Inc. became the execution squad for the national crime syndicate.

Authors Turkus and Feder in *Murder, Inc.* declared, "From courtroom testimony and sworn statements we obtained. . .from gangsters who were on the inside. . .the evidence clearly showed the modern underworld organization in this country to be one huge syndicate, one single powerful syndicate of many gangs." And, they said, "the single national syndicate is bound by a government of its own, just as tightly as General Motors or the National Baseball League, and. . .this government has absolute power." Earlier in the same book while discussing the Unione Siciliana, Turkus and Feder warned that no knowledgeable person "would ever attempt to attribute to any one group the control over the whole." This admonition would appear to have validity also when considering the proposition that the governing board of the national crime syndicate has "absolute power" over organized crime in the United States.[17]

Countless references to the national crime syndicate have appeared in books and articles dealing with organized crime. Although there are discrepancies in these stories, many appear to have been repeating the account provided by Reles.

Joseph Valachi's sensational testimony in 1963 provided detailed information regarding an underworld organization called La Cosa Nostra, a name very likely coined by Valachi himself. Membership in La Cosa Nostra is restricted to full-blooded Italians, who are subjected to elaborate initiation rites that include holding burning paper in cupped hands, bloodletting, and formal oath taking. A godfather is named for each initiate. Making up the organization, he explained, are twenty-four Cosa Nostra core families (criminal groups or gangs), each of which is headed by a boss. At the time of

Valachi's testimony five families were located in New York City. No other city has more than one family.

According to Valachi, in September 1931 Salvatore Maranzano, then the Boss of Bosses, was murdered in his office at 210 Park Avenue. The assassins were four Jewish gunmen who posed as policemen. Valachi learned that one of the killers was Red Levine, a Meyer Lansky man. Lucky Luciano became the boss of the most prestigious family in New York City and, in effect, the overall boss of La Cosa Nostra. Luciano initiated some reforms in the organization and abolished the Boss of Bosses system. It was under Luciano's leadership that a confederation of all Cosa Nostra families became a reality. Reputedly, this confederation controls organized crime in America today.

Ultimate authority over the Cosa Nostra organization was vested in a commission composed of nine family bosses, of whom five were from New York City. Thus, as a practical matter, the balance of power to control organized crime nationally rested in the hands of the five New York City bosses. However, the evidence is convincing that the five New York City bosses engaged in internecine struggles for power and often resorted to double-crossing one another. It would appear obvious that a commission unable to control its own members in New York City would meet with little success in exercising effective authority over underworld bosses throughout the nation.

Some of Valachi's revelations concerning the organization he called La Cosa Nostra have been corroborated. Through the use of electronic eavesdropping devices the FBI recorded conversations that occurred in the plumbing shop of Simone Rizzo (Sam the Plumber) DeCavalcante in Kenilworth, New Jersey, from 1961 to 1965. From these recordings, it appears that at least in the New York City area the Italian underworld has a formalized structure. Each Italian Cosa Nostra family has a boss, an underboss, a consigliere, lieutenants, and soldiers. The recorded conversations also verified the existence of a commission. But they also revealed clearly that the commission was helpless in attempting to exercise any meaningful control over the five New York City bosses, even though they were members of the commission itself.

For many years Valachi's testimony has been regarded in many circles as the gospel on organized crime in America. Much of the literature on the subject has religiously followed Valachi's version of the structure of organized crime locally and nationally. This has been true even though Valachi's firsthand knowledge was limited to New York and his ignorance about places beyond was abysmal. An examination of Valachi's testimony also discloses that at least on some occasions he either was ignorant of the facts or deliberately lied.

The versions of organized crime as provided by the three informers—Davis,

Reles, and Valachi—have many differences, but also a few general similarities. Each of the three informants depicts a national underworld organization that controls organized crime throughout the nation. To Davis, that organization was the Unione Siciliana; to Reles, the national crime syndicate; and to Valachi, La Cosa Nostra. Particularly noteworthy, however, is the obvious fact that there are irreconcilable fundamental differences in the versions of the three informants.

Criminals who have been converted into informers often provide a valuable insight into the affairs of the underworld. But information received from such sources should be viewed with a certain amount of skepticism and scrutinized carefully. The same informant may provide information that is a mixture of truth and falsehood. Men whose lifestyles embrace killing, maiming, cheating, stealing, and lying do not suddenly become paragons of virtue. Usually such men become informers as a means of aiding themselves or to gain revenge. Often they have axes to grind. Many are opportunists who attempt to give the kind of information they believe their interrogators wish to hear. Some retell previously published stories and add embellishments of their own.

Indications are that, at times, underworld figures attempt to emulate patterns of life attributed to them in the press. Luigi Barzini has written about a prevailing myth that certain American criminal groups are branches of the Mafia and take orders from Sicily. Singled out by Barzini as being a gullible American criminal was Lucky Luciano. Widespread newspaper publicity had deluded Luciano into assuming that he was actually a member of the Mafia and had achieved high status in the Honored Society. When Luciano arrived in Sicily, following his deportation, he sought out some of the real Mafia leaders, whom he wined and dined. But they looked upon Luciano as a rank outsider—an easy mark with lots of money. They persuaded him to make a big investment in a deal that was rigged and Luciano was swindled out of fifteen million lire.[18]

On some occasions, members of the underworld have attempted to imitate the conduct attributed to them in the various articles, books, and movies that followed in the wake of Joseph Valachi's celebrated testimony in 1963. This phenomenon was borne out in the highly significant testimony given by New Jersey State Police detective Robert Delaney before a U.S. Senate subcommittee in February 1981.

For two and a half years Delaney had worked on an undercover assignment in the Newark Port area where he posed as the owner and president of a trucking firm. The company started business in 1976 in Jersey City. Working with Delaney on this undercover assignment were two other New Jersey State Police officers, three FBI agents, and a successful businessman who was on intimate terms with several of the most prestigious organized crime figures in the New York–New Jersey waterfront. Because of this man,

Delaney was accepted by the same criminals and thus "had the unique opportunity to see firsthand the problems of organized crime and labor racketeering in New Jersey and elsewhere."

Delaney observed, "The movies *Godfather I* and *Godfather II* have had an impact on these crime families." One young man said he had seen the movie ten times. Other crime family members reported having seen it three or four times. On one occasion, Delaney, accompanied by his business associate, and Joseph Doto, the son of Joseph Adonis, were dining together in a restaurant. "Joe Adonis, Jr. gave the waiter a pocketful of quarters and told him to play the jukebox continuously and to play the same song, the theme music from *The Godfather*. All through dinner, we listened to the same song, over and over." Senator Sam Nunn inquired, "You are saying sometimes they go to the movie to see how they themselves are supposed to behave, is that right?" Delaney replied, "That is true. They had a lot of things taught to them through the movie. They try to live up to it. The movie was telling them how."

Delaney spoke of the frequent "blurring of family lines" and noted that in some instances members of one family worked "closer and more effectively with members of another family than they worked with members of their own." It was apparent, he noted, that "the conventional and popular perception of the family members working only with each other does not always apply." When asked if members of organized crime identified themselves by family, Delaney replied, "I think we in law enforcement have a tendency to structure organized crime so that we are able to understand it. We make the. . .table of organization because we are used to tables of organizations and we are used to being identified by uniform or by credentials. That does not take place in organized crime. It is a thing that is understood, it is a way of life with them." Delaney asserted, "The truth of the matter is that the crime families are. . .not nearly as highly structured as the media and popular writers have portrayed them."[19]

In literature dealing with organized crime, one of the most widely used—and abused—terms is *Mafia*. The frequently held belief that various Italian or Sicilian criminal organizations in this country actually are branches of the Honored Society in Sicily and take orders from Palermo is without foundation.

Most serious students of the Honored Society agree that even in Sicily the Mafia has never been a highly formalized, rigidly structured, monolithic organization. Instead, the Mafia consists of many relatively small autonomous associations (gangs or groups), each of which is called a *cosca*. Each is headed by a boss and ordinarily his influence is limited to his own cosca. Only rarely does the boss of a cosca become sufficiently prestigious that his influence is felt over a wide area in western Sicily. The numerous cosche are not brought together in one compact organization. At times, two cosche in the same community are bitter enemies and engage in warfare resulting in numerous murders.

During the period of great immigration of Sicilians to America, the majority were illiterate peasants of limited intelligence. Most were men with provincial horizons, having spent their entire lifetime in small villages in which they were reared. They would have been ill equipped to serve as a vanguard for an international criminal organization about to establish itself on American shores. Most of these immigrants settled in sections of American cities known as Little Sicily or Little Italy. The Sicilians brought with them their own culture, which had developed over a period of several centuries of oppression. That culture included an innate distrust of government, a refusal to cooperate with law-enforcement authorities, an honor that required a wrong to be avenged personally, and a code of silence. It was this culture that Sicilian immigrants imported to this country—not an international conspiratorial organization.

Nevertheless, the myth persists that organized crime in the United States is controlled by a mystical and somewhat romantic Sicilian Mafia with secret initiation rites that include bloodletting, holding a burning paper in cupped hands, and oath taking.

A *Time* cover story on May 16, 1977, depicted the Mafia as a feudal society that was going through its most bloody internal struggles since 1931, when a nationwide commission of Mafia dons was established to "coordinate criminal operations." Only then, said the article, "did the closed brotherhood, which was imported by Sicilian immigrants in the 1860s, begin dominating the American underworld." It was conceded, properly, that organized crime "knows no ethnic limits" and mentioned the involvement of Jews, Irish Americans, Greeks, Chinese, blacks, and Hispanics. Yet, said the *Time* article, "The Mafia is by far the best organized criminal group in the U.S. and the only one with a national structure. . . ."

The organizational structure of the Mafia as reported in the *Time* article was basically identical with that advanced in 1963 by Joseph Valachi when describing what he called La Cosa Nostra. It has become rather commonplace for journalists to treat the Mafia and La Cosa Nostra as being one and the same thing. Actually, the Mafia originated in Sicily and membership is limited to Sicilians. On the other hand, the organization known as La Cosa Nostra purportedly started in New York City and membership includes all Italians, Neapolitans as well as Sicilians. The commission was established by the American Cosa Nostra and has never been a part of the Mafia in Sicily. In response to a specific question during his testimony before a Senate subcommittee, Valachi stated, "As long as I belong to this Cosa Nostra. . .they never express it as Mafia."

Some aspects of La Cosa Nostra, as described by Valachi, resemble the romanticized version of the Mafia. This is true of the elaborate initiation rites that require the novitiate to hold a burning paper in cupped hands, submit to bloodletting, and take a formal oath. Although such initiation rites and formal oaths have been described in fictionalized accounts of the Mafia, they in truth have no place in the genuine Mafia in Sicily.

Valachi's firsthand information was limited to New York City and environs. He was woefully ignorant about most places beyond. Assuming that the highly formalized structure of Italian organized crime groups, as described by Valachi, was accurate for New York, is it valid throughout America? Probably not.

In April 1978 a U.S. Senate subcommittee in Washington conducted hearings regarding the infiltration of organized crime into labor unions. Appearing before the subcommittee was Peter Vaira, head of the U.S. Department of Justice Organized Crime Strike Force in Chicago. Vaira testified, "I would say in Chicago organized crime differs from the classic pattern, which you find in the eastern part of the U.S. There you see various families, six or seven different families in an area with their own internal structure. In Chicago it is much more loosely associated. . . ."[20]

According to Valachi, one of the principal Cosa Nostra families is located in Chicago. However, some of the highly important posts in the Chicago crime syndicate have always been filled by non-Italians and therefore ineligible for membership in La Cosa Nostra. During the regimes of Al Capone, Frank Nitti, and Tony Accardo, the Jewish mobster Jack Guzik functioned for many years as the equivalent of general manager of the organization. During a bugged conversation in 1962 between Jackie Cerone, righthand man to Accardo, and other members of the Chicago organization, Cerone was heard to say, "We got Jews and Pollacks also."

It is quite probable that many, if not most, of the American criminal syndicates, including those with Italian leadership, are much more loosely organized than the rigid structures depicted by Valachi's testimony. In any event, it is virtually a certainty that each of the significant criminal organizations insists upon maintaining its own autonomy. And it would never willingly surrender any of its sovereignty to a national commission.

From time to time, in various places, meetings of numerous gangland bigwigs have been disrupted by the authorities and given wide publicity. The purpose of such conclaves is known only by those in attendance. It would be reasonable to assume, however, that at such get-togethers the mob bosses discuss criminal projects and perhaps formulate plans for intermob cooperative efforts.

It is known that underworld bosses from various cities keep in touch with one another. Sometimes these gangland contacts embrace the entire nation. In 1950 the Los Angeles police arrested Giroloma (Mo Mo) Adamo, principal lieutenant of West Coast mob boss Jack Dragna. Seized from Adamo was a confidential address book containing the names, addresses, and telephone numbers of some of the nation's most prominent underworld characters. Among those listed in the address book were Tony Accardo, Murray Humphreys, and Charles Fischetti, top figures in the ruling hierarchy of the Chicago Capone organization; Joseph Profaci and Joseph Bonanno, leaders of two of the most powerful Italian criminal gangs in Brooklyn; Pete Licovoli, Joe Zerilli, and William (Black Bill) Tocco, gangland bosses and numbers racket kings in Detroit; Santo Trafficante, organized crime boss in Tampa, Florida; Allen Smiley, intimate associate of Bugsy Siegel; Charles (Babe) Baron, Chicago gambler associated with Meyer Lansky in gambling operations in Cuba and the Bahamas; Carl Cascio and Charles Blanda, big-time gambling operators in Colorado.[21]

Many underworld leaders began their criminal careers in New York City before moving to other locales. Friendships they had developed with New York gangsters were retained and probably served to encourage intermob cooperation. Johnny Torrio and Al Capone, while heading the Chicago underworld, maintained cordial relations for some time with their former associate Frankie Yale in New York. At Torrio's behest, Yale visited the Windy City, where he handled gang assassinations for the Chicago mob boss.

Before moving to Hot Springs, Arkansas, Owney Madden had gained enormous prestige as an underworld leader in New York City. Dandy Phil Kastel, as Frank Costello's partner, also became influential in the New York City underworld before moving to New Orleans. For decades a steady stream of important gangland bigwigs from all parts of the nation visited Madden in Hot Springs and Kastel in New Orleans. It is reasonable to assume that many of these visits were related directly to underworld affairs and, at times, to collaboration in profitable criminal ventures. But it cannot be concluded from such intermob contacts alone that all are part of a single organization.

In Gaia Servadio's history of the Mafia in Sicily, she has pointed out that organization in the true sense is limited to the level of the gang, known as the cosca. The Mafia, as a single entity, an organization or secret society, embracing all cosche, does not exist in Sicily. And some efforts to repress the Mafia, she declares, have failed because they were based on the erroneous assumption that the Mafia is a single organization.[22]

In a somewhat similar manner, efforts are made in the United States to depict the underworld as being under the control of one powerful and sophisticated organization—the Mafia, La Cosa Nostra, Unione Siciliana, or the national crime syndicate. As a result, a distorted and oversimplified picture emerges, which in turn gives rise to unrealistic measures intended to cope with the problem. In the aftermath of the furor created by Valachi's testimony, a bill designed to outlaw the Mafia was introduced in the U.S. Senate in 1965. One section of the bill provided that "Mafia means a secret society whose members are pledged and dedicated to commit unlawful acts against the United States or any state thereof in furtherance of their objective to dominate organized crime. . . .''

Responding to an inquiry from the chairman of the Subcommittee on Criminal Laws and Procedures of the U.S. Senate Judiciary Committee, the author of this book wrote on December 17, 1965: "As a practical matter, I question the enforceability of this proposed law. . . .I would. . .question the advisability of using the term Mafia, a strictly Sicilian organization, in the provisions of the bill as a synonym for organized crime. . . .''

Organized crime in its totality is composed of numerous diverse units scattered throughout the length and breadth of the land. Even when loose alliances are formed, each organized crime group insists upon retaining its autonomy and each boss jealously guards his sovereignty over his domain. It is unrealistic to assume that the modern underworld organization can be reduced to one powerful syndicate with a government of its own that exercises absolute power over organized crime throughout the nation. Some underworld leaders are more prestigious than others, to be sure, but it is a certitude that no single gangland boss occupies the position of top man or boss of organized crime in the United States.

Although there is no single syndicate that controls the underworld in America, the principles that govern organized crime are everywhere the same.

Organized crime groups are conspiratorial in character. Their major goals are economic—profits. They attempt to perpetuate their existence through violence or threat of violence and by making arrangements for immunity by corrupting officials. As a result, criminal-political alliances are formed that enable the underworld to exert a tremendous influence on government in general and on the administration of justice in particular.

In 1970 Attorney General William C. Sennett, chairman of the Pennsylvania Crime Commission, submitted the commission's *Report on Organized Crime* to the governor. Included in the report was a study of ten cases involving criminal offenses, deportation hearings, and extradition proceedings against organized crime leaders. In each case, public officials came to the front as witnesses in behalf of the racketeers. The witnesses included a mayor and a tax collector of a Pennsylvania town, police officers and the chiefs of police of two other towns, a county commissioner, a Philadelphia county court president, a common pleas court judge, several Philadelphia county court judges, Philadelphia city councilmen, a former city solicitor, a representative of the Pennsylvania General Assembly, and a justice of the Pennsylvania Supreme Court. The report also related that during a hearing for the reduction of a sentence that had been imposed on a notorious organized crime figure, "numerous prominent political leaders and public officials appeared." All represented the racketeer as a law-abiding citizen with a reputation for honesty, even though he had a criminal record with fifteen arrests, of which three were for murder. The so-called law-abiding citizen was also a partner of notorious organized crime bosses in Reading, Pennsylvania, and in New York City. His criminal records had mysteriously disappeared from four police departments and a county Bureau of Criminal Identification. Several organized crime characters had been the beneficiaries of pardons from Pennsylvania governors. "The only logical conclusion. . . ," said the report, "is that organized criminals in Pennsylvania have benefited from the method of administering criminal justice. Whether through bribery, political influence, or subtle manipulation of its processes, the criminal justice system has operated more to the advantage of the racketeer than for justice and the safety of society."[23]

Conditions described in the Pennsylvania Crime Commission report are typical of those in many sections of the country. In numerous places a well-organized underworld has exercised an insidious influence over political leaders, city officials, the police, prosecutors, and the judiciary. In some instances the same basic criminal organization has flourished in a city continuously for nearly a half century. But its subversive effect on the entire web of government is what makes organized crime one of America's greatest problems today.

APPENDICES

Appendix 1

ORIGIN AND DEVELOPMENT OF THE MAFIA

The term most commonly associated with organized crime in the United States is *Mafia*. A public opinion poll conducted by Louis Harris in 1971 revealed, by a decisive seventy-eight to seventeen percent, that a majority of Americans believe "there is a secret organization engaged in organized crime in this country which is called the Mafia." Although the Mafia is restricted exclusively to Sicilians, the same public opinion poll disclosed that a majority of Americans, by a margin of fifty-seven to twenty-four percent, denied an ethnic association with those who run the Mafia organization.[1] The results of this public opinion poll emphasize the confusion that exists in the mind of the average citizen regarding the Mafia.

The Mafia originated in Sicily and has no valid application to any people other than Sicilians. Giovanni Schiavo, author of numerous volumes on Italians in America and a student of the Mafia, has written: "If there is a Mafia, then its members must be perforce nothing but Sicilians, exclusively Sicilians. . . .If, on the other hand, the so-called Mafia is not confined to Sicilians. . .then it is not a Mafia. Call it what you may, 'mob,' 'syndicate,' or 'Bird Watchers' Society'. . .but do not call it Mafia."[2]

Almost daily, newspaper stories, as well as numerous magazine articles and books, deal with the Mafia, without regard to its real meaning or character. Countless officials, including reputed authorities on organized crime, have loosely used the term, thus adding to general misunderstanding.

In 1963 federal prisoner Joseph Valachi appeared before a U.S. Senate subcommittee and gave his celebrated testimony regarding an underworld organization which he called the Cosa Nostra. The name Cosa Nostra, as an organization, was unheard of before Valachi's revelations. Although membership is limited to Italians, it is not restricted to Sicilians. And, said Valachi, members of Cosa Nostra never referred to their organization as the Mafia. Appearing before the same subcommittee was the late Robert F. Kennedy, then attorney general of the United States. When asked about the organization described by Valachi, Attorney General Kennedy replied, "It is Mafia. It is Cosa Nostra. There are other names for it, but it all refers to the same operation."[3] Such statements are inaccurate, and instead of helping to clarify merely add to the haziness and confusion that surround the concept of the Mafia.

Historically, the origin of the term *Mafia* is unknown. It did not appear in any Sicilian dictionary before 1868. One often-repeated legend traces the origin of the term *Mafia* to the Sicilian Vespers, which took place in 1282 as a result of the unpopularity of the French government. According to this legend, as the vespers were being rung on March 30, 1282, a girl and her lover had gone to the church to be married. The young man left his bride-to-be while he went to get the priest. During his absence a drunken French sergeant, Pierre Drouet, assaulted the girl. As she struggled to extricate herself from his grasp, she tripped and fell, crushing her head against a sharp projection on the church wall. The incident caused thousands of angered Sicilians to shout "Morte Alla Francia Italia Anela," which means "Death to the French is Italy's cry!" The acronym Mafia became the name of a secret organization formed by the Sicilians to fight the French. Its password was Mafia, the initial letters in their embittered slogan.[4] This version is without historical foundation. In fact, the Sicilians did not even consider themselves Italians in 1282.

Some writers have indicated that possibly the word *Mafia* is derived from the quarries or pits in the Trapani district of Sicily called the Mafie.[5] Others have suggested that it comes from the name of an Arabic tribe, Ma-Afir, which settled in Palermo in ancient times. Still others have suggested that the word may have come from the Tuscan *Maffia*, a synonym for misery and distress.

The foremost authority on Sicilian folklore, Giuseppe Pitre, states that the word *Mafia* was virtually unknown before 1860. However, in Il Borgo, a district of Palermo, the word implied beauty, grace, and excellence. An object of superior quality was described as *Mafiusa*. In 1863 a playwright of Palermo, Giuseppe Rizzoto, wrote a two-act melodrama depicting aspects of life in the great prison at Palermo. Originally the play was called *I Mafiusi della Vicaria (The Heroes of the Penitentiary)*. Subsequently, two acts were added to the play, and under the title *I Mafiusi* it was performed about three thousand times over a thirty-year period. The names and deeds of I Mafiusi in the Palermo prison became widely known and the words *Mafia* and *Mafioso* naturally found their way into the common speech of the people.[6] This version appears to be the most plausible to explain the origin and development of the term *Mafia* as a designation of a certain type of Sicilian criminal. However, this is mere speculation.

Luigi Barzini, the noted Italian author and onetime member of Parliament, states that "nobody really knows what the word means, where it came from, where the thing originated. . . ." Sicilians, he said, prefer to allude to the Mafia as the *onorata societa* ("honored society") and its members are known as *gli amici*, ("the friends,") or *gli amici degli amici*, ("the friends of friends.").[7]

Although it is impossible to determine the origin of the term *Mafia*, or its meaning, there is almost complete agreement as to *why* it developed. The Honored Society is the product of centuries of oppression of an impoverished people by a succession of invaders who were interested only in exploiting the island.

Centuries before Christendom, the Phoenicians settled the west coast of Sicily in what is now the province of Palermo. The Carthaginians founded the present area of Trapani. Between the eighth and sixth centuries B.C., the Greeks located on the east and southeast coasts of Sicily and established Syracuse, Catania, and Zancle (now Messina), Acragas (which became Agrigento), and other cities. A century of strife between the Greeks and Carthaginians gave way to warfare between the Romans and Carthaginians culminating in the First Punic War (264–241 B.C.). By the end of the First Punic War all of Sicily except Syracuse and a few other cities had passed into Roman hands. Syracuse was taken and sacked about 212 B.C.

The Romans, now in control of Sicily, milked its resources dry. They formed huge landed estates that were in the hands of the rich and tilled by serfs. The landed estates established a pattern that has prevailed until modern times and that has been a major economic evil in the island ever since. The serfs on the estates were so ill treated that they engaged in two major revolts, the first in 135–132 B.C. and the second in 104–100 B.C. These uprisings were cruelly and ruthlessly suppressed by the Romans, who virtually devastated the countryside.

Following the barbarian invasion, Sicily passed from the Vandals to the Goths, and in A.D. 535 to the Byzantines. In the ninth century Sicily fell to the Arabs, who were later displaced by the Norman Conquest (1061–91). The Norman army and its leaders ruled over the people on the island, who were of mixed origins—Sicilian, Phoenician, Carthaginian, and Arab.

In 1266 Pope Clement IV crowned Charles I (Charles of Anjou) king of Sicily and Naples. Because of the unpopularity of the French rule, an insurrection broke out on Easter Monday,

1282. As the revolt spread throughout the island, most of the French were massacred. The Sicilians chose Peter III of Aragon as king.

Following a brief rule by the House of Aragon, the House of Hapsburg acceded to the Spanish throne. Spanish governors were dispatched to Sicily. Corruption flourished and the island passed into the hands of a few powerful nobles and ecclesiastics.

In 1713 the Peace of Utrecht gave Sicily to Savoy and seven years later (1720), under the terms of the Treaty of Hague, Sicily passed into the control of Austria. The Austrian rule was bitterly detested in Sicily. Austrian domination of the island ended during the War of Polish Succession, when both Sicily and Naples were placed under the rule of the Spanish Bourbon prince, Don Carlos (later Charles III of Spain). The Sicilian nobles resisted the centralizing policies of the Bourbons and welcomed British intervention in 1811. Feudal privileges were formally renounced in 1812 but, because of deeply embedded traditions, neither the social nor the economic conditions were altered very much.

Over Sicilian protests, Naples and Sicily were merged in 1816 and Ferdinand I, son of Charles III of Spain, proclaimed himself king of the Two Sicilies. The reactionary policies of his reign led to a Sicilian revolt in 1820. When the regime of Ferdinand I ended in 1825, he was succeeded by his son, Francis I, who reigned until 1830. The son of Francis I, Ferdinand II, ruled from 1830 until 1859, when he was succeeded by Francis II, son of Ferdinand II. Francis II was the last king of the Two Sicilies. All of the regimes were highly oppressive and corrupt.

The Bourbons thus maintained their long rule over Sicily until 1860. For public security, the island depended upon the services of hired contractors. The feudal landowners, to safeguard their interests, employed strong-arm men to protect themselves and their estates.

In 1860, with the tacit consent of Victor Emmanuel II, Giuseppe Garibaldi embarked on his successful conquest of the Two Sicilies. In 1861 Victor Emmanuel II was proclaimed king of a united Italy but the plight of the Sicilians, many of whom had come to the aid of Garibaldi, remained much the same. The national government in Rome cast covetous eyes on Sicily, seeing it as an opportunity for ruthless exploitation. Oppressive measures against the island were as severe as those under the Bourbon kings.

A century later archaeologist Vincenzo Tusa observed: "The history of Sicily as a whole, and of Palermo in particular, is one long story of occupation, oppression, favoritism, patronage, and clientship. . . .there has never been any government in Sicily that was genuinely concerned with the good of the citizens: they have always been regarded as a more or less amorphous mass to be exploited in the interests of the various rulers who at various times have controlled the destiny of the island. . . .In this situation it is only natural. . .that the citizen, despairing of getting any help from his fellow man, should always have acted on his own behalf, trying to work on his own, and defending himself from injustice. . . ."[8]

Having endured the heavy hand of oppression for centuries, Sicilians understandably have never developed a patriotism. Instead, there had always been a deep-seated mistrust of government at all levels. Personal honor must be maintained or avenged personally without recourse to the authorities. Loyalties are confined to family and friends. Blood relationships are of primary importance. As a result a Sicilian culture developed in which the family reigned supreme, a supremacy that cannot be challenged by the state or the church. And in this context the Mafia emerged, one of many secret societies formed on the island and in southern Italy.

Under the Italian constitution of 1947, Sicily is an autonomous region with Palermo as capital. It is divided into the provinces of Palermo, Agrigento, Caltanissetta, Catania, Enna, Messina, Ragusa, Syracuse, and Trapani, each province named after its chief city. The Mafia has always been confined to the western provinces of Palermo, Trapani, and Agrigento, and to the province of Caltanissetta. It never penetrated or became influential in the island's eastern provinces.

The pattern of huge landed estates, called latifundia, established by the Roman invasion of Sicily, remained almost unchanged under the domination of the island by the Goths, Byzantines, and Arabs. In the center of the latifundium was a farmhouse. Nearby were large fortified storehouses surrounded by the humble dwellings of the owner's guards and serfs, who were required to live on the estate throughout the year. During the peak seasons of planting, plowing, and harvesting of crops, the services of a large number of additional laborers were required. Some of these seasonal workers were housed in wattle and daub shacks on the estate, but most of them spent the night in nearby villages and towns, walking to and from the estate each day.

With the arrival of the Normans the territory of Sicily was divided into seigniories, patterned after the feudal system of France. As a practical matter feudalism prevailed almost without interruption from the Norman invasion until a little over a century ago. A succession of uprisings by peasants and serfs made little impact on the feudal system, still deeply rooted in the island's economic and social structure at the time of Giuseppe Garibaldi's conquest of Sicily in 1860.

A baron, who resided in a coastal town such as Palermo, was given one or more feudi in the interior. Each feudal estate, which contained not less than five thousand acres, corresponded with the latifundium and serf economy that existed previously. The baron had unlimited power over his feudi. Living in the farmhouse on the latifundium were the baron's overseer and armed guards, who had delegated to them the absolute power of their lord in administering and protecting the estate.[9]

At least until after 1812 there were no public institutions or governmental authorities. The rule of the baron, through his henchmen, was absolute. From the earliest times, the landowners established small private armies, *compagnie d'armi,* to protect their estates. These companies of armed guards were recruited from the criminal classes. An English scientist, Patrick Brydone, who visited Sicily in 1770 described these private gudards employed by the nobility as "the most daring, and most hardened villains, perhaps, that are to be met with upon earth, who, in any other country, would have been broken upon the wheel, or hung in chains, but are here publicly protected and universally feared and respected."[10]

Since the barons who owned the feudi were far away in Palermo, or in some instances in Naples, the compagnie d'armi could function quite largely as they pleased. In payment for their services, the landowner gave the compagnie d'armi a share of the crops and conveniently overlooked the crimes they committed. Frequently they came to an agreement with other outlaws which permitted these desperadoes to rob and kill with impunity as long as their crimes were committed beyond the limits of the estate the armed guards were hired to protect. Such arrangements were satisfactory to the landowner, who saw no reason to become perturbed if it was his neighbor's cattle that were being stolen or crops destroyed.[11] Occasionally, struggles for political power between two or more barons broke out and they spilled over into the feudi as rival compagnie d'armi battled one another.

The origin of the Mafia is traceable to these small private armies that were employed for centuries by landowners to protect their estates from marauding bandits.[12] Since there were no public authorities or legal machinery for the administration of justice, the functions of the police, prosecutors, and courts were handled by the compagnie d'armi. The so-called justice meted out by the armed guards was harsh, cruel, and primitive—but certain. If someone wronged a woman, committed a robbery, or theft, the compagnie d'armi would hunt down the offender and kill him on the spot. The bands of armed guards themselves engaged in cattle rustling, extortion, and kidnapping. Other bands were engaging in the same offenses and rivalry between the various compagnie d'armi resulted in many murders.

In some respects the compagnie d'armi were not totally dissimilar to the vigilantes who have been immortalized in the folklore of the early American western frontier. The absence of government institutions and duly constituted authorities created a vacuum in which crime and disorder flourished with impunity. Into this breach stepped the vigilantes. In some instances the ranks of the vigilantes included lawless elements that were little, if any, better than the offenders they sought and punished. Nevertheless, they meted out their own brand of justice. It was frequently harsh and uncivilized but it was always certain and final. As the western communities achieved stability and government institutions gained the confidence of the people, the vigilantes gradually disappeared. In Sicily, however, the people underwent centuries of oppression. Total distrust of government remained and the compagnie d'armi, representing private interests, the landowners, became deeply entrenched as the protectors of many communities and the administrators of their type of justice.

The entire economic and social system in Sicily was one of tyranny imposed through violence and ruthless exploitation. It bred complete disrespect for any authority as well as mistrust of neighbor. It instilled the need to adopt and follow a code of silence; to obtain justice or vengeance by one's own hand—Omerta.

The sad lot of the people was not always accepted with abject docility. Numerous servile insurrections arose which were usually suppressed with harshness and cruelty. Nevertheless, they were credited with having brought about the formal renunciation of feudal privileges and the elimination of serfdom in 1812 and the abolishment of the compagnie d'armi by royal decree in 1837. Eleven years later, in 1848, a revolt by peasants and a general insurrection caused the government to institute La Guardia Nationale. During this period, local governmental institutions, although weak and ineffective, were established and there developed a system of land tenancy.

Overall, however, the so-called reforms did not basically alter the economic and social structure of the island. The barons who owned the latifundia in the interior still lived in Palermo. Running the latifundium for the baron was his tenant, the *gabellotto*. The gabellotto, who rented the whole feudo, was required to guarantee an income to the absentee owner. Sometimes the gabellotto sublet part of the land he had rented and was able to impose oppressive dues. Because of the ineffectiveness of local governmental institutions, the protection of the estate, its crops, buildings, and cattle, as well as the security of the gabellotto, his family, and stewards, was placed in the hands of private guards known as *campieri*. The campieri, like the compagnie d'armi before them, were recruited from bandits and criminals. They were accustomed to violence and were expert in its use to accomplish their ends or to impose their will.

The gabellotto and his campieri have been described by one observer as "the industry of violence."[13] The peasant had to find work on the feudo to survive. Through violence and fear of violence he was kept in a state of economic subjection. The gabellotto, aided by his campieri, also exacted tribute for protection from small landowners in his locality who were not under his tenancy. If a small landowner did not see fit to make protection payments, he soon discovered that his cattle were being killed or stolen, his crops destroyed, his vineyards slashed, and the lives of himself and members of his family threatened with kidnapping or murder.

The baron landlord was also the target of the gabellotto's criminal machinations. To keep him away from his latifundium, the landlord was sent dire threats or attempts were made to kidnap or murder him. Invariably the baron turned to the gabellotto for protection. In the end, the landlord would find it necessary to renounce the dues coming to him for the rental of the estate. Since he could get no income from the latifundium, he was forced to sell it. And the only buyer for the estate at an absurdly low price was the gabellotto. In this fashion, one gabellotto after another replaced the nobility as the owners of the landed estates in Sicily.[14]

With the replacement of the nobility by the gabellotto as the landed bourgeoisie in Sicily, the first stage in the development of the Mafia was completed. The gabellotto, his campieri, and other henchmen formed the nucleus of an efficient organization. Such groups, with the gabellotto as boss, increasingly took the place of all legitimate authority.

The second stage in the development of the Mafia occurred when these groups began to turn their attention to every aspect of rural life that could be exploited for blackmail. And it was this second stage that led to the real organization of crime and violence as an industry controlled by groups eventually known as the Mafia. Until recent times, most of the more powerful Mafia leaders in Sicily launched their careers in the organized crime industry as a gabellotto.

With the unification of Italy, following Garibaldi's Sicilian conquest in 1860, came universal suffrage. Conditions were thus created that were to give the Mafiosi greater influence and power than ever. Before unification and universal suffrage, the gabellotti and campieri on the various latifondo were able to engage in violence and achieve their ends through blackmail, extortion, and murder with very little to fear from weak, ineffective, and practically nonexistent governmental institutions. After unification the organizations of gabellotti and campieri were able to control elections and place in office men friendly to them, men who would give legal protection to their criminal activities and punish their rivals and enemies. The gabellotti became the intermediaries between the government and the peasants. Favors would be granted or denied according to the will of the gabellotti. The role of the gabellotti as intermediaries was made easy by virtue of the Sicilian's innate mistrust of government, a mistrust based on centuries of governmental abuse and exploitation. With the alliance among the gabellotti, the campieri and their henchmen, and politics (government), the Mafia emerged as organized crime in its most powerful, insidious, and real sense.

The alliance between the Mafia and politics was not a phenomenon peculiar to western Sicily, however. The alliance between crime and politics has always been a basic element of organized crime. Before the unification of Italy in 1861—thus before the wedlock of the Mafia and politics in Sicily—organized crime flourished in a number of American cities, notably New York City and Chicago. And these powerful organized crime groups, together with their political allies, were non-Sicilian and non-Italian. To attribute the origin and development of organized crime in the United States to the Sicilian Mafia, as some observers have suggested, is a myth, and any objective study of history will explode it.

After Sicily became a part of Italy in 1861, the lot of the average citizen of the island was little better than before. The Italian central government neglected the island, and its social and economic problems were given little if any attention. The Italian government resorted to savage repressive measures against any who resisted. In 1866 serious revolts broke out and mobs ran wild for seven days in Palermo and nearby towns as well as in the province of Trapani. By this time, and particularly after 1874, the Mafia as a political phenomenon was in full swing, having established itself as an invisible government.[15]

Before long, in Palermo, the capital of Sicily for centuries and the center of political and economic life, Mafiosi engaged in racketeering and blackmail against commercial enterprises. However, the Mafia was confined largely to the rural areas of Sicily, where its principal targets were landowners and tenants. The penalties for failing to comply with a Mafioso's extortionary demands were burning of crops, theft of cattle, slashing of grapevines, destruction of fruit or olive trees, and frequently kidnapping and murder.

As late as 1900, two thirds of all landlords in Sicily were absentees who spent their time reveling in the pleasures of Rome or other European cities while management of their estates was placed in the hands of their representatives.[16] Many were gabellotti with Mafia affiliation. Almost all fell under Mafia domination. A peasant farmer who wished to enter into an agreement to cultivate certain land on a sharecropping basis was required to have his contract approved by a Mafia chief. And, of course, the Mafia chief was promised a fixed percentage of the sharecropper's income from the land. Any tenant or landowner who refused to accept guardianship of his crops by the Mafia or had the temerity to report any attempted blackmail or extortion to the police would be subjected to the usual reprisals.

The Mafia resorted to savage and barbaric methods to maintain discipline in its role of affording protection to its clients. If a man under the guardianship of the Mafia found on his premises a corpse with his hand cut off, that indicated the deceased was a thief. If the genitals of a corpse had been cut off and stuffed in his mouth, it was a sign that the murdered man had offended the woman of a Mafia client. If a tongue was cut off, that man had witnessed a crime and had not followed the strict code of Omerta.[17] Under the code of Omerta, demanded by the Mafia, a person must exhibit his manliness by refusing to recognize legal power or authority, by taking direct action to avenge any wrong, and by maintaining complete silence.

In the rural districts key figures in the Mafia's industry of crime and violence were the campieri, the watchmen or guards of the landed estates. The latifondi were usually in isolated and unprotected areas, and the services of the campieri were essential to their protection. But all landowners or tenants were required to employ only campieri designated by Mafiosi. By this means the Mafia found remunerative employment for many of its most vicious members. It could distribute them among the latifondi throughout western Sicily and thus keep the landed interests in complete subjugation. As a result, an organization was created enabling the Mafia to maintain absolute control over crime in the rural areas. Under this system, dozens of wagonloads of stolen grain or thousands of stolen cattle could be moved from place to place with complete assurance that the thieves would not be caught or the property recovered. Such loot could even be transported from one province to another, across closed frontiers, as long as a Mafia campiere had given his orders and approval. The absence of roads and the lack of communication facilities also greatly aided the Mafia in its control of crime in the rural areas of western Sicily.

Constantly roaming around the solitary and somewhat boundless tracts of the latifondi were various criminals, fugitives who were in flight to prevent arrest on warrants which had been issued for them (*latitanti*) and others who had gone into hiding for offenses they had committed but with which they had not yet been identified. These fugitives were in constant touch with the campieri, who gave them full protection as long as they were in the good graces of the Mafia. Many bandits roaming the countryside were given aid by the campieri. If the outlaw had Mafia affiliation, a campiere would offer him protection as long as he committed his crimes outside the campiere's domain. An outlaw or thief working on his own without Mafia backing would be shot instantly.[18]

The Mafia was still primarily rural in scope when the big exodus of Sicilians and southern Italians to the United States began in the late 1800s. Particularly after 1870, hordes of Sicilians and southern Italians left their native land to settle in American cities where they filled the need for cheap labor. Many were men who left their families behind expecting to return to Sicily after they had made their fortunes in the New World. Overwhelmingly, they were peasants, illiterate day laborers. Before coming to the United States many had seldom strayed beyond the limits of the villages in which they had been born and reared.

Upon arriving in the United States, they settled in communities composed of inhabitants of the same ethnic background—Little Italies. As late as 1930, roughly seventy-five percent of the Italian-American population lived in the Little Italy sections in urban centers of six Middle Atlantic and northeastern states. Within the Italian communities, the immigrants tended to congregate with people who had originated from the same locality in their native land. At times, an entire street was made up of persons who had hailed from the same Sicilian province. Another street was inhabited solely by Neapolitans. All brought with them the culture of the Old World, and this culture, even in the United States, was not appreciably diluted by exposure to the outside. They continued to live in surroundings similar to those they had left behind. As was observed by a distinguished sociologist in Chicago, the Little Sicily section of that city remained until World War I "relatively untouched by American custom, a transplantation of Sicilian village life into the heart of a hurrying American city." It was the same in Little Sicilies elsewhere in the United States.

Loyalties were based on family ties. As in the past, they viewed all government with hostility and were baffled by U.S. laws and customs. Crimes of violence committed in the Italian communities were not looked upon as offenses against the state. They were regarded as personal crimes demanding personal vengeance or at times retaliation by a form of spontaneous group action. The innate hatred that existed between Sicilians and Neapolitans in the Old World continued to manifest itself in American Little Italies by frequently erupting into blood feuds.[19]

The murders, extortion plots, and vendettas that took place in the Italian communities were not the product of organized crime. They were crimes largely committed by Italians against Italians. The illiterate peasants frequently involved in such offenses were hardly capable of serving in the United States as a vanguard of a sophisticated international conspiracy. Yet, when crimes of violence were committed in the Little Italy sections of American cities, the belief was often expressed that the dreaded Mafia had been transplanted to this country. Actually, it was a culture, not an organization, that had been transplanted.

In New Orleans, a city noted for political and police corruption throughout much of its history, Italians controlled the business of loading and unloading ships transporting fruit from South and Central America. Two factions of Italians became engaged in a bitter fight to monopolize this business on the docks. A vendetta broke out and there were several shootings. The leadership of one faction had the friendship and backing of New Orleans Chief of Police David C. Hennessy. While the vendetta between the rival Italian factions was raging, Hennessy was shot and killed. Several Italians were arrested and charged with Hennessy's murder. When the jury failed to convict any of the men brought to trial, a mob stormed the parish prison on March 14, 1891, and murdered eleven Italians.

It was widely believed that the Mafia was responsible for the chief's murder and numerous citizens as well as segments of the American press condoned the mob action. Even today the 1891 incident is frequently cited as proof that the Mafia had become established in the United States.

This commonly held version loses some of its validity when all of the facts are considered. The central figure in the drama was the New Orleans chief of police, David C. Hennessy. Some writers have described Hennessy as a popular and respected chief, others have labeled him capable and courageous.[20] However, New Orleans in 1891, as in many other periods of its history, was steeped in political and police corruption. And the credentials of Chief Hennessy were less than impeccable.

Born on March 4, 1857, Hennessy was thirty-three years old at the time of his murder. His father, also a policeman, had been murdered in a New Orleans coffeehouse when the chief was a young lad. Feuding among New Orleans policemen over the spoils and power was not uncommon. David C. Hennessy was appointed chief of police by Mayor Joseph Shakespeare in 1888. Before his elevation to the chief's post, he had worked for a time as an aid (detective) and was teamed with his cousin, Mike Hennessy, a former cab driver, who was also a detective. Bitter enmity broke out between the Hennessys and the chief of aids (detectives), Thomas Devereaux. On October 31, 1881, when David and Mike Hennessy met Devereaux on a New Orleans street, gunplay erupted. Chief of Detectives Devereaux was killed and Mike Hennessy wounded. Both David and Mike Hennessy were charged with the killing. They pleaded self-defense and were acquitted. However, they were dismissed from the police department and David was affiliated with a private harbor protection agency when Mayor Shakespeare appointed him chief of police. Subsequently, Mike Hennessy was murdered on September 29, 1886, in Houston, reputedly by a man dispatched from New Orleans for the express purpose of killing him.

For several years three brothers, George, Joseph, and Peter Provenzano, had a monopoly of the unloading of fruit ships that arrived in New Orleans from South and Central America. They had become rich and influential politically. They were also friends of Chief of Police

Hennessy. In fact, Chief Hennessy and George Provenzano frequented the Red Light Club, a place that featured wide-open gambling and prostitution. And rumor had it that they may have been partners in a joint business venture.

The unloading of fruit ships in New Orleans was sufficiently lucrative that a rival faction headed by Charles and Tony Matranga cast covetous eyes on the Provenzano monopoly. Tony Matranga operated a disreputable saloon and there were allegations that Charles Matranga dominated the Mafia in New Orleans. Eventually the Matranga group succeeded in taking over the business of unloading the fruit ships and the Provenzanos were ordered off the docks. About the time that David C. Hennessy was appointed chief of police in New Orleans a vendetta was raging between the Provenzano and Matranga factions.

On May 6, 1890, Tony Matranga and two of his men were ambushed and wounded on a New Orleans street. The Matrangas, it is reported, appealed to the authorities. If the Matrangas were leaders of the Mafia, as alleged, it would appear that their pleas to officials for action against their enemies would have violated the strict code of Omerta, to which all Mafiosi are bound. At any rate, Joe and Peter Provenzano, as well as three other men of their faction, were arrested. At the end of their trial on July 15, 1890, the Provenzanos were found guilty but on August 9, 1890, the judge ordered a new trial because he did not believe the identifications were conclusive.

Following several delays, the trial of the Provenzano brothers and their allies was set for October 17, 1890. Chief Hennessy, friend of the Provenzanos, publicly declared that he intended to give testimony against the Matrangas at the trial. He indicated that he would show the connections of the Matranga gang with the Mafia in New Orleans and its responsibility for a number of fatal shootings in the city. In other words, the chief admittedly was going to aid the defendants, the Provenzanos, in gaining an acquittal on the charges that they had ambushed and shot members of the Matranga gang.

On October 15, 1890, just two days before the trial was to begin, Chief Hennessy left his office in the Central Police Station and headed home. He was accompanied by Captain William J. O'Connor of the Boylan Protective Police, a private agency. Shortly after O'Connor left Chief Hennessy on a New Orleans street, he heard a burst of shotgun fire. He ran back to the scene of the shooting and asked Hennessy who shot him. Replied Chief Hennessy, "Dagos." Hennessy was rushed to a hospital where he died the following morning.

The murder of the chief of police outraged the citizens of New Orleans. On October 18, 1890, Mayor Joseph Shakespeare appointed a Committee of Fifty citizens to assist the authorities in collecting evidence to convict those responsible for the crime. Fourteen men were subsequently indicted and on February 16, 1891, nine men were placed on trial for Chief Hennessy's murder. On March 13, 1891, the jury found six of the nine men not guilty and could not come to an agreement on the remaining three defendants. Hence a mistrial was declared as to them. Incensed because the jury had not found anyone guilty of Chief Hennessy's murder, a mob was formed on March 14, 1891. Leaders of the mob stated that since justice could not be obtained in the courts, the citizens would have to take action themselves. Led by a politician, W.S. Parkerson, the angry citizens marched on the parish prison. Meeting no resistance, about twenty men entered the prison and shot to death ten Italian prisoners. Another wounded Italian was given to the mob outside the prison walls. A rope was placed around his neck and as he was pulled up to the cross bars, numerous men took aim and fired bullets into his body. The dead body dangled in midair for several hours before it was removed.

The killing of the eleven by mob action was approved by many citizens as a necessary step to wipe out the dreaded Mafia. Parkerson, who led the mob to the prison, received congratulatory messages from all sections of the country. The *New York Times,* which deplored the "lawless and uncivilized" mob action, nevertheless condemned the "sneaking and cowardly Sicilians" who had transported their "oath-bound societies" to this country.

The *Times* suggested that there would be greater respect for life and property in New Orleans as a result of the lynchings.

A mass meeting of Italians held in the Cooper Union in New York City denounced the New Orleans lynchings. The Italian government minister in Washington, Baron Fava, was recalled and the prime minister of Italy, Antonio DiRudini, demanded an indemnity as well as the prosecution of the mob leaders. At the urging of President Benjamin Harrison, Congress awarded $25,000 to the families of the three men killed who were citizens of Italy. The families of the remaining eight Italians killed by the mob received no compensation.[21]

The New Orleans affair is still cited frequently as proof that the Honored Society of Sicily had by then established branches in the United States. However, the U.S. attorney in his official report to the attorney general stated that "he had been unable to obtain any direct evidence connecting these persons with the Mafia or any other association of a similar character in the city." Although the public generally believed that such an association existed, the U.S. attorney asserted that only George and Joseph Provenzano, the bitter enemies of the Matranga faction, had been willing to "divulge the truth in an affidavit."[22]

The Italian consul was quoted in an interview in the *Eco d'Italia* on March 19, 1891, that the murder of Hennessy "could be attributed to diverse causes which were not brought out at the trial." These motives were known to the authorities, he said. Admittedly, Chief Hennessy had many enemies. The foreman of the jury at the murder trial reportedly had remarked before he was called for jury duty that the killing of Chief Hennessy was no worse then the earlier killing of Chief of Detectives Thomas Devereaux by David and Mike Hennessy in 1881.[23]

In the *Weekly Post,* New York, March 18, 1891, a former New Orleans police lieutenant, J.H. Moore, stated that the murder of Chief Hennessy stemmed from "an old feud between the detectives of the city, which had its foundation. . .in the famous Whiskey Ring and Sugar Ring excitement" twenty years earlier. It was the same bitter fight in the department, he asserted, that was the cause of the killing of Chief Hennessy's father, also a policeman, in 1872. He had no doubt, he said, that Chief Hennessy's murder resulted from this old detective feud, which had been a main issue in local politics for years and which was simply a quarrel over the spoils.[24]

The New Orleans lynching took place during the same era that the Black Hand flourished in many Italian communities in the United States. A threatening letter bearing the symbol of a Black Hand would be sent to a victim demanding money. Failure to meet the payoff terms in the letter would result in violence, often murder.

A major center of Black Hand operations in the United States at the turn of this century was New York City. Highly successful in coping with the Black Hand as well as other offenses committed by Sicilian and Italian criminals in New York was an Italo-American police detective, Lieutenant Joseph Petrosino. Born in Padula, in the province of Salerno, Italy, in 1860, Petrosino made an outstanding record in apprehending Italian criminals who were wanted in their native land. On September 30, 1908, the Italian consul general in New York City and the government of Italy presented gold watches to Joseph Petrosino and another Italian detective, Anthony Vachris, for "fearless and active work in the detection and arrest of fugitives from Italian justice."[25]

On February 19, 1909, Theodore Bingham, New York City commissioner of police, announced that he had established a secret-service branch that was to be used to crush the Black Hand and anarchists in the city. These men had been recruited outside the police department and were to work independently of the force. Placed in charge of this special squad was a New York City Police Department detective, Lieutenant Joseph Petrosino. The announcement was reported in a *New York Herald* editorial on February 20, 1909, which also advised that "as a first step in the undertaking Lieutenant Petrosino has gone to Italy and Sicily, where he will procure important information about Italian criminals who have come to this country.'' The *New York Herald* also published a Paris edition of the paper at that time.[26]

Arriving in Rome on February 21, 1909, Lieutenant Petrosino had an audience with the Italian minister of the interior, who was briefed on the activities of Italian criminals in the United States. Based on his conference with Petrosino, the minister of the interior instructed Francisco Leonardi, director of the police force throughout Italy, to issue a strict order to prefects, underprefects, and mayors throughout the kingdom of Italy not to issue passports to Italian criminals and to take steps to prevent Italian criminals from immigrating to the United States. The minister of the interior also gave Petrosino a letter addressed to all the prefects in Sicily, Calabria, and Naples directing them to aid the New York detective as much as they could. These facts were reported to New York City Commissioner of Police Theodore Bingham in a letter written by Petrosino from Rome on February 24, 1909. Another letter was written by Petrosino to Commissioner Bingham on March 1, 1909, advising that he had arrived in Palermo, Sicily, on February , 1928, and had established an address at the Banca Commerciala in Palermo. Petrosino was registered, however, at Weinen's Hotel de France in Palermo under the name of Guglielmo DeSimoni.[27]

On March 12, 1909, Joseph Petrosino was standing near the base of the Garibaldi statue in the Piazza Marina waiting for a trolley when two men fired four shots at him. According to the report of the American consul in Palermo to the New York City police commissioner, three of the four shots found their mark. Bullets struck the right side of Petrosino's back, his left temple, and pierced both lungs. He died instantly. The New York policeman was unarmed at the time he was assassinated. However, a Smith & Wesson revolver was found in his valise in the hotel where he had been staying. A Belgian revolver was discovered near the scene of the shooting.[28]

A frequently repeated version of Joseph Petrosino's assassination relates that on the day the New York policeman's ship was to land in Palermo, Don Vito Cascio Ferro, then head of the Mafia in Sicily, was dining with a member of Parliament. The all-knowing Mafia, it was said, mysteriously knew of the day and exact hour that Petrosino would disembark at Palermo. At the appropriate time, Don Vito borrowed his host's carriage, and drove to the Piazza Marina where he waited outside the Courts of Justice near the port. When Petrosino, who had just disembarked, made an appearance, Don Vito Cascio Ferro fired one deadly shot that killed the New York City police officer instantly. Don Vito then got in the awaiting carriage and drove back to the house of the member of Parliament. Later, this man asserted that Don Vito had never left his home on the fateful day and thus could not have been at the Piazza Marina when Petrosino was assassinated.[29]

This dramatic version is at considerable variance with the official correspondence and reports in the files of the New York Police Department. Instead of having been assassinated just after he disembarked, Petrosino had been in Palermo for nearly two weeks—since Frbruary 28, 1909. And Petrosino's presence in Palermo was not the secret that has been indicated. As early as February 20, 1909, the *New York Herald* had announced his trip to Italy and Sicily. After arriving in Rome on February 21, 1909, Petrosino had conferred with the minister of the interior, who gave him a letter which directed all prefects in Sicily, Calabria, and Naples to give the New York police lieutenant so much aid as they could. Although Don Vito reputedly killed Petrosino by firing a single shot, the report of the American consul in Palermo stated that two men fired four shots and three of them found their target.

It is entirely possible, however, that Don Vito Cascio Ferro was responsible for the assassination of Petrosino. He was then the reputed head of the Honored Society in Sicily and was credited with having been the first to adapt the archaic ways of the rural-oriented Mafia to complex city life. Under his leadership, the Mafia controlled all crime and forced almost everyone to pay tribute. Nothing was overlooked. The Mafia even extracted its pittance from lovers who then followed the practice of walking back and forth under their sweetheart's windows as a means of expressing their ardor. The lovers were required to pay tribute to symbolize the price of a candle, which a Mafioso had held up to facilitate the lovemaking demonstration. Even beggars were forced to pay a percentage of their collections to the Mafia. Every phase of Sicilian life was subjected to Mafia exploitation. Obviously, when a rank outsider, Lieutenant Petrosino of New York, began sticking his nose into the Sicilian underworld, he was invading the domain of Don Vito Cascio Ferro, He was presenting a challenge that Don Vito could not overlook. At any rate, Don Vito reputedly once remarked that during his long career he had killed only one man, Lieutenant Petrosino. And since the lieutenant had threatened the Mafia as a whole, he had to be killed by the Mafia chief personally. Although established facts are at variance with the popular version, it is possible that Don Vito personally engineered Petrosino's murder and was one of the assassins who fired the fatal shots.[30]

Don Vito Cascio Ferro has been called the "greatest" head of the Mafia of all time and is credited with having brought the Honored Society to its highest state of perfection and power. He was born in Palermo on June 25, 1862. His father, an illiterate man, was a campiere of Baron Inglese at Bisacquino. Don Vito's criminal career started early. Between 1884 and 1893 Don Vito was charged with assault, bankruptcy, threats against public officials, arson, and attempted extortion. In 1899 he was accused of participating in the kidnapping of a baroness. However, Don Vito always escaped punishment for his crimes.

In 1900 Don Vito left Sicily temporarily and came to New York City, where he lived with a sister who ran a shop on 103d Street. The police believed that Don Vito was responsible for the murder of an Italian man in New York City. The victim was stabbed to death, after which his body was chopped into pieces and stuffed into a barrel. Don Vito fled New York City before the police could arrest him. After spending some time in New Orleans, Don Vito returned to Palermo.

Don Vito was a masterful organizer. Under his direction shopkeepers and businessmen of every type were required to make regular payments for protection. Those who refused to become a part of the system were ruined. Shops, homes, and crops were destroyed. Thus, criminals, under the direction of Don Vito, were able to gain domination over the business community.

Some writers have credited Don Vito with having established the system of protection payoffs in the United States. However, similar systems of extortion and regular payments for protection had been flourishing in New York City long before the arrival of Don Vito in America. It is within the realm of conjecture that Don Vito may have been impressed with the efficient system of extortion then prevailing in New York City. And his later operations in Sicily may have been influenced somewhat by what he had observed in New York City.

Don Vito was an impressive man physically—tall, lean, elegantly attired, and with a face adorned by a white flowing beard. He was almost illiterate but his manners were those of royalty. When he left Palermo and traveled in Sicily, mayors would meet him at the entrances of their villages, kiss his hand, and render homage due a king. Eventually, during the purge of the Mafia by Mussolini's fascist regime, Don Vito was arrested and thrown into prison where he died. For many years, those confined in the Ucciardone Prison considered it a great honor to be assigned to the cell in which Don Vito spent the last years of his life.[31]

By the beginning of the twentieth century in western Sicily, the Mafia was flourishing in all urban centers and in the rural areas. The Mafia in Palermo, the base of Don Vito's operations, was dominant. The Mafia had succeeded in infiltrating and controlling all spheres of the economy in western sicily—from sulfur mines to cemetery lots to rock-salt and building contracts.

During World War I (1915–18) the Mafia continued to grow in power and arrogance. It reaped huge profits by entering the black market in scarce foodstuffs. It sold horses and mules to the army at inflated prices. Many of the animals had been stolen; others were too old to be of much use to the armed services.[32]

In 1922, during the reign of King Victor Emmanuel III, Benito Mussolini led his followers on the noted march on Rome that led to his designation as prime minister of Italy. Before he started his drive against the Mafia in Sicily, the Honored Society had taken over virtually all of the functions of government on the island. The conditions that prevailed during the 1920s were described in an official report made by the king's procurator-general of the Sicilian Court of Appeal. The report asserted that "the Mafia dominated and controlled the whole social life, it had leaders and followers, it issued orders and decrees, it was to be found equally in big cities and in small centers, in factories and in rural districts, it regulated agricultural and urban rents, forced itself into every kind of business, and got its way by means of threats and intimidation or of penalties imposed by its leaders and put into execution by its officers. Its orders had the force of laws and its protection was a legal protection, more effective and secure than that which the state offers to its citizens. . . ."

The report indicated that owners of property and businessmen would pay sums of money to the Mafia as a form of insurance to make certain that their property would be protected from theft and their lives be free from attack. In some parts of Sicily, a man traveling by night or day was better protected "accompanied by two associates of the Mafia than by two or more members of the police force." The Mafia associations "of the small centers ordinarily exercised jurisdiction in them, or in the adjoining communes: those of the more important centers were in communication with one another and with those in adjacent provinces, and lent one another mutual assistance."

Sometimes the same commune had two Mafias, and that resulted in a bitter, violent struggle and "the mortal conflict would continue for generations till whole families had been extinguished. . .Murder was the expression of vengeance to be carried out at all costs. . . ." The vengeance was directed against the offending person or other members of the family and pursued in a savage and barbarous manner. The report of the king's procurator-general stated that victims were attacked "by surprise, by ambush, with stones, with razors, with scythes, with arms, by poisoning, by beheading, by strangling and then dishonoring the corpse, by soaking with paraffin and then setting alight, or by mutilation or horrible disfigurement as a mark of the terrifying power of the Mafia."[33]

The Honored Society controlled all crime that it directed and exploited. It was able to substitute itself for the government in relations between criminals and the people. Victims of crime fared better by appealing to the Mafia than by seeking the aid of the government. If persons robbed of valuable property reported their losses to the government, in only ten percent of the cases were they successful in recovering the stolen property; in fifteen percent the perpetrators of the crimes were discovered but no stolen property was located; and in seventy-five percent of the cases, the authorities found out nothing about the offenders or the property stolen. By ignoring the government and appealing to the Mafia, the stolen property was recovered in approximately ninety-five percent of the cases and was returned to the victims upon payment of a fee of about one third of its value. The advantage in ignoring the government and appealing to the Mafia was evident. The Mafia could offer robbed persons a ninety-five percent chance of recovery of the property by paying a fee of one third of its value as against a ninety percent chance of total loss by reporting the crimes to the authorities. And it frequently took years to conclude cases handled by the government, whereas the Mafia was able to complete its services within a matter of a few days.[34]

The insolent power of the Mafia in western Sicily was more than the prime minister of Italy, Benito Mussolini, could stomach. He saw in the Honored Society a threat to his fascist regime on the island. In 1924 Mussolini paid a visit to Sicily, where arrangements for his trip were made by his prefect of Palermo, Cesare Mori. The prefect had been sent to Sicily to establish fascist order there. Mori, an ex-police officer, was already noted for his excessive zeal and unscrupulous methods.

In Palermo, Mussolini was welcomed by Vittorio Emanuele Orlando, who had served as premier of Italy from 1917 to 1919. Orlando had risen to political heights mainly through the electoral support given him by his Mafia clients in Palermo and Partinico.

After touring Palermo, Mussolini visited the nearby town of Piana dei Greci (later renamed Piana degli Albanesi), which was under the control of a powerful Mafia chieftain, Don Ciccio Cuccia, the podesta or mayor of the town. Prefect Mori had ordered a strong escort of police mounted on motorcycles to accompany the dictator's car. Riding in Mussolini's automobile was Don Ciccio Cuccia. When in Piana dei Greci, Cuccia turned to Mussolini and remarked that there was no necessity to have so many policemen to guard him. Said Cuccia, "Your Excellency has nothing to fear when you are by my side." Then in a loud voice he issued a command to his men standing nearby, "Let no one dare touch a hair of Mussolini's head. He is my friend and the best man in the world!" The implication was clear: ultimate power in the land, power even to ensure the safety in Sicily of Prime Minister Mussolini, reposed in the hands of the Mafia. Inwardly, Mussolini was seething with anger. About two months later, Prefect Mori, on Mussolini's instructions, had Cuccia arrested and lodged in the Ucciardone Prison. The drive to stamp out the Mafia was now launched in earnest.[35]

The methods used by Mori were savage and brutal. The rights of those arrested were wantonly disregarded, confessions were extorted by torture, and many innocent people were thrown in jail. In some instances people were tried and convicted for crimes that never actually took place. In other instances two separate gangs were tried and convicted in different courts for the same offense. Although Prefect Mori resorted to means that were inexcusable in a civilized society, they were effective in destroying much of the Mafia's power. Only a few of the oldest and strongest Mafia groups survived, principally those engaged in the traditional activities of the gabellotti. Some Mafia chiefs were converted to fascism, whereas others were still in confinement when World War II broke out. Mussolini's attack on the Mafia left it weaker than at any other time in its history, and as an organization the Honored Society largely disappeared. The citizens, unaware of the true nature of Mori's methods, were grateful. For the first time, they enjoyed a genuine sense of security against criminal attack.[36]

The drive by Cesare Mori to smash the Mafia threw the Honored Society into a state of disarray. Even the most powerful Mafia leader of all time, Don Vito Cascio Ferro, had been sent to prison, where he eventually died. Nevertheless, some of the big fish were able to escape Prefect Mori's net and later emerge as influential Mafia chiefs, particularly after the invasion of Sicily by the Allied armed forces in World War II. This was certainly true of Calogero Vizzini, commonly known as Don Calo, of Villalba, a village in the Sicilian province of Caltanissetta. His career affords an insight into the genesis and development of a Mafia chief.

Calogero Vizzini was born on July 24, 1877, in Villalba, where he spent his entire lifetime of seventy-seven years. His father, Beniamino, was a laborer and small farmer and his mother, Turidda Scarlata, came from a family with influence in the church. Her brother became the titular bishop of Muro Lucano. Don Calo had two younger brothers, Giovanni and Salvatore, who also entered the church but through fascist government influence on the Vatican they fell into disfavor because of brother Calogero's misdeeds.[37]

Don Calo himself shunned all schooling and was illiterate. He first ran afoul of the law in 1898 on charges of instigating murder for robbery. Thereupon a pattern emerged that was to prevail in all his future clashes with authority—witnesses refused to testify and he was acquitted because of the absence of evidence. He became a member of a band of brigands led by the fearsome Paolo Vassalona. In 1903 Don Calo was arrested with other members of the gang and again won an acquittal because of lack of evidence.

Calogero Vizzini rented land and became a gabellotto active in Mafia affairs. When rent was not paid, the landowner was forced to sell his estate. No one, except the gabellotto, would dare to bid on the land and his offer would be absurdly low. At one such public auction Calogero Vizzini bought the Suora Marchesa feudo of some twelve hundred and fifty acres. Don Calo was the sole bidder.

At the outbreak of World War I, Don Calo spent only a few days in the armed service, then was exempted. Whereupon he embarked on a program designed to amass a fortune for himself and his cosca. (In the Mafia the nucleus is the family, each of which has a chief or boss. A group of families, belonging to the same district and pursuing identical or related activities, is a cosca.) Through the protection of Don Calo and his cosca, owners of good sound animals needed by the army were able to keep them without fear of having them requisitioned. Old and sick animals were sold at prices fixed by the Mafia. Also many sound animals were stolen and sold to the government. Don Calo and his cosca accumulated a great fortune in wartime transactions with the government.

Charges were filed against Calogero Vizzini and his confederates, and they were brought to trial before a military court at Palermo. At the trial, witnesses, including military judges, retracted previous statements they had made and no one could be persuaded to testify against the Mafia chief. Nine persons were sentenced on the spot for perjury and related offenses. Again, Don Calo was acquitted; his power and prestige had reached unprecedented heights throughout the province.[38]

Mussolini's fascist regime was deemed invincible in 1929 when charges of criminal conspiracy were brought against Calogero Vizzini. Nevertheless, he won an acquittal. As usual there was a lack of evidence at the trial. Don Calo exhibited a high degree of cunning, as well as duplicity, by moving warily between groups of fascists—some of whom were formerly Mafiosi who had expediently defected—and the gabellotti, who were still aspiring to positions of power. By the time World War II arrived, Don Calo controlled a close network of cosche.[39]

On July 10, 1943, the Allied armies landed on the south coast of Sicily to begin a conquest of the island. Important Italian-German defense lines were stationed in the area of Monte Cammarata near the towns of Villalba and Mussomeli. On July 14, 1943, an American airplane flew over Villalba. Fluttering from the cockpit of the plane was a yellowish gold pennant with a large black L in the middle. A nylon bag was dropped from the plane as it flew over the house of Monsignor Giovanni Vizzini, a priest and the brother of Don Calo. The bag was retrieved by Private Raniero Nuzzolese, who gave it to Angelo Riccioli, a lance corporal of the Carabinieri. On the following day, July 15, a plane flying the same yellowish gold pennant with a black L dropped another bag in front of the Vizzini family home. The words *zu Calo* (uncle Calo) were written on the bag, which was recovered by a servant of the Vizzini home, Carmelo Bartolomeo, who delivered it to Calogero Vizzini. The same evening, Don Calo directed a peasant called Mangiapane to deliver a secret message written in code to the Mafia chief Giuseppe Genco Russo of Mussomeli,. This message reputedly concerned proposed movements of Allied troops on July 20, 1943, and instructed Russo as to the role he was to play in aiding the invasion forces, including the establishment of centers of revolt.[40]

On the afternoon of July 20, three American tanks rolled into Villalba. In the center of the turret of one tank was a yellowish-gold flag with a black letter L in the middle. Calogero Vizzini appeared on the scene with his nephew Damaniano Lumia, who had once spent some time in the United States. Both Don Calo and his nephew climbed into one of the tanks, which then lumbered out of Villalba.

During the night Mafiosi reputedly approached soldiers under the command of Lieutenant Colonel Salemi, who was charged with defending the left wing of the Italian-German positions at Monte Cammarata. They were warned of the hopelessness of their situation. By the morning of July 21, 1943, two thirds of Salemi's forces had deserted. The same day a Sicilian agent from Mussomeli gave the signal for the Allied forces to advance and the battle of Monte Cammarata was ended without a shot having been fired. After an absence of six days, Calogero Vizzini returned to Villalba in a big American automobile.[41]

Adding to the drama surrounding the invasion of Sicily was the contention that the black L on the yellowish-gold pennants was intended to identify the notorious American gang leader Charles (Lucky) Luciano. His real name was Salvatore Lucania and he was born on November 24, 1897, in Lercara Friddi, located on the main road between Villalba and Palermo in Sicily. At the age of ten Salvatore was brought to America by his father, Antonio Lucania. Progressing from perpetual truancy to a life of crime and rackets, he eventually became one of the most powerful underworld bosses in America. In 1936 he was convicted in New York of compulsory prostitution, sentenced to a prison term of thirty to fifty years, and lodged in the maximum-security penitentiary at Dannemora, New York.[42]

In 1942 the American war effort was being hindered by sabotage on the New York docks. Much of the sabotage stemmed from the activities of criminals and racketeers plying their trade as usual. It was suggested to U.S. Navy personnel that perhaps Lucky Luciano, because of his control over important segments of the underworld, could be helpful in reducing thievery and other crimes on the docks. Luciano appeared to be receptive to the idea and arrangements were made to have him transferred from Dannemora to the Great Meadow prison at Comstock, New York, where he would be more readily available for naval officials to meet with him. Late in the summer of 1942 plans were being formulated by the Allied armies to invade Sicily. Included in these plans was the identification of persons in Sicily who could be helpful to the invading forces. And Luciano reputedly gave naval officials the names of Sicilian Mafiosi who might assist them.[43]

The exact nature of Luciano's assistance to the U.S. Navy officials in New York has never been officially disclosed. It is significant, however, that the state of New York granted him a parole and in 1946 he was deported to Italy. Favorable action on his parole is said to have been based on Luciano's cooperation in aiding the war effort. Nevertheless, his release from prison and deportation created a controversy that continued for many years.

The account of the Allied invasion of Sicily, aided by Mafiosi and American underworld boss Lucky Luciano, reads like a movie script of a thrilling spy mystery instead of factual history. It has been related by such distinguished Sicilian authors and political leaders as Michele Pantaleone, who was born in Villalba and grew to manhood there. Because of the official secrecy that has surrounded the incident, it is difficult to separate fact from fiction, truth from rumor and legend. Nevertheless, certain facts are irrefutable. Luciano was born in Lercara Friddi, located near Villalba. Although nothing indicates that he knew Calogero Vizzini, his father and relatives undoubtedly knew of him and his prestige in the community. It is also known definitely that Calogero Vizzini emerged from the Allied invasion with immeasurable power and prestige. On the day following his return to Villalba, after a six-day journey with the armed services, he was appointed mayor of the town by an American lieutenant in charge of civil affairs.[44] Under the Allied occupation, Vizzini regained all the powers he had lost under the fascist regime. He restructured the Honored Society and became its last chief comparable in power to that of Don Vito Cascio Ferro.[45]

Following the invasion, many key positions fell into the hands of Mafiosi. The mayors of some towns were actually designated by Calogero Vizzini, and his nephew, Damiano Lumia, served as a trusted interpreter in the Allied government headquarters.

Between 1943 and 1946, Mafiosi made fortunes from large-scale black-market operations in Sicily. Truckloads of scarce foodstuffs and other commodities regularly left Villalba for Palermo and for the Italian mainland, where it was sold at exorbitant prices.

Aiding in the disposition of black-market goods on the mainland was the notorious American gang leader Vito Genovese, who was held in high esteem by Allied military government officials in Nola, Italy. Among such officials was Colonel Charles Poletti, a former lieutenant governor of the state of New York. After the war Poletti was a man of power in governing Sicily. A year before the war ended, Poletti had quietly spent much time in Palermo, where he stayed in the home of a Mafia lawyer.[46]

In view of the high regard in which Genovese was held by high Allied officials, it is not surprising that he was able to build up a huge smuggling ring. Vast quantities of sugar, oil, flour, and other foodstuffs were stolen and sold in neighboring Italian towns.

Vito Genovese, a naturalized citizen of the United States, was born in Risigliano, Italy, on November 21, 1897, and immigrated to America in 1913. Four years later he was arrested in New York for carrying a gun. This was the first of several conflicts with the law in New York, where he was arrested on charges ranging from assault to robbery and murder. About 1934 Genovese fled from America to Italy. There he reputedly became a confidant of the dictator, Benito Mussolini.[47]

In 1934 Genovese and his lieutenant, Mike Miranda, were ringleaders in a crooked card game and a confidence operation that defrauded a New York merchant out of $166,000. One member of the plot, Ferdinand (the Shadow) Boccia, demanded $35,000 as his share of the loot. Genovese and Miranda had no intention of coming to terms with the Shadow. Instead, they hired two New York hoodlums, Ernest (the Hawk) Rupolo and William Gallo, to kill him. After he had been stalked by the Genovese men for several weeks, Boccia was slain, although Rupolo and Gallo were not the killers. About two years earlier, Gallo and Boccia had been involved in the holdup of Anthony Strollo, a pal of Genovese. Hence, Genovese had a score to settle with Gallo. He offered Rupolo $175 to murder Gallo. While in the company of his so-called friend Gallo, Rupolo fired three shots at him. The gun misfired twice and the third attempt only wounded Gallo. Gallo identified Rupolo to the authorities as his would-be assailant and the Hawk was sentenced to a prison term of nine to twenty years. After gaining a parole in 1944, Rupolo engaged in another shooting. Again he muffed the job. Although he fired five shots, his victim recovered and identified him. At this point Rupolo decided to talk to the authorities about the murder of Boccia several years earlier. The New York law requires the testimony of a corroborating witness not implicated in the crime. Rupolo provided the prosecutor with such a witness, Peter LaTempa, and an indictment was returned in New York in 1944. The indictment charged Vito Genovese with the murder of Ferdinand Boccia in 1934.[48]

Julius Helfand, assistant district attorney in Brooklyn, learned that Vito Genovese was then being used as an interpreter for the Allied military government in Italy under a former New York lieutenant governor, Charles Poletti, then a colonel in the U.S. Army. An appeal was made to the War Department for assistance in arresting Genovese and having him returned to New York on the murder indictment. The case was assigned to O. C. Dickey, an agent of the Criminal Investigation Division of the U.S. Army. His inquiry established that Vito Genovese was a big black-market operator in Italy and controlled the sale of wheat and olive oil in Allied-held territory. Two Canadian soldiers who had been implicated with the American gangster confessed that the gang headed by Genovese had stolen U.S. Army trucks from the docks at Naples. The stolen vehicles were then driven to the quartermaster's supply depot and loaded with army sugar, flour, and other commodities that the gang sold in nearby towns. After disposing of the loot, the trucks were destroyed. By the time the Canadians confessed, Genovese had been relieved of his duties as an interpreter for the Allied military government.[49]

On August 27, 1944, Vito Genovese was sitting in his chauffeur-driven automobile in Nola, Italy, when agent Dickey located and arrested him. Both Genovese and his chauffeur were heavily armed. In the apartment of Genovese officers discovered a powerful radio receiver and large quantities of army PX supplies—articles hard to get and in big demand on the black market. In the wallet of the gangster were letters of recommendation signed by three Allied military government officers. The letters described Genovese as "absolutely honest" and "trustworthy, loyal, and dependable." He was also praised for his efforts in exposing several cases of bribery and black-market operations among so-called trusted civil personnel. One document authorized the American gang leader to make an investigation of the mayor of Castello di Cisterna.

Following extradition proceedings initiated by the district attorney in Brooklyn, orders were issued on January 8, 1945, to return Genovese to New York to stand trial for the murder of Ferdinand Boccia. A few days later, on January 16, Peter LaTempa, the all-important witness who was to testify in the trial, asked for some pain-killing tablets to alleviate his suffering from gallstones. His custodians in New York handed him a glass inexplicably containing an overdose of dissolved tablets. He promptly died, and to all practical purposes Genovese's murder trial also died.

In Italy no steps were taken to prosecute Genovese for his theft of army supplies or black-market operations, although it was not until May 17, 1945, that the gangster was placed on a boat to take him back to the United States. When he beat the murder rap in New York on June 11, 1946, the presiding judge told Genovese, "By devious means, among which were the terrorizing of witnesses, kidnapping them, yes, even murdering those who could give evidence against you, you have thwarted justice time and again."[50]

Back in America Genovese would become one of the most powerful underworld leaders in the country and the central figure in Joseph Valachi's celebrated revelations before a U.S. Senate subcommittee in 1963.

In Sicily, the rejuvenated Mafia was increasing in power and arrogance. Occasionally there were voices of protest. A socialist leader in Villalba, Michele Pantaleone, published reports denouncing the Mafia. In August 1944, following his article "Mafia, Fascism and Separatism in Central Sicily" and an open letter to Honorable Salvatore Aldisio, high commissioner of Sicily, which appeared in *Voce Socialista,* an attempt was made on his life and some of the olive trees on his estate were cut down. When it was announced that a public meeting would be held in Villalba, Calogero Vizzini ordered it stopped. In defiance of Don Calo, on September 16, 1944, a meeting was scheduled to take place on the piazza of Villalba. Following remarks by Pantaleone, the principal speaker, Girolamo LiCausi, a veteran communist hero of Sicily, began to talk to the crowd. Don Calo and his henchmen were carefully watching the proceedings. When LiCausi referred to the poverty-stricken conditions of the Villalba peasants, Don Calo shouted, "What you are saying is a lie!" This appeared to be a prearranged signal. Immediately shots were fired and hand bombs thrown. In addition to LiCausi, eighteen persons were wounded. The assailants, including Don Calo, were charged with massacre. However, not until fourteen years later, 1958, were the legal proceedings in the case concluded. By that time Don Calo had died from natural causes; although found guilty, none of the accused has ever spent a day in jail.[51]

Calogero Vizzini, who died in Villalba on July 12, 1954, was given a funeral that revealed his enormous power and prestige. His remains were placed in a hearse drawn by jet-black horses, lines of priests and monks were chanting, and all the village officials were present to pay their respects. Officials and politicians from Agrigento, Palermo, and other cities of Sicily, as well as from Rome, came to honor this man. For eight days the municipal offices of Villalba and the headquarters of the Christian Democrat political party were closed, and black mourning crepe hung from the office windows. The men chosen to carry the tasseled cords of the coffin included Giuseppe Genco Russo, chief of the feudo Mafia, and Paola Bonta, the reputed head of the Mafia in Palermo. Russo was considered the successor to Don Calo as chief of the Sicilian Mafia.

During his lifetime Don Calo had been on trial for robbery, massacre, cattle stealing, bribing civil servants, aggravated fraud, and instigation of murder. Luigi Barzini, editor of several newspapers and onetime member of Parliament from Milano, knew this humble-appearing man well. Barzini said, "You could not imagine the amount of fear he could generate." Yet, his elaborate funeral, swarming with dignitaries and officials to honor him, suggested the passing of an honored and beloved prince. The estate left by Calogero Vizzini included sulfur mines, land, houses, and other investments worth two billion lire (roughly equivalent to $4 million).[52]

The long, eventful career of Don Calo, including the homage paid him at death, emphasizes a frequently overlooked fact. To most Sicilians, neither the Honored Society nor most of its ruthless chiefs are monsters. Instead, the Mafia is regarded by many as the protector of the weak and the source of favors, legal as well as illegal. This was particularly evident on those days when Don Calo held "court" in Villalba. People of all descriptions—young men, old women with shawls over their heads, peasants, politicians—lined up to await their turn to have a word with their "great benefactor." An aura of magnanimity was about him as he administered a primitive justice easily understood by the peasants. Little wonder the Mafia's tradition of omnipotence is accepted by countless Sicilians and successfully blunts most efforts to eradicate it.

In the postwar period two rival Mafia groups were ofttimes in the same town vying for supremacy. This was true in Corleone, Sicily. The leader of the traditional Mafia in Corleone was Dr. Michele Navarra. Through Mafia manipulation and graft he became medical officer for health, chairman of the hospital, medical officer for a health insurance scheme, chairman of the Christian Democrat party, and had an interest in a slaughterhouse that specialized in butchering stolen cattle. The chief of the newer, rival Mafia group was Luciano Liggio, originally a cattle thief. Liggio gained distinction by becoming a Mafia chieftain at the age of nineteen. Following the cutomary tradition, he became a gabellotto and protector of a huge estate. Tenants of the estate who had sharecropping contracts were driven off by Liggio's cohorts. Their houses were burned down and their livestock killed. The Mafia headed by Liggio, who has been described as an American-style gangster, and the one dominated by Dr. Navarra engaged in a bitter vendetta. Between 1944 and 1948, 153 murders were committed in the town of Corleone. Many were traceable to the warfare between the two Mafia groups. The vicious conflict continued into the 1950s, when an unsuccessful attempt was made on Liggio's life. Liggio responded by murdering Dr. Navarra in 1958.[53]

The notorious American underworld leader Lucky Luciano, who was deported in 1946 to Italy, lived in Naples. Between 1953 and 1958 he frequently visited Palermo, Sicily, where he stayed at the Albergo Sole or the Hotel delle Palme. Among those meeting with Luciano was Giuseppe Genco Russo of Mussomeli. In America Luciano had known the value of alliances with important political figures in New York. In fact, some New York officials owed their positions to him. On one of his visits to Palermo in 1958, Luciano contributed three hundred thousand lire to the election campaign of Senator Santi Savarino of Partinico.[54]

In the United States the press had often labeled Luciano a Mafia chief. Luigi Barzini cites Luciano as a classical example of many gullible American underworld characters of Sicilian descent who actually believe their press clippings and expect to hold a high rank in the Honored Society when they return to their native land. A police officer in Italy assigned to watch Luciano's movements remarked: "He believes he is a big shot in the Mafia, the poor innocent man." Luciano often associated with influential Mafia leaders and entertained them but he was never accepted as a member of the society. In fact, Barzini asserted that Mafia chieftains actually swindled the American gang leader out of fifteen million lire by inducing him to invest in a caramel factory. The deal was rigged in such a way by his so-called friends that the more money the factory made, the greater were Luciano's losses. This was the nature of the treatment he received at the hands of the real Mafia in Sicily.

It is Barzini's conviction that, at best, American criminals like Luciano are *uomini rispettati*, like all foreigners with money, but they are deemed outsiders or strangers by the genuine Mafiosi in Sicily. The often-expressed belief that various Italian or Sicilian criminal groups in the United States are, in effect, branches of the Honored Society in Sicily and take orders from Palermo is a myth. Actually, even in Sicily, the Mafia is not a tight, efficiently run organization. Its influence has always been limited to the western part of the island and in the central Caltanissetta area. If the Mafia has never been able to control the entire underworld in the relatively small island of Sicily, it is highly unlikely that it can control and direct organized crime thousands of miles away in the United States.[55]

In the area of its influence in Sicily, however, Mafia power has been frightening, all-pervasive. It has controlled elections, ruled over the landed estates, dominated business and the professions, kept thousands of peasants and laborers in a state of virtual serfdom, and controlled law enforcement. Gaspare Pisciotta, second in command of the notorious gang of bandits led by Salvatore Guliano, observed, "We were a single body. . .bandits, police, and Mafia, like the Father, the Son, and the Holy Ghost." Another member of the gang stated that an inspector general himself informed Guliano when a police drive was in progress. He said, "The same people who gave us our orders gave the police theirs."[56]

When Guliano was killed in the early morning hours of July 5, 1950, it was at the hands of his chief aide and cousin, Gaspare Pisciotta, who betrayed him. In a letter written by his hand, Pisciotta stated, "The moment has come to inform you. . .[that] by a personal agreement reached with the minister of the interior, Mario Scelba, Guliano was killed by me. . . ."[57]

In Sicily the Mafia has been a principal obstacle to progress. From time immemorial it has flourished by controlling scarcity. In poor rural sections the people suffered and were impoverished because of poor water supply. When proposals were made to build dams, the Mafia often blocked the efforts because it made huge profits by controlling water pumped from artesian wells. Mafia chiefs vigorously fought the development of labor unions. They looked upon labor union leaders as bitter rivals who might weaken their hold over working-men.

The strong influence of the Honored Society was even felt in education. In a recorded statement made to a fearless reformer, Danilo Dolci, a Mafioso explained, "Tomorrow, I must leave the threshing, my cattle, all my things, in order to go to Agrigento. I have been asked to recommend a student to his teachers, so that he may surely pass his examinations. . . ." The teacher was aware that his advancement or chance for favorable assignment depended on Mafia influence, so when a Mafioso interceded in behalf of students, as he frequently did, passing marks were given regardless of how ignorant they might be.[58]

On December 12, 1962, the Chamber of Deputies of Italy, by a vote of 478 to 35, approved the appointment of a commission to investigate the Mafia and determine how it could be eradicated. The change in public attitudes that made the formation of the parliamentary Anti-Mafia Commission possible traced in no small measure to the leadership of Danilo Dolci, and Michele Pantaleone of Villalba, the home of Calogero Vizzini. Pantaleone, who had survived attempts on his life, was once a socialist deputy in the regional assembly in Palermo, and for a time was vice president of the regional Institute for Agrarian Reform.[59]

A stepped-up drive against the Mafia resulted in many arrests but the power of the Honored Society was far from broken. In November 1969 Mafia chieftain Luciano Liggio of Corleone, Sicily, who had been arrested, escaped while under police surveillance when he was in a Rome clinic. The Anti-Mafia Commission asserted that it had evidence of collusion between Liggio and the law-enforcement officers. On May 1, 1970, the Constitutional Court in Rome issued a decree ordering the provisional release of defendants who had been held without bail for four to six years and whose sentences had not yet become final. This court action met with the approval of the press and civil libertarians. But many citizens were outraged when important Mafiosi were among the first to benefit from the order. Only twelve days after the decree was made public, the bosses of two Mafia factions in Palermo—Angelo

LaBerbera and Pietro Torretta—were released from a penitentiary. They had been sentenced in December 1968 to twenty-two and a half and twenty-seven years on many counts of murder and other serious crimes. The appeals of their cases are pending still.[60]

In October 1970 Candido Ciuni, a Palermo hotel manager, was attacked on the street by two men armed with knives. He was rushed to the hospital. Four men dressed in doctors' garb, with surgeons' masks hiding their faces, entered the hospital room where Ciuni was receiving treatment, shot him to death, and fled in a waiting car. The assassination, according to the police, was committed by a Mafia commando team.[61]

On May 5, 1971, Sicily's chief prosecutor, Pietro Scaglione, a prominent foe of the Mafia, was ambushed and slain shortly after he had placed flowers on his wife's grave in a Palermo cemetery. Both Scaglione and the chauffeur of his car were mowed down by machinegun bullets on a narrow street near the cemetery. The slaying caused a great public outcry and precipitated a determined campaign against the Honored Society. By July 1971 over forty suspected Mafia bosses were serving long-term exile sentences on small Mediterranean islands. Police reports in western Sicily during 1969 and 1970 accused the Mafia of carrying out sixty-five slayings by shotguns, thirty-three by dynamite and bombings, six by submachine guns, and five by knifings. During the same period, twenty-six more Sicilians, including a well-known Palermo newspaper crime reporter, had mysteriously disappeared.[62]

The Italian Parliament's Anti-Mafia Commission in 1971 filed a three-hundred-page report which asserted that Sicily's Mafia bosses, many of whom were ruthless killers, had continually evaded conviction through the connivance of the authorities. The Mafia had been able to penetrate and influence almost every level of government. And there were indications that the Anti-Mafia Commission itself had been infiltrated, thereby greatly reducing its effectiveness.

In May 1972 a forty-four-year-old Palermo attorney, Giovanni Matta, a Christian Democrat, had been elected in Sicily to serve as a member of Italy's Chamber of Deputies in Rome. A short time later he was assigned to the parliamentary Anti-Mafia Commission. Two years earlier Matta, a former public-works commissioner of Palermo, had been called as a witness before the Anti-Mafia Commission and questioned about an alleged Mafia scandal that had erupted in connection with the Sicilian capital's shortage of school buildings. The central government in Rome had earmarked $20 million for school construction in Palermo. Yet only one tenth of that amount had been spent while Palermo had been paying exorbitant rentals—an average of $1 million annually for makeshift classrooms in private buildings. Most of the rent was paid to Francesco Vassallo, a Palermo real estate developer, whom the Anti-Mafia Commission had listed in a published document as a top Mafioso. In Matta's testimony before the commission, he praised this reputed Mafioso "as a builder and also as a benefactor."

In January 1973 Senator Carlo Torelly, in protest, resigned from the Anti-Mafia Commission. He stated that Matta's membership on the commission was "juridically and morally incompatible" with his role as a former witness. Most of the other members of the commission also resigned in protest. Matta resisted pressure from Italy's dominant political party, the Christian Democrats, to relinquish his place on the Anti-Mafia Commission. He asserted that he intended to defend "myself and my friends," a peculiar choice of words since in Sicily "friends" is commonly used to denote Mafiosi.[63]

Appendix 2

THE MAFIA'S SOURCE OF POWER

The Mafia—its power and perpetuity—subsists by two principal sources: (1) fear generated through violence and threat of violence, and (2) control of public officials, which results in a blanket of immunity for lawlessness. These same principles govern organized crime wherever it exists.

The origin of the Mafia, as noted earlier, is traceable to the compagnie d' armi, abolished by royal decree in 1837, and development was gradual. The renunciation of feudal privileges in 1812 and the abolishment of the compagnie d'armi did not basically alter conditions. Subsequently, the gabellotto who rented the entire feudo placed the protection of the estate into the hands of private guards, the campieri, who, like the compagnie d'armi, were recruited from the criminal classes. The gabellotto, his campieri, and henchmen formed the nucleus of an efficient organization that ruled, and exploited, its jurisdiction through violence—blackmail, robbery, murder.

With the unification of Italy in 1860 came a new element—universal suffrage. Naturally, the Mafia gabellotto was able to impose his will on the many families living on his latifundium and in neighboring towns. The gabellotto became the "chief elector" for the candidate of the majority party. His control of votes ensured the election of any candidate he supported. And once elected, the official could be relied upon to give the Mafia chief full protection for the criminal activities of his organization. Significantly, not until after 1860, when the Mafia became a political force, did it rise to the height of its power, a power not diminished or seriously threatened until the advent of Mussolini's fascist regime shortly after World War I. Many competent observers have concluded that the dominating factor in the very existence and rise of the Mafia in Sicily was politics.[1]

The Mafia had now emerged as organized crime in its most powerful and insidious sense. Now rife was not only fear of violence, but fear and distrust of governmental officials controlled by the Mafia—the invisible government, a state within a state.

In a speech before the Chamber of Deputies on June 11, 1875, Diego Tajani, the general prosecutor at the Palermo Court of Appeals in 1868 and later the minister of justice, charged that the Mafia was the instrument of local government. He said he had documents to prove that of six Mafia chieftains of Monreale, one was the commander of the rural national guard and the five others were captains of the national guard. Almost all crimes in the Monreale country district, he asserted, were committed with their complicity or with their permission.[2]

The Mafia, wrote William Agnew Paton in 1897, "enters into affairs of all kinds; it busies itself to secure verdicts in the courts in favor of its friends, and to secure the condemnation of its enemies; it terrorizes witnesses on the stand and closes their mouths, or compels them, by the silent, unspoken threat of its existence, to commit perjury. . . . Judges on the bench feared to deliver just verdicts with the vengeance of La Mafia hanging over their heads like the sword of Damocles."[3]

At the turn of this century, Bolton King and Thomas Okey, in their book *Italy Today,* wrote:

The Mafia, like the Camorra, has made good use of the ballot box. . . .Where the Mafia is strong, it is impossible for a candidate to win a parliamentary or local election unless he promises it his protection. Thus, it has its patrons in the Senate and Chamber, who use it for political and worse ends; and the government has its well-understood relations with the Mafiosi grand-electors. The gangs are allowed free rein; they have licenses to carry arms, while honester citizens are denied them; they know that there will be no interference with a discreet blackmailing, provided that they terrorize the opposition voters at election time and keep the seats under their control safe for the ministerial candidates. It is this unseen hand at Rome that paralyzes the police. . . .But when a police officer or magistrate, more honest or more energetic than his fellows, tries to lay a strong hand on the Mafia, he finds himself discountenanced by his superiors, or removed to a distant post. . . .Nothing is more sinister in Italian life than the alliance of Mafia and government.[4]

Before Benito Mussolini's march on Rome in 1922 and the establishment of his fascist regime, the politico who arranged a candidate's election in Sicily was invariably a Mafioso. In local government the mayor's righthand man, who dispensed jobs, was a Mafioso. And it was the Mafia's political influence that made it possible for members of the Honored Society to engage in all kinds of criminal acitvities with the assurance of immunity from prosecution and punishment. The repressive measures taken by the fascist regime against the Mafia in Sicily were only partially responsible for the temporary demise of the Honored Society during Mussolini's rule. The death blow was delivered when the fascist regime abolished elections and thus deprived the Mafia of its true source of power—its alliance with, and control over, political leaders and elections. When it lost control of the political machinery, the Mafia was virtually destroyed.[5]

Significantly, the power of the Mafia did not emerge in Sicily again until its political influence was restored following World War II. And since that time, the Mafia has had a hand in government at every level, "from the local council to the provincial administration, the regional government, and right up to the very highest levels."[6]

At least one prime minister of Italy owed much of his success in politics to the active and open support of the Mafia. Vittorio Emanuele Orlando came from Partinico, Sicily, a Mafia stronghold near Palermo. When he was elected to public office for the first time in 1897, he had Mafia support. Between 1903 and 1907 Orlando held several cabinet posts, and was premier of Italy from 1917 to 1919. At the Paris Peace Conference in 1919, Orlando, Georges Clemenceau of France, David Lloyd George of England, and Woodrow Wilson of the United States constituted the Big Four. In 1925 Orlando, who opposed fascism, gave up his seat in Parliament, and as a writer and teacher was deemed a foremost Italian authority on constitutional law. After the fall of Mussolini, Orlando again entered politics and served as a senator from 1948 until his death in 1952. During the first free election held in Italy following World War II, a large canvas campaign poster was prominently displayed in Partinico; it read, "Vote for Vittorio Emanuele Orlando, l'amico degli amici, the friend of friends." Obviously, this poster clearly indicated that Orlando's backing by the Mafia, the friend of friends, was open and notorious.[7]

A candidate for public office needs votes and in the Mafia-dominated areas of western Sicily, the Honored Society can ensure the necessary votes for election. In the early part of this century, the homage paid Mafia chief Don Vito Cascio Ferro by the mayors and leading officials of the villages and towns he visited evidenced the political power he wielded. Succeeding Ferro as the most influential Mafia chief in Sicily was Don Calogero Vizzini of Villalba. The elaborate funeral given the seventy-seven-year-old Don Calo in 1954 revealed the close ties existing between the Honored Society and politics. To pay their respects to this deceased Mafia chief, dignitaries, politicians, and officials poured into Villalba from Agrigento, Palermo, and other cities in Sicily, as well as from Rome.

The history of the Mafia has been one of political collusion, based not on ideological grounds but on expediency. It has embraced whatever party aids and protects it. Between 1943 and 1946 Mafiosi penetrated virtually all political parties in Sicily. In the provinces of Agrigento and Caltanissetta, strongholds of the Honored Society, Mafiosi affiliated with the socialist and communist parties. When the political star of separatist leader Andrea Finocchiaro Aprile began to dim, the Mafia turned to the Christian Democrat party as the one that could best serve its interests.

In Caltanissetta, the provincial secretary of the Christian Democrats was Giuseppe Alessi, who had enjoyed the support of Don Calogero Vizzini. In 1946, however, Alessi threatened to resign from his post and party if Mafia infiltration was not checked. In the Regional Assembly the Mafia was then well entrenched among the deputies. Eventually Allesi did resign as president of the region and was replaced by Professor Franco Restivo, a right-wing Christian Democrat. Restivo's political forces had allied themselves with those of Giuseppe LaLoggia, who had Mafia connections, particularly in the province of Agrigento. Through the Restivo-LaLoggia combination, the Mafia grew in strength politically in the provinces of Caltanissetta, Agrigento, and Trapani. Since 1948 the Mafia has given almost all its political support to the Christian Democrats.[8]

On rare occasions voices within the Christian Democrat party have decried Mafia influence. Young Christian Democrats led by Dottor Gullotti and Nene Gioia urged a fight against the Honored Society. They soon perceived, however, that Mafia cosche had control of the electors and found it expedient to abandon the fight.

In 1953 the leaders of the Christian Democrat party in western Sicily included Franco Restivo, Giuseppe LaLoggia, Giuseppe Alessi, Bernardo Mattarella, Calogero Volpe—all with strong ties with the Mafia. Naturally, the Honored Society continued to gain in strength from its connections with the Christian Democrat party, which in turn benefited from the solid support it received from most of the Mafia chiefs.[9]

One leader of the Christian Democrat party, Calogero Volpe, had been the doctor of Mafia chief Calogero Vizzini. Beginning in 1946, Volpe was elected as a Christian Democrat in the electoral college of western Sicily for over two decades. The national and foreign press labeled him the deputy for the rural Mafia. In the late 1960s Volpe was undersecretary of state to the Ministry of Health. Previously, he had served as undersecretary to the Ministry of Transport. Volpe was the godfather to the daughter of the notorious Mafioso Calogero Castiglione of Mussomeli. And Castiglione was a brother-in-law of Giuseppe Genco Russo, reputed successor to Don Calogero Vizzini, who was the most puissant Mafia chief in Sicily.[10]

For many years, until about 1966, the government minister from western Sicily was Bernardo Mattarella. He was born on September 15, 1905, in Castellammare del Golfo, one of the most important Mafia centers in Sicily, particularly before World War I. Mattarella served as secretary and minister several times after his political career was launched with Mafia support immediately following World War II.

During the election campaign of 1946, Mattarella arrived in Salemi with several carloads of supporters. Among those meeting the Mattarella group in the Piazza Liberta were Santo Robino, Mafia boss of Salemi; Vincenzo Mangogna, a violent Mafioso who had served a sentence for murder; Mariano Licari, an important Mafioso from Marsala who was later sent to prison for kidnapping; Alberto Agueci, a Mafioso dealer in drugs who was later murdered in America. All were present to aid Mattarella's election campaign.

Testimony taken by the parliamentary Anti-Mafia Commission revealed that Mattarella's subsequent political campaigns followed the same pattern. Whenever he came to Alcamo for a rally he was accompanied by Castellammare Mafiosi. The Alcamo police officers were subservient to Mattarella, granting gun licenses and permits to Mafiosi, who were allowed to go about unmolested.

In the 1953 election campaign rallies in Villafrati, Mattarella was in the company of some of the most dangerous Mafiosi of the area. The Mafiosi with whom Mattarella associated openly boasted, even to the carabinieri, that it would be a waste of time to arrest them since they would be freed immediately. In the 1958 elections in Alia, Mafia bosses were the chief campaigners for Mattarella.[11]

It was during 1958 that deported American gang leader Lucky Luciano met with Senator Santi Savarino of Partinico in the Hotel delle Palme in Palermo and contributed 300,000 lire to help finance Savarino's election campaign. Previously, the chief campaigner for Savarino had been the notorious Mafioso Frank Coppola. However, in 1958, Frank Coppola, as chief campaigner for Girolamo Messeri, appeared in Partinico and recommended the election of Messeri as the new Christian Democrat to replace Senator Savarino. With Coppola as Messeri's chief campaigner and with the solid support of the Mafia, the success of Messeri at the polls was ensured.[12]

Francesco Paola Coppola, sometimes known as Three-Fingers Frank and Trigger-Happy, had a long history of criminal activity. In 1926 he went to the United States. He spent much time in Kansas City, Missouri, where he was a friend of underworld chief and political boss Charles Binaggio. Many years later, on April 6, 1950, Binaggio and his pal Charles Gargotta were mowed down by gangland bullets in Binaggio's political headquarters.

During 1946 and 1947 violent gang warfare was waged throughout the United States between Continental Press and a Chicago-based Capone syndicate horse-race wire service called Trans-American Publishing and News Service, Inc. In New Orleans Frank Coppola was one of the operators of the Southern News Publishing Company, which was affiliated with the Capone syndicate wire service. Associated with Frank Coppola in Southern News were men allied with the New Orleans underworld boss, Carlos Marcello, and with Ralph Emery, son of Jim Ammeratto, alias Jim Emery, important crime syndicate boss in Chicago Heights, Illinois. In Louisiana, Coppola was also engaged in the coin-machine racket, then dominated by Frank Costello, underworld leader of New York City, and his allies Dandy Phil Kastel and Carlos Marcello.

While in the United States, Coppola made trips to Mexico in connection with narcotics operations. In Tijuana, he conferred with several prominent gangland figures from Missouri, California, and other states. In December 1947 Coppola was arrested in a Kansas City hotel, where he was registered as Francesco Coppola of Detroit, and on January 11, 1948, he was ordered deported from the United States as an undesirable. He located in Anzio, Italy.

A 1952 report presented by Lieutenant Colonel Vittorio Montanari of the Customs and Excise at the attorney's office in Trapani asserted that evidence collected at Anzio and Aprilia established Francesco Paola Coppola as the head of a drug-traffic organization engaged in smuggling large quantities of narcotics to America. On August 1, 1965, as a result of an antidrug operation carried out by the Palermo police in collaboration with Interpol, Frank Coppola was one of several individuals arrested along with the notorious Genco Russo of Mussomeli. During this period, Coppola's two nephews, the brothers Domenico and Giacomo Coppola, were involved in a one-arm bandit and pin-table racket in western Sicily which was headed by Luciano Liggio, Mafia boss of Corleone. A large number of machines located in Partinico and other towns were controlled by Coppola's nephews.[13]

Notwithstanding his long criminal history, Frank Coppola was so important to the political affairs of Partinico, Sicily, that before every election he would journey from his home in Italy to Partinico to give open support to the Christian Democrats. On one occasion he was met at the Partinico station by a brass band along with Padre LaRocca, priest of the Church of the Holy Sufferers, and other prominent civic authorities.[14]

With Frank Coppola as his chief campaigner and with the support of other Mafiosi as well, Senator Girolamo Messeri became a man of great political influence. He was appointed undersecretary of state to the Ministry of Foreign Trade and became chairman of the Interministerial Committee for the Examination of Temporary Import and Export Licenses. In September 1966 Messeri was in Washington, D.C., where he met with high officials of the United States government to exchange ideas on NATO. The minister of defense of Italy did not learn of these meetings until some time later and they became the subject of bitter debates in the Italian Parliament in January 1967.[15]

During the 1950s and 1960s, numerous Christian Democrat candidates for public office were either notorious Mafiosi or were closely allied with them. In several municipalities the Mafia succeeded in having its members elected to town councils. In 1960 the infamous Giuseppe Genco Russo became a candidate for the town council of Mussomeli. In a television appearance on October 11, 1960, Mario Scelba, minister of interior, urged the voters to elect Christian Democrat candidates. He was taken aback when a representative of the Palermo daily L'Ora confronted him with the charge that coinciding with the candidacy of Mafia chief Genco Russo, there had been an alarming recrudescence of violence against left-wing candidates. The television confrontation created a furor. A few days later, Benedetto del Castillo, provincial secretary of the Christian Democrat branch at Caltanissetta, asserted that Genco Russo was a citizen and therefore had a right to stand as a Christian Democrat candidate at Mussomeli.[16]

Genco Russo had long been active in politics and his candidacy should not have caused great surprise. In previous elections, he had served as the chief canvasser to procure votes for the Christian Democrat party in his area. And the chief canvassers for the Christian Democrats for the provinces of Palermo, Trapani, and Caltanissetta were under the domination of the Honored Society.

Anyone elected with Mafia support owed blind allegiance to the Honored Society. Deputies who failed to protect the Mafia in every respect were defeated at the next election. Francesco Pignatone, a member of the Chamber of Deputies, agreed to a proposal for a parliamentary inquiry into the Mafia. At a meeting in the home of Genco Russo in Mussomeli it was decreed that Pignatone must be ousted at the next election. In towns controlled by the Mafia, Pignatone received virtually no votes and his defeat became a foregone conclusion.

For several years, the Christian Democrat party was the dominant political organization and the Honored Society gave it solid backing. As time went on, however, deputies elected to the Italian Parliament and Sicilian Regional Assembly with Mafia support were at liberty to join any party of their choosing provided their allegiance was to the Honored Society. The Mafia transcended party lines.[17]

Following World War II political crimes perpetrated by the Mafia in Sicily increased dramatically. The attack at Villalba on September 16, 1944, when eighteen persons were wounded, was merely the forerunner of numerous similar incidents. Several trade unionists, deemed rivals by the Mafia, were killed. Within a sixteen-day period in 1946, the mayors of Naro and Favara were assassinated. In March 1948 Vincenzo Campo, provincial secretary of the Christian Democrat party and a candidate for reelection to the national Parliament, was murdered in the province of Agrigento. The Mafia wanted his place in Parliament filled by another candidate upon whom it could rely more completely.

In March 1951, during the election campaign for the Second Regional Assembly, the Christian Democrat leader Eraclide Giglio was murdered at Alessandria della Rocca. He had once been a notorious Mafia chief and had received promotions to highly responsible posts in the government. The old Mafia insisted upon his candidacy, but another Mafia group was backing a young candidate in the same party and reputedly instigated the killing.

In 1947 Accursio Miraglia, the secretary of the Sciacca Camera del Lavoro, was murdered and the police commissioner Cataldo Tandoy accused three Mafiosi of the crime. The suspects retracted confessions they had made to Tandoy and were acquitted. Tandoy was subsequently appointed chief of the Agrigento flying squad. While he served in this capacity from April 1956 to March 1960, there were twelve political assassinations, including five Christian

Democrat political leaders, of whom three were candidates for Parliament. During this period there were also eight attempted murders of trade union leaders and thirty-one alleged Mafia killings. On March 30, 1960, Tandoy was murdered, the victim of a political assassination. The Honored Society had succeeded in demobilizing law enforcement and was able to commit the most vicious crimes with the assurance of immunity.[18]

Also aiding the Mafia in neutralizing police effort has been the system itself. Law enforcement in Italy, including Sicily, rested in two national agencies: the polizia and the carabinieri. Both function under the ultimate control and direction of the minister of interior. Detachments of carabinieri maintained in the villages and towns engage in antiseditious investigations and enforcement activities. Although its budget is under the minister of defense, the carabinieri, like the police, function at the orders of the minister of interior. Yet, rivalry between the two police forces is often intense. As pointed out by Barzini, "The polizia and the carabinieri have been carrying on a running feud for more than a century." Naturally, such a situation frequently aids the criminal elements. But the people are convinced that each force keeps an eye on the other, thus preserving individual liberties.[19]

Some alliances between the Mafia and police are encouraged on the basis of raw expediency. The minister in Rome holds the chiefs of police responsible for maintaining law and order in their jurisdictions. Ironically, the Honored Society abhors hippies, left-wing extremist agitators, and other dissidents who may upset the status quo. By ridding the community of such elements, the Mafia preserves a brand of law and order that helps keep the police chief in the good graces of the minister. And the ties between the police and the Mafia are thus further strengthened.

Mafia control of the criminal justice system even extended to penal institutions. In fact, one of the principal strongholds of the Honored Society in western Sicily was the Ucciardone Prison at Palermo. At times, large-scale illegal operations were directed from within the prison itself. On occasion, an incarcerated Mafia chief was permitted to leave the institution and continue his underworld activities on the outside. The official records carried him as an inmate and the state continued to pay for his keep during his absence. Robberies were committed in several towns by Mafiosi at the same time they were listed as prisoners in jails and prisons in western Sicily.

Violence within prison walls was commonplace. Following the poisoning of two inmates in the Ucciardone Prison, the Ministry of the Interior ordered an inquiry. A search of the cells uncovered knives, daggers, and other weapons. Between 1947 and 1957 the records of the Ucciardone Prison had implausibly accounted for the injuries to some five hundred prisoners by "falling from the stairs." Actually, these injuries had been inflicted by weapons used during fights, brawls, and duels among prisoners. Some injuries were penal, ordered by Mafiosi from within and without prison walls.

On July 7, 1958, some prisoners who had engaged in an uprising in the Palermo prison were brought to trial in the courts at Brindisi. In a statement to the judges, the prison governor revealed that as a means of maintaining discipline he had found it necessary to appeal to Mafia chiefs who were serving sentences in the institution. When he first took over the management of the prison he received threats from persons on the outside as well as from inmates. The governor was warned that if he expected to remain in his post, he must leave things alone in the prison. The prison governor's statement clearly revealed that the Mafia maintained control over the affairs of the institution. Although the governor informed the judges in Brindisi that he could identify about fifty Mafia chiefs in the various prison wards, he was never asked to disclose their names.[20]

The collusion of the Mafia with officials at every level of government has served as a main source of its power and of its perpetuation as a conspiracy. Violence and threats of violence have been component parts of its power base. But no group of criminals could continually organize and engage in murder, robbery, extortion, and blackmail if responsible officials were unhampered by political interference. Fear generated by the Mafia has become more and more potent as victims of crimes realize the utter futility of turning to the authorities for protection of their lives and property. The mere reporting of a crime to officials, many of whom are under Mafia rule, often results in violence against the victim. Silence has thus become the code of the average citizen as well as Mafiosi themselves, who are universally bound by Omerta.

In achieving its political influence, the Mafia has relied on a simple formula: the office seeker, whether a regional or national candidate, needs votes. The Honored Society can produce votes to ensure victory at the polls. But the votes are delivered only for a consideration—the protection of the Mafia and its activities.

Direct alliances, consummated before an election, between office seekers and Mafiosi are commonplace. In other instances, candidates willingly accept the support of well-known Mafiosi to gain electoral victory. But that acceptance means the official incurs obligations to the Mafia that he must fulfill. Sometimes Mafiosi enter the political arena directly. They become candidates for public office and hold highly responsible positions in government. At times, aspirants for public office are avowed enemies of a system based on Mafia-political alliances. They soon learn, however, that to oppose the system is to deal a death blow to their political advancement. Frequently, they give up the fight and resign themselves to the system. Whatever the case, the Honored Society almost always wins, and its members and activities continue unmolested. The Mafia has been a major ingredient in the bloodstream of Sicilian political life.

Appendix 3

ORGANIZATIONAL STRUCTURE OF THE MAFIA

Although the insidious influence of the Mafia on the social, economic, and political life in Sicily has been fully documented, considerable confusion, as well as dispute, exists regarding the exact nature of the organizational structure of the Honored Society. Adding to the confusion has been the frequent and improper identification of the Mafia with separate and distinct criminal operations or associations.

In 1951 the Kefauver committee asserted that the Mafia that originated in Sicily is known in America as the Black Hand and the Unione Siciliana. A few years later, in 1958, a district supervisor of the Federal Narcotics Bureau, when testifying in New York, stated that the Black Hand, Unione Siciliana, and Mafia are synonymous. The same assertions have been voiced by numerous officials and writers from time to time. They are inaccurate.[1]

The Black Hand, which flourished in American cities during the late 1800s and the early years of this century, was not an organization but a method of extortion. A threatening letter bearing the sinister symbol of a Black Hand, signifying death, was sent to a victim with the demand for money. Failure to meet the extortioner's terms meant violence, often death. Frequently, the blackmail plot was initiated and carried out by a single man. At other times the scheme was perpetrated by several individuals.

In the nineteenth century there was an anarchist society in Spain called the Black Hand. Numerous members of the Spanish Black Hand settled in the United States. However, Black Hand extortion plots in American cities took place largely in Sicilian and Italian communities. Both the extortionists and the victims were Italians and Sicilians. In some instances Sicilian Mafiosi who had immigrated to America engaged in Black Hand extortion schemes when preying on their countrymen in the United States. In Zorbaugh's classic sociological study of Chicago's near North Side, he discusses the violence that prevailed in the 1920s in the section of the city known as Little Sicily. Many of the crimes, including murder, were committed by Black Handers. However, Zorbaugh accurately pointed out, "The Black Hand is not an organization. Its outrages are the work of lawless individuals or of criminal gangs. But it trades upon the reputation of the Mafia, the fear of which is deeply ingrained in the Sicilian heart."[2]

Unlike the Black Hand, which was merely a method of extortion, the Unione Siciliana was a fraternal organization which originated in Chicago during the late 1800s. Official records reveal that the secretary of state in Springfield, Illinois, on September 17, 1895, certified the Unione Siciliana di Mutuo Soccorso Negli State America as a legally organized corporation. The objective of the Unione Siciliana, as stated in the official records, was "the voluntary and charitable benevolence and assistance of a member toward the other in case of sickness." On November 9, 1910, the Illinois Department of Insurance approved the certificate of association of the Unione Siciliana and it began operating as a fraternal beneficiary society under the supervision of the Department of Insurance. A charter amendment changing the name of the society to the Italo-American National Union was approved and filed on February 8, 1926.

At times, particularly during Prohibition, notorious gangsters vied with one another in attempting to gain control of the Unione Siciliana by having their representatives elected to high offices in the organization. During one ten-year period in Chicago, six presidents of the Unione Siciliana were murdered in gangland style. Obviously, gangsters were then attempting to use the Unione Siciliana for their own illicit purposes and they succeeded.

J. Richard (Dixie) Davis, onetime lawyer for the notorious New York numbers racket king Dutch Schultz, asserted that Charles (Lucky) Luciano became the leader of the Unione Siciliana in 1931. Said Davis, "A man no longer had to be a Sicilian to be in the Unione. Into its highest councils came such men as Meyer Lansky and Bugsy Siegel, leaders of a tremendously powerful mob, who were personal partners in the alcohol business with Lucky and Joe Adonis of Brooklyn. . . ."[3] The close association of Luciano, Adonis, Lansky, and Siegel in organized crime operations has been fully established. Quite likely they used the Unione Siciliana to further their criminal activities. Perhaps, as Davis stated, they were accepted into the highest councils of the Unione Siciliana. But by no stretch of the imagination could the infamous Jewish gangsters Meyer Lansky and Bugsy Siegel have gained membership into the Sicilian Mafia, much less been accepted into its highest councils. The Unione Siciliana, which originated in America as a fraternal beneficent society, and the Sicilian Mafia were certainly not one and the same organization, as has been frequently stated.

The Mafia is commonly portrayed as having a monolithic, highly formalized, rigid structure with membership in the society involving elaborate, mysterious initiation rites, which include bloodletting, the burning of a bloodstained effigy of a saint, and the taking of solemn oaths.[4] Based in Sicily, this secret organization is believed by many to control or dominate organized crime in the United States. And whenever there are gatherings of Sicilian or Italian criminals in America, such as the highly publicized conclave in Apalachin, New York, on November 14, 1957, they are promptly labeled meetings of the Grand Council of the Mafia.[5] In fact, so loosely and inaccurately has the word *Mafia* been used that some meetings of important underworld figures have been characterized as sessions of the Grand Council of the Mafia even though large numbers of Jewish as well as other non-Sicilian and non-Italian gangsters attended.[6] Actually, there is no evidence of a Grand Council of the Mafia in Sicily. The term is an American invention to describe—and sensationalize—meetings of gangsters.

In relating the organizational structure of the Honored Society, writers and officials in the United States have casually assumed that the title *Don* is a designation of a particular position in the Mafia hierarchy. Some journalists have at times reported that a certain Italian or Sicilian underworld character had advanced in Mafia leadership, as evidenced by his having been made a Don. A Don is recognized, it is said, as the most capable leader of a group, one who has proven his worth as an organizer or executive on a large scale. He is the head of his local complex, is responsible for its welfare, is the coordinator of his area, and arranges meetings with other Dons. And the Honored Society is reputedly held together by the Dons, the important elders of the organization.[7]

The host at the Apalachin crime conference in 1957 was Joseph Barbara and one of the more important guests was Vito Genovese. Published accounts of the meeting referred to them as Don Giuseppe and Don Vito. Others present were also characterized as Dons in the Mafia. As a matter of fact, *Don* is a title of honor and respect in southern Italy, including Sicily, as well as in Spain. It has nothing to do with a position in the organizational structure of the Mafia.[8]

In the early 1700s, Sicily was placed under the rule of the Spanish Bourbon prince Don Carlos (later Charles III of Spain). In Sicily, *Don* is frequently used as a title before the names of princes, priests, and others held in honor and high respect. In the same manner, the title *Don* has been used with reference to some Mafia chiefs, not because they hold a position in the Honored Society but because they are held in high respect and are influential in their communities. Thus, two of the most powerful Mafia chiefs of all time, Vito Cascio

Ferro and Calogero Vizzini, were known as Don Vito and Don Calo. Their power and influence were recognized throughout much of Sicily. They were respected and, in the minds of Sicilians, were deemed worthy of the title Don. Lesser Mafia chiefs have been accorded the same title of respect. They may have climbed to positions of influence and power through the Mafia, but that was of little concern to many Sicilians. Instead, they have looked upon them as their patrons, the source of favors, jobs, and protection. As such, they are deemed worthy of honor in their communities and the title Don.

The concept of the Mafia as a monolithic organization having bloodletting initiation rites and directing and controlling a worldwide criminal conspiracy varies much with known facts, facts uncovered by exhaustive investigations and research.

On February 1, 1893, it was learned that the president of the Bank of Sicily, Marquis Emanuele Notarbartolo di San Giovanni, had been assassinated. Just before his stab-riddled body was found, he was about to announce the discovery of irregularities in his bank. The victim's son, Leopoldo Notarbartolo, a young lieutenant in the Italian navy, determined to bring his father's murderer to justice. He spent the greater part of a decade investigating the case, in which the Mafia was inextricably involved.

Accused of the murder was Raffale Palizzolo, a Mafia leader on the board of directors of the Bank of Sicily and a member of Parliament. Through Mafia influence, Palizzolo went scot-free. Relevant documents mysteriously disappeared from police stations and various public offices, including a ministry in Rome. Witnesses committed perjury.

Based on his investigation, Leopoldo Notarbartolo subsequently wrote a book, *Memorie della Vita di Mio Padre,* in which he described the Mafia and how it functioned. Each cosca, he said, was headed by a chief, a man who had invariably shed blood. And each cosca always had a protector, a man with political influence, such as a member of Parliament. This protector was "as necessary to the gang as the tusk is to an elephant." He led the gang to the polls during elections and bargained for a share of the patronage; he obtained gun permits and issued warnings. But, said Notarbartolo, the Mafia is not a society. Rather, it is a "mosaic of little tiny republics or *cosche* with clearly defined topographical boundaries. . . ."[9]

Writing in 1897, William Agnew Paton stated that the ablest Mafioso in a district—the one most daring and most truculent—is known as the Capo Mafioso. He rules despotically until someone stronger than he kills him or usurps his authority. Each Capo Mafioso seeks to secure as his partisans the assassins and malefactors of his district. He also invites alliances with the Mafia bosses of other districts. These alliances continue only so long as they are useful in promoting joint interests or defeating common enemies. The Mafia "infects and affects the whole social and political life of Sicily. . .it is accepted as a matter of course, and it involves all classes of society, it pervades every department of life." But, said Paton, "La Mafia is not a compact association, and so far as Sicily at large is concerned there is no general organization of Mafiosi." It is a phase of Sicilian society and "not a compact organization of individuals bound together by oaths, a secret society of members who recognize one another by grips and passwords."[10]

At the turn of the century, Bolton King and Thomas Okey, in their book *Italy Today,* wrote: "In its true sense the Mafia means a number of small gangs, the *cosche* (artichokes), whose members hold to one another closely as the artichoke's leaves. A gang seldom consists of more than a dozen members led by some accomplished criminal. . . .The Mafia is hardly a secret society, for it almost certainly has no rites or formulas of initiation, and there is little or no organization common to the different gangs."[11]

In 1916 Alexander Nelson Hood, in his *Sicilian Studies,* wrote on the vast Mafia power in Sicily, a power knowing no obstacles, not even at the hands of government. The Mafiosi, he said, are to be found among smugglers and small proprietors. In the city they are visible everywhere and many congregate "in the antechambers of the prefectures, of senators and deputies, of those who occupy positions of power and profit.'' He said that Mafiosi engage in cattle stealing on a large scale, obtain control of public funds as well as of many charitable institutions, which they employ for their own purposes, and dominate the administration of justice [which] offers opportunity for their machinations.

But, wrote Hood, "La Mafia is no elaborate secret society with its written code of laws and solemn initiation into its mysteries. It has probably no list of members sworn to obey the orders of a chief, with periodic meetings of its followers in remote hiding places to decree vengeance on its enemies. It is better defined as a sentiment of opposition to social and moral obligations; in short, an extended conspiracy against the community on the part of individuals to impose their will arbitrarily and violently on others.''[12]

In the 1920s Benito Mussolini, fascist prime minister of Italy, ordered Prefect Cesare Mori to wipe out the Mafia in Sicily. Mori pursued his mission with a vengeance. Following several years of investigating the Honored Society and waging a ruthless battle to suppress it, Mori wrote that the Mafia is not an "association in the sense of being a vast aggregate organized and incorporated on regular principles.'' The Mafia, he said, has no statutes, no rules of admission, and no election of chiefs. The chiefs arise of their own accord and impose themselves on others. As for admission into the Honored Society, a candidate with necessary qualifications is absorbed automatically and if need be is automatically expelled or done away with. The rule for the division of profits is the right of the strongest. In some instances, he did find that Mafiosi habitually met in groups, and had secret laws, concealed marks of recognition, and election of chiefs. But, he said, these were exceptional cases or cases of a special and sporadic nature. Mori described the Mafia as "a potential state which normally takes concrete form in a system of local oligarchies, closely interwoven, but each autonomous in its own district.''[13]

In a somewhat similar vein, Gaetano Mosca has pictured the Mafia as consisting of many small autonomous associations each of which is called a cosca. Relations between neighboring cosche may be cordial or bitterly antagonistic, erupting in violent warfare. The Mafia, said Mosca, has never been a vast association of malefactors with a hierarchy of leaders. The activities of a cosca usually are confined to a limited district. Chiefs are not elected. Instead, authority over a cosca is wielded by a member whose prestige is based on a long history of criminal activity. Thus, like Mori, Mosca emphasizes the autonomous character of each cosca.[14]

Gaia Servadio, in her history of the Mafia, has concluded that the Mafia is not really an organization but a way of thinking. Organization exists only at the level of the cosca. The Mafia, she says, cannot be eliminated because as a single entity, a secret society, it does not exist.[15]

Henner Hess, in his scholarly study of the Mafia, has pointed out that from centuries of oppression and exploitation there evolved in Sicily a Mafia mentality—a deep-seated distrust of constituted authority and the concept of a man of honor personally avenging wrongs committed against himself, members of his family, or his property. From this Mafia mentality emerged small groups of malefactors, more or less organized, who obeyed leaders. Each of these small groups is called a cosca and is independent of the other. At times, various cosche may support one another and cooperate in joint action, but on other occasions they may engage in bloody battles. The concept of the Mafia in Sicily as a big, single organization is erroneous. No such organization, says Hess, has ever existed.[16]

A different version of the nature of the Mafia was given in a confession purportedly made to police in 1937 by Dr. Melchiorre Allegra, then involved in a highly publicized murder case. The confession did not come to light until 1962, when the newspaper L'Ora published it in three installments. Allegra asserted that in 1916 he was a medical officer in a military hospital in Palermo. A Miafioso, Giulio D'Agate, approached him with the request to ''cover up'' for a patient who was malingering to avoid war service. Dr. Allegra granted the favor.

A few days later, D'Agate met Allegra outside the hospital and accompanied him to a fruit shop where D'Agate and two other men described in detail the Mafia, an association to which they belonged. These men invited him to join the Mafia and since he had been given an inside account of Mafia secrets, he did not dare to decline membership. Allegra related that at the admission rites, the tip of his middle finger was pierced by a needle, blood was squeezed from his finger to soak a small paper image of a saint, the image was burned, and while holding the ashes in his hand he was required to take an oath of loyalty to his brother members. If he failed to uphold his oath he was to be turned into ashes similar to those of the image. After the initiation rites Dr. Allegro's sponsors took him on a tour of the neighborhood in Palermo and at the Birreria Italia Cafe he was introduced to Mafioso chief Don Vito Cascio Ferro and had lunch with Don Calogero Vizzini.[17]

The Mafia initiation rites for Dr. Allegra took place in 1916. It was twenty-one years later, 1937, when he made his confession to the police at a time when he was involved in a murder investigation and during a period when the fascist authorities were waging a vigorous fight against the Mafia. The confession was reportedly mislaid in the police records office and did not come to light until 1962, almost a half century after the initiation ceremonies. These facts do not automatically discredit the details of Allegro's confession, but they naturally arouse serious doubts as to its credibility. It may be, of course, that Allegro was truthfully dscribing one of the "exceptional" or "sporadic" Mafia groups mentioned by Cesare Mori.

In Dr. Allegra's confession, he stated that when D'Agate and his two associates approached him in 1916 to become a member of the Honored Society, they explained that the Mafia was divided into families, each headed by a chief. When a family's membership became too large, it split up into groups of ten, each with a subordinate chief. Insofar as the relationship between provinces was concerned, independence was the rule. However, informal liaison was maintained between the provinces. The chiefs of the families were elected. They were assisted by counselors who served as substitutes for chiefs during their absence. Before a chief could take action on a matter of high policy it was incumbent on him to consult his counselor. Dr. Allegra was told that, in general, the Mafia was not interested in politics. From time to time, however, a family might decide to support a candidate for Parliament to obtain the benefit of his influence in securing firearm permits and tax favors, in facilitating the issuance of passports, and in aiding in matters of criminal justice.[18]

In September 1963 Nicola Gentile, onetime American gangster, made a statement to the Italian press in which he described the organizational structure of the Mafia. After jumping bail on a narcotics charge in New Orleans, Gentile returned to his native Sicily. According to Gentile, the Mafia is a very democratic organization and elections are held regularly. Groups of ten selected a chief. These groups of ten, in turn, elected the boss of the family. The bosses of families, their deputies, and their counselors then elected the head of the Mafia in Sicily, who was known as the *Capo dei Capi*. ("Boss of Bosses"). In America, said Gentile, the head was known as the king. However, the systems in Sicily and the United States are identical.[19]

The structure of the Mafia as described by Allegra and Gentile differs in fundamental respects. Gentile's description clearly depicts the Mafia as a monolithic organization with the heads of families and their deputies and counselors electing the chief of the Honored Society for Sicily as a whole. Allegra states that as between provinces the Mafia groups retained their independence with only an informal liaison being maintained. Thus, highly different versions of the organizational structure of the Honored Society in Sicily have been given by two informants who said they were members of the Mafia.

Two highly respected authorities on the Mafia, Luigi Barzini and Michele Pantaleone, have provided similar outlines of the basic structure of the Honored Society in Sicily. In the first place, the Mafia is subdivided into specialized groups concerned with one activity.

Thus, there are the Mafia of the landed estates (that is, the feudo Mafia), the Mafia of the fruit plantations, the Mafia of the taxi drivers, the Mafia of the fish markets, and innumerable other specialized Mafia groups.

The nucleus of the Mafia is the family (criminal gang), usually composed of persons with blood relationships or those related through marriage or "friends." Each family confines itself to a particular activity, such as slaughterhouses, the awarding of public-works contracts, or kidnapping. Several families can exist on good terms in the same center if their activities do not compete. The man who emerges as the most capable and authoritative is accepted as the chief of the family. On rare occasions, the youngest member of the family may be accepted as chief although it is common for a family chief to turn over his domain eventually to his eldest son.

The second stage in the Mafia organization is the cosca, which consists of a group of families from the same district all pursuing identical or related activities. One family in the cosca is recognized as more powerful and influential than the others. And the chief of that family is recognized as the leader or chief of the cosca. A cosca usually maintains good relations with cosche engaged in other types of activity; and generally, competing cosche enter into working agreements in which territories and boundaries are fixed and respected. Occasionally warfare breaks out between cosche. This may occur when a member of one cosca is slain; in revenge, a member of another cosca is killed and a traditional feud is the result.

The third step in Mafia organization is the consorteria, an alliance within a district of all cosche engaged in identical or related activities. There may be a consorteria for fruit plantations, another for fish markets, and others for various specialized criminal activities. Again, each consorteria recognizes one cosca as the most powerful and influential. The leader of this cosca automatically is accepted as the chief of the consorteria. On some occasions, two consorterie may have a disagreement that results in a series of murders and violence affecting the entire province of Sicily. Sometimes the warfare between consorterie lasts many years.

Finally, the Honored Society is made up of all of the consorterie in Sicily. The chief of the Mafia in Sicily is not chosen through election or a conclave of big chiefs or any other formal meeting. Instead, he emerges by being commonly recognized as the most powerful, ruthless, and influential of all chiefs. Thus, he gains acceptance as the head of the Mafia in Sicily. This was true of Don Vito Cascio Ferro and Don Calogero Vizzini, each of whom became so powerful and influential as to be considered the chief of the Sicilian Mafia. Few Mafia bosses have reached such positions of eminence. At times the Mafia has been without a single head. During such periods, a number of chiefs have been equally respected and reverenced.

Actually, the Mafia in Sicily does not adhere to a highly formalized rigid structure. Barzini, once a member of Italy's parliamentary Anti-Mafia Commission, has emphasized that the Mafia is not a strictly organized association, with hierarchies, written statutes, headquarters, a ruling elite, and an undisputed chief. On the contrary, says Barzini, the Honored Society is a fluid and incoherent association with vague boundaries and various degrees of affiliation. At times, he says, a family may operate for years without having become affiliated with other families in a cosca, a cosca may likewise carry on its activities without joining other cosche in a consorteria, and a consorteria may control its territory and function independently of all other Mafia groups. The Mafia has been described by Barzini as a "spontaneous formation. . .a loose and haphazard collection of single men and heterogeneous groups. . .each group uppermost in its tiny domain, independent, submitted to the will of its own leader, each group imposing its own rigid form of primitive justice. Only in rare times of emergency does the Mafia mobilize and become one loose confederation."[20]

Since its early development, the gabellotto has been a key figure in the Sicilian Mafia. Many, if not most, Mafia chiefs started out as gabellotti. In the 1800s the majority of the absentee landlords lived in Palermo, a center of political activity and intrigue and long a principal Mafia power base. Professor Francis A. J. Ianni, a highly respected research student of the Honored Society, has pointed out that it was natural for the gabellotti to congregate in Palermo where they had intercourse with one another. These gabellotti-Mafiosi had a common purpose and concern that served to draw them together. Yet, never was there a fusion of Mafia groups into a tightly knit organization. The systematic coercion that the Honored Society imposed throughout Sicily was potent but decentralized.

The basic organizational unit has always been the Mafia family, which, at first, was composed of blood or marriage relations. As the family grew in size and strength, friends became associated with it. "By 1900," says Ianni, "a loose confederation of the local gangs began to emerge, bound together by a complex policy of infiltration into all spheres of activity." However, Ianni emphasizes, the Sicilian Honored Society is actually a collection of independent Mafia groups. It is not an organization that could have made a decision to export the Mafia to the United States for criminal or other purposes.[21]

Evidence clearly reveals the autonomous existence of many Mafia groups in Sicily. During election campaigns one Mafia group has sometimes supported one candidate while a second Mafia group has supported another. Occasionally, political assassinations have stemmed from such action. In some localities, two traditional Mafia groups have waged warfare against each other over a period of years in a struggle for power. There are indications of a tendency in Sicily to pin the label Mafia on all organized crime groups. Following an exhaustive research study, Joseph L. Albini of Wayne State University concluded that the Mafia in Sicily is not an association in the real sense but a "synonym for syndicated crime."[22] The cohesiveness found among many Mafia groups in Sicily is based largely rather on expediency and necessity than on a formalized, rigid organizational structure.

Far more significant than organizational structure is the long-standing tradition of the Mafia's omnipotence, an omnipotence that is feared and respected by Sicilians throughout the western provinces of the island.

Many Sicilian immigrants to the United States are baffled by the American language, laws, and customs. Since they distrust all government, which they believe oppressive, they turn for aid and protection to the type of spontaneous organization to which they were accustomed in Sicily. This has certainly been true of the numerous Mafiosi who have emigrated from Sicily to the United States where they have become affiliated with organized crime groups in American cities. In some instances, the leaders in these organized crime groups may have ties, through blood or marriage relationships, to Mafiosi in Sicily. But there is little, if any, evidence to suggest that the crime syndicates in the United States receive direction from the Mafia in Sicily or are branches of the Sicilian Mafia.

For many years, among the official agencies, the Federal Bureau of Narcotics was the principal exponent for the proposition that the Sicilian Mafia is a dominant force in organized crime in America. A former U.S. commissioner of narcotics, Harry J. Anslinger, was impatient with those who failed to accept this premise. He said that the Federal Bureau of Narcotics had "revealed the existence of the Mafia when many officials insisted that the organization, its rituals and rules and punishments were largely myths. . ."[23] However, certain statements made by high officials of the Federal Bureau of Narcotics indicate that the bureau did not possess specific information, much less concrete evidence, regarding the Mafia as an organization in the United States.

Following the celebrated Appalachian crime conference in 1957, the New York State Joint Legislative Committee on Government Operations conducted hearings. Testifying before this committee on January 9, 1958, was John T. Cusack, district supervisor for the Federal Bureau of Narcotics. He said that over a thirty-year period his agency had amassed evidence regarding the Mafia as a secret international society. The Federal Bureau of Narcotics, he said, regards "the Mafia as a well organized secret fraternal order originating and probably still controlled from the Palermo area of Sicily. Its members, with few exceptions, are all of Sicilian origin and are located in every prosperous city in the world. . . .The Mafia, as a secret society, has never been completely uncovered or exposed. . . .It is difficult to say who is eligible to join the Mafia or who joins it today, whether there is a formal joining or whether members through family tradition are just born into the Mafia. However, it appears to us that one becomes a member only through family sponsorship, such as father sponsoring son, uncle sponsoring nephew, father-in-law sponsoring son-in-law, and brother sponsoring brother. . . .With the coming of Prohibition, no group was better qualified to assume a dominant role in the golden age of crime in America than the Mafia.''

Regarding the nature of the organization, Cusack stated, ''The Mafia, throughout the United States, Canada, Mexico, Cuba, Italy, and France, is a fraternal organization divided into many different mobs, gangs, rings, syndicates, or conspiracies. Members of the fraternity belong to one or more such groups, which are often temporary in nature, organized usually to carry out one particular enterprise or venture, such as the importation of narcotics or the operation of a gambling casino. . . .Rather than being one unified crime syndicate, the Mafia is a union or association of many syndicates composed of Mafia members adhering to the tradition and policy-making directives of the order.''

As to the organizational breakdown, Cusack testified, ''We are informed that the Mafia society is divided into units of ten men. The unit is supervised by a group chief and group chiefs, in turn, by an area chief. The area chief would, in all probability, be a member of the Grand Council,'' which, he said, formulates policy for the organization. The witness also made the erroneous assertion that the Mafia, Black Hand, and Unione Siciliana are synonymous.

Based on this testimony, the Federal Bureau of Narcotics has conceded that after thirty years of inquiry the Mafia as a secret society has never been completely uncovered; it is not known who is eligible to become a member or who actually joins the Mafia today; it is not known whether there are formal induction rites or whether membership is gained through family relationships or individuals are just born into the organization. The qualifying word ''probably'' is used when mentioning the control of the Mafia in the United States from Palermo, Sicily, and the phrase ''we are informed'' precedes a description of the organizational breakdown into units, group chiefs, and area chiefs. Thus, many pertinent data on the Mafia as an organization in the United States were admittedly unknown or based on conjecture.

Criminal conspiracies involving American-based underworld characters have been hatched by Mafiosi in Sicily. And criminal conspiracies involving Mafiosi in Sicily have been initiated by crime syndicates in the United States. But such plots do not mean that the Sicilian Mafia, as an organization, is in control of such international conspiracies. Similar conspiracies involve American crime syndicate figures and underworld characters of many other nations in the world.

International conspiracies are particularly prevalent in the area of illicit narcotics. Mafiosi in Sicily, including such prominent bosses as Frank Coppola and Genco Russo, have been deeply involved in narcotics trafficking to the United States. Some of their coconspirators have been based in the United States. It does not follow, however, that the Mafia in Sicily, as an organization, has monopolized the distribution of drugs to the United States. In fact, in 1973 the government asserted that Auguste Joseph Ricord, a sixty-two-year-old man of French Corsican extraction, was the largest trafficker in heroin ever brought to trial in this country. On January 29, 1973, Ricord was sentenced to a twenty-year prison term by a federal court in New York City. Originally a pimp in Marseilles, France, he fled his native land after World War II and at the time of his apprehension was operating a many-tentacled narcotics ring from his headquarters on the outskirts of Asunción, Paraguay.

On August 16, 1972, in Washington, D.C., the Cabinet Committee on International

Narcotics Control, headed by Secretary of State William P. Rogers, released a report covering a worldwide survey of drugs. The report noted that the "primary complex" that leads to the largest deliveries of narcotics into the United States begins in Turkey, encompasses many countries in the Western Hemisphere, and terminates in the United States. The principal production center for most of the heroin entering this country is France, which, the report estimated, has been responsible for as much as eighty percent of American heroin. Said the report, "The most common factor in virtually every major trafficking group over the last twenty years is the preponderance of French Corsicans. It is this ethnic group above all others that has controlled the heroin traffic in France." Heroin bound for the United States was routed directly from France or through Italy, Spain, or Germany. Italy was described as a transshipment point for heroin and other drugs to America. In this phase of the international heroin traffic, some organized groups of Mafiosi in Italy maintain close ties to their Corsican counterparts as well as to their American confederates.[24]

Not long after the release of the Cabinet Committee's report in 1972, there was a marked change in the ethnic background of those engaged in the importation and distribution of drugs in this country. Because of a shortage of heroin during the 1970s, the demand for cocaine rose sharply. To meet this demand highly organized rings composed of Cubans, Colombians, and Mexicans, as well as some black groups, emerged. Colombia, in particular, became a major source of supply in the United States. The cocaine was turned over to Latin American distribution rings located primarily in New York and New Jersey. Mexico became the principal source of heroin, and it was estimated that in the 1970s Mexican sources accounted for seventy to ninety percent of the supply of heroin in the United States.[25]

In contemporary literature on organized crime, the term *Mafia* has been loosely and improperly applied to various crime syndicates in the United States. In some instances, underworld leaders whose ethnic background would preclude them from being Mafiosi have nevertheless been designated Mafia bosses. The indiscriminate use of the label *Mafia* has distorted the picture of organized crime in this country.

Organized crime in the United States definitely is not the product of the Mafia in Sicily. Organized crime became established, and flourished, in a number of cities before either Sicilians or Italians played any significant role in the underworld in this country. At no time, including the present, has the Mafia or any other ethnic group or organization controlled organized crime in America.

NOTES

Chapter 1

Tammany Hall—Origin and Early Corruption

1. Maud Wilder Goodwin, Alice Carrington Royce, Ruth Putnam, and Eva Palmer Brownell, eds., *Historic New York* (New York: G. P. Putnam's Sons, 1899), vol. 2, pp. 45, 46; Gustavus Myers, *The History of Tammany Hall,* 2nd ed. (New York: Boni & Liveright, 1917), p. 4.
2. Goodwin et al., op. cit., pp. 45, 47, 49.
3. John S. Jenkins, *History of Political Parties in the State of New York* (Auburn, N.Y.: Alden & Markham, 1846), pp. 155–56.
4. Jabez D. Hammond, *The History of Political Parties in the State of New York* (Syracuse: Hall, Mills, 1852), vol. 1, pp. 340–42.
5. Goodwin et al., op cit., pp. 53–55; Myers, op. cit., pp. 11, 31.
6. M. R. Werner, *Tammany Hall* (Garden City, N.Y.: Doubleday, Doran, 1928), p. 25; Meyers, op. cit., pp. 1, 12, 13.
7. Myers, op. cit., pp. 18, 58.
8. Ibid., pp. 15, 16; Goodwin et al., op. cit., pp. 57, 58.
9. Myers, op. cit., pp. 23–25.
10. Ibid., p. 37; A. E. Costello, *Our Police Protectors,* 2d ed. (New York, 1885), p. 73.
11. Myers, op. cit., pp. 32, 33, 34.
12. Werner, op. cit., pp. 36, 37; Myers, op. cit., pp. 38–41; Jenkins, op. cit., pp. 291–93.
13. Myers, op. cit., p. 46.
14. Ibid., pp. 50, 51, 60, 63; John Samuel Ezell, *Fortune's Merry Wheel: The Lottery in America* (Cambridge, Mass.: Harvard University Press, 1960), p. 187–91.
15. Myers, op. cit., p. 77.
16. Hammond, op. cit., pp. 129, 130.
17. Myers, op. cit., pp. 96, 97.
18. Ibid., pp. 44, 78.
19. Ibid., pp. 53, 68.

Chapter 2

Gangs of the Five Points and the Bowery

1. Maud Wilder Goodwin, Alice Carrington Royce, Ruth Putnam, eds., *Historic New York* (New York: G. P. Putnam's Sons, 1898), vol. 1, pp. 371–73.
2. *The Old Brewery and the New Mission House at the Five Points,* by ladies of the mission (New York: Stringer & Townsend, 1854), pp. 33, 49.
3. Herbert Asbury, *The Gangs of New York* (New York: Alfred A. Knopf, 1937), pp. 5–9.
4. Ibid., pp. 21, 22.
5. A. E. Costello, *Our Police Protectors,* 2d ed. (New York, 1885), pp. 69, 72, 73.
6. Gustavus Myers, *The History of Tammany Hall,* 2d ed. (New York: Boni & Liveright, 1917), pp. 40, 65, 66.
7. Goodwin et al., pp. 359–84.
8. Asbury, op. cit., pp. 26–28.
9. Goodwin et al., op. cit., p. 389; Asbury, op. cit., pp. 28, 29, 32.
10. Herbert Asbury, *Sucker's Progress* (New York: Dodd, Mead, 1938), pp. 156, 157.

Chapter 3

The Immigrant Vote—Fraud and Violence

1. Gustavus Myers, *The History of Tammany Hall,* 2d ed. (New York: Boni & Liveright, 1917), pp. 52. 73, 74.
2. Ibid., pp. 63, 75, 76.
3. Maud Wilder Goodwin, Alice Carrington Royce, Ruth Putnam, and Eva Palmer Brownell, eds.,

Historic New York (New York: G. P. Putnam's Sons, 1899), vol. 2, pp. 97–99; Myers, op. cit., p. 95.
4. Myers, op. cit., pp. 85, 86.
5. Philip Hone, *The Diary of Philip Hone, 1828–1851,* ed. Bayard Tuckerman (New York: Dodd, Mead, 1889), vol. 1, pp. 56–58, 64.
6. Alexis de Tocqueville, *Democracy in America,* Henry Reeve Text, rev. Francis Bowen and ed. Phillips Bradley (New York: Alfred A. Knopf, 1945), vol. 1, pp. 289, 290.
7. Hone, op. cit., pp. 39, 40.
8. Ibid., pp. 208, 209.
9. Ibid., p. 109.
10. Herbert Asbury, *The Gangs of New York* (New York: Alfred A. Knopf, 1937), pp. 39, 40.
11. Ibid., p. 37.
12. A. E. Costello, *Our Police Protectors,* 2d ed. (New York, 1885), p. 80; Hone, op. cit., pp. 99, 100.
13. John S. Jenkins, *History of Political Parties in the State of New York* (Auburn, N.Y.: Alden & Markham, 1846), pp. 401, 402; Jabez D. Hammond, *The History of Political Parties in the State of New York* (Syracuse: Hall, Mills, 1852), vol. 2, pp. 489–503.
14. Hone, op. cit., pp. 153–55, 180–86.
15. Ibid., pp. 239, 241, 242.
16. Ibid., pp. 248, 250, 251, 256; George Templeton Strong, *The Diary of George Templeton Strong,* ed. Allan Nevins and Milton Halsey Thomas (New York: Macmillan Co., 1952), vol. 1, pp. 48, 49, 51, 55, 62.
17. Myers, op. cit., pp. 109, 110.
18. Ibid., pp. 117, 118.
19. Ibid., pp. 91, 118, 119.
20. Goodwin et al., op. cit., vol. 2, p. 64; Hone, op. cit., pp. 332, 333, 338, 339; M. R. Werner, *Tammany Hall* (Garden City, N. Y.: Doubleday, Doran, 1928), p. 33; Myers, op. cit., pp. 123, 124; Marquis James, *The Life of Andrew Jackson* (Garden City, N.Y.: Garden City Publishing, 1940), pp. 122, 412, 504, 704.
21. Herbert Asbury, *Sucker's Progress* (New York: Dodd, Mead, 1938), p. 158.
22. Robert M. Coates, *The Outlaw Years* (New York: Macaulay, 1930), pp. 276–80, 296–98.
23. Asbury, *Sucker's Progress,* pp. 159, 161.
24. "Tammany and Vice," *The Independent,* 1900, vol. 52, p. 2924.
25. Costello, op. cit., p. 82.
26. Strong, op. cit., p. 110.
27. Myers, op. cit., p. 122.
28. Strong, op. cit., pp. 128, 129; Myers, op. cit., pp. 131, 132.
29. Myers, op. cit., pp. 121, 122.
30. Ibid., pp. 128, 129.
31. Hone, op. cit., vol. 2, pp. 50, 51.

Chapter 4

Gangs Achieve Political Importance

1. Gustavus Myers, *The History of Tammany Hall,* 2d ed. (New York: Boni & Liveright, 1917), p. 130; George Templeton Strong, *The Diary of George Templeton Strong,* ed. Allan Nevins and Milton Halsey Thomas (New York: Macmillan Co., 1952), vol. 1, pp. 177, 178.
2. Myers, op. cit., pp. 130, 131.
3. Herbert Asbury, *The Gangs of New York* (New York: Alfred A. Knopf, 1937), p.43; M. R. Werner, *Tammany Hall* (Garden City, N. Y.: Doubleday, Doran, 1928), p.65; Myers, op. cit., pp. 136, 137.
4. Philip Hone, *The Diary of Philip Hone, 1828–1851,* ed. Bayard Tuckerman (New York: Dodd, Mead, 1889), vol. 2, pp. 144, 145, 161, 162; Strong, op. cit., p. 186; Herbert Asbury, *Sucker's Progress* (New York: Dodd, Mead, 1938), pp. 178–80.
5. Werner, op. cit., p. 65; Myers, op. cit., p. 136.

6. Raymond B. Fosdick, *American Police Systems* (New York: Century, 1920), pp. 63–68; A. E. Costello, *Our Police Protectors,* 2d ed. (New York, 1885), pp. 87, 88.
7. Hone, op. cit., vol. 2, p. 234; Myers, op. cit., pp. 133–36, 141.
8. Hone, op. cit., vol. 2, pp. 293–95, 297, 301; Myers, op. cit., pp. 154, 155.
9. *The Old Brewery and the New Mission House at the Five Points,* by ladies of the mission (New York: Stringer & Townsend, 1854), pp. 32, 33, 45–49.
10. Strong, op. cit., pp. 354, 358, 361, 362.
11. Myers, op. cit., pp. 145, 146.
12. Strong, op. cit., pp. 352, 353; Hone, op. cit., vol. 2, pp. 359–62; Asbury, *Gangs,* pp. 44.
13. Asbury, *Sucker's Progress,* pp. 97, 98, 162–65, 167, 169–71, 178, 185–87, 194–96.
14. Strong, op. cit., vol. 2, pp. 56, 57.

Chapter 5

Emergence of the Bosses

1. Samuel Augustus Pleasants, *Fernando Wood of New York* (New York: Columbia University Press, 1948), pp. 11, 12, 13, 14, 17, 18, 24, 25, 26; Donald MacLeod, *Biography of Hon. Fernando Wood* (New York: O. F. Parsons, 1856), pp. 40, 46, 47, 58; Denis Tilden Lynch, *Boss Tweed* (New York: Boni & Liveright, Blue Ribbon Books, 1927), pp. 25, 110–13.
2. Philip Hone, *The Diary of Philip Hone, 1828–1851,* ed. Bayard Tuckerman (New York: Dodd, Mead, 1889), vol. 2, p. 393; Gustavus Myers, *The History of Tammany Hall,* 2d ed. (New York: Boni & Liveright, 1917), pp. 150–52.
3. Myers, op. cit., pp. 157–59.
4. George Templeton Strong, *The Diary of George Templeton Strong,* ed., Allan Nevins and Milton Halsey Thomas (New York: Macmillan Co., 1952), vol. 2, p 99.
5. Myers, op. cit., pp. 167–71.
6. Raymond B. Fosdick, *American Police Systems* (New York: Century, 1920), pp. 70, 71.
7. Strong, op. cit., pp. 114, 118, 123.
8. Fosdick, op. cit., pp. 78, 80, 81.
9. A. E. Costello, *Our Police Protectors,* 2d ed. (New York, 1885), pp. 126, 129.
10. M. R. Werner, *Tammany Hall* (Garden City, N.Y.: Doubleday, Doran, 1928), pp. 255, 256; Herbert Asbury, *Sucker's Progress* (New York: Dodd, Mead, 1938), p. 361; Lynch, op. cit., p. 119.
11. Herbert Asbury, *The Gangs of New York* (New York: Alfred A. Knopf, 1937), pp. 90–93; Werner, op. cit., p. 67; Lloyd Morris, *Incredible New York* (New York: Random House, 1951), p. 33.
12. Lynch, op. cit., pp. 119, 120.
13. Asbury, *Sucker's Progress,* p. 371.
14. Lynch, op. cit., pp. 115, 118, 119.
15. Strong, op. cit., pp. 195, 196.
16. Pleasants, op. cit., pp. 49–51; Lynch, op. cit., pp. 120, 121.
17. Lynch, op. cit., pp. 127, 128; Asbury, *Gangs,* p. 105.
18. Lynch, op. cit., pp. 143, 144, 145; Asbury, *Gangs,* pp. 96–99; Strong, op. cit., pp. 214, 215.
19. Werner, op. cit., pp. 81–83.
20. Myers, op. cit., pp. 176, 177.
21. Lynch, op. cit., pp. 152, 154, 155.
22. Pleasants, op. cit., pp. 63, 64.
23. Ibid., p. 68.
24. Strong, op. cit., p. 320.
25. Ibid., pp. 341, 342.
26. Pleasants, op. cit., p. 77; Costello, op. cit., pp. 137–39.
27. Pleasants, op. cit., p. 73.
28. Ibid., pp. 78–80; Costello, op. cit., pp. 140–42.
29. Pleasants, op. cit., p. 80.
30. Ibid., pp. 80–82; Strong, op. cit., pp. 346, 347, 348; Myers, op. cit., p. 186.
31. Strong, op. cit., pp. 347, 348.
32. Ibid., pp. 316, 353–55, 358, 359, 361, 362; Lynch, op. cit., p. 169.

33. Strong, op. cit., pp. 370, 373, 374.
34. Ibid., 374; Myers, op. cit., pp. 187, 188.
35. Lynch, op. cit., pp. 202, 203.
36. Pleasants, op. cit., pp. 89, 90; Myers, op. cit., p. 190.
37. Strong, op. cit., pp. 408, 410, 417.
38. Ibid., p. 418; Asbury, *Gangs,* p. 100.
39. Strong, op. cit., p. 425.
40. Costello, op. cit., p. 151.
41. Mel Heimer, *Fabulous Bawd: The Story of Saratoga* (New York: Henry Holt, 1952), pp. 73, 74.
42. Lynch, op. cit., p. 215; Myers, op. cit., pp. 192, 193.
43. Lynch, op. cit., pp. 218, 219, 220.
44. Ibid., p. 217; Myers, op. cit., pp. 194, 195; Strong, op. cit., vol. 3, pp. 39, 120, 256.
45. Strong, op. cit., vol. 3, pp. 32, 46–49.
46. Pleasants, op. cit., p. 104.

Chapter 6

The Civil War Era

1. Samuel Augustus Pleasants, *Fernando Wood of New York* (New York: Columbia University Press, 1948), pp. 113, 114, 115; Denis Tilden Lynch, *Boss Tweed* (New York: Boni & Liveright, Blue Ribbon Books, 1927), p. 222.
2. Pleasants, op. cit., pp. 134, 135, 136; Gustavus Myers, *The History of Tammany Hall,* 2d ed. (New York: Boni & Liveright, 1917), pp. 196, 197, 201, 202, 204.
3. George Templeton Strong, *The Diary of George Templeton Strong,* ed. Allan Nevins and Milton Halsey Thomas (New York: Macmillan Co., 1952), vol. 3, pp. 264, 270.
4. Stewart Mitchell, *Horatio Seymour of New York* (Cambridge, Mass.: Harvard University Press, 1938), pp. 303–5.
5. Strong, op. cit., pp. 331–37; A. E. Costello, *Our Police Protectors,* 2d ed. (New York, 1885), pp. 160–77; Herbert Asbury, *The Gangs of New York* (New York: Alfred A. Knopf, 1937), pp. 118–47; William Harlan Hale, *Horace Greeley: Voice of the People* (New York: Harper & Brothers, 1950), pp. 271–74.
6. Mitchell, op. cit., pp. 306–9; Strong, op. cit., p. 345.
7. Strong, op. cit., pp. 337–42; vol. 4, p. 25; Costello, op. cit., pp. 177–200; Asbury, op. cit., pp. 148–71; Mitchell, op. cit., pp. 308–36; Edward Robb Ellis, *The Epic of New York City* (New York: Coward-McCann, 1966), pp. 297–316.
8. Asbury, op. cit., p. 170.
9. Strong, op. cit., vol. 3, pp. 345, 369, 502, 509, 512; vol. 4, p. 9.
10. Ibid., vol. 3, p. 561.
11. Ibid., pp. 579, 582, 583.
12. Ibid., pp. 571, 572.
13. Ibid., vol. 4, pp. 166, 171.
14. Ibid., p. 11.
15. Ibid., p. 80; Edward Crapsey, *The Nether Side of New York; or the Vice, Crime, and Poverty of the Great Metropolis* (New York: Sheldon, 1872), p. 114.
16. Strong, op. cit., vol. 4, pp. 222, 223; Myers, op. cit., pp. 216, 217.
17. Myers, op. cit., p. 217.

Chapter 7

The Tweed Ring

1. Matthew P. Breen, *Thirty Years of New York Politics* (New York, 1899), pp. 45–49; Denis Tilden Lynch, *Boss Tweed* (New York: Boni & Liveright, Blue Ribbon Books, 1927), pp. 51, 53, 58, 66, 67.
2. Lynch, op. cit., pp. 67, 68, 75.

3. Alexander B. Callow, Jr., *The Tweed Ring,* (New York: Oxford University Press, 1966), pp. 8, 21, 29, 31, 75, 169.
4. Breen, op. cit., p. 52; Myers, op. cit., pp. 247, 248; James Bryce, *The American Commonwealth,* 3d ed. (New York: Macmillan Co., 1898), vol. 2, p. 384.
5. Croswell Bowen, *The Elegant Oakey* (New York: Oxford University Press, 1956), p. 40; Bryce, op. cit., pp. 385, 386.
6. Bowen, op. cit., pp. 17, 18, 19, 21, 22, 24, 25, 26, 28, 31, 32, 33; Werner, op. cit., p. 118.
7. Bowen, op. cit., pp. 32, 34, 37, 39, 74; Lynch, op. cit., pp. 293, 294.
8. Callow, op. cit., pp. 135–38; Werner, op. cit., pp. 124, 125; Breen, op. cit., pp. 318, 319, 386–88; Lynch, op. cit., p. 292; George Templeton Strong, *The Diary of George Templeton Strong,* ed. Allan Nevins and Milton Halsey Thomas (New York: Macmillan Co., 1952), vol. 4, pp. 263, 264.
9. Callow, op. cit., pp. 138, 139, 151; Strong, op. cit., pp. 263, 264; Bernard Schwartz, *The American Heritage History of the Law in America* (New York: American Heritage Publishing Co., 1974), pp. 174, 200, 201.
10. Callow, op. cit., pp. 139, 140; Strong, op. cit., pp. 263, 264.
11. Callow, op. cit., pp. 224, 225, 227.
12. Werner, op. cit., pp. 179–85; Lynch, op. cit., pp. 331–33; Callow, op. cit., pp. 236, 238; Bowen, op. cit., pp. 60, 61, 62, 63; Breen, op. cit., p. 316; Bryce, op. cit., pp. 387–89; Myers, op. cit., p. 227.
13. A. E. Costello, *Our Police Protectors,* 2d ed. (New York, 1885), pp. 239, 240, 241.
14. Meyer Berger, *The Story of the New York Times, 1851–1951* (New York: Simon & Schuster, 1951), p. 36; Myers, op. cit., pp. 234, 235.
15. Callow, op. cit., pp. 222, 223; Myers, op. cit., pp. 225, 226.
16. Berger, op. cit., pp. 33, 35; Callow, op. cit., pp. 256, 257.
17. Breen, op. cit., pp. 325, 326, 333, 334; Berger, op. cit., pp. 33, 35, 36, 38, 39.
18. Myers, op. cit., p. 233.
19. Breen, op. cit., pp. 341, 342, 343; Callow, op. cit., pp. 247, 248, 249, 250.
20. Berger, op. cit., pp. 40, 41; Callow, op. cit., pp. 259, 260.
21. Berger, op. cit., pp. 41, 42; Breen, op. cit., pp. 334, 335; Strong, op. cit., p. 381.
22. Lynch, op. cit., pp. 363, 364.
23. Strong, op. cit., pp. 370, 371; Costello, op. cit., pp. 244, 245, 246.
24. *One Hundred Years of Famous Pages from the New York Times, 1851–1951* (New York: Simon & Schuster, 1951), p. 21.
25. Berger, op. cit., pp. 48, 49, 50; Breen, op. cit., pp. 335–36; William Thompson Bonner, *New York: The World's Metropolis, 1623-4–1923-4* (New York: R. L. Polk, 1924), p. 449.
26. Bowen, op. cit., pp. 109, 110.
27. Myers, op. cit., p. 240.
28. Lynch, op. cit., p. 385; Myers, op. cit., pp. 244, 245; Bowen, op. cit., p. 131; Callow, op. cit., p. 283.
29. Breen, op. cit., pp. 386, 397, 403, 404, 405.
30. Callow, op. cit., p. 288.
31. Breen, op. cit., pp. 457, 459, 468–71, 569; Callow, op. cit., pp. 288–98; Lynch, op. cit., pp. 389, 390, 393, 394, 396, 397, 401; Myers, op. cit., pp. 245, 246; Strong, op. cit., pp. 467, 468, 502.
32. Bowen, op. cit., pp. 156, 158, 180, 192; Lynch, op. cit., pp. 389, 390.
33. Bowen, op. cit., pp. 199–201, 208, 216, 218, 219, 232, 234, 236, 237, 264, 265, 267, 271, 272.
34. Callow, op. cit., pp. 238, 239, 254.
35. Berger, op. cit., p. 38; Callow, op. cit., p. 58.
36. Strong, op. cit., pp. 264, 265, 271.
37. Callow, op. cit., p. 145.
38. Herbert Asbury, *Sucker's Progress* (New York: Dodd, Mead, 1938), pp. 358, 360, 372, 373, 386, 391, 392; Edward Crapsey, *The Nether Side of New York: or the Vice, Crime, and Poverty of the Great Metropolis* (New York: Sheldon, 1872), p. 100.
39. Mel Heimer, *Fabulous Bawd: The Story of Saratoga* (New York: Henry Holt, 1952), pp. 74, 76, 77, 79, 90; Werner, op. cit., p. 85; Strong, op. cit., p. 159.
40. Asbury, op. cit., pp. 386, 402, 403.
41. Werner, op. cit., pp. 255, 256.

42. Asbury, op. cit., pp. 98–101, 103.
43. Herbert Asbury, *The Gangs of New York* (New York: Alfred A. Knopf, 1937), pp. 174, 175; Callow, op. cit., p. 145.
44. Asbury, *Gangs,* pp. 175–77, 235, 236.
45. Ibid., pp. 190, 201, 202; Asbury, *Sucker's Progress,* p. 103; Costello, op. cit., p. 369.

Chapter 8

Tammany Dabbles in Reform

1. M. R. Werner, *Tammany Hall* (Garden City, N.Y.: Doubleday, Doran, 1928), pp. 277–79; Gustavus Myers, *The History of Tammany Hall,* 2d ed. (New York: Boni & Liveright, 1917), p. 251.
2. Edward C. Mack, *Peter Cooper: Citizen of New York* (New York: Duell, Sloan, & Pearce, 1949), p. 174; Allan Nevins, *Abram S. Hewitt: With Some Account of Peter Cooper* (New York: Harper & Brothers, 1935), pp. 265, 266; Myers, op. cit., p. 252.
3. Myers, op. cit., pp. 254, 255; Werner, op. cit., 278, 279.
4. Nevins, op. cit., pp. 293, 295, 296, 298; Werner, op. cit., pp. 308–10.
5. A. E. Costello, *Our Police Protectors,* 2d ed. (New York, 1885), pp. 265–70.
6. Werner, op. cit., pp. 286, 288, 291.
7. Myers, op. cit., pp. 258, 259; Nevins, op. cit., pp. 306, 312.
8. Mack, op. cit., pp. 294, 295.
9. Nevins, op. cit., p. 433.
10. Ibid., pp. 438–40.
11. Myers, op. cit., pp. 262, 263, 264, 266.
12. Werner, op. cit., pp. 291, 293; Myers, op. cit., p. 258; Frederick Shaw, *The History of the New York City Legislature* (New York: Columbia University Press, 1954), p. 5; Cleveland Rodgers and Rebecca B. Rankin, *New York: The World's Capital City* (New York: Harper & Brothers, 1948), p. 80.
13. Myers, op. cit., p. 267.
14. Alfred Henry Lewis, *Richard Croker* (New York: Life Publishing Co., 1901), pp. 4, 5, 8, 16, 30, 36, 40, 44, 128; Lothrop Stoddard, *Master of Manhattan: The Life of Richard Croker* (New York: Longmans, Green, 1931), pp. 20, 24, 25, 29, 30, 40, 45–47, 52.
15. Nevins, op. cit., pp. 460–68; Myers, op. cit., pp. 269, 270.
16. Nevins, op. cit., pp. 472, 473; Costello, op. cit., pp. 307, 308, 309, 312.
17. Nevins, op. cit., pp. 473, 474.
18. Ibid., pp. 474, 475.
19. Ibid., pp. 480, 481.
20. Ibid., pp. 475, 476, 511, 521, 525; Myers, op. cit., p. 271.

Chapter 9

Croker Rule—A Decade of Investigations

1. M. R. Werner, *Tammany Hall* (Garden City, N.Y.: Doubleday, Doran, 1928), p. 313.
2. Gustavus Myers, *The History of Tammany Hall,* 2d ed. (New York: Boni & Liveright, 1917), pp. 272, 273.
3. Lothrop Stoddard, *Master of Manhattan: The Life of Richard Croker* (New York: Longmans, Green, 1931), pp. 115–17.
4. Myers, op. cit., p. 274.
5. Stoddard, op. cit., pp. 128, 129.
6. C. H. Parkhurst, *My Forty Years in New York* (New York: Macmillan Co., 1923), pp. 106, 107, 108, 109, 112, 120.
7. Ibid., pp. 126, 127, 129, 130.
8. Ibid., pp. 135–45.
9. Myers, op. cit., p. 281.

10. Charles H. Parkhurst, *Our Fight with Tammany* (New York: Charles Scribner's Sons, 1895), pp. 96, 97; Myers, op. cit., p. 277.
11. Alexander Gardiner, *Canfield: The True Story of the Greatest Gambler* (Garden City, N.Y.: Doubleday, Doran, 1930), pp. 114, 115.
12. Werner, op. cit., pp. 356, 357, 360, 361, 364, 367–70.
13. Louise Ware, *Jacob A. Riis: Police Reporter, Reformer, Useful Citizen* (New York: D. Appleton-Century, 1939), pp. 112–14.
14. Myers, op. cit., pp. 278, 279.
15. Jacob A. Riis, *Theodore Roosevelt the Citizen* (New York: Macmillan Co., 1904), pp. 129–31; Gardiner, op. cit., p. 117.
16. Stoddard, op. cit., pp. 159, 162, 163.
17. William Thompson Bonner, *New York: The World's Metropolis, 1623-4–1923-4* (New York: R. L. Polk, 1924), pp. 357, 358; Stoddard, op. cit., pp. 169, 170, 171.
18. Werner, op. cit., pp. 451–56; Stoddard, op. cit., pp. 168, 172.
19. Myers, op. cit., pp. 282, 283; Stoddard, op. cit., pp. 182, 183; Virgil W. Peterson, *Barbarians in Our Midst* (Boston: Little, Brown, 1952), pp. 74, 75.
20. Myers, op. cit., pp. 282, 289; Stoddard, op. cit., pp. 178, 185.
21. Gardiner, op. cit., p. 121.
22. Franklin Matthews, " 'Wide Open' New York: What Renewed Croker Government Means and What Is to Be Expected," *Harper's Weekly,* October 22, 1898; Gardiner, op. cit., pp. 123, 124; Herbert Asbury, *Sucker's Progress* (New York: Dodd, Mead, 1938), pp. 103, 104.
23. Myers, op. cit., pp. 285, 287, 288; Stoddard, op. cit., p. 120; Werner, op. cit., p. 336.
24. Werner, op. cit., pp. 396, 410–14, 416.
25. Stoddard, op. cit., p. 143; Myers, op. cit., p. 287.
26. Stoddard, op. cit., p. 214; Myers, op. cit., p. 286.
27. Stoddard, op. cit., pp. 211, 212.
28. Werner, op. cit., pp. 416, 417; Asbury, op. cit., p. 456; Gardiner, op. cit., pp. 180, 181, 183, 184, 185; Myers, op. cit., p 288.
29. Gardiner, op. cit., pp. 76, 78, 79, 95–97, 100–102, 116, 117, 124–29, 164, 165, 238.
30. Stoddard, op. cit., pp. 228–30, 235, 236; Myers, op. cit., pp. 292, 293.
31. Werner, op. cit., p. 438; Herbert Asbury, *The Gangs of New York* (New York: Alfred A. Knopf, 1937), pp. 225–29; Stoddard, op. cit., p. 231.
32. Stoddard, op. cit., pp. 232–35; Werner, op. cit., pp. 439, 508.
33. Stoddard, op. cit., pp. 236, 237, 239; Werner, op. cit., p. 466.
34. Werner, op. cit., pp. 471–73; Stoddard, op. cit., pp. 243–246.
35. Werner, op. cit., p. 473; Stoddard, op. cit., pp. 252, 253.
36. Myers, op. cit., p. 295; Stoddard, op. cit., pp. 256–58; Werner, op. cit., p. 476.
37. Myers, op. cit., pp. 296, 297; Werner, op. cit., pp. 482, 483.
38. Myers, op. cit., pp. 297–302.
39. Werner, op. cit., pp. 478–81.
40. Jack McPhaul, *Johnny Torrio* (New Rochelle, N.Y.: Arlington House, 1970), pp. 42, 45, 46, 49, 50; Asbury, *Gangs,* pp. 252, 253, 273.
41. Lewis J. Valentine, *Autobiography, Night Stick* (New York: Dial Press, 1947), pp. 124, 125; Asbury, *Gangs,* pp. 274, 275, 278–82.
42. Valentine, op. cit., pp. 126, 127; Asbury, *Gangs,* pp. 285, 286.
43. Craig Thompson and Allen Raymond, *Gang Rule in New York* (New York: Dial Press, 1940), pp. 18–20, 360–63.

Chapter 10

Early 1900s—A Policeman Executed, a Governor Impeached

1. George B. McClellan, Jr., *Autobiography: The Gentleman and the Tiger,* ed. Harold C. Syrett, from original manuscript in possession of New York Historical Society (Philadelphia: J. B. Lippincott, 1956), pp. 16, 22, 87, 88, 180.
2. Ibid., pp. 176, 213, 214.
3. Ibid., pp. 23, 181, 190, 198.

4. Ibid., pp. 185, 199.
5. Gustavus Myers, *The History of Tammany Hall*, 2d ed. (New York: Boni & Liveright, 1917), pp. 309–12; McClellan, op. cit., pp. 214, 251, 252.
6. Myers, op. cit., pp. 312, 313.
7. McClellan, op. cit., pp. 201, 202; William McAdoo, *Guarding a Great City* (New York: Harper & Brothers, 1906), pp. 242–47.
8. McClellan, op. cit., p. 256.
9. Merlo J. Pusey, *Charles Evans Hughes* (New York: Macmillan Co., 1951), vol. 1, pp. 140, 141, 144, 145, 147, 148, 150, 166; Earl Chapin May and Will Oursler, *The Prudential* (Garden City, N.Y.: Doubleday, 1950), pp. 129–41.
10. Myers, op. cit., pp. 322, 323; McClellan, op. cit., pp. 221, 222, 230.
11. McClellan, op. cit., pp. 231–4.
12. McAdoo, op. cit., p. 52.
13. Myers, op. cit., pp. 339, 340; McClellan, op. cit., pp. 234, 295.
14. McAdoo, op. cit., pp. 146, 147.
15. Ibid., pp. 148, 151, 154.
16. Ed Reid, *Mafia* (New York: Random House, 1952), pp. 163, 164, 172; Michele Pantaleone, *The Mafia and Politics* (New York: Coward-McCann, 1966), pp. 40, 41.
17. Lewis J. Valentine, *Autobiography, Night Stick* (New York: Dial Press, 1947), pp. 126, 127, 128; Herbert Asbury, *The Gangs of New York* (New York: Alfred A. Knopf, 1937), pp. 295–8.
18. Asbury, op. cit., pp. 287, 288, 289, 290.
19. Ibid., pp. 290, 291, 292.
20. Craig Thompson and Allen Raymond, *Gang Rule in New York* (New York: Dial Press, 1940), pp. 360, 361, 363; Asbury, op. cit., 295, 296.
21. Asbury, op. cit., pp. 292–95.
22. Ibid., pp. 325, 328, 329.
23. Thompson and Raymond, op. cit., pp. 3, 228; Asbury, op. cit., pp. 329, 330.
24. Pusey, op. cit., pp. 225, 226; Harold Seidman, *Investigating Municipal Administration* (New York: Institute of Public Administration, Columbia University, 1941), pp. 48, 49, 51; Myers, op. cit., pp. 324–30.
25. Myers, op. cit., pp. 343, 344.
26. Pusey, op. cit., pp. 226, 227, 228, 229, 232; Myers, op. cit., pp. 348, 349.
27. McClellan, op. cit., p. 285.
28. Ibid., p. 289.
29. Robert M. Thornton, "William Jay Gaynor, Libertarian Mayor of New York," *The Freeman* 20, no. 3, (March 1970): 156–64; McClellan, op. cit., p. 301; Myers, op. cit., pp. 340, 341; Mortimer Smith, *William Jay Gaynor* (Chicago: Henry Regnery, 1951), p. 132.
30. Smith, op. cit., pp. 104–8.
31. Ibid., pp. 128, 129, 131; Myers, op. cit., p. 356.
32. Ransom McCarthy, "A Murder Has Been Arranged—The Story of the Rosenthal-Becker Case," *Harper's*, January 1935, p. 181; Asbury, op. cit., pp. 336, 340.
33. Walter Chambers, *Samuel Seabury: A Challenge* (New York: Century, 1932), p. 161; M. R. Werner, *Tammany Hall* (Garden City, N.Y.: Doubleday, Doran, 1928), p. 521; Smith, op. cit., p. 128.
34. Chambers, op. cit., p. 162.
35. Asbury, op. cit., pp. 341, 342; Myers, op. cit., p. 356.
36. Werner, op. cit., pp. 520, 521.
37. McCarthy, op. cit., pp. 176, 177; Chambers, op. cit., pp. 153–55.
38. Chambers, op. cit., p. 155; Myers, op. cit., pp. 356, 357; McCarthy, op. cit., p. 182.
39. McCarthy, op. cit., pp. 188, 189; Chambers, op. cit., pp. 155, 156, 157; Valentine, op. cit., pp. 32, 33, 34; Myers, op. cit., pp. 359, 360; Warren Moscow, *Politics in the Empire State* (New York: Alfred A. Knopf, 1948), p. 156.
40. Werner, op. cit., pp. 509, 510; Myers, op. cit., p. 345.
41. Smith, op. cit., pp. 177–83.
42. Myers, op. cit., p. 354.
43. Ibid., pp. 361, 362.
44. Werner, op. cit., pp. 531, 532.

45. Jay W. Forrest and James Malcolm, *Tammany's Treason: Impeachment of Governor William Sulzer* (Albany, N.Y., 1913); Werner, op. cit., pp. 534, 535, 536.
46. Werner, op. cit., pp. 536, 537, 538, 550; Forrest and Malcolm, op. cit., pp. 132–42.
47. Myers, op. cit., pp. 375–78; Forrest and Malcolm, op. cit., pp. 168–80.
48. Forrest and Malcolm, op. cit., pp. 189–201.
49. Myers, op. cit., 388, 389.

Chapter 11

The Rise of Jimmy Hines

1. Edward Robb Ellis, *The Epic of New York City* (New York: Coward-McCann, 1966), p. 499.
2. Gustavus Myers, *The History of Tammany Hall*, 2d ed. (New York: Boni & Liveright, 1917), pp. 396, 397.
3. Ellis, op. cit., pp. 501, 502.
4. Craig Thompson and Allen Raymond, *Gang Rule in New York* (New York: Dial Press, 1940), pp. 360, 362.
5. Gene Fowler, *The Great Mouthpiece: A Life Story of William J. Fallon* (New York: Grosset & Dunlap, 1931), pp. 326, 327; Lothrop Stoddard, *Master of Manhattan: The Life of Richard Croker* (New York: Longmans, Green, 1931), pp. 241–46; Thompson and Raymond, op. cit., pp. 19, 20.
6. Fowler, op. cit., p. 327; Thompson and Raymond, op. cit., p. 18.
7. Thompson and Raymond, op. cit., pp. 136–39.
8. Ibid., pp. 140–42.
9. Roy V. Peel, *The Political Clubs of New York City* (New York: G. P. Putnam's Sons, 1935), pp. 138, 238, 239; Thompson and Raymond, op. cit., pp. 143, 144.
10. Thompson and Raymond, op. cit., p. 62.
11. Donald Henderson Clarke, *In the Reign of Rothstein* (New York: Grosset & Dunlap, 1929), pp. 13, 14, 20, 25, 31, 296.
12. Ibid., pp. 34–39.
13. Ibid., pp. 40, 41, 42, 43, 45, 47, 49, 50.
14. Ibid., pp. 55, 82, 168; Thompson and Raymond, op. cit., p. 53.
15. Sid Feder and Joachim Joesten, *The Luciano Story* (New York: David McKay, 1954), pp. 48, 49, 54; Burton B. Turkus and Sid Feder, *Murder, Inc.* (New York: Farrar, Straus & Young, 1951), p. 77; David Hanna, *Frank Costello: The Gangster with a Thousand Faces* (New York: Belmont Tower Books, 1974), pp. 19, 20; Thompson and Raymond, op. cit., pp. 4, 5; *New York Times*, June 4, 1922; July 19, 1936; February 23, 1938; *New York Evening Sun*, February 24, 1938.
16. Thompson and Raymond, op. cit., pp. 5–7.
17. Turkus and Feder, op. cit., pp. 78, 79, 80; Feder and Joesten, op. cit., pp. 54, 55; Thompson and Raymond, op. cit., pp. 17, 18.
18. Ellis, op. cit., p. 509.
19. George Walsh, *Gentleman Jimmy Walker* (New York: Praeger, 1974), pp. 61, 109; Harold Seidman, *Investigating Municipal Administration* (New York: Institute of Public Administration, Columbia University, 1941), p. 8; Ellis, op. cit., pp. 499, 500.
20. Ellis, op. cit., p. 509; Walsh, op. cit., p. 109.
21. Ellis, op. cit., pp. 509, 510.
22. Ibid., p. 511.
23. Thompson and Raymond, op. cit., pp. 144–47; M. R. Werner, *Tammany Hall* (Garden City, N.Y.: Doubleday, Doran, 1928), pp. 559–61.
24. Clarke, op. cit., pp. 1–6, 270, 271; Thompson and Raymond, op. cit., pp. 21, 22.
25. Thompson and Raymond, op. cit., pp. 148, 149.
26. Werner, op. cit., pp. 558, 559; Thompson and Raymond, op. cit., pp. 152, 153.
27. Clarke, op. cit., pp. 91–99.
28. Thompson and Raymond, op. cit., pp. 57, 58; Clarke, op. cit., pp. 145, 146.
29. Fowler, op. cit., pp. 317–22; Clarke, op. cit., pp. 145, 146.
30. Fowler, op. cit., p. 326; Thomspon and Raymond, op. cit., p. 21.
31. Fowler, op. cit., pp. 331, 332, 336; 337; Thompson and Raymond, op. cit., p. 21.

32. Thompson and Raymond, op. cit., pp. 58, 59.

Chapter 12

The Rothstein Era

1. George Wolf with Joseph DiMona, *Frank Costello: Prime Minister of the Underworld* (New York: William Morrow, 1974), pp. 24, 25, 26.
2. Ibid., p. 28; Craig Thompson and Allen Raymond, *Gang Rule in New York* (New York: Dial Press, 1940), p. 66.
3. David Hanna, *Frank Costello: The Gangster with a Thousand Faces* (New York: Belmont Tower Books, 1974), pp. 19, 26; Wolf, op. cit., pp. 29, 30, 31.
4. Hanna, op. cit., pp. 27, 28; Wolf, op. cit., p. 30.
5. Wolf, op. cit., p. 31.
6. Ibid., pp. 32, 33.
7. Ibid., p. 38; Thompson and Raymond, op. cit., p. 66.
8. U.S., Congress, Senate, Special Committee to Investigate Crime in Interstate Commerce, *Investigation of Organized Crime in Interstate Commerce: Hearing on S. 202*, 81st Cong., 2d sess., pt. 2, pp. 131, 159; pt. 7, pp. 1630, 1631; Martin A. Gosch and Richard Hammer, *The Last Testament of Lucky Luciano* (Boston: Little, Brown, 1974), p. 95; Thompson and Raymond, op. cit., pp. 62, 63.
9. Sid Feder and Joachim Joesten, *The Luciano Story* (New York: David McKay, 1954), pp. 39, 40, 43, 45, 46, 55, 57, 58, 59; Gosch and Hammer, op. cit., pp. 40, 41, 57, 87, 88; Burton B. Turkus and Sid Feder, *Murder, Inc.* (New York: Farrar, Straus & Young, 1951), pp. 81, 82; Thompson and Raymond, op. cit., pp. 25, 26, 70.
10. Lloyd Morris, *Incredible New York* (New York: Random House, 1951), pp. 342, 343; Thompson and Raymond, op. cit., p. 3.
11. Hank Messick, *Secret File* (New York: G. P. Putnam's Sons, 1969), pp. 58, 59; *Lansky* (New York: G. P. Putnam's Sons, 1971), pp. 23, 24.
12. Messick, *Secret File*, op. cit., p. 59.
13. Morris, op. cit., p. 343.
14. Thompson and Raymond, op. cit., pp. 63, 64.
15. Messick, *Secret File*, op. cit., p. 59; Lewis J. Valentine, *Autobiography, Night Stick* (New York: Dial Press, 1947), pp. 49, 51.
16. Messick, *Secret File*, op. cit., pp. 59, 60; Thompson and Raymond, op. cit., pp. 26, 45; Valentine, op. cit., p. 48.
17. M. R. Werner, *Tammany Hall* (Garden City: N.Y.: Doubleday, Doran, 1928), p. 564; George Walsh, *Gentleman Jimmy Walker* (New York: Praeger, 1974), pp. 6, 7, 8, 38, 40.
18. Thompson and Raymond, op. cit., pp. 22, 360, 362, 363.
19. Walsh, op. cit., pp. 45, 46.
20. Ibid., pp. 4, 5, 44, 45.
21. Ibid., p. 47; Charles W. Van Devander, *The Big Bosses* (New York: Howell, Soskin, 1944), p. 17.
22. Gene Fowler, *Beau James* (New York: Viking Press, 1949), pp. 144, 145; Walsh, op. cit., p. 48.
23. Fowler, op. cit., pp. 145-9; Walsh, op. cit., pp. 32, 33.
24. Walsh, op. cit., p. 54.
25. Edward Robb Ellis, *The Epic of New York City* (New York: Coward-McCann, 1966), p. 525; Fowler, op. cit., p. 153.
26. Walsh, op. cit., pp. 12, 15, 16, 17; Fowler, op. cit., pp. 18, 48, 49.
27. Walsh, op. cit., pp. 18, 19, 20, 21, 22.
28. Fowler, op. cit., pp. 65, 68, 69.
29. Ibid., pp. 74, 77, 97; Walsh, op. cit., pp. 29, 32.
30. Walsh, op. cit., pp. 65, 67.
31. Valentine, op. cit., pp. 102, 103.
32. Ibid., pp. 104, 105, 106, 107.
33. Walsh, op. cit., pp. 104, 105, 107.
34. Thompson and Raymond, op. cit., pp. 363, 364.

35. Walsh, op. cit., p. 107.
36. Valentine, op. cit., pp. 107, 108; Walsh, op. cit., p. 108.
37. Walsh, op. cit., p. 104.
38. Fowler, op. cit., pp. 190, 191; Walsh, op. cit., pp. 111, 120, 135.
39. Ellis, op. cit., pp. 525, 526.
40. Fowler, op. cit., p. 166.
41. Ibid., p. 190; Walsh, op. cit., p. 110.
42. Walsh, op. cit., pp. 38, 110, 111, 324, 325.
43. Ibid., pp. 36–38; Fowler, op. cit., pp. 131, 132; Thompson and Raymond, op. cit., pp. 231, 232.
44. Thompson and Raymond, op. cit., p. 359.
45. Ibid., pp. 234, 235.
46. Ibid., pp. 236, 237, 238, 239.
47. John Kobler, *Capone: The Life and World of Al Capone* (New York: G. P. Putnam's Sons, 1971), pp. 34, 35; Turkus and Feder, op. cit., p. 80.
48. Jack McPhaul, *Johnny Torrio* (New Rochelle, N.Y.: Arlington House, 1970), p. 204; Thompson and Raymond, op. cit., p. 116; Kobler, op. cit., p. 34.
49. McPhaul, op. cit., pp. 50, 51; Kobler, op. cit., pp. 23, 36.
50. McPhaul, op. cit., p. 121; Kobler, op. cit., p. 37.
51. Kobler, op. cit., p. 72; Virgil W. Peterson, *Barbarians in Our Midst* (Boston: Little, Brown, 1952), p. 108.
52. Kobler, op. cit., pp. 128–33; Peterson, op. cit., pp. 125, 126.
53. Peterson, op. cit., p. 127.
54. Herbert Asbury, *The Great Illusion: An Informal History of Prohibition* (Garden City, N.Y.: Doubleday, 1950), pp. 203, 253, 254; Kobler, op. cit., p. 223.
55. Kobler, op. cit., pp. 146, 223, 224.
56. Thompson and Raymond, op. cit., pp. 115, 116, 117.
57. Ibid., pp. 355, 395; Turkus and Feder, op. cit., p. 80.
58. Paul Sann, *Kill the Dutchman! The Story of Dutch Schultz* (New Rochelle, N.Y.: Arlington House, 1971), pp. 105, 109–19.
59. Donald Henderson Clarke, *In the Reign of Rothstein* (New York: Grosset & Dunlap, 1929), pp. 284, 285, 286.
60. Valentine, op. cit., pp. 109, 110; Clarke, op. cit., pp. 286, 291.
61. Valentine, op. cit., p. 110.
62. Thompson and Raymond, op. cit., pp. 67, 68.
63. Fowler, op. cit., pp. 230, 231, 232.
64. Valentine, op. cit., pp. 110, 111; Fowler, op. cit., pp. 147, 186, 232, 233, 234; Walter Chambers, *Samuel Seabury: A Challenge* (New York: Century, 1932), pp. 214, 215.
65. Thompson and Raymond, op. cit., pp. 53, 65, 66, 69; Walsh, op. cit., p. 200.
66. Clarke, op. cit., pp. 8, 291; Thompson and Raymond, op. cit., pp. 70, 71.
67. McPhaul, op. cit., pp. 233, 234, 235.
68. Elmer L. Irey as told to William J. Slocum, *The Tax Dodgers* (Garden City, N.Y.: Garden City Publishing, 1948), pp. 159, 160.
69. Gosch and Hammer, op. cit., pp. 91, 93, 94, 95; Thompson and Raymond, op. cit., pp. 358, 359; Messick, *Secret File*, pp. 96, 97, 100; Hank Messick, *The Silent Syndicate* (New York: Macmillan Co., 1967), pp. 55, 56, 98.
70. Wolf, op. cit., pp. 74, 87, 88, 89; Thompson and Raymond, op. cit., pp. 356, 357.
71. Messick, *Secret File*, pp. 137, 138, 139.
72. Messick, *Lansky*, pp. 35–40; Gosch and Hammer, op. cit., pp. 103–8.
73. Wolf, op. cit., p. 91; Kobler, op. cit., pp. 259, 260, 261, 262; McPhaul, op. cit., pp. 252–55.
74. Kobler, op. cit., p. 264.

Chapter 13

The Seabury Investigations

1. George Walsh, *Gentleman Jimmy Walker* (New York: Praeger, 1974), pp. 182, 183, 185–87; Gene

Fowler, *Beau James* (New York: Viking Press, 1949), pp. 238–40; Walter Chambers, *Samuel Seabury: A Challenge* (New York: Century, 1932), pp. 212, 213.

2. Fowler, op. cit., pp. 239, 240.
3. Walsh, op. cit., pp. 189–91.
4. Ibid., p. 208.
5. Fowler, op. cit., pp. 243, 244.
6. Walsh, op. cit., pp. 198, 199; Fowler, op. cit., p. 245.
7. Walsh, op. cit., pp. 196, 197.
8. Fowler, op. cit., p. 255; Walsh, op. cit., p. 204.
9. Walsh, op. cit., pp. 200–202, 204; Fowler, op. cit., p. 255.
10. Chambers, op. cit., pp. 213, 214; Norman Thomas and Paul Blanshard, *What's the Matter with New York* (New York: Macmillan Co., 1932), p. 338.
11. Samuel Eliot Morison, *The Oxford History of the American People* (New York: Oxford University Press, 1965), pp. 940–43.
12. Craig Thompson and Allen Raymond, *Gang Rule in New York* (New York: Dial Press, 1940), pp. 200, 207.
13. Ibid., pp. 204–6, 318, 319; Paul Sann, *Kill the Dutchman! The Story of Dutch Schultz* (New Rochelle, N.Y.: Arlington House, 1971), pp. 127–32.
14. Thompson and Raymond, op. cit., p. 201; Walsh, op. cit., pp. 205, 206.
15. Thompson and Raymond, op. cit., pp. 203, 204, 212, 213, 214, 368; Walsh, op. cit., pp. 206, 207.
16. Chambers, op. cit., pp. 216, 217; Fowler, op. cit., p. 270.
17. Thompson and Raymond, op. cit., pp. 215, 216.
18. Fowler, op. cit., pp. 269–71.
19. Ibid., pp. 272, 273; Walsh, op. cit., pp. 223, 224.
20. Walsh, op. cit., pp. 224–26; Fowler, op. cit., pp. 273, 274; Chambers, op. cit., p. 223.
21. Chambers, op. cit., pp. 221–23; Charles Garrett, *The LaGuardia Years* (New Brunswick, N.J.: Rutgers University Press, 1961), p. 66.
22. Fowler, op. cit., p. 271.
23. Garrett, op. cit., pp. 70–76, 81–83.
24. Ibid., pp. 66, 67.
25. Ibid., pp. 68–70; Chambers, op. cit., pp. 245, 251, 252.
26. Chambers, op. cit., pp. 232, 250, 251.
27. Ibid., pp. 265, 266, 268–70, 274.
28. Ibid., pp. 275–82.
29. Garrett, op. cit., p. 69; Walsh, op. cit., p. 240.
30. Garrett, op. cit., pp. 64, 71.
31. Herbert Mitgang, *The Man Who Rode the Tiger* (New York: J. B. Lippincott, 1963), pp. 208, 209; Garrett, op. cit., pp. 71, 72.
32. Thompson and Raymond, op. cit., pp. 224, 263–67.
33. Mitgang, op. cit., pp. 209, 210.
34. Chambers, op. cit., p. 292.
35. Mitgang, op. cit., p. 221; Chambers, op. cit., pp. 299, 300; Garrett, op. cit., pp. 72, 73.
36. Garrett, op. cit., p. 73.
37. Chambers, op. cit., pp. 325–29; Mitgang, op. cit., pp. 240, 241.
38. Chambers, op. cit., p. 325.
39. Milton Mackaye, *The Tin Box Parade* (New York: Robert M. McBride, 1934), pp. 188–97; Mitgang, op. cit., p. 241; Chambers, op. cit., pp. 330–32.
40. Mitgang, op. cit., pp. 234–36; Chambers, op. cit., pp. 334–38.
41. Chambers, op. cit., pp. 333, 334.
42. Mitgang, op. cit., p. 228; Garrett, op. cit., p. 74.
43. Mitgang, op. cit., pp. 222–27.
44. Sid Feder and Joachim Joesten, *The Luciano Story* (New York: David McKay, 1954), pp. 75, 76.
45. Martin A. Gosch and Richard Hammer, *The Last Testament of Lucky Luciano* (Boston: Little, Brown, 1974), pp. 131, 132; Feder and Joesten, op. cit., pp. 75–78.
46. Feder and Joesten, op. cit., pp. 79–83.
47. Gosch and Hammer, op. cit., pp. 138–43; Feder and Joesten, op. cit., pp. 83, 84; U.S., Congress,

Senate, Subcommittee on Investigations of the Committee on Government Operations, *Organized Crime and Illicit Traffic in Narcotics: Hearings on S. 17*, 88th Cong., 1st sess., 1963, pt. 1, pp. 228–33; N.Y., Crime Commission, *Public Hearings, No. 4* (pursuant to governor's executive order of March 29, 1951), November 14, 1952, vol. 2, pp. 308–11.

48. Feder and Joesten, op. cit., pp. 82, 83; Gosch and Hammer, op. cit., pp. 143, 144; Sann, op. cit., p. 143; J. Richard (Dixie) Davis, "Things I Couldn't Tell Till Now," *Collier's*, August 5, 1939, p. 44.

49. Davis, op. cit., p. 44.

50. Warren Moscow, *The Last of the Big-Time Bosses* (New York: Stein & Day, 1971), p. 45; Thompson and Raymond, op. cit., p. 364.

51. Thompson and Raymond, op. cit., pp. 363, 365, 394.

52. Ibid., pp. 367–71; Feder and Joesten, op. cit., pp. 52, 53.

53. George Wolf with Joseph DiMona, *Frank Costello: Prime Minister of the Underworld* (New York: William Morrow, 1974), pp. 104, 105; Sann, op. cit., p. 72; Thompson and Raymond, op. cit., pp. 12, 104, 105, 131, 356, 378–81; "Kingpin Costello, Gamblers' Gambler," *Newsweek*, November 21, 1949, pp. 27–33.

54. Stanley Walker, *The Night Club Era* (New York City: Blue Ribbon Books, 1933), pp. 104, 122, 124.

55. Ibid., pp. 103, 113, 117–20; Thompson and Raymond, op. cit., pp. 32–37.

56. Walker, op. cit., pp. 113–15.

57. Thompson and Raymond, op. cit., pp. 47, 96, 97, 130, 167; Wolf, op. cit., pp. 63, 64, 68, 71; Herbert Asbury, *The Great Illusion* (Garden City, N.Y.: Doubleday, 1950), pp. 254, 255; "Kingpin Costello, Gamblers' Gambler," *Newsweek*, November 21, 1949, pp. 28, 31.

58. Walker, op. cit., pp. 105, 108-11; Thompson and Raymond, op. cit., pp. 67, 105, 312; Sann, op. cit., pp. 114; Asbury, op. cit., p. 202.

59. Sann, op. cit., pp. 144, 145.

60. Walker, op. cit., pp. 111, 124–27; *Chicago Tribune*, April 24, 1965.

61. Davis, op. cit., July 29, 1939, pp. 37, 38; Sann, op. cit., pp 159–63, 180, 181.

62. Davis, op. cit., August 5, 1939, p. 44; Sann, op. cit., pp. 171, 172.

63. Davis, op. cit., July 29, 1939, p. 40; Sann, op. cit., pp. 150, 186, 187.

64. Sann, op. cit., pp. 147, 148; Davis, op. cit., July 29, 1939, p. 40.

65. Martin M. Frank, *Diary of a D.A.* (New York: Henry Holt, 1957), pp. 139, 140, 147–56; Sann, op. cit., pp. 138, 149.

66. Sann, op. cit., pp. 152–55; Davis, July 29, 1939, p. 40.

67. Lewis J. Valentine, *Autobiography, Night Stick* (New York: Dial Press, 1947), pp. 47, 48; Davis, op. cit., July 29, 1939, p. 40.

68. Walsh, op. cit., p. 302.

69. Garrett, op. cit., p. 75; Walsh, op. cit., p. 305.

70. Mackaye, op. cit., pp. 284–91.

71. Walsh, op. cit., pp. 306–8; Mitgang, op. cit., p. 252.

72. Garrett, op. cit., p. 76.

73. Walsh, op. cit., pp. 279, 280, 281; Mitgang, op. cit., p. 252.

74. Garrett, op. cit., p. 76; Walsh, op. cit., p. 280.

75. Garrett, op. cit., p 76; Walsh, op. cit., p. 311; Mitgang, op. cit., p. 253.

76. Garrett, op. cit., p. 77; Walsh, op. cit., pp. 315, 316.

77. Thomas and Blanshard, op. cit., pp. 350–55; Mitgang, op. cit., pp. 263, 264.

78. Thomas and Blanshard, op. cit., p. 178; Mitgang, op. cit., p. 265.

79. Mitgang, op. cit., p. 264.

80. Thompson and Raymond, op. cit., pp. 244, 366, 367; Gosch and Hammer, op. cit., pp. 162, 163.

81. Virgil W. Peterson, *Barbarians in Our Midst* (Boston: Little, Brown, 1952), p. 158.

82. Mitgang, op. cit., pp. 282–84, 293, 295–97; Walsh, op. cit., p. 327.

83. Walsh, op. cit., pp. 327, 329, 333–36, 338–40.

84. Garrett, op. cit., pp. 91–93; Walsh, op. cit., pp. 330–32; Mackaye, op. cit., pp. 322, 323.

Chapter 14

The Downfall of Dutch Schultz, Lucky Luciano, and Jimmy Hines

1. Edward J. Flynn, *You're the Boss* (New York: Viking Press, 1947), pp. 133–38.
2. Charles Garrett, *The LaGuardia Years* (New Brunswick, N.J.: Rutgers University Press, 1961), p. 171; Warren Moscow, *Politics in the Empire State* (New York: Alfred A. Knopf, 1948), p. 120.
3. Thomas E. Dewey, *Twenty Against the Underworld*, ed. Rodney Campbell (Garden City, N.Y.: Doubleday, 1974), pp. 329, 330.
4. Edward Robb Ellis, *The Epic of New York City* (New York: Coward-McCann, 1966), p. 550.
5. Fiorello H. LaGuardia, *The Making of an Insurgent: An Autobiography, 1882–1919* (New York: J. B. Lippincott, 1948), pp. 17, 19, 20, 24, 25.
6. Ibid., pp. 33, 34, 38, 39, 62, 63, 70, 71.
7. Ibid., pp. 77, 96, 100, 101, 106, 117, 119, 127, 146, 165, 169–71, 182, 183, 196.
8. George Walsh, *Gentleman Jimmy Walker* (New York: Praeger, 1974), p. 336; Garret, op. cit., p. 305.
9. Lewis J. Valentine, *Autobiography, Night Stick* (New York: Dial Press, 1947), pp. 119, 120, 121; Lowell M. Limpus, *Honest Cop Lewis J. Valentine* (New York: E. P. Dutton, 1939), p. 163.
10. Newbold Morris with Dana Lee Thomas, *Let the Chips Fall* (New York: Appleton-Century-Crofts, 1955), p. 117; Garrett, op. cit., pp. 159, 160.
11. George Wolf with Joseph DiMona, *Frank Costello: Prime Minister of the Underworld* (New York: William Morrow, 1974), pp. 105, 107; Garrett, op. cit., p. 160.
12. Harnett T. Kane, *Louisiana Hayride* (New York: William Morrow, 1941), pp. 397–402; Wolf, op. cit., p. 108.
13. Hank Messick, *Secret File* (New York: G. P. Putnam's Sons, 1969), p. 242; Wolf, op. cit., p. 109.
14. Hank Messick, *Lansky* (New York: G. P. Putnam's Sons, 1971), pp. 84, 85, 86.
15. T. Harry Williams, *Huey Long* (New York: Alfred A. Knopf, 1970), p. 825.
16. Messick, *Secret File,* p. 242.
17. Dewey, op. cit., pp. 149, 150.
18. Ibid., pp. 150–52; Garrett, op. cit., pp. 165, 166.
19. Dewey, op. cit., pp. 72, 74, 75, 78, 80.
20. Ibid., pp. 98–101.
21. Craig Thompson and Allen Raymond, *Gang Rule in New York* (New York: Dial Press, 1940), p. 294; Garrett, op. cit., p. 163; Dewey, op. cit., pp. 109, 110.
22. Dewey, op. cit., p. 117.
23. Ibid., pp. 121, 122.
24. Ibid., pp. 119–21, 125, 126, 138; Elmer L. Irey as told to William J. Slocum, *The Tax Dodgers* (Garden City, N.Y.: Garden City Publishing, 1948), pp. 140, 147–53.
25. Dewey, op. cit., pp. 142, 143, 150–52, 161.
26. Ibid., pp. 13, 156, 157, 161, 162.
27. Ibid., p. 158; Garrett, op. cit., p. 167.
28. Paul Sann, *Kill the Dutchman! The Story of Dutch Schultz* (New Rochelle, N.Y.: Arlington House, 1971), p. 74.
29. Dewey, op. cit., pp. 278–82; Thompson and Raymond, op. cit., pp. 252–60.
30. Sann, op. cit., pp. 241–54; Dewey, op. cit., pp. 271, 272.
31. Sann, op. cit., pp. 256–59.
32. Ibid., pp. 11–17.
33. Ibid., pp. 22–29, 31–39, 314–18; Burton B. Turkus and Sid Feder, *Murder, Inc.* (New York: Farrar, Straus & Young, 1951), pp. 141–45, 150; Dewey, op. cit., pp. 276, 277.
34. Sann, op. cit., pp. 40–46.
35. Ibid., pp. 51, 68, 297.
36. Turkus and Feder, op. cit., pp. 134–41; Dewey, op. cit., p. 276.
37. Sann, op. cit., pp. 20, 293, 313, 314; Turkus and Feder, op. cit., pp. 131, 132.
38. Sann, op. cit., pp. 313, 314, 318.
39. Ibid., pp. 324, 325, 326, 328, 335; Turkus and Feder, op. cit., pp. 159, 160.

40. Dewey, op. cit., pp. 180–83.
41. Ibid., pp. 186, 188, 189.
42. Ibid., p. 190.
43. Ibid., pp. 186, 193, 198, 203, 204.
44. Ibid., pp. 194, 202, 203.
45. Ibid., pp. 205, 206; Messick, *Lansky,* p. 86; Martin A. Gosch and Richard Hammer, *The Last Testament of Lucky Luciano* (Boston: Little, Brown, 1974), pp. 193–97.
46. Dewey, op. cit., pp. 207, 208, 221, 223, 227.
47. Ibid., pp. 214, 215, 245, 246, 247.
48. Ibid., pp. 263–6; Garrett, op. cit., p. 169; Gosch and Hammer, op. cit., pp. 201–25.
49. Dewey, op. cit., pp. 269, 270; Gosch and Hammer, op. cit., p. 189.
50. Dewey, op. cit., p. 294.
51. Garrett, op. cit., pp. 169, 170; Virgil W. Peterson, "Citizens Crime Commissions," *Federal Probation* 17, no. 1 (March 1953).
52. Garrett, op. cit., p. 259; Moscow, op. cit., pp. 102–3.
53. Dewey, op. cit., pp. 286, 287, 291; Thompson and Raymond, op. cit., pp. 252–60.
54. Dewey, op. cit., p 297; Valentine, op. cit., p. 133; Turkus and Feder, op. cit., pp. 331–33; John Starr, *The Purveyor* (New York: Holt, Rinehart & Winston, 1961), pp. 137, 138.
55. Turkus and Feder, op. cit., pp. 348, 349; Dewey, op. cit., p. 460.
56. Turkus and Feder, op. cit., p. 350; Garrett, op. cit., p. 170; Starr, op. cit., p. 138.
57. Dewey, op. cit., pp. 299–304.
58. N.Y. Crime Commission, *Public Hearings, No. 4* (pursuant to governor's executive order of March 29, 1951), November 23, 1952, vol. 1, pp. 93–97; Starr, op. cit., p. 139; Turkus and Feder, op. cit., pp. 386, 387.
59. Dewey, op. cit., pp. 324, 325.
60. Moscow, op. cit., pp. 25, 26.
61. Dewey, op. cit., pp. 326, 333; Garrett, op. cit., pp. 261, 266, 267; Moscow, op. cit., p. 75.
62. Garrett, op. cit., pp. 305, 306; Thompson and Raymond, op. cit., p. 360.
63. Morris op. cit., pp. 121, 122.
64. Dewey, op. cit., pp. 353–55.
65. LaGuardia, op. cit., p. 96.
66. Dewey, op. cit., p. 380.
67. Ibid., pp. 320, 321, 372–75, 382–85, 387–89, 447, 451; Garrett, op. cit., p. 172.
68. Dewey, op. cit., pp. 384–87; Ralph Salerno and John S. Tompkins, *The Crime Confederation* (Garden City, N.Y.: Doubleday, 1969), p. 348. Reportedly, telephone taps revealed that Jimmy Hines was sharing in the profits of the Schultz policy operations. However, the statement that Hines and Schultz actually met only once was solidly controverted by a number of witnesses at the Hines trial.
69. Dewey, op. cit., pp. 385, 386, 463–65, 470, 471.
70. Ibid., pp. 386, 461; Garrett, op. cit., pp. 171, 172.
71. Dewey, op. cit., pp. 386, 387.
72. Ibid., pp. 386, 452, 461.
73. Ibid., pp. 465, 474, 475.
74. Ibid., pp. 475, 476; Turkus and Feder, op. cit., pp. 360, 361, 363, 364, 369, 371–74, 410–15; Valentine, op. cit., p. 138.
75. Thompson and Raymond, op. cit., p. 131.
76. Garrett, op. cit., pp. 173–75.
77. Morris, op. cit., pp. 215–16; Ellis, op. cit., pp. 565, 566.
78. Daniel Bell, *The End of Ideology* (New York: Free Press, 1962), pp. 144, 145; Garrett, op. cit., pp. 304, 305.

Chapter 15

The O'Dwyer Years—Costello Influence

1. Burton B. Turkus and Sid Feder, *Murder, Inc.* (New York: Farrar, Straus & Young, 1951), p. 55; Lewis J. Valentine, *Autobiography, Night Stick* (New York: Dial Press, 1947), p. 141.
2. Turkus and Feder, op. cit., pp. 51, 53–8, 62, 70; Valentine, op. cit., p. 146.

3. Valentine, op. cit., pp. 141, 142.
4. Turkus and Feder, op. cit., pp. 216, 217, 220, 229, 231, 235–37, 259, 262, 263, 324, 325, 358.
5. Ibid., pp. 302–4, 307, 309, 310, 319, 323, 324, 325, 329.
6. Ibid., pp. 4, 22, 67, 332; U.S., Congress, Senate, Committee to Investigate Organized Crime in Interstate Commerce, *Investigation of Organized Crime in Interstate Commerce: Hearing on S. 202*, 81st Cong., 2d sess., and 82d Cong., 1st sess., 1951, pt. 7, pp. 1342, 1364, 1365. Hereafter referred to as Kefauver Committee Hearings.
7. Hank Messick, *Lansky* (New York: G. P. Putnam's Sons, 1971), pp. 72–77.
8. Malcolm Johnson, *Crime on the Labor Front* (New York: McGraw-Hill, 1950), p. 192; N.Y. Crime Commission, *Public Hearings, No. 5* (pursuant to governor's executive orders of March 29, 1951, and November 13, 1952), vol. 3, pp. 1590, 1592, 1593, 1695–99, 1704; vol. 5, pp. 3654, 3655; Kefauver Committee Hearings, pt. 7, p. 1575.
9. Kefauver Committee Hearings, pt. 7, pp. 1363, 1571–73.
10. Turkus and Feder, op. cit., pp. 436, 437.
11. Ibid., pp. 437–40; Kefauver Committee Hearings, pt. 7, pp. 1348, 1349.
12. Turkus and Feder, op. cit., pp. 443, 453–58.
13. Charles Garrett, *The LaGuardia Years* (New Brunswick, N.J.: Rutgers University Press, 1961), pp. 271, 272, 273; Kefauver Committee Hearings, pt. 7, pp. 572, 854, 855.
14. Edward Robb Ellis, *The Epic of New York City* (New York: Coward-McCann, 1966), p. 559.
15. Kefauver Committee Hearings, pt. 7, pp. 1351, 1352, 1355, 1359, 1360, 1525, 1526.
16. Ibid., pp. 621, 628; Daniel Bell, *The End of Ideology* (New York: Free Press, 1962), p. 145.
17. Kefauver Committee Hearings, pt. 7, pp. 1161, 1162.
18. Garrett, op. cit., p. 295; Ellis, op. cit., p. 568; Kefauver Committee Hearings, pt. 7, pp. 1287, 1369, 1370.
19. Kefauver Committee Hearings, pt. 7, pp. 1393, 1394, 1578.
20. Ibid., pt. 7, pp. 635, 1066, 1068–71, 1297, 1395.
21. N.Y., Crime Commission, *Public Hearings, No. 4*, vol. 2, pp. 390, 391; Kefauver Committee Hearings, pt. 7, pp. 1426–32.
22. George Wolf with Joseph DiMona, *Frank Costello: Prime Minister of the Underworld* (New York: William Morrow, 1974), pp. 125, 221; Kefauver Committee Hearings, pt. 7, pp. 629–32, 722–24, 1370–73, 1378, 1379, 1383, 1384, 1536, 1538, 1539, 1622–24. See page 1371 for O'Dwyer's recollection that Irving Sherman, at O'Dwyer's request, arranged the meeting with Frank Costello. That recollection is undoubtedly correct. Moran's account of the affair is faulty in several respects.
23. N.Y., Crime Commission, *Public Hearings, No. 4*, vol.1, pp. 192, 194; Kefauver Committee Hearings, pt. 7, p. 1429.
24. N.Y., Crime Commission, *Public Hearings, No. 4*, vol. 1, pp. 195–98.
25. Ibid., pp. 153, 157, 161–63, 169–72.
26. Robert H. Prall and Norton Mockridge, *This Is Costello* (New York: Fawcett, 1951), pp. 44–46; Wolf, op. cit., pp. 134–37, 140–43, 148, 221, 226; Kefauver Committee Hearings, pt. 7, pp. 1008, 1391, 1432, 1433, 1561.
27. N.Y., Crime Commission, *Public Hearings, No. 4*, vol. 2, pp. 397, 398, 404–6, 408, 409, 446; Kefauver Committee Hearings, pt. 7, pp. 1436, 1691.
28. Wolf, op. cit., pp. 153–56; Prall and Mockridge, op. cit., pp. 49, 50.
29. Kefauver Committee Hearings, pt. 7, pp. 3, 125, 126, 129, 131, 135, 136, 298, 299, 301, 302, 316, 1658, 1659; N.Y., Crime Commission, *Public Hearings*, No. 5, vol . 3, pp. 1702, 1703; Fred J. Cook, *The Secret Rulers* (New York: Duell, Sloan & Pearce, 1966), pp. 103, 109, 122, 123, 168, 170, 216, 248, 249.
30. Ellis, op. cit., p. 564.
31. Garrett, op. cit., p. 285; Newbold Morris with Dana Lee Thomas, *Let the Chips Fall* (New York: Appleton-Century-Crofts, 1955), pp. 202, 204.
32. Valentine, op. cit., pp. 29, 188, 288, 289.
33. Morris, op. cit., p. 216; Kefauver Committee Hearings, pt. 7, p. 1367.
34. Kefauver Committee Hearings, pt. 7, pp. 1620, 1692, 1693.
35. Ibid., pp. 1389, 1578.
36. Garrett, op. cit., pp. 295, 296; Morris, op. cit., pp. 206–8.
37. Garrett, op. cit., p. 287; Kefauver Committee Hearings, pt. 7, p. 1394.

38. Garrett, op. cit., pp. 297, 298; Morris, op. cit., pp. 216, 217.
39. Garrett, op. cit., p. 299; Kefauver Committee Hearings, pt. 7, pp. 1297, 1392, 1393.
40. Editorial, *Boston Globe*, September 20, 1947; Ellis, op. cit., p. 569; Garrett, op. cit., pp. 300, 301.
41. Morris, op. cit., p. 234.
42. Kefauver Committee Hearings, pt. 7, pp. 1349, 1495–98, 1500–1503.
43. Ibid., pp. 564, 570, 852, 854, 855, 1564.
44. Ibid., pp. 1678, 1679, 1682, 1683, 1685, 1686.
45. Morris, op. cit., p. 226; Fulton Oursler, "The Remarkable Story of William O'Dwyer," *Reader's Digest*, May 1952, p. 9.
46. Kefauver Committee Hearings, pt. 7, pp. 636, 637, 1299, 1300, 1313, 1542, 1543.
47. N.Y., Crime Commission, *Public Hearings, No. 4*, vol. 2, pp. 398, 399; Kefauver Committee Hearings, pt. 7, pp. 1560–62; Wolf, op. cit., p. 221.
48. Kefauver Committee Hearings, pt. 7, p. 1558.
49. Martin A. Gosch and Richard Hammer, *The Last Testament of Lucky Luciano* (Boston: Little, Brown, 1974), pp. 276, 277.
50. Kefauver Committee Hearings, pt. 7, pp. 606, 607.
51. Sid Feder and Joachim Joesten, *The Luciano Story* (New York: David McKay, 1954), pp. 221–27; Wolf, op. cit., pp. 168, 169; Gosch and Hammer, op. cit., pp. 281–88; N.Y., Crime Commission, *Public Hearings, No. 4*, vol. 1, pp. 172–73.
52. Kefauver Committee Hearings, pt. 7, pp. 610–12; Gosch and Hammer, op. cit., pp. 305–7.
53. Gosch and Hammer, op. cit., p. 311; Kefauver Committee Hearings, pt. 7, pp. 609, 611, 650, 651, 1662, 1663.
54. Gosch and Hammer, op. cit., pp. 306–19, 330; Kefauver Committee Hearings, pt. 2, p. 189; pt. 10, pp. 46, 47, 85, 86.
55. Feder and Joesten, op. cit., pp. 230–47; Gosch and Hammer, op. cit., pp. 322–27.
56. Kefauver Committee Hearings, op. cit., pt. 7, pp. 1436, 1556, 1599, 1600; N.Y., Crime Commission, *Public Hearings, No. 4*, vol. 1, p. 167; vol. 2, pp. 520–24.
57. Kefauver Committee Hearings, pt. 7, p. 1620.
58. Ibid., pp. 1550–53.
59. N.Y., Crime Commission, *Public Hearings, No. 4*, vol. 2, pp. 528, 529.
60. *New York Times*, January 26, 1949; Wolf, op. cit., pp. 150, 151.
61. N.Y. County, Report of the District Attorney, 1946–48, pp. 43–46; Johnson, op. cit., p. 176; Kefauver Committee Hearings, pt. 7, pp. 305, 306, 860, 861; William J. Keating with Richard Carter, *The Man Who Rocked the Boat* (New York: Harper & Brothers, 1956), pp. 81–83, 91, 94, 95, 109, 110.
62. Johnson, op. cit., pp. 177–83; N.Y., Crime Commission, *Public Hearings, No. 5*, vol. 5, pp. 3619, 3620.
63. *New York Sun*, October 28, 1949.
64. Norton Mockridge and Robert H. Prall, *The Big Fix* (New York: Henry Holt, 1954), pp. 212, 220–23.
65. Walter Arm, *Pay-Off* (New York: Appleton-Century-Crofts, 1951), pp. 1–11; Ed Reid, *The Shame of New York* (New York: Random House, 1953), pp. 18, 19.
66. Arm, op. cit., pp. 203, 208; Cook, op. cit., pp. 273, 274.
67. Arm, op. cit., pp. 100, 101, 131; Mockridge and Prall, *Big Fix*, p. 248.
68. Arm, op. cit., pp. 43–47, 49, 52, 53, 55; Mockridge and Prall, *Big Fix*, pp. 94, 180–83, 187, 188, 257.
69. Mockridge and Prall, *Big Fix*, pp. 235–37.
70. Ibid., pp. 244, 245, 309–12; *New York Times*, March 23, 1951; October 15, 1952; Kefauver Committee Hearings, pt. 7, p. 1563.
71. *New York Times*, September 27; October 1, 1950; Arm, op. cit., p. 134; Mockridge and Prall, *Big Fix*, p. 250.
72. Mockridge and Prall, *Big Fix*, p. 251.
73. Arm, op. cit., pp. 164, 166, 167.
74. Ibid., pp. 255–61; Keating, op. cit., pp. 182–96.
75. Arm, op. cit., pp. 169–86; Mockridge and Prall, *Big Fix*, pp. 306, 307, 330, 334.

Chapter 16

The Kefauver Committee Hearings

1. *New York Times,* December 3, 1949; *Chicago Herald-American,* December 2, 1949; *Cleveland Plain Dealer,* December 3, 1949; *American City,* January 1950; William Howard Moore, *The Kefauver Committee and the Politics of Crime, 1950–1952* (Columbia: University of Missouri Press, 1974), p. 38, 39.
2. Moore, op. cit., pp. 43, 44, 49–53; Virgil W. Peterson, *Barbarians in Our Midst* (Boston: Little, Brown, 1952), p. 257.
3. U.S., Congress, Senate, Special Committee to Investigate Organized Crime in Interstate Commerce, *Third Interim Report on S. 202,* 82d Cong., 1st sess., Senate Report No. 307, pp. 20, 21. Hereafter referred to as *Third Interim Report.* Peterson, op. cit., p. 258; Moore, op. cit., pp. 59–66.
4. U.S., Congress, Senate, Subcommittee of the Committee on Interstate and Foreign Commerce, *Transmission of Gambling Information: Hearings on S. 3358,* 81st Cong., 2d sess., 1950, pp. 472, 477, 479, 482.
5. *New York Times,* May 18–20; June 20, 1950; N.Y., Crime Commission, *Public Hearings, No. 4,* vol. 1, p. 202.
6. *Third Interim Report,* pp. 110, 111; Moore, op. cit., p. 181.
7. Estes Kefauver, *Crime in America* (Garden City, N.Y.: Doubleday, 1951), p. 283; Moore, op. cit., p. 184.
8. Kefauver Committee Hearings, pt. 7, pp. 915, 918, 929, 930, 933, 964, 1658, 1659; *Third Interim Report,* p. 112.
9. Kefauver Committee Hearings, pt. 2, p. 189; pt. 7, pp. 602–6, 1635, 1636; pt. 10, pp. 46, 47; *Third Interim Report,* p. 112; Virgil W. Peterson, *The Juke Box Racket* (Chicago: Chicago Crime Commission, 1954), pp. 28–30.
10. Kefauver Committee Hearings, pt. 7, pp. 941–60; *Third Interim Report,* pp. 113–15.
11. Kefauver Committee Hearings, pt. 7, pp. 966–68, 970, 1018.
12. *Third Interim Report,* pp. 111, 121–24.
13. Ibid., p. 116; George Wolf with Joseph DiMona, *Frank Costello: Prime Minister of the Underworld* (New York: William Morrow, 1974), pp. 73, 74, 80, 143.
14. *Third Interim Report,* pp. 115–17.
15. Kefauver Committee Hearings, pt. 7, p. 309; Moore, op. cit., pp. 189, 190.
16. Kefauver Committee Hearings, pt. 7, p. 1326; *Third Interim Report,* pp. 124, 125; Moore, op. cit., p. 196; Kefauver, *Crime in America,* pp. 288, 289.
17. Kefauver Committee Hearings, pt. 7, pp. 580, 853, 854, 1563, 1564; *Third Interim Report,* p. 139; Fred J. Cook, *The Secret Rulers* (New York: Duell, Sloan & Pearce, 1966), p. 108.
18. Kefauver Committee Hearings, pt. 7, p. 1575; *Third Interim Report,* p. 139.
19. *Third Interim Report,* pp. 126–29; Kefauver Committee Hearings, pt. 7, pp. 1355, 1356; Burton B. Turkus and Sid Feder, *Murder, Inc.* (New York: Farrar, Straus & Young, 1951), pp. 464–67.
20. *Third Interim Report,* pp. 129, 130; Kefauver Committee Hearings, pt. 7, pp. 1371, 1543, 1544.
21. Kefauver Committee Hearings, *Final Report,* pp. 62–65; *Third Interim Report,* pp. 138, 139.
22. *Third Interim Report,* pp. 141, 142.
23. Ibid., pp. 143, 144.
24. Ibid., pp. 1, 2.
25. Ibid., pp. 2, 149, 150.
26. Ibid., pp. 1–5.

Chapter 17

The New York Waterfront Hearings

1. N.Y., Crime Commission, *Public Hearings, No. 5,* vol. 5, pp. 3620, 3622, 3623; N.Y., Crime Commission, *Fourth Report to the Governor, the Attorney General, and the Legislature of the State of New York,* May 20, 1953, Legislative Document no. 70, p. 7. Hereafter referred to as *Fourth Report.*
2. *Third Interim Report,* p. 132.
3. Kefauver Committee Hearings, pt. 7, pp. 673, 674, 678, 1487–89; N.Y., Crime Commission,

Public Hearings, No. 5, vol. 1, p. 275; vol. 3, pp. 1594, 1697.

4. N.Y., Crime Commission, *Public Hearings, No. 5,* vol. 1, pp. 276, 318, 319; vol 3, p. 1694; Kefauver Committee Hearings, pt. 7, pp. 1487, 1488; *New York Times,* December 14, 1952.

5. Kefauver Committee Hearings, pt. 7, p. 683; N.Y., Crime Commission, *Public Hearings, No. 5,* vol. 3, pp. 1595, 1596, 1705, 1706; Malcolm Johnson, *Crime on the Labor Front* (New York: McGraw-Hill, 1950), p. 192.

6. Kefauver Committee Hearings, pt. 7, pp. 673, 675, 680.

7. *Annual Report for the Year 1952,* New York City Anti-Crime Committee, pp. 12, 13.

8. *Fourth Report,* pp. 5, 6; N.Y., Crime Commission, *Public Hearings, No. 5,* vol. 1, p. 1.

9. Johnson, op. cit., pp. 91, 92; *Fourth Report,* p. 7.

10. Johnson, op. cit., pp. 112, 113; *Fourth Report,* pp. 37, 39–41.

11. N.Y., Crime Commission, *Public Hearings, No. 5,* vol. 1, pp. 64, 68–72, 109–13; vol. 4, pp. 2616, 2617; Johnson, op. cit., p. 139.

12. N.Y., Crime Commission, *Public Hearings, No. 5,* vol. 1, pp. 158–160.

13. U.S., Congress, Senate, Subcommittee of the Committee on Interstate and Foreign Commerce, *Waterfront Investigation: Hearing on S. 41,* 83d Cong., 1st sess., 1953, pt. 1, pp. 462, 560, 561. Hereafter referred to as *Waterfront Investigation. Annual Report,* Waterfront Commission of New York Harbor, 1954–55, p. 4.

14. N.Y., Crime Commission, *Public Hearings, No. 5,* vol. 5, p. 3629; Johnson, op. cit., pp. 156, 157.

15. N.Y., Crime Commission, *Public Hearings, No. 5,* vol. 5, pp. 3607, 3608, 3612, 3613, 3615, 3616, 3619; Johnson, op. cit., pp. 150, 152, 153, 162, 163.

16. N.Y., Crime Commission, *Public Hearings, No. 5,* vol. 3, pp. 1589, 1590, 1591, 1596–98; vol. 5, pp. 3630, 3635–39, 3641–44, 3646, 3647, 3654; Johnson, op. cit., pp. 98, 101, 102.

17. N.Y., Crime Commission, *Public Hearings, No. 5,* vol. 2, p. 1477; *Waterfront Investigation,* p. 453; Johnson, op. cit., pp. 210, 211.

18. N.Y., Crime Commission, *Public Hearings, No. 5,* vol. 5, pp. 3649, 3650; *Waterfront Investigation,* pp. 453, 454; Johnson, op. cit., pp. 206–9; *New York Times,* December 16, 1952.

19. N.Y., Crime Commission, *Public Hearings, No. 5,* vol. 2, p. 1478; *Waterfront Investigation,* pp. 134–37, 184, 185, 215; *New York Times,* January 8, 1953.

20. *Waterfront Investigation,* pp. 175, 218, 219, 454, 455.

21. Ibid., pp. 178, 184, 185, 224–26.

22. N.Y., Crime Commission, *Public Hearings, No. 5,* vol. 2, pp. 1425, 1478.

23. Ibid., pp. 1310, 1396–1400, 1416–20, 1481, 1482; *Waterfront Investigation,* p. 666.

24. N.Y. Crime Commission, *Public Hearings, No. 5,* vol. 2, pp. 1485, 1486, 1496; *Waterfront Investigation,* p. 666.

25. N.Y., Crime Commission, *Public Hearings, No. 5,* vol. 2, pp. 1453, 1454; *Waterfront Investigation,* p. 666.

26. N.Y., Crime Commission, *Public Hearings, No. 5,* vol. 2, pp. 1423–25, 1448–51; *Waterfront Investigation,* pp. 154, 234, 455, 456.

27. N.Y., Crime Commission, *Public Hearings, No. 5,* vol. 2, pp. 1308, 1429, 1430; *Waterfront Investigation,* pp. 154, 159–61, 233.

28. N.Y., Crime Commission, *Public Hearings, No. 5,* vol. 2, pp. 1291, 1302, 1310, 1415, 1431, 1438, 1440; *Waterfront Investigation,* pp. 244, 669.

29. N.Y., Crime Commission, *Public Hearings, No. 5,* vol. 5, pp. 3703, 3704.

30. Ibid., vol. 1, pp. 163, 164, 270, 271; Johnson, op. cit., pp. 105, 106.

31. Johnson, op. cit., pp. 110, 111; *New York Times,* January 24, 1953.

32. N.Y., Crime Commission, *Public Hearings, No. 5,* vol. 1, pp. 15, 86, 87, 89, 107, 255–61; William J. Keating with Richard Carter, *The Man Who Rocked the Boat* (New York: Harper & Brothers, 1956), pp. 205, 206; *Waterfront Investigation,* pp. 54, 55.

33. N.Y., Crime Commission, *Public Hearings, No. 5,* vol. 2, pp. 1398, 1399; vol. 4, pp. 2790, 2791; Johnson, op. cit., pp. 166, 176; Keating, op. cit., pp. 95, 110.

34. N.Y., Crime Commission, *Fifth and Final Report to the Governor, the Attorney General, and the Legislature of the State of New York,* July 15, 1954, Legislative Document no. 52, pp. 24–26; N.Y., Crime Commission, *Public Hearings, No. 5,* vol. 3, pp. 1707, 1709; *New York Times,* December 5, 20, 22, 1952; January 22, 1953.

35. N.Y., Crime Commission, *Fifth and Final Report,* pp. 21–23.

36. *New York Times,* August 16; November 19, 1953.

37. Ibid., November 19, 1953.
38. Ibid., December 24, 29, 1953; editorial, "Action on the Piers," April 2, 1954.
39. Ibid., March 17, 28, April 5, 1954; editorial, "The Pier Strike Ends," April 3, 1954.
40. *New York Times,* November 17, 1954; September 17, 1955.
41. Ibid., September 28, 1955.

Chapter 18

Tammany Boss DeSapio's Heyday—Era of Gangland Turbulence

1. Kefauver Committee Hearings, *Final Report,* p. 1.
2. *Chicago Daily Tribune,* April 5, 1952; *Chicago Sun-Times,* April 5, 1952; *New York Times,* January 17, 1953; May 14, 1954.
3. *New York Times,* February 18, 21, 1953; *Newark News,* July 16, 1953; *New York Times,* June 2, 3; July 17; August 6, 1953; March 20, 1954.
4. *New York Times,* February 18, 19; May 3; December 30, 1953.
5. *New York Times,* September 9; December 2, 1952; February 12, 1954.
6. N.Y., Crime Commission, *Public Hearings, No. 4,* vol. 2, pp. 301–3, 305, 314–18; *New York Times,* November 22, 1952.
7. Kefauver Committee Hearings, pt. 7, pp. 1086–90, 1184; N.Y., Crime Commission, *Public Hearings, No. 4,* vol. 2, pp. 219–24, 340–44, 347, 351, 352; vol. 3, pp. 652–53; *New York Times,* November 22, 1952.
8. N.Y., Crime Commission, *Public Hearings, No. 4,* vol. 2, pp. 237–39, 296, 297, 300, 321, 323–27, 368, 370–72; *New York Times,* November 22, 1952.
9. Warren Moscow, *The Last of the Big-Time Bosses* (New York: Stein & Day, 1971), pp. 67, 68; *Report of the District Attorney,* County of New York, 1946–1948, pp. 116–19; *New York Times,* August 10; November 3, 1954.
10. Moscow, op. cit., pp. 58–60, 62–64.
11. N.Y., Crime Commission, *Public Hearings, No. 4,* vol. 2, p. 371; Moscow, op. cit., pp. 91, 97, 98; Ed Reid and Neal Patterson, "Who Is Three Finger Brown?" *Chicago Daily News,* November 12, 1952.
12. Moscow, op. cit., pp. 89–93.
13. N.Y., Crime Commission, *Public Hearings, No. 4,* vol. 1, pp. 160–63; Moscow, op. cit., pp. 94, 95, 98; see also George Wolf with Joseph DiMona, *Frank Costello: Prime Minister of the Underworld* (New York: William Morrow, 1974), pp. 161–64. (Frank Rizzo, long-time friend and confidant of Costello, wrote a letter in which he related how Mancuso was ousted from his leadership because he double-crossed Costello by working for Impellitteri. Rizzo asserted that he delivered a message to Mancuso in which Costello threatened to throw Mancuso out the window if he ever showed up at the Costello residence. Wolf's book indicates the incident occurred during the 1949 mayoral election, but it actually took place in 1950.)
14. Reid and Patterson, op. cit.; *New York Times,* December 22, 1953.
15. *New York World Telegram,* October 21, 1952.
16. *New York Times,* September 3, 26, 1953; April 21; August 21, 1954.
17. Ibid., September 24, 26, 28; December 17, 1953; December 9, 1954.
18. Ibid., September 21; October 2, 17, 1953; March 2, 10, 14, 1954; Kefauver Committee Hearings, pt. 7, pp. 510–26.
19. *New York Times,* March 4, 14; April 10, 1954.
20. Ibid., December 10, 1953; March 2, 4, 10, 14; June 30, 1954.
21. Ibid., December 22, 1953; February 3, 1954.
22. Ibid., December 23, 29, 1953.
23. Moscow, op. cit., pp. 110, 113, 114; editorial, "New York's Primary," *New York Times,* August 31, 1953.
24. *New York Times,* September 2, 1953; editorial, "Disinterested Voters," September 9, 1953.
25. Moscow, op. cit., pp. 115, 116; editorial, "The Wagner Landslide," *New York Times,* September 17, 1953.
26. Editorial, "Tammany and Mutual Aid," *New York Times,* January 3, 1954; *New York Times,* January 7; August 2, 1954; Moscow, op. cit., p. 119;

27. Mocsow, op. cit., pp. 115, 121, 122, 124, 125, 126; *New York Times,* December 15, 1954; *Chicago Daily Tribune,* May 25, 1955.

28. Editorial, "Governor Dewey's Service," *New York Times,* December 27, 1954.

29. *New York Times,* July 5, 1954; *Chicago Daily Tribune,* May 25, 1955.

30. Malcolm Johnson, *Crime on the Labor Front* (New York: McGraw-Hill, 1950), pp. 34–39.

31. *New York Times,* May 18; July 31, 1954; May 18, 1955; Kefauver Committee Hearings, pt. 7, pp. 288, 293, 350, 652, 1641.

32. *New York Journal,* March 11, 1956; *New York Times,* March 13, 1956; *New York Daily News,* January 22, 1970; Clark R. Mollenhoff, *Strike Force* (Englewood Cliffs, N.J.: Prentice-Hall, 1972), pp. 29–33, 143, 144.

33. Editorial, "Street Attack," *New York Times,* April 6, 1956; *New York Times,* April 7, 1956.

34. *New York Times,* August 18, 19, 30; November 16, 1956.

35. Ibid., September 8; November 20, 21, 1956; *Chicago Daily Tribune,* May 28, 1957.

36. Wolf, op. cit., pp. 248, 250; *New York Times,* April 26, 1956.

37. *Newark Ledger,* March 14, 1956; *New York Times,* May 24; June 4, 1955; *Newark News,* May 23, 1955.

38. *New York Times,* March 26, 1954; November 15, 1955; January 4, 1956; *Newark News,* January 3, 1956.

39. Wolf, op. cit., pp. 251, 252; *Chicago Daily News,* December 18, 1957; January 3, 1962; *Chicago Sun-Times,* May 3, 1957; *Chicago American,* May 27, 1957; *New York Times,* June 29, 1961.

40. N.Y., Crime Commission, *Public Hearings, No. 4,* vol. 1, p. 194; vol. 3, pp. 559–61; *New York Times,* April 8, 9, 12 , 13, 22, 24, 1957.

41. *New York Times,* April 22, 27; May 1, 2, 7; November 13, 1957.

42. Ibid., April 22; May 10, 16, 1957.

43. Ibid., April 22; May 18, 1957.

44. Ibid., April 19; May 7, 9, 10, 18, 1957.

45. Virgil W. Peterson, *A Report on Chicage Crime for 1957* (Chicago Crime Commission, May 29, 1958), pp. 30–32; *New York Times,* May 8, 1957; Wolf, op. cit., pp. 253–57; Peter Maas. *The Valachi Papers* (New York: G. P. Putnam's Sons, Bantam Book, 1968), pp. 252–55; *Chicago Sun-Times,* May 3, 1957.

46. Peterson, op. cit., p. 32; Maas, op. cit., pp. 256–57; Ralph Salerno and John S. Tompkins, *The Crime Confederation* (Garden City, N.Y.: Doubleday, 1969), p.297.

47. *New York Times,* October 26, 1957; Wolf, op. cit., pp. 258, 259; Frederic Sondern, Jr., *Brotherhood of Evil* (New York: Farrar, Straus & Cudahy, 1959), pp. 14, 15; Hank Messick, *Lansky* (New York: G. P. Putnam's Sons, 1971), pp. 211, 216, 217.

48. U.S., Congress, Senate, Committee on Improper Activities in the Labor or Management Field, *Hearing on S. 74 and 221,* 85th Cong., 2d sess., 1958, pt. 32, pp. 12202–206, 12209–215.

49. Ibid., pp. 12194–219; Sondern, op. cit., pp. 3–17; Peterson, op. cit., pp. 32–34; *A Report on Chicago Crime for 1959* (Chicago Crime Commission, July 26, 1960), pp. 39–42; Dwight C. Smith, Jr., *The Mafia Mystique* (New York: Basic Books, 1975), pp. 163, 180, 200–216.

50. Moscow, op. cit., pp. 132–34.

Chapter 19

End of Line for Boss DeSapio

1. Barry Cunningham with Mike Pearl, *Mr. District Attorney* (New York: Mason/Charter, 1977), pp. 120–24, 149, 150; Edward N. Costikyan, *Behind Closed Doors* (New York: Harcourt, Brace & World, 1966), p. 159–63; Warren Moscow, *The Last of the Big-Time Bosses* (New York: Stein & Day, 1971), pp. 139–41, 144, 148, 152, 158–61; editorial, *New York Times,* January 24, 1959.

2. Moscow, op. cit., pp. 162–64.

3. *New York Times,* February 21, 1959. Subsequently, Costello was ordered deported, but on February 17, 1964, the U.S. Supreme Court set aside the deportation order in a decision criticized by the *New York Times* editorially as a "strained and distorted interpretation of the law"—see *New York Times,* February 18, 1964; editorial, "Reward for Deceit," February 22, 1964.

4. Virgil W. Peterson, *A Report on Chicago Crime for 1959,* Chicago Crime Commission, July 26, 1960, p. 34.

5. Hank Messick, *Lansky* (New York: G. P. Putnam's Sons, 1971), p. 218; Kefauver Committee Hearings, pt. 7, pp. 1630, 1631; Peterson, *Chicago Crime for 1959*, p. 35; Virgil W. Peterson, *A Report on Chicago Crime for 1966*, Chicago Crime Commission, August 11, 1967, p. 79.
6. *New York Times*, April 18, 1959.
7. U.S., Congress, Senate, Subcommittee on Antitrust and Monopoly of the Committee on the Judiciary, *Professional Boxing: Hearings on S. 238*, 86th Cong., 2d sess., 1961, pt. 2, p. 280. Hereafter referred to as *Professional Boxing.* Barney Nagler, *James Norris and the Decline of Boxing* (Indianapolis: Bobbs-Merrill, 1964), pp. 181, 224–27.
8. *Professional Boxing*, pp. 279, 280; Burton B. Turkus and Sid Feder, *Murder, Inc.* (New York: Farrar, Straus & Young, 1951), pp. 274–83; Nagler, op. cit., pp. 227–30.
9. *Professional Boxing*, pp. 550, 551, 561–64.
10. Ibid., pp. 284, 551, 572, 577, 578; Nagler, op. cit., 27, 231; Virgil W. Peterson, *A Report on Chicago Crime for 1960*, Chicago Crime Commission, May 31, 1961, pp. 65–68.
11. *Professional Boxing*, pp. 282, 560; Nagler, op. cit., pp. 114, 161–67, 186; *New York Times*, January 13, 1959.
12. Nagler, op. cit., pp. 123, 196–223, 240–247.
13. *New York Times*, January 2, 1959; Messick, op. cit., pp. 221, 222.
14. *New York Times*, April 23; July 7, 1967.
15. Messick, op. cit., pp. 228, 229, 231–34; *New York Times*, April 19, 22, 23; July 7; August 25; September 2, 1967.
16. *New York Times*, June 8, 1960; Moscow, op. cit., p. 170.
17. Mocow, op. cit., pp. 167, 168, 171–74.
18. *New York Times*, June 1, 4, 30, 1961; Moscow, op. cit., p. 178.
19. Alfred Connable and Edward Silberfarb, *Tigers of Tammany: Nine Men Who Ran New York* (New York: Holt, Rinehart & Winston, 1967), pp. 299, 325; Moscow, op. cit., pp 177, 180.
20. *New York Times*, September 8, 1961; editorial, "Victory for Mayor Wagner," September 8, 1961; Costikyan, op. cit., p. 29; Moscow, op. cit., pp. 180–84.
21. Editorial, "A New Mayor for New York," *New York Times*, October 19, 1961; *New York Times*, November 8, 1961.
22. *New York Daily News*, December 22, 1961; *New York Mirror*, December 18–20, 1961.
23. Kefauver Committee Hearings, pt. 7, pp. 264, 295, 684, 743–51; Ed Reid, *The Grim Reapers* (Chicago: Henry Regnery, 1969), pp. 33–35; *New York Times*, June 8, 1962; *New York Post*, December 10, 1963; Peterson, *Chicago Crime for 1959*, p. 41.
24. *New York Times*, June 16, 1962.
25. U.S., Congress, Senate, Committee on Improper Activities in the Labor or Management Field, *Hearing on S. 74 and 221*, 85th Cong., 2d sess., 1958, pt. 32, p. 12191; *New York Times*, December 22, 1967.
26. *Chicago Tribune*, January 11, 26, 1961; *Chicago Sun-Times*, January 26, 1961.
27. *New York Times*, June 17; August 3, 1962.
28. Ibid., January 27, 28; March 3, 1962; *Washington Post*, February 27, 1962; *1963 Britannica Book of the Year* (Chicago: Encyclopaedia Britannica, 1963), pp. 298, 299.
29. Reid, op. cit., pp. 34, 35; Virgil W. Peterson, *A Report on Chicago Crime for 1962*, Chicago Crime Commission, June 28, 1963, pp. 66, 67, 68.
30. *Wall Street Journal*, January 19, 1961; Peterson, *Chicago Crime for 1959*, p. 40; *The Loan Shark Racket*, a report by the New York State Commission of Investigation, April 1965, pp. 57, 58, 63, 65; *New York Times*, July 13, 21, 1962.
31. U.S., Congress, Senate, Subcommittee on Investigations of the Committee on Government Operations, *Organized Crime, Stolen Securities: Hearings on S. 31*, 92d Cong., 1st sess., 1971, pt. 3, pp. 843, 847, 849, 852–57, 868.
32. *New York Times*, May 22; July 23; November 27, 1963; Virgil W. Peterson, *A Report on Chicago Crime for 1963*, Chicago Crime Commission, July 14, 1964, p. 62.
33. *The Loan Shark Racket*, pp. 10, 11, 12, 27.
34. Ibid., pp. 17–20.
35. Ibid., p. 20–32.
36. Ibid., pp. 52, 68–76.
37. *New York Times*, March 3, 1962.
38. Ibid., September 6, 1963; editorial, "DeSapio Defeated," September 6, 1963.

39. *New York Times,* September 27, 1963; November 6, 1964.
40. Moscow, op. cit., pp. 184, 186; *New York Times,* February 9, 1965; Costikyan, op. cit., pp. 22, 23, 25; Connable and Silberfarb, op. cit., pp. 13, 17.
41. *New York Times,* December 4, 1964; July 8, 1967; Moscow, op. cit., pp. 128, 186.
42. *New York Times,* November 3, 1965; Moscow, op. cit., pp. 200, 201.
43. Moscow, op. cit., pp. 201, 202; *New York Times,* November 15, 1969.
44. *New York Times,* December 19, 1967; Cunningham, op. cit., pp. 144–49; Moscow, op. cit., pp. 202–5; *Chicago Tribune,* June 20, 1968; July 9, 1969; *New York Times,* November 19, 1969; Ralph Salerno and John S. Tompkins, *The Crime Confederation* (Garden City, N.Y.: Doubleday, 1969), pp. 256–60.
45. Cunningham, op. cit., pp. 149, 150; Moscow, op. cit., pp. 205, 206.
46. *New York Times,* December 21, 1968; November 15, 1969.
47. Ibid., November 15, 19, 25; December 2, 1969; Moscow, op. cit., pp. 206, 207.
48. *New York Times,* December 21, 1968; November 15, 18, 1969.
49. Ibid., November 19, 20, 1969.
50. *Wall Street Journal,* December 15, 1969; *New York Times,* May 25; June 26, 1971; Moscow, op. cit., pp. 213–15.
51. Connable and Silberfarb, op. cit., p. 309.

Chapter 20

Joseph Valachi's Background

1. U.S., Congress, Senate, Permanent Subcommittee on Investigations of the Committee on Government Operations, *Organized Crime and Illicit Traffic in Narcotics: Hearings on S. 17,* 88th Cong., 1st sess., 1963, pt. 1, pp. 24, 31. Hereafter referred to as Organized Crime Hearings.
2. Ibid., pp. 78, 79.
3. Ibid., pp. 134, 135.
4. Ibid., pp. 105, 106, 107.
5. Ibid., p. 6.
6. Ibid., p. 121.
7. Ibid., pp. 136–39.
8. Ibid., pp. 134, 135, 140–43.
9. Ibid., pp. 144, 146, 148–50.
10. Ibid., pp. 150–52, 154, 155.
11. Ibid., pp. 83, 84, 155, 156.

Chapter 21

Castellammarese War

1. Organized Crime Hearings, pp. 162, 163, 166, 167, 174.
2. Ibid., pp. 180–84.
3. Ibid., pp. 185, 186.
4. Ibid., p. 210.
5. Ibid., pp. 188, 191, 192, 193.
6. Ibid., pp. 193, 194, 198.
7. Ibid., pp. 198, 199, 210, 211, 212.
8. Ibid., pp. 212, 214.
9. *Chicago Daily News,* October 24, 1930; *Chicago Tribune,* October 28, 1930; *Chicago Examiner,* October 29, 1930; John Kobler, *Capone* (New York: G. P. Putnam's Sons, 1971), pp. 205, 206.
10. Organized Crime Hearings, p. 215.
11. Ibid., p. 216.
12. Ibid., pp. 217, 218.
13. Ibid., pp. 220, 221.
14. Craig Thompson and Allen Raymond, *Gang Rule in New York* (New York: Dial Press, 1940), pp. 68, 110, 314, 315.

15. Organized Crime Hearings, pp. 228–34.
16. Ibid., p. 229.
17. Thompson and Raymond, op. cit., pp. 358, 359; Hank Messick, *Secret File* (New York: G. P. Putnam's Sons, 1969), p. 96; Messick, *The Silent Syndicate* (New York: Macmillan Co., 1967), p. 98.
18. Paul Sann, *Kill the Dutchman! The Story of Dutch Schultz* (New Rochelle, N.Y.: Arlington House, 1971), p. 143.
19. Organized Crime Hearings, p. 226.
20. Ibid., pp. 205, 237, 238.
21. Ibid., pp. 227, 234, 235.
22. Ibid., pp. 235–37, 251.

Chapter 22

Cosa Nostra Membership

1. Organized Crime Hearings, p. 238.
2. Ibid., p. 210.
3. Ibid., p. 367.
4. Ibid., pp. 81, 82, 111, 271, 386.
5. Ibid., pp. 240, 241, 323.
6. Ibid., pp. 83, 109, 115, 116.
7. Ibid., pp. 239, 240.
8. Ibid., p. 239.
9. Ibid., pp. 239, 297, 298.

Chapter 23

Cosa Nostra Family

1. Organized Crime Hearings, pp. 81, 82.
2. Ibid., pp. 205, 236, 386–88.
3. Ibid., p. 309.
4. Ibid., pp. 259, 262.
5. Ibid., pp. 81, 236, 237.
6. Ibid., pp. 210, 301.
7. Ibid., pp. 6, 7, 237.

Chapter 24

The "No-Narcotics" Rule

1. Organized Crime Hearings, pp. 319, 320.
2. Ibid., pp. 320, 321, 322.
3. Ibid., pp. 321–23.

Chapter 25

Narcotics Conspiracy

1. Organized Crime Hearings, pt. 3, pp. 630, 631, 639.
2. Ibid., pp. 632, 633, 634, 639.
3. Ibid., pp. 635, 636, 639, 640.
4. Sid Feder and Joachim Joesten, *The Luciano Story* (New York: David McKay, 1954), pp. 16–23.
5. Through correspondence with the U.S. Bureau of Narcotics and Dangerous Drugs, the author established that the Dominick Petrelli arrested with Eugene Giannini in Milan, Italy, was in fact Valachi's intimate friend.

6. Organized Crime Hearings, pt. 1, pp. 350–56.

Chapter 26

Valachi—Man of Many Talents

1. Organized Crime Hearings, pt. 1, pp. 234, 235, 283, 284, 289.
2. Vincent Teresa with Thomas C. Renner, *My Life in the Mafia* (Garden City, N.Y.: Doubleday, 1973), pp. 42, 43, 44, 86, 87, 93, 317.
3. Organized Crime Hearings, pt. 1, pp. 289, 305, 306.
4. Ibid., pp. 129, 130, 131, 277, 278.
5. Ibid., pp. 186–88.
6. Ibid., pp. 342, 392, 393.
7. Ibid., pp. 391, 392.
8. Ibid., pp. 267, 268, 363, 364.
9. Ibid., pp. 348, 349.
10. Ibid., pp. 268, 326.

Chapter 27

New Jersey Rackets

1. Organized Crime Hearings, pt. 1, p. 324.
2. Ibid., p. 329.
3. Ibid., pp. 324, 329–32.
4. Ibid., p. 325.

Chapter 28

Luciano–Costello–Genovese Family

1. Organized Crime Hearings, pt. 1, pp. 162, 251, 252, 255, 256, 275, 296, 364.
2. Ibid., pp. 221, 323, 324; Robert H. Prall and Norton Mockridge, *This Is Costello* (New York: Fawcett, 1951), pp. 15, 16.
3. Organized Crime Hearings, pt. 1, pp. 257, 271, 275, 324, 348.
4. Ibid., pp. 249, 365, 366.
5. Ibid., pp. 162, 252, 324, 364.
6. Ibid., pp. 95, 227, 234, 235.
7. Ibid., p. 249.
8. Ibid., pp. 118, 323.
9. Ibid., pp. 248, 249.
10. Ibid., p. 159.
11. Ibid., p. 250.
12. Ibid., pp. 291, 292, 365.
13. Ibid., pp. 81, 301, 366.
14. Ibid., pp. 86, 87, 88.
15. Ibid., pp. 94, 95.
16. Ibid., pp. 99, 102, 104–7, 112.
17. Ibid., pp. 250, 251, 293.
18. Ibid., p. 88.
19. *Newark Ledger,* February 15, 17, 1969; *New York Daily News,* February 18, 1969.
20. *New York Times,* July 17, 1972.
21. Ibid., February 19, 1973.

Chapter 29

Albert Anastasia–Carlo Gambino Family

1. Organized Crime Hearings, pt. 1, pp. 164–66, 168, 173.
2. Ibid., pp. 118, 378–80.
3. Ibid., pp. 348, 349.
4. Ibid., p. 304.
5. Ibid., pp. 388, 389.
6. Ibid., p. 7.
7. Ibid., pp. 349, 350, 361.
8. Ibid., pp. 294, 306.
9. Ibid., pp. 294, 302, 304, 305, 306; Paul Meskil, *Don Carlo: Boss of Bosses* (New York: Popular Library, 1973), pp. 60, 61.

Chapter 30

Lucchese Family

1. Organized Crime Hearings, pt. 1, pp. 164, 168, 174–76.
2. Ibid., pp. 156, 193, 194, 216, 246.
3. Ibid., p. 275, 276.
4. Ibid., pp. 282, 283, 284.
5. Ibid., pp. 177, 276, 285.
6. *Chicago Tribune,* July 14, 1967.

Chapter 31

Joseph Profaci Family

1. Organized Crime Hearings, pt. 1, p. 88.
2. Ibid., pp. 369, 371, 372, 374, 377.
3. Ibid., pp. 371, 375–78.
4. *The Loan Shark Racket,* a report by the New York State Commission of Investigation, April 1965, pp. 18, 19.
5. Organized Crime Hearings, pt. 1, pp. 308, 310, 311.
6. Gay Talese, *Honor Thy Father* (New York: World Publishing, 1971), pp. 93, 95, 96, 386, 393.
7. *Time,* July 12, 1971, pp. 14–19; *New York Times,* May 24, 1978.
8. *New York Times,* April 8, 1972.

Chapter 32

Joseph Bonanno Family

1. Gay Talese, *Honor Thy Father* (New York: World Publishing, 1971), p. 205.
2. Organized Crime Hearings, pt. 1, pp. 184, 246.
3. Ibid., p. 313.
4. Talese, op. cit., pp. 170–72, 204, 211.
5. Organized Crime Hearings, pt. 1, p. 314.
6. Talese, op. cit., pp. 94, 95, 186, 211, 380, 393.
7. Joseph Volz and Peter J. Bridge, *The Mafia Talks* (Greenwich, Conn.: Fawcett, 1969), pp. 147, 149.
8. Ibid., pp. 153, 154, 161.
9. Ibid., pp. 166, 185.
10. Paul Meskil, *Don Carlo: Boss of Bosses* (New York: Popular Library, 1973), pp. 100, 103–5.
11. Talese, op. cit., pp. 179, 181.
12. Meskil, op. cit., p. 105.
13. Ibid., pp. 231, 232; *New York Times,* October 16, 18, 1976; July 13, 1979.

Chapter 33

Valachi's Knowledge Limited to New York

1. Organized Crime Hearings, pt. 1, pp. 263, 264.
2. Vincent Teresa with Thomas C. Renner, *My Life in the Mafia* (Garden City, N.Y.: Doubleday, 1973), pp. 320, 322, 325.
3. Organized Crime Hearings, pt. 1, p. 205.
4. Ibid., pp. 205, 206.

Chapter 34

President's Commission on Law Enforcement

1. President's Commission on Law Enforcement and Administration of Justice, *Task Force Report: Organized Crime* (Washington, D.C.: Government Printing Office, 1967), pp. 6, 7.
2. Ibid., p. 31.
3. Ibid., pp. 7, 8.

Chapter 35

Organized Crime in U.S. Not Controlled by One Group

1. Peter Maas, *The Valachi Papers* (New York: G. P. Putnam's Sons, Bantam Books, 1968), p. 253.
2. *New York Times,* February 27, 1973.
3. For a history of the Cleveland syndicate, see Hank Messick, *The Silent Syndicate* (New York: Macmillan Co., 1967).
4. Pennsylvania Crime Commission, *Report on Organized Crime* (Harrisburg: Office of the Attorney General, 1970), pp. 1, 16, 17, 76.
5. Organized Crime Hearings, pt. 1, p. 7.
6. "Winning the War Against Organized Crime," interview with Henry E. Petersen, head of Justice Department's Criminal Division, *U.S. News & World Report,* June 5, 1972, p. 65.
7. Paul Meskil, *Don Carlo: Boss of Bosses* (New York: Popular Library, 1973), pp. 98, 99, 100.
8. Ibid., pp. 200, 201; Gay Talese, *Honor Thy Father* (New York: World Publishing, 1971), p. 385.

Chapter 36

Conclusion: Organized Crime in America—An Overview

1. *Organized Crime,* Report of the Task Force on Organized Crime, National Advisory Committee on Criminal Justice Standards and Goals, Law Enforcement Assistance Administration, Washington, D.C., 1976, p. 23.
2. Alfred Connable and Edward Silberfarb, *Tigers of Tammany: Nine Men Who Ran New York* (New York: Holt, Rinehart & Winston, 1967), p. 114.
3. Pennsylvania Crime Commission, *Report on Organized Crime* (Harrisburg: Office of the Attorney General, 1970), pp. 16, 31, 32, 33, 53, 68; U.S., Congress, Senate, Committee to Investigate Crime in Interstate Commerce, *Final Report,* 82d Cong., 1951, pp. 60, 61. John A. Gardiner, *The Politics of Corruption: Organized Crime in an American City* (New York: Russell Sage Foundation, 1970), pp. 1–129. This book provides a detailed, long-term study of corruption and organized crime in Reading, Pennsylvania. The book uses fictitious names for the city and individuals mentioned. The city called Wincanton in the book is actually Reading and the organized crime boss called Irving Stern was actually Abe Minker.
4. Edward N. Costikyan, *Behind Closed Doors* (New York: Harcourt, Brace & World, 1966), pp. 40, 298, 306, 307, 352, 353.
5. *Chicago Tribune,* April 30, 1978.
6. *Time,* March 5, 1979.

7. Steven Brill, *The Teamsters* (New York: Simon & Schuster, 1978), pp. 24, 132–37, 139, 140, 149, 150; *New York Times,* June 22, 1978.
8. Brill, op. cit., pp. 14, 24, 35, 201, 210, 211, 215, 216.
9. *New York Times,* October 14, 1969.
10. National Advisory Committee on Criminal Justice Standards and Goals, *Report of the Task Force on Organized Crime,* Washington, D.C., 1976, pp. 89, 90.
11. Frederic M. Thrasher, *The Gang: A Study of 1,313 Gangs in Chicago* (Chicago: University of Chicago Press, 1936), pp. 328, 351, 352.
12. Ibid., pp. 288–93, 417, 418.
13. Gus Tyler, *Organized Crime in America: A Book of Readings* (Ann Arbor, University of Michigan Press, 1962), pp. 91, 325, 326.
14. Ed Reid and Ovid Demaris, *The Green Felt Jungle* (New York: Pocket Books, 1964), photograph with text between pp. 116 and 117.
15. Humbert S. Nelli, *The Business of Crime: Italians and Syndicate Crime in the United States* (New York: Oxford University Press, 1976), pp. 182, 183.
16. Burton B. Turkus and Sid Feder, *Murder, Inc.* (New York:, Farrar, Straus & Young, 1951), p. 75; J. Richard (Dixie) Davis, "Things I Couldn't Tell Till Now," *Collier's,* August 5, 19, 1939.
17. Turkus and Feder, op. cit., pp. 75, 97–106, 424, 425.
18. Luigi Barzini, *The Italians* (New York: Atheneum, 1965), pp. 270, 271.
19. U.S., Congress, Senate Subcommittee on Investigations of the Committee on Governmental Affairs, *Waterfront Corruption: Hearings,* 97th Cong., 1st sess., February 17–19, 25–27, 1981, pp. 349, 350, 351, 352, 354, 372, 382. Mario Puzo's bestselling novel *The Godfather* (New York: G. P. Putnam's Sons, 1969) was made into a motion picture; both the novel and the film vividly portray a highly organized Italian underworld.
20. *Chicago Tribune,* April 30, 1978.
21. Kefauver Committee Hearings, pt. 2, pp. 134, 135, 141, 162, 196.
22. Gaia Servadio, *Mafioso: A History of the Mafia from Its Origins to the Present Day* (New York: Stein & Day, 1976), pp. 29, 73, 222, 268.
23. Pennsylvania Crime Commission, *Report on Organized Crime,* pp. 68–72.

Appendix 1

Origin and Development of the Mafia

1. Louis Harris, "The Harris Survey: Most Believe There's a Mafia," *Chicago Tribune,* May 17, 1971.
2. Giovanni Schiavo, *The Truth About the Mafia and Organized Crime in America* (New York: Vigo Press, 1962), p. 101.
3. U.S., Congress, Senate, Subcommittee on Investigations of the Committee on Government Operations, *Organized Crime and Illicit Traffic in Narcotics: Hearings on S. 17,* 88th Cong., 1963, pt. 1, p. 21.
4. Ed Reid, *Mafia* (New York: Random House, 1952), pp. 25, 26; Nicholas Gage, *The Mafia Is Not an Equal Opportunity Employer* (New York: McGraw-Hill, 1971), p. 30.
5. Schiavo, op. cit., p. 35.
6. William Agnew Paton, *Picturesque Sicily* (New York: Harper & Brothers, 1897), pp. 359, 360.
7. Luigi Barzini, *The Italians* (New York: Atheneum, 1965), p. 257.
8. Danilo Dolci, *The Man Who Plays Alone,* trans. Antonia Cowan (New York: Pantheon Books, 1968), pp. 103, 104.
9. Michele Pantaleone, *The Mafia and Politics* (New York: Coward-McCann, 1966), pp. 24, 25.
10. Schiavo, op. cit., p. 36.
11. Barzini, op. cit., pp. 257, 258, 259.
12. Luciano J. Iorizzo and Salvatore Mondello, *The Italian-Americans* (New York: Twayne Publishers, 1971), pp. 6, 7.
13. Joseph L. Albini, *The American Mafia: Genesis of a Legend* (New York: Appleton-Century-Crofts, 1971), p. 129.
14. Pantaleone, op. cit., pp. 27, 28, 29.
15. Schiavo, op. cit., pp. 38, 42, 44.

16. Bernard A. Weisberger, *The American Heritage History of the American People* (New York: American Heritage Publishing Co., 1970), p. 196.
17. Pantaleone, op. cit., pp. 29, 30.
18. Cesare Mori, *The Last Struggle with the Mafia,* trans. Orlo Williams (New York: Putnam, 1933), pp. 92, 108, 109, 110.
19. Francis A. J. Ianni with Elizabeth Reuss-Ianni, *A Family Business, Kinship and Social Control in Organized Crime* (New York: Russell Sage Foundation, 1972), pp. 43, 44, 45, 47, 49; Richard Gambino, "The Italian-Americans," *Chicago Tribune,* May 7, 1972; Harvey Warren Zorbaugh, *The Gold Coast and the Slum* (Chicago: University of Chicago Press, 1929), pp. 161–67.
20. Joseph E. Persico, "Vendetta in New Orleans," *American Heritage, the Magazine of History,* June 1973, pp. 65–72; Fred J. Cook, *Mafia!* (Greenwich, Conn.: Fawcett, 1973), pp. 34–36.
21. Herbert Asbury, *The French Quarter: An Informal History of the New Orleans Underworld* (Garden City, N.Y.: Garden City Publishing, 1938), pp. 405–22; Iorizzo and Mondello, op. cit., pp. 67–73.
22. Schiavo, op. cit., pp. 147, 148.
23. Ibid., p. 152.
24. Ibid., p. 154.
25. Reid, op. cit., p. 163.
26. Ibid., pp. 163, 164.
27. Ibid., pp. 164, 165, 172.
28. Ibid., p. 172.
29. Norman Lewis, *The Honored Society* (New York: G. P. Putnam's Sons, 1964), pp. 78, 79; Pantaleone, op. cit., pp. 40, 41.
30. Barzini, op. cit., p. 265.
31. Ibid., pp. 263–66; Gaia Servadio, *Mafioso: A History of the Mafia from Its Origins to the Present Day* (New York: Stein & Day, 1976), pp. 57–60.
32. Pantaleone, op. cit., p. 43.
33. Mori, op. cit., pp. 1–6.
34. Ibid., pp. 36, 50–52, 67.
35. Pantaleone, op. cit., pp. 47–49; Lewis, op. cit., pp. 69–72.
36. Pantaleone, op. cit., pp. 49, 50, 52; Lewis, op. cit., pp. 14, 15.
37. Pantaleone, op. cit., pp. 80, 81.
38. Ibid., pp. 82–85.
39. Ibid., pp. 86, 87.
40. Ibid., pp. 54, 55; Lewis, op. cit., pp. 10–12.
41. Pantaleone, op. cit., pp. 56–58; Lewis, op. cit., pp. 13–15.
42. Sid Feder and Joachim Joesten, *The Luciano Story* (New York: David McKay, 1954), pp. 7, 39, 160–62.
43. Ibid., pp. 190, 194, 195, 207–17.
44. Pantaleone, op. cit., p. 61.
45. Barzini, op. cit., pp. 268, 270.
46. Pantaleone, op. cit., pp. 60, 61, 63.
47. Reid, op. cit., pp. 100, 101.
48. Peter Maas, *The Valachi Papers* (New York: G. P. Putnam's Sons, Bantam Books, 1968), pp. 155, 156, 201, 202.
49. Reid, op. cit., pp. 109, 110.
50. Ibid., pp. 104, 105, 110–13.
51. Pantaleone, op. cit., pp. 12, 18, 87, 88; Lewis, op. cit., pp. 109–11.
52. Barzini, op. cit., pp. 267–69; Pantaleone, op. cit., pp. 80, 81.
53. Lewis, op. cit., pp. 121–24; Ianni, op. cit., pp. 37, 38.
54. Dolci, op. cit., pp. 330, 331.
55. Barzini, op. cit., pp. 270–72.
56. Lewis, op. cit., p. 249.
57. Ibid., p. 248.
58. Barzini, op. cit., pp. 267, 268.
59. Pantaleone, op. cit., pp. 17, 18.
60. Paul Hoffman, *New York Times,* June 11, 1970 (Palermo dateline, June 6, 1970).

61. *Chicago Tribune,* October 29, 1970.
62. Ibid., May 6, 1971.
63. *New York Times,* January 21, 1973.

Appendix 2

The Mafia's Source of Power

1. Joseph L. Albini, *The American Mafia: Genesis of a Legend* (New York: Appleton-Century-Crofts, 1971), p. 132, also pp. 89, 126, 127; Michele Pantaleone, *The Mafia and Politics* (New York: Coward-McCann, 1966), pp. 32, 33; Giovanni Schiavo, *The Truth About the Mafia and Organized Crime in America* (New York: Vigo Press, 1962), pp. 40, 41; Francis A. J. Ianni with Elizabeth Reuss-Ianni, *A Family Business, Kinship and Social Control in Organized Crime* (New York: Russell Sage Foundation, 1972), pp. 28, 29.
2. Schiavo, op. cit., pp. 47, 48.
3. William Agnew Paton, *Picturesque Sicily* (New York: Harper & Brothers, 1897), p. 368.
4. Bolton King and Thomas Okey, *Italy Today*, 2d ed. (London: James Nisbet, 1904), pp. 121, 122.
5. Pantaleone, op. cit., p. 46; Schiavo, op. cit., pp. 39, 44, 69, 83; Norman Lewis, *The Honored Society* (New York: G. P. Putnam's Sons, 1964), pp. 43, 84.
6. Danilo Dolci, *The Man Who Plays Alone,* trans. Antonia Cowan (New York: Pantheon Books, 1968), p. ix.
7. Luigi Barzini, *The Italians* (New York: Atheneum, 1965), p. 256; Dolci, op. cit., p. 40.
8. Pantaleone, op. cit., pp. 195–98.
9. Ibid., pp. 199–201.
10. Dolci, op. cit., pp. 92, 93.
11. Ibid., pp. 203, 207, 208, 213, 216, 218, 219, 227, 228, 230.
12. Ibid., pp. 73–76, 330, 331.
13. *Kansas City Star,* April 8, 1952; August 2, 1965; *Newsweek,* August 16, 1965; U.S., Congress, Senate, Special Committee to Investigate *Investigation of Organized Crime in Interstate Commerce: Hearing on S. 202,* 81st Cong., 2d sess., and 82d Cong., 1st sess., pt. 4A—Missouri, pp. 772, 773, 774, pt. 8—Louisiana, pp. 45, 92, 93, pt. 10, Nevada-California, pp. 340, 341, 343; Dolci, op. cit., pp. 78, 79, 82, 83.
14. Dolci, op. cit., p. 73.
15. Ibid., pp. 80, 85.
16. Pantaleone, op. cit., pp. 218–21.
17. Ibid., pp. 223–25.
18. Ibid., pp 202–4, 215, 216.
19. Barzini, op. cit., p. 215.
20. Pantaleone, op. cit., pp. 157–59, 161.

Appendix 3

Organizational Structure of the Mafia

1. Giovanni Schiavo, *The Truth About the Mafia and Organized Crime in America* (New York: Vigo Press, 1962), pp. 111–13, 133, 134, 135, 138; Joseph L. Albini, *The American Mafia: Genesis of a Legend* (New York: Appleton-Century-Crofts, 1971), pp. 206–8.
2. Harvey Warren Zorbaugh, *The Gold Coast and the Slum* (Chicago: University of Chicago Press, 1929), p. 171; Albini, op. cit., pp. 191–95.
3. Donald R. Cressey, *Theft of the Nation* (New York: Harper & Row, 1969), pp. 55, 56.
4. Ed Reid, *Mafia* (New York: Random House, 1952), pp. 31, 32; Nicholas Gage, *The Mafia Is Not an Equal Opportunity Employer* (New York: McGraw-Hill, 1971), pp. 28–31.
5. Frederic Sondern, Jr., *Brotherhood of Evil: The Mafia* (New York: Farrar, Straus & Cudahy, 1959), pp. 3–17. Sondern states that the Mafia "is not a rigid, monolithic organization. . . .There is no president, no formal roster; there is no initiation or oath" (p. 5).
6. Fred J. Cook, *Mafia!* (Greenwich, Conn.: Fawcett, 1973), pp. 67, 68.
7. Sondern, op. cit., pp. 6–16.

8. Schiavo, op. cit., pp. 15, 16, 117–29; Mario Pei, *The Story of Language* (New York: J. B. Lippincott, 1965), p. 79.
9. Schiavo, op. cit., pp. 58, 59.
10. William Agnew Paton, *Picturesque Sicily* (New York: Harper & Brothers, 1897), pp. 361, 367, 368.
11. Bolton King and Thomas Okey, *Italy Today,* 2d ed. (London: James Nisbet, 1904), pp. 120, 121.
12. Alexander Nelson Hood (Duke of Bronte), *Sicilian Studies* (New York: Dodd, Mead, 1916), pp. 74, 80, 81.
13. Cesare Mori, *The Last Struggle with the Mafia,* trans. Orlo Williams (New York: Putnam, 1933), pp. 39, 40.
14. Gaetano Mosca, "Mafia," *Encyclopaedia of the Social Sciences* (New York: Macmillan Co., 1933), vol. 10, p. 37.
15. Gaia Servadio, *Mafioso: A History of the Mafia from Its Origins to the Present Day* (New York: Stein & Day, 1976), pp. 222, 268.
16. Henner Hess, *Mafia & Mafiosi: The Structure of Power,* trans. Ewald Osers (Lexington, Mass.: D. C. Heath, Lexington Books, 1973), pp. ix, 10, 11, 14.
17. Norman Lewis, *The Honored Society* (New York: G. P. Putnam's Sons, 1964), pp. 84–92.
18. Ibid., pp. 87–89.
19. Ibid., pp. 89–90. For a detailed account of Nicola Gentile's statement regarding certain aspects of organized crime in the U. S., see Hank Messick, *Lansky* (New York: G. P. Putnam's Sons, 1971), pp. 49–63.
20. Luigi Barzini, *The Italians* (New York: Atheneum, 1965), pp. 254, 259–62; Michele Pantaleone, *The Mafia and Politics* (New York: Coward-McCann, 1966), pp. 34–36.
21. Francis A. J. Ianni with Elizabeth Reuss-Ianni, *A Family Business, Kinship and Social Control in Organized Crime* (New York: Russell Sage Foundation, 1972), pp. 28, 29, 30, 43.
22. Albini, op. cit., p. 126.
23. Harry J. Anslinger and Will Oursler, *The Murderers* (New York: Farrar, Straus & Cudahy, 1961), p. 79.
24. Cabinet Committee on International Narcotics Control, *World Opium Survey 1972,* Washington D.C., July 1972, pp. 17, 22, 47, A47, A48, A49.
25. National Advisory Committee on Criminal Justice Standards and Goals, *Organized Crime: Report of the Task Force on Organized Crime,* Washington, D.C., 1976, pp. 223, 224.

Index

Bonta, Paola, 468
Bonventre, John, 320
Bonventre, Pietre, 409
Booth, Willie, 133
Boran, Jon, 342
Bottler, the, 110
Bowers, Harold, 284, 292-93
Bowers, Mickey, 284
Bowery Boys Gang, 13, 14, 18, 23, 28, 30, 39, 42, 102
Bowery District, 96, 97
Bowery Lane, 13
Bowery Theater, 13, 17
Boyle, James, 231
Boyel, Joseph, 256
Bozzuffi, Tony, 127
Braden, Spruille, 258
Bradley, Mary L., 71
Bradley, William V., 292
Brannigan, James E., 253
Braunell, Ltd., 297
Breckinridge, Lucian S., 122
Brice, Fannie, 131
Brickman, Harry, 249
Bridges, Harry, 282
Briguglio, Salvatore, 432
Brill, Steven, 433
Broadway Tabernacle, 31
Brocato, James a.k.a. Moran, Jimmy, 202
Brooks Brothers Clothing Store, 53
Brooks, Danny see Gentile, Daniel
Broome, John L., 5, 7, 8
Brothwell, Dudley, 207
Brown, Florence (cokey Flo), 214
Brown, James W., 172
Brown, Joe—see Lucchese, Joe
Brown, Tommy (Three Finger)—see Lucchese, Thomas
Brownell, Herbert Jr., 295
Bruccola, Philip (Buccola), 384
Brudner, Charles, 334
Brunder, Wilfred Adolphus, 187, 204-05
Bruno, Angelo, 343, 424
Bruno, Joe, 383
Bruno Vincent J., 431
Bruno, Vinney—see Mauro, Vincent
Brunswick Laundry, 409
Brush, Charley, 384
Brydone, Patrick, 454
Bubona, Phil, 383
Buccieri, Fiore, 416
Buchalter, Louis (Lepke), 112, 137-38, 148-49, 158, 179, 190, 195, 208, 210, 211, 216-20, 223, 227-30, 272, 296, 303, 308-09, 311, 329, 369, 428, 435, 438-40
Buchanan, James, 44

Buckley, Charles A., 313
Buckley, William F. Jr., 348
Building Service Employees Union, AFL, Local 32-E, 301-02, 308
Building Service Employees International Union, 308
Bull's Head Tavern, 13
Bureau of City Betterment, 112
Bureau of Fire Prevention, 177
Bureau of Municipal Research, 112
Bureau of Standards and Appeals, 161
Burran, Nathan, 201
Burns, Tom, 36
Burr, Aaron, 4-6, 8, 12, 20
Burton, Mary, 10
Buster from Chicago, 364, 396, 415
Butler, General Benjamin F., 56
Bye, Wilbur A., 264
Byk, Leo P., 184, 224
Byrnes, Thomas, 89, 90

Caesar's Palace, 433
California Dried Fruit Importers, 402
Callace, Frank (chick 99), 363-64
Calo, Don—see Vizzini, Calogero
Camara, Michael, 124
Camarado, Carmine, 373
Camarda, Anthony, 291
Camarda, Emil, 229-30
Camp, Vincenzo, 476
Camporetto, Mike, 346
Canfield, Richard A., 94-96
Cantor, Maurice, 156
Capishaw, Hulon, 222
Capodichino Airport, Naples, 340
Capone, Al, 101, 149-52, 157-60, 187, 367, 391, 415, 425, 434, 445-46
Capone, Louis, 223
Capone, Ralph, 434
Cappola, Anthony, 398
Cappozzoli, Louis, 297
Capri Casino, Havana, 385
Capuzzi, Nick, 364, 396
Carbo, Frank, 328-32, 334
Carbo, John Paul—see Carbo, Frank
Carfano, Anthony, 152, 229, 240, 248, 286, 308, 327, 334, 391
Carlino, Charles, S., 311
Carlino, Joseph Peter, 311
Carlton Securities, 342
Carnera, Primo, 186
Carpenter, Daniel, 45
Cardozo, Albert, 61-62
Cardozo, Benjamin Nathan, 62, 68
Carter, Jimmy, 331
Caruso, Angelo, 367